D1269156

Microsoft Press

Building Applications with
Microsoft **Outlook** 2000
Technical Reference

Randy Byrne
Micro Eye, Inc.

Foreword by Sue Mosher
Slipstick Systems

T Professional

PUBLISHED BY
Microsoft Press
A Division of Microsoft Corporation
One Microsoft Way
Redmond, Washington 98052-6399

Copyright © 1999 by Microsoft Corporation

All rights reserved. No part of the contents of this book may be reproduced or transmitted in any form
or by any means without the written permission of the publisher.

Library of Congress Cataloging-in-Publication Data
Byrne, Randy.
    Building Applications with Microsoft Outlook 2000 Technical Reference / Randy Byrne.
        p. cm.
    ISBN 0-7356-0581-5
    1. Microsoft Outlook.   2. Time management--Computer programs.
    3. Personal information management--Computer programs.
    I. Microsoft Press.   II. Title.
    HD69.T54B97   1999
    005.369--dc21   99-20170
                                                              CIP

Printed and bound in the United States of America.

1 2 3 4 5 6 7 8 9   WCWC   4 3 2 1 0 9

Distributed in Canada by Penguin Books Canada Limited.

A CIP catalogue record for this book is available from the British Library.

Microsoft Press books are available through booksellers and distributors worldwide. For further information about international editions, contact your local Microsoft Corporation office or contact Microsoft
Press International directly at fax (425) 936-7329. Visit our Web site at mspress.microsoft.com.

ActiveX, BackOffice, Developer Studio, FrontPage, IntelliSense, JScript, Microsoft, Microsoft Press,
Outlook, PowerPoint, Visual Basic, Visual C++, Visual FoxPro, Visual InterDev, Visual J++, Visual
Studio, Windows, and Windows NT are either registered trademarks or trademarks of Microsoft Corporation in the United States and/or other countries. Other product and company names mentioned herein may
be the trademarks of their respective owners.

The example companies, organizations, products, people, and events depicted herein are fictitious. No
association with any real company, organization, product, person, or event is intended or should be
inferred.

Acquisitions Editor: David Clark
Project Editor: Maureen Williams Zimmerman

Dedication

I dedicate this book to my parents, Marie and Warren Byrne. My father, who died suddenly just before this book became a reality, would have been very proud. I thank them both for their love and support.

Acknowledgments

This book represents a substantial revision of Peter Krebs's pioneering effort, *Building Applications with Microsoft Outlook 97*. Jaye Colorado and Carola Klass revised Peter's work in the second edition to accommodate the changes introduced by Outlook 98. Since I was one of the first individuals outside of Microsoft to write about the Outlook object model, I had the good fortune (at times I thought it was the misfortune) to be asked to write the completely revised edition of this book.

First and foremost I want to acknowledge the tireless hours devoted to this book by David Kane, the Vice-President of Micro Eye, Inc. David, your contributions have been invaluable. I could not have completed this book on schedule without your help. Your sense of humor and perspective has kept me sane during this project.

I want to thank Darrique Barton of Microsoft for giving me the opportunity to make this contribution to the Outlook developer community. Darrique, I hope that your hand has healed from your energetic efforts to ensure that critical features did not get cut from Outlook 2000 during the product design stage. The wait for the "wish list" I presented to you when we spoke at Tech Ed 1997 has been well worth it.

Florian Voss, also an Outlook Program Manager, created the initial version of the Northwind Contact Management application and provided me with critical feedback. Florian, get some sleep, and again, danke!

Other members of the Microsoft Outlook team in Redmond also deserve special mention. Thanks to Ramez Naam, who always took the time to respond to my nagging about loose ends. Don Mace took time away from his busy schedule to educate me about Folder Home Pages. Thanks also go to Kevin Kahl, Jay Abbott, Bill Jacob, and Frank Lee. On the Exchange side of the house, I offer thanks to Charles Eliot, Tom Rizzo, and Jim Reitz.

Apart from the Outlook team, my debt of gratitude is to all the Microsoft Most Valued Professionals (MVPs) on the Outlook newsgroups who volunteer their time and effort to make Outlook a better product. Thanks to Don Adams, Jay B. Harlow, Vince Averello,

Ken Slovak, Jessie Louise McClennan, and Ben M. Schorr. Other frequent and invaluable contributors to the Outlook newsgroups are Rick Spiewak, Hollis D. Paul, Jan R. Cirpka, Per Winkvist, Chris Burnham, and Diane Poremsky. You have helped me to comprehend pieces of Outlook that escaped my notice or understanding. In the MVP community, I send an immense thank-you to Sue Mosher of Slipstick Systems, whose energy and commitment to Outlook and Exchange is unsurpassed. For those of you who live by Outlook (both literally and figuratively), you know that there aren't enough superlatives to describe Sue's contributions.

There are peers and customers who also enriched my knowledge of Outlook. I'd like to thank Robert Ginsburg and Andy Sakalian of ECMS, Inc., Tom Howe of Control Center Computing, Dan Desmond of The SIMI Group, Phil Seeman of Catalyst Innovations, and Siegfried Weber of CDOLive. For their early commitment to Outlook as a sales force automation platform, thanks to Yvonne Risch, Susan Briscoe, Kim Salisbury, Pat McNeil, Patti Rabe, and Mark Simko of Vision Service Plan, Inc.

Since a book of this type is by its very nature a group effort, I want to thank the team behind this book. Thanks to David Clark, my acquisitions editor, and Maureen Zimmerman of Microsoft Press, who supervised this long effort. Jan Benes kept the production team chugging along and prevented us from falling behind schedule. Paul Green did the copyediting and Jo-Anne Rosen served as the principal compositor. Sally Neuman, my technical editor, deserves special praise and gratitude for going the extra mile to get things right. Sally, your commitment to this project went way beyond the call of a paycheck.

Since I'm writing this acknowledgment during Oscar season, I can also thank everyone in my immediate and extended family without a great deal of guilt. Thanks to my daughters, Lily and Zoe, for putting up with Dad when he was holed up in "the cave." Both of you are the light at the end of the tunnel. For encouragement and support during what sometimes appeared to be the marathon writing of this book, I want to thank Lou and Harriet Cohen; Marie Byrne; Barry Byrne, MD; Davide Atenoux; Didar Khalsa; Andre Ptaszynski; Chuck Schultz; Susan Brown; Steve Ekstrom; Steve Cohen; Laura Hogan; Karen Kane; Ursula (the Leek) and Peter Labermeier; Fern Friedman; Billy Rosen, MD; Julia Levine; Steve Stombler; and Debbe Heller-Lewkowicz.

Finally, I want to thank my wife Susan Cohen Byrne for putting up with me during a time when I could be by turns ecstatic and irritable. Your therapeutic powers kept me calm when the going was rough and the end nowhere in sight. Once again, you helped to guide me through a difficult time.

Randy Byrne
Esparto, CA
March 1999

Contents

PART III Building Blocks of Applications

5   Forms   99

6 Controls, Fields, and Properties 137

7 Actions 185

8 Folders 217

PART IV **Beyond the Basics**

11 **Using VBA and VBScript with Outlook   361**

PART V Advanced Topics

Foreword

History seems to repeat itself in the programming world, as well as in every other walk of life. The first application I ever wrote was a scheduling program. It checked the weekly shifts for the 80 people working in a newsroom against a fairly complex set of union rules that governed how long each shift could be, what start times were allowable, and how much time off was required between shifts. Any mistake violating one of those rules could result in the company paying a fine. I didn't have very sophisticated tools, but managed to put something together with VisiCalc and Basic that ran well on my RadioShack TRS-80. (I remember those good old days fondly indeed.)

After a long detour through the world of news technology, I've come full circle to spend much of my time working with sophisticated scheduling and messaging applications that collate information across an enterprise using Microsoft Outlook and Microsoft Exchange Server. One of my allies and mentors in this arena is Randy Byrne, founder of Micro Eye, Inc., one of the leading Exchange/Outlook development firms, and author of this book.

Building Applications with Microsoft Outlook 2000 represents another instance of programming history repeating itself. It's the third *Building Applications with Microsoft Outlook* volume, the previous two having covered Outlook 97 and Outlook 98. However, Outlook 2000 represents a sea change for Outlook developers, and this book follows suit, introducing a whole new range of topics—application-level events, Folder Home Pages, VBA for Outlook, data access strategies, Exchange Server scripting, and so on. In fact, it's so big that it doesn't all fit between two covers; you'll find some prime sample projects in three E-Chapters on the accompanying CD.

I encouraged Randy to take on the project of updating *Building Applications* because I don't know anyone with more patience to explain things clearly, more insight into the Outlook application design process, and more knowledge of the intricacies of the Outlook Object Model. Who else has the eye for detail required to build a wall chart of the object model in full color, suitable for framing?

That sense of detail pervades this new edition of *Building Applications*. Don't expect to find a simple code cookbook that you can copy and paste into your own projects. Instead, you need to work through the examples, read the explanations, and grasp the goals that Microsoft set in designing Outlook 2000. If you stick with this program, you'll emerge with an in-depth understanding of what you can accomplish with Outlook—and how to get the job done with the variety of tools and technologies available. Chances are, you'll also catch Randy's enthusiasm for Outlook as a development focus. I guarantee you that it's highly contagious.

Sue Mosher
Slipstick Systems, Moscow
http://www.slipstick.com/

Introduction

In This Chapter

Who Should Use This Book

This book is designed primarily for Outlook application developers using Microsoft Exchange Server. Although there are plenty of programming samples that will benefit Internet Only developers, many of the examples assume that you will be deploying workgroup applications in a Microsoft Exchange Server environment using both public and private folders. It's also assumed that you will be using Outlook 2000 to run the applications in this book. Although many of the techniques discussed in this book can be used in Outlook 97 and Outlook 98, you won't be able to take full advantage of the code examples and sample applications unless you have installed Outlook 2000. New features that are specific to Outlook 2000 are identified with the following graphic:

In Part II, "Quick Guide to Building Applications," both programmers and non-programmers can pick up this book and find the information they need to develop groupware applications. Part III, "Building Blocks of Applications," gives you a solid foundation on which to build more complex Outlook applications. You'll understand that Outlook applications are developed using the core objects of messages and folders. You'll go beyond this core understanding to learn about the important new events in Outlook 2000 and your greatly expanded ability to customize the Outlook application using Command Bars, the Outlook Bar, and the Office Assistant.

In Part IV, "Beyond the Basics," you will learn how to write Visual Basic for Applications or VBScript code to create more sophisticated applications than you can using Outlook's built-in modules. We'll also cover some new ideas about distributing your application using Folder Home Pages. Part V, "Advanced Topics," is for developers who are at an intermediate or advanced level in Visual Basic. Step-by-step instructions are included that show you how to create COM Add-ins that replace Exchange Client Extensions and provide Outlook functionality that you only dreamed of in the past. You'll learn about Folder Home Pages, the Outlook Team Folder Wizard, and Visual Basic DHTML applications. An entire chapter is devoted to data access strategies for Outlook, a popular and confusing topic on the Outlook newsgroups. This chapter also includes several data-aware ActiveX controls that you can distribute with your applications. For the developers who need to scale their application, we'll cover using Microsoft Transaction Server and ActiveX components to extend Outlook. Finally, you'll learn how to use Microsoft Exchange Server scripting agents to synchronize customer data in SQL Server and Outlook forms in an Exchange public folder.

How This Book Is Organized

This book consists of the following six parts.

Part I Introducing Outlook

Chapter 1, "Applications You Can Create with Outlook," discusses the processes and problems best suited for Outlook solutions and shows you the kind of Request, Discussion, Tracking, and Reference applications you can build to streamline communications in your organization. Chapter 2, "Outlook Design Tools," showcases the tools available for creating Outlook forms and for building COM Add-Ins and Folder Home Pages using Microsoft Office Developer, Microsoft Visual Basic, and Microsoft Visual InterDev.

Part II Quick Guide to Building Applications

Chapter 3, "Customize Built-In Modules," shows you how to create instant groupware applications by modifying the built-in Contacts application, customizing it for tracking customer correspondence related to a beta program, and then copying it to Public Folders on Microsoft Exchange Server. Chapter 4, "Design a Custom Application," shows you how to build a Discussion application called Product Ideas that makes it possible for users to submit, read, and respond to new products ideas.

Part III Building Blocks of Applications

Chapter 5, "Forms," introduces the form design process, and covers fundamental form design tasks such as adding controls and fields, creating new actions, setting form properties, and publishing forms. Chapter 6, "Controls, Fields, and Properties," covers the fundamental skills and information you need to effectively use controls, fields, and properties on a form. It also explains the unique features of each commonly used control, and then offers some strategies for implementing these controls and fields in an application. Chapter 7, "Actions," discusses the easiest way to create responses for Message forms, explains how to create custom Reply actions for Message forms, and then shows how to create custom Reply To Folder actions for Post forms. Chapter 8, "Folders," takes an in-depth look at the folder design process, discusses how to manage forms, and explains how to create custom views and folder home pages. It also covers setting folder permissions and building rules. Chapter 9, "Raise Events and Move to the Head of the Class," explains how you can use all the new events in the Outlook 2000 object model to write Outlook VBA code or create a COM Add-In. Chapter 10, "Outlook Bar, Command Bars, and the Assistant" shows you how to program the new Outlook Bar objects. You'll also learn how to program Office 2000 objects such as the Command Bar and the Assistant. With your ability to control the command bars in Outlook, you can customize Outlook menus and toolbars in ways that were impossible in previous versions.

Part IV   Beyond the Basics

Chapter 11, "Using VBA and VBScript with Outlook," introduces VBScript and provides a wide variety of code examples for the most commonly performed tasks using VBScript in Outlook. Chapter 12, "Distribute and Maintain Applications," shows you how to distribute forms in folders and provides some techniques for maintaining applications. It also covers how mobile users can use off-line folders, increasing the effectiveness of using applications in collecting and recording information while in the field.

Part V   Advanced Topics

The Advanced Topics chapters are primarily for developers who want to use Visual Basic to extend Outlook in a corporate environment where Microsoft Exchange Server is installed. Chapter 13, "Creating COM Add-Ins with Visual Basic," provides you with practical templates for Visual Basic COM Add-In component creation and discusses some of the security issues associated with COM Add-ins. You'll also learn how to use Visual Basic to create an ActiveX control that serves as a property page in the Outlook Tools Options dialog box. Chapter 14, "Customizing Folder Home Pages," gives you a quick tour of the Outlook Team Folder Wizard and then introduces you to a Visual Basic DHTML application that serves as the Folder Home Page for the Customers folder in the Northwind Contact Management application. In Chapter 15, "Outlook Data Access Strategies," we'll look at several options you can use to bring legacy data into Outlook. Chapter 16, "Using ActiveX DLLs and Microsoft Transaction Server with Outlook," considers how you can use remote components and MTS to your advantage when you attempt to scale your Outlook application to hundreds or thousands of users. Finally, Chapter 17, "Extending Outlook Using Exchange Server Scripting and Routing Objects," offers a practical example using VBScript and Visual Basic to accomplish bilateral data synchronization between a SQL Server database and the Customers public folder in the Northwind Contact Management application.

Part VI   Sample Applications

The sample applications for this book are in the Building Microsoft Outlook 2000 Applications personal folders (.pst) file on the CD-ROM that accompanies this book. You can modify these sample applications for use in your organization. Each sample application is discussed in detail in a matching E-Chapter. The three E-chapters accompanying this book are located in the E-Chapters folder under the 6. Sample Applications folder in the Building Microsoft Outlook 2000 Applications personal folders (.pst) file. If you prefer a printed copy, you can open an E-Chapter in Word 2000 and print the chapter in its entirety. From this point on, these chapters will be referred to as E-Chapters.

> **Note** Figure I.1 shows the Customers folder in the Northwind Contact Management Application folder under 6. Sample Applications. You should be aware that the chapters that explain the sample applications are located in separate E-Folder chapters in the 6. Sample Applications folder. You can open the documents in these E-chapter folders using Word 2000 or a browser of your choice.

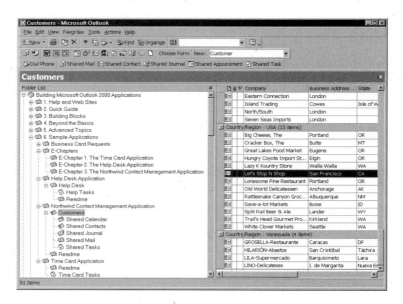

Figure I.1 *Chapters explaining the Sample Applications are located in the E-Chapters folder.*

E-Chapter 1, "The Time Card Application," takes you step-by-step through the process of building an application that automates employee timekeeping tasks with VBA code in both Excel and Outlook. E-Chapter 2, "The Help Desk Application," is a revised example of the Help Desk application that shipped with previous editions of this book. It showcases a variety of design techniques, including how new Outlook 2000 application-level events and Collaboration Data Objects can be used to route help requests. E-Chapter 3, "The Northwind Contact Management Application," is the showcase application for this book. It uses the new Links collection object in Outlook 2000 to provide tracking of shared activities for customers and customer contacts. In the "Advanced Topics" section of the book, you'll learn how to customize a Folder Home Page for this application and how to use Exchange Server scripting agents to create bilateral synchronization between the Customers public folder in the Northwind Contact Management application and the Customers table in Microsoft SQL Server.

Use the Companion CD-ROM

The companion CD-ROM contains all the code necessary to run the sample applications discussed in this book, including compiled ActiveX DLLs if you don't have Visual Basic to open the included source code, the help file for Collaboration Data Objects, white papers, several ActiveX controls that will help you to develop forms that access external data, and sample COM Add-Ins. It also includes a sample personal folders (.pst) file, which contains all of the applications and sample code covered in this book.

You might want to make a copy of the applications and dissect the ones you're most interested in to see how they're developed. You can also customize these applications and put them to work in your organization.

> **Important** Many of the examples on the CD-ROM and in this book require that you connect to Microsoft Exchange Server to use Public Folders in Corporate/ Workgroup mode. Several of the advanced topics applications are not suitable for use in an Internet Only environment. See the Readme file on the companion CD-ROM for a list of software installation requirements.

Run the Setup Program for Building Applications with Microsoft Outlook 2000

> **Caution** The Setup program requires that you have already installed Microsoft Outlook 2000 on your computer. Unlike the previous edition of this book, Microsoft Outlook 2000 is not included on the companion CD-ROM. You must install Microsoft Outlook 2000 before you proceed.

To install Building Applications with Microsoft Outlook 2000 program files

1. Insert the CD-ROM accompanying this book into your CD-ROM drive.

2. If your computer does not launch the Setup program automatically, double-click Setup.exe in your CD-ROM directory.

3. In the Welcome dialog box, click Next.

4. In the Select Directory dialog box, select the folder where you will install the Building Microsoft Outlook 2000 Applications personal folders (.pst) file. The default is the same location where Office 2000 is installed. Click the Browse button if you want to select an alternate folder.

5. Click Next to begin the installation process.

6. If Setup detects that you already have a VBAProject.otm file on your system, you will see an Alert message box that informs you that the VBAProject.otm accompanying this book has been renamed and the location of the renamed file. See "Installing VBAProject.otm" later in the Introduction if you see this alert message box during installation. Click OK to dismiss the VBAProject.otm Warning alert box if it appears during installation.

7. Click Finish to complete the installation.

Using the Building Microsoft Outlook 2000
Applications Personal Folder (.pst) File

The Setup program installs a Building Microsoft Outlook 2000 Applications file in the destination folder you specified during installation and adds this file as a personal folders file to your current profile. The Building Microsoft Outlook 2000 Applications file is actually a personal folders (.pst) file that contains sample forms and files, information on where to access help files, shortcuts to Web sites, and all the files necessary to run the sample applications and code examples.

While it's not required that you add the Building Microsoft Outlook 2000 Applications file to your system, it serves as a valuable reference tool, and the sample applications can be used as a starting point for building applications that can be customized for your environment.

Installing VBAProject.otm

Outlook 2000 supports Visual Basic for Applications as an integral component of the Outlook application environment. All the code for Outlook Visual Basic for Applications is stored in a single file, VBAProject.otm. This file is stored in the following locations depending upon operating system and whether user profiles are operational on your system. If your operating system is installed on a drive other than drive c:\, adjust the location accordingly.

Operating System	Location for VBAProject.otm
Windows 95 and 98 without UserProfiles	C:\Windows\Application Data\Microsoft\Outlook
Windows 95 and 98 with UserProfiles	C:\Windows\Profiles*UserName*\Application Data\Microsoft\Outlook
Windows NT 4.0 or Windows 2000	C:\Winnt\Profiles*UserName*\Application Data\Microsoft\Outlook

If you already have a VBAProject.otm on your system, the installation program will display an alert message informing you that it has detected an existing VBAProject.otm. In this instance, the VBAProject.otm that accompanies this book will be renamed to VBABAO2K.otm and copied to the location of your existing VBAProject.otm. In order for you to use the sample code in the VBAProject.otm that accompanies this book, you will have to rename your existing VBAProject.otm to a name such as MyVBAProject.otm and then rename VBBAO2K.otm to VBAProject.otm. If you don't have an existing VBAProject.otm, the VBAProject.otm that accompanies this book will be installed automatically and you can ignore the following steps.

To install VBAProject.otm that accompanying this book if you already have VBAProject.otm installed on your system

1. If Outlook is running, quit Outlook using the Exit And Log Off command on the File menu. You must exit Outlook completely or you will receive a sharing violation when you attempt to rename VBAProject.otm.

2. Click the Start button on the Windows Task bar, click Find, and select Files Or Folders.

3. Type *vba*.otm* in the Named drop-down combo box.

4. Select Local Drives in the Look-In drop-down combo box.

5. Make sure that the Include Subfolders box is checked.

6. Click Find Now.

7. When VBAProject.otm and VBABAO2K.otm are found on your system, right-click VBAProject.otm and select Rename on the shortcut menu. Type *MyVBAProject.otm* as the new name. Press Enter.

8. Right-click VBABAO2K.otm and select Rename on the shortcut menu. Type *VBAProject.otm* as the new name. Press Enter.

9. Restart Outlook. The VBAProject.otm that accompanies this book is now the operational VBA Project for Outlook.

Outlook Macro Security

If Outlook security is set to Medium (the default), you will be prompted to trust the macros installed with this book in VBAProject.otm. You will see the dialog box shown in Figure I.2 asking you to trust the macros in ThisOutlookSession. In order for the code in the VBAProject.otm file accompanying this book to run correctly, you must click the Enable Macros button in the Macro warning dialog box. If you change your security settings to Low, you will not see the Macro Warning dialog box when you start Outlook. If you want to change your Outlook Macro security settings, follow the steps outlined next.

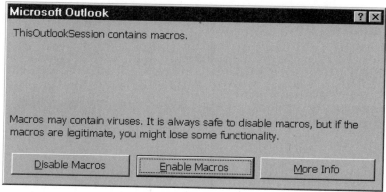

Figure I.2 *The Outlook Macro Warning dialog box for ThisOutlookSession.*

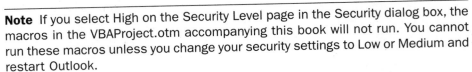

To change Outlook Security settings

1. Select Macro from the Tools menu.
2. Select Security from the Macro submenu.
3. Select a security option on the Security Level page.
4. Click OK to accept your selection.

Note If you select High on the Security Level page in the Security dialog box, the macros in the VBAProject.otm accompanying this book will not run. You cannot run these macros unless you change your security settings to Low or Medium and restart Outlook.

Important Because Outlook Visual Basic for Applications code is loaded on demand, you must press Alt+F11 to open the Visual Basic Editor the first time you launch Outlook after you install the VBAProject.otm that accompanies this book. Once you press Alt+F11, you will see the Macro Warning dialog box illustrated in Figure I-2. Select the Enable Macros button to run the code in VBAProject.otm.

Technical Support for the Companion CD-ROM

Every effort has been made to ensure the accuracy of this book and the contents of the companion CD-ROM. Microsoft Press provides corrections for books through the World Wide Web at the following address:

http://mspress.microsoft.com/support/sup_er.htm/

If you have comments, questions, or ideas regarding this book or the companion CD-ROM, please mail or e-mail them to Microsoft Press at the following addresses:

Postal Mail

Microsoft Press
Attn: Building Applications with Microsoft Outlook 2000 Editor
One Microsoft Way
Redmond, WA 98052-6399

E-mail

mspinput@microsoft.com

Please note that product support is not offered through the above mail addresses. For support information on Outlook, see the documentation for the appropriate product support phone number.

Part I
Introducing Microsoft Outlook 2000

Chapter 1, "Applications You Can Create with Outlook," discusses the processes and problems best suited for Outlook solutions and shows you the kind of Request, Discussion, Tracking, and Reference applications you can build to streamline communications in your organization. Chapter 2, "Outlook Design Tools," showcases the tools available for creating Outlook forms and for building COM Add-ins and Folder Home Pages using Microsoft Visual Studio.

Chapter 1
Applications You Can Create with Outlook

In This Chapter

Outlook 2000 offers some wonderful new features that help users communicate and collaborate more effectively. It is now possible to selectively synchronize items to offline folders for mobile users, and the ability to customize the Outlook environment has been extended by improved shortcuts on the Outlook Bar and complete control over Outlook command bars. These changes, however, are incremental improvements in comparison to previous versions of Outlook, where totally new user interface changes were introduced.

The real revolution in Outlook 2000 is in the area of programmability. Although there are still certain areas of Exchange that are inaccessible from the Outlook 2000 object model, the improvements in the development environment for Outlook are monumental. First, Outlook supports Visual Basic for Applications 6.0. No longer do Outlook developers have to dream of a professional editor and debugger. The full Visual Basic object browser is only a keystroke or mouse click away. Performance improves with strongly typed variables and early binding. ActiveX property pages created in Visual Basic can replace Exchange custom extensions written in C++. Folder Home Pages and the Outlook View Control offer a means of scripting Active Server Pages to provide Web-based views into Exchange and Outlook public and private folders. COM Add-ins allow you to create commercial or corporate versions of Outlook. The list goes on, and it is extensive. For developers who are familiar with the constraints of VBScript in Outlook forms, Outlook 2000 represents a major advance in functionality, productivity, and creativity. Here are just a few of the things you can accomplish with Outlook 2000:

Share information   You can build applications that allow users to share all types of information, including schedules, tasks, contacts, distribution lists, documents, product ideas, and customer feedback.

Structure information   You can build forms and folders to structure information so it's both easy to read and easy to find. For example, you can create a Preferred Vendors public folder so managers can quickly find qualified vendors that have been referred by other managers in the organization, or you can use the Product Ideas application supplied with this book to enable users to submit, organize, and view new product ideas in a public folder.

Distribute information   You can create forms that enable users to send announcements, sales reports, documents, and request-for-services items. For example, you can create a Bulk Mailer form so you can automatically notify all users in a particular distribution list when a product update is available. Outlook 2000 features a new distribution list item in a Contacts folder that replaces distribution lists in the Personal Address Book.

Collect information   You can create forms and folders for collecting information. For example, you can create a User Response Form and public folder for collecting information about a product under development. Or you can use the Classified Ads application supplied with this book to allow users to submit and respond to classified ads.

Collaborate on information   One of the benefits of Outlook is that it allows each user to collaborate on the same item. For example, with the Product Ideas application, users from different locations can all participate in an online discussion about a particular product feature. With the Contact Management application, users can collaborate on the pursuit of new customers in a set of linked public folders.

Streamline processes   You can create applications that are modeled on paper-based processes in your organization. For example, you can create forms and folders that allow users to electronically submit vacation requests, travel plans, copier requests, purchase orders, time cards, status reports, classified ads, and training class registration.

Work offline   One of the advantages of Outlook over a pure Web mail interface is the ability of mobile users to work offline and consolidate their work later. Remote users can update custom forms and then synchronize their changes when they return to the office.

Types of Applications You Can Create

The two main building blocks of Outlook applications are forms and folders. From an object model perspective, all Outlook applications consist of message and folder containers. Advanced applications elaborate this core model by either presenting data in departmental or corporate databases or by maintaining links to Web documents stored with Office Server Extensions.

The design tools described in this book allow you to create a wide variety of Outlook and Exchange applications, ranging from rudimentary applications that leverage the basic Outlook forms to more complex collaboration and tracking applications that are multitiered.

- **Applications that consist entirely of forms** These are forms that are not associated with a specific folder, such as the While You Were Out form.
- **Applications that consist of a custom folder and standard forms** When you create a folder, you often will create custom views for that folder while still using the standard Outlook forms. For example, you might create a Contacts folder in a public folder and create custom views for the folder, but not change the standard forms supplied with the folder.
- **Applications created with the Team Folder Wizard** The Team Folder Wizard lets you create the following types of applications with the ease of a wizard: discussion, frequently asked questions, document library, issue tracking, team calendar, team contacts, team project, and team tasks. Folder Home Pages for these applications can be customized to go beyond what the Wizard provides.
- **Applications that consist of a custom folder and custom forms** In many cases, you customize both the folder and the form to build an application. For example, the Training Management, Classified Ads, and Contact Management applications all consist of customized forms and folders.
- **Applications that use Folder Home Pages** Outlook 2000 allows developers to combine the power and flexibility of Web pages with Outlook views and offline support for mobile users. Folder Home Pages provide users with a graphical way to organize their Outlook information with Web links to related content on either the Internet or a corporate intranet. Active Server Pages and the new Outlook View Control let you combine Outlook views with Active Server Page scripting. You can create HTML-based Web views of Exchange folders with links to user instructions, frequently asked questions, or component downloads. Folder Home Pages can also provide data or pivot table analysis to the user with the new Office 2000 PivotTable List control. See Figure 1.1 for an example of a Folder Home Page in the parent folder of the Northwind Contact Management Application.
- **Applications that use Exchange public folders and Outlook forms through a browser** Outlook Web Access provides a means for Internet users to access public folders that contain discussions or customer service applications, for example. Outlook Web Access lets users send e-mail, manage appointments and contacts, and access Exchange public folders and Outlook forms using a browser.
- **Applications that modify the Outlook user interface through COM Add-Ins** These applications could best be described as custom Outlook applications that change the normal appearance and functionality of Outlook. COM Add-ins allow you to modify the command bars, toolbars, and the Outlook Bar to suit specific application requirements. Other programs can be launched from a COM Add-in, such as retrieving data from corporate databases or providing other custom functions.

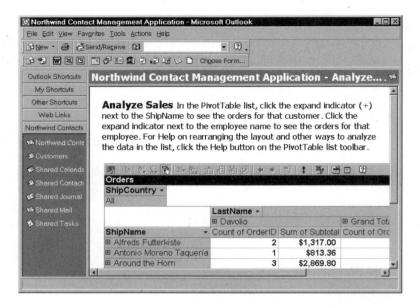

Figure 1.1 *Folder Home Page uses Sales Analysis Data Access Page created in Access 2000.*

- **Applications that use Exchange agents to extend a custom folder or custom forms** Certain advanced applications require the use of either Exchange server scripting or routing on private and public folders. For example, scripting agents are essential when you want to synchronize the contents of an Exchange public folder with a corporate database. Users can create workflow processes for documents and forms (voting, routing) that improve business processes by automating the transfer of information with Exchange Routing Objects available with Exchange Server 5.5 Service Pack 1 or later.

- **Applications that provide custom functionality built on Exchange and Outlook** Knowledge Management, Sales Force Automation, and Document Management applications provide customizations of Exchange and Outlook for their target customers. These applications will become increasingly prevalent with Outlook 2000 COM Add-ins and the integration of Office 2000 with Microsoft BackOffice.

Forms You Can Create

With the Outlook form in Design mode, you can create a wide spectrum of forms to perform a variety of tasks. When you create forms with Outlook, you never start from scratch. Instead, you base the forms you create on a standard form of a specific type supplied with Outlook. Standard form types include Message, Post, Office Document, and built-in modules, such as Appointment, Contact, Distribution List, Journal, and Task. Because most of the functionality is already available in these forms, you can often create custom forms by adding additional fields and controls to the standard forms, or by removing any controls you do not need. You can also create custom forms that bear little resemblance to the base form, such as a Post or Contact form.

In this section, we look at the different types of forms you can create or customize in Outlook. For more information, see "Outlook Form Design Mode" in Chapters 2 and 5.

Message Forms

Message forms are forms that are based on the Outlook Mail Message form. As such, Message forms allow users to send information to other users or to a public folder. Message forms are often used to streamline a request or approval process. Here are some examples of Message forms.

Vacation Request   The Vacation Request application, covered in Part 3, "Building Blocks of Applications," contains a Vacation Request form as shown in Figure 1.2. The Vacation Request form allows a user to send a vacation request to a manager. The Vacation Request application also contains a Vacation Approved form and a Vacation Denied form so a manager can respond to a request.

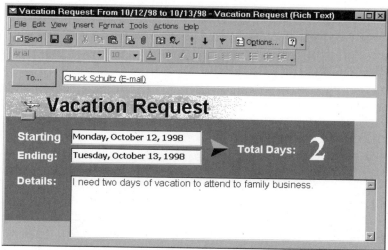

Figure 1.2 *The Vacation Request form.*

Status Report   You can also create a form that enables users to send weekly or monthly status reports to their managers. Submitted status reports can be stored in a personal folder or public folder and used for reference at review time.

Mileage Report   Forms can be created to make it possible for a user to submit monthly mileage reports to a manager for approval. When approved, the information in the Mileage Report item can be written to a database. This report can be extended to a management-type application with Exchange routing agents.

Post Forms for Posting Items in a Folder

Post forms are used to post items, as well as responses to items, to a folder. Post forms are used in applications that enable users to conduct online discussions, such as the Product Ideas folder discussed in Chapter 4, "Design a Custom Application." As such, Post forms serve as the foundation for creating threaded conversations in views. Post forms are also used for applications that require users to respond to a particular item, such as the Training Management application, in which the Evaluation form is used to post a response to a Course Offering item.

Here are a few ideas for creating Post forms using Outlook in Design mode:

Product Ideas The Product Ideas application consists of a Product Idea form and a Product Idea Response form, both of which are posted to a public folder as shown in Figure 1.3. Innovative, new ideas are readily shared and recorded in a public folder for all to access.

More Info For more information, see Chapter 4, "Design a Custom Application."

Job Posting You can also create a Job Posting form that structures information and makes it possible for Human Resources to post a job opening in the Job Postings folder.

Job Candidate You can also create a Job Candidates application, which consists of a Job Candidate form and a Response form. A manager or human resources administrator can submit a Job Candidate item to the Job Candidates public folder.

Each user, after interviewing the candidate, uses the Response form to submit hiring recommendations to the Job Candidates folder, where the manager can review the summary of opinions.

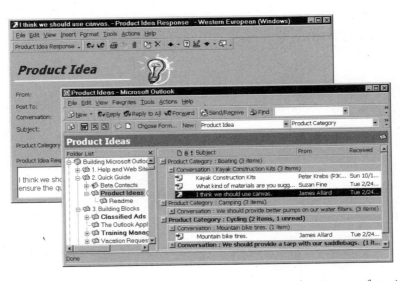

Figure 1.3 *The Product Ideas folder with the Product Idea Response form in the background.*

Office Document Forms

With Office Document forms, you can create forms using Office 2000 applications such as Microsoft Access, Microsoft Excel, Microsoft Word, or Microsoft PowerPoint. For example, you might want to streamline the process of creating and approving a sales document by creating a Word 2000 sales document template for authors so they can create sales documents using the template and then route the document to appropriate coworkers for editorial and legal review.

Here are a few more examples of the kinds of Office Document forms you can create:

Time Card   As shown in Figure 1.4, you can create a Time Card form based on a Microsoft Excel document. To record employee time card information, the user opens the Time Card form from the Organizational Forms Library; the form automatically collects task information from the user's task folder, and, finally, the user clicks the Send button on the form. The form is sent to the employee's manager for approval. If approved, the form is forwarded to the Timekeeper mailbox, which opens the time card and inserts the information contained on the form into a database for additional processing.

Micro Eye
EMPLOYEE TIME CARD

Approve	Record			

Name:	Help Manager	Report Date:	Thursday Jan 14, 1999	
Employee ID:	ME-10233	Period Covered:	Jan 1, 1999 Jan 14, 1999	
Department:	Help Desk	Approval Date:		
Job Title:	Help Desk Manager	Recorded Date:		
Manager:	David Kane	Total Hours:	42	

Project	Task	Start Time	End Time	Current Work
BAO 2K	Time Card	Dec 29, 1998		15
BAO 2K	Time Sheet Task form	Dec 28, 1998		7
OL 2K Data Ac	Data Synch Exchange/SQL	Dec 28, 1998		20

Summary / Detail

Figure 1.4 *The Time Card form uses the Exchange Directory and the user's Tasks folder.*

Sales Report   You can create a Sales Report form based on a Microsoft Excel chart for mailing weekly sales reports to a distribution list. Using Exchange Server scripting, you can write a scripting agent to create the report automatically at a specified time interval and then send it to an Exchange distribution list.

Invoice   You can create an Invoice form based on a Microsoft Excel worksheet for mailing invoices or for posting them in a folder.

Service Contract   You can create forms based on Microsoft Word documents for service contract agreements, exit interviews, or a variety of other purposes that require semi-structured information in a form.

More Info For more information on integrating Office Document forms into Outlook, see Chapter 5, "Forms."

Built-in Module Forms

You can customize forms based on the forms in the built-in modules—Appointment, Task, Contacts, and Journal—to take advantage of the specific functionality of the module.

Here are a few ideas for the types of forms you can create based on the forms in the Outlook built-in modules:

Assigned Help Task form You can create forms such as the Assigned Help Task form, as shown in Figure 1.5, to make it possible to update and track the progress of a task. As shown here, the standard Task page is hidden, and a custom page is added to the form. The standard Status and % Complete fields are added to the custom page.

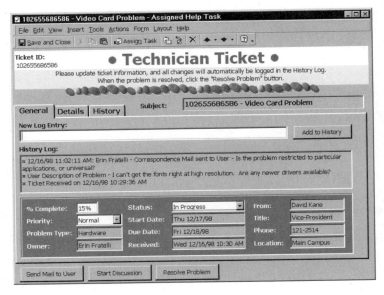

Figure 1.5 *The Assigned Help Task form.*

Folder Applications

Folders in Outlook are generally used for the following purposes:

- To facilitate online discussions about a particular topic, as demonstrated with the Product Ideas folder.

- To store, organize, and share information, as demonstrated with the Classified Ads, Training Management, and Web Sites folders.

- To record and track information that is constantly updated, as demonstrated with the Help Desk, Time Card, and Northwind Contact Management applications.

Folders Based on Built-in Modules

With built-in modules such as Appointments, Tasks, and Contacts, instant workgroup solutions can be created simply by creating a folder in public folders. The folder can then be modified for the specific purpose of your workgroup or organization. Here are a few ideas for the types of applications you can build based on built-in module folders:

Beta Contacts folder   With the Beta Contacts folder, managers can post contacts for a beta testing program. The Beta Contacts folder, as shown in Figure 1.6, is based on the built-in Contacts module.

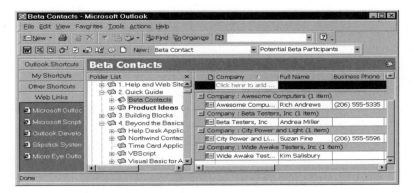

Figure 1.6 *The Beta Contacts folder based on the built-in Contacts module.*

Shared Calendar Application   You can create a custom Calendar folder in Public Folders, so events relating to a particular group can be easily recorded and shared. For example, you might want to create a shared Calendar that contains events related to the product development cycle so that product announcements, press releases, trade shows, and shipping dates are accessible to the entire workgroup.

Discussion Folders

Most often, Discussion folders serve as a central location for users to submit, share, and respond to ideas and information. Discussion folders feature views with threaded conversations, so users can view the history of responses to a particular item.

Product Ideas folder   The Product Ideas folder makes it possible for users to post and respond to new product ideas. In addition, users can post responses to product idea responses. Responses to a particular item are indented and placed underneath the original item, creating the threaded conversation view.

Training Management folder   The Training Management folder makes it possible for training personnel to post Course Catalog items in the folder, as shown in Figure 1.7. After a Course Catalog item is posted, training personnel can post a Course Offering item as

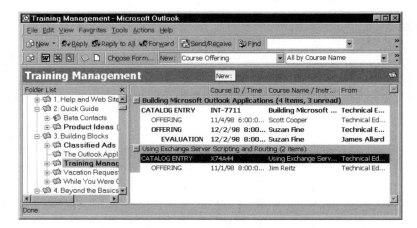

Figure 1.7 *The Training Management folder.*

a response to the Course Catalog item. Users completing a course can post an Evaluation item as a response to the Course Offering item.

Tracking Folders

Tracking folders allow users to record and review information that is constantly updated.

Northwind Customers folder and related activities subfolders   This folder contains Customer items that allow the sales force to keep track of activity involving key customer contacts. Separate subfolders record customer-related activities and use new Outlook 2000 links to tie public folder Appointment, Task, Contact, E-Mail, and Journal items to customer items. See Figure 1.8.

Help Manager Tasks folder   This folder, as shown in Figure 1.9, allows a Help Desk technician or manager to view the status of a Help Desk Request. When a technician changes the status of a task or completes a task, the status is updated in the By Status view in the Tasks folder of the Help Manager mailbox.

Reference Applications

You can store just about any kind of information in a folder, including product specifications, feature proposals, sales reports, software prototypes, employee status reports, Web site addresses, and training materials. With the addition of the new Folder Home Pages feature in Outlook 2000, a folder gains a Web interface, as shown in Figure 1.10. Web views of a folder can be customized with Microsoft Visual InterDev 6.0 or any other Web development tool. You can use Microsoft Site Server to create powerful reference applications that locate information on both your public folders and your corporate intranet.

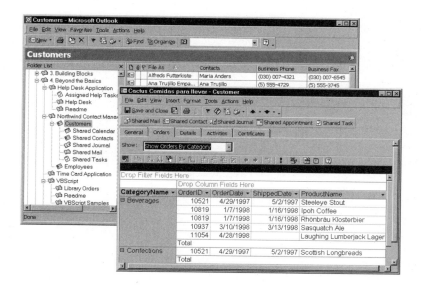

Figure 1.8 *Customer Form with PivotTable List of recent orders in Northwind Customers folder.*

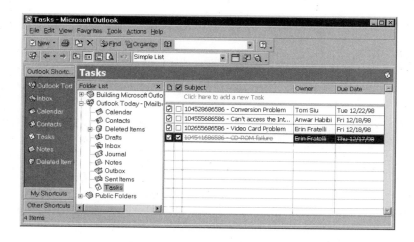

Figure 1.9 *The Tasks folder in the Help Manager mailbox.*

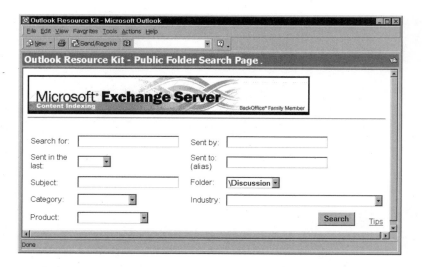

Figure 1.10 *A Folder Home Page powered by Site Server lets users search across multiple Exchange folders.*

Specification Library As development team members work on a project, individuals can store product specifications in a public folder so other members of the team, as well as sales and marketing personnel, can have access to the documents.

Status Reports Managers, as well as employees, may want to store weekly status reports in a public folder for reference at review time.

Web Sites These folders are great for storing Web addresses. Web Site folders can be personal folders for private use or public folders to which the entire workgroup can contribute.

VBScript Samples These folders provide a good medium for collecting communal sample scripts. As shown in Figure 1.11, the VBScript Samples folder contains sample procedures for a variety of commonly performed tasks that can be accomplished using VBScript.

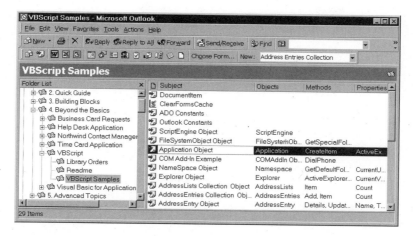

Figure 1.11 *The VBScript Samples folder.*

For More Form and Folder Ideas

For additional information about the types of applications you can create, visit the following Web sites:

http://www.microsoft.com/outlook/

http://technet.microsoft.com/reg/download/exchange/

http://officeupdate.microsoft.com/downloadCatalog/dldoutlook.htm

Chapter 2
Outlook Design Tools

In This Chapter

Microsoft Outlook offers easy-to-use design tools for creating custom forms and folders. For example, in Design mode, Outlook provides an AutoLayout feature that automatically positions controls as you add them to a form. In addition, a Script Editor window is provided in Design mode, so you can use Microsoft Visual Basic Scripting Edition (VBScript) in your forms to control folders, forms, fields, and controls. And when working with Outlook folders, you can create custom views directly in the folder by dragging fields to or from the column heading row. In many cases, you don't even need to open a dialog box to create a view.

I'll also introduce you to some important new programming tools that are available with the appearance of Visual Basic for Applications in Outlook 2000. These tools are available only if you purchase Microsoft Office 2000 Developer. The additional ActiveX controls that ship with Office Developer, and Visual Basic for Applications add-ins such as the Code Librarian make Office Developer well worth the additional cost involved.

In this chapter, you'll get a quick introduction to the tools that you use to design Outlook applications. Along the way, you'll see some of the features that you can use to make designing applications quicker and easier.

Help and Web Sites

In the Building Microsoft Outlook 2000 Applications folder supplied on the CD that comes with this book, you'll find a Help And Web Sites folder, as shown in Figure 2.1. In this folder, you'll find Readme files with information on how you can install Microsoft Outlook Visual Basic Reference Help, in case you didn't install this file while installing Outlook. You can also click an item in the Microsoft Web Sites folder or the Third Party Web Sites folder to open the URL in a separate browser window.

Important If you have not added the Building Microsoft Outlook 2000 Applications folder, see the Introduction of this book for instructions.

To open the Help And Web Sites folder

- Click Folder List on the View menu. Select the Building Microsoft Outlook 2000 Applications folder, and then open Folder 1. Help And Web Sites folder, as shown in Figure 2.1.

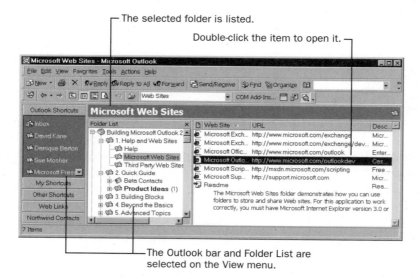

Figure 2.1 *The contents of the Help And Web Sites folder in the Building Microsoft Outlook 2000 Applications folder.*

Here is a quick summary of the contents of the Help And Web Sites folder.

Help folder This folder contains information about Microsoft Outlook Visual Basic Reference Help. Microsoft Outlook Visual Basic Reference Help includes the Outlook Object Model and descriptions of supported Outlook objects, methods, properties, and events. It also provides comprehensive information about supported properties and methods for Microsoft Forms 2.0 controls—the intrinsic controls for Outlook forms development. You'll also find valuable tips and techniques supplied by the Outlook development team.

Microsoft Web Sites folder This folder contains shortcuts you can click to go to the following sites:

- *http://msdn.microsoft.com/scripting/* The Scripting Technologies Web site contains information on hosting scripting with Microsoft Visual Basic Scripting Edition, script control for VBScript, runtime VBScript objects, free downloads, and a script debugger.

- *http://www.microsoft.com/outlookdev/*   The Outlook Developer Forum Web site contains case studies, VBScript samples, form samples, free downloads, training information, and valuable tips and techniques for creating Outlook applications.

- *http://www.microsoft.com/outlook/*   The Microsoft Office Outlook Web site contains templates, converters, add-ins, troubleshooting tips, product and pricing information, a feature matrix, and configuration guides.

- *http://www.microsoft.com/exchange/developers/*   The Microsoft Exchange Developers' Resources Web Site contains valuable tips and techniques for creating Outlook applications on Exchange Server. It offers essential information on Exchange server scripting and routing, public folder applications, Collaboration Data Objects, Outlook Web Access, and Exchange application development in general.

Third Party Web Sites folder   This folder contains shortcuts you can click for third-party Web sites that offer information relating to Outlook and Exchange development. Microsoft is not responsible for the content or the availability of these sites. However, these sites contain additional information that will be useful to you when you develop applications with Microsoft Outlook.

To visit a Web site

1. In the Folder List, open the appropriate Web Sites folder.
2. Double-click an item in the folder to go to the Web site you want.

Note Use Microsoft Outlook 2000 Web Views to browse Web pages directly within Outlook without launching your Web browser. Figure 2.2 shows the Microsoft Office Web page displayed in an Outlook Web view. You can view Web pages directly in the Outlook window. Click on sites listed on your Favorites menu, or create shortcuts to Web pages that you visit frequently and add them to your Outlook Bar.

To open a Web page directly in Outlook

1. Click the View menu, select the Toolbars command, and then click Web on the Toolbars submenu.
2. Type the URL for the Web page in the Address box of the Web toolbar.
3. Press the Enter key.

To add a page opened in a Web View to your Outlook Bar

1. Use the steps outlined above to display a Web page in Outlook.
2. Right-click in the gray area of the Outlook Bar. Do not right-click on an Outlook Bar shortcut.

Use the Web toolbar to navigate to a URL.

Web Views display HTML directly in Outlook.

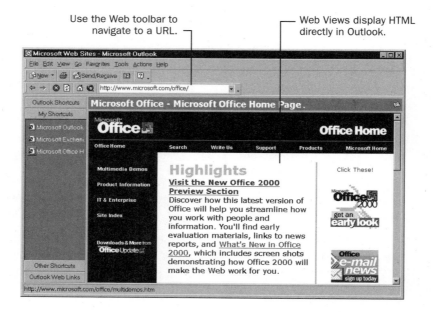

Figure 2.2 *The Microsoft Office Home Page displayed directly in Outlook.*

3. Select the Outlook Bar Shortcut To Web Page command. Outlook will place an Outlook Bar shortcut for the active Web page in the My Shortcuts group on your Outlook Bar.

4. If you want to rename the shortcut, right-click the Shortcut icon and click the Rename Shortcut command.

Outlook Form Design Mode

The ability to customize and create forms is built directly into Outlook, so opening a form in Design mode is as easy as opening a new form, choosing Forms on the Tools menu, and then clicking Design This Form. When the form is in Design mode, the Form Design toolbar and the Field Chooser appear. As shown in Figure 2.3, you can add fields and controls to the form by dragging the fields from the Field Chooser to the form. When you add a field to a form using the Field Chooser, Outlook automatically creates a control and a label for the field and binds the control to the field. With the Outlook AutoLayout feature, the controls are automatically aligned with existing controls on the form. To enter Run mode, you click Run This Form on the Form menu. In this way, you can easily switch back and forth between Design and Run mode to check the layout of a form at run time.

When the form is in Design mode, the
Outlook Form Design toolbar appears.

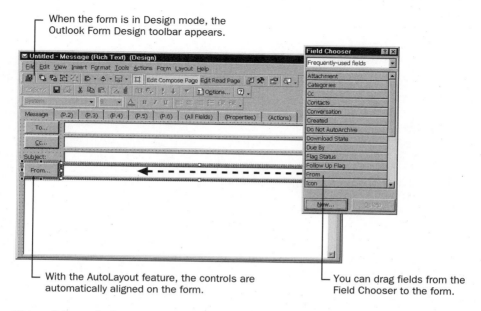

With the AutoLayout feature, the controls are
automatically aligned on the form.

You can drag fields from the
Field Chooser to the form.

Figure 2.3 *Outlook Design mode tools.*

To view an Outlook form in Design mode

1. On the Outlook Actions menu, click New Mail Message, or click the New Mail Message icon on the Standard toolbar. You may also select a form, such as Appointment, which most closely resembles your end application.

2. On the form Tools menu, choose Forms and then click Design This Form.

Note Message and Discussion/Post forms are fully customizable. While Office Document forms can't be directly modified, you can add VBScript code to the form's Inspector and VBA code to the Office document itself. See E-Chapter 1, "The Time Card Application," in the E-Chapters folder on the companion CD for an example of VBA code behind an Office document in an Outlook application. You can customize Task, Distribution List, Appointment, and Journal forms by adding additional pages to the forms, but the existing built-in pages cannot be modified. This constraint also applies to the Contact form, but you can modify the first page of a Contact form. See Chapter 5, "Forms," for more information.

Here are just a few advantages of developing forms using Outlook design capabilities.

Outlook forms are fully 32-bit forms   so they're fast, and perhaps equally important, they're small, averaging about 1 KB. Attachments and shortcuts add to the average size of the form.

Outlook forms are interpreted so they're easy for designers to keep track of and update. With Outlook forms, designers don't need to worry about searching through folders or directories to find uncompiled source files to make changes to a form.

In Design mode, an Outlook form provides a grid and a variety of alignment tools, including AutoLayout, to make sure your forms have a professional appearance.

Properties Dialog Box

To set properties for controls and fields that you add to forms, you use the Properties dialog box, which is accessible while Outlook is in Design mode, as shown in Figure 2.4.

To view the Properties dialog box

- With the form in Design mode, right-click an existing control on the form. For this example, you can right-click the Subject control, and then click Properties on the shortcut menu.

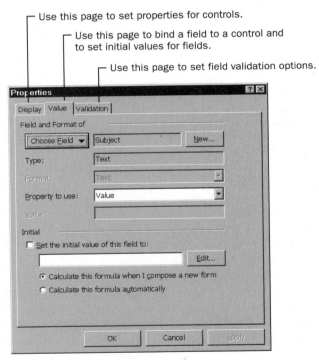

Figure 2.4 *The Properties dialog box available in Design mode.*

Advanced Properties Dialog Box

With the Advanced Properties dialog box, you can set properties for controls. As shown in Figure 2.5, the Advanced Properties dialog box is used to set the ControlTipText property for a control.

To view the Advanced Properties dialog box

- With the form in Design mode, right-click an existing control (the Subject control in this example), and then click Advanced Properties on the shortcut menu.

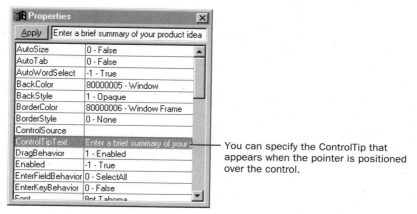

You can specify the ControlTip that appears when the pointer is positioned over the control.

Figure 2.5 *The Advanced Properties dialog box available in Design mode.*

More Info For more information about using the Properties dialog box or the Advanced Properties dialog box, see Chapter 6, "Controls, Fields, and Properties."

The Visual Basic Expression Service

Using the Visual Basic Expression Service provided in Outlook, you can create validation criteria for fields, you can create formulas to calculate field values, and you can create formulas that combine text strings in a field.

To explore this capability using the Business Card Request form, open the form in Design mode.

To open the Business Card Request form in Design mode

1. In the Folder List, select the Business Card Request folder under 4. Beyond The Basics.

2. On the Actions menu, select New Business Card Request.

3. To get into Design mode, select Forms on the Tools menu, and then click Design This Form.

To open the Visual Basic Expression Service

1. With the form in Design mode, right-click an existing control (in this example, the CardAddress control), and then click Properties on the shortcut menu.

2. Click the Value tab, and then click Edit.

As shown in Figure 2.6, the Visual Basic Expression Service is used to create a formula for a field in the Business Card Request form.

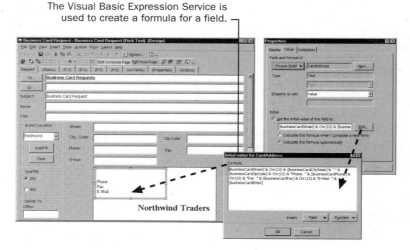

Figure 2.6 *With the Visual Basic Expression Service, you can create formulas for fields.*

With the Visual Basic Expression Service, you can:

- **Validate fields** You can create validation formulas to ensure that a specific value or a value range is entered in a field, or to ensure that a field value is not exceeded.

- **Create formulas for calculating values in fields** For example, you can create a formula for a Total field that multiplies hours by hourly rate.

- **Create Combination fields** You can create formulas that combine field values and text fragments together or you can create combination fields that show the value of the first non-empty field in the item.

More Info For more information about the Visual Basic Expression Service, see Chapter 6, "Controls, Fields, and Properties."

Script Editor and VBScript

With the Script Editor, available in Design mode, you can program Outlook forms using VBScript. VBScript is a subset of the Visual Basic language and is designed to be a small, lightweight interpreted language. Using VBScript, the Outlook 2000 Object Model, and the Forms 2.0 Object Library you can accomplish a wide variety of programming tasks. For example, you can set the current form page when the form opens in Compose mode. Or you can create a procedure that automatically sends a notification message to a distribution list when a new item is posted in a folder.

To view the Script Editor

- With the form in Design mode, click View Code on the Form menu.

The Script Editor has templates for all the item events. To add an event template to your script in the Script Editor, click Event Handler on the Script menu, click an event name in the list, and then click Add. The appropriate Sub...End Sub or Function...End Function statement is inserted. As shown in Figure 2.7, the *Item_Open* function is added to the Script Editor window for the Business Card Request form, and code is added to the event to hide the Status page of the form when the form is in Compose mode. This code also resolves the hard-coded Business Card Requests recipient address and displays a critical error message box if the address cannot be resolved.

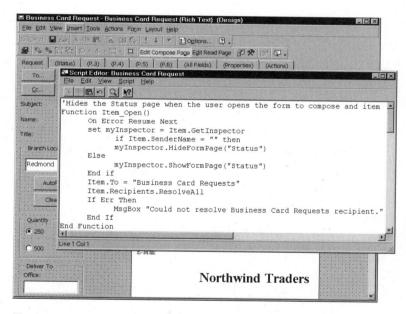

Figure 2.7 *The Script Editor window shows the* Item_Open *function.*

More Info For more information about using VBScript, see Chapter 11, "Using VBA and VBScript with Outlook."

Folder View Design Tools

With Outlook, you can create custom views by adding, removing, and rearranging fields in the Column Heading row of the folder. For example, you can create a column by dragging a field from the Field Chooser to the Column Heading row.

To add or remove a column using the Field Chooser

1. Select a folder on the Folder List. Click Toolbars on the View menu, and then click Advanced.

2. Select Field Chooser from the Advanced toolbar.

3. Drag the field you want to add as the new column to the Column Heading row, as shown in Figure 2.8. Use the double-arrow marker to position the new column heading in the Column Heading row.

4. To remove the column heading, drag the column heading you added away from the Column Heading row until an X appears, and then release the mouse button.

As shown in Figure 2.8, the Business Phone 2 column is created by dragging the Business Phone 2 field from the Field Chooser to the Column Heading row.

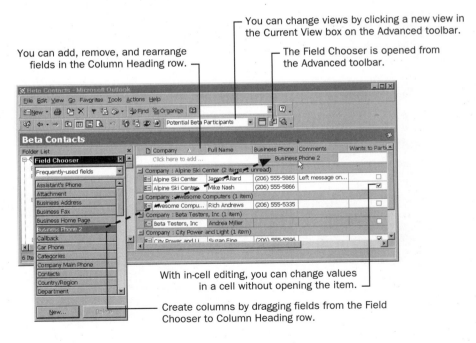

Figure 2.8 *The Beta Contacts folder and the Field Chooser.*

Drag and Drop Grouping   You can group items in a folder by a particular field simply by dragging the field you want to group by above the Column Heading row. On the Advanced toolbar, click the Group By icon. Click and drag a field from the Field Chooser to the area above the Column Heading row. You cannot group or sort by combination or formula fields.

Format Columns   The ability to format columns gives you great flexibility in designing views. For example, in many cases, you want the column label to be different than the name of the field the column is based on. To format a column, right-click the column heading, and then click Format Columns on the shortcut menu. You can then choose the options you want.

In-Cell editing   When the in-cell editing option is turned on for a folder, users can edit and enter information in cells within the folder without opening a form. For example, in the Beta Contacts folder, as shown earlier in Figure 2.8, users can click in a Wants To Participate cell on the far right to add or remove a check box icon in the cell. To activate in-cell editing, select Current View on the View menu, and then click Customize Current View. Click Other Settings, and then choose the Allow In-Cell Editing check box in the Rows box.

Best Fit feature   This feature automatically arranges the column size to fit the text in the column heading label. To choose the Best Fit option for a column, right-click the column heading, and then click Best Fit on the shortcut menu.

Show Only Custom Views   Quite often, users are confused by the large number of views available in a folder. To alleviate this problem, Outlook makes it possible to show only the custom views created for the folder. To select this option, select Current View on the View menu, and then click Define Views. Then select the Only Show Views Created For This Folder check box.

Folder Properties Dialog Box

With the folder Properties dialog box, as shown in Figure 2.9, you define folder attributes and behavior. For example, you can define who can access the folder and the functions they can perform, and you can create rules that automatically process items as they arrive in a folder.

To view the folder Properties dialog box

Right-click the folder, and then click Properties on the shortcut menu.

Note   To view all available Properties dialog box pages for a folder, the folder must be located in your Mailbox or in a public folder where you have owner permissions. Also note that the Outlook Address Book page is only available for contact-type folders.

More Info   For more information about designing folders or designing folder views, see Chapter 8, "Folders" and Chapter 14, "Customizing Folder Home Pages."

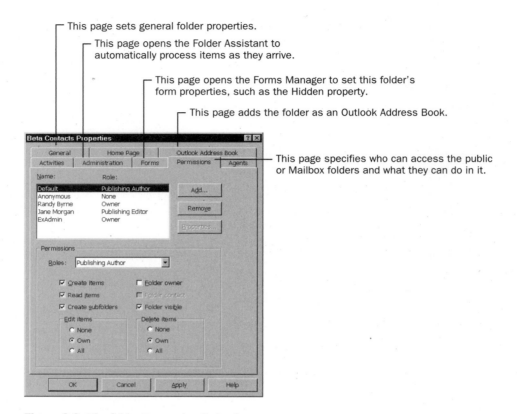

This page sets general folder properties.

This page opens the Folder Assistant to automatically process items as they arrive.

This page opens the Forms Manager to set this folder's form properties, such as the Hidden property.

This page adds the folder as an Outlook Address Book.

This page specifies who can access the public or Mailbox folders and what they can do in it.

Figure 2.9 *The folder Properties dialog box.*

Outlook Visual Basic for Applications Design Tools

In case you were marooned on a desert island and didn't hear the news, the most important design tool addition to Outlook 2000 is Visual Basic for Applications. VBA brings many features to the design environment of Outlook, including the ability to display UserForms, create custom command bars for the Outlook Inspector and Explorer windows, and write code in standard and class modules. I want to emphasize that Outlook VBA does not replace the design tools used in Outlook forms development. You cannot use VBA to program Outlook forms directly. However, VBA provides you with the ability to design new features in the Outlook application environment and to customize the Outlook experience for yourself and your users. Corporate users will prototype COM Add-ins, a new ActiveX component that replaces obsolescent Exchange Client Extensions, using Outlook VBA code and design tools.

Visual Basic Editor

The Visual Basic Editor gives you an integrated design environment for writing and debugging your code. You can now enjoy the same feature-rich editor that users of other Office applications such as Word and Excel have used for quite some time. We'll tour some of the important VBA features in this chapter. In later chapters, I'll drill down into the addition of new objects, properties, and events in the Outlook 2000 object model.

To open the Visual Basic for Applications Editor window

1. On the Explorer or the Inspector Tools menu, click Macro.
2. Click the Visual Basic Editor command. You can also press Alt+F11 to open the VBA Editor window as shown in Figure 2.10.

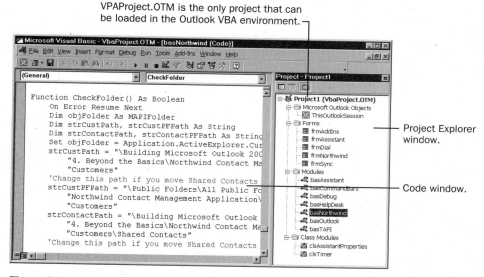

Figure 2.10 *The Outlook Visual Basic Editor window.*

Auto List Members and Context-Sensitive Help

When you write code in a code window, you can use the Auto List feature to display the properties and methods of objects as you type your code in the code window. Auto List Members enhances your productivity and cuts down on the tedium of debugging typing errors. When you place the cursor under a Visual Basic keyword or an object type, property, or method and press the F1 key, you'll see context-sensitive help. Figure 2.11 illustrates the pop-up Auto List window that appears after you type the dot operator. It also shows help in the new HTML-based format used by all Office 2000 applications.

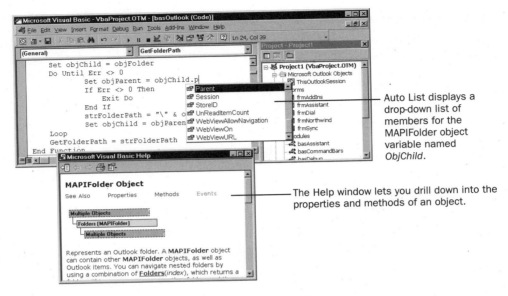

Auto List displays a drop-down list of members for the MAPIFolder object variable named *ObjChild*.

The Help window lets you drill down into the properties and methods of an object.

Figure 2.11 *Auto List Members saves on typing and reduces errors.*

The Object Browser

Unlike the VBScript code environment, where all variables are Variants by default, Outlook VBA encourages you to declare strongly typed variables. Early binding of these variables speeds up the execution of your code. You can use the Tools References command to set references to other object libraries such as ActiveX Data Objects so that you can use those libraries in your code. The Visual Basic Object Browser helps you add additional object libraries to your project and lets you quickly find class members and their properties, methods, and events.

To open the Visual Basic for Applications Object Browser

1.   On the Visual Basic View menu, click Object Browser.

2.   Select the object library that you want to browse in the Object/Library drop-down list.

UserForms

Visual Basic UserForms provide dialog boxes in the Outlook application environment. The intrinsic controls that you place on UserForms are the same as the Forms 2.0 controls used with Outlook custom forms. In Outlook VBA, all the properties, methods, and events of the control are exposed when the controls are placed on a UserForm. No longer are you limited to just the click event of Forms 2.0 controls on an Outlook form. You can also place extrinsic ActiveX controls on your UserForm. Figure 2.12 depicts a UserForm that uses the Outlook View control, a new ActiveX control that ships with the Microsoft Team Folder Wizard. The versatile View control lets you display views on forms or HTML pages.

➲ **To add a Userform to your Outlook VBA Project**

1. On the Visual Basic Insert menu, click UserForm.
2. On the Visual Basic View menu, click Toolbox.
3. Drag and drop controls from the Control Toolbox onto the UserForm.
4. Select the control on the UserForm and press F4 to display the Properties window.
5. Set UserForm and control properties in the Properties window.

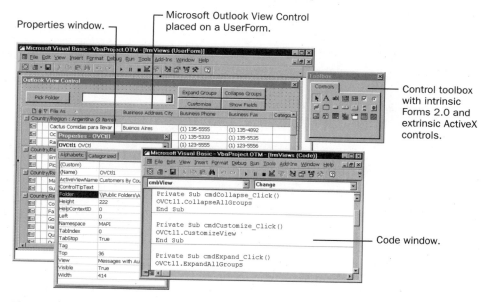

Figure 2.12 *VBA UserForms and ActiveX controls let you create complex Application dialog boxes.*

Command Bars

Although you might not think of command bars as design tools, they are essential to the design of a custom user interface for Outlook. Command bars are now completely programmable in both the Explorer and Inspector windows. You can program an Outlook command bar to display built-in or custom dialogs, launch other applications, or open custom forms. Figure 2.13 shows two custom command bars in the Outlook Explorer window. The New Call dialog that you see in Figure 2.13 appears when a user clicks the Dial Phone command bar button on the Create Shared Items toolbar. We'll examine both of these command bars in detail in subsequent chapters.

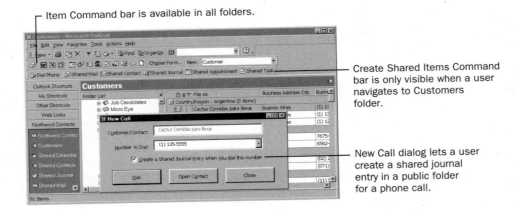

Figure 2.13 *Command bars are an essential element of custom application design.*

Outlook Bar

Like command bars, the Outlook Bar is also completely programmable in Outlook 2000. While not a design tool per se, you should think of the Outlook Bar as a design element when you create a custom application. Outlook Bar shortcuts can go to a URL, open a file on a local or networked drive, or launch an application. Figure 2.13 shows a custom Outlook Bar group that works in conjunction with the displayed Customers folder.

Add-Ins and Other Design Tools

Microsoft Office Developer

We've just covered some of the basic design tools in Outlook Visual Basic for Applications. Since Visual Basic for Applications supports an add-in extensibility model, there are add-ins available for the VBA environment that provide you with additional tools to complete your application design quickly and effectively. VBA add-in design tools are available from Microsoft or from third-party vendors. Microsoft offers its add-in design tools in a special version of Microsoft Office 2000 known as Microsoft Office Developer. You might also see Microsoft Office Developer referred to by its acronyms, MOD or ODE. Figure 2.14 shows the Code Librarian database window and a procedure named *LinkExchangeFolder* that creates an Access table linked to the Outlook Contacts folder.

The following add-ins are available when you install Office Developer:

- Code Librarian
- Code Commentor
- Error Handler
- Multi-code Import/Export
- Package and Deployment Wizard

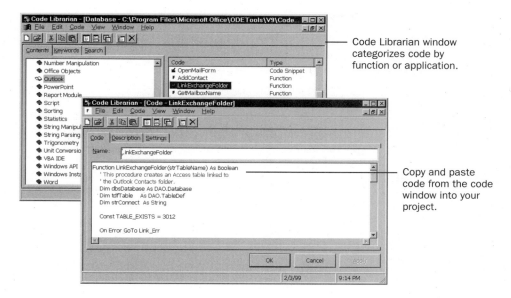

Figure 2.14 *The Code Librarian add-in contains VBA procedures for use in Outlook and other Office applications.*

- Source Code Control
- String Editor
- Win API Viewer

Office Developer also includes several extrinsic ActiveX controls that you can add to your Outlook forms and distribute with your solution. Noteworthy is the DTPicker control that duplicates the functionality of the drop-down calendar control on Outlook appointment and task items.

Microsoft Visual Studio

Discussion of Outlook design tools now must include Microsoft Visual Studio in addition to the Office Developer product. Outlook's development stage has expanded to such an extent that you should now consider Microsoft Visual Studio 6.0 or later as part of your Outlook development toolbox. The table below illustrates how you gain additional design resources when you obtain Visual Studio.

Function	Visual Studio Component
Author custom ActiveX controls for use on Outlook forms	Visual Basic 6.0
Create COM Add-ins that replace Exchange Client Extensions	Visual Basic 6.0
Create ASP pages and write VBScript to enhance and extend Team Folder Home Pages.	Visual InterDev 6.0
Debug Exchange Server Scripting Agents with Microsoft Script Editor	Visual InterDev 6.0
Develop DHTML applications that serve as Folder Home Page	Visual Basic 6.0

Part II
Quick Guide to Building Applications

Chapter 3, "Customize Built-In Modules," shows you how to create instant groupware applications by modifying the built-in Contacts application, customizing it for tracking customer correspondence related to a beta program, and then copying it to public folders on Microsoft Exchange Server. Chapter 4, "Design a Custom Application," shows you how to build a Discussion application called Product Ideas that makes it possible for users to submit, read, and respond to new product ideas.

Chapter 3
Customize Built-In Modules

In This Chapter

As a desktop information manager, Outlook provides built-in personal management tools such as Calendar, Tasks, Contacts, and Journal that can significantly increase user productivity. While these modules work great for individual use, their value is dramatically increased when they're located in an Exchange public folder because they allow users to share calendars, schedules, task lists, and customer information among workgroups or across the organization. In fact, with the built-in modules in Outlook, creating groupware is as simple as creating a module in public folders.

> **Note** The examples in this book, and in the companion CD-ROM, require Microsoft Exchange to create and access public folders.

This chapter is designed to show you how to easily customize built-in Outlook modules to suit the needs of your workgroup or organization. You will learn how to transform the Contacts module into a groupware application that allows users to record, share, and track the history of customer correspondence. When you're finished with this chapter, you should have a better understanding of both the limits and possibilities of customizing built-in modules. Perhaps equally important, you should have a whole new set of ideas about the kinds of applications you can create using these modules as a starting point. Here are a few ideas:

Calendar can be created in public folders and used to post, share, and update schedules for activities such as training classes, sporting events, and company functions. For a product launch, you might want to post milestone events such as trade shows, press tours, and the product ship date to the Calendar folder.

Tasks can be created in public folders and used to post and track the tasks completed by each member of a project team. For example, the Tasks folder can be used to delegate responsibilities to a staff of temporary workers or to track workgroup members' hours, billing information, and mileage.

Contacts can be created in public folders and used to post contact names, phone numbers, addresses, and company information that can then be shared by a workgroup. With Contacts, users can post and track correspondence with sales contacts, potential customers, vendors, contractors, and coworkers.

Distribution Lists can be created in either the Contacts folder of a user's mailbox or in a public folder that contains Contact items. A distribution list can contain multiple recipients, and is used to send messages to all members of the list. Outlook 2000 Distribution List items are meant to replace distribution lists maintained in the Personal Address Book.

Journal can be created in public folders and used to log and track information such as the amount of time an individual or workgroup spends on a particular task, on a project, or with a specific customer.

Note For the Notes module, you can add custom views to the folder, but you cannot modify the built-in form.

Overview of the Folder You Create

The Contacts module is designed primarily for individuals to keep track of their personal contacts. As such, it offers a built-in Contact form and a variety of views, including an Address Cards view, a Phone List view, and a By Company view. In this chapter, you transform the Contacts module into the Beta Contacts application, shown in Figure 3.1.

In this chapter, you also transform the Contacts module into a groupware application that is used to track correspondence with participants in a beta software program. (For those of you not involved in the software industry, most software companies send early copies of their software to their preferred customers for early testing and feedback. This process, known as beta testing, usually involves close communication between the people running the beta program and the beta participants.)

To build the Beta Contacts application based on the Contacts module, you first create a new Contacts folder in public folders. Then you rename the folder and add custom views

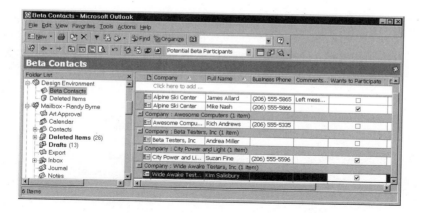

Figure 3.1 *The Beta Contacts folder you can create.*

to it. Next, you modify the built-in Contacts form. Finally, you set permissions on the folder so only those individuals involved in the beta program can have access to it.

The Beta Contacts folder   This folder is based on the built-in Contacts module. The Beta Contacts folder is created in public folders so that the information in the folder can be shared among members of a workgroup. In this chapter, you first create the Design Environment folder so you have a place for creating and testing applications, as shown in Figure 3.2.

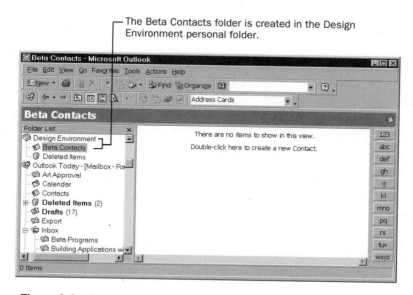

Figure 3.2 *The Beta Contacts folder is created in the Design Environment personal folder (.pst) file.*

The Potential Beta Participants view   As part of the customization process, you create a Potential Beta Participants view. This view groups contacts by company and enables users of the Beta Contacts application to select a check box in a column to specify that the contact wants to participate in the beta program. The Potential Beta Participants view is shown in Figure 3.3.

The Potential Beta Participants
view is applied to the folder.

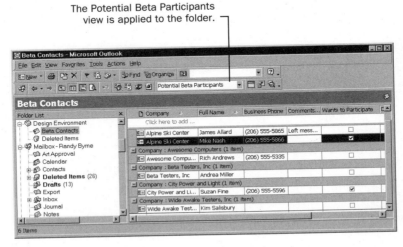

Figure 3.3 *The Beta Contacts folder with the Potential Beta Participants view selected.*

The Beta Participants view   You also add to the Beta Contacts folder a view that uses a filter to show only the contacts that have agreed to participate in the beta program. In addition, you add fields to the Beta Participants view that enable users of the Beta Contacts folder to update and track the status of correspondence either sent to or returned by customers, as shown in Figure 3.4.

The Beta Contacts form   Finally, you customize the form that comes with the Contacts module by adding a page to the form. You then add controls to the page and bind the controls to custom fields that you add to the Beta Contacts folder. Figure 3.5 shows the additional page you design for the Beta Contacts form.

Create New Folders

To start, you create a new personal folder (.pst) file called Design Environment. This is the folder you use throughout this book for creating and testing folders. We recommend you start building your Outlook applications by creating forms and views in a personal folder (.pst) file. After you've tested the forms and views, you can then copy the folder to a public folder, if necessary.

The Beta Participants view
is applied to the folder. ─┐

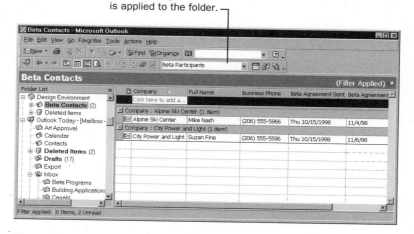

Figure 3.4 *The Beta Contacts folder with the Beta Participants view selected.*

┌─ The Company Profile page is added to the Beta Contact form.

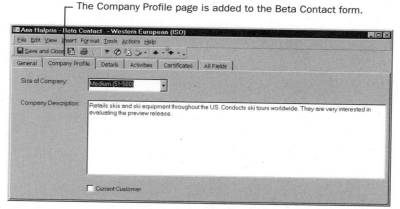

Figure 3.5 *The Beta Contacts form with the Company Profile page selected.*

Create the Design Environment Personal Folder (.pst) File

The Design Environment personal folder (.pst) file you create is a private folder, which means that only you can view its contents. This secure environment is ideal for building applications. A personal folder file can reside on either your local drive or a network drive. In either case, it is always best to back up your Design Environment personal folder file on a regular basis.

To create the Design Environment folder

1.   On the File menu, click New, and then select Personal Folders File (.pst).

2. In the Create Personal Folders dialog box, select a location for the .pst file from the Save In folder drop-down list box. This is the folder in which the .pst file will be stored on the file system.

3. In the File Name text box, type *Design Environment*, and then click Create. This is the name of the .pst file on the file system.

4. The Create Microsoft Personal Folders dialog box opens. In the Name text box, type *Design Environment*, and then click OK. This is the name of the personal folder, as it appears on the Folder List in Outlook.

Create the Beta Contacts Folder

Now you create the Beta Contacts folder as a subfolder of the Design Environment folder. When you create the Beta Contacts folder, you specify that the folder contains Contact items, so the folder automatically inherits the properties and functionality of the built-in Contacts module.

To create the Beta Contacts folder

1. In the Folder List, right-click the Design Environment folder.

2. Click New Folder.

3. In the Name text box, type *Beta Contacts*.

4. In the Folder Contains drop-down list box, select Contact Items.

    When you click Contact Items, the folder automatically takes on the characteristics of the Contacts module.

5. Click OK.

6. If a prompt appears, select your choice in the Add Shortcut To Outlook Bar dialog box.

7. Right-click the Beta Contacts folder, and then click Properties.

8. In the Description text box, type the following:

    This folder contains beta program contacts. It also contains beta program status that shows whether the company is a beta customer, and whether they have returned their beta material.

Create Custom Views

With Outlook, you can create custom views to organize and show information in the folder so users can easily find the information they want. For the Beta Contacts folder, you create two views:

The Potential Beta Participants view lets users keep track of those people who agree over the telephone to participate in the beta program.

The Beta Participants view   lets users view only those contacts who have agreed to participate in the beta program.

Create the Potential Beta Participants View

Let's assume that you and a few others in your workgroup are responsible for contacting a list of companies to see if they want to participate in the beta program. To keep track of who agrees to participate, you can create the Potential Beta Participants view. To create this view, you add user-defined fields to the Beta Contacts folder. Once you create these fields, you build a view with columns based on these fields.

To create the Potential Beta Participants view

1. In the Folder List, click the Beta Contacts folder in the Design Environment folder.
2. On the View menu, select Current View, and then click Define Views.
3. In the Define Views For "Beta Contacts" dialog box, click By Company, and then click Copy.

    In this case, you save time by creating the new view based on the existing By Company view.
4. In the Name Of New View text box, type *Potential Beta Participants*.
5. Click This Folder, Visible To Everyone, and then click OK.
6. In the View Summary box, click OK.
7. In the Define Views For "Beta Contacts" list box, click Apply View.

Remove Fields

Many of the fields in the By Company view aren't necessary for the Potential Beta Participants view, so you can remove them by dragging them from the Column Heading row.

To remove fields

*   Drag the following column headings away from the Column Heading row until an X appears through the column heading, and then release the mouse button.
    *   Attachment (shown as a paper clip in the column heading)
    *   Job Title
    *   File As
    *   Department
    *   Business Fax
    *   Home Phone
    *   Mobile Phone
    *   Categories

Add New Fields

Next you add the Wants To Participate, Does Not Want To Participate, and Primary Contact fields to the view.

To add new fields

1. Right-click anywhere in the Column Heading row, click Field Chooser, and then click New.

2. In the Name text box, type *Wants to Participate*.

3. In the Type drop-down list box, click Yes/No, and then click OK.

4. Click New.

5. In the Name text box, type *Does Not Want to Participate*.

6. In the Type drop-down list box, click Yes/No, and then click OK.

7. Repeat steps 4, 5, and 6 to add the Primary Contact field, but in step 5, type *Primary Contact* in the Name text box. Make sure you choose a Yes/No type field.

8. Repeat steps 4 through 6 to add the Comments Or Issues field, but in step 5, type *Comments or Issues* in the Name box. Make sure you choose a Text type field.

Change the Order of the Company and Full Name Columns

With Outlook, you can change the order of column headings by dragging them to new locations.

To drag the Company column heading

- Drag the Company column heading, as shown in Figure 3.6, until a red double-arrow marker appears over the border where you want to place the column.

Add the Column Headings to the Column Heading Row

To add column headings, you drag the fields you created earlier from the Field Chooser to the Column Heading row.

To drag the fields to the Column Heading row

1. From the Field Set drop-down list box on the Field Chooser, select User-Defined Fields In Folder.

2. Drag the Comments Or Issues field from the Field Chooser to the Column Heading row and position it to the right of the Business Phone column heading. The red double-arrow marker shows you where the new column heading will be inserted in the Column Heading row.

3. Drag the Wants To Participate field from the Field Chooser to the Column Heading row and position it to the right of the Comments Or Issues column heading.

The Company column heading is dragged to a new location in the Column Heading row.

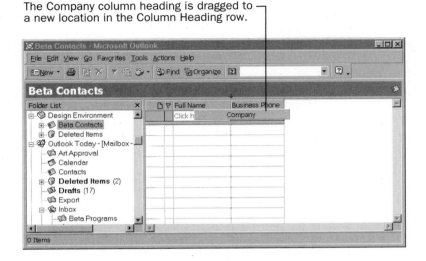

Figure 3.6 *The Company column is placed in front of the Full Name column.*

4. Drag the Does Not Want To Participate field from the Field Chooser to the Column Heading row and position it to the right of the Wants To Participate column heading.

5. Drag the Primary Contact field from the Field Chooser to the Column Heading row and position it to the right of the Does Not Want To Participate column heading.

Adjust the Column Widths to Best Fit

To resize columns, you can right-click the column heading, and then click Best Fit.

To adjust the column widths

1. Right-click the Comments Or Issues column heading, and then click Best Fit.

2. Repeat for the Wants To Participate, Does Not Want To Participate, and Primary Contact column headings.

The view should now look similar to the view shown in Figure 3.7.

Create the Beta Participants View

Next, you create a view that shows only the people who are primary contacts and who have agreed to participate in the beta program. This view enables folder users to track what has been sent by beta coordinators and returned by beta participants. For example, once a contact agrees to participate in the beta program, you send him a beta agreement to read and sign. Then, once the beta agreement has been returned, you send him a beta package, complete with the product and necessary feedback forms.

The Current View box is available on the Advanced toolbar.

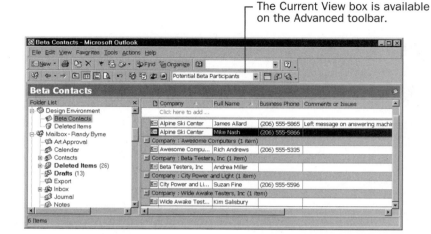

Figure 3.7 *The column widths are adjusted for Best Fit in the Potential Beta Participants view.*

To create the Beta Participants view

1. In the Folder List, click the Beta Contacts folder.
2. On the View menu, choose Current View, and then click Define Views.
3. In the Define Views For Folder "Beta Contacts" list box, click Potential Beta Participants, and then click Copy.
4. In the Name Of New View text box, type *Beta Participants*.
5. Click This Folder, Visible To Everyone, click OK twice, and then click Apply View.

To remove fields from the view

- Drag the following column headings away from the Column Heading row until an X appears through the column heading, and then release the mouse button.
  - Comments Or Issues
  - Wants To Participate
  - Does Not Want To Participate
  - Primary Contact

Add New Fields

Next you add the Beta Agreement Sent, Beta Agreement Returned, and Beta Package Sent fields to the view. The user can enter information directly in these fields without opening the form.

To add new fields

1. On the Outlook Advanced toolbar, click the Field Chooser icon.
2. Click New on the Field Chooser.
3. In the Name text box, type *Beta Agreement Sent*.
4. In the Type drop-down list box, click Date/Time.
5. In the Format field, click a date format, and then click OK.
6. Repeat steps 2 through 5 for both the Beta Agreement Returned and Beta Package Sent fields.
7. Click OK.

Add the Column Headings to the Column Heading Row

Now you add the new fields to the Column Heading row.

To drag the fields to the Column Heading row

1. Drag the Beta Agreement Sent field from the Field Chooser to the Column Heading row and position it to the right of the Business Phone column heading. The double-arrow marker shows you where the new column heading will be inserted in the Column Heading row.
2. Drag the Beta Agreement Returned field from the Field Chooser to the Column Heading row and position it to the right of the Beta Agreement Sent field.
3. Drag the Beta Package Sent field from the Field Chooser to the Column Heading row and position it to the right of the Beta Agreement Sent field.

Adjust the Column Widths to Best Fit

Next, you adjust the column widths for the Beta Agreement Sent, Beta Agreement Returned, and Beta Package Sent column headings.

To adjust the column widths

1. Right-click the Beta Agreement Sent column heading, and then click Best Fit.
2. Repeat for the Beta Agreement Returned and Beta Package Sent column headings.

Your Beta Participants view should now look similar to the view shown in Figure 3.8.

Create a Filter for the Beta Participants View

With a filter, you can create a set of criteria that determines the items that are shown in a view. For the Beta Participants view, you create a filter that displays only items that have a check in the Wants To Participate and Primary Contact fields.

To create a filter

1. On the View menu, select Current View, click Customize Current View, and then click Filter.

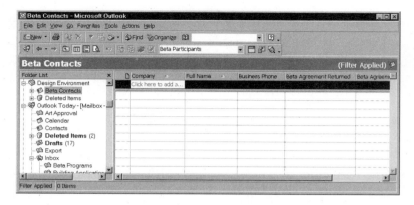

Figure 3.8 *The Beta Participants view.*

2.   In the Filter dialog box, click the Advanced tab.

3.   Click Field, point to User-Defined Fields In Folder, and then select Wants to Participate.

4.   In the Value text box, select Yes from the drop-down list box, and then click Add To List.

5.   Click Field, point to User-Defined Fields In Folder, and then click Primary Contact.

6.   In the Value text box, select Yes from the drop-down list box, and then click Add To List.

7.   Click OK twice.

Create Items for the Beta Contacts Folder

Now let's assume you're ready to call potential beta participants and you want to keep track of those customers who agree to participate and those who do not. You might also want to type the results of your calls, such as "Left message on answering machine," in the Comments field.

Before you create items, you switch to the Potential Beta Participants view. This is the view in which you enter new contacts.

To switch to the Potential Beta Participants view

- On the Outlook Advanced toolbar, select Potential Beta Participants in the Current View drop-down list box.

To create a Beta Contacts item

- In the folder view, click the Click Here To Add A cell in the Company column as shown in Figure 3.9, and then fill in the cells. After you finish typing in an

Click in this row to create a new Beta Contacts item.

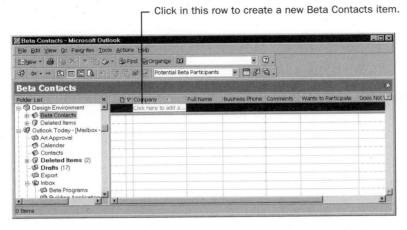

Figure 3.9 *The top row in the view lets you create a new item for the view.*

item, click outside the cell. The item is then added to the folder. The values for the cells are shown in the table below.

Cell Column	Value
Company	*Alpine Ski Center*
Full Name	*James Allard*
Business Phone	*(206) 555-5865*
Comments	*Left message on answering machine 7-10*
Wants To Participate	
Does Not Want To Participate	
Primary Contact	

Now, let's assume you talked to Mike Nash, and he agreed to participate in the program and to be the primary contact for the beta program for Alpine Ski Center.

To create a second Beta Contacts item

- In the folder view, click the Click Here To Add A cell in the Company column, and then fill in the cells with the values shown in the following table.

Cell Column	Value
Company	*Alpine Ski Center*
Full Name	*Mike Nash*
Business Phone	*(206) 555-5866*

(continued)

Cell Column	Value
Comments	
Wants To Participate	X
Does Not Want To Participate	
Primary Contact	X

To keep things interesting, let's create another item.

To create third and fourth Beta Contacts items

- In the folder view, click the Click Here To Add A cell in the Company column, and then fill in the cells with the values shown in the following table.

Cell Column	Value
Company	*Awesome Computers*
Full Name	*Rich Andrews*
Business Phone	*(206) 555-5335*
Comments	
Wants To Participate	
Does Not Want To Participate	X
Primary Contact	

- Here's one more to create.

Cell Column	Value
Company	*City Power and Light*
Full Name	*Suzan Fine*
Business Phone	*(206) 555-5596*
Comments	
Wants To Participate	X
Does Not Want To Participate	
Primary Contact	X

Your view should now look like the view shown in Figure 3.10.

Enter Dates in the Beta Participants View

Now let's assume you want to send beta agreement contracts to those people who agree to participate in the program. To do this, you use the Beta Participants view to enter the date that the beta agreement contracts are sent.

Beta Contact items are added to the folder.

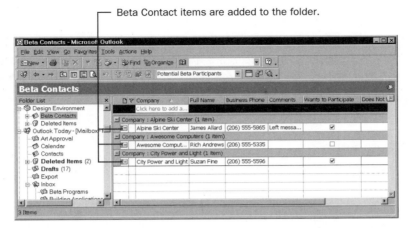

Figure 3.10 *The Potential Beta Participants view with the Beta Contact items.*

→ **To switch to the Beta Participants view**

- On the Outlook Advanced toolbar, click Beta Participants in the Current View drop-down list box.

→ **To enter the Beta Agreement Sent date in the fields**

- Click the Beta Agreement Sent field for Mike Nash and then type the date, as shown in Figure 3.11.

Dates can be entered directly into the cells.

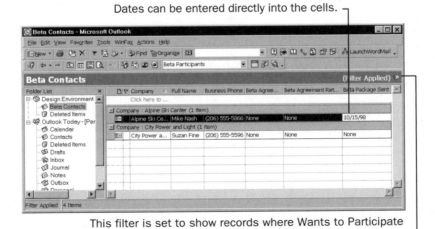

This filter is set to show records where Wants to Participate
and Primary Contact fields' values are checked.

Figure 3.11 *The Beta Participants view with dates entered directly in the Beta Agreement Sent fields.*

Customize the Contacts Form

Up to this point, we've focused on modifying the Beta Contacts application by adding custom views. Now we'll further customize the Beta Contacts application by modifying the built-in Contacts form.

In this example, you add a Company Profile page to the Contacts form, as shown in Figure 3.12.

Open the Contacts Form

To customize a built-in form, first open it as you would to create a new contact. After the form is open, you switch between Design mode and Run mode.

To open the Contacts form in Design mode

1. While in the Beta Contacts folder, click the New Contact icon on the Outlook Standard toolbar.

2. On the Tools menu of the Untitled - Contact window, select Forms, and then click Design This Form.

To switch from Design mode to Run mode

1. On the Form menu, click Run This Form.

2. Close the Run mode window to return to Design mode.

Rename the New Page

The Contacts form provides several additional pages to which you can add controls. Notice that the additional pages are in parentheses; this indicates that the pages are hidden at run time. When you add controls to a page, the parentheses are automatically removed, so the page is visible at run time. For this example, you rename (P.2) to Company Profile.

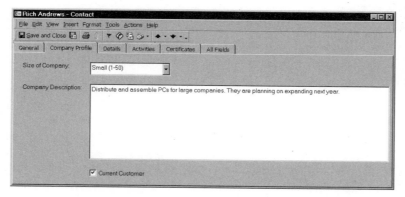

Figure 3.12 *The Company Profile page you add to the Contacts form.*

⊃   **To rename and show the page**

1. In Design mode on the Contacts form, click the (P.2) tab.
2. On the Form menu, click Rename Page.
3. In the Page Name text box, type *Company Profile,* and then click OK.
4. On the Form menu, click Display This Page.

Add Controls to the Form

Now you use the Control Toolbox to add controls to the Company Profile page. After you add a control, you create a new field, and then bind the control to the field. In Outlook, a control is the physical component on the form in which the user enters, views, or clicks values. The field is the storage area in which the values from the controls are saved or loaded.

⊃   **To show the Control Toolbox**

• On the Form Design toolbar, click Control Toolbox.

Add a ComboBox Control

The ComboBox control you add to the Company Profile page allows users to select and view the size of a company, such as Small (1 – 50), Medium (51 – 500), or Large (501 – 1000+).

⊃   **To add the ComboBox control**

• From the Control Toolbox, drag a ComboBox control to the form. Then drag the sizing handle on the right border of the control until the field is approximately the size of the field shown in Figure 3.13.

The Control Toolbox from which you drag controls. ⌐

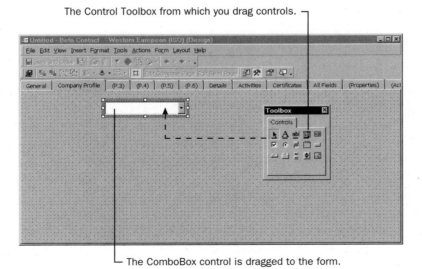

└ The ComboBox control is dragged to the form.

Figure 3.13 *The ComboBox control is added to the Company Profile page.*

Set Properties for the ComboBox Control

When you set properties for the ComboBox control, you create a Size Of Company field. When you create a new field for a control from the Properties dialog box, the field is automatically bound to the control. When a control is bound to a field, the values in the control are saved to the field when an item is composed. When an item is opened in a folder, the values from the fields are loaded into the controls.

To set properties for the ComboBox control

1. Right-click the ComboBox control, click Properties, and then click the Value tab, as shown in Figure 3.14.

2. Click New.

3. In the Name text box, type *Size of Company,* and then click OK.

4. In the List Type drop-down list box, select Droplist.

   With a Droplist ComboBox control, the user must select a value from the list. A Dropdown ComboBox control, on the other hand, allows the user to type in the value or choose from the list. If you intend to group fields (for example, by company size) based on values in a combo box, it's usually best to specify that the combo box is a Droplist so that you can control the values by which you group items in the folder.

5. In the Possible Values text box, type the following:

   Small (1 – 50); Medium (51 – 500); Large (501 – 1000+)

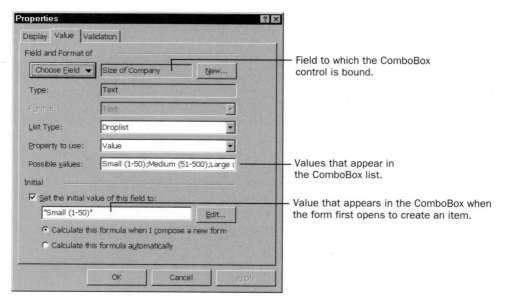

Figure 3.14 *Properties for the ComboBox control.*

6.   Select the Set The Initial Value Of This Field To check box, and in the text box below it, type *"Small (1 – 50)"* and then click OK.

Add a Label for the ComboBox Control

Now you add a label for the ComboBox control to identify the control and to help the user understand the purpose of the control.

To add a label

1.   From the Control Toolbox, drag a Label control to the form.

2.   In the label, select the word Label1 and then type *Size of Company:*, as shown in Figure 3.15.

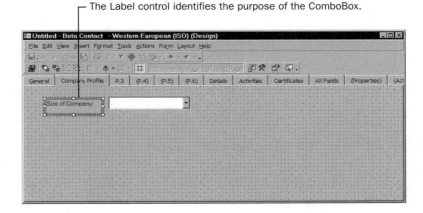

Figure 3.15 *A label is added for the ComboBox control to identify its purpose.*

Add a TextBox Control

Now you add a TextBox control to the Company Profile page. This control allows users to enter and view a company description on the Company Profile page.

To add a TextBox control

•   From the Control Toolbox, drag a TextBox control to the form. Then drag the sizing handle on the right border of the control until the field is approximately the size of the field shown in Figure 3.16.

Set Properties for the TextBox Control

Now you create a Company Description field that is automatically bound to the TextBox control. In addition, you select the Multi-line check box for the control so the user can enter multiple lines of text in it. You also select the Resize With Form check box so the control size is adjusted to the size of the form.

A TextBox control is added to the form.

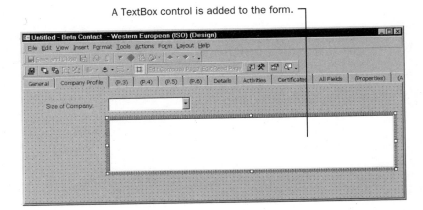

Figure 3.16 *A TextBox control is added to the Company Profile page.*

To set properties for the TextBox control

1. Right-click the TextBox control, click Properties, and then click the Value tab.
2. Click New.
3. In the Name text box, type *Company Description*, and then click OK.
4. Click the Display tab.
5. Select the Resize With Form check box.
6. Select the Multi-Line check box.
7. Click OK.

Add a Label for the TextBox Control

Now you add a label for the TextBox control so users know the purpose of the control.

To add a label

1. From the Control Toolbox, drag a Label control to the form, and position it to the left of the TextBox control.
2. In the label, select the word Label2, and then type *Company Description:*.
3. To resize the label, drag the sizing handle on the right border of the label until all text in the label is visible.

Add a CheckBox Control

Finally, you add a CheckBox control to the form. This control allows users to specify that a company is a current customer.

To add a CheckBox control

1. From the Control Toolbox, drag a CheckBox control to the form.

2.   Click the CheckBox control, and then type *Current Customer*, as shown in Figure 3.17.

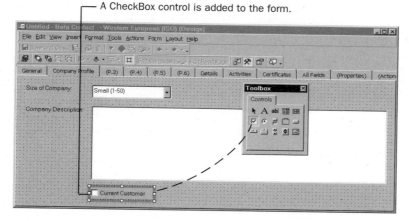

Figure 3.17 *A CheckBox control is added to the Company Profile page.*

Set Properties for the CheckBox Control

Next, you create a Current Customer field to which the CheckBox control is bound.

To create the Current Customer field

1.   Right-click the CheckBox control, and then click Properties.
2.   Click New.
3.   In the Name text box, type *Current Customer*.
4.   In the Type drop-down list box, click Yes/No.
5.   In the Format drop-down list box, click Icon, and then click OK twice.

Set Form Properties

The Properties page of the form shown in Figure 3.18 lets you name the form and specify a contact in case someone has suggestions for improvements or problems with the form.

To set form properties

1.   Click the Properties tab.
2.   In the Version text box, type *1.0*.
3.   In the Form Number text box, type *1.1*.
4.   In the Contact text box, type your name, and in the Description text box type the following:

     Use this form to post, view, and update Beta Contact items in the Beta Contacts folder.

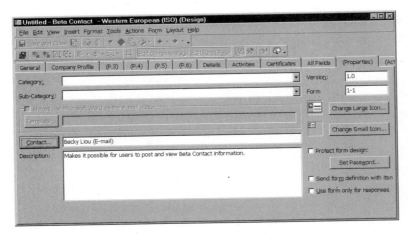

Figure 3.18 *The Properties page of the Beta Contact form.*

More Info For more information about setting form properties, see Chapter 5, "Forms."

Test the Form at Design Time

Before you save a form or publish a form to a folder, it's a good idea to run the form to see how the form layout appears at run time. With Outlook, you can easily switch between Design mode and Run mode for the form.

To switch from Design mode to Run mode

1. With the Compose page in Design mode, click Run This Form on the Form menu. View the Compose page of the form.

2. To test the Read page, send the form to your Inbox. Double-click the item in your Inbox to view the Read page of the form.

3. To return to Design mode, close the Run mode window.

Publish the Form

After you run the form and you're satisfied with its layout, you can publish the form in the Beta Contacts folder. When you publish the form, it is saved and registered in the Beta Contacts folder Form Library. Also, a menu item appears for the form on the Actions menu of the folder.

Forms with the same name, but different contents, may produce unpredictable results. For example, the Beta Contacts form in the Beta Contacts folder (Building Outlook 2000 Applications) and the Beta Contacts form in the Beta Contacts folder (Design Environment) should be identical. If they are not, unique names should be assigned, or the forms should be updated using Forms Manager. For further information, see "The Forms Manager" in Chapter 12, "Distribute and Maintain Applications."

To publish the form to the Beta Contacts folder Form Library

1. On the Tools menu, choose Forms, and then click Publish Form As.

2. In the Display text box and the Form Name text box, type *Beta Contact,* as shown in Figure 3.19.

   If for some reason the Beta Contacts folder is not selected (in the Look In box), click in the Look In drop-down list box and select the Beta Contacts folder.

3. Click Publish.

4. Close the form. When the message box appears, click No for Do You Want To Save Changes? in most cases. Click Yes if you want to save a backup copy to the Beta Contacts folder.

5. Click the Actions menu to verify that the form is published and available for use.

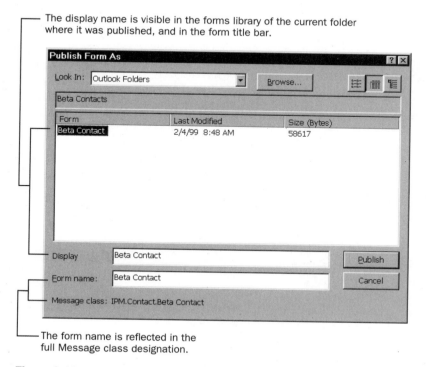

The display name is visible in the forms library of the current folder where it was published, and in the form title bar.

The form name is reflected in the full Message class designation.

Figure 3.19 *The Publish Form As dialog box is automatically filled in for you.*

Specify the Default Form for the Folder

Now that you've created a custom form, you may want to run it to see if it works as expected. However, at this point, there are two possible forms that you can open. One form is the built-in Contacts form that's provided with Outlook. The other is the Beta Contacts form you created. If you click the New Contact button on the Standard toolbar, the built-in Contacts form appears. You must click New Beta Contact on the Outlook Actions menu to open the Beta Contacts form you created.

To avoid this step, make the Beta Contacts form the default form for the folder. Then, when the user clicks the New Contact button, the Beta Contacts form will appear.

To make the Beta Contacts form the default form

1. In the Folder List, right-click the Beta Contacts folder, and then click Properties.
2. Click the General tab.
3. In the When Posting To This Folder, Use list box, click Beta Contacts, and then click OK.

Test the Application

Let's test the Beta Contacts application to make sure the Beta Contact form opens when you click the New Contact button. But first, let's switch to the Potential Beta Participants view.

To select the Potential Beta Participants view

-   In the Current View drop-down list box on the Advanced toolbar, click Potential Beta Participants.

To test the Beta Contact form

1. While in the Beta Contacts folder, click the New Contact button on the Standard toolbar.

    You should see the Beta Contact form with the Company Profile tab.
2. Fill in the form, and then click Save and then Close.

    The new item is posted in the Beta Contacts folder.

More Info For more information about how forms and views work together, see Chapter 8, "Folders."

Delete the Items You Created

Before you make the form available to other users, delete the items you created earlier in this chapter. You do this because the items you created earlier in the chapter without the Beta Contacts form will show in the Contacts form when opened.

To delete the items in the Beta Contacts folder

1. Hold down the Shift key, and then click the items in the Beta Contacts folder.
2. Press the Delete key.
3. Click OK in the message box.

Copy the Folder to Public Folders

Now that you've created forms and views for the Beta Contacts folder, and you've tested the folder to make sure it works as planned, you copy the folder from the Design Environment personal folder (.pst) file to public folders so the folder can be shared by a workgroup or across the entire organization. Before you copy the folder, you might want to check with your administrator to determine the best location for the folder. In addition, you might need to get administrative permission to copy the folder to its destination in Public Folders.

To copy the Beta Contacts folder

1. In the Folder List, click the Beta Contacts folder.
2. On the File menu, point to Folder, and then click Copy Beta Contacts.
3. In the Copy The Selected Folder To The Folder box, click the location you want the folder copied to, such as All Public Folders, and then click OK.

More Info For more information about distributing folders, see Chapter 12, "Distribute and Maintain Applications."

Set Permissions

With Permissions, you define who can open the folder and what functions they can perform in the folder. When you create a folder in Outlook, you are automatically given an Owner role for the folder. This means you have full permissions to create, edit, and delete items in the folder, and you have full permissions to change any folder properties.

When you create a public folder under All Public Folders, the Default role is set to Author. If the public folder is a subfolder of an existing public folder, the Default role is inherited from the Default role in the parent folder. The Author default role assignment means that all users in the Microsoft Exchange Server system are automatically given permissions to create and open items in the folder and to delete and edit their own items. The Author role does not have the ability to create subfolders.

The Anonymous role should be set to None in the Beta Contacts folder. The anonymous role assignment means that users who open public folders through the Outlook Web Access—under the anonymous Internet Information Server Internet guest account—have no access to the Beta Contacts public folder.

For the Beta Contacts folder, you limit access to the folder to only a few users by first setting the Default role to None. You then give a few of your coworkers a Publishing Author role so they can create, edit, and delete items in the folder.

To set permissions for the Beta Contacts folder

1. In the Folder List, right-click the Beta Contacts folder, and then click Properties.

2. Click the Permissions tab. This tab is only available if the folder is an Outlook Mailbox folder or a public folder.

3. In the Name list box, click Default, and then, in the Roles drop-down list box, click None.

   This prevents all users on the Microsoft Exchange Server from opening the folder.

4. Click Add, select several of your coworkers' names from the list, click Add, and then OK.

5. In the Name list box, hold the Ctrl key down and click each name you want to select. In the Role drop-down list box, click Publishing Author.

   The Permissions page should now look similar to the illustration shown in Figure 3.20.

Release the Application

Before you release the application, set the Initial View On Folder property to Potential Beta Participants. This will be the view users first see when they open the Beta Contacts folder.

To set administration properties

1. In the Folder List, right-click the Beta Contacts folder, and then click Properties.

2. Click the Administration tab.

3. In the Initial View On Folder drop-down list box, click Potential Beta Participants, and then click OK.

Now that the folder is ready for use, send a message to your coworkers to notify them that the application is available.

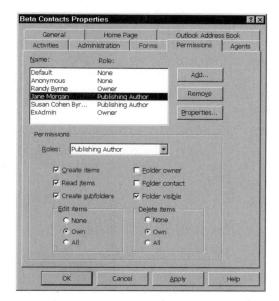

Figure 3.20 *The Permissions page for the Beta Contacts folder in Public Folders.*

What's Next

In this chapter, we covered how to build a groupware application based on a built-in module. With built-in modules, most of the functionality is already defined, so usually all you need to do is make a few modifications to create an application with a specific purpose.

In the next chapter, we'll take a look at building a custom discussion application based on the Post To Folder form supplied with Outlook. Unlike the forms in built-in modules, the Post To Folder form can be completely customized, so you can use it for building a wide range of applications. To begin working with the Post To Folder form, you'll design a Product Ideas application that lets users post, read, and respond to new product ideas in a public folder.

Chapter 4
Design a Custom Application

In This Chapter

The Microsoft Outlook Post form can be used in conjunction with a public folder to build custom discussion applications that let users submit, share, and collaborate on ideas and information. Discussion applications provide a great way to facilitate communication in your organization because they enable users across the enterprise to conduct online conversations. Perhaps equally important, the history of correspondence is saved and organized in a public folder, so important ideas or critical conversations are always available for viewing at a later date. Discussion applications are especially useful for virtual corporations or flexible workgroups where members collaborate on a project, but work different hours or in different locations.

In this chapter, you will build a Product Ideas application that lets users submit, read, and respond to new product ideas in a public folder. This application provides a good example of how a discussion application can be used in your organization both to collect, store, and organize ideas, and to foster enterprise-wide dialogue about subjects that are vital to your company's interests.

By the end of this chapter, you should have the basic skills and concepts you need to build one of the most common types of groupware applications—the discussion application. As a result, you will be able to build a wide variety of new applications to foster communication in your company. In addition, you should also have a working discussion application that you can use as a basis for building other information-sharing applications.

Here are just a few suggestions for the types of discussion applications you can build:

Product Feedback   Allows users to post comments about existing products and features in a public folder. Other users, such as product developers, marketing, or sales personnel, can then respond to existing comment items, thus creating an online discussion. Product planners can review the folder on a periodic basis to get an overall idea of what users like and dislike about a particular product.

Technical Users Group   Serves as a forum for posting issues and problems, as well as solutions to problems. For example, users who are having difficulty with particular tasks can post problems to the Technical Users Group public folder. In turn, another user can post a solution to the problem item, perhaps suggesting an alternative discovered by working on a similar task.

Vendor Services Application   Allows members of your organization to post, respond to, and read reviews of professional services provided by your company's vendors. For example, a supervisor looking for temporary word-processing help can search the folder for a highly recommended vendor who has previously been employed by the company.

Restaurants and Accommodations Application   Allows users to post, read, and respond to restaurant and hotel/motel reviews in a public folder. With this application, your company can quickly develop an online travel guide to help business travelers plan where to eat and stay when they're working away from the office.

Overview of the Product Ideas Application

The Product Ideas application consists of a Product Ideas folder and two forms: the Product Idea form and the Product Idea Response form. Here is an example of how the Product Ideas application might by used by a sports equipment manufacturer to help generate new ideas for products.

Let's assume Peter Krebs in Seattle opens the Product Ideas public folder, and then uses the Product Idea form to post an idea for a wooden kayak construction kit. Suzan Fine in Boston reads the idea, and then uses the Product Idea Response form to post a response asking what kind of wood is best to use. A few minutes later, James Allard reads the items posted by Peter Krebs and Suzan Fine and uses the Product Idea Response form to post a response to Suzan Fine's item. As shown in Figure 4.1, the resulting conversation is stored and organized in the folder.

The Product Category view   As part of the application design process, you add a custom view to the Product Ideas folder that groups items first by Product Category field, then by the Conversation field, as shown in Figure 4.2.

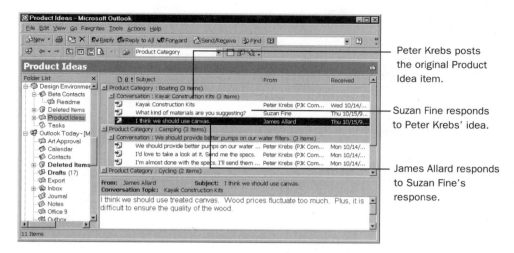

Peter Krebs posts the original Product Idea item.

Suzan Fine responds to Peter Krebs' idea.

James Allard responds to Suzan Fine's response.

Figure 4.1 *The Product Ideas folder.*

Items are grouped by Product Category.

The custom Product Category view is selected in the Current View box, on the Advanced toolbar.

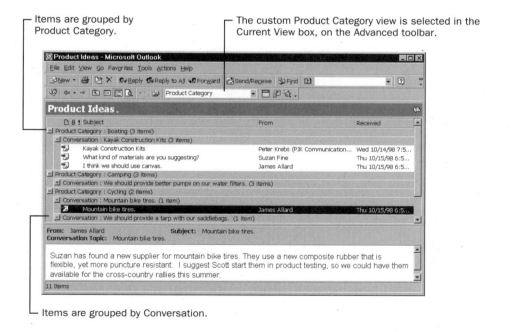

Items are grouped by Conversation.

Figure 4.2 *The Product Category view in the Product Ideas folder.*

The Product Idea form The Product Idea form is a modified Post To Folder form. The New Product Idea form has both a Compose page and a Read page. With the Compose page, as shown in Figure 4.3, the user posts a new item in the Product Ideas folder. With the Read page, the user opens and views a posted item.

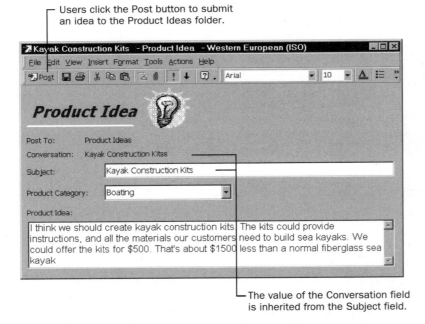

Users click the Post button to submit an idea to the Product Ideas folder.

The value of the Conversation field is inherited from the Subject field.

Figure 4.3 *The Compose page of the Product Idea form.*

The Product Idea Response form The Product Idea Response form, as shown in Figure 4.4, serves two purposes. It lets users post a response to a product idea. It also lets users post a response to the response. We'll take a look at how this is done later in this chapter.

Create the Product Ideas Folder

To get started, you create the Product Ideas folder in the Design Environment personal folder, as shown in Figure 4.5.

If you haven't yet created the Design Environment folder, refer to "Create the Design Environment Personal Folder (.pst) File" in Chapter 3, "Customize Built-In Modules."

To create the Product Ideas folder

1. In the Folder List, right-click the Design Environment folder, and then click New Folder on the shortcut menu.

2. In the Name text box of the Create New Folder dialog box, type *Product Ideas*.

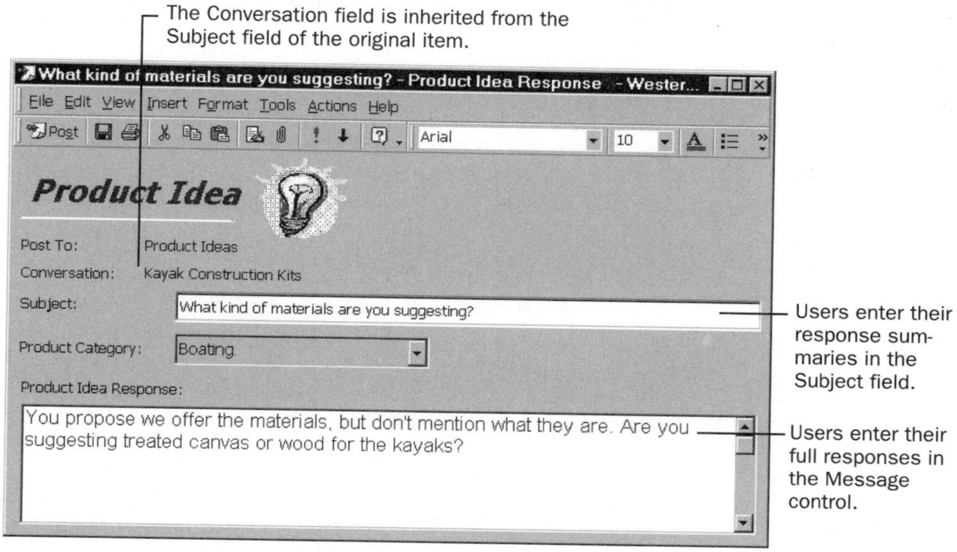

The Conversation field is inherited from the Subject field of the original item.

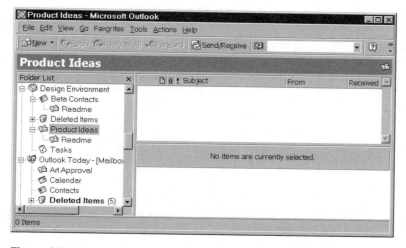

Users enter their response summaries in the Subject field.

Users enter their full responses in the Message control.

Figure 4.4 *The Compose page of the Product Idea Response form.*

Figure 4.5 *The Product Ideas folder is created in the Design Environment personal folder.*

3.   In the Folder Contains list box, click Mail Items.

4.   Choose the Design Environment folder in the Select Where To Place The Folder drop-down list box.

5.   If a prompt appears, click your desired response in the Add A Shortcut To Outlook Bar? message box.

Create the Product Idea Form

The Product Idea form that you create will enable users to post new ideas to the Product Ideas folder. The Product Idea form is based on the standard Outlook Post form. The Outlook Post form supplies most of the required functionality, so all you need to do to build the Product Idea form is add and remove some controls, and then set a few properties for the controls and the form. To design the Product Idea form, you'll modify the Compose page of the Post form, as shown in Figure 4.6.

Open the Post To Folder Form

To build the Product Idea form, you open the Post form in the Product Ideas folder, and then switch to Design mode to modify the form.

To open the Post form in Design mode

1. In the Folder List, click the Product Ideas folder.
2. On the File menu, select New and click Post In This Folder.
3. On the Tools menu of the form, select Forms, and then click Design This Form.

Edit the Compose Page

Most forms consist of two pages—a Compose page for submitting items and a Read page for opening and viewing items. In most cases, the Compose page is slightly different from the Read page. For example, the Compose page has a Post To control that shows where the item is posted, while the Read page has a From control that shows who posted the item.

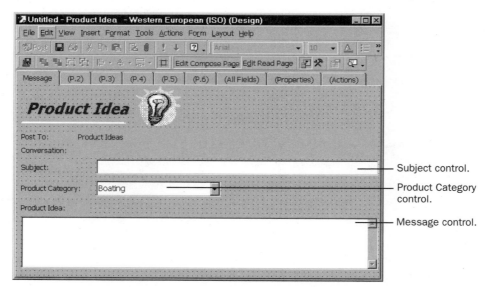

Figure 4.6 *The finished version shows the Compose page of the form in Design mode.*

To edit the Compose page, remove the Categories control, resize the Message control, and then add a Product Category control plus a label, a frame, and an image control to give visual impact to the form. The associated labels for the controls will also be removed.

Remove the Categories Control

For the form you're creating, the Categories control serves no purpose, so you can remove it from the Compose page.

To remove the Categories control and its label

- Click the Categories control, and then press Delete.

Adjust the Message Control

Now move the Message control and resize it to make room for the Product Category control that you add to the form.

To adjust the Message control

1. Drag the Message control bottom border until it resizes to fill to nearly the bottom of the Compose page.
2. Drag the Message control top border until it is approximately the size and at the location of the control shown in Figure 4.7.

To center the Message control horizontally

- On the Layout menu, point to Center In Form, and then click Horizontally.

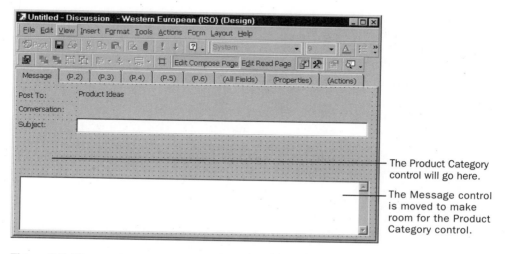

Figure 4.7 *The Message control is adjusted to make room for the Product Category control.*

Add the Product Category Control

The Product Category control is a ComboBox control that lets users select a product category, such as Boating or Fishing, or enter a new product category. Later in this chapter, you will build a view that groups items in the Product Ideas folder by product category. When product ideas are grouped in the folder by product category, it becomes much easier for the user to find ideas about a particular product.

To add the Product Category control

1. On the Form Design toolbar, click the Control Toolbox button.

2. From the Control Toolbox, drag a ComboBox control to the form. Then place the pointer over a sizing handle on the right border of the control and drag the border until the field is approximately the size and at the position of the control shown in Figure 4.8.

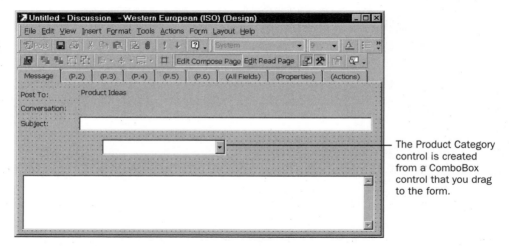

The Product Category control is created from a ComboBox control that you drag to the form.

Figure 4.8 *The Product Category control is added to the Compose page.*

Set the Properties for the Product Category Control

When you set properties for the Product Category control using the Properties dialog box, as shown in Figure 4.9, you name the control, and then you create a Product Category field for the control. When you create the field from the Properties dialog box, you automatically bind the field to the control. When a field is bound to the control, the value in the control at run time is saved to the field when the item is posted. The value is loaded into the control from the field when a posted item in a folder is opened.

To set the properties for the Product Category control

1. Right-click the ComboBox control you added to the form, and then click Properties on the shortcut menu.

2. Click the Display tab.

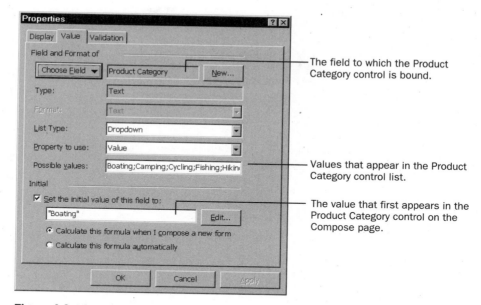

The field to which the Product Category control is bound.

Values that appear in the Product Category control list.

The value that first appears in the Product Category control on the Compose page.

Figure 4.9 *The Properties dialog box for the Product Category control.*

3.   In the Name text box, type *Product Category*.

4.   Click the Value tab.

5.   Click New.

6.   In the Name text box, type *Product Category*, and then click OK.

The Product Category control is now bound to the Product Category field.

7.   In the Possible Values text box, type:
Boating;Camping;Cycling;Fishing;Hiking;Running

8.   Select the Set The Initial Value Of This Field To check box, and then type *"Boating"* in the text box.

The initial value is the value that appears first in the control when the form first opens at run time.

9.   Click OK.

Add a Label for the Product Category Control

Now add a label for the Product Category control so users know the purpose of the control.

➲ To add a Label control

1.   From the Control Toolbox, drag a Label control to the Compose page, as shown in Figure 4.10.

2.   Click the Label control, and then change its text to Product Category.

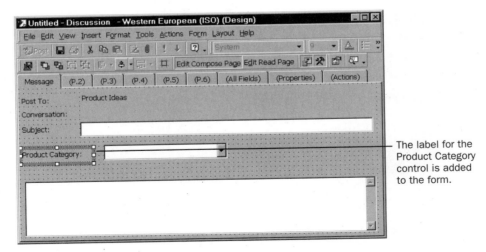

Figure 4.10 *The Product Category label is added to the form.*

Align the Subject and Product Category Control

One way to make sure your forms have a professional look is to align the controls on the form. Outlook offers a variety of layout options, but in most cases you can align items simply by dragging the borders of controls until they are aligned the way you want. For example, on the Compose page, you can align the Subject and Product Category controls by dragging the left edge of the Subject control until it is aligned with the left edge of the Product Category control. Because the Snap To Grid option is on by default, the Subject control is automatically adjusted for you.

➡ **To align the Subject and Product Category controls**

- Click the Subject control, and then drag the left border of the Subject control to the right until it is aligned with the left border of the Product Category control, as shown in Figure 4.11.

Add a Label for the Message Control

Now add a label for the Message control to indicate to users the type of information they're supposed to type into the control. To make room for the label, you may need to make the Message control slightly smaller.

➡ **To add a Label control**

1. Drag a Label control from the Control Toolbox to the Compose page.
2. Click the Label control, and then type *Product Idea:*.

Subject and Product Category controls are aligned.

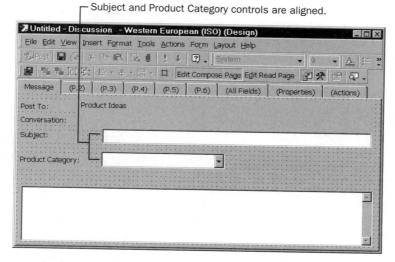

Figure 4.11 *The Subject control is aligned with the Product Category control.*

Move Controls and Add Form Graphics

Next, move controls down to make room for the form graphic that consists of a Label, Frame, and Image control. You will need to resize the form vertically to add more room at the bottom of the Message tab.

To move controls

1. Click the Selector tool in the Control Toolbox.
2. Click in the top left corner of the Compose page and drag the selector box to the lower-right corner of the page. All controls on the page should be selected. Start again and reselect all the controls if they are not selected.
3. Drag the selected controls to the bottom of the form. When you have finished dragging the controls, they will be positioned as shown in Figure 4.12.

To add a form graphic using a label control

1. Drag a Label control from the Control Toolbox to the Compose page.
2. Click the Label control, and then type *Product Idea*.
3. Right-click the Label control, and select Properties on the shortcut menu.
4. Click the Display tab and then click the Font button on the Properties dialog box.
5. Set the font to 16 pt Tahoma, Bold Italic, color Maroon and click OK twice.
6. Drag the Product Idea label to the approximate position shown in Figure 4.12.

Label, Frame, and Image controls provide form graphic.

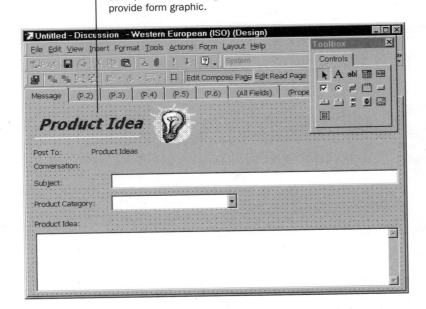

Figure 4.12 *The Compose page shows the form graphic consisting of a Label, a Frame, and an Image control.*

To add a form graphic using a Frame control

1. Drag a Frame control from the Control Toolbox to the Compose page.
2. Right-click the Frame control, and then select Advanced Properties on the shortcut menu.
3. Double-click the BackColor property and select White Color Box from Basic Colors. Click OK.
4. Double-click the Caption property, press the Delete key, and then click Apply.
5. Double-click the Height property, type *3* in the edit box, and then click Apply.
6. Double-click the Width property, type *180* in the edit box, and then click Apply.
7. Close the Advanced Properties window. The Frame control is now masquerading as a white line. Select and drag the line to the approximate position shown in Figure 4.12 under the Product Idea label.

To add a form graphic using an Image control

1. Navigate to the Product Ideas Readme folder. This folder is a subfolder of the Product Ideas folder.
2. Open the Readme post item in the Readme folder.

3.   Right-click the attachment icon for idea.gif and select the Save As command. Navigate to the Desktop folder and click the Save button to save the file on your desktop.

4.   Drag an Image control from the Control Toolbox to the Compose page.

5.   Right-click the Image control, and then select Advanced Properties on the shortcut menu.

6.   Double-click the Picture property, and then use the Load Picture dialog box to select a picture for the Image control. Click the Desktop folder in the Folder drop-down list box, select idea.gif from the File Name list box, and click OK to confirm your selection. You can delete idea.gif using Windows Explorer or move it to a storage folder for graphics files.

7.   Double-click the BorderStyle property to change it to None. Click the Apply button.

8.   Double-click the PictureSizeMode property and the property should change to Stretch. Click the Apply button.

9.   Close the Advanced Properties window. Select and drag the image to the position shown in Figure 4.12, just to the right of the Product Idea label. You might need to resize the Image control by selecting and then resizing the control.

To save the form graphic for reuse on other pages

1.   Click the Selector tool in the Control Toolbox.

2.   Click in the top-left corner of the Compose Page and drag the selector box to the right of the Image control until all the form graphic controls are selected.

3.   Drag the selection from the Compose page to the Control Toolbox.

Set the Tab Order for the Compose Page

The tab order defines the sequence in which the controls become active on the form when the user presses the Tab key. When you add controls to the form, the control name is added to the bottom of a list of controls in the Tab Order box. For the Compose page, you must move the Product Category control up the list so it follows directly after the Subject control.

To set the Tab Order for the Compose page

1.   On the Layout menu, click Tab Order.

2.   In the Tab Order dialog box, click Product Category, and then click Move Up until Product Category is above Message.

3.   Click OK.

Note Label controls, such as *ConversationLabel* and *SubjectLabel*, are listed in the Tab Order box, but are not included in the tab order.

Edit the Read Page

To edit the Read page, you copy the controls you added to the Compose page. Before you do this, however, you must switch to the Read page, adjust the grid settings, and delete existing controls to make room for new controls.

To switch to the Read page

- On the Form Design toolbar, click Edit Read Page, as shown in Figure 4.13.

To delete controls to make room for new controls

1. Click the Selector tool on the Control Toolbox. Click on the Read page just above and to the left of the Post To label and drag the selection box to the lower right corner of the form so that all controls on the Read page are selected except for the From label, the From control, the Posted label, and the Posted control. If these controls are selected accidentally, you can deselect them by holding down the Ctrl key and then clicking the control that you want to deselect.

2. Press Delete.

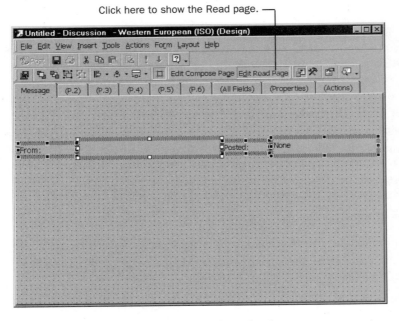

Figure 4.13 *The Read page of the Product Idea form.*

➥ **To adjust the From and Posted controls**

    1. Use the Selector tool to select the remaining From and Posted controls on the Read page.

    2. Drag the selected controls until the position of the controls is approximately the same as the controls shown in Figure 4.13.

Copy Controls from the Compose Page

Now switch to the Compose page and copy the controls required to complete the Read page. Then switch back to the Read page, and paste the controls.

➥ **To copy the controls from the Compose page**

    1. On the Form Design toolbar, click Edit Compose Page.

    2. Click the Selector tool in the Control Toolbox. Click just to the top and left of the Post To label and drag the selection box to the lower right of the page so that all controls on the page—including and below the Post To control—are selected.

    3. On the Standard toolbar, click Copy.

    4. On the Form Design toolbar, click Edit Read Page.

    5. When the Read page appears, click Paste, and then position the pasted controls on the page as shown in Figure 4.14.

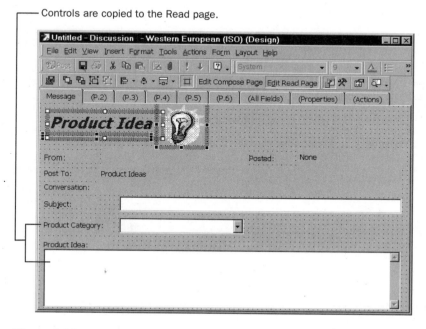

Figure 4.14 *The Read page of the Product Idea form.*

6. On the Form Design toolbar, click Edit Compose Page again.

7. Use the Selector tool to select the form graphic controls (Product Idea label, Frame control line, and Image control).

8. On the Standard toolbar, click Copy.

9. On the Form Design toolbar, click Edit Read Page.

10. When the Read page appears, click Paste, and then position the pasted controls on the page as shown in Figure 4.14.

11. Change the caption of the Product Ideas label to Product Ideas Response.

12. Right-click the Product Category ComboBox and check the Read Only check box in the Properties dialog box.

Set the Tab Order for the Read Page

In designing forms, it is important to remember that, when you change a design element on the Compose page, you often need to make the same change on the Read page.

> **To set the tab order**

1. On the Layout menu, click Tab Order.

2. In the Tab Order dialog box, click Product Category, and then click Move Up until Product Category is below Subject.

Set Product Idea Form Properties

The Outlook Properties tab lets you define the overall attributes for the form, including the Caption property, which appears in the title bar of the form window, and the Contact property, which specifies the individual to contact for upgrades or form maintenance. There are a variety of other properties you can set for the form, but for now, set only the properties listed below.

> **To set Product Idea form properties**

- Click the Properties tab, and then fill in the values shown below.

Property	Value
Contact	*Your name*
Description	*Use this form to post and view product ideas in the Product Ideas folder.*
Version	*1.0*
Form Number	*1*

 More Info For more information about how to set form properties, see Chapter 5, "Forms."

Test the Form at Design Time

Before you save a form or publish it to a folder, it's a good idea to run the form to see how the form layout appears at run time. It's also a good idea to test both the Read page and the Compose page of the form.

To switch between Design mode and Run mode when testing

1. With the Compose page in Design mode, click Run This Form on the Form menu.
2. To test the Read page, send the form to yourself and view the received item in your Inbox.
3. To return to Design mode, close the Run mode window of the Compose page.

Make a Backup Copy of the Product Idea Form

Although it's not absolutely necessary, it is a good idea to make a backup copy of the form before you publish it to a form library.

To save the Product Idea form

1. With the form open, click Save As on the File menu.
2. In the Save In drop-down list box, select the default Outlook template folder, such as C:\Program Files\Microsoft Office\Templates.
3. In the File Name text box, type *Product Idea* as the name for the form.
4. In the Save As Type drop-down list box, select Outlook Template.
5. Click Save.

To open your backup copy of a form

1. Select New on the File menu, and then click Choose Form.
2. Click User Templates In File System in the Look In drop-down list box, and then click on the form you'd like to open.

Publish the Product Idea Form

When you publish the Product Idea form to the Product Ideas folder, you register the form definition in the folder. As a result, a menu command appears on the Actions menu of Outlook when the user opens the Product Ideas folder. This is the menu command that enables users to open the Product Idea form and create a new Product Idea item.

To publish the form to the Product Ideas folder

1. Choose Forms on the Tools menu, and then click Publish Form As.
2. In the Form Name text box and the Display Name text box, type *Product Idea*.
3. If the text in the Look In drop-down list box is not Product Ideas, click the drop-down list box, select the Product Ideas folder, and then click OK.
4. Click Publish.

5. In the Send Form Definition With Item message box, choose Yes if this form will be sent to someone without access to your forms library system. That way, recipients will have a self-contained form that can be viewed independently. Select No if the recipient has the form published in Personal Forms Library, Organizational Forms Library, or has access to the forms library of the folder. This keeps form size down and speeds form opening. For more information, see Chapter 12, "Distribute and Maintain Applications."

Tip Click the Outlook Actions menu. You'll notice that the New Product Idea command is added to the menu. Outlook automatically constructs the menu command by combining the word New with the Display Name property Product Idea.

Create the Product Idea Response Form

The Product Idea Response form, as shown in Figure 4.15, is very similar to the Product Idea form. Therefore, to create the Product Idea Response form, all you need to do is modify a few properties of the original Product Idea form, change the form name, and then publish the form in the Product Ideas folder.

Edit the Compose Page

To edit the Compose page, you change several properties for the control, and you change the label associated with the Message control. First, however, you must switch from the Read page to the Compose page.

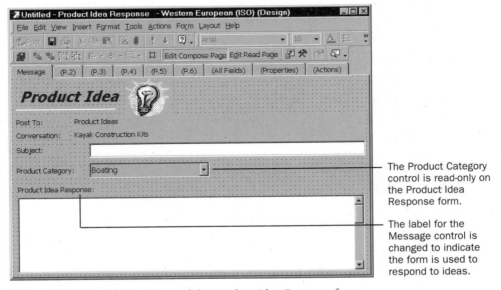

Figure 4.15 *The Compose page of the Product Idea Response form.*

To switch to the Compose page

- On the Form Design toolbar, click Edit Compose Page.

Make the Product Category Control Read-Only

On the Product Idea Response form, you make the Product Category control a read-only control so the product category selected by the person who posted the new idea cannot be changed by individuals responding to the idea.

To make the Product Category control read-only

1. On the Compose page, right-click the Product Category control, and then click Properties.
2. Click the Display tab, and then select the Read Only check box.
3. Click OK to close.

Clear the Initial Value Property for the Product Category Field

Now specify that the Initial Value property for the Product Category field is cleared. This ensures that the value from the Product Category field in the Product Idea item is copied to the Product Category field in the Product Idea Response item.

To clear the Initial Value property

1. Right-click the Product Category control, and then click Properties.
2. Click the Value tab, clear the Set The Initial Value Of This Field To check box, and then click OK.

Change the Product Idea Label

Now change the label above the Message control from Product Idea: to Product Idea Response: to clarify the purpose of the Message control on the Product Idea Response form.

To change the label

1. Click the Product Idea label (located above the Message control), and then click it again.
2. Change the text in the label to Product Idea Response:.
3. Resize the label.

Edit the Read Page

Now switch to the Read page, set the Product Category control to read-only, and then change the Product Idea label to Product Idea Response.

To switch to the Read page

- On the Form Design toolbar, click Edit Read Page.

To make the Product Category control read-only

1. Right-click the Product Category control, and then click Properties.
2. Click the Display tab, select the Read Only check box, and then click OK.

To change the Product Idea label

1. Click the Product Idea label (above the Message control), and then click it again.
2. Change the label to Product Idea Response:.
3. Resize the label.

Set the Form Properties

Now set the form properties for the Product Idea Response form.

To set the form properties

- Click the Properties tab, and then fill in the values shown in the following table.

Property	Value
Contact	*Your name*
Description	*Use this form to post or view a response to a product idea or to post or view a response to a product idea response.*
Version	*1.0*
Form Number	*2*
Use Form Only For Responses	*True (checked)*

Make a Backup Copy of the Product Idea Response Form

Now save the Product Idea Response form in the folder where you saved the Product Idea form.

To make a backup copy of the Product Idea Response form

1. With the form open, click Save As on the File menu.
2. In the Save In drop-down list box, select the default Outlook template folder, such as C:\Program Files\Microsoft Office\Templates.
3. In the File Name text box, type *Product Idea Response* as the name for the form.
4. In the Save As Type drop-down list box, select Outlook Template.
5. Click Save.

To open your backup copy of a form

1. Select New on the File menu, and then click Choose Form.

2. Click User Templates In File System in the Look In drop-down list box, and then click on the form you'd like to open.

Publish the Product Idea Response Form

Before you publish the Product Idea Response form, change the Form Name option in the Publish Form As dialog box to Product Idea Response. Then, publish the Product Idea Response form to the Product Ideas Form Library.

To publish the Product Idea Response form

1. On the Tools menu, select Forms, and then click Publish Forms As.
2. In the Display Name text box and Form Name text box, change the name to Product Idea Response.

   The Message Class property automatically updates when you change the Form name.

   The Display Name field reflects both the form name on the Actions menu of the folder and the caption on the title bar of the published form.
3. Click Publish.
4. Close the Product Idea Response form. In the Save Changes? message box, select No in most cases. Select Yes if you want a backup item in the current folder.

Set the Actions

Actions determine how a form handles responses. For example, the action you create for the Product Idea form will allow users to respond to a Product Idea item with the Product Idea Response form. In addition, the action you create for the Product Idea Response form will enable users to respond to a Product Idea Response item with the Product Idea Response form. In essence, the form will call itself for a response.

Set the Actions for the Product Idea Form

First, open the Product Idea form in the Product Ideas folder. Then, switch to Design mode for the form and set its actions.

To open the Product Idea form in Design mode

1. Locate the Product Ideas folder in the Folder List and click once to open it.
2. On the Outlook Actions menu, hold down the Shift key and click New Product Idea.

Tip Holding down the Shift key when you open a form for design purposes is a good practice because it prevents any code in the form from executing when the form is opened. Note that the Product Ideas folder must be open for the New Product Idea command to appear on the Actions menu.

3. On the Tools menu of the Product Idea form, select Forms, and then click Design This Form.

Make the Reply To Folder Action Unavailable

When you create a new action for a Post form, you usually make the standard Post To Folder action unavailable. You do this for two reasons. First, you don't want standard Post items in the Product Ideas folder because they won't group correctly in custom views. Second, you want to avoid the confusion of presenting the user with two commands—New Post In This Folder and New Product Idea—that allows them to post an item in the folder.

To make the Reply To Folder action unavailable

1. On the Product Idea form, click the Actions tab.
2. Double-click the Reply To Folder action.
3. Clear the Enabled check box, and then click OK.

   The Actions page should now look like the Actions page shown in Figure 4.16.

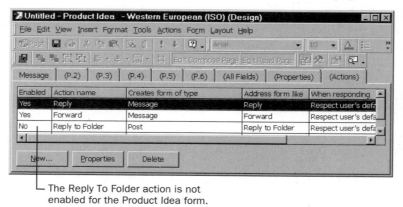

The Reply To Folder action is not enabled for the Product Idea form.

Figure 4.16 *The Reply To Folder action is made unavailable for the Product Idea form.*

Create a New Action

Now create a new action that specifies that a Product Idea Response button appears on the Product Idea form when the user opens a posted Product Idea. When the user clicks the Product Idea Response button, as shown in Figure 4.17, the Product Idea Response form appears, which can then be used to post a response in the folder.

To create a new action

1. Click New on the Actions page of the Product Idea Response form.
2. In the Action Name text box, as shown in Figure 4.18, type *Product Idea Response*.

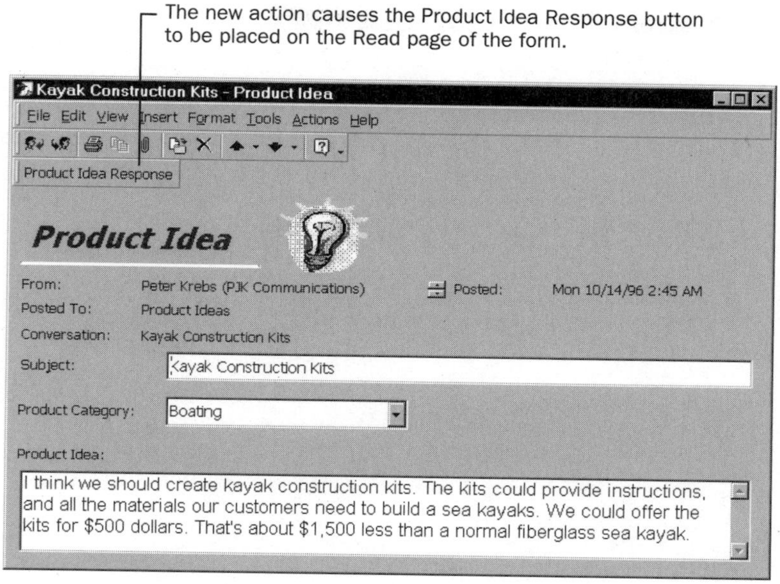

The new action causes the Product Idea Response button
to be placed on the Read page of the form.

Figure 4.17 *The Product Idea Response button is added to the Product Idea
form when a Product Idea item is opened in the folder.*

The Product Idea Response command appears on the Product Idea Response
button on the Product Idea form when a posted item is opened. The Product
Idea Response command also appears on the Actions menu of the folder when
a Product Idea item is selected in the Product Ideas folder.

3.   In the Form Name drop-down list box, click Product Idea Response.

4.   In the Address Form Like A drop-down list box, click Reply To Folder, and
     then click OK.

Make a Backup Copy of the Product Idea Form

Before you republish the form, it's a good idea to make a backup copy of the modified form.

➡ **To make a backup copy of the Product Idea form**

1.   With the form open, click Save As on the File menu.

2.   In the Save In drop-down list box, select the default Outlook template folder,
     such as C:\Program Files\Microsoft Office\Templates.

3.   In the File Name text box, double-click on Product Idea.

4.   In the Save As Type drop-down list box, select Outlook Template.

5.   Click Save.

6.   Select Yes to replace the existing file.

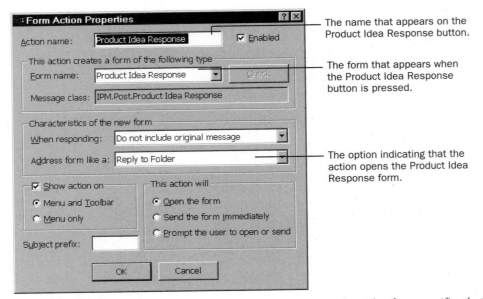

Figure 4.18 *The Form Action Properties dialog box for the Product Idea form specifies that the Product Idea Response form opens when the user clicks the Product Idea Response button.*

Republish the Product Idea Form

To republish the form

1. On the Tools menu, select Forms, and then click Publish Form As.
2. In the window with the list of published forms, double-click Product Idea.
3. If you are prompted to replace the existing form, click Yes.
4. Close the Product Idea form. Click No to save changes. Click Yes if you want a backup draft saved to the current folder.

Set the Actions for the Product Idea Response Form

Now open the Product Idea Response form and create a new Product Idea Response action so users can respond to a Product Idea Response item. In effect, users can create a response to a response by opening another instance of the Product Idea Response form. When you create the new action, the Product Idea Response button is added to the form when a posted Product Idea Response item is opened in the Product Ideas folder, as shown in Figure 4.19.

Open the Product Idea Response Form

To create a new action for the Product Idea Response form, you first open the form in Run mode, and then switch to Design mode so you can add the new actions to the form.

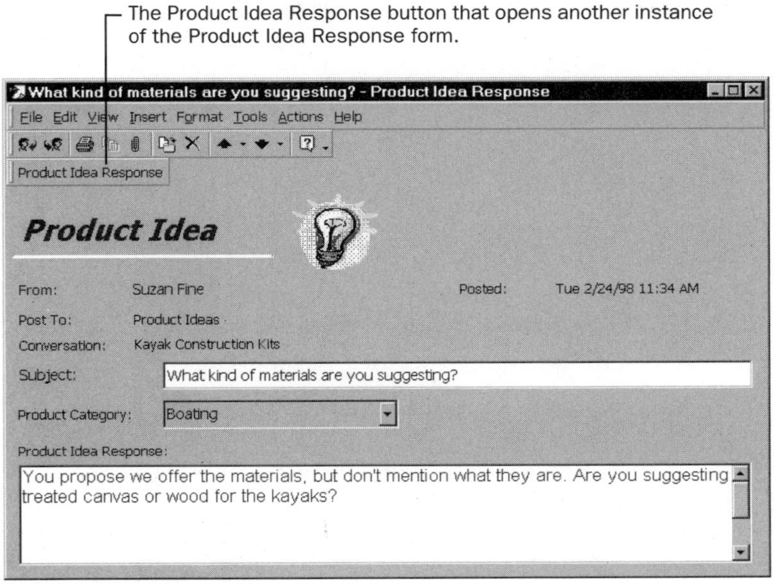

The Product Idea Response button that opens another instance
of the Product Idea Response form.

Figure 4.19 *The Product Idea Response button appears on the form when
the user opens a Product Idea Response item in the folder.*

Note that the Product Ideas folder must be open for the New Product Idea Response
command to appear on the Actions menu.

To open the Product Idea Response form in Design mode

1. On the Outlook Actions menu, hold down the Shift key and click New Product
    Idea Response.

2. On the Tools menu of the Product Idea form, select Forms and then click
    Design This Form.

Make the Reply To Folder Action Unavailable

Just as you made the Reply To Folder action unavailable for the Product Idea form, you
make it unavailable for the Product Idea Response form.

To make the Reply To Folder action unavailable

1. On the Product Idea Response form, click the Actions tab.

2. Double-click the Reply To Folder action.

3. Clear the Enabled check box, and then click OK.

Create a New Action

Now create a new action that causes the Product Idea Response button to appear on the
Product Idea Response form when the user opens a posted Product Idea Response item.

To create a new action

1. On the Product Idea Response form, click the Actions tab.
2. Click New.
3. In the Action Name text box, type *Product Idea Response.*
4. In the Form Name drop-down list box, click Product Idea Response.
5. In the Address Form Like A drop-down list box, click Reply To Folder, and then click OK.

Make a Backup Copy of the Product Idea Response Form

It's always a good idea to have a backup copy of the form.

To make a backup copy of the Product Idea Response form

1. With the form open, click Save As on the File menu.
2. In the Save In drop-down list box, select the default Outlook template folder, such as C:\Program Files\Microsoft Office\Templates.
3. In the File Name drop-down list box, double-click on Product Idea Response.
4. In the Save As Type drop-down list box, select Outlook Template.
5. Click Save.
6. Select Yes to replace the existing file.

Publish the Product Idea Response Form

To publish the Product Idea Response form

1. On the Tools menu, select Forms, and then click Publish Forms As.
2. Double-click on Product Idea Response in the forms window.
3. Close the Product Idea Response form. Close the form and select No in the Save Changes? message box.

Create the Product Category View

Custom views organize information in folders so the information is meaningful and can be analyzed more quickly. For example, take a look at the Messages view in Figure 4.20. In this view, items are listed chronologically according to the order in which they were posted in the folder. With this flat presentation of information, you'd never know that discussions are taking place within the folder.

Now take a look at the same information in Figure 4.21. With the custom Product Category view applied to the folder, items are grouped first by the Product Category field, and then by the Conversation field. In addition, each item in a conversation group is sorted by the Conversation Index field, so you can see the history of responses to each item.

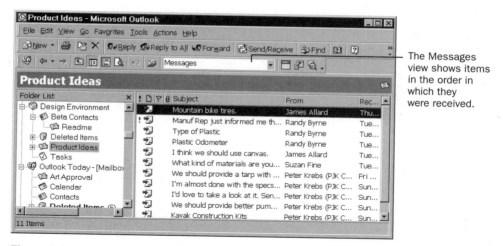

Figure 4.20 *The Product Ideas folder with the Messages view selected.*

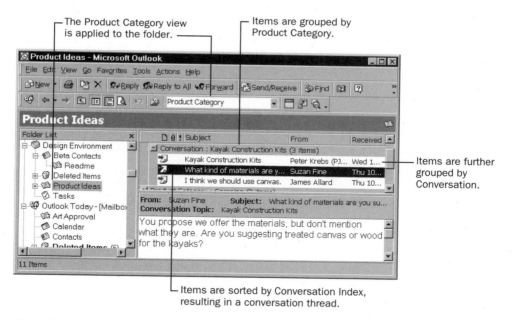

Figure 4.21 *The Product Ideas folder with the Product Category view selected.*

To create the Product Category view

1. Click the Product Ideas folder in the Folder List.

2. On the View menu, select Current View, and then click Define Views.

3. Click New.

4. In the Name Of New View text box, type *Product Category*, click OK twice, and then click Apply View.

Remove Fields

Now remove the fields that aren't necessary for the Product Category view.

➡ **To remove fields**

- Drag the Flag Status column heading (the column heading with the flag symbol) away from the Column Heading row until an X appears through the column heading, and then release the mouse button.

Group Items

For the Product Category view, you group items first by the Product Category field, and then by the Conversation Topic field.

When you group items in a view by product category, all items in the Product Ideas folder that have the value *Camping* selected in the Product Category drop-down list box are grouped together. Similarly, all items that have the value *Fishing* selected in the Product Category drop-down list box are grouped together.

When a user first submits a Product Idea item, the subject of the item becomes the Conversation Topic property. Any response items to the item, whether it is a direct response or a response to a response, inherit this Conversation Topic property value. As a result, all items about a particular conversation topic are grouped together.

➡ **To group items by Product Category, then by Conversation**

1. On the View menu, select Current View, and then click Customize Current View.

2. Click Group By in the View Summary box.

3. In the Select Available Fields From drop-down list box near the bottom, click User-Defined Fields In Folder.

4. In the Group Items By drop-down list box, click Product Category.

5. In the Select Available Fields From drop-down list box, click Frequently-Used fields.

6. In the Then By drop-down list box, click Conversation.

7. Click OK twice.

Sort Items

The Conversation Index field is the field that makes threaded conversations come to life. When you group items by conversation topic, and then sort them by conversation index, you can see the relationships between items in a discussion application because a response to an item immediately follows the item. Plus, the response is indented from the associated item, so it's easy for a user who hasn't been part of the online conversation to quickly become familiar with an issue by simply following the thread of conversation up to the last posted item.

To sort items by the Conversation Index field

1. On the View menu, select Current View, and then click Customize Current View.
2. Click Sort in the View Summary box.
3. In the Select Available Fields From drop-down list box, click Frequently-Used Fields.
4. In the Sort Items By drop-down list box, click Conversation Index, and then click OK twice.

Arrange the Column Heading Order

For discussion applications, the Subject column heading usually precedes the From column heading. In Outlook, you can make adjustments to the view directly in the folder, so changing the column heading order is a simple matter of drag-and-drop editing.

To arrange the column heading order

- Drag the Subject column heading to the left until the double arrow appears, and then drop the column heading.

Specify the Default Form for the Folder

Now make the Product Idea form the default form for the Product Ideas folder so that when the user clicks the New button on the Outlook Standard toolbar, the Product Idea form appears.

To specify that the Product Idea form is the default form

1. In the Folder List, right-click the Product Ideas folder.
2. Click Properties.
3. Click the General tab.
4. In the When Posting To This Folder, Use drop-down list box, click Product Idea, and then click OK.

Set the Hidden Property for the Product Idea Response Form

Before you test the Product Ideas application to make sure it's working as expected, you set the Hidden property for the Product Idea Response form. This ensures that users can only open the Product Idea Response form by first selecting or opening a posted item.

Therefore, the Product Idea Response form can be used only for posting responses, not for creating new items to start a conversation topic.

When you set the Hidden property of the Product Idea Response form, you remove the Product Idea Response command from the Outlook Actions menu. With the Hidden property set, the Product Idea Response form can only be opened by clicking one of the action commands you specified for the Product Idea and Product Idea Response forms.

To set the Hidden property for the Product Idea Response form

1. In the Folder List, right-click the Product Ideas folder.
2. Click Properties.
3. Click the Forms tab, and then click Manage.
4. In the Forms list box on the right, click Product Idea Response, and then click Properties.
5. Select the Hidden check box, and then click OK.
6. Click Close twice.

Test the Application

Before you copy the Product Ideas application to public folders and make it available to other users, it's a good idea to test the application to make sure everything is working as expected.

To test the Product Ideas application

1. With the Product Ideas folder open, click New Product Idea on the Outlook Actions menu.
2. Fill in the form, and then click Post.
3. The new item is posted in the Product Ideas folder.
4. Double-click the Product Idea item you posted.
5. When the Product Idea form appears, click the Product Idea Response button on the form.
6. Fill in the Product Idea Response form, and then click Post.
7. Close the Product Idea form.
8. In the Product Ideas folder, double-click the Product Idea Response item you just posted.
8. When the Product Idea Response form appears, click the Product Idea Response button.
9. Fill in the Product Idea Response form, and then click Post.
10. Close the Product Idea Response form.

11.   Repeat Steps 1 through 7 several times. Each time you perform step 2, click a different value in the Product Category box and enter different text in the Subject text box.

Copy the Folder to Public Folders

Now you've created forms and a custom view for the Product Ideas folder. You've also tested the folder to make sure it works as planned. Now copy the folder from the Design Environment personal folder to public folders so the folder can be shared by a workgroup or across the entire organization. Before you copy the folder, you might want to discuss with your administrator the best location for the folder. In addition, you might need to get the appropriate permissions to copy the folder to its destination in public folders.

To copy the Product Ideas folder

1.   In the Folder List, click the Product Ideas folder.

2.   Delete any test items or draft forms from the folder, before copying. Select the items and press the Delete key.

3.   On the File menu, point to Folder, and then click Copy Product Ideas.

4.   In the Copy The Selected Folder To The Folder list box, click the location you want the folder copied to, such as All Public Folders.

5.   Click OK.

About Folder Permissions

When you create the Product Ideas folder, you are automatically given owner permissions for the folder. In addition, all users are given Publishing Author permissions so they can post and open items in the folder, and modify and delete items they create. At this time, you can leave the folder permissions alone.

> **More Info** For more information about how to set permissions, see Chapter 8, "Folders."

Release the Application

Before you make the application available to coworkers, you set the Initial View On Folder property to Product Category. This is the view users first see when they open the folder.

To set Administration properties

1.   In the Folder List, right-click the Product Ideas folder, and then click Properties.

2.   Click the Administration tab.

3. In the Initial View On Folder drop-down list box, select Product Category. Click OK.

Now that the folder is ready for use, you can send a message to your coworkers to notify them that the application is available.

More Info For more information about releasing applications, see Chapter 12, "Distribute and Maintain Applications."

What's Next

In this chapter, we've taken a quick look at how to build an information-sharing groupware application based on the Post form. In the next chapter, "Forms," we'll take an in-depth look at the forms design environment, the different types of forms you can create, how forms work, and how to set form properties.

Part III
Building Blocks of Applications

Chapter 5, "Forms," introduces the form design process, and covers fundamental form design tasks such as adding controls and fields, creating new actions, setting form properties, and publishing forms. Chapter 6, "Controls, Fields, and Properties," covers the fundamental skills and information you need to effectively use controls, fields, and properties on a form. It also explains the unique features of each commonly used control, and then offers some strategies for implementing these controls and fields in an application. Chapter 7, "Actions," discusses the easiest way to create responses for Message forms, explains how to create custom Reply actions for Message forms, and then shows how to create custom Reply to Folder actions for Post forms. Chapter 8, "Folders," takes an in-depth look at the folder design process, discusses how to manage forms, and explains how to create custom views and Folder Home Pages. It also covers setting folder permissions and building rules. Chapter 9, "Raise Events and Move to the Head of the Class," explains how you can use all the new events in the Outlook 2000 object model to write Outlook VBA code or create a COM Add-in. Chapter 10, "Out-

look Bar, Command Bars, and the Assistant" shows you how to program the new Outlook Bar objects. You'll also learn how to program Office 2000 objects such as the CommandBar and the Assistant. With your ability to control the command bars in Outlook, you can customize Outlook menus and toolbars in ways that were impossible in previous versions.

Chapter 5
Forms

In This Chapter

With Outlook forms in Design mode, you can build custom forms to streamline request processes, collect and distribute information, and save and show information that is structured so that it's both easy to find and easy to read. For example, you can create travel request forms to automate the approval of business travel plans. You can create product response forms to collect valuable information from your customers. Or you can create job candidate forms to post information about a potential employee, so that other members of your organization can view the candidate's background before interviewing the candidate. After the interview, interviewers can post their impressions of the candidate in a public folder, so a manager can quickly get an overall impression of the candidate.

This chapter discusses form design concepts, introduces the form design process, and then covers fundamental form design tasks such as adding controls and fields, creating new actions, setting form properties, and publishing forms. When you have completed this chapter, you should have the basic knowledge and skills you need to create and publish forms in your organization.

Become Familiar with Designing Forms and Form Components

This section covers the components of forms in Design mode and discusses the parts of an Outlook form.

Outlook Forms in Design Mode

The following elements are available while Outlook forms are in Design mode:

- **Form Design** window, to show the various pages of the form and the form properties and actions
- **Toolbox** to add new controls (such as buttons) to the form
- **Field Chooser** to select fields for the form
- **Properties** dialog box, to modify a control or field
- **Script Editor** to program or automate the forms

The last four elements are shown in Figure 5.1. For more information on how to open a form in Design mode, see "Outlook Forms Design Mode" in Chapter 2, "Outlook Design Tools."

Types of Forms

Outlook provides four basic types of forms to use as starting points for all forms that you build. To design forms effectively, you need to know the basic characteristics of these four types: Message, Post, Office Document, and built-in forms.

Message and Post forms can be fully customized. Although Office Document forms can't be directly modified, you can add VBScript to the form to customize it. Task, Appointment, and Journal forms can be customized by adding additional pages to the forms, but the existing pages cannot be modified. This also applies to the Contact form, but you can modify the first page of a Contact form.

For a detailed description of form components, see "Parts of a Form" later in this chapter.

Message Form

Use the Message form shown in Figure 5.2 as a starting point for building forms that allow users to send information to other users, to a distribution list, or to a folder. The Message form can be fully customized. When Message forms are sent, they travel through the messaging transport system and are then routed to the specified address. Examples of Message forms are the Vacation Request form, the While You Were Out form, and the Business Card Request form.

Post Form

Use the Post form shown in Figure 5.3 as a starting point for building forms that allow users to post, open, and respond to information in a personal or public folder. The Post form can be fully customized. Post forms submit items directly to the active folder. As

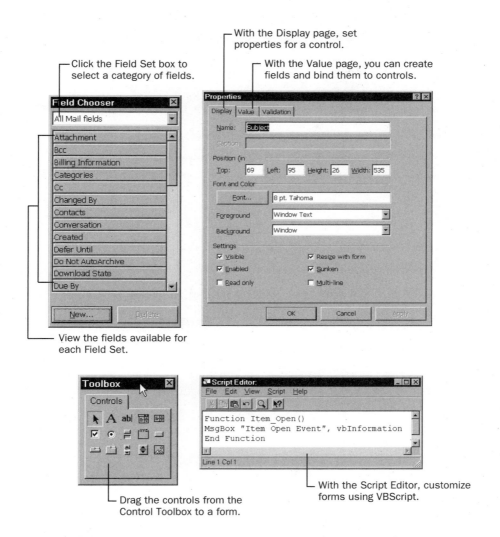

With the Display page, set properties for a control.

Click the Field Set box to select a category of fields.

With the Value page, you can create fields and bind them to controls.

View the fields available for each Field Set.

Drag the controls from the Control Toolbox to a form.

With the Script Editor, customize forms using VBScript.

Figure 5.1 *These elements are available while Outlook forms are in Design mode.*

such, Post forms are tightly integrated with folders. Examples of Post forms are the Product Idea and Product Idea Response forms found in the Product Ideas application, which is discussed in Chapter 4, "Design a Custom Application."

Office Document Form

Use the Office Document form shown in Figure 5.4 as a starting point for building forms that have an Office 2000 document—Word, PowerPoint, or Excel—embedded in them. Office Document forms are essentially Office documents wrapped in either a Message

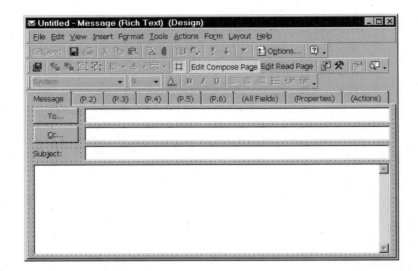

Figure 5.2 *The Mail Message form is the starting point for Message forms.*

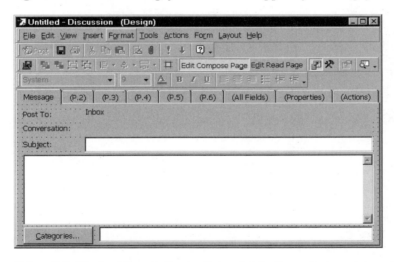

Figure 5.3 *The Post form is the starting point for forms that are integrated with a personal or public folder.*

or a Post form. You can create Office Document forms to send documents to other users and to post documents in a folder. For instance, expense reports may be sent to your accounting department on Microsoft Excel spreadsheets embedded in an Outlook form.

Important Office Document forms do not offer Outlook pages that you can customize. However, you can customize the document embedded in the Document

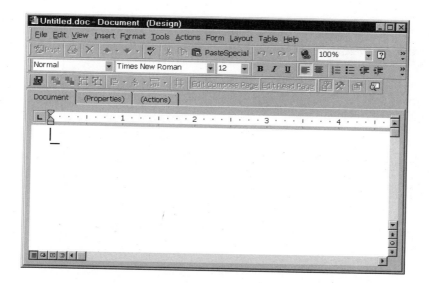

Figure 5.4 *The New Office Document form is the starting point for Office Document forms.*

page of the form. For example, you can create sheets on an embedded Excel document that mimic the functionality of pages. To create a form in a Microsoft Office 2000 document, see Help for the specific application for which you want to create a form.

Built-In Forms

You can modify built-in forms in Calendar, Contacts, Distribution List, Journal, and Task modules by showing additional pages on the form. You can then add controls and fields to the form to suit the needs of your application (see Figure 5.5). The default page cannot be modified, with the exception of the Contact form's default page.

The characteristics of each built-in form vary, depending on the application. For example, with the Task Request form, users send a Task Request to other users. With the Task form, however, users save the task in the current folder.

Parts of a Form

Before you get started designing forms, you need to know about the different components of a form and what each component is used for. This section dissects a form and discusses the purpose of each of its components.

The Compose and Read Pages

An Outlook form can consist of a single page, but in most cases, it consists of two pages: a Compose page and a Read page, as shown in Figure 5.6. Although the Compose and

You can show additional pages and add controls to them.

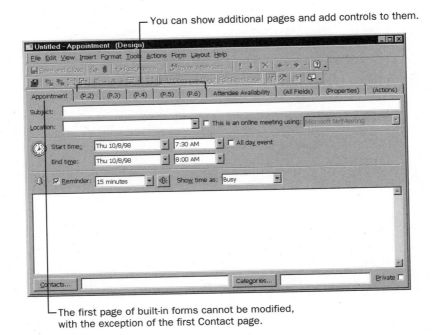

The first page of built-in forms cannot be modified,
with the exception of the first Contact page.

Figure 5.5 *The built-in Appointment form can be customized to meet your personal needs or those of your workgroup or organization.*

With the Compose page, users can create an item and send or post it.

With the Read page, users view and respond to information.

Users enter information on the Compose page.

Users view submitted information on the Read page.

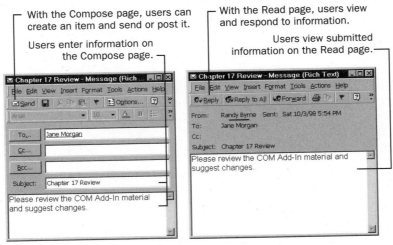

Figure 5.6 *The Outlook form consists of a Compose page and a Read page.*

Read pages are often similar in appearance, they serve very different purposes. The Compose page enables users to create items and to send or post items. The Read page lets users open and read submitted items in a folder, and to respond to items.

Pages

Forms also have a series of pages that you view by clicking their respective tabs. In addition to the default Message or General page, forms have five custom pages that you can add controls to. Forms also have pages such as the Properties and Actions pages that enable you to set properties for the form to define how it functions, as shown in Figure 5.7. The All Fields page allows you to view all fields and field values for the form. You can even update some of these properties, which is useful for testing.

Controls

Controls are the components of a form that allows users to enter and view information. Controls are the means through which users interact with the form. You add controls to the form by dragging them from the Control Toolbox. (See Figure 5.8.)

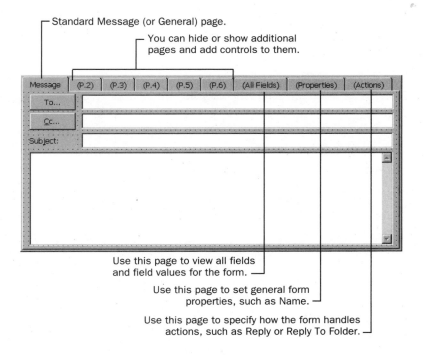

Figure 5.7 *Pages of the Message form.*

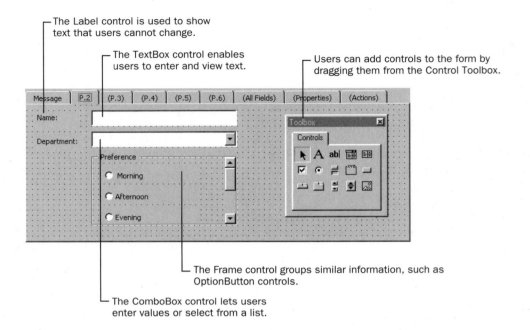

Figure 5.8 *Controls and the Control Toolbox.*

Fields

A form field is a field that defines how information in a control or in a folder is saved and displayed in messaging applications. In addition, the field is a physical storage location in the item where the specified data is saved. To specify that the information in a control is to be saved, you bind the control to a field. For example, as shown in Figure 5.9, the TextBox control is bound to the Name field, so that the information in the control is saved to the field when an item is sent, saved, or posted. When the item is opened, the information is loaded from the field into the control.

Properties

Properties define the characteristics of form components. With Outlook, you can define properties for forms, controls, and fields. Figure 5.10 shows display properties that are set for the Name control.

Control properties are accessed by right-clicking on the control or field, and then selecting Properties. Form properties are modified in the Properties dialog box while in Design mode.

The TextBox control is bound to the Name field.

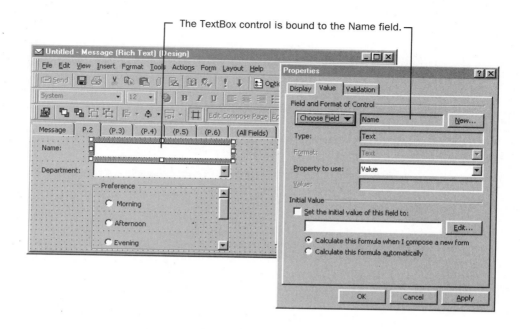

Figure 5.9 *The TextBox control is bound to the Name field.*

Display properties define the name and appearance of a control.

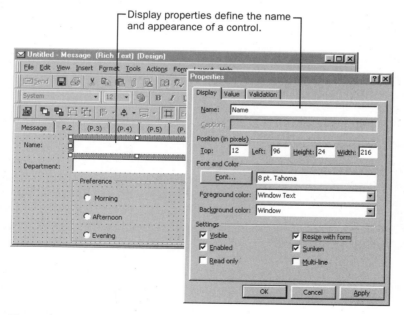

Figure 5.10 *Properties of the Name control.*

Actions

Actions define how a form handles responses. You can modify existing actions or create new actions. For example, you can modify an action to specify that a custom form is opened when the user clicks the Reply button on a form. You can also create a new action that adds a custom response button to the form. As shown in Figure 5.11, new actions have been created for the Vacation Request form that allow users to respond to a Vacation Request item by clicking an Approve Vacation or Deny Vacation button on the form.

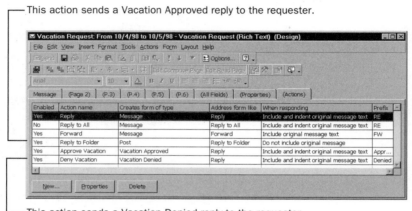

This action sends a Vacation Approved reply to the requester.

This action sends a Vacation Denied reply to the requester.

Figure 5.11 *The Actions page for the Vacation Request form.*

Form Scripts

With the Script Editor, you can use Microsoft Visual Basic Scripting Edition (VBScript) to add functionality to a form. You can add code for a command button that creates and sends a response item, call the properties and methods of an ActiveX component, launch other applications from a form using Automation, or create procedures that automatically fill in or clear values on the form, as shown in Figure 5.12.

Important Outlook 2000 includes a COM Add-in that allows you to use Visual Basic for Applications (VBA) to program the running instance of Outlook. VBA is especially useful when you want to respond to events that occur within the Outlook application environment. However, VBA is not available for Outlook forms. You still must use VBScript to program Outlook custom forms. See Chapter 11, "Using VBA and VBScript with Outlook."

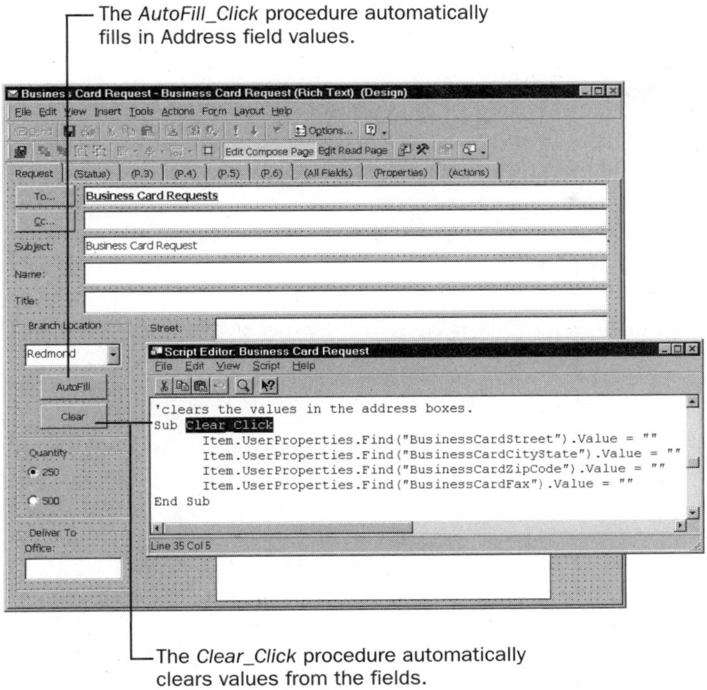

The *AutoFill_Click* procedure automatically fills in Address field values.

The *Clear_Click* procedure automatically clears values from the fields.

Figure 5.12 *The Script Editor shows code that automates a Business Card Request form.*

Learn How Forms Work

This section briefly covers some fundamental form concepts, such as the meaning of the term item, how saving the form definition with an item affects the form, and how shared fields work.

What Is an Item?

Throughout the book, the term item is used often. In the past, an item was simply called a message. So why change the terminology? Because the term message can no longer encompass the vast array of information that can be included in an item. In Outlook, an item is a container for information. In addition to text and number values entered by users, this container can hold just about anything, including Uniform Resource Locators (URLs), voice mail, office documents, video clips, PowerPoint presentations, and so on. An item also contains properties that define the item—such as message class—and that associate the item with a specific form.

Note You may be wondering where items are stored. If you are running Outlook in Corporate/Workgroup (C/W) mode as a client for Microsoft Exchange Server, public folder items are stored in a public information store on an Exchange Server. If you run Outlook in either Internet Mail Only (IMO) or Corporate/Workgroup mode, personal folder items are stored on a local or network drive in a container known as a personal information store or a .pst file. Mailbox items are stored either in a .pst file or in a private information store on an Exchange Server. The important point to remember is that both .pst files and public and private stores on Exchange Server are containers for a collection of items with diverse message classes. In all cases, you cannot access a message item in a public or private folder by simply opening a file on drive C:, as you would with a Word document.

What Happens When the Form Definition Is Saved with the Item?

In Design mode, Outlook provides an option on the form Properties page called Send Form Definition With Item. The Send Form Definition With Item option serves two purposes:

- **It enables users to send Message forms to other users** When the Send Form Definition With Item option is selected for a Message form, the form definition is included in the item. This allows users who receive the item to view the item in the custom form, even though they do not have the custom form published in a forms library on their system. As such, it provides a useful way to send items created with custom forms to locations outside your immediate system. For example, you may want to send a customer response item over the Internet to a customer site. If the Send Form Definition With Item option is selected, customers see the item in the custom form when they open it, even though they do not have the form published on their system. Saving the form definition with the item also has a side effect of not giving your item a unique message class.

- **It provides a security measure** If a user opens a Message form that has the Send Form Definition With Item option selected, and the form is not available on the server or on the user's Outlook system, and the form has VBScript included with it, then the user sees the Warning message box, as shown in Figure 5.13. In this case, the Send Form Definition With Item option provides a security measure to prevent a user from opening a potentially harmful form. When you finish designing a Message form, you can:
    - Clear the Send Form Definition With Item option and publish the form in the Personal Forms Library or in a forms library in a folder.
    - Submit the form to an Exchange administrator who checks it for harmful macros. If none exist, the administrator clears the Send Form Definition With Item check box and then publishes the form to the Organizational Forms Library.

Important By default, the Send Form Definition With Item option is turned off to keep form size small and reduce network traffic and form loading time. Users are given the choice to turn it on when the form is published.

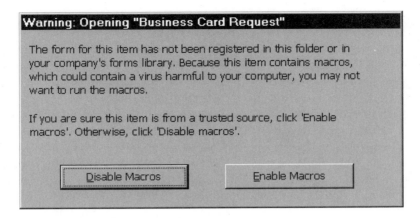

Figure 5.13 *Users see this message box when they try to open an item that contains the form definition and VBScript.*

More Info For more information about the Send Form Definition With Item option, see "Set Form Properties" later in this chapter.

How Is a Form Opened?

By default, the Send Form Definition With Item check box is cleared. The question then arises: If the form definition doesn't travel with the item, how is the form opened? The answer is that the form is launched from a Personal or Organizational Forms Library, or from the forms library of a folder, when the user attempts to create or view an item associated with the form. The form is associated with the item by its message class. Each form has a message class that identifies it internally to the Outlook messaging system. For example, the standard Post form has the message class IPM.Post, while the standard Contact form has the message class IPM.Contact. When an item is created, the message class of the form used to create the item is saved as one of the attributes of the item. When the user double-clicks an existing item to open it, the form definition for the message class of the item is retrieved from a personal folder, or Organizational Forms Library, and and is then used to display the form associated with the item within Outlook.

Publishing a form registers its definition. If the form definition doesn't exist in the user's forms libraries, Outlook will substitute the next class in common. For example, if IPM.Note.Myform.ThisForm does not exist, Outlook will try to open IPM.Note.Myform. If that does not exist, IPM.Note will load and the user will see a standard message form.

As shown in Figure 5.14, when a user opens the form to create a Volunteer Registration item, the form is launched from the Organizational Forms Library. The item, and not the form, is then sent to a recipient. When the recipient opens the item in his or her Inbox, the Volunteer Registration form is launched and the information from the item is shown in the form.

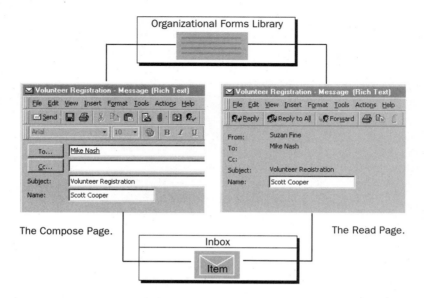

Figure 5.14 *The Compose page creates and sends the item. The Read page shows the item. The form is loaded from the Organizational Forms Library.*

For More Information About	See
Sending the form definition with an item	"Set Form Properties" later in this chapter
Submitting a form to an administrator	Chapter 12, "Distribute and Maintain Applications"
How forms are cached	Chapter 12, "Distribute and Maintain Applications"

How Do Shared Fields Work?

If you're new to designing forms, it helps to understand how the form saves information in the item and how it loads information from the item to the form. One of the central concepts behind the storing and loading of information is shared fields. A shared field is a field that is bound to controls on both the Compose and Read pages of a form. As shown in Figure 5.15, the Name control is bound to the Name field on the Volunteer Registration form.

Shared fields can also be used between forms. For example, when a user creates a response to an item, the information in fields that are common to both forms is copied from the first-opened form to the response form.

More Info For more information about creating shared fields, see Chapter 6, "Controls, Fields, and Properties."

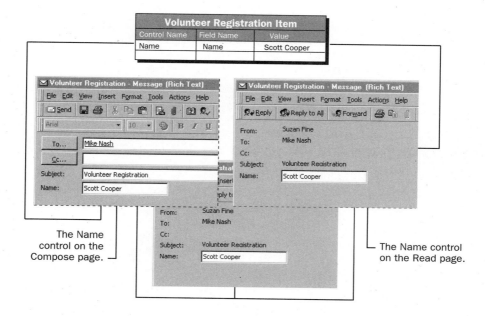

Figure 5.15 *When the item is created and sent, the information is saved from the control to the field. When the item is opened, the information is loaded from the field into the control.*

Create a Folder

Generally, it is a good idea to create a form in a personal folder. This method offers a couple of advantages. First, it lets you store forms in a central and private location while you're designing them. Second, it makes it easy to test the form. To test the form, open the form by clicking the menu command that Outlook adds to the Actions menu of the folder when you publish the form in the folder's forms library.

More Info If you have not yet created a personal folder (.pst) file, see "Create New Folders" in Chapter 3, "Customize Built-In Modules."

To create a personal folder

1. In the Folder List, right-click a personal folder under which you want to create a folder, and then click New Folder.

2. In the Name text box, enter a name for the folder.

3. In the Folder Contains drop-down list box, do one of the following:

    *   Click Mail Items to create a folder that will contain items created with Message, Post, or Office Document forms.

- Click Appointment Items, Contact Items, Journal Items, Note Items, or Task Items to create a folder for items of that type. For example, if you click Appointment Items, Outlook creates a Calendar folder.

4. Click OK.

More Info For more information about creating folders, see Chapter 8, "Folders."

Open the Form and Switch to Design Mode

When you design an Outlook form, you always start with an existing form. Outlook lets you choose from a variety of standard and custom forms. In addition to forms supplied in Outlook, you can design forms based on custom templates created by others in your organization.

- To open a form and switch to Design mode, first select the folder in which you want to create the form. Then select the type of form you want to open, such as those in the following sections.
- To close a form, click the Close button. When you save Message, Post, or Office Document forms, they become items in the Drafts folder of your mailbox. Other forms are saved to the current folder.

To create a Message form

1. On the Outlook Actions menu, click New Mail Message.

   To create a Message form, you must be in the Inbox folder or a folder that contains Mail items.

2. On the Tools menu of the form, select Forms, then click Design This Form.

To create a Post form

1. On the Outlook File menu, select New, and then click Post In This Folder.

   To create a Post form, you must be in the Inbox folder or a folder that contains Mail items.

2. On the Tools menu of the form, select Forms, and then click Design This Form.

To create an Office Document form

1. Click the folder in which you want to create the form.
2. On the File menu, select New, and then click Office Document.
3. Select the document type—for example, a Word document—and then click OK.
4. Do one of the following:
   - To create an Office Document form for posting items, click Post The Document In This Folder. Reply items will be posted to the current folder.

- To create an Office Document form for sending items, click Send The Document To Someone. Reply items will be sent as mail messages.

To modify the Office Document form, the Lock button on the Forms toolbar should be off.

To create a Calendar, Contact, Distribution List, Task, or Journal form

1. Select the folder in which you want to create the form. Typically you will create a custom item in a folder that is designed to hold items of the same message class. For example, you would create a Contacts folder to hold custom contact items. However, folders that contain mail or post items are generic containers—they can contain items of any message class.

2. On the File menu, point to New, and then click the appropriate form type. You can also click the New button on the Standard toolbar. The New button defaults to the item type that is the default item type for the current folder.

3. On the Tools menu of the form, select Forms, and then click Design This Form.

Important If you want to design a custom Distribution List, you must first switch to a Contacts folder. Distribution List items can reside only in Contact folders.

Caution You cannot design a custom Notes form. Be sure not to confuse the sticky notes form, using a message class of IPM.StickyNote, with the standard mail message form, using a message class of IPM.Note.

To create a form based on a custom Outlook template

1. On the File menu, select New, and then click Choose Form.

2. In the Look In drop-down list box, select Templates In File System.

3. Double-click the template you want.

4. If the template is a Post template, select the folder with which the form will be associated.

5. On the form Tools menu, select Forms, and then click Design This Form.

For More Information About	See
Creating a Message form	Chapter 8, "Folders"
Creating a Post form	Chapter 4, "Design a Custom Application," and E-Chapter 2, "The Help Desk Application" in the E-Chapters folder on the companion CD
Modifying a built-in form	Chapter 3, "Customize Built-In Modules"

Edit Form Pages

Forms usually consist of two pages: a Compose page and a Read page. There are other pages contained within the Compose or Read pages, such as (P.2)–(P.6), that you can customize or use to set properties on the form. These pages are covered later in the chapter. Each of these individual pages of the form has its own Compose and Read pages, depending on whether Separate Read Layout has been selected for that page.

The Compose page appears when the user opens the form to create an item. The Read page appears when the user double-clicks an existing item and opens it. When you create forms, you usually edit both the Compose and Read pages. In fact, when you first start designing forms, it's a common mistake to make adjustments to the Compose page, but fail to make the same adjustments to the Read page. When working with forms, you can switch back and forth between the Read and Compose pages by clicking the Edit Compose Page or Edit Read Page button on the Form Design toolbar, as shown in Figure 5.16. Although the Compose and Read pages look very similar, they each have unique characteristics that you need to be aware of.

Click here to show the Compose page. ⌐   ⌐ Click here to show the Read page.

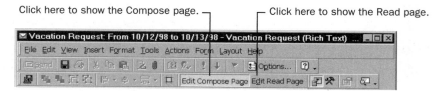

Figure 5.16 *The Edit Compose Page and Edit Read Page buttons.*

The Compose Page

The Compose page of a form contains controls in which the user enters information. For example, in Figure 5.17, the user can enter information in the Starting and Ending text boxes of the Vacation Request form. When the item is sent or posted, the information in these controls is saved in the item. In addition, the Compose page of Message forms provides controls such as the To button and To text box that allow users to specify an address for an item.

The Read Page

The Read page of a form lets the user open and read an item. Quite often, many controls on the Read page are read-only, especially when the form involves financial or sensitive information. As shown in Figure 5.18, the Starting and Ending text boxes on the Read page of the Vacation Request form are read-only, so the reader cannot change them.

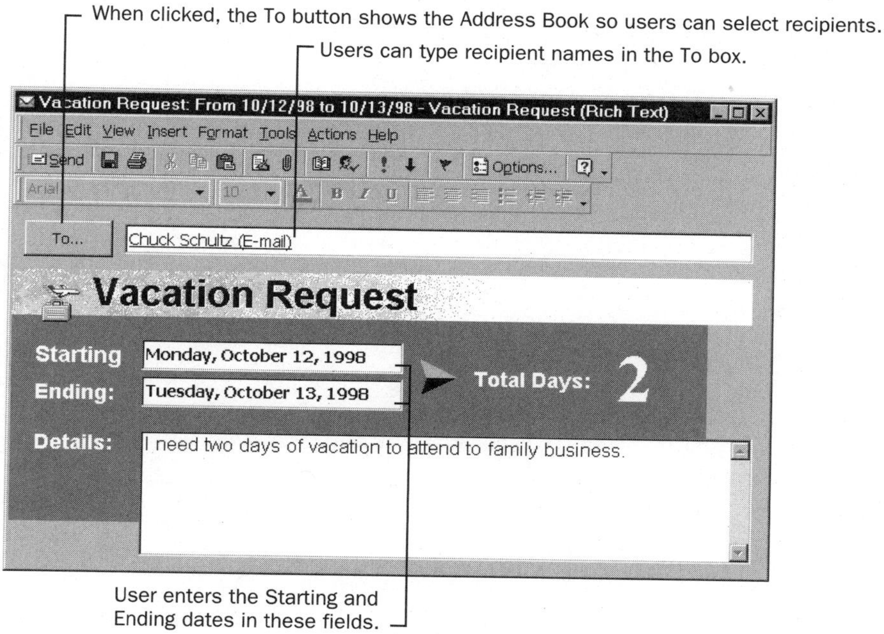

When clicked, the To button shows the Address Book so users can select recipients.

Users can type recipient names in the To box.

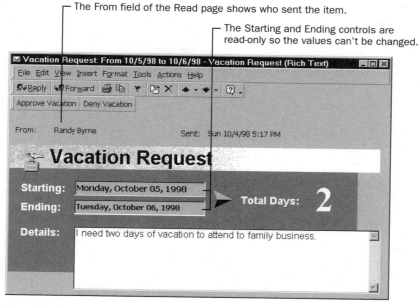

User enters the Starting and
Ending dates in these fields.

Figure 5.17 *The user enters information in the controls on the Compose page.*

The From field of the Read page shows who sent the item.

The Starting and Ending controls are
read-only so the values can't be changed.

Figure 5.18 *The Read page of the Vacation Request form. Many of the controls
on the Read page are read-only, so they cannot be changed by the reader.*

About Separate Read Layout

While a form is in Design mode, Outlook provides a Separate Read Layout option that lets you specify if an individual form page has a Read page layout that is different than the Compose page layout. By default, the Separate Read Layout option, located on the Form menu, is selected for the Message page of Message and Post forms. However, for a custom page, this option is not automatically selected.

Most often when designing forms, you edit the Compose page first, and then edit the Read page. When you open a Message or Post form, the Message page is visible. For many of the forms you create, the Message page may be the only page you edit. However, you can also edit pages P.2 through P.6, as shown in Figure 5.19.

Important If you decide to add controls to a custom form page, you must select the Separate Read Layout option (Form menu) if you want the Compose layout of this page to be different from the Read layout of the form page, as shown in Figure 5.19.

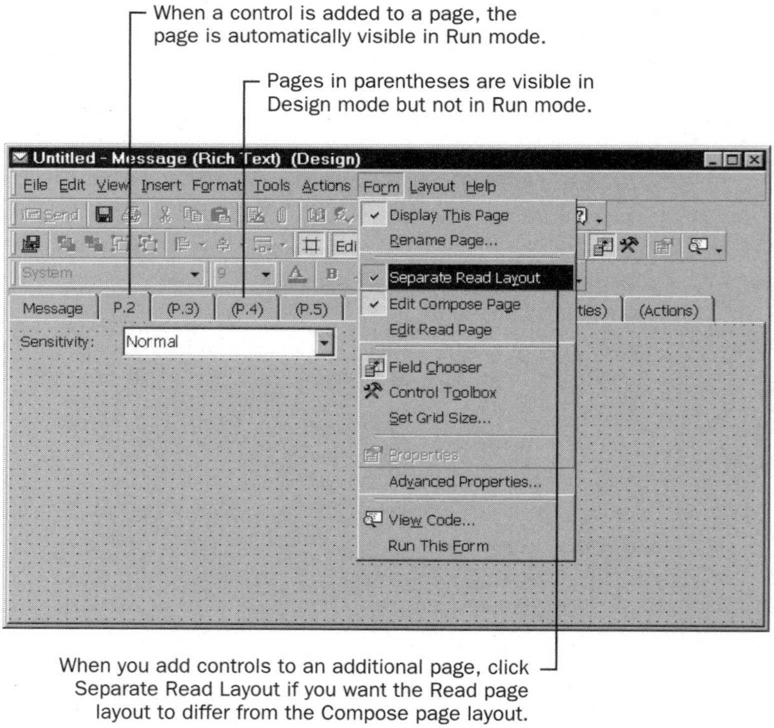

When a control is added to a page, the page is automatically visible in Run mode.

Pages in parentheses are visible in Design mode but not in Run mode.

When you add controls to an additional page, click Separate Read Layout if you want the Read page layout to differ from the Compose page layout.

Figure 5.19 *For the Message form, the Separate Read Layout option is selected for the custom page.*

Note If the Separate Read Layout option is not selected for a page, then you can-not switch between the Compose and Read pages when the individual page is active.

To view either the Read or Compose page

1. Open the form and put it in Design mode.
2. Click the Edit Compose Page or Edit Read Page button on the Form Design toolbar.

To specify the Separate Read Layout option for a page

1. Click the page for which you want to specify the Separate Read Layout option.
2. On the Form menu, click Separate Read Layout.
3. Repeat for each individual page of the form.

Hide or Show a Page

Outlook uses parentheses to designate the pages that are hidden at run time. For example, in the preceding Figure 5.19, notice that the tab label text for pages 3 through 6 is in pa-rentheses to indicate that these pages will be hidden at run time.

The ability to hide and show pages gives you great flexibility in designing forms. For ex-ample, quite often there isn't enough room on the Message page for all the controls you need to add. In this case, you can add additional controls to a custom form page. When you add controls to a page, the parentheses are removed from the text on the page's tab, indicating that the page will be visible at run time.

For some forms, you may want to hide the Message page. This can be especially useful for pre-addressing forms. For example, you can specify an address in the To field of a form at design time, and then hide the page. This prevents the user from changing the address and also lets users submit items without ever seeing the destination address on the form. In addition, you may also want to hide a second page of the form. Keep in mind, however, that at least one page must be visible on the form.

To hide or show a page at run time

1. In Design mode, click the desired page.
2. On the Form menu, click Display This Page.

Note If you drag a field or a control to a hidden page, Display This Page will turn on automatically. To hide the page, deselect Display This Page on the Form menu.

For More Information About	See
Pre-addressing forms	"To" Field in Chapter 6, "Controls, Fields, and Properties"
Hiding and showing pages	"Hiding and Showing a Form Page" in Chapter 11, "Using VBA and VBScript with Outlook," and E-Chapter 2, "The Help Desk Application," in the E-Chapters folder on the companion CD

Rename a Page

When you make a page visible, you should rename it to convey the purpose of the page.

To rename a page

1. In Design mode, click the page.
2. On the Form menu, click Rename Page.
3. Type the new name for the page.

Add Controls

Controls are the means through which users enter and view information on the form. When creating forms with Outlook, you usually add controls to the Compose page of the form first. Then, if you want the information in the controls to be saved to the item, you create a field for the control and bind the field to the control.

To add controls to the form, you use the Control Toolbox.

To show the Control Toolbox

- In Design mode, on the Form Design toolbar, click the Control Toolbox icon.

With Outlook, you can add third-party .ocx controls and Microsoft ActiveX controls to the toolbox to provide added flexibility on your forms. Figure 5.20 illustrates the addition of several Microsoft ActiveX controls to the Outlook Control Toolbox.

Note Be aware that almost all of the events for third-party ActiveX controls do not fire within the Outlook forms container. However, the properties and methods of those controls are accessible using Outlook VBScript. See Chapter 6, "Controls, Fields, and Properties."

Caution If you add ActiveX controls to your custom form, you must ensure that those controls are correctly installed and registered on your user's system. If the controls are not registered properly, an error message will appear when the user opens the form containing the embedded custom control.

Chapter 5   Forms | 121

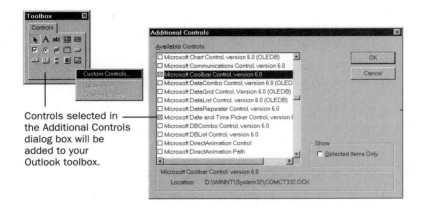

Controls selected in the Additional Controls dialog box will be added to your Outlook toolbox.

Figure 5.20 *You can add additional controls to the Outlook Control Toolbox by using the Custom Controls command and selecting controls in the Additional Controls dialog box.*

To add additional controls to the Control Toolbox

1. Right-click the bottom of the Controls page on the Control Toolbox, and then click Custom Controls on the shortcut menu.
2. Under Available Controls, click the controls you want to enable, and then click OK.

To add a control to a form

- Drag the control from the Control Toolbox to the form

To set Display properties for a control

1. Right-click the control, and then click Properties.
2. On the Display page, set the properties you want.

To set Advanced Properties for a control

1. Right-click the control, and then click Advanced Properties.
2. In the Properties window, set the properties you want and then close the window.

Create and Bind Fields

Fields are the means through which information in a control gets saved and shown in an item. Therefore, you only need to create fields for those controls containing information that you want to save in the item. For example, you generally don't need to create an associated field for a Label control, as shown in Figure 5.21, because there's no reason to save the values in such controls to the item. However, for controls in which users enter

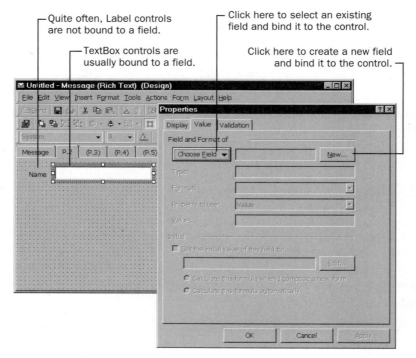

Quite often, Label controls are not bound to a field.

TextBox controls are usually bound to a field.

Click here to select an existing field and bind it to the control.

Click here to create a new field and bind it to the control.

Figure 5.21 *Fields in which the user enters or selects information are generally bound to fields. Label and Image controls are usually not bound to fields.*

information, such as the TextBox and ComboBox controls, you usually create a new field or bind an existing field to the control so that the value in the control is saved to the item.

Create a New Field and Bind It to a Control

When you create a new field by using the Properties dialog box, the field you create is automatically bound to the currently selected control. In addition, the field you create is automatically added to the User-Defined fields in the Folder field set.

To create a new user-defined field

1. Right-click the control, and then click Properties.
2. Click the Value page.
3. Click New.
4. In the Name text box, type the field name.
5. If necessary, change the Type and Format of the field, and then click OK twice.

More Info For more information about specifying the type and format for a field, refer to Chapter 6, "Controls, Fields, and Properties."

Bind a Control to an Existing Field

In addition to the user-defined fields that you create, Outlook supplies several different sets of fields that you can use. These field sets include Frequently-Used fields, Address fields, Date/Time fields, and All Mail fields. These are built-in fields that, in most cases, perform advanced functions not easily attained with user-defined fields. To select an existing field to bind to a control, you use the Properties dialog box, as shown previously in Figure 5.21.

To bind a control to an existing field

1. Right-click the control, and then click Properties.
2. Click the Value tab.
3. Click Choose Field, point to the set of fields you want, and then click the field.
4. If necessary, change the format and set the initial value of the field, and then click OK.

Select Fields from Other Forms

Outlook conveniently categorizes fields by the forms with which they're associated. This is often useful if you want to create a form that has many of the same fields as another form. Rather than looking through the User-Defined fields in the Folder field set, you can view a shortened list of fields for a form.

To add a field set from a form to the field list

1. Right-click the control, and then click Properties.
2. Click the Value tab.
3. Click Choose Field, and then click Forms.
4. In the upper left-hand library drop-down list box, click the forms library that contains the forms you want, as shown in Figure 5.22.
5. In the left-hand forms list box, double-click the form to add it to the Selected Forms box.
6. Click Close and then click OK.

When To Use the Field Chooser

The Field Chooser allows you to view, add, and delete fields. You add a field by dragging it from the Field Chooser to the form. When you drag a field from the Field Chooser, Outlook adds a control and a control label to the form, and automatically binds the control to the associated field. It then automatically positions the controls on the form if the AutoLayout option is selected on the Layout menu. The control added to the form depends on the field you add. For example, if you add a Yes/No type field to a form from the Field Chooser, a CheckBox control is added to the form. If you add a Text type field, a TextBox control is added to the form.

In addition to providing a shortcut for adding TextBox and CheckBox controls to a form, the Field Chooser serves several other purposes.

- If you accidentally delete a standard control such as Message, To, or From on a form, you can add it back to the form by dragging it onto the form from the Field Chooser.
- The Field Chooser allows you to delete fields.
- The Field Chooser allows you to view fields available in the active folder and in other forms, as shown in Figure 5.23.

To add a field from the Field Chooser

1. On the Field Chooser, click the set of fields you want.
2. Drag the field from the Field Chooser to the form.

Delete a Field

To delete a field, you use the Field Chooser.

To delete a field

1. On the Field Chooser, click the set of fields you want from the drop-down list box.
2. Click the field you want to delete, and then click Delete.
3. In the message box, click Yes.

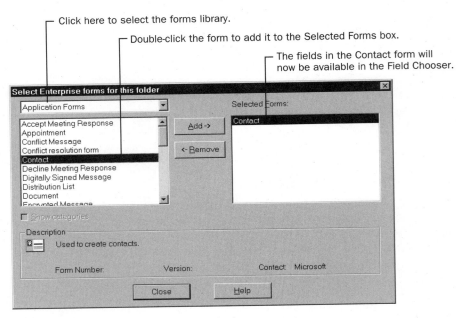

Figure 5.22 *You can add a field set from another form to the field list.*

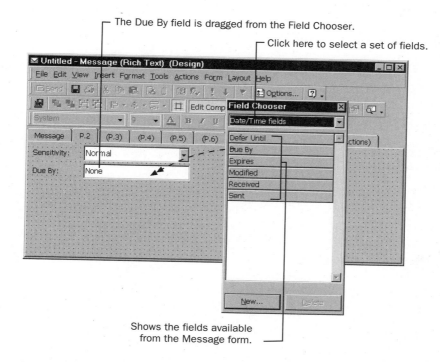

Figure 5.23 *You can drag fields directly from the Field Chooser to the form.*

Polish the Layout

After you add controls to the form, you can use Outlook's layout options to add professional polish to your forms. Outlook provides a great set of layout options that will save you countless hours of finish work. This section covers how to select, edit, align, and space controls. You are encouraged to experiment with the remainder of the layout options.

Select and Edit Controls

To select a control on a form, click the control. To edit the control, click it again. For example, to select a Label control, click it once. To type text into the label, click it again and then type the text. To exit Edit mode, click outside the Label control.

Align Controls

With Outlook alignment options, you can align the borders of a control. When you align controls, the alignment is always based on the last control selected. The sizing handles of the last control selected are white, as opposed to black sizing handles on the other controls, to indicate the control on which the alignment is based.

⊃ **To align controls**

1. Hold down the Ctrl key and then click each of the controls you want to align.
2. On the Layout menu, point to Align, and then click one of the alignment menu commands from the Align submenu.

Space Controls

After you align the controls, you can space them so they are evenly separated.

⊃ **To space controls**

1. Hold down the Ctrl key and then click each of the controls you want to space.
2. On the Layout menu, point to Horizontal Spacing or Vertical Spacing, and then click one of the spacing options from the menu.

Set Tab Order

The tab order defines the sequence in which the controls become active on the form when a user presses the Tab key. When you add controls to the form, the control name is added to the bottom of a list of controls in the Tab Order dialog box, as shown in Figure 5.24.

Label controls, such as *ConversationLabel* and *SubjectLabel,* are listed in the Tab Order dialog box but are not included in the tab order at run time. Also, when the Message control is active, pressing the Tab key will cause the insert bar to advance to the next tab stop in the control. If possible, it's usually best to place the Message control as the last control in the tab order.

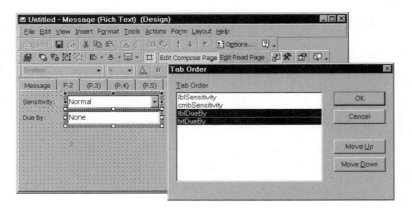

Figure 5.24 *Use the Tab Order dialog box to change the tab order of controls on a page.*

To set the tab order for the Compose page

1. In Design mode, on the Layout menu, click Tab Order.
2. In the Tab Order list box, click Move Up or Move Down to put the controls in the proper tab sequence and then click OK.

Tip You can select more than one control at a time in the Tab Order dialog box. To move multiple controls, hold down the Ctrl key, click the controls you want in the Tab Order list box, and then click the Move Up or Move Down button.

Note If you intend to use the Tab Order dialog box to rearrange the tab order, it is good form design practice to use a standard naming convention to name the controls on your form. Otherwise, you will be confused as to the identity of the controls referenced by *TextBox1, TextBox2*, and so forth. Consider adopting a standard control-naming convention that is used throughout your organization. Figure 5.24, shown previously, uses a typical Visual Basic naming convention.

View the Form in Run Mode

When you've finished with the layout of a page, it's a good idea to switch from Design mode to Run mode to see how the form will look at run time.

To switch between Design mode and Run mode

1. On the Form menu, click Run This Form.
2. Click the Close button to return a form to Design mode.

Create Help (Optional)

Not all forms require TipText help. In fact, most forms should be simple enough that TipText help is not required. In some cases, however, you may want to specify ControlTipText for a control. With ControlTipText, the TipText appears when the user positions the pointer over the control.

To create ControlTipText

1. In Design mode, right-click the control you want to specify ControlTipText for, and then click Advanced Properties on the shortcut menu.
2. Double-click the ControlTipText cell, and then type the text you want in the text box next to the Apply button.
3. Click the Apply button to insert the text into the cell.
4. Close the Advanced Properties dialog box.

Edit the Read Page

Quite often, the Compose and Read pages of a form are very similar. As a result, you can design most of the Read page by copying controls from the Compose page. As a rule, you must edit the pages of the Read page if the page has a separate read layout.

Important Each individual page of the form has its own Read or Compose page if Separate Read Layout was selected for that page.

To copy controls to the Read page

1. On the Form Design toolbar, click Edit Read Page.
2. Click the individual page you want to edit.
3. Adjust or remove any unnecessary controls on the page to make room for the controls you want to copy from the Compose page.
4. On the Form Design toolbar, click Edit Compose Page.
5. Click the individual page that contains the controls you want to copy.
6. Hold down the Ctrl key and click the fields that you want to copy, or use the selector tool to select a group of fields.
7. Click the Copy button.
8. Click Edit Read Page.
9. Click the Paste button.
10. Repeat steps 2 through 9 for each Read page you want to edit.

Set Properties for Controls on the Read Page

Quite often, you make many of the controls on the Read page read only. This prevents readers from changing the contents of an item after it has been sent or posted.

To make a control read only

1. Right-click a control, and then click Properties.
2. On the Display page, check the Read Only box.

Set the Tab Order for the Read Page

With Outlook forms, you must set the tab order for the Compose and Read pages separately. In addition, you must the set the tab order for each individual page separately. For instructions on setting the tab order for a page, see "Polish the Layout" earlier in this chapter.

About Viewing the Read Page in Run Mode

To view the Read page in Run mode, you must first send or post an item with the form. For some built-in forms, you must save an item. Consequently, you should test the Read page after you publish the form. Publishing and testing the Read page of the form is discussed later in this chapter.

To switch between Design mode and Run mode

1.   On the Form menu, click Run This Form.

2.   Close the form in Run mode to return to the form in Design mode.

Set Action Properties

With form action properties, you specify how a form handles responses. Form actions are one of the most important aspects of Outlook because they enable users to respond to existing items in an Outlook folder.

> **Important** Throughout this book, the term response is used to encompass Reply, Forward, Reply To All, Reply To Folder, and all user-defined response actions.

With Outlook actions, you can specify

- Whether a Reply, Reply To All, Forward, Post To Folder, or custom menu command appears on the Outlook Actions menu and the form Actions menu
- Whether an Action button appears on the form toolbar
- The form to activate to enable the user to send or post a response
- Whether the action opens the response form, sends the response immediately, or whether the user is prompted to open the response form

To create actions

- See "Create a New Action" in Chapter 4, "Design a Custom Application."

To set actions

- See Chapter 7, "Actions," which provides a detailed discussion on how to set actions for Message and Post forms, and provides several detailed examples to help you understand how actions can be applied in applications.

Set Form Properties

With the form's Properties page, you give the form a name and a description and you specify whom to contact with questions about the form.

To set form properties

- With the form open in Design mode, click the Properties page, as shown in Figure 5.25.

Category   Allows you to create or specify a category for forms to help organize the forms in the New Form dialog box.

Sub-Category   Allows you to create or specify a subcategory for the form.

Always Use Microsoft Word As The E-Mail Editor   Allows you to specify that Microsoft Word runs in the Message control of the form, so users have spell checking, thesaurus, and full formatting options that are available with Microsoft Word. The Word editing features are available only to recipients who use Word as their e-mail editor.

Template   Allows you to specify the Microsoft Word template that is used to format the text in the Message control of the form.

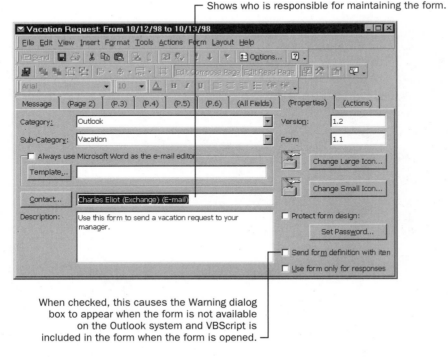

Shows who is responsible for maintaining the form.

When checked, this causes the Warning dialog box to appear when the form is not available on the Outlook system and VBScript is included in the form when the form is opened.

Figure 5.25 *The form's Properties page.*

Word Templates and Outlook Default Mail Format

The Always Use Microsoft Word As The E-Mail Editor option and the Template edit box are disabled on the Properties page of your custom form if your default mail format is either Plain Text or HTML. You can only specify a Word template for use in the message body of your custom form if you have selected Microsoft Outlook Rich Text as the default mail format for outgoing messages. To change the default mail format, select the Options command from the Tools menu and click the Mail Format page in the Tools Options dialog box.

Contact   Click the Contact button to select the names of those people who are responsible for maintaining and upgrading the form. When the form is published, contact information shows in the form's Properties page and the form's Properties dialog box selected from the Form Manager.

Description   Type a description for the form. The form description shows in the form's About dialog box on the Help menu and also in the Properties dialog box for the form.

Change Large Icon   Click to change the icons for the form. Large icons appear in the form Properties dialog box.

Change Small Icon   Click to change the icons that appear in the Outlook folder to represent an item of the type created with the form.

> **Note** Outlook 2000 provides both large and small icons for all the built-in Outlook forms in a language-specific folder under the Forms folder. For example, if you are using the U.S. English version of Outlook, the language-specific identifier is 1033. Look for the icons in C:\Program Files\Microsoft Office\Office\Forms\1033.

Protect Form Design   Select this check box to have password protection enabled for your form. This prevents other users from changing the form after you've published it.

Send Form Definition With Item   Specifies that the form definition is included with the item. To speed opening the form, this check box is cleared by default. However, it may be selected when the form is published.

This option provides convenience and security for forms. It provides convenience because it enables you to send items to other users. Those users can then open the item in the form on their computers, even though the form is not installed on their Outlook system.

It provides a security measure for this reason: If a form contains VBScript and is not available on the user's Outlook system, and the Send Form Definition With Item option is checked, the user sees a Warning dialog box, as shown earlier in this chapter in Figure 5.13. It prevents users from opening a form containing macros that might potentially delete or copy their mail, or that might send mail from their mailbox to another user without their knowledge.

After you create a Message form that is intended for general use, you submit it to an administrator for approval. The administrator checks the form for viruses and potentially harmful code. If the administrator approves the form, she then clears the Send Form Definition With Item check box and publishes the form in the Organizational Forms Library.

More Info For more information about form security and managing forms in your organization, see Chapter 12, "Distribute and Maintain Applications."

Use Form Only For Responses   Certain forms, such as the Approve Vacation and Deny Vacation forms, are used solely for responding to existing items. As a result, these forms are opened only if a related item is first selected or opened. They also don't appear in the dialog boxes allowing you to compose a new form.

More Info For more information about this option and creating response forms, see Chapter 7, "Actions."

Publish the Form

When you finish designing a form, you publish it to a forms library. Optionally, you can make a backup copy of the form, although it is not required.

- When you publish a form, you register the form in a forms library and expose the form to the Outlook user interface. For example, after the form is published, the form menu commands and form name are visible in the Outlook user interface.

- When you make a backup copy of the form, you save the form definition as an Outlook Form Template or .oft file.

Outlook forms are interpreted, not compiled. Therefore, there's no source code to worry about. Since only the form definition is saved, rather than the form and all of its associated controls, the message size for forms where the form definition is not saved with the item averages 1 KB per item. If your custom form contains one or more file attachments, the message size will increase accordingly.

Make a Backup Copy of the Form

Before you publish the form, you may want to make a backup copy of the form on your hard disk or on your organization's server. When you make a copy of the form, you save it as an .oft file in much the same manner as you would save a Microsoft Word template.

To make a backup copy of a form

1. With the form open, click Save As on the File menu.
2. In the Save In drop-down list box, select the default Outlook template folder, such as C:\Program Files\Microsoft Office\Templates.
3. In the File Name text box, type a name for the form.
4. In the Save As Type drop-down list box, select Outlook Template (.oft).
5. Click Save.

To open your backup copy of a form

1. Select New on the File menu, and then click Choose Form.
2. Click User Templates In File System in the Look In drop-down list box, and then click on the form you'd like to open.

Publish the Form

When you publish a form, you accomplish three things:

- You make the form available to be run in Outlook.
- You register the form in the designated form library.
- You expose the form's properties, such as form name, description, and menu commands in Outlook.

About the Form Name and Message Class

When you click the Publish Form button on the Form Design toolbar and type a name in the Display name text box, Outlook automatically adds the name to the Form Name text box and sets the message class for the form by appending the form name to IPM.*xxx*. For example, if the form is a Message form and you type *Business Card Request* in the Form Name text box, Outlook constructs the message class for the form by appending the form name to IPM.Note. Thus, the message class would become IPM.Note.Business Card Request. The message class is the internal identifier of the form and is used to locate and activate a form when an item associated with the form is created or opened.

To specify the form name

1. On the Form Design toolbar, click Publish Form.
2. Type a name in the Display Name text box.

To change the message class

- In the Form Name text box, change the name of the form
  The Message class is automatically updated.

Publish to a Forms Library

When you publish a form, you publish it to a forms library. After the form is published in a library, you can then open the form to compose, submit, and read items in a folder. Where you publish the form determines how the form will be available to other users. The following table provides a description of the forms libraries where you can publish forms.

> **Important** When publishing and naming forms, the form names should be unique, or unpredictable results may occur. Also, if the form is published in more than one forms library and you make changes to the form, the form must be updated in all the forms libraries in which it is published, unless the form definition is sent

with the item. To update forms libraries, use the Forms Manager. To synchronize offline forms libraries, use Synchronize on the Tools menu. For more information, see the sections "Forms Manager" and "How folders are synchronized" in Chapter 12, "Distribute and Maintain Applications."

Location	Description	Advantage
Organizational Forms Library	A public container of forms that is located on an Exchange Server. It is not connected with a specific application folder.	Allows forms to be used by anyone who has access to the Exchange Server.
Personal Forms Library	A private container of forms. It is not connected with a specific application folder.	Allows forms to be available for personal use. Also handy for designing and testing forms.
Public Folder Forms Library	A public container of forms. Each public application folder has its own forms library. The container exists in the folder in a Public Information Store on an Exchange Server.	Allows forms to be used by anyone with access to the Exchange Server and whoever has permission to use the application folder.
Personal Folders Forms Library (in a .pst file)	A private container of forms. Each application folder has its own attached forms library located on a local or network hard disk drive. Can be opened only by one user at a time.	Allows forms to be organized in a personal folder. Also allows designers to distribute a large number of forms and folders by using a .pst personal folder or file.
Offline Folder Forms Library (in an .ost file)	A private container of forms that is associated with the security context of a mailbox account, located on a local hard disk drive. Each folder has its own attached forms library. Synchronized manually or programmatically with an Exchange Server.	Allows forms to be organized in an offline store folder. Users in remote locations can use forms as if they were connected directly to the server. Folders can then be synchronized between the local hard disk and the server.

 More Info For more information on updating or synchronizing forms published in multiple locations, see Chapter 8, "Folders." For more information on publishing and distributing forms, see Chapter 12, "Distribute and Maintain Applications."

To publish a form

1. In Design mode, select Forms on the Tools menu, and then click Publish Form As.

2. In the Display Name text box and Form Name text box, type the name for the form.

3. To change the location (library) where the form is stored, click Look In, and then do one of the following:

- To publish a form in the Organizational Forms Library, click Organizational Forms Library in the Look In drop-down list box, and then click OK.

- To publish a form in the Personal Forms Library, click Personal Forms Library in the Look In drop-down list box, and then click OK.

- To publish a form in a public or personal folder, choose Outlook Folders, click the Browse button, select the folder in the Look In drop-down list box, and then click OK.

4. Click Publish.

5. In the message box, choose No for most cases where users have access to the same libraries as you. Choose Yes if this form will be sent to someone outside your system who needs the definition to view the form.

More Info For more information about how to make forms available to users, see Chapter 12, "Distribute and Maintain Applications."

Test and Release the Form

After you publish the form, you need to test it to make sure it works as expected.

To test a Message form in the Personal or Organizational Forms Library

1. On the Folder List, click Inbox.

2. On the Outlook Tools menu, select Forms and then click Choose Form.

3. Select the forms library from the Look In drop-down list box, then double-click the form in the list.

4. Fill out the form options and then send the form to yourself.

5. When the item arrives in your Inbox, double-click it to make sure the Read page of the form works as expected.

To test a Post form in a forms library in a folder

1. In the Folder List, click the folder that contains the form you want to test.

2. On the Outlook Actions menu, click the form's associated menu command to open the form.

3. Fill out the form options and then click Post.

4. After the item is posted in the folder, double-click it to open it and make sure the Read page of the form works as expected.

Release the Form

 More Info For more information about releasing forms, see Chapter 12, "Distribute and Maintain Applications."

Chapter 6
Controls, Fields, and Properties

In This Chapter

In this chapter, you'll get the fundamental skills and information you need to use controls, fields, and properties effectively on a form. In addition, you'll take a look at the unique features of each commonly used control and then learn some strategies for implementing these controls and fields in an application.

Specifically, we'll cover how to

Set display properties for controls   including foreground and background colors.

Set advanced properties   such as the BackStyle, BorderStyle, ControlTipText, and WordWrap properties for a control.

Create combination fields   that show the results of combined text strings.

Create formula fields   that automatically perform calculations and show the results in the field. For example, for a Grand Total field, you can create a formula to show the result of adding the value of the Total field to the value of the SubTotal field.

Set initial values   in a field to determine the value that appears in the field when the form first appears at run time.

Validate and restrict information in a field   and learn how to create validation formulas that Microsoft Outlook checks before it closes the form. For example, you can create a validation formula that shows a message box if a value in a field exceeds a certain number.

Use the To, Subject, and Message fields and see how to preaddress a form by setting the initial value of a To field. You will also look at how the Subject field works, and how to insert files, items, and hyperlinks to Web pages in the Message field.

Set control-specific properties and learn how to create check boxes, bind option buttons to a field, and create list boxes so users can select multiple values.

Set Control Display Properties

Each control, regardless of whether it is bound to a field, has a unique set of display properties that you can change. With display properties, you can change the name of the control, specify its exact position on the form, set its foreground or background color, and specify settings such as read-only or multi-line, as shown in Figure 6.1.

Since the Vacation Request form is the example used in this chapter, select the Vacation Request folder from the Folder List. To do this, click the Actions menu, and choose the Vacation Request form from those listed at the bottom of the menu.

To view the display properties for a control on the Vacation Request form

1. In Design mode, right-click the control, and then click Properties on the shortcut menu.
2. Click the Display tab.

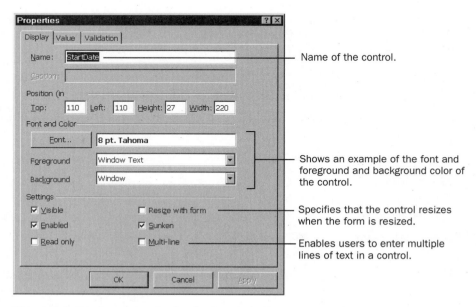

Figure 6.1 *Display properties for the StartDate TextBox control.*

Tip When you add a control to a form, the control is given a default name such as TextBox1, Label1, and so on. If you'll be referencing the control in Microsoft Visual Basic Scripting Edition (VBScript) procedures for the form, it's a good idea to give the control a unique name, as shown previously in Figure 6.1.

Change Foreground and Background Colors

The background or foreground color for a control corresponds to the color specified for the component on the Appearance tab of the Display icon in Windows Control Panel. As shown earlier in Figure 6.1, the foreground color of the StartDate control is set to Window Text, so the color of the foreground text in the StartDate control matches the color of Window text in the Display Properties dialog box. Similarly, the background color of the StartDate control matches the color defined for Window. If you have Window defined as green on your system, the background of the control is green.

To set foreground and background colors for a control

1.   Right-click the control, and then click Properties.
2.   Click the Display tab.
3.   In the Foreground Color or Background Color drop-down list box, click the component to which you want to map the control.

The Vacation Request form shown in Figure 6.2 provides a good example of how color effects can be achieved on a form. The background color for the Label8 control is set to Button Shadow so that it will have a dark gray color for almost all users. Also, many of the controls on the form have a white background. In this case, the background color is set to Window, which maps to white in the Windows Control Panel. Notice that most of the controls actually sit on top of the Label8 control. Controls are layered in Design mode, using Bring To Front and Send To Back options from the icons in the Form Design toolbar. For this form, the Label8 control is sent to the back layer of the page.

Tip Generally, you can make a dark gray background for a control by setting the background color to Button Shadow. You can make a white background by setting the background color to Window.

Layer Controls

The Label8 control on the Vacation Request form provides a good example of how you can layer controls on a form. As shown in Figure 6.2, several controls, such as StartDate and EndDate, are located on top of the Label8 control. This is done by using the Send To Back and Bring To Front buttons on the Form Design toolbar. With these buttons, you can layer controls by bringing them to the front layer or sending them to the back layer.

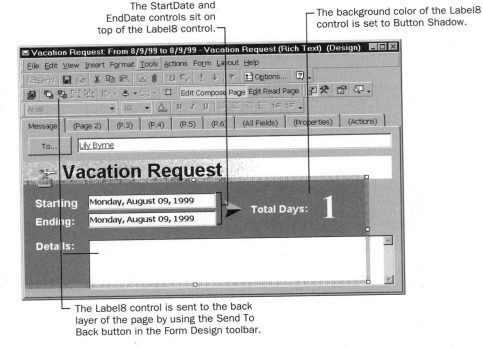

The StartDate and EndDate controls sit on top of the Label8 control.

The background color of the Label8 control is set to Button Shadow.

The Label8 control is sent to the back layer of the page by using the Send To Back button in the Form Design toolbar.

Figure 6.2 *The Vacation Request form.*

To send a control to a back layer

- Click the control, and then click the Send To Back button on the Form Design toolbar, or select Order from the Layout menu.

To bring a control to a front layer

- Click the control, and then click the Bring To Front button on the Form Design toolbar, or select Order from the Layout menu.

More Info For more information about setting control display properties, see "Set Control-Specific Properties" later in this chapter.

Set Advanced Control Properties

The Advanced Properties window provides even more ways to customize a control. For example, with the Advanced Properties window, you can

- Define a transparent background for a control.
- Specify the ControlTipText property—the text that appears when the user moves the pointer over the control.

- Specify whether the control has the WordWrap property turned on.
- Specify the BorderStyle property for the control.

To open the Advanced Properties window

- Right-click the control, and then click Advanced Properties on the shortcut menu.

In the example shown in Figure 6.3, the Label2 control sits on top of the textured Image1 control. However, the text appears to be part of the image because the Label2 BackStyle property is set to Transparent. The BackStyle property for a control can only be set in the Advanced Properties dialog box.

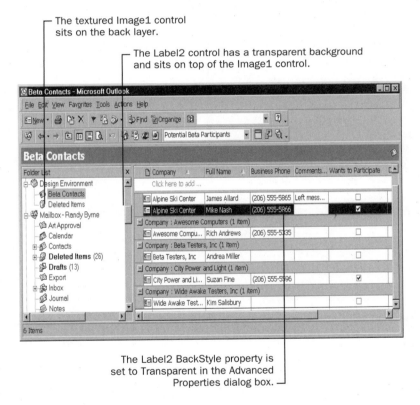

Figure 6.3 *The BackStyle property of the Label2 control is set to Transparent so the control appears to be part of the Image1 control behind it.*

Bind a Control to an Existing Field

In many cases, you can bind a control to an existing field, rather than creating a new field. For example, you can bind a control to a field supplied by Outlook, or you can bind a control to an existing user-defined field. You can view a list of available fields in the field list in the Properties dialog box, as shown in Figure 6.4.

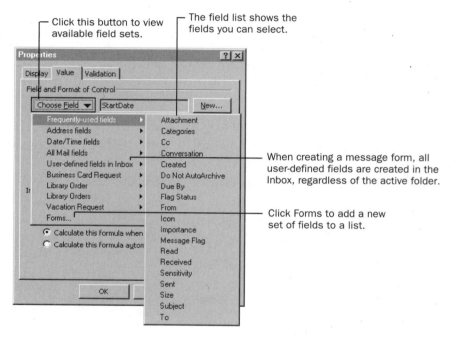

Figure 6.4 *The field set and field list in the Properties dialog box.*

⊃ **To bind a control to an existing field**

1. Right-click the control you want to define a field for, and then click Properties on the shortcut menu.

2. Click the Value tab.

3. Click Choose Field, point to the set of fields you want, and then click the field.

The sets of fields available in the field list in the Properties dialog box differ for each type of form. For example, if you create a Message form, the field list does not show the field categories for built-in forms, such as All Contact fields, All Appointment fields, and All Task fields. In addition, when you create a Message form, all user-defined fields are created in the Inbox, regardless of the active folder.

The following table shows the field sets that are available for each type of form, and where the user-defined fields are created for the form. It also shows whether the Field Chooser is available for the form type.

Form Type	Available Field Categories	User-Defined Fields Are Created In	Field Chooser Available
Message	Field sets from built-in forms, such as Appointment, are not available	Inbox	Yes
Post	All Post fields	Active folder	Yes
Office Document	Not applicable	Active folder	Yes
Built-in	All	Active folder	Yes

Important For Office Document forms or Office documents posted directly to an application folder, you must create fields in the document itself using the built-in or custom document properties of the application (Microsoft Word, Microsoft Excel, or Microsoft PowerPoint). For example, you would use the Word Forms toolbar in a Word document to add linked fields to a bookmark in the document. You can then use the Properties command on the File menu to add built-in or custom document properties and link them to the bookmarks in the Word document. In a similar manner, you can link defined names in an Excel workbook to custom document properties that you define for the Excel document. Any built-in or custom document properties you create in the document are exposed as user-defined fields in the folder containing the document. However, you must explicitly create those built-in or custom document properties; they are not created automatically.

More Info For more information about creating built-in or custom document properties in an Office 2000 document, see the online Help for the specific application.

Create User-Defined Fields

There are two ways to create fields with Outlook. You can use the Field Chooser, which offers the advantage of automatically creating and positioning controls for you when you drag fields onto the form. You can also use the Properties dialog box, which enables you to edit field properties. In this section, we explain how to use the Properties dialog box to create new user-defined fields. Before you can create a field using the Properties dialog box, however, you must first select a control on the form to which you want to bind the field.

Note When creating a Message form, all user-defined fields are created in the Inbox, regardless of which folder is active.

↪ **To create a user-defined field**

1. Right-click the control you want to define a field for, and then click Properties on the shortcut menu.

2. Click the Value tab.

3. Click New.

4. In the Name text box, type a name for the field.

5. In the Type drop-down list box, click a field type.

6. In the Format drop-down list box, click a format, as shown in Figure 6.5.

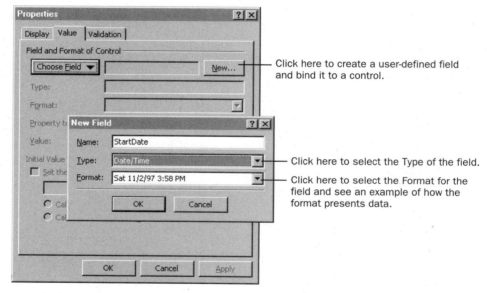

Figure 6.5 *You can create user-defined fields from the Properties dialog box.*

Note After you create a field, you cannot change its type. Rather, you must create a new field with a different name and with the desired properties. You can then delete the old field. To delete a field, use the Field Chooser.

Location of User-Defined Fields

A user-defined field can be created in several different locations depending on how you create the field. The following table specifies where user-defined fields are created.

Action	Field Added To
Use the New button on the Field Chooser in a view	Folder
Use the New button on the Field Chooser in form Design mode	Folder
Drag a field from the Field Chooser to a form	Item
Use the New button in the Properties dialog box of a control when binding the control to a field	Item and Folder

Specify Field Type

When you create a new field, you use the Type property to specify the type of data stored in a field in the item. The following table describes the uses for the various field types:

Field Types	Description
Combination	Fields that show the result of combined text strings. Combination fields are read only.
Currency	Numeric data as currency or mathematical calculations that involve money.
Date/Time	Date and time data.
Duration	Use to show time expired. This control has no inherent intelligence built in.
Formula	Fields that show the result of a formula. For example, a Totals field might contain a formula that multiplies the value of the Hours field by the Hourly Rate field. Formula fields are read only.
Integer	Nondecimal numeric data.
Keywords	Fields that are bound to a ListBox control from which the user can select multiple values.
Number	Numeric data used in mathematical calculations, with the exception of currency.
Percent	Numeric data as a percentage.
Text	Text or numbers that don't require calculations, such as phone numbers.
Yes/No	Fields that are bound to a CheckBox control.

Changing Field Type

After you create a field, its Type drop-down list box is disabled so you cannot easily change its type. When you create a user-defined field with the Properties dialog box, it is created in the folder where you are creating the form and with a user-defined field in your custom form. If you haven't specifically defined a folder for the form by publishing the form in the folder's forms library, you will create the folder-level user-defined field in your Inbox. Even if you delete the control containing the user-defined field from your form page, a copy remains at the folder level. Any attempt to delete the control and then redefine the user-defined field with the same name and a different field type will result in an error message informing you that a user-defined field with this name already exists in the folder. You can circumvent this problem by following these steps.

To change the type of a user-defined field

1. Select the control bound to the user-defined field that you want to change and press Delete to delete the control.

2. In the Field Chooser window, select User-Defined Fields In Folder from the drop-down list box at the top of the Field Chooser.

3. Select the user-defined field that you want to redefine.

4. Click the Delete button.

5. You will see a prompt stating "The field <Name> will be removed from the list of available fields but will remain in all items in which it was used. Do you want to continue deleting the field from the available fields?" Select Yes to delete the user-defined field on the assumption that you have not published your form and are still in the initial design phase. If you are deleting a user-defined field in a form that has been published to a folder and which contains data in the form, select No. You will have to write VBA code to perform the type conversion.

You can now recreate the user-defined field that you removed in step 2, and use a different field type for the field.

Specify Field Formats

Field formats determine how information is saved and shown in a control. Each field type has a different set of formats that you can choose from. Each format in the Field Format drop-down list box, as shown earlier in Figure 6.5, includes an example of how the format displays information in the control.

Create Combination Fields

With Combination fields, you can create a formula for a field that combines string values from other fields and then shows the results in the control bound to the field. This section describes the general procedure for creating Combination fields and provides several examples of the types of Combination fields you can create.

To create a Combination field

1. Right-click the control that you want to bind to a Combination field, and then click Properties on the shortcut menu.

2. Click the Value tab.

3. Click New.

4. In the Name text box, type a name for the field.

5. In the Type drop-down list box, click Combination.

6. Click Edit.

7. Do one of the following.

- Click Joining Fields And Any Text Fragments To Each Other to show combined string values in the field.
- Click Showing Only The First Non-Empty Field, Ignoring Subsequent Ones if you want only the first value entered in the specified fields to show in the Combination field.

8. Type text in the Formula text box or click Field to specify the fields you want inserted in the expression. Click OK.

9. To make the formula update automatically, select the Calculate This Formula Automatically button on the Value page.

Note The Showing Only The First Non-Empty Field, Ignoring Subsequent Ones option is generally used in the context of folder fields. For example, when you have a folder that contains different types of items, one type of item may have the user name in the Author field, while another type of item may have the user name in the From field. To combine these two field values into one field in the folder, you can use the Showing Only The First Non-Empty Field, Ignoring Subsequent Ones option.

Combine Field Strings

With the Visual Basic Expression Service provided with Outlook, you can easily build expressions for Combination fields without worrying about concatenating values. As shown in Figure 6.6, the FullName control shows the combined values from the FirstName and LastName fields.

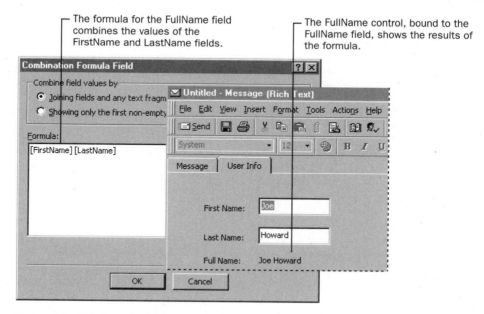

Figure 6.6 *The formula for the FullName field combines the values from the FirstName and LastName fields and shows the results in the FullName control. Notice that the field is read only.*

Combine Field Value Strings with Text Fragments

Quite often, you combine text fragments that you type into the Formula text box with string values from other fields. In the following example, the Combination field named UserName is located on the Read page of a form. At run time, when the user opens a submitted item, the value of the From field is combined with the User Name: fragment to create the result shown in Figure 6.7.

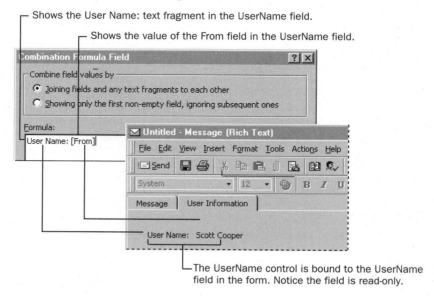

Shows the User Name: text fragment in the UserName field.

Shows the value of the From field in the UserName field.

The UserName control is bound to the UserName field in the form. Notice the field is read-only.

Figure 6.7 *The User Name: [From] formula automatically combines the text fragment with the value in the From field.*

Combine Field Values by Showing Only the First Non-Empty Field

In general, this option makes more sense when applied to a folder than when applied to a form. In fact, it is described in detail in Chapter 8, "Folders." However, it can have some use when applied to a form. For example, let's assume a folder contains items created with a form having a variety of phone number fields, such as home phone, car phone, business phone, and fax number. Also assume that you want to create a new form that consolidates the numbers so that only the primary phone number shows on the form. To do this, you can create a Combination field named Primary Phone that combines the phone numbers, but only displays the value in the first non-empty phone field in the item.

More Info For more information about using Combination fields in folders, see Chapter 8, "Folders."

Create Formula Fields

With Formula fields, you can create formulas that automatically calculate values and show the result in a control. Here are a few examples:

- **For a Time Card form,** you can create a formula for a field that totals the hours for the day, and then totals the hours for the week, showing the results in the Totals field.

- **For the sample While You Were Out form,** the Subject field contains a formula that combines the values from several fields into a message that shows in the Subject field.

- **For the Vacation Request form,** the TotalDays field contains a formula that automatically calculates the number of vacation days by finding the difference between the Starting date and the Ending date.

- **For an Invoice form,** you can create a Totals field that contains a formula that shows the results of the number of hours multiplied by the hourly rate.

Although you can create a Formula field using the Type property, it's just as easy to create a formula for a Text, Number, or Currency field. As a result, there is no compelling reason to create a Formula field. Instead, it's preferable to create the type of field you want, and then create the formula for the field. As you'll see in the examples in this section, the fields include formulas but are not defined as Formula fields.

To create a Formula field when you create the field

1. In Design mode, right-click the control you want to bind to the Formula field, and then click Properties on the shortcut menu.
2. Click the Value tab.
3. Click New.
4. In the Name text box, type a name for the field.
5. In the Type drop-down list box, click the type of field you want. You do not have to select Formula. You can select any type of field—Currency, Number, Date/Time—and then click OK.
6. On the Value page, click Edit.
7. In the Formula text box, type in the formula or use the Field or Function button to insert the field or function you want. Some samples follow.

Specify That the Field Automatically Calculates the Results

After you create the formula for the field, you must set the Calculate This Formula Automatically option so the field is updated when field values referenced in the formula are changed. For example, for the Invoice form shown in Figure 6.8, the TOTAL field automatically updates when the values in the Hours or Hourly Rate controls change.

To specify that the field automatically calculates the result

1. Right-click the control that you want to create a formula for, and then click Properties on the shortcut menu.

2. On the Value page, select the Set The Initial Value Of This Field To check box.

3. Click Calculate This Formula automatically.

4. To make the control read only, click the Display tab, and then select the Read Only check box.

Calculate Totals

In Figure 6.8, the TOTAL field is a formula field that shows the result of the expression:

```
[Hours] * [Hourly Rate]
```

This expression multiplies the number of hours in the Hours field by the value in the Hourly Rate field and shows the result in the TOTAL field.

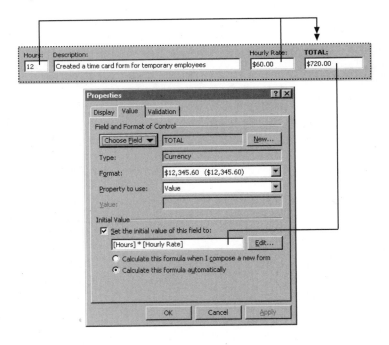

Figure 6.8 *The TOTAL field automatically multiplies the hours by the hourly rate and shows the results.*

Build Text Strings

The While You Were Out form shown in Figure 6.9 gives an example of a Formula field showing the results of combined values in the Subject field—which is not visible on the form at run time. When the While You Were Out item is created, the values from the You Received and Please Contact fields are combined with the You Received text fragment to create the value in the Subject field. This is the value that appears in the user's Inbox when they receive the message.

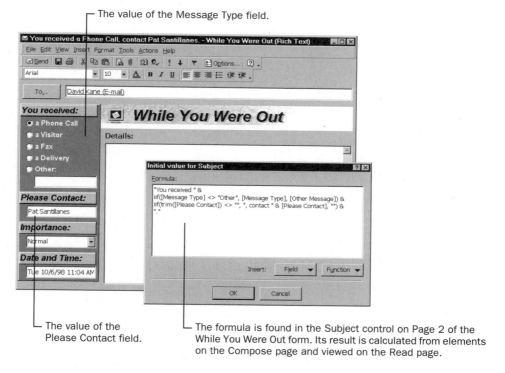

The value of the Message Type field.

The value of the Please Contact field.

The formula is found in the Subject control on Page 2 of the While You Were Out form. Its result is calculated from elements on the Compose page and viewed on the Read page.

Figure 6.9 *The While You Were Out form. The Subject field is hidden on the form at run time.*

When the item arrives in the user's Inbox, the Subject field shows the following result:

You received a Phone Call; contact Joe Howard. ·

In the formula, as shown earlier in Figure 6.9, the *IIf* function evaluates the expression and returns one of two parts, based on whether the expression evaluates as *True* or *False*. For example, if the Message Type field value is not *Other*, then the Subject field shows the value of the Message Type field (a phone call). In the next line, if the Please Contact field is not empty, then the value of the Please Contact field is added to the Subject field.

For more information, see the Microsoft Outlook Visual Basic Reference Help.

Calculate Date Differences

On the Vacation Request form, as shown in Figure 6.10, the TotalDays field contains a formula that automatically calculates the difference between the Starting and Ending date fields and shows the result.

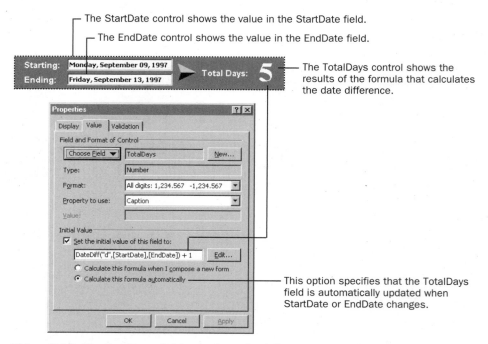

Figure 6.10 *The TotalDays field calculates the difference between the StartDate and EndDate fields and adds 1.*

Tip The StartDate and EndDate fields in the Vacation Request form offer Microsoft IntelliSense. For example, if you enter Next Tuesday into the EndDate field, Outlook translates Next Tuesday into the correct date.

Set Initial Field Values

When you create an initial value for a field, you specify the values that are available in the field when the user opens the form to create a new item. With Outlook, the way the initial value is set varies somewhat depending on the control to which the field is bound. As a result, we'll cover the general concept of initial values in this section, and then cover how to set initial values for each control separately.

Here are a few examples of why you set initial values for fields.

- To set the default values in Label, TextBox, ComboBox, ListBox, CheckBox, and OptionButton controls.

- To set the initial value of the Subject field of a form to summarize the content of the form. For example, for an Art Approval form, you can set the initial value of the Subject field to Art Approval.

- To set the initial value of the To field on a Message form to preaddress the form. For example, for an Employee Feedback form, you can preaddress the To field to an Employee Feedback public folder so that all responses are automatically routed to that folder.

The following table lists the sections in this chapter that explain how to set initial values for the control to which the field is bound. Therefore, each control contains a separate section on how to set the initial value.

To Set the Initial Value For a	See Later in This Chapter
To field	To Field
Subject field	Subject Field
Message field	Message Field
Field bound to a Label control	Label Controls
Field bound to a TextBox control	TextBox Controls
Field bound to an OptionButton control	OptionButton Controls
Field bound to a CheckBox control	CheckBox Controls
Field bound to a ComboBox control	ComboBox Controls
Field bound to a ListBox control	ListBox Controls

Validate and Restrict Data

Outlook provides a couple of ways to validate and control how information is entered into a form.

- At the simplest level, you can specify that a value is required for a field. As a result, if the user tries to submit or save the item and no value is in the field, a message box appears saying that a value is required in the field.

- You can create a validation formula for a field. If the field validation fails, a message box appears showing the types of values allowed in the field.

Specify That a Value Is Required for a Field

Many forms contain Text fields in which the user is required to enter information. For example, on the Business Card Request form, as shown in Figure 6.11, the Name field requires a value. If a value is not entered in the Name field when the user attempts to

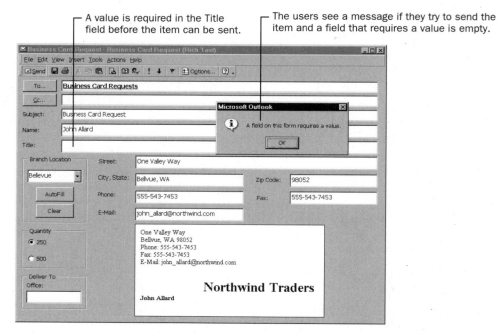

A value is required in the Title field before the item can be sent.

The users see a message if they try to send the item and a field that requires a value is empty.

Figure 6.11 *On the Business Card Request form, a value is required in the Title field. If no value is entered, users see a message when they attempt to send the item.*

send the form, Outlook shows a message box that tells the user that a field on the form requires a value.

 To specify that a value is required for a text field

1. Right-click the control that is bound to the field, and then click Properties on the shortcut menu.

2. Click the Validation tab.

3. Select the A Value Is Required For This Field check box.

Important Many of the Outlook field types automatically supply a value in the field by default. For example, the Date field has the value None by default. For field types such as Date, Currency, and Number that automatically supply a value, you must create a formula or use a script to validate that the field contains the specified information.

Create Validation Formulas

Outlook performs field validation when users attempt to save, send, or post an item. In addition, Outlook performs field validation when users attempt to close a form. With validation formulas, you can limit the type of information that can be saved to the item. For example, you can define

```
>=10 And <=100
```

as the validation formula for a Number field that accepts only values from 10 to 100. When users attempt to submit or save the item, they see a message only if the number entered in the field does not fall within the range of 10 to 100.

> **Tip** If you want to validate the field immediately after users enter information in the field, you can do so by writing VBScript code for your form and using the PropertyChange event or CustomPropertyChange event. For more information, see Chapter 11, "Using VBA and VBScript with Outlook." Samples are also given in "The PropertyChange Event" and "The CustomPropertyChange Event" in E-Chapter 2, "The Help Desk Application," in the E-Chapters folder on the companion CD.

To create a validation formula

1. Right-click the control you want to create a validation expression for, and then click Properties on the shortcut menu.
2. Click the Validation tab and then, under Validation Formula, click the Edit button.
3. Type the validation formula or use the Field or Function button to build the formula and then click OK.
4. In the Display This Message If The Validation fails text box, type the message you want to appear in the message box the user will see if the validation fails.

Formulas That Validate Amounts

For many forms, you can create field validation formulas to check whether a value in the field is more or less than a specified value. For example, in Figure 6.12, the validation formula for the Amount field in the Charity Donation form specifies that the value in the field must be at least $1. If the user enters a value less than $1 in the Amount field, a message appears.

> **More Info** Note that the *CCur* function (Currency Conversion) is used in the validation formula. For more information on the *CCur* function, see Microsoft Visual Basic Help.

Validation Formulas That Compare One Field Value with Another

In some cases, you might want to create a validation formula that compares one field value against another field value. For example, for the Vacation Request form shown in Figure 6.13, the value of the StartDate field is compared with the value of the EndDate field to make sure the EndDate value falls after the StartDate value.

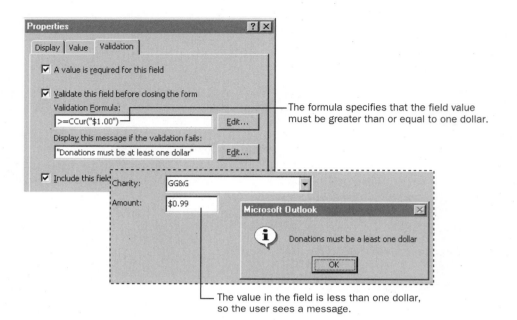

The formula specifies that the field value must be greater than or equal to one dollar.

The value in the field is less than one dollar, so the user sees a message.

Figure 6.12 *The Amount field contains a value that is less than one dollar. When the user attempts to send the form, a message box appears indicating what is acceptable in the field.*

The validation formula for the EndDate field compares the value of the EndDate and StartDate field values.

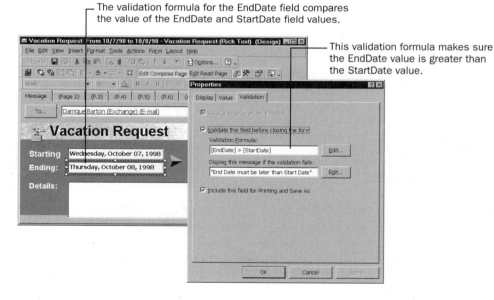

This validation formula makes sure the EndDate value is greater than the StartDate value.

Figure 6.13 *The validation formula for the EndDate field specifies that the validation passes if the value is greater than the StartDate field.*

Caution Validation formulas can sometimes cause unexpected results in your forms. If you delete a bound control that uses a validation formula but then fail to delete the underlying user-defined field in the folder, you may experience validation messages that don't appear to have a source. Normally, the focus changes to the control that has triggered the validation error. However, if the control is not on the form page that has the focus, the user will not be able to determine which field value is causing the error. Writing VBScript code to control validation is more difficult than using validation formulas, but it can lead to a more consistent experience for your users and it can accommodate more complex validation scenarios.

Set Field-Specific Properties

The Message page of standard Message and Post forms contains three Outlook-supplied fields that provide fundamental functionality on the form. These fields are

To field   Used to address the form.

Subject field   Used to summarize the message. The text in the Subject field appears in the Title bar of the Form window. The value in the Subject field also sets the value of the Conversation field in the item.

Message field   Used to enter text or insert files, items, or objects or insert shortcuts to them.

This section describes how the To, Subject, and Message fields work, and then describes strategies for effectively using these fields in a form.

To Field

With Outlook, you can preaddress forms by setting the initial value of the To field. Preaddressing a form is much like providing a self-addressed envelope. Because the address is already provided on the form, the user just fills in the form and clicks the Send button.

Preaddress a Form to a Distribution List or Person

In some cases, you want to preaddress a Message form to a distribution list or to a user. For example, you want to preaddress a form such as a Weekly Schedule form to a distribution list. In addition, you may want to preaddress a Reply form so that the item created with the form is sent to your Inbox.

To set the initial value of the To field

1.   On the Outlook Actions menu, click New Mail Message.
2.   On the form, click the To button.
3.   Double-click the desired names or distribution list name to select recipients, and then click OK.

If the distribution list you want to specify does not exist, you must ask your administrator to create it. If you create a Personal Distribution List or use an existing Personal Distribution List, the form will work correctly only on your computer.

4. On the Tools menu, select Forms, and then click Design This Form to switch to Design mode.

5. Make additional modifications to your form, and then save and exit.

Preaddress a Form to a Folder

In some cases, you might want to preaddress a form to a folder. For example, the Business Card Request form, as shown in Figure 6.14, can be opened from the Organizational Forms Library. However, the form is preaddressed to the Business Card Request folder, so the user can submit the item automatically by simply clicking the Send button.

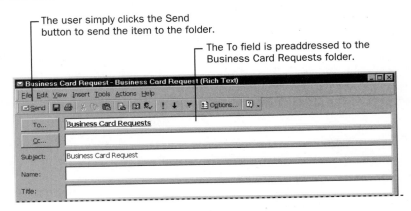

Figure 6.14 *The Business Card Request form is preaddressed to the Business Card Request folder.*

Before you can preaddress a form to a folder, the folder address must exist in the Global Address Book or in an Address Book in your profile. If the folder address does not exist in the Global Address Book, you can ask your administrator to make the folder address available in the Global Address Book, or you can publish the folder address to an Address Book in your profile.

 Important To publish a folder address in an Address Book in your profile, the folder must be located in Public Folders.

To add a folder address to an Address Book in your profile

1. In the Folder List, right-click the folder, and then click Properties on the shortcut menu.

2.   Click the Administration tab (you will see the Summary tab if you do not have owner permissions to modify this folder).

3.   Click Personal Address Book to add this item to a Personal Address Book in your profile. Unlike previous versions of Outlook, which would add a public folder address only to your Personal Address Book when you clicked the Personal Address Book button, Outlook 2000 will add the folder address to the Address Book selected in the Keep Personal Addresses In drop-down list box on the Addressing page of the Services dialog box for your Exchange profile.

To Preaddress the To field to a folder

1.   On the Outlook Actions menu, click New Mail Message.

2.   On the Message form, click the To button.

3.   In the Show Names From The drop-down list box, click the name of the Address Book that you've selected to keep personal addresses in on the Adressing page in the Services dialog box for your Exchange profile.

4.   Double-click the folder name in the list, and then click OK. The folder name should appear in the To field.

5.   On the Tools menu, select Forms, and then click Design This Form to switch to Design mode.

6.   Modify the form as desired, then save and exit.

More Info For more information, see "Add Folder Address to Personal Address Book" in Chapter 8, "Folders."

Subject Field

The Subject field provides several important functions on a form:

- It summarizes the information in the item.
- It sets the value of the Conversation field. The Conversation field is the field used to create threaded conversations in views.
- The value in the Subject field appears in the title bar of the window.

Set the Initial Value of the Subject Field

In some cases, you may want to set the initial value of the Subject field. For example, for single-purpose forms such as the Business Card Request form, you can set the initial value of the Subject field to Business Card Request.

To specify the initial value of the Subject field

1.   Right-click the Subject control, and then click Properties on the shortcut menu.

2.   Click the Value tab.

3. In the Value text box, type a value or click Edit to build an initial value formula for the Subject field as shown in Figure 6.15.

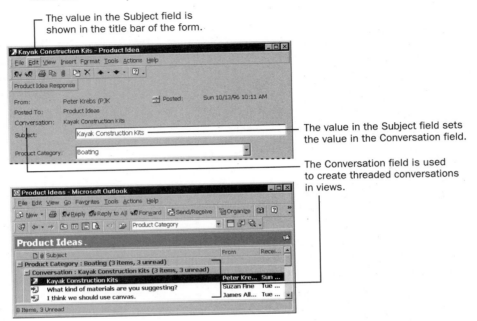

Figure 6.15 *Shows how the Subject field functions in the New Product Idea form.*

Message Field

With the Message field shown in Figure 6.16, you can insert the following types of items. Each of these scenarios is covered in more detail in later sections.

- **File attachments and shortcuts** For example, for a Copier Request form, the user can insert attached files into the Message field. If the files are too large to send through the Microsoft Exchange Server system, the user can insert shortcuts to the attached files instead. In addition, you—the designer—can insert files, file shortcuts, and hyperlinks. For example, you may want to insert attachments for ReadMe files that explain how to use the form or application. Or you may want to insert a hyperlink to a file or folder address.

- **Item attachments and shortcuts** This allows users to insert messages from other users into the Message field.

- **Shortcut to a World Wide Web page** Recipients must have a Web browser installed on their computer to use the shortcut.

- **Linked or embedded objects**   These objects can be Word documents, Excel workbooks, PowerPoint presentations, or any other valid ActiveX object supporting object linking and embedding.

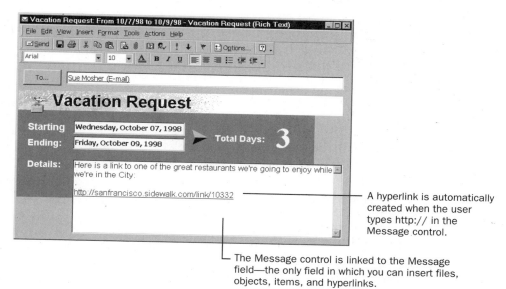

A hyperlink is automatically created when the user types http:// in the Message control.

The Message control is linked to the Message field—the only field in which you can insert files, objects, items, and hyperlinks.

Figure 6.16 *At design time or run time, you can insert files, items, hyperlinks, and objects in the Message field. You can also insert shortcuts.*

Restrictions and Rules for the Message Control Usage

When working with the Message field and Message control, there are a few guidelines you should be aware of:

- The Message control is automatically bound to the Message field.
- Each form can contain only one Message control per page. For example, the Compose page of a form can contain a Message control and the Read page can contain a Message control.
- You cannot have a Message control on the Message page and a duplicate control on page 2 or following the Compose or Read pages.
- If the form does not have the Separate Read Layout option selected on the Form menu for the page that contains the Message control, the form can contain only one Message control.
- The Message control is the only control on a form in which you or the user can insert files, items, or objects.
- The form must be in Run mode to enter information into the Message control.

To insert a file attachment or shortcut in the Message control

1. In Run mode, click in the Message control where you want to insert the file attachment or shortcut.
2. On the Insert menu, click File.
3. Locate and click the file you want to insert.
4. Under Insert As, click an option.
5. Click OK.

To insert an item in the Message control

1. In Run mode, click in the Message control where you want to insert the item.
2. On the Insert menu, click Item.
3. In the Look In drop-down list box, click the folder that contains the item you want to insert, and then click the item.
4. Under Insert As, click an option.
5. Click OK.

To insert a folder shortcut in the Message control

- In Run mode, using the right mouse button, drag the folder from the Folder List to the Message control.

To insert a URL shortcut in the Message control

1. First create a Uniform Resource Locator (URL) shortcut on the Windows desktop using your Web browser.
2. In Run mode, drag the URL shortcut from the desktop to the Message control.

To insert a hyperlink in the Message control

- In Run mode, type the hyperlink in the Message control. When you type *http://* or one of the supported protocols, the text is automatically underlined and the color is changed to blue by default. For example, to create a hyperlink to the Building Microsoft Outlook 2000 Applications root folder using the Outlook protocol, you specify the following hyperlink in the Message control:

    <Outlook://Building Microsoft Outlook 2000 Applications/>

Important If the hyperlink includes spaces, you must enclose the entire address in angle brackets <>. Notice in the examples below that file names use the forward slash (/) instead of the traditional backslash (\). If you want the hyperlink to open an item in the folder rather than in an Outlook Explorer displaying the hyperlinked folder, place a tilde character (~) in front of the subject for the item that you want to open. Duplicate subjects in the folder can yield unpredictable results. Valid examples are as follows.

<file://c:/program files/microsoft office/office/msowcvba.hlp/>

<outlook://public folders/all public folders/ITSD/Y2K/~Solutions for the Year 2K Problem/>

<outlook:inbox/>

<file:////ServerName/ShareName/exchsrvr/bin/cdo.hlp/>

Note If you want the hyperlink to point to default folders in the current user's mailbox, don't add the double forward slash (//) after outlook:protocol. Valid examples are *outlook:Contacts* or *outlook:Tasks*.

Here are the supported protocols:

Protocol	Description
file://	A protocol used to open files on an intranet.
ftp://	File Transfer Protocol (FTP), the most common method used to transfer files over the Internet.
gopher://	Gopher protocol, by which hyperlinks and text are stored separately.
http://	Hypertext Transfer Protocol (HTTP).
https://	Hypertext Transfer Protocol Secure; a protocol designed to provide secure communications using HTTP over the Internet.
mailto://	A protocol used to send mail to an e-mail address. When the recipient clicks this hyperlink, a new message opens with the mailto e-mail address filled in.
news://	A protocol used to open an Internet newsgroup for recipients who are connected to an NNTP server.
nntp://	Network News Transfer Protocol, a protocol used to distribute, inquire about, retrieve, and post Usenet articles over the Internet.
outlook://	A protocol used to open an Outlook folder or an item or file in Outlook. This protocol is supported only in Outlook.
prospero://	A protocol used to organize Internet resources in your personal set of hyperlinks that go to information on remote file servers; for your personal virtual file system.
telnet://	The Internet standard protocol for logging on from remote locations.
wais://	Wide Area Information Servers protocol, a distributed information system used to retrieve documents based on keywords you supply.

To insert an object in the Message control

1. In Run mode, click in the Message control where you want to insert the object.
2. On the Insert menu, click Object.
3. In the Insert Object dialog box, click the Create From File button.
4. In the Create From File text box, type the name of the file that you want to link or embed in the Message control, or click Browse to select from a list.

- To create a linked object, select the Link To File check box.
- To show the object as an icon, select the Display As Icon check box.

You can see the Link To File check box when Create From File is selected.

About the Control Toolbox

The Control Toolbox identifies the controls you can add to a Frame or page of a form. You can customize the Control Toolbox in many ways, including the following:

- Add pages to the Control Toolbox. Right-click on Control Toolbox page tab and select the New Page command.
- Move controls from one page in the Control Toolbox to another. Right-click on Control Toolbox page tab and select the Move command.
- Rename Control Toolbox pages. Right-click on Control Toolbox page tab and select the Rename command.
- Change the properties of a control in the Control Toolbox. Right-click on the icon for the control and select the Customize ControlName command. You can change the ToolTip text for the control and the image that represents the control.
- Add other controls—including ActiveX controls—to the Control Toolbox. Right-click in the body of the Control Toolbox and select Custom Controls command.
- Copy modified controls from a form to the Control Toolbox. Use the selection tool to select a group of controls and drag them to the Control toolbox to create a controls template. Drag the controls template from the Control Toolbox to a form in design mode to recreate the controls.
- Import or export all the controls on a page on the Control Toolbox. Right-click on Control Toolbox tab and select the Import Page or Export Page command. Toolbox pages are saved with the .pag extension.

Note When you add a control to a form by using the Control Toolbox, the control is not initially bound to a field.

Set Control-Specific Properties

Each of the controls in the Outlook Control Toolbox serves a unique purpose. As a result, the properties for each control are set in a slightly different way. This section covers setting the properties for the most commonly used controls.

More Info For more information about all Outlook intrinsic controls, see the Microsoft Outlook Visual Basic Reference Help. The Microsoft Outlook Visual Basic Reference Help (vbaoutl.chm) is available on the Microsoft Office 2000 installation CD. If the Outlook Visual Basic Reference Help is not available, follow these steps to install it.

⭢   **To install Microsoft Outlook Visual Basic Reference**

1. Click the Start button, select Settings, and then select Control Panel.
2. Double-click the Add/Remove Programs icon.
3. Select Microsoft Office 2000 in the list of installed programs and click the Add/ Remove button.
4. Click the Add Or Remove Features button.
5. Open the Microsoft Outlook for Windows item under the Microsoft Office root item.
6. Click the Visual Basic Scripting Support item.
7. Select Run From My Computer.
8. Click Update Now.

⭢   **To use controls**

1. Open the form in Design mode by selecting Forms on the Tools menu, and then clicking Design This Form.
2. Click the Control Toolbox button on the Advanced toolbar.
3. Drag the desired control to the form page.
4. Modify the control using the following guidelines.

Label Controls

Label controls can be used to show text on the page. As such, they are useful for company logos, address information, or a heading on a form page, as shown in Figure 6.17.

When To Bind a Label Control

Generally, you bind Label controls to fields when you want to save the value to the item. For example, in the Vacation Request form, as shown in Figure 6.17, the Total Days label is bound to the TotalDays field. In this way, the value in the field is saved to the item when the item is saved or sent. However, also notice that Label2 and Label5 are not bound. As a result, the value in the Vacation Request field is not saved to the item. Rather, it exists in the form definition and is recreated each time an instance of the form is activated.

Set the Initial Value of a Label Control

In some cases, you may want to set the initial value of a Label control. For example, in the Vacation Request form, the TotalDays Label control on the Compose page contains a formula that automatically shows the result in the field.

⭢   **To set the initial value of a Label control**

1. In Design mode, right-click the control, and then click Properties on the shortcut menu.

The Label3 control is not bound.

The Label2 control is not bound.

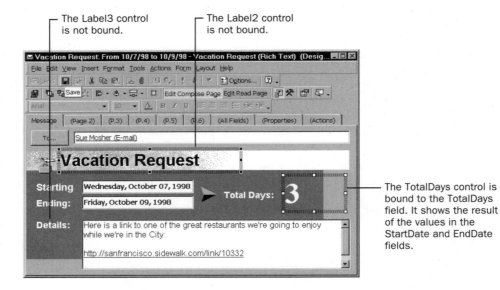

The TotalDays control is bound to the TotalDays field. It shows the result of the values in the StartDate and EndDate fields.

Figure 6.17 *Label controls on the Vacation Request form.*

2. Click the Value tab, and then type the initial value in the Initial Value text box, or click Edit to create an initial value formula.

- To automatically calculate a formula, click Calculate This Formula Automatically.

- To show the initial value in the Label control when the form is opened to create an item, click Calculate This Formula When I Compose A New Form.

Note Before you can set the initial value of a Label control, the control must be bound to a field. For more information, see "Bind a Control to an Existing Field," earlier in this chapter.

TextBox Controls

Use TextBox controls on a form to let the user enter, edit, and view information, as shown in Figure 6.18. For example, you can place a TextBox control on a Compose page to let the user enter information and on the Read page to let the user view information.

Note In some cases, you may want to insert attachments, shortcuts, or hyperlinks. To do this, you must use the Message control. For more information about the Message control, see "Message Field" earlier in this chapter.

The TextBox control has a variety of display properties that give you great flexibility in determining how the TextBox control looks and functions. For example, you can specify the Multi-Line property so the user can enter more than one line of text in the control. Before you can specify the initial value for a control, it must be bound to a field.

TextBox controls on the Business Card Request form.

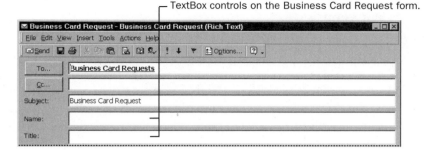

Figure 6.18 *TextBox controls on the Business Card Request form.*

To specify the Multi-Line option for a TextBox control

1. In Design mode, right-click the control, and then click Properties on the short-cut menu.

2. Click the Display tab, and then select the Multi-Line check box.

Initial values for text boxes can be specified on the Value page of the Properties dialog box for that control.

To specify the initial value for a TextBox control

*   On the Value page, type a value in the Initial Value text box or click Edit to build an initial value formula for the field.

Frame Controls

Use the Frame control to contain controls that are logically related, as shown in Figure 6.19. Frame controls are often used to contain OptionButton controls, but they can also contain other controls such as CheckBox, ComboBox, Label, and TextBox controls.

Tip You can use the Frame control to create a line on the form. Set the height or width to 2, depending on whether it is a horizontal or vertical line.

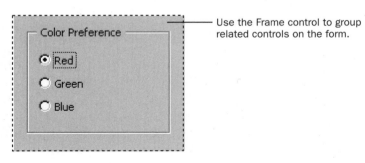

Use the Frame control to group related controls on the form.

Figure 6.19 *The Frame control.*

➲ **To add a Frame control**

- Drag the control from the Control Toolbox to the form.

Controls within the Frame can be easily removed by dragging and deleting.

➲ **To add or remove controls from a Frame control**

- To add a control, drag the control into the frame. To remove a control, drag it outside the border of the frame, right-click the control, and then choose Delete on the shortcut menu.

➲ **To change the caption of the Frame control**

1. Right-click the border of the Frame control, and then click Properties on the shortcut menu.
2. In the Caption text box on the Display page, type a new caption for the Frame control.

OptionButton Controls

Use OptionButton controls on a form when you want to give the user a limited number of choices. For example, on the Business Card Request form, OptionButton controls are used to enable users to select the quantity of cards they want, as shown in Figure 6.20.

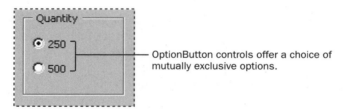

Figure 6.20 *OptionButton controls on the Business Card Request form.*

➲ **To specify a caption for an OptionButton control**

1. In Design mode, drag the OptionButton control from the Control Toolbox to the form.
2. Click the OptionButton control. When the insertion pointer appears, type a caption for the control.

Set Value Properties for an OptionButton Control

To group OptionButton controls together, you bind the controls to the same field. For example, the OptionButton controls in Figure 6.20 are bound to the Quantity field. When you bind one OptionButton control to a field, all other option buttons in the group are automatically bound to the same field. Option buttons on a page that are not included in a container, such as a Frame or MultiPage control, are grouped together automatically.

Option buttons in a Container control are grouped with the option buttons in that container.

To bind an OptionButton control to a field

1. Right-click the control, and then click Properties on the shortcut menu.
2. Click the Value tab.
3. Do one of the following:
   - Click New to create a new field. You can create a Currency, Text, or Number field. Choose the type of field to match the data in the control. In this example, the Quantity field is a Number field.
   - Click Choose Field, point to User-Defined Fields In Folder, and then click the field to which you want to bind the OptionButton control. In this example, the OptionButton control is bound to the Quantity field. The folder name changes depending on which form is being designed.

When you bind one option button in the group to a field, all option buttons in the group are bound to the same field automatically.

Set the Value Property of Each Option Button Separately

After you bind the option buttons in a group to an existing field, you must set the Value property of each option button separately. The Value property is the value that is written to the field when the option button is selected at run time. As such, this value appears in folder views to represent the option button if it is selected in an item.

To set the Value property of an OptionButton control

1. Right-click the OptionButton control that you want to set the Value property for, and then click Properties on the shortcut menu.
2. Click the Value tab.
3. In the Initial Value text box, type a value for the option button.
4. Click OK.

To set the initial value of an OptionButton control

1. Right-click the OptionButton control that you want as the default button when the form first appears at run time. Then, click Advanced Properties on the shortcut menu.
2. Click the Value cell, and then type *True*.
3. Click Apply, and then close the Advanced Properties window.

CheckBox Controls

Use CheckBox controls to give the user an On/Off or Yes/No choice, as shown in Figure 6.21. Because check boxes work independently of each other, the user can select any number of check boxes at one time.

⊃ **To bind a CheckBox control to a field**

1. Right-click the CheckBox control, and then click Properties on the shortcut menu.

2. On the Value page, do one of the following:

   - Click New to create a new field. You can create a Yes/No, On/Off, True/False, or Icon field. When you select a Yes/No field, the selected value appears in the cell in the folder. If you select Icon, the CheckBox icon appears in the folder as selected or cleared.

   - Click Choose Field, point to User-Defined Fields In Folder, and then choose the field to which you want to bind the CheckBox control. In this example, the CheckBox control in Figure 6.21 is bound to the Corporate field.

Figure 6.21 *A CheckBox control.*

Note The CheckBox control must be bound to a Yes/No field type for the check box to operate properly.

⊃ **To set the initial value of a CheckBox control**

1. Right-click the CheckBox control, and then click Advanced Properties on the shortcut menu.

2. Click the Value cell, and then type *True*.

3. Click Apply, and then close the Advanced Properties window.

ComboBox Controls

Use ComboBox controls so users can either choose a value from the list portion of the control or enter text in the edit box portion of the control, as shown in Figure 6.22. When working with the ComboBox control, you create the control, bind it to a field, and then specify the values for the items in the combo box list.

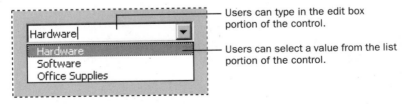

Figure 6.22 *A Dropdown ComboBox control.*

To bind the ComboBox control to a field

1. Right-click the ComboBox control, and then click Properties on the shortcut menu.
2. On the Value page, do one of the following:
   - To create a new field, click New.
   - To bind the ComboBox control to an existing field, click Choose Field, point to User-Defined Fields In Folder, and then click the field to which you want to bind the ComboBox control.

To select a list type

- In the List Type drop-down list box on the Value page, click either Dropdown or Droplist.

  Outlook provides two types of combo boxes that you can use. You can set the combo style at design time on the Value page of the field's Properties dialog box, or you can set the style at run time by programmatically setting the Style property. The ComboBox also supports the same ListStyle property as the ListBox control. See the ListStyle table under "ListBox" later in this chapter.

Style	Description
DropDownCombo	Users can either select a value from the list or type a new value in the combo box.
DropDownList	Users must select a value from the list. Users cannot type a new value in the combo box.

To add values to the combo box list

- In the Possible Values text box on the Value page, type the values you want to appear in the list. Separate each value with a semicolon (;), as shown in Figure 6.23.
- You can also programmatically add items to the ComboBox. See Chapter 11, "Using VBA and VBScript with Outlook" for examples. Use any of the following programmatic methods:
  - The *AddItem* method allows you to loop through a collection and add the items one at a time. This method works well for a small number of items.
  - The List and Column properties let you set or retrieve an array of values. List and Column properties are especially useful when you want to create multi-column lists or combo boxes. If you assign a variant array to the List property of the control, you will enhance the performance of programmatically populating controls.

To set the initial value of a ComboBox control

- In the Initial Value text box on the Value page, type in the value that you want to appear in the edit box portion of the control when the form first appears, as shown in Figure 6.23.

You can set the MatchEntry property to determine how a ListBox or ComboBox responds to user input at the keyboard. Use the Advanced Properties dialog box at design time to set the MatchEntry property for a selected control or programmatically set the property at run time.

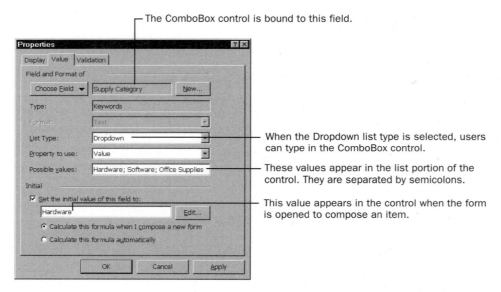

Figure 6.23 *Properties of a ComboBox control.*

Set the MatchEntry Property To	To
None	Provide no matching.
FirstLetter	Compare the most recently typed letter to the first letter of each entry in the list (the first match in the list is selected).
Complete	Compare the user's entry and an exact match in an entry from the list.

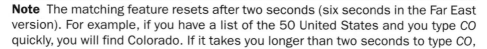

Note The matching feature resets after two seconds (six seconds in the Far East version). For example, if you have a list of the 50 United States and you type *CO* quickly, you will find Colorado. If it takes you longer than two seconds to type *CO*, however, you will find Ohio first because the auto-complete search resets between letters.

ListBox Controls

Use ListBox controls to show a list of values from which the user can select one or many values. To create a list box that enables users to select more than one value, you must bind the ListBox control to a Keywords field. List boxes that are bound to Keywords fields have check boxes that allow users to select multiple values, as shown in Figure 6.24. When the user selects multiple values in the ListBox control, the values appear in the view in an Outlook folder as comma-separated values.

Outlook provides two presentation styles for the ListBox control. You can set the style at design time by using the Advanced Properties dialog box for the control or at run time by programmatically setting the ListStyle property.

List Style	Description
Plain	Each item in the list box is in a separate row. Depending on the setting of the MultiSelect property, the user can select either one row or multiple rows in the control.
Option	An OptionButton or CheckBox appears at the beginning of each row. With this style, the user selects an item by clicking the option button or check box. Check boxes appear only when the MultiSelect property is set to either Multi or Extended.

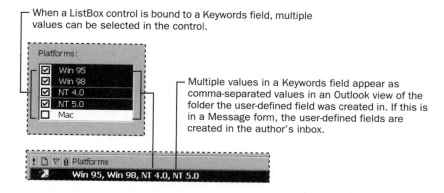

When a ListBox control is bound to a Keywords field, multiple values can be selected in the control.

Platforms:
- ☑ Win 95
- ☑ Win 98
- ☑ NT 4.0
- ☑ NT 5.0
- ☐ Mac

Multiple values in a Keywords field appear as comma-separated values in an Outlook view of the folder the user-defined field was created in. If this is in a Message form, the user-defined fields are created in the author's inbox.

! ▯ ⏳ 𝟢 Platforms
Win 95, Win 98, NT 4.0, NT 5.0

Figure 6.24 *Values selected in a list box bound to a Keywords field are shown as comma-separated values in an Outlook view.*

To bind the ListBox control to a field

1. In Design mode, right-click the control, and then click Properties on the shortcut menu.

2. On the Value page, do one of the following:

   • To bind the ListBox control to an existing field, click Choose Field, point to User-Defined Fields In Folder, and then click the field to which you want to bind the ListBox control. Items selected from this list will appear in the field to which this list is bound.

   • To create a Keywords field, click New, and then click Keywords in the Type drop-down list box. With Keywords you can place several values in a single field, depending on what the user selects. These values can be used to group items within a folder, similar to the Categories field of Task items.

   • To create a ListBox control without a Keywords field, click Text, Number, Currency, or Date/Time in the Type drop-down list box and then, in the Format dialog box, click to select a format. This information is transient and not stored in a field, but it can be accessed and manipulated by VBScript code. For more information, see Chapter 11, "Using VBA and VBScript with Outlook."

Note Do not bind the ListBox control to a Yes/No, Combination, or Formula field.

To add values to the ListBox control

   • In the Possible Values text box on the Value page, type the values you want to appear in the list. Separate each value with a semicolon, as shown in Figure 6.25. You can also use the *AddItem* method or the List and Column properties to add items programmatically to the control.

To set the initial value of a ListBox control

   • In the Initial Value text box on the Value page, do one of the following:

   • To set the initial value to a single value, type the value that you want to appear as checked in the ListBox control when the user opens the form to compose an item, as shown in Figure 6.25.

   • To set the initial value to multiple values, type the values that you want to appear as checked in the ListBox control when the user opens the form to compose an item. Separate each value in the Initial Value text box with a semicolon.

Note The ListBox control can also display multiple columns, at which point it behaves more like a grid than a list box. For an example of an ActiveX Flex Grid placed on a form, see E-Chapter 3, "The Northwind Contact Management Application," in the E-Chapters folder on the companion CD.

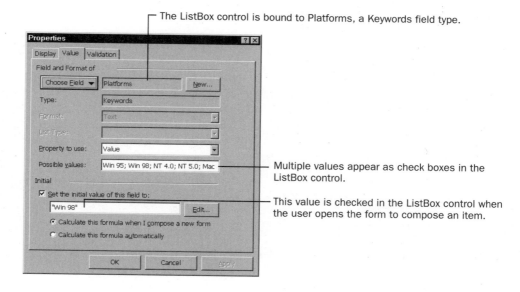

The ListBox control is bound to Platforms, a Keywords field type.

Multiple values appear as check boxes in the ListBox control.

This value is checked in the ListBox control when the user opens the form to compose an item.

Figure 6.25 *The values that you want to appear in the list are typed in the Possible Values text box.*

CommandButton Controls

The CommandButton control, when clicked, triggers the Click event. As such, you can write VBScript Click event procedures in the Script Editor for each CommandButton control, as shown in Figure 6.26.

Important Outlook only supports the Click event for most of its instrinsic controls. Some third-party extrinsic ActiveX controls might not support even the Click event, but most extrinsic ActiveX controls do support this event.

To add a CommandButton control

1. In Design mode, drag the control from the Control Toolbox to the form.
2. To set the caption for a CommandButton control, click the control. When the edit pointer appears, type the name in the control.
3. To specify a name for the CommandButton control, right-click the control, and then click Properties on the shortcut menu.
4. In the Name text box on the Display page, type a name, and then click OK.

To create a procedure for a CommandButton control

1. Click the View Code button on the Form Design toolbar.
2. In the Script Editor window, type *Sub* followed by a space, followed by *CommandButton1_Click*, where *CommandButton1* is the name of the control.

Users click the CommandButton control to trigger VBScript procedures.

With the Script Editor, you can create procedures using VBScript.

The AutoFill_Click procedure for the AutoFill CommandButton control automatically fills the address fields in the form.

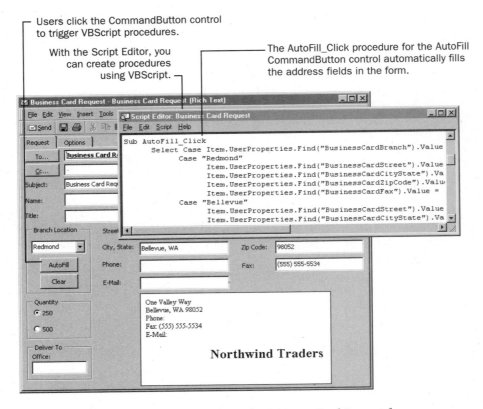

Figure 6.26 *CommandButton controls on the Business Card Request form.*

Add the necessary code to the procedure. End the procedure with an End Sub statement, as shown in the following example:

```
Sub CommandButton1_Click
    MsgBox "This is a procedure for a CommandButton control"
End Sub
```

3. Close window.

To test a CommandButton control Click procedure

1. On the Form menu, click Run This Form to switch the form into Run mode.

2. Click the command button.

3. To switch back to Design mode, close the Run window.

More Info For more information about creating procedures for forms using Visual Basic Scripting Edition, see Chapter 11, "Using VBA and VBScript with Outlook."

MultiPage Controls

Use MultiPage controls to provide multiple pages of information on a form, as shown in Figure 6.27.

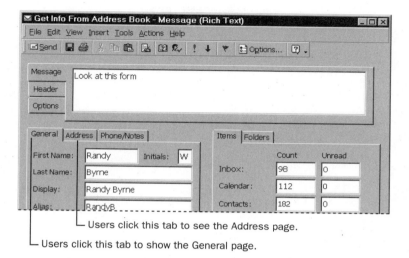

Users click this tab to see the Address page.

Users click this tab to show the General page.

Figure 6.27 *The MultiPage control on the Compose page of the Get Info From Address Book form.*

⮕ **To add a MultiPage control**

- Drag the MultiPage control from the Control Toolbox to the form.

⮕ **To add controls to the MultiPage control**

- Switch to the page you want to add controls to, and then drag the controls you want from the Control Toolbox to the MultiPage control.

⮕ **To insert, rename, delete, or move a page**

- Right-click a tab on the MultiPage control, and then click Insert, Delete, Rename, or Move on the shortcut menu, as shown in Figure 6.28.

How the TabStrip Control Differs from the MultiPage Control

With a MultiPage control, each page on the control usually contains a different set of controls. With the TabStrip control, however, each page contains the same controls. For example, you might use a TabStrip control to display the addresses of various companies. You set the title of each tab to the name of the company, and then you write code that, when you click a tab, updates the controls to show the address of that company.

Right-click on a tab on the MultiPage control to
show the shortcut menu.

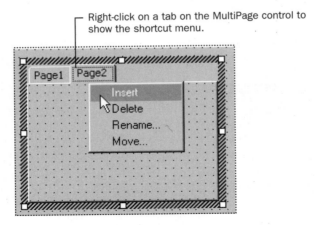

Figure 6.28 *The shortcut menu of the MultiPage control.*

Image Controls

Use Image controls to contain graphic images, as shown in Figure 6.29.

➲ **To add a picture to an Image control**

1. Right-click the Image control, and then click Advanced Properties on the short-cut menu.

2. Double-click the Picture cell, and then select the image.

The Image2 control.   The Image1 control on the Vacation Request form.

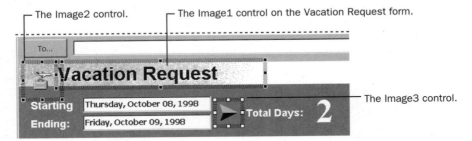

The Image3 control.

Figure 6.29 *Image controls on the Vacation Request form*

➲ **To delete the picture in the Image control**

- You must delete the Image control, so click to select the Image control, and then press the Delete key.

➲ **To size an image in the Image control**

1. Right-click the Image control, and then click Advanced Properties.

2. Do one of the following.

To	Do This
Automatically size the control to the picture	In the AutoSize cell, click True.
Maintain the size of the picture, regardless of the size of the Image control	In the PictureSizeMode cell, click Clip.
Stretch the picture to fill the Image control	In the PictureSizeMode cell, click Stretch.
Enlarge the picture, but still maintain the PictureAlignment property setting	In the PictureSizeMode cell, click Zoom.

Tip The Click event fires for Image controls. You can create large command buttons containing graphics by using the Image control as shown in Figure 6.30. Drop an image on your form using the Control Toolbox, add a picture, and then stretch the picture using the PictureSizeMode property above. The image will have the appearance of a command button if you set the SpecialEffect property to Raised in the Advanced Properties dialog box. Write code for the image's Click event and the job is complete.

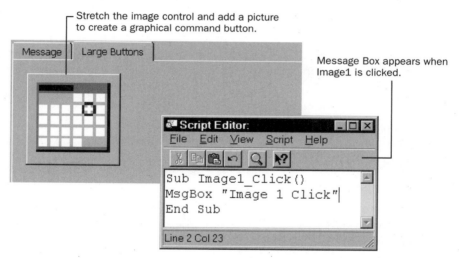

Figure 6.30 *Use an Image control to create the equivalent of a large command button.*

SpinButton Control

Use the SpinButton control to enable the user to increase or decrease numbers in a control. Although you can write script for the SpinButton control, it is not required to create a SpinButton control. To create a spin button for a control, you can bind the spin button to the same field that a TextBox control is bound to. Here is an example of how you can create a SpinButton control.

To add the TextBox control and bind it to a field

1. From the Control Toolbox, drag a TextBox control to the form.
2. Right-click the TextBox control, and then click Properties on the shortcut menu.
3. Click the Value tab, and then click New.
4. In the Name text box, type a name for the field.
5. In the Type drop-down list box, click Number.
6. Click OK. If desired, select Calculate This Field Automatically, and then click OK again.

To add the SpinButton control and bind it to a field

1. From the Control Toolbox, drag a SpinButton control to the form and position it to the right of the TextBox control you just added.
2. Right-click the SpinButton control, and then click Properties on the shortcut menu.
3. Click the Value tab.
4. Click Choose Field, point to User-Defined Fields In Folder, and then click the field you just added.
5. Click OK.
6. Hold down the Ctrl key, and then right-click the SpinButton and TextBox controls.
7. On the shortcut menu, point to Make Same Size, and then click Height.
8. To test the SpinButton control, click Run This Form on the Form menu to enter Run mode, and then click the SpinButton control to increase or decrease the number in the TextBox control.

Controls That Require VBScript

In addition to the CommandButton control, the Control Toolbox provides several other controls that require VBScript to operate. These are the ToggleButton, TabStrip, and ScrollBar controls.

More Info For more information about these controls, see the Microsoft Outlook Visual Basic Reference Help.

Using Custom ActiveX Controls

If the Microsoft Forms controls that are available in the Outlook Control Toolbox do not satisfy your requirements, you can add either Microsoft or third-party ActiveX controls to your Outlook form. You can also use Visual Basic 5.0 or 6.0 to create your own custom ActiveX controls for use in Outlook forms. However, this strategy presents several problems that must be addressed in your solution.

- The ActiveX control must be installed and registered properly on every machine where you intend to run the custom form.

- You must possess a valid license to set the properties of the control in Design mode.

- None of the events supported by the ActiveX control—except the Click event—will fire in a custom Outlook form. For example, you cannot write VBScript code in your Outlook form to respond directly to the DblClick event if the user double-clicks a row in a data-bound grid.

- Not every ActiveX control can be bound to an Outlook user-defined field. You should test the ActiveX control's ability to bind its default property to an Outlook user-defined field.

One of the most frequent questions seen in the Outlook newsgroups is how to duplicate the date and time selection controls on the first page of the Appointment, Task, and Journal item forms. If you have purchased Microsoft Office 2000 Developer, you can use the ActiveX controls that ship with Office 2000 Developer. You can also obtain the same controls if you have a license for Microsoft Visual Studio 98. The control that specifically replaces the Outlook date and time selection controls is the Microsoft DTPicker control. The following procedure list assumes that you have installed either Microsoft Office 2000 Developer or Visual Studio 98 on your system.

To add a Date Selection control to your custom Outlook form

1. In form design mode, right-click the Controls Toolbox and select the Custom Controls command.

2. Check the Microsoft Date And Time Picker Control, Version 6.0 in the drop-down list box of available controls in the Additional Controls dialog box.

3. Click OK.

4. Drag the DTPicker control from the Control Toolbox to your form.

5. Resize the control on your form, if necessary.

6. Set the properties of the control using the Properties dialog box to bind the control to a user-defined or default field.

7. Set the Format property of the control using the Advanced Properties dialog box to specify how the control displays the date or time field to which it is bound.

8. Setting the UpDown property of the control to *True* provides spin buttons for date or time modification. If the UpDown property is *False*, then the control will use a drop-down calendar that mimics the Outlook calendar control.

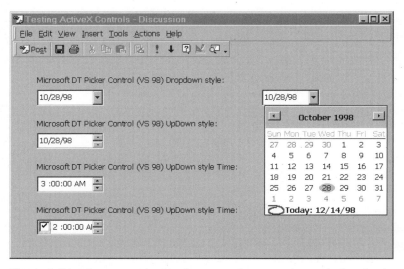

Figure 6.31 *The Microsoft DTPicker control mimics the Outlook calendar control.*

Select Multiple Controls and the Dominant Control

You can select multiple controls in three ways. In addition, when you select more than one control, one of the controls becomes a reference for the other controls and is called the dominant control. The sizing frame of the dominant control has black handles. Any other selected controls have white handles.

Selection Method	What Is Selected	Dominant Control
Shift+Click	All controls in an invisible rectangle around the selected controls.	First control you select
Ctrl+Click	Individual controls, one at a time.	Last control you select.
Select Objects pointer in Control Toolbox	All controls that fall within or touch a rectangle you draw.	Control nearest the mouse pointer when you begin drawing the rectangle.

Tip Use the following special tips when selecting controls on a form page:

- The Ctrl+Click method may occasionally select additional controls that are near to or adjacent to the selected controls. For more accuracy, use the Select Objects pointer method.
- If you Ctrl+Click twice on a selected control, that control becomes the dominant control.
- If you select a group of controls and then drag the selection to the Control Toolbox, the selected controls will be available as an item to drag from the

Control Toolbox to another page on this form or on a different form. When you drag the icon for these controls to a page, the alignment and size of the controls is maintained.

Where To Go from Here

There are many resources that can help you deepen your understanding of the material in this chapter. For additional information, see the following resources:

ActiveX Components

Appleman, Dan. *Developing COM/ActiveX Components with Visual Basic 6.0— A Guide to the Perplexed*. Indianapolis, IN: Macmillan Computer Publishing, 1998.

Eddon, Guy, and Henry Eddon. *Programming Components with Microsoft Visual Basic 6.0*. Redmond, WA: Microsoft Press, 1998.

The ActiveX Components Web site *http://www.microsoft.com/com/activex.asp/*.

ActiveX Components Tools Guide

Microsoft Visual Basic 6.0 Programmer's Guide. Redmond, WA: Microsoft Press, 1998. An online version of this book is included with Visual Basic 6.0 and is also available on the MSDN Online Web site at *http://msdn.microsoft.com/developer/*.

Chapter 7
Actions

In This Chapter

Action properties make it possible for you to define custom responses for forms, instead of using the standard Reply and Reply To Folder actions. For example, with the Vacation Request form, a supervisor can reply to a vacation request item by choosing an Approve Vacation or Deny Vacation action, rather than using the standard Reply action.

This chapter describes the different ways of creating responses for forms. Specifically, topics include

Voting Buttons for Message Forms   The easiest way to create responses for Message forms is to use voting buttons. An example shows how voting buttons are created for an Art Approval form.

Reply Actions for Message Forms   As an example, you'll look at how Reply actions are implemented for the Vacation Request form.

Reply To Folder Actions for Post Forms   As an example, you'll look at how custom responses are designed for the Course Catalog Entry in the Training Management folder.

Voting Buttons for Message Forms

Voting buttons, which are only available with Message forms, provide an easy way for users to collect quick feedback from other users. When you specify voting button options for a form, two important things happen:

- Voting buttons are added to the Read page, as shown in Figure 7.1.
- The location of the Tracking item is specified. The Tracking item contains the voting results and shows them on the Tracking page, as shown in Figure 7.2.

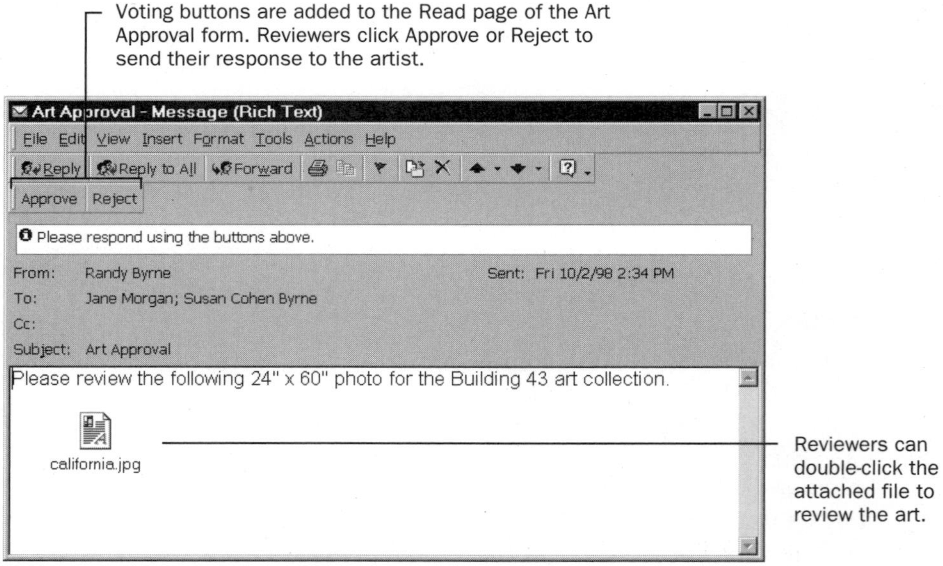

Voting buttons are added to the Read page of the Art Approval form. Reviewers click Approve or Reject to send their response to the artist.

Reviewers can double-click the attached file to review the art.

Figure 7.1 *The Read page of the Art Approval form. This page is used by members of the Art Approval Committee to approve or reject the art submitted by the artist.*

In the following section, you create an Art Approval form that has voting buttons and a Tracking item. When you're done, you will understand how voting buttons work and how they can be used to collect feedback from other users.

Overview of the Art Approval Form

The Art Approval form illustrates the easiest way to create responses for Message forms. It uses voting buttons, which send responses to a folder for review. The Art Approval form, as shown in Figure 7.3, is used by an artist to send an attached file of electronic art to users on the Art Approval Committee distribution list for review. The recipients review the attached file, and then vote to approve or reject. To see the voting results, the artist opens the Art Approval Tracking item in the Art Approval folder.

Create the Art Approval Folder

Before you create the Art Approval form, create an Art Approval folder in your Mailbox folder. This is where you'll store the Tracking item that tallies responses.

To create the Art Approval folder

1. In the Folder List, right-click the Mailbox folder, and then click New Folder.
2. In the Name text box, type *Art Approval*, and then click OK.

The Tracking item is stored in the Art Approval folder in the user's Mailbox folder.

The Tracking item tallies the responses. The user double-clicks the Tracking item to open it.

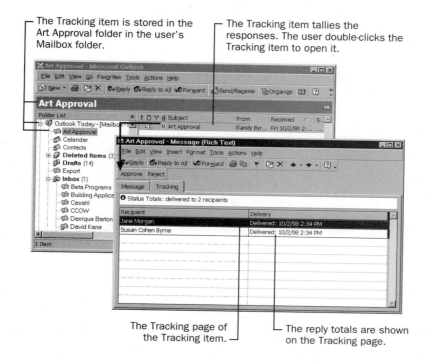

The Tracking page of the Tracking item.

The reply totals are shown on the Tracking page.

Figure 7.2 *The Tracking page of the Art Approval form tallies the results of the responses from the Art Approval Committee members.*

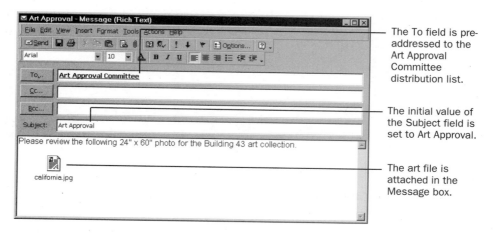

The To field is pre-addressed to the Art Approval Committee distribution list.

The initial value of the Subject field is set to Art Approval.

The art file is attached in the Message box.

Figure 7.3 *The Compose page of the Art Approval form.*

3. If a dialog box appears asking if you want to Add A Shortcut To Outlook Bar?, click No.

Create the Art Approval Form

To create the Art Approval form, first open the standard Message form. Set the initial value of the To and Subject fields. Next, specify voting button options for the form. Finally, publish the form in your Personal Forms Library.

Open the Form in Run Mode

This form should be built entirely in Run mode.

To open the standard Message form

1. In the Folder List or from the Outlook Shortcut bar, click Inbox.
2. Select New Mail Message from the Outlook Actions menu.

Preaddress the To Field

Quite often, you'll want to preaddress a form to the people you send the form to on a regular basis. To preaddress a form, you set the initial value of the To field. In this chapter's example, the initial value of the To field is set to the Art Approval Committee distribution list. For the form that you create, however, you will preaddress the form to your own address. You must set the initial value of the To field at run time because you cannot open the Address Book from the To field at design time.

More Info To create a distribution list, see Microsoft Outlook Help.

To pre-address the form

1. On the opened form, click the To button.
2. Double-click the address you want to set as the initial value in the To field. (For this example, you can select your own address.)
3. Click OK.

Set the Initial Value of the Subject Field

For forms that serve a specific purpose, such as the Art Approval form, it makes sense to set the initial value of the Subject field. This saves the user the time of filling in the field and ensures that recipients see a consistent subject field each time they receive an Art Approval item in their Inboxes.

To set the initial value of the Subject field

- Type *Art Approval* in the Subject text box.

You won't see the initial value in the Subject field immediately. It appears only when the form is opened to compose an item at run time.

Set Options for the Art Approval Form

Options are set by clicking the Options icon on the form's Standard toolbar, which opens the Message Options window. Here, you specify voting button and menu options and desired tracking and tallying information. Remember, the Options icon is available only in Message forms.

Set Voting Button Options

Voting buttons appear on the Read page of the form and allow the user to respond to the Art Approval item by clicking the Approve or Reject button. The Read page of the form appears when the user double-clicks an Art Approval item in the Inbox.

To specify voting buttons

1. Select the Use Voting Buttons check box.
2. In the Use Voting Buttons text box, type the text you want to appear on the voting buttons or select the values from the list. If you type values, you must separate each value with a semicolon.

Specify Recipients of the Replies

When you select the Have Replies Sent To check box, your address is automatically added to the text box. You can add additional addresses to the text box or you can replace your address with another.

To specify the reply address

1. Select the Have Replies Sent To check box.
2. To specify additional names, click Select Names, and then double-click the names you want.
3. When the appropriate addresses appear in the Message Recipients box, click OK.

Note When the approval committee votes, their replies will go to the Inbox(es) specified here. The tally of votes (tracking) will be stored in the folder specified in the Save Sent Message To text box.

Specify Where the Tracking Item Is Stored

With forms that have voting buttons, Outlook provides an automatic tally of the voting button responses in a saved item in a folder. This folder must be located in your Mailbox folder. The default folder is the Sent Items folder, but you can change it.

To specify where the Tracking item is stored

1. On the Message Options window, choose Save Sent Message To, and then click Browse.
2. In the Folders list box, click the Art Approval folder, and then click OK.
3. Click Close to save your options.

As shown in Figure 7.4, the Save Sent Message To option is set to the Art Approval folder. So when an Art Approval item is sent, an Art Approval item is also saved in the Art Approval folder in your Mailbox folder. After you receive and open voting responses in your Inbox, the responses are written to the Tracking item in the Art Approval folder. If this seems a little confusing right now, don't worry. You'll go through the process step by step.

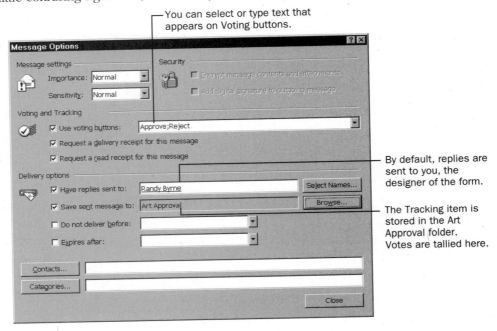

Figure 7.4 *Voting button options for the Art Approval form.*

Publish the Form to the Personal Forms Library

After the form is created and modified, you publish the form to your Personal Forms Library so that you can open and test the form.

To publish the form

1. Select Forms on the Tools menu, and then click Publish Form As.

2. If Personal Forms Library does not appear in the Look In drop-down list box, click the drop-down list box and select Personal Forms Library from the box.

3. In the Display Name text box and the Form Name text box, type *Art Approval* or whatever you want to name the form, and then click Publish.

4. If the Save Form Definition With Item message box appears, choose No for the Do You Want This Checkbox Selected? prompt.

5.   Close the form. At the Do You Want To Save Changes? prompt, choose No for most cases, or Yes if you want a backup copy saved in the Drafts folder.

The form is saved in its final form by publishing it. The Save prompt, on the other hand, creates a copy in the Drafts folder.

> **More Info** For more information about where to publish forms, see Chapter 12, "Distribute and Maintain Applications."

How Actions Are Automatically Set for Voting Buttons

When you specify voting buttons and publish a form, Outlook automatically adds custom actions to the Actions page. There are two important points to remember about these actions. First, when you specify voting buttons, the Creates Form Of Type property is set to the standard Message form (IPM.Note). Second, the Address Form Like property is set to Response, as shown in Figure 7.5.

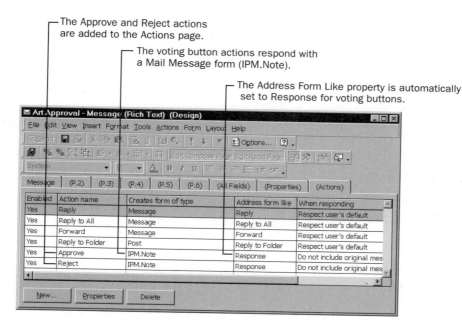

Figure 7.5 *The Actions page of the Art Approval form. Approve and Reject actions are automatically added when you specify the voting buttons on the Options page.*

Test the Art Approval Form

Now you open the Art Approval form and then send an Art Approval item to your Inbox.

Send an Art Approval Item

Open the Art Approval form from your Personal Forms Library. When you open the form, you will see the Compose page of the form. Using the Compose page, you send an Art Approval item to your Inbox.

To send the Art Approval form

1. On the Outlook File menu, select New, and then click Choose Form.
2. In the Look In drop-down list box, click Personal Forms Library, and then double-click Art Approval.
3. On the Insert menu, click File, and then double-click a file to insert in the message box on the Art Approval form.
4. Click the Send button.

Use the Voting Buttons To Respond

Now you open the Art Approval item in your Inbox. Then you click one of the voting buttons.

To vote in the item

1. Double-click the Art Approval item in the Inbox to which the form was addressed in the To box.
2. Normally, you open the attached item to review it. In this case, however, there is no need to.
3. Click Approve.
4. Click Send The Response Now, and then click OK.
5. Close the Art Approval form.

Review Replies

Open the Art Approval Reply in your Inbox. Then, you open the Tracking item in the Art Approval folder.

> **Important** The voting button responses are tallied in the Tracking item only after the response items are opened in your Inbox. If the items are not opened, the results are not tallied in the Tracking item. If no response items are opened, the Tracking page is not available on the Tracking form.

To open the response item in your Inbox

- In your Inbox, double-click the Art Approval item.

⊃   **To open the Tracking item**

1.   In the Folder List, open the Art Approval folder.
2.   Double-click the Tracking item, as shown in Figure 7.2, earlier in this chapter.
3.   The Tracking item is identified by an information icon, as shown in Figure 7.6.
4.   Click the Tracking tab.

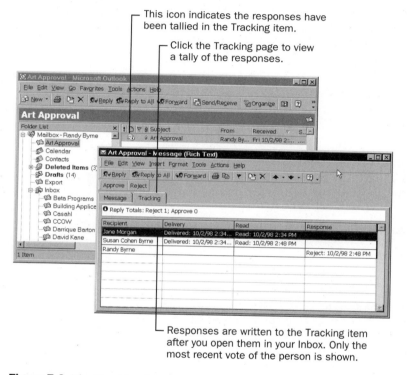

This icon indicates the responses have been tallied in the Tracking item.

Click the Tracking page to view a tally of the responses.

Responses are written to the Tracking item after you open them in your Inbox. Only the most recent vote of the person is shown.

Figure 7.6 *The Tracking item is opened in the Art Approval folder.*

Reply Actions for Message Forms

When creating applications with Message forms, you often create Reply actions that open custom forms instead of the standard Message form. For example, the Vacation Request form has two custom actions: the Approve Vacation action activates the Vacation Approved form and the Deny Vacation action activates the Vacation Denied form.

In this section, we create custom Reply actions for Message forms. Throughout this section, we use the Vacation Request application for examples of how to implement Reply actions with Message forms.

> ### To open the Vacation Request folder
>
> - In the Folder List, expand the Building Microsoft Outlook 2000 Applications folder, and then expand the Building Blocks folder. Then click the Vacation Request folder.

Note If you haven't installed the Building Microsoft Outlook 2000 Applications folder, see the Introduction of this book for instructions.

Overview of the Vacation Request Application

The Vacation Request application consists of four forms: Vacation Request, Vacation Approved, Vacation Denied, and Vacation Report. All forms are intentionally left unhidden in this folder so you can view them.

> ### To view a Vacation Request form
>
> 1. On the Actions menu, view the forms at the bottom of the menu.
> 2. Click New Vacation Request.

Vacation Request form   The form opens in Compose page. The user can compose a Vacation Request item and send it to his supervisor. When the receiving supervisor opens the form from her Inbox, she sees the Vacation Request Read page. It contains the Approve Vacation and Deny Vacation buttons, as shown in Figure 7.7.

Vacation Approved form   The supervisor sees the Compose page of the Vacation Approved form when she clicks the Approve Vacation button on the Vacation Request form. She then clicks Send to route the approved vacation request to the user.

Vacation Denied form   The supervisor sees the Compose page of this form when she clicks the Deny Vacation button on the Vacation Request form. She can then click Send to route the denied vacation request to the user.

Vacation Report form   This form lets the user send the supervisor a report of the vacation days taken. The supervisor can then track the days available for each employee.

Here the discussion focuses primarily on the Vacation Request form and its associated actions. Along the way, you will also take a look at a custom Reply action.

Actions for the Vacation Request Form

To get familiar with actions, take a look at the Actions page for the Vacation Request form, as shown in Figure 7.8.

> ### To view the Actions page for the Vacation Request form
>
> - In the Design mode of the Vacation Request form, click the Actions page.

This action button opens
the Vacation Approved form.

This action button opens
the Vacation Denied form.

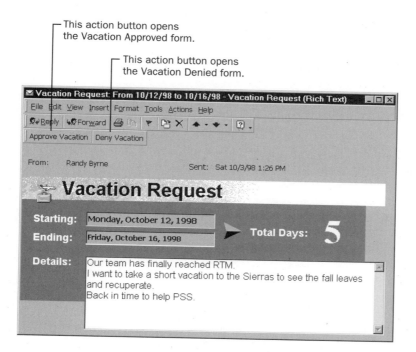

Figure 7.7 *The Read page of the Vacation Request form.*

This action places an Approve Vacation button on the Read page.
When the button is clicked, it opens the Vacation Approved form.

This action places a Deny Vacation button on the Read page.
When the button is clicked, it opens the Vacation Denied form.

Click here to show the Actions page.

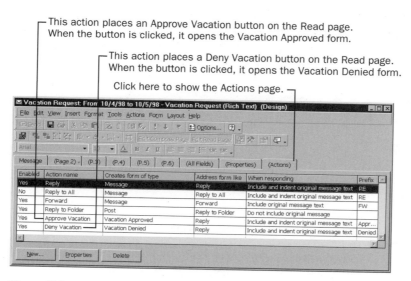

Figure 7.8 *The Actions page for the Vacation Request form.*

New Reply Actions

When you create new Reply actions, you specify that custom command buttons and menu commands are added to the form. The menu commands and buttons, when clicked, activate a custom form that lets the user reply to an item. For example, the Vacation Request form has a custom Approve Vacation action. When a supervisor opens a Vacation Request form, he or she can click the Approve Vacation button to open the Vacation Approved form, as shown in Figure 7.9.

The supervisor can then click the Send button to send the Vacation Approved item to the person who requested it. When the Vacation Approved form is opened, the original message is copied from the Vacation Request form to the message box of the Vacation Approved form. Likewise, the From field is copied to the To field, and the values in the StartDate, EndDate, and TotalDays fields are copied from the Vacation Request form to the Vacation Approved form.

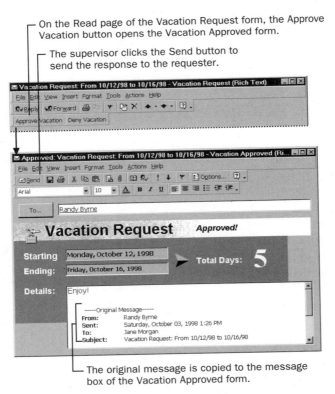

On the Read page of the Vacation Request form, the Approve Vacation button opens the Vacation Approved form.

The supervisor clicks the Send button to send the response to the requester.

The original message is copied to the message box of the Vacation Approved form.

Figure 7.9 *The Read page (partial) of the Vacation Request form and the Compose page of the Vacation Approved form.*

Approve Vacation Action

Now let's take a look at the properties associated with the Approve Vacation action.

To view the Approve Vacation action

1. Open the Vacation Request form by selecting the Vacation Request folder from the Folder List. Then, click New Vacation Request on the Actions menu.

2. In Design mode, click on the Actions page, and then double-click the Approve Vacation action.

The Form Action Properties dialog box, as shown in Figure 7.10, allows you to create new actions and to modify existing actions. With this dialog box, you specify the text that appears on the action button and menu, the form that appears when the button is clicked, and whether the original message is copied to the Reply item.

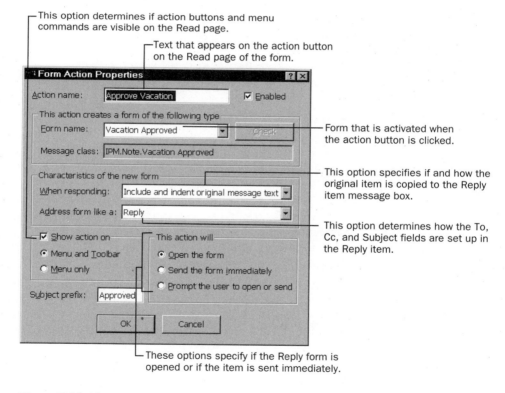

Figure 7.10 *The Form Action Properties dialog box.*

More Info To create a new Action Item, see "Create a New Action" in Chapter 4, "Design a Custom Application."

Action Name

The Action Name text box, as shown in the preceding Figure 7.10, defines the name of both the menu command and command button that open the associated custom Reply form. The custom action button appears on the Read page of the form.

The custom menu command appears in two places:

- On the Outlook Actions menu when an item created with the associated form is selected in a folder. For example, with the Vacation Request form, the Approve Vacation command appears on the Actions menu when a Vacation Request item is selected in the Inbox.
- On the Form Actions menu of the Read page.

Form Name and Message Class

The Form Name box contains the name of the form that is opened when the menu command or command button is selected. The Message Class box contains the internal identifier for the form. When you select a form in the Form Name box, the message class automatically appears in the Message Class box.

The Form Name combo box contains the names of the forms published in the active folder. In addition, it contains a Forms value that you can use to select from forms in the Organizational, Personal, or Standard Forms Libraries.

To specify a form name

Do one of the following:

- In the Form Name combo box, type a form name, and then click Check to search for the form.

  If Outlook cannot find the form, you see a message box. If this happens, you should create the form before you specify the form name. After you create the form and publish it in a forms library, you can return to the original form and click the name of the form in the Form Name combo box.

- In the Form Name combo box, click a Form Name from the drop-down list.
- In the Form Name combo box, click Forms on the drop-down list. In the Choose Form box, double-click the form you want.

Characteristics Of The New Form

Under Characteristics Of The New Form, you can specify whether the original message is copied to the message box of the Reply form. In addition, you can specify how the values in the From, cc, and Subject fields are copied from the original form to the Reply form.

When Responding

For Reply actions, you can specify if the contents of the original item are copied to the message box of the Reply item. You can also specify how the contents of the message box are copied. The default setting for this property is Respect User's Default. In Outlook, the user can set the When Replying To A Message option on the Email Options page of the Options dialog box (Tools menu). By default, this property is set for the user to Include And Indent Original Message Text. Therefore, if you have Respect User's Default selected in the When Responding drop-down list box, you can assume that for most users the message box on the Reply form includes and indents the original message. If you want to override the user's When Replying To A Message preference, click another option in the When Responding drop-down list box to define explicitly how you want the contents of the message box to appear on the Reply form.

Here are a few general guidelines for setting the When Responding option for Message forms.

- If the original message is brief, click Include And Indent Original Message Text. As shown in the preceding Figure 7.10, this is the option that is selected for the Approve Vacation action in the Vacation Request form.

- If you want to include a shortcut to the message in the response item, click Attach Link To Original Message.

Address Form Like A

For Message forms, you almost always choose Reply for this option. When you choose Reply, the To field of the Reply form contains the contents of the From field of the original item, and the cc field is empty. The Subject field, unless otherwise specified, contains RE:, followed by the contents of the Subject field of the original item.

The following table describes how the Address Form Like A options set up the Reply form.

Option	Description
Reply	This sets up the Reply form so the To field contains the contents of the From field of the original item. The cc field is empty. The Subject field contains whatever is specified in the Subject Prefix box of the Form Action Properties dialog box, such as RE:. It is followed by the contents of the Subject field of the original item.
Reply to All	This sets up the Reply form so the To field contains the contents of the From and cc fields of the original item. The Subject field contains RE:, or whatever you specify, followed by the contents of the Subject field of the original item.
Forward	This sets up the form so the To and cc fields are empty and the Subject field contains FW:, or whatever you specify, followed by the contents of the Subject field of the original item.
Reply To Folder	This sets up the Reply form so the Post To field contains the active folder address, the Conversation field contains the subject of the original item, and the Subject field is empty. In most cases, the Conversation field is not visible on a form. The Conversation field contains the value of the Subject of the original item.
Response	This is used exclusively for voting button actions.

Show Action On

Most of the time, you can leave the default Menu and Toolbar options for a form. However, there may be times when you want to control the placement of the custom action buttons on the form. For example, you may want to add a command button to the bottom of the form and then write a macro for the command button to activate the Reply form when the button is clicked. If this is the case, you can click the Menu Only option, or uncheck the Show Action On box so it will not show in either the menu or the toolbar.

This Action Will

For the Vacation Request form, the Approve action, when initiated, opens the Vacation Approved form. For most actions, under This Action Will you should specify Open The Form. However, there might be cases when you choose the Send The Form Immediately option. For example, you might send a form to a user requesting an updated phone number and address. Rather than opening a Reply form, the user can fill in the fields on the original form, and then click the custom action button. The Reply form is then activated, but isn't visible to the user. Values from the originating form are then copied to the Reply form. If you specify the Send The Form Immediately option, you must still create the Reply form. Also, you must ensure that the fields you want filled in on the invisible Reply form are included on the original form.

Subject Prefix

This shows the prefix that appears in the Subject text box of the Reply form. The prefix is RE: by default. For example, for the Approve Vacation action, the Approve prefix appears in the Subject text box of the Vacation Approved form. When the person who requested the vacation receives the Approved Vacation item in his Inbox, the text in the Subject column in the folder tells him his vacation is approved.

How Field Values Are Copied to the Reply Form

Outlook does not provide a way to explicitly define the field values that are copied from custom fields on the original form to custom fields on the Reply form. Rather, you accomplish this by using the same fields for both forms, as shown in Figure 7.11. When the field is shared between the original and Reply forms, the values are automatically copied from the original form to the Reply form at run time.

For example, the following fields are located on both the Vacation Request form and the Vacation Approved form. When an Approve Vacation action is initiated, the values in these fields are copied from the Vacation Request form to the Vacation Approved form.

- Subject
- TotalDays
- StartDate
- EndDate

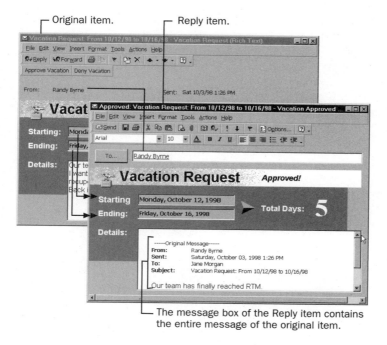

The message box of the Reply item contains the entire message of the original item.

Figure 7.11 *Values between fields common to both the original and Reply forms are copied to the Reply form.*

Important To ensure that field values are copied between the original form and the Reply form, use the same fields for both forms. For example, for the Vacation Request application, the TotalDays, StartDate, and EndDate fields are used for the Vacation Request form.

Note In Figure 7.11, the Subject field is not visible. Instead, it is located on page 2, a hidden page. The Subject text, however, is copied from the original item to the Reply item and does appear in the Subject box on the Read page of the Reply item.

Vacation Request Reply Forms

In most cases, the custom Reply form is very similar to the original form. Quite often, you can use the original form as a template for the Reply form. For example, the Vacation Approved form is a Reply form based on the Vacation Request form. Only a few modifications have been made:

- The custom Reply actions are removed.
- The form description is changed, as shown in Figure 7.12.

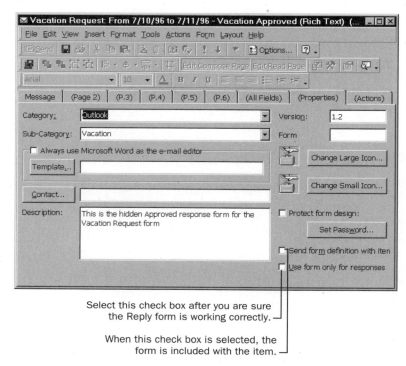

Figure 7.12 *The form description is changed for the Reply form.*

 More Info For more information on creating and modifying forms, see "Open the Form and Switch to Design Mode" in Chapter 5, "Forms."

Publish Reply Forms

For Reply forms to work correctly, they must be available on the user's system. Before you publish the forms, however, it's a good idea to make a backup copy.

To make a backup copy of a form

1. With the form open, click Save As on the File menu.
2. In the Save In drop-down list box, select the default Outlook template folder, such as C:\ Program Files\Microsoft Office\Templates.
3. In the File Name text box, type a name for the form.
4. In the Save As Type drop-down list box, select Outlook Template (.oft).
5. Click Save.

To open your backup copy of a form

1. Select New on the File menu, and then click Choose Form.

2. Click User Templates In File System in the Look In drop-down list box, and then click the form you'd like to open.

After you make a backup copy of the form, you can publish it to one of the following forms libraries:

Organizational Forms Library   Publish the form in this library if you want the form to be available to all users in your organization.

Personal Forms Library   Publish the form in this library if you intend to use the form for personal use. The Personal Forms Library is also a good place to publish forms when you want to test them.

The forms library of a folder   Publish the form in the forms library of a folder if the form is integrated with the folder.

More Info For more information about where to publish forms, see Chapter 12, "Distribute and Maintain Applications."

To publish a form

1. On the Tools menu, select Forms, and then click Publish Form As.
2. Click the Look In drop-down list box, and select the forms library you want to publish in.
3. In the Display Name text box and the Form Name text box, type a name for the form, and then click Publish.

Test the Forms

After you publish the forms to a forms library, you should run the forms to make sure they work as expected. For example, here's how you publish and test the Vacation Request forms.

To publish the Vacation Request forms

1. In the Vacation Request folder, click New Vacation Request on the Actions menu.
2. On the Tools menu, select Forms, and then click Design This Form to switch to Design mode.
3. On the Tools menu, select Forms, and then click Publish Form As.
4. Click the Look In drop-down list box and then click Personal Forms Library.
5. Type a name for the form in the Display Name text box. The Form Name will be identical by default, but can be changed if you wish.
6. Click Publish.
7. Close the form.

8. On the Actions menu, click New Vacation Approved, and then repeat steps 2 through 7.

9. On the Actions menu, click New Vacation Denied, and then repeat steps 2 through 7.

To test the Vacation Request forms

1. Select New on the File menu, and then click Choose Form.

2. In the Look In drop-down list box, select Personal Forms Library and click Vacation Request.

3. Address the form to yourself, and then click the Send button.

4. When the Vacation Request item arrives in your Inbox, double-click it to open it.

5. Click the Approve Vacation button.

6. Click Send.

7. When the Approved Vacation item arrives in your Inbox, double-click it to open it.

Note Remember to keep forms updated and synchronized with each other by performing forms maintenance:

- Keep fields uniform on both Compose and Read pages.
- If form names are changed, update the links between the action and form. See the section "The Create Offering Action" later in this chapter.

Set the Hidden Properties for Response Forms

After you publish and test the forms, you select the Hidden option for response forms so that the response forms can only be opened as a response to an item. For example, if the Hidden check box is selected for the Vacation Approved form and the form is published in the Personal Forms Library, the Vacation Approved form name does not appear in the forms list in the New Form dialog box. Users can only open the form when an associated Vacation Request item is selected in the Inbox or when the Vacation Request item is opened in Read mode.

To set the Hidden property for the Vacation Approved form and the Vacation Denied form

1. On the Outlook Tools menu, click Options, and then click the Other tab.

2. Click the Advanced Options button.

3. Click the Custom Forms button.

4. Click the Manage Forms button.

5. Note that the right-hand Form Library text box is set to Personal Forms.

6. In the right-hand Library list box, click Vacation Approved, and then click Properties.

7. Select the Hidden check box, and then click OK.

8. Repeat steps 6 and 7 for the Vacation Denied form.

9. Click Close and then click OK.

Note After forms are hidden, they are no longer visible in the following places:

- The Choose Form dialog box selected from New on the File menu
- The Actions menu for that folder

Custom Reply Forms for Users Not on Your Microsoft Exchange Server System

You may occasionally want to create forms that are used between your company and another company over the Internet. For example, let's assume you have a Legal Approval form and a Legal Approval Response form and you want to use the forms between your company and an attorney's office. Also assume that the attorney has Outlook, but is not on your Microsoft Exchange Server system. For this scenario to work correctly, the attorney must have both the Legal Approval form and the Legal Approval Response form installed on his or her system—either in the Organizational Forms or Personal Forms Library.

Note If the Reply form specified by an action is not available on the user's system, Outlook opens the standard Message form in its place.

More Info For more information about where to publish forms, see Chapter 12, "Distribute and Maintain Applications." For information on sending forms to other people, see "Learn How Forms Work" in Chapter 5, "Forms."

Reply To Folder Actions for Post Forms

When creating applications with Post forms, you can create custom actions so users can reply to items in a folder using custom forms, rather than the standard Post form. In this section, we use the Training Management application for examples of how to implement Reply To Folder actions for Post forms.

To open the Training Management folder

- In the Folder List, expand the Building Microsoft Outlook 2000 Applications folder, and then expand the Building Blocks folder. Then click the Training Management folder.

Overview of the Training Management Application

The Training Management application allows training personnel to create an entire course catalog in the Training Management folder. To create the catalog, administrators first post Course Catalog Entry items in the folder. Course Catalog Entry items contain a general description of the course. After Course Catalog Entry items have been posted, training administrators can post Course Offering items as responses to the Course Catalog Entry items, as shown in Figure 7.13. After students complete a course, they can post an Evaluation item as a response to the Course Offering item.

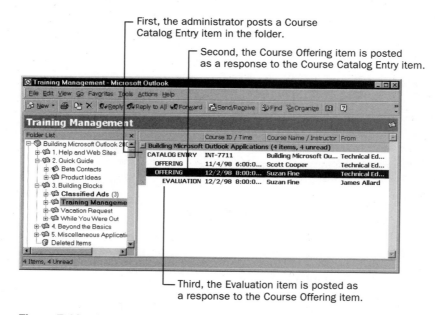

First, the administrator posts a Course Catalog Entry item in the folder.

Second, the Course Offering item is posted as a response to the Course Catalog Entry item.

Third, the Evaluation item is posted as a response to the Course Offering item.

Figure 7.13 *The Training Management folder.*

The Training Management application contains the following forms:

Course Catalog Entry form   This form allows the administrator to post an item that contains general information about a course, such as the Course ID, Cost, Name, Target Audience, and Course Description. The Read page of the form, shown in Figure 7.14, allows an administrator to view the course offering information and to open a Course Offering Response item.

Course Offering form   The Course Offering form allows an administrator to post a Course Offering item in the Training Management folder. The Course Offering item, which contains specifics about the course such as class time and instructor, is posted as a response to the Course Catalog Entry item. The Read page of the Course Offering form shows two custom buttons: a Signup button that lets students register for a class and a Course Evaluation button that lets students post a course evaluation in the Training Management folder. The Compose page, shown in Figure 7.15, shows a Post button that sends the form to the specified folder for public viewing.

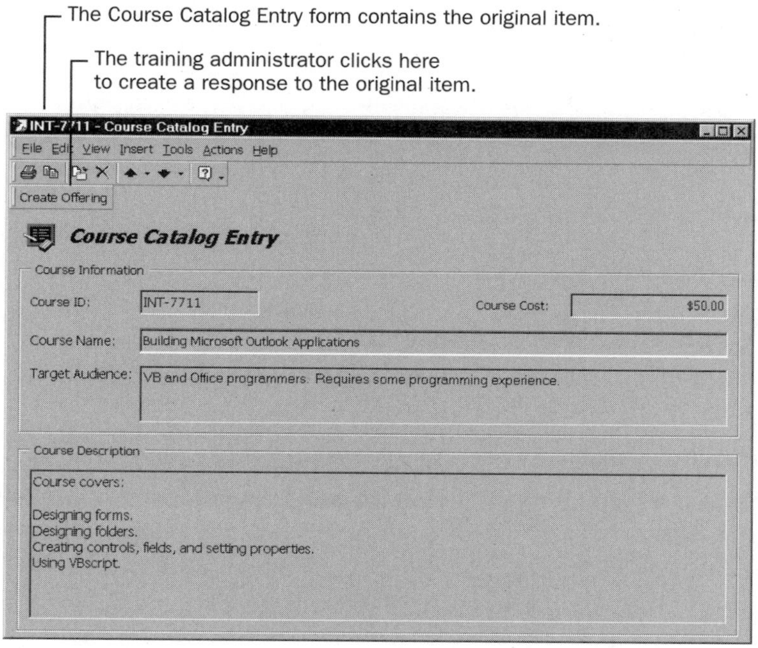

The Course Catalog Entry form contains the original item.

The training administrator clicks here
to create a response to the original item.

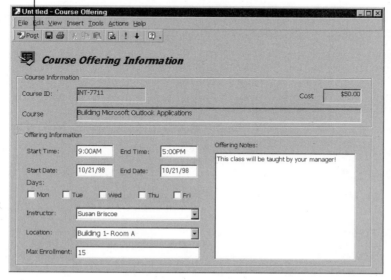

Figure 7.14 *The Read page of the Course Catalog Entry form.*

The administrator clicks here to post the Course Offering
Response item in the Training Management folder.

Figure 7.15 *The Compose page of the Course Offering form.*

Signup form   This form enables a student to send a Signup item to the Course Registration folder. This part of the application is not covered in this section.

Evaluation form   This form allows students to post an Evaluation item as a response to a Course Offering item. This part of the application is not covered in this section.

In the rest of this section, we look at the custom actions of the Course Catalog Entry form. First, we examine how the actions work in the folder. Then, we look at how the fields are copied from the Course Catalog Entry form to the Course Offering form. Finally, we look at how response items are organized in a custom view in the Training Management folder.

Actions for the Course Catalog Entry Form

Now let's take a look at the Actions page for the Course Catalog Entry form, as shown in Figure 7.16.

To view the Actions page of the Course Catalog Entry form

1. On the Actions menu of the Training Management folder, click New Course Catalog Entry.

2. On the form's Tools menu, select Forms, and then click Design This Form.

3. Click the Actions tab, as shown in Figure 7.16.

┌─ The Reply To Folder action is not enabled
│ for the Course Catalog Entry form.

┌─ The Create Offering action is a custom action that
│ causes a Create Offering command button to be placed
│ on the Read page of the Course Catalog Entry form.

The Actions page. ─┐

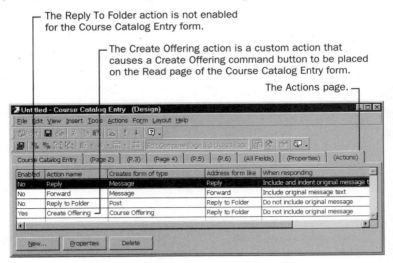

Figure 7.16 *The Actions page for the Course Catalog Entry form.*

Make the Reply To Folder Action Unavailable

Here is a simple rule to remember.

As shown in Figure 7.16, the Reply To Folder command is not available for the Course Catalog Entry form. This is done to prevent the user from posting standard Post form items in the Training Management folder. You can also do this for the Reply and Forward actions.

> **Tip** If you create a custom Reply To Folder action for a form, set the Enabled option to No for the standard Reply To Folder so the action is not available.

➔ To make the Reply To Folder action unavailable

1. On the Actions page, double-click the Reply To Folder action.
2. Clear the Enabled check box.

New Post To Folder Actions

With New Post To Folder actions, you can specify that custom command buttons and menu commands are added to the form. The menu commands or buttons, when clicked, open a custom form that enables the user to post a response item to the folder. For example, the Course Catalog Entry form has a custom Create Offering action. When an administrator opens a Course Catalog Entry item in his Inbox, he can click the Create Offering button as shown in Figure 7.17.

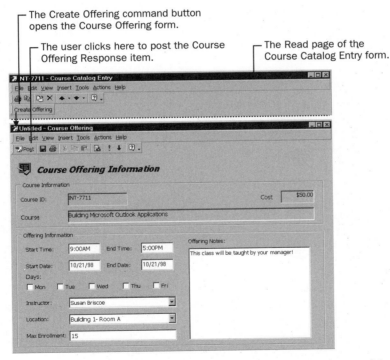

Figure 7.17 *The Create Offering button is added to the Read page of the Course Catalog Entry form. When clicked, it opens the Compose page of the Course Offering form.*

The Create Offering Action

Now let's take a look at the options that make up the Create Offering action, as shown in Figure 7.18.

To view the Create Offering action options

1. In the Design mode of the Course Catalog Entry form, click the Actions page.

2. Double-click the Create Offering action to open the Form Action Properties dialog box.

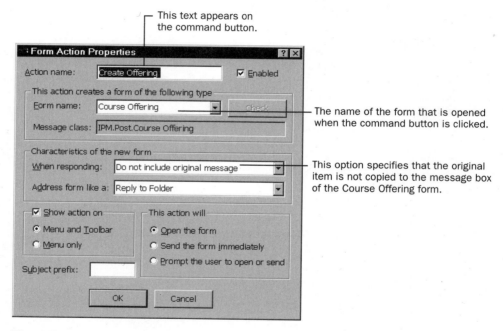

Figure 7.18 *The properties for the Create Offering action*

Action Name

On Post forms, the Action Name option defines the name of the menu command and action button that open the associated Reply To Folder form.

The custom Create Offering command button appears on the Read page of the Course Catalog Entry form. The custom menu command appears in the following places:

- On the Outlook Actions menu when an item created with the associated form is selected in a folder. For example, the Create Offering command appears on the Actions menu when a Course Catalog Entry item is selected in the Training Management folder.

- On the Context menu when you right-click on an item created with the associated form.
- On the Actions menu of the Read page of the Course Catalog Entry form.

Form Name and Message Class

The Form Name option holds the name of the form that opens when the command button or menu command is clicked. The Message Class, the internal identifier for the form, is automatically supplied for you in the Message Class text box. The Form Name combo box contains the names of the forms published in the current folder, so you see the Training Management forms in the Form Name combo box.

To specify a form name

Do one of the following:

- In the Form Name combo box, type a form name, and then click Check to search for the form.

  If Outlook cannot find the form, you will see a message box that explains that Outlook can't find the form. If this happens, you should create the Response form before you specify the Form Name option. After you create the Response form and publish it in a forms library, you can then return to the original form and click the name of the Response form in the Form Name combo box.

- In the Form Name combo box, click a form name to specify the form that is activated when the user clicks an action menu command or command button.

- In the Form Name combo box, click Forms to open the Choose Form dialog box. In the first box, click the library, and then click the form you want in the box below it.

Characteristics Of The New Form

Under Characteristics Of The New Form, you specify how values from the original item are copied to the Response item.

When Responding

When creating actions, remember that the original message can be copied only to the message box of the Response item. If the Response form does not have a message box, as is the case with the Course Offering form, then the message cannot be copied.

Tip If the Response form does not have a message box, then specify Do Not Include Original Message in the When Responding box.

Generally, with Post forms, you should be very careful about including the original message, especially if the message is very large.

Address Form Like A

For Post forms, you always choose Reply To Folder for the Address Form Like A option. Reply To Folder sets up the response form so the Post To field of the Response form contains the active folder address, the Conversation field contains the subject of the original item, and the Subject field is empty.

Show Action On

Most of the time, you can specify the default Menu And Toolbar option. However, there may be times when you want to place action buttons in a custom location on the form. To do this, you can add a command button to the form, and then create a procedure for the command button to open the Response form when the command button is clicked. If this is the case, you can click the Menu Only option or uncheck Show Action On.

> **More Info** For more information about creating procedures for forms, see Chapter 11, "Using VBA and VBScript with Outlook."

This Action Will

For the Course Catalog Entry form, when the Create Offering action is initiated, it opens the Course Offering form. For most Reply To Folder actions, under This Action Will you should specify Open The Form.

Subject Prefix

When the Reply To Folder option is selected in the Address Form Like A box, the Subject field of the Response item is cleared. So, in most cases, you leave the Subject Prefix box blank when Reply To Folder is selected.

How Field Values Are Copied to the Response Form

Earlier in this chapter, we learned that values from shared fields—those fields that are common between the original item and the Response item—are copied from the original item to the Response item.

When the Reply To Folder option is selected in the Address Form Like A box for an action, the same principles apply. Values from shared fields are copied from the original item to the Response item. However, there is one important exception.

> **Important** When the Reply To Folder option is selected in the Address Form Like A box, the value from the Subject field is not copied from the original item to the Response item. Instead, the value of the Subject field of the original item is copied to the Conversation field of the Response item and the Subject field in the Response item is blank.

In Figure 7.19, there is no Subject field visible on either form. Instead the Subject field is hidden (on page 2) and bound to the CourseID field, so when a form is opened, the value of the CourseID field appears in the title bar of the form. This is done because the value in the item's Subject field always appears in the title bar of the form. Also, there is no message box on either form, so the original message is not copied to the Response message.

When the Create Offering action is started, as shown in Figure 7.19, the values in these fields are copied from the Course Catalog Entry form to the Course Offering form.

- CourseID
- CourseCost
- CourseName

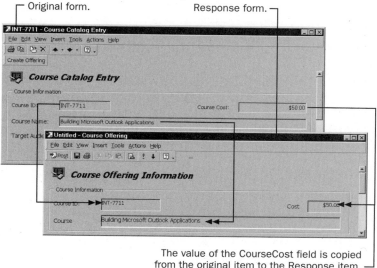

Original form.

Response form.

The value of the CourseCost field is copied from the original item to the Response item.

Figure 7.19 *Values between fields common to both the original and Response form are copied to the Response form.*

Tip To make sure field values are copied between the original form and the Response form, use the same fields for both forms. For example, for the Training Management application, the CourseID, CourseCost, and CourseName fields are used for both the Course Catalog Entry form and the Course Offering Information form.

Create Response Forms

Generally, it is recommended that you create all Response forms for an application before you create form actions. For example, for the Training Management application, you create the Course Catalog Entry form, and then you create the Course Offering form. After you've created the Course Offering form, you then return to the Course Catalog Entry form and create a Create Offering action that specifies the Course Offering form as the Form Name option.

In some cases, the Response form is very similar to the original form, so you can use the original form as a template. At other times, it's quicker to start from scratch. In the case of the Course Offering Response form, either approach can be used.

> **More Info** For more information on creating and modifying forms, see Chapter 5, "Forms."

Publish the Forms to the Forms Library of the Folder

When you create actions for a form, you must make sure that the forms that are opened as a result of the action are published in the forms library of the folder. Before you publish the forms, however, it's a good idea to make backup copies of them.

To make a backup copy of a form

1. With the form open, click Save As on the File menu.
2. In the Save In drop-down list box, select the default Outlook template folder, such as C:\Program Files\Microsoft Office\Templates.
3. In the File Name text box, type a name for the form.
4. In the Save As Type drop-down list box, select Outlook Template (.oft).
5. Click Save.

To open your backup copy of a form

1. Select New on the File menu, and then click Choose Form.
2. Click User Templates In File System in the Look In drop-down list box, and then click the form you'd like to open.

To publish a form in the forms library of a folder

1. On the Tools menu, select Forms, and then click Publish Form As.
2. If the text in the Look In box does not reflect the active folder, click Browse, select the forms library you want, and then click OK.
3. Type the name of the form in the Display Name text box and the Form Name text box.
4. Click Publish.

Test the Forms

After you create actions and custom forms to respond to the actions, you should run the forms to make sure they work as expected. For example, here is a quick way to test the forms and their actions in the Training Management application.

To test the forms in the Training Management application

1. In the Folder List, click the Training Management folder.

2. On the Actions menu, click New Course Catalog Entry.

3. Fill in the Course Catalog Entry form, and then click Post.

4. In the Training Management folder, double-click the Course Catalog Entry item you just posted.

5. Click the Create Offering button.

6. Fill in the Course Offering form, and then click Post.

7. The Course Offering item is posted as a response to the Course Catalog Entry item. As such, it is indented in the folder.

8. Alternatively, you can double-click the Course Offering item, and then click Create Evaluation or Signup on the form. Click Post to put it in the folder.

9. The Signup form is a Message form that routes course registration information to a course administrator or public folder. If you like, you can send the message to your Inbox as a test. The Course Evaluation form is a custom Response form that posts a Response Evaluation item in the Training Management folder.

Set the Hidden Property for Response Forms

After you publish and test forms, you set the Hidden property for the Response forms. For example, the following procedure sets the Hidden property for the Response forms in the Training Management folder.

 To set the Hidden property for the Training Management Response forms

1. In the Folder List, right-click the Training Management folder, and then click Properties on the shortcut menu.

2. Click the Forms page, and then click Manage.

3. In the right-hand drop-down list box, click Course Offering, and then click Properties.

4. Select the Hidden check box, and then click OK.

5. In the right-hand drop-down list box, click Course Evaluation, and then click Properties.

6. Select the Hidden check box, and then click OK.

7. In the right-hand drop-down list box, click Signup, and then click Properties.

8. Select the Hidden check box, and then click OK.

9. Click Close, and then click OK.

Note After forms are hidden, they are no longer visible in the following places:

- From the Choose Form dialog box selected from New on the File menu
- From the Actions menu for that folder

Chapter 8
Folders

In This Chapter

With Outlook, you can create a wide variety of folders to help users share, organize, and track information in your organization. Here are just a few examples:

- **Discussion folders that provide a public forum for users to submit, share, and respond to ideas and information**   For example, you can create a discussion folder for posting job openings, job candidate information, and interview responses for a candidate. Or you can create a Technical Users Group folder, such as the HTML folder at Microsoft, where writers and designers can post, read, and share information and solutions to problems.

- **Placeholder folders that provide a logical hierarchy for your application folders**   Public folder applications sometimes include placeholder folders that provide a logical means of organizing the application folders that actually hold the documents that are manipulated by a user. Assign permissions to a placeholder folder, which prevents users from adding, editing, or deleting items in the folder. For example, you might have a top-level placeholder folder named Sales with regional placeholder folders for East, West, South, and Midwest. Under the regional folders you would add application folders named Current Customers and Prospective Customers that contain items holding the data for your application.

- **Reference folders that provide a place to store and organize information**   For example, you can create a Product Specification Library that stores Microsoft Word documents. You can use the built-in or custom document properties of those Word documents to create views in the folder. In addition, you can create a Reference Library that stores Web addresses or a Project Library that stores a variety of materials such as Visio documents, PowerPoint presentations, Visual Basic prototypes, or Microsoft Excel workbooks.

- **Tracking folders that allow users to record and review information that is constantly updated**   For example, you can create an application such as the sample Help Desk application, so users and help desk technicians can schedule appointments and track the status of help desk requests.

This chapter takes an in-depth look at creating public folders, discusses how to manage forms, and looks at creating custom views. It also covers how to set folder permissions, create rules for a folder, and establish Folder Home Pages. Folder Home Pages are a new feature of Outlook 2000 that allows you to specify a URL displaying a Web page in place of a normal Outlook view of those folder items. Using Visual InterDev 6.0 and the new Outlook View Control, you can also create custom HTML-based views of a folder's contents.

For the majority of examples in this chapter, the sample Classified Ads folder is used, as shown in Figure 8.1.

To open the Classified Ads folder

- In the Folder List, expand the Building Microsoft Outlook 2000 Applications folder, expand the Building Blocks folder, and then click the Classified Ads folder.

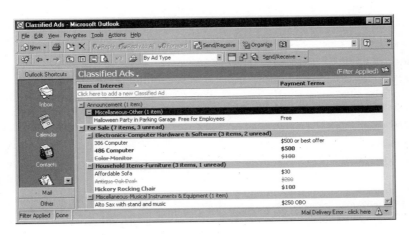

Figure 8.1 *The Classified Ads folder.*

An Important Reminder About Planning

To create folders that meet the needs of your users, it is essential to plan them first. If you dive head first into creating a folder hierarchy and its contents, you might have to redesign both your folder structure and the custom forms contained in those folders if business rules change or design requirements are overlooked. Careful planning avoids expensive, time-consuming redesigns. Your motto when you approach folder design should be to plan, plan, and plan again. Although planning processes differ with each organization and application, there are general steps you should follow when planning a public folder:

- Determine who will plan, design, and implement the folder.
- When you identify folder users and their needs, evaluate their requirements in terms of public folder roles and permissions. For example, what is the default permission on the application folder? Can your users modify the folder items created by other users? Create a list of user groups that will have access to your folder and determine whether they have permission to create, edit, or delete folder items. You also need to consider which forms will be available in your folders and which users can modify those forms.
- Be aware that folder users do not have to correspond to individual mailbox accounts. Exchange Distribution Lists provide a convenient way for you to manage the users who have been assigned to a public folder permissions role such as editor or author.
- Create a design plan that identifies the problems to be solved and how the folder will solve them. The design plan should include preliminary graphics of form windows or views to be created.

Create or Select a Folder

With Outlook, you can design a folder by using one of three methods.

Method	Use When
Create a new folder from scratch.	You cannot find an existing folder in your organization that closely matches the folder you want to create. In this case, it's quicker to start from scratch.
Modify an existing folder that is in public use.	You want to make minor changes to a folder, such as adding permissions or a view.
Copy the design of an existing folder to a new folder, and then modify the new folder.	You want to create a new folder based on the design of an existing folder, or you want to make changes to an existing folder and those changes will disrupt users' work.

Choose Where To Design the New Folder

If the method of folder design you choose requires that you create a new folder, you can create the folder in Public Folders, your Outlook Mailbox, or Personal Folders. The location determines whether the folder is public or private and determines the design properties you can set for the folder.

Designing new folders in a personal folder is recommended for most public folder application designs. After you have tested and refined your application, you can copy the private folders to Public Folders on an Exchange Server. At this point you should set permissions and go through another round of testing before you publish your application.

In a personal folder (.pst), you can create forms and design views, and then test them to make sure they work as expected. After you create forms and design views, you or the administrator can copy the folder to Public Folders, where you can complete the design of the folder by setting permissions and administration properties. At this point you will also publish your custom forms, if any, to an application folder or to the organizational forms registry.

You should be aware that some organizations require that you deploy your public folder application on a test Exchange Server before you move your application to a production server in your Exchange site.

The following table shows the attributes that you can set in each folder location.

Option	In a Personal folder	In a Mailbox Folder	In a Public Folder
Activities tab and Outlook Address Book tab on Contact Folders only	X	X	X
Create Exchange Server scripting and routing agents with appropriate permissions		X	X
Copy or install forms	X	X	X
Define rules		Set rules with the Rules Wizard	Set rules with the Folder Assistant
Design views	X	X	X
Designate the types of items allowed in the folder	X		X
Set administration properties	Can only set the initial view on folder	Can only set the initial view on folder	All
Set Folder Home Page	X	X	X
Set permissions		X	X

> **Note** Personal folders appearing on the Folder List are attached to personal folder (.pst) files saved on your hard disk drive. For more information on creating a personal folder (.pst) file, see "Create New Folders" in Chapter 3, "Customize Built-In Modules."

Create a Folder from Scratch

One way to design a folder is to create a new folder. After you create the folder, you can follow the design process outlined in this chapter, beginning with step 2, "Publish Forms in the Folder."

To create a folder

1. In the Folder List, right-click a personal folder you want to create a folder in, and then click New Folder on the shortcut menu.

2. In the Name text box, enter a name for the folder.

3. In the Folder Contains A drop-down list box, do one of the following:

   - Click Mail Items to create a folder that will contain items created with Message, Post, or Office Document forms.

   - Click Appointment Items, Contact Items, Journal Items, Note Items, or Task Items to create a folder that will contain items of the associated type. For example, if you click Appointment Items, Outlook creates a Calendar folder.

4. Click OK to close. If a dialog box appears asking if you want to Add A Shortcut To Outlook Bar?, click No if you do not want to add a shortcut to the current group in your Outlook Bar. Otherwise, click Yes to add a shortcut to this folder in the currently selected group.

Directly Modify a Folder

If a folder is in public use, it's best to directly modify the folder only if the changes are minor and will not disrupt another user's work. Minor changes include adding permissions, adding a view, or changing a folder contact.

To make more significant changes—such as modifying forms or rules—copy the design of the folder to another folder, modify the design, as described in "Copy a Folder Design" later in this chapter, and then copy the modified design back to the original folder.

> **Note** To modify a folder, you must have owner permissions for the folder. To check your permissions for a folder, right-click the folder, and then click Properties on the shortcut menu. You can view your permissions on the Permissions page of a Mailbox or Public Folder. If you are viewing subfolders of your Exchange mailbox, you are the folder owner by default. If you cannot see the Permissions page of a Public Folder, you do not have permissions as a folder owner. If you need to acquire owner permissions, contact your Exchange administrator.

⮕ To directly modify a Mailbox or Public folder

1. In the Folder List, right-click the folder, and then click Properties on the shortcut menu. You can also right-click the shortcut for the folder if it exists on your Outlook Bar.

2. In the Properties dialog box, make the changes, and then click OK.

Copy a Folder Design

To create or modify a folder, you can copy the design of an existing folder to a new folder. You can then customize the design of the new folder.

Copying a folder design involves copying design components, such as forms and views, from one folder to another. When a folder design is copied, the folder permissions and rules are always maintained, regardless of whether the folder design is copied to or from a folder in a personal or a public folder.

When Outlook copies the design to a folder, it merges the design components of the source folder with design components of the destination folder. If two properties conflict—for example, the permissions for a user in the source folder are different from the permissions in the destination folder—the properties in the source folder take precedence. All of the design components in the destination folder are overwritten.

Note To modify a Mailbox or Public Folder, you must have owner permissions for the folder. To check your permissions for a folder, right-click the folder, and then click Properties on the shortcut menu. You can view your permissions on the Permissions page. To copy permissions, rules, forms, and views, you must have owner permissions for the folder.

⮕ To copy a folder design

1. In the Folder List, select the folder to which you want to copy the design. Remember that you are copying the folder design to the selected target folder from a source folder that you will specify in step 3.

2. On the File menu, point to Folder, and then click Copy Folder Design.

3. In the Copy Design From This Folder drop-down list box, select the folder you want to copy the design from.

4. Under Design Copy Of, select one or more of the following:

To Copy	Select
Permissions from the source folder	Permissions
The rules associated with the source folder	Rules
The description of the source folder	Description
Forms and views that are stored in the source folder	Forms & Views

5. Click OK.

Publish Forms in the Folder

Not all folders require custom forms. For those folders that do, however, you must first design the forms, and then publish them in an Outlook folder, such as a Mailbox folder, a public folder, or a personal folder. When you publish a form in a folder, you accomplish two things:

- You make the form available in the folder so it can be opened by users to compose and view items in the folder.

- You expose the form properties, such as form name, description, and menu commands, in Outlook.

To publish a form in an Outlook folder

1. With the form open, select Forms on the Tools menu, and then click Publish Form As. If you have already published your form to either the personal or Organizational Forms Library, select the Tools menu, then click the Select Form command to open the form in order to publish the form to your application folder.

Tip If the form you wish to publish contains VBScript code, select the Tools menu, click the Choose Form command, select the form in the Choose Form dialog box, and hold down the Shift key in order to disable macros when the form opens. If you run macros and then publish the form, you might unintentionally create default values for some of the user-defined fields in the form.

2. In the Display Name text box, type in the name of the form that will appear in the form caption, forms list, and menu command.

   In the Form Name text box, type the name reflected in Message Class, if different.

   To change the location (library) where the form is published, click the Look In drop-down list box, and then select the folder where you want to publish the form.

3. Click Publish.

More Info For more information about creating and publishing forms, see Chapter 5, "Forms."

Manage Forms

With the Forms page of the folder's Properties dialog box, as shown in Figure 8.2, you can see the forms that are published in the forms library of the folder. In addition, you can specify the types of items that can be created in the folder. You can also use the Forms page to access the Forms Manager. With the Forms Manager, you can copy and delete forms, and view form properties.

To view the Forms page

1. In the Folder List, right-click the folder, and then click Properties on the short-cut menu.

2. Click the Forms page.

Click here to open the Forms Manager.

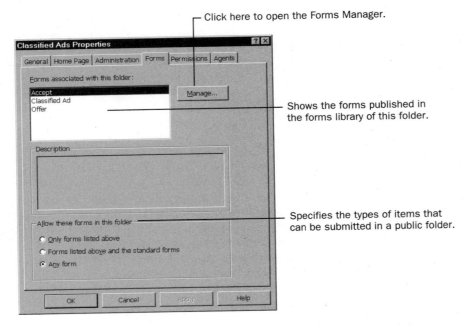

Shows the forms published in the forms library of this folder.

Specifies the types of items that can be submitted in a public folder.

Figure 8.2 *The Forms page shows the forms that are published in the current folder.*

Tip You can also access the Forms Manager by clicking Options on the Outlook Tools menu. This allows access to all forms, not just those in the current folder. Click the Other tab, then click the Advanced Options button, and then click the Custom Forms button. Finally, click the Manage Forms button to get to the Forms Manager.

Specify the Types of Items Allowed in the Folder

In many folders, you may want to control the types of items that can be submitted. For example, in the Classified Ads folder, you want to prevent the user from submitting standard Post items to the folder because they are out of context and do not appear correctly in the custom views created for the folder.

To specify the types of items allowed in a public folder

- On the Forms page of the folder's Properties dialog box, under Allow These Forms In This Folder, click one of the following.

To Specify That	Click
Only items created with the forms specified in the Forms Associated With This Folder drop-down list box can be submitted in the folder.	Only Forms Listed Above
Only items created with the forms in the Forms Associated With This Folder drop-down list box and standard Post and Message forms can be submitted in the folder.	Forms Listed Above And The Standard Forms
Any type of item can be created in the folder.	Any Form

Copy and Delete Forms or Set the Hidden Property for a Form

You can use the Forms Manager, as shown in Figure 8.3, to copy and delete forms and to view form properties.

To open the Forms Manager

- On the Forms page of the folder's Properties box, click Manage.

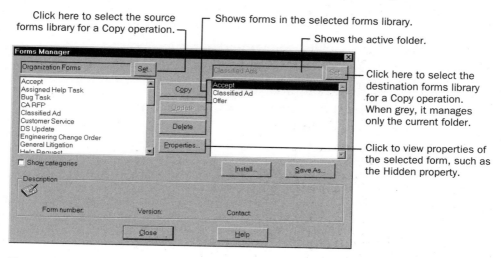

Figure 8.3 *The Forms Manager dialog box.*

If the form you want to use already exists in your organization and is published in a forms library, you can copy it to the forms library of the folder you're designing. By default, the left drop-down list box in the Forms Manager dialog box shows the contents of the Organization Forms library and the right list box shows the contents of the active folder's forms library. The left list box shows the source forms library from which you can copy forms. The right list box shows the destination forms library to which you copy the forms. You can easily change the libraries shown in these boxes.

To change the library in the left or right drop-down list boxes of the Forms Manager

1. Choose Set for the list box that contains the library you want to change.
2. Do one of the following:
   - In the Forms Library drop-down list box, click the library you want.
   - In the Folder Forms Library drop-down list box, select the folder you want.

To copy a form to a folder

- In the left drop-down list box, click the form you want to copy, and then click Copy.

   You can copy a form from one forms library to another. You can delete any form from either forms library.

To delete a form

- In the left or right drop-down list box, click the form you want to delete, and then click Delete.

   To synchronize a form with an updated version, select the one you wish to update. For the update process to work properly, the form must be visible in both forms libraries (in both the left and right drop-down list boxes).

To update forms published in different forms libraries

- In the right drop-down list box, click the form, and then click Update. Although you won't see an action, the forms will now be updated.

View Forms Properties or Set the Hidden Property for a Form

With the Properties dialog box, you can view a form's properties, and you can set the Hidden property for a form. When you select the Hidden property for a form, you specify that the form's associated menu command is not visible in the Outlook user interface, so users can only create response items with the form or view items with the form. In addition, forms published in the Personal Forms Library or the Organization Forms Library with the Hidden property selected will not be visible to the user in the Choose Form dialog box. The Choose Form dialog box is available by selecting New on the File menu.

To view the properties of a form

- In the right list box of the Forms Manager dialog box, click the form whose properties you want to view, and then click Properties.

To set the Hidden property for a form

1. In the right drop-down list box of the Forms Manager dialog box, click the form that you want to set the Hidden property for, and then click Properties.
2. Select the Hidden check box, and then click OK.

Important The Install and Save As buttons are not valid for Outlook forms. They are intended for use with forms created for Microsoft Exchange Client.

Design Folder Views

To help users organize and manage the information stored in folders, you can create folder views. With views, users can organize and view the same information in different ways within the folder. With Outlook, you can create table, timeline, card, day/week/month, and icon view types.

A new feature in Outlook 2000 is the ability to set a Folder Home Page for a public or private folder. A Folder Home Page displays a Web view provided by a URL to an external Web site on the Internet, an intranet link, or an Active Server Page. Using Visual InterDev 6.0 and the Outlook View Control, you can create a Folder Home Page that renders an HTML-based custom view of your folder. With Microsoft Site Server 3.0, you can link a Folder Home Page that provides custom searching capabilities for a target folder and its subfolders. For information on programming Folder Home Pages and the new Outlook Team Folder Wizard, see Chapter 14, "Customizing Folder Home Pages."

- **Columns**   As shown in Figure 8.4, columns show values for a particular field in an item under the column heading.
- **Groups**   With groups, you can create categories of items that share a common field value. Items in the By Category view are grouped by the type of ad, as Figure 8.4 shows. Groups can be expanded or collapsed.

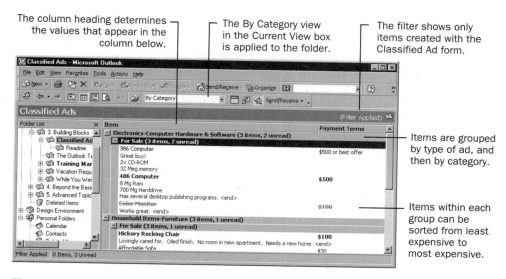

Figure 8.4 *The view chosen by the user determines how items are organized in the folder.*

- **Sort** You can sort the items in a group based on the criteria you specify. For example, you can sort items by the date received, field values, or alphabetically.
- **Filter** With Outlook filters, you create criteria to specify the items to be shown in the folder. For example, in Figure 8.4, the filter applied to the folder specifies that only items created with the Classified Ad form are shown in the folder.
- **Format** With the Format dialog box, you can specify fonts, grid lines, and in-cell editing for a folder. With in-cell editing, users can change information in a cell in the folder.

Create a New View

Each view you create is given a name that appears in the Current View drop-down list box on the Advanced toolbar, as shown earlier in Figure 8.4. When the view name is clicked in the Current View drop-down list box, the view is applied to the folder and the items in the folder are arranged according to the criteria specified in the view.

To create a new view

1. On the View menu, select Current View, and then click Define Views.
2. Click New.
3. In the Name Of New View text box, type a name.
4. In the Type Of View text box, click the type of view you want.
5. Under Can Be Used On, verify that This Folder, Visible To Everyone is selected.
6. Click OK twice.
7. Click Apply View.

Show Only the Views Created for the Folder

For each folder you create, Outlook provides several standard views in the Current View drop-down list box. In many cases, these views are not relevant to your folder, so you can remove them from the Current View drop-down list box. If you want to remove the standard views from the Current View drop-down list box and show only the custom views you create, you can select the Only Show Views Created For This Folder check box, as shown in Figure 8.5.

To show only the custom views created for the folder

1. On the View menu, select Current View, and then click Define Views.
2. Select the Only Show Views Created For This Folder check box.
3. Click Close.

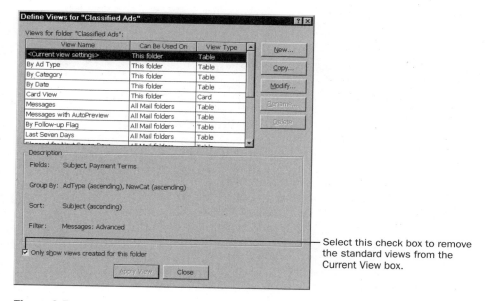

Figure 8.5 *The Only Show Views Created For This Folder check box specifies that the standard views are not shown in the Current View drop-down list box on the Standard toolbar.*

Create Columns

With Outlook, you can create columns by dragging fields from the Field Chooser to the Column Heading row. When you add a column to a view, the column shows the value of the field for each of the items in the view, as shown in Figure 8.6.

To add a column to a view

1. On the Advanced toolbar, click the Field Chooser icon.

2. In the Field Set drop-down list box in the Field Chooser, click the field set from which you want to choose fields.

3. Drag the field you want as the new column heading to the Column Heading row, as shown in Figure 8.7. Use the red double-arrow marker to position the new column heading in the Column Heading row.

To remove a column from a view

- Drag the column heading away from the Column Heading row until an X appears through the column heading, and then release the mouse button.

Format Columns

By default, a column heading has the same label as the field on which it is based. For example, the Payment Terms column heading is identical to the Payment Terms field. In some cases, you may want to change the column heading label so it is different from the

Under this column heading, you see the values from the Subject field of each item.

Under this column heading, you see the values from the Payment Terms field of each item.

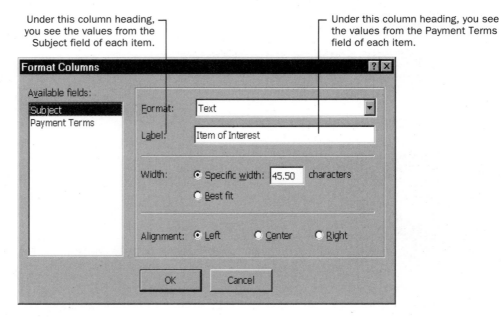

Figure 8.6 *Columns for the By Ad Type view in the Classified Ads folder.*

Fields can be dragged from the Field Chooser to the column heading row to create columns.

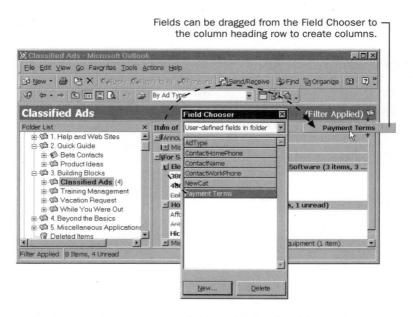

Figure 8.7 *The Payment Terms field is added to the Column Heading row.*

field name. The Item Of Interest column heading in the By Ad Type view shows an example of a changed column heading label.

On the Classified Ads form, the Subject field on the form is labeled Item Of Interest, as shown in Figure 8.8. In this example, the Subject field is used for the form because it provides the unique ability to display its value in the caption on the form window. Just as the label for a field can be changed on the form, the label can also be changed in the column heading of the view. For example, for the By Ad Type view, as shown earlier in Figures 8.6 and 8.7, the column heading for the Subject field is Item Of Interest. To change the column heading label, you change the label for the field in the Format Columns dialog box.

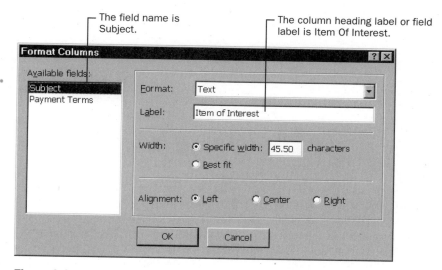

Figure 8.8 *The Subject field is labeled Item Of Interest. The value of the field appears in the window caption.*

To change the format properties of a column

1. Right-click the column heading you want to format, and then click Format Columns on the shortcut menu.

2. In the Available Fields list box, click the field you want to format, and then make the changes you want.

3. Click OK.

Create Combination Columns

In some cases, you may want to add Combination fields to a view. To help demonstrate the point, this section shows you an example of a Volunteer Registration application. Note that this application is merely an example and is not included in the Building Microsoft Outlook 2000 Applications folder.

With the fields on the Volunteer Registration form, as shown in Figure 8.9, a user can enter his or her first name, last name, address, city, and postal code in separate fields.

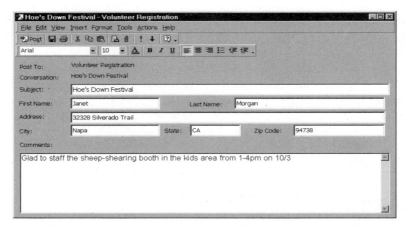

Figure 8.9 *The Volunteer Registration form.*

Now, assume you want to create a column in the Volunteer Registration view that combines the Fname and Lname field values and shows them in a single Name column, as shown in Figure 8.10. To do this, you create a combination column.

Create a Combination Column That Combines Text Fragments

There are two kinds of Combination fields you can create: those that combine text fragments and those that show the value of the first non-empty field. This section shows you how to create a combination column that combines text fragments. The next section shows you how to create a combination column that shows only the value of the first non-empty field.

 To create a combination column

1. On the Advanced toolbar, click the Field Chooser icon.
2. Click New.
3. In the Name text box, type the column name.
4. In the Type drop-down list box, click Combination.
5. Click Edit.
6. Click Field to add the fields you want to combine, and then click OK twice.
7. From the Field Chooser, drag the field you want as the new column heading to the Column Heading row. Use the red double-arrow marker to position the new column heading in the Column Heading row.

Note Message forms save user-defined fields in the Inbox. Other forms save User-defined fields in the current folder.

The Name column combines values
from the Fname and Lname fields.

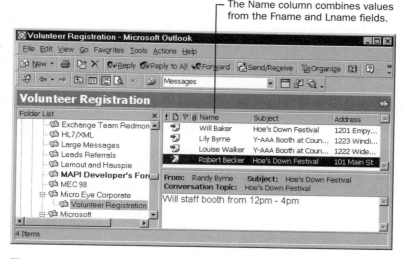

Figure 8.10 *The Volunteer Registration folder.*

In some cases, you may want to change the label of the combination column so it is different from the field name. In addition, you may want to change the formula specified for the combination column. To do this, you use the Format Columns dialog box, as shown in Figure 8.11.

To change a combination column label or formula

1. Select the folder, right-click the column heading, and then click Format Columns on the shortcut menu.

2. In the Available Fields list box, select the combination field whose properties you want to set, and do one or both of the following:

   • To change the formula, click the button next to the Formula text box.

   • To change the column label, change the text in the Label text box.

3. Click OK.

Create a Combination Column That Shows Only the Value of the First Non-Empty Field

In some cases, you may want to create a column that shows only the value of the first non-empty field in the item. For example, you may want to create a combination column if you have multiple item types in the folder and the items have fields with similar values but different field names. Assume you have documents and standard post items in a folder and you want to create an Author column. Rather than creating a From column for post items and an Author column for document items, you can create an Author/From field, and then click the Showing Only The First Non-Empty Field, Ignoring Subsequent Ones option.

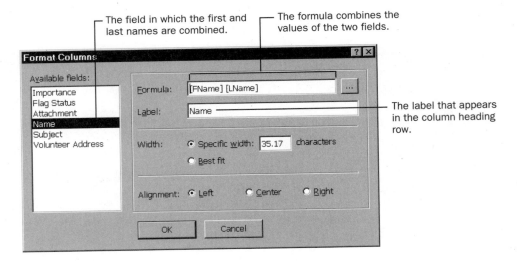

Figure 8.11 *The format properties for the Name column in the Volunteer Registration folder.*

To create a Combination Column that shows only the value of the first non-empty field

1. On the Advanced toolbar, click the Field Chooser icon.
2. Click New.
3. In the Name text box, type a name.
4. In the Type drop-down list box, click Combination.
5. Click Edit.
6. Click Showing Only The First Non-Empty Field, Ignoring Subsequent Ones.
7. Click Field to add the fields you want to combine, and then click OK twice.
8. From the Field Chooser, drag the field you want as the new column heading to the Column Heading row. Use the double-arrow marker to position the new column heading in the Column Heading row.

Create Formula Columns

For some views, you may want to show different field values in the folder. For example, in the sample Training Management folder, as shown in Figure 8.12, the Course ID/Time and Course Name/Instructor columns are formula columns. In the Course ID/Time column, the value of the CourseID field is shown in the column if the item is a Catalog Entry item. If the item is a Course Offering item, the value of the StartTime field is shown in the column.

To create a formula column

1. On the Advanced toolbar, click the Field Chooser icon.

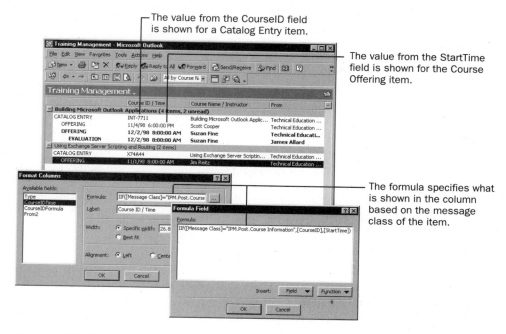

Figure 8.12 *The formula for the Course ID/Time column shows a different field value for each message class.*

2. Click New.

3. In the Name text box, type a name.

4. In the Type drop-down list box, click Formula.

5. Click Edit.

6. In the Formula box, specify the formula you want for the column, and then click OK twice.

7. From the Field Chooser, drag the field you want as the new column heading to the Column Heading row. Use the red double-arrow marker to position the new column heading in the Column Heading row.

    You may want to change the label of the formula column so it reflects the field values shown in the column. In addition, you may want to change the formula specified for the column.

To change a formula column label or formula

1. Right-click the column heading, and then click Format Columns on the shortcut menu.

2. In the Available Fields list box, select the field whose properties you want to set, and do one or both of the following:

- To change the formula, click the button next to the Formula text box.
- To change the column label, change the text in the Label text box.

3. Click OK.

Group Items

Groups provide a convenient way to organize items that have the same field values in a folder. For example, in the By Ad Type view in the Classified Ads folder, items are grouped by ad type, and then by category. So items that have a *For Sale* value in the AdType field, as shown in Figure 8.13, are grouped together. In addition, items that have an *Electronics-Computer Hardware & Software* value in the Category field are grouped together.

If your application makes use of custom forms, you should consider enforcement of validation rules to ensure that views are complete and logical for the user. A validation rule on a user-defined field requires that a given field have a value, or one value from a range of possible values.

To group items using Customize Current View

1. On the View menu, select Current View, click Customize Current View, and then click Group By.
2. In the Select Available Fields From drop-down list box, click the field set containing the field you want to group by.
3. Under Group Items By, click the field you want to use to group items.
4. Alternatively, you can click the Show Field In View check box. This option shows the field in the view above the column heading.
5. Click Ascending or Descending. When Ascending is selected, the groups are arranged alphabetically, starting with "A" at the top.
6. To group items into further subsets, click a field in the next available Then By drop-down list box, as shown in Figure 8.14.
7. Click OK twice.

Show or Hide the Group By Box

An easy way to create groups for a view is to show the Group By dialog box, and then drag column headings to the Group By box. You can then hide the Group By box.

To create groups by using the Group By box

1. On the Advanced toolbar, click the Group By icon. The Group By box appears above the column heading area.
2. Drag the fields you want to group by from the Field Chooser, or from the Column Heading row, to the Group By box above the Column Heading row.
3. After you create the groups you want, click the Group By Box icon on the Advanced toolbar to hide the Group By box.

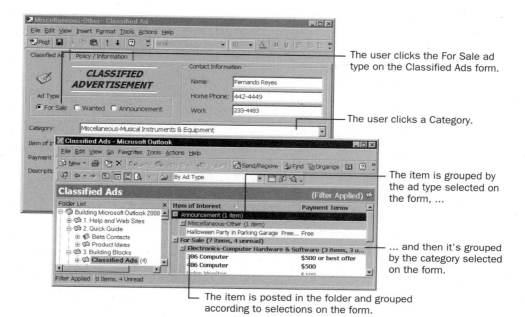

The user clicks the For Sale ad type on the Classified Ads form.

The user clicks a Category.

The item is grouped by the ad type selected on the form, ...

... and then it's grouped by the category selected on the form.

The item is posted in the folder and grouped according to selections on the form.

Figure 8.13 *The Classified Ads form.*

Items are grouped by the AdType field.

Items are further grouped into subsets in the NewCat (Category) field.

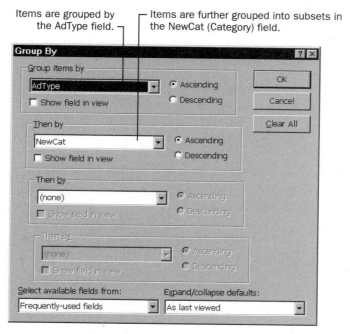

Figure 8.14 *The Group By dialog box for the By Ad Type view.*

Sort Items

Sorting items provides a convenient way to organize information within a group. For example, you can sort items in a group by the date the items were received, or you can sort items alphabetically. When you specify a field to sort by, you can specify ascending or descending order. Ascending order sorts items in alphabetical order, with the oldest date (or the lowest value) at the top of the list. Descending order sorts items in alphabetical order, with the most recent date (or highest value) at the top of the list. Figure 8.15 shows the items in the By Ad Type view sorted by Subject. Remember that the label for the Subject field is changed in the column heading from Subject to Item Of Interest, as discussed earlier in "Format Columns."

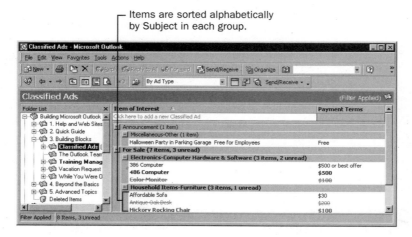

Figure 8.15 *Items in each group are sorted alphabetically by Subject in the Item Of Interest column.*

To sort items

1. On the View menu, click Current View, and then click Customize Current View.

2. Click Sort.

3. In the Select Available Fields From drop-down list box, click the category of fields containing the field you want to use for sorting.

4. Under Sort Items By, click the field you want to use to sort items by.

5. Click either Ascending or Descending to choose the sort order.

6. To sort items into further subsets, click a field in the next available Then By drop-down list box, as shown in Figure 8.16.

7. Click OK twice.

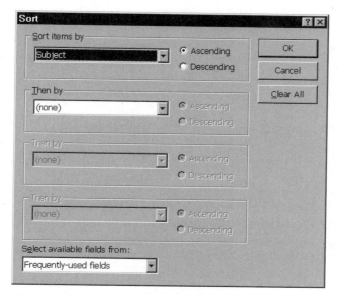

Figure 8.16 *Items are sorted alphabetically by the value in the Subject field.*

Group by Conversation, Sort by Conversation Index

Conversation and Conversation Index are unique properties that you can use to create views for discussion folders so people can view the history of responses to an item, also known as a conversation thread. For this section, the Product Ideas folder covered in Chapter 4, "Design a Custom Application," is used to provide an example of grouping by Conversation and sorting by Conversation Index.

Grouping by Conversation

Conversation is a unique property that is inherited from the Subject field. For example, if you submit a standard Post item to a folder, the Conversation field of the item is set to the value of the Subject field. Thereafter, any responses made to the item automatically inherit the value of the Conversation field. As shown in Figure 8.17, the items in the Product Ideas folder are grouped by Product Category, and then by Conversation.

To group items by Conversation

1. On the View menu, select Current View, and then click Customize Current View.
2. Click Group By.
3. In the Select Available Fields From drop-down list box, click Frequently-Used Fields.
4. Under Group Items By, click the field that you want to use to group items by.
5. In the Then By drop-down list box, click Conversation, as shown in Figure 8.18.
6. Click OK twice.

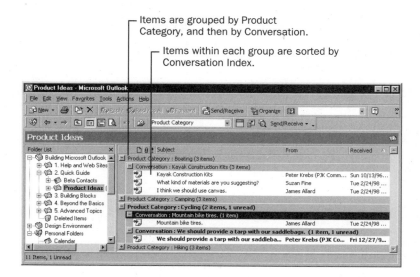

Figure 8.17 *Items are grouped by Product Category, and then by Conversation. They are sorted by Conversation Index.*

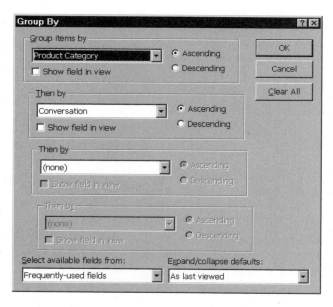

Figure 8.18 *Items are grouped by Product Category, and then by Conversation.*

Sorting by Conversation Index

The Conversation Index property is a way of keeping track of responses. When you sort by Conversation Index, the responses to each item are indented from, and follow directly after, the original item. In this way, users can track the history of responses to an item.

To sort items by Conversation Index

1. On the View menu, select Current View, and then click Customize Current View.
2. Click Sort.
3. Under Sort Items By, click Conversation Index, as shown in Figure 8.19.
4. Click OK twice.

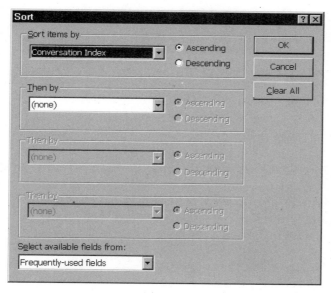

Figure 8.19 *When items are sorted by Conversation Index, response items are indented and follow the original item.*

Filter Items

Filters provide a way to find information quickly and easily in a folder. When a filter is applied in a view, only the items that meet the filter conditions show in the folder. For example, as shown in Figure 8.20, the filter created for the By Ad Type view shows only items created with the Classified Ad form (IPM.Post.CreateAd) in the folder.

Filters consist of a condition or set of conditions that determine what items are shown in a folder. For example, a condition may be From:Jim Hance. Conditions can have multiple arguments. For example, From:Jim Hance;Don Funk. Here are a few simple guidelines to follow when creating conditions:

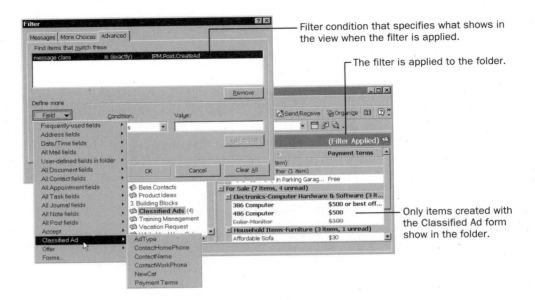

Figure 8.20 *The filter for the By Ad Type view shows only items created with the Classified Ad form (IPM.Post.CreateAd) in the folder.*

- **Multiple conditions are logical AND values** For example, the condition From:Jim Hance;Subject:GG&G is *True* if the From field of the incoming item contains *Jim Hance* and the Subject field contains *GG&G*.

- **Multiple arguments within a condition are logical OR values** For example, the condition From:Jim Hance;Karl Buhl;Don Funk;Max Benson is *True* if the From field contains any of the names included in the expression.

Specify Simple Filter Conditions

In some cases, you may want to filter messages that meet specific criteria. For example, you may want to filter all incoming messages from a particular user or about a particular subject.

➡ **To filter simple message properties**

1. On the View menu, select Current View, and then click Customize Current View.
2. Click Filter.
3. On the Messages page, specify the properties you want for the filter. For example, to create a filter that shows only messages from a particular person, click From, and then double-click the person's name in the list.
4. Click OK twice.

Specify Advanced Filter Conditions

On the Advanced page, you can create a variety of filter conditions. For example, you can specify that only items with a specific message class show in the view. In addition, you can specify that only items with a specific value in a field show in the view.

Filter By Message Class

When you filter on message class, you specify that only items created with a particular form are visible in the folder. For example, in the By Ad Type view in the Classified Ads folder, only items created with the Classified Ad form show in the view.

To filter by message class

1. On the View menu, select Current View, and then click Customize Current View.
2. Click Filter.
3. Click the Advanced tab.
4. Click Field, point to All Mail fields, and then click Message Class.
5. In the Condition drop-down list box, click Is (Exactly).
6. In the Value text box, type the message class, as shown in Figure 8.21.
7. Click Add To List.
8. Click OK twice.

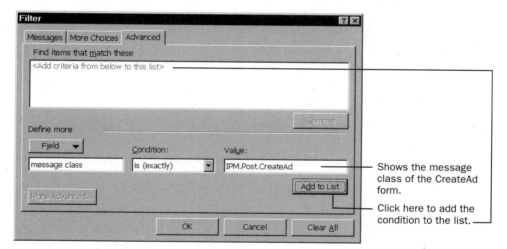

Figure 8.21 *The condition for the filter in the By Ad Type view specifies that only items with the message class IPM.Post.CreateAd show in the folder.*

Filter By Field Values

You can create a filter that shows only items that have a specific value in a field. For example, as shown in Figure 8.22, the conditions for the filter specify that only items created with the Classified Ad form and that have the value *For Sale* in the AdType field and the value *Transportation-Cars* in the NewCat field show in the view.

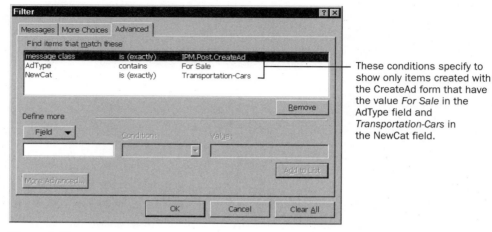

These conditions specify to show only items created with the CreateAd form that have the value *For Sale* in the AdType field and *Transportation-Cars* in the NewCat field.

Figure 8.22 *Advanced filter conditions for the Ad Type view.*

To filter on a field value

1. On the View menu, select Current View, and then click Customize Current View.
2. Click Filter.
3. Click the Advanced page.
4. Click Field, point to the field set you want, and then click the field you want.
5. Do one of the following:
    -   To filter a single field value, click Is (Exactly) in the Condition drop-down list box, and then type the value you want in the Value text box.
    -   To filter multiple values in a field, click Contains in the Condition drop-down list box, and then type the values you want, separated by a comma, in the Value text box.
6. Click Add To List.
7. Click OK twice.

Format Views

By using the Other Settings dialog box, accessible from the View Summary dialog box, you can change the fonts in the view, specify grid lines for the view, specify whether group headings are to be shaded, and turn on in-cell editing so users can enter and edit information in the cells in the folder, as shown in Figure 8.23.

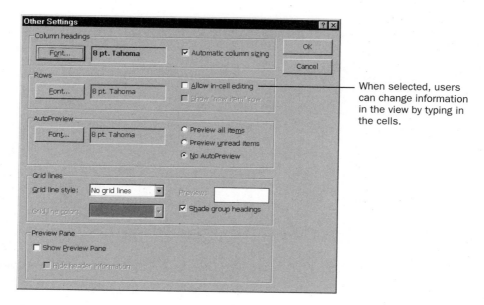

When selected, users can change information in the view by typing in the cells.

Figure 8.23 *Format options for the By Ad Type view.*

To format a view

1. In the Current View drop-down list box on the Advanced toolbar, switch to the view you want to change.

2. On the View menu, select Current View, and then click Customize Current View. You can also right-click a field heading in the current view and select Customize Current View from the shortcut menu.

3. Click Other Settings.

4. Select the options you want, and then click OK twice.

In-Cell Editing Views

If you check Allow In-Cell Editing in the Other Settings dialog box, users can edit item information directly from the view. The Beta Contacts sample application discussed in Chapter 3, "Customize Built-In Modules," has both in-cell editing and Show "New Item" Row enabled in the Potential Beta Contacts view shown in Figure 8.24. Users do not have to open the form to change field values. You can also expose a new item row so that users can enter new information from the view rather than using the Actions menu to open a new form instance.

To enable in-cell editing and a new items row

1. In the Current View drop-down list box on the Advanced toolbar, switch to the view you want to change.

2. On the View menu, select Current View, and then click Customize Current View.

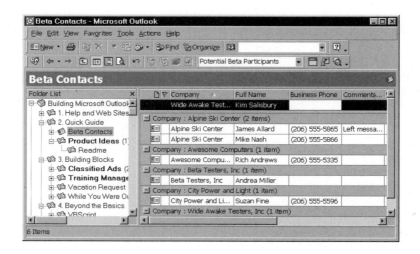

Figure 8.24 *In-cell and new item editing allow item creation and modification directly in the view without opening an item.*

3. Click Other Settings.
4. Check the Allow In-Cell Editing box.
5. Check the Show "New Item" Row box.
6. Click OK twice.

Note Use in-cell editing and the new items row with caution in a public folder. If you are using a custom form (IPM.Contact.Beta Contact) rather than a built-in form (IPM.Contact or IPM.Post), you could experience problems with one-off form creation and the firing of CustomPropertyChange events in VBScript code when you enable in-cell editing. For a detailed explanation of these issues, search for the following articles on *http://support.microsoft.com/support/*.

Working with User-Defined Fields in Solutions
http://support.microsoft.com/support/kb/articles/q201/4/38.asp/

Working with Form Definitions and One-Off Forms
http://support.microsoft.com/support/kb/articles/q207/8/96.asp/

Automatic Formatting

You can format the font of the individual items in the row on the basis of built-in rules such as whether the item has been read. You can create your own rules for automatic formatting of an item that depend on a custom set of conditions. Figure 8.25 illustrates a custom condition to highlight items according to special rules in the Classified Ads folder. Custom automatic formatting rules use the Filter dialog box explained earlier to set con-

Click the Font button to set font
name, size, style, and effects.

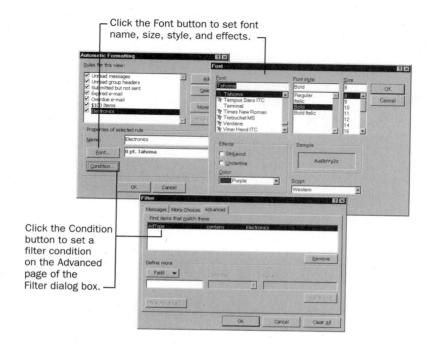

Click the Condition
button to set a
filter condition
on the Advanced
page of the
Filter dialog box.

Figure 8.25 *The Automatic Formatting dialog box lets you establish font colors and sizes for a Folder View.*

ditions for the rule. Follow the guidelines shown in this chapter's "Filter Items" section to create rules in a folder to produce automatic formatting.

To create automatic formatting for individual messages in a view

1. In the Current View drop-down list box on the Advanced toolbar, switch to the view you want to change.

2. On the View menu, select Current View, and then click Customize Current View.

3. Click Automatic Formatting.

4. Click Add.

5. Type a name for the automatic formatting rule in the Name edit box.

6. Click Font and select the font name, size, weight, and special effects in the Font dialog box. Click OK to confirm your font selection.

7. Click Conditions to establish a filter for your automatic formatting rule. Use the guidelines for filters discussed earlier. Click OK to confirm your filter.

8. Click Move Up or Move Down to change the order of precedence by which your rule will be applied to an item for automatic formatting. Note that you

cannot move your automatic formatting rule above the default formatting rules for the folder. Each folder type has a given set of automatic formatting rules.

9. Click OK twice.

View Performance

When you design a public folder application, you should consider the time that will be required to build views and present the view to the user in Outlook. Not all views render instantly, especially when there are thousands of items in the application folder. View performance depends on several factors, including the number of items in the folder and the time interval between the current time and the time when the user last inspected the folder using the current view.

Here are some general rules to follow when you design views for an application folder:

- Don't create so many views for the folder that the users have difficulty selecting the correct view for the information they are seeking to display.
- Name your views clearly so that their purpose is clearly understood by the user.
- If possible, create the folder views you will need when the number of items in the folder is small. This reduces the time needed to create the original view index.
- Views for on-line users are cached on the Exchange Server where the public folder is stored. If the view is not used within an eight-day default cache interval, the view must be refreshed and view indices rebuilt when an Outlook client requests a folder view. Your Exchange Server administrator can change the cache interval to a longer interval, if necessary.
- See Q159197 at *http://support.microsoft.com/support/kb/articles/q159/1/97.asp/* for details on modifying the registry to control folder index aging.
- Views for offline users will be slower than views for on-line users. Use filtered synchronization to reduce the number of items in an offline public folder. The Outlook client supports only one index at a time, so it may take a long time to change views offline if the number of folder items is large.

 ## Folder Home Pages

Folder Home Pages are a powerful means to extend views for application folders. Folder Home Pages let you set a default view on a folder based on a Home Page URL that points to a page on your Web server containing custom script to render the view in the Outlook Web view pane. See Chapter 14, "Customizing Folder Home Pages," for a complete discussion on programming custom Folder Home Pages.

Think of a Folder Home Page as a customizable Outlook Today page for a given folder or a hierarchy of subfolders. You can establish Folder Home Pages for folders in a personal information store, a private mailbox, or Exchange public folders. Folder Home Page views are available only if you are using Outlook 2000 or later. Users of Outlook 97 and Outlook 98 will see the normal default view on the folder.

Figure 8.26 shows a Folder Home Page that serves as the default view for the FAQ folder in a Team Project application created by the Team Folder Wizard. Notice that the Folder Home Page provides functionality not available in conventional Outlook views. New Question and Mark All As Unread hotspots let you embed commands directly into your view. By pointing and clicking, a user can change views without resorting to the Advanced toolbar. Find and Advanced Find functionality is simplified in the FAQ Folder Home Page.

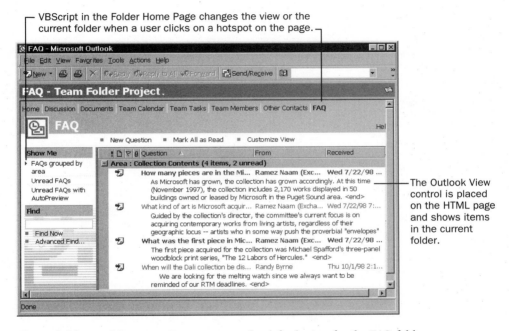

Figure 8.26 *A Folder Home Page serves as the default view for the FAQ folder.*

Folder Home Pages can also provide special functionality in a parent folder that contains many subfolders. Figure 8.27 illustrates a Folder Home Page in the Outlook Resource Kit public folder. This folder is actually a placeholder folder containing many subfolders relating to Microsoft Outlook. The default permission on this folder is none; users are not allowed to post items in this folder.

A user navigating to the Outlook Resource Kit folder will encounter a Folder Home Page allowing her to search all the items in the subfolders of the Resource Kit folder. Unlike traditional views that display all or a subset of the items in a folder, this view lets a user search across multiple public folders, providing functionality that is not possible with the built-in search capabilities of Microsoft Exchange Server and Outlook.

Microsoft Site Server lets you create customized searches across Exchange public folders.

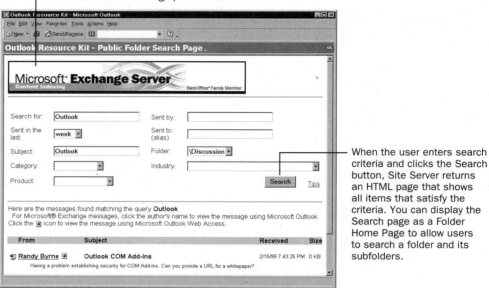

When the user enters search criteria and clicks the Search button, Site Server returns an HTML page that shows all items that satisfy the criteria. You can display the Search page as a Folder Home Page to allow users to search a folder and its subfolders.

Figure 8.27 *Search.asp allows searching across multiple Exchange Server public folders. A Search Catalog has been established using Microsoft Site Server 3.0.*

To set a Folder Home Page

1. In the Folder List, right-click the folder you want to set properties for, and then click Properties on the shortcut menu.

2. Click the Home Page tab.

3. Check the Show Home Page By Default For This Folder box.

4. Enter the URL for the Folder Home Page in the Address edit box as shown in Figure 8.28. You must enter a valid URL that points to either a page on your intranet or a page on an external site. External site pages are not recommended because the page may be unavailable. If you enter an invalid URL, your browser will report that it could not open the URL.

5. Click OK.

Tip If you want to reset a Folder Home Page view to the default Outlook view on the folder, single-click the folder's icon in the Folder List. To return to the Folder Home Page view, you must click a different folder in the folder list and then reselect the folder where you want to redisplay the Folder Home Page view. Clicking the folder icon in the Folder List acts only as a one-way toggle from a Folder Home Page view to a native Outlook view.

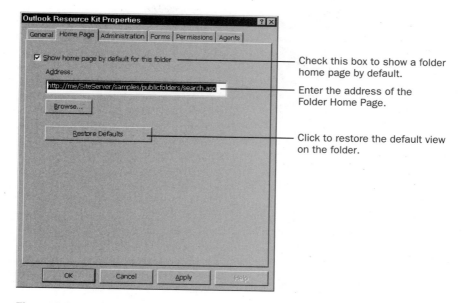

Figure 8.28 *Set a Folder Home Page using the Home Page tab of the Folder properties dialog box.*

Set General Properties

On the General page of the Properties dialog box, as shown in Figure 8.29, you can specify the default form that appears when a user creates a new item in a folder. For example, for the Classified Ads folder, the Classified Ads form appears when the user clicks the New Post In This Folder command on the Actions menu.

To set general properties

1. In the Folder List, right-click the folder you want to set properties for, and then click Properties on the shortcut menu.
2. Click the General page.

To specify the form that appears when the user clicks the New Post In This Folder command

- In the When Posting To This Folder, Use drop-down list box, click the form that you want to appear when the user clicks Post In This Folder after selecting New on the File menu.

  If you do not want a custom form to appear, click Post in the When Posting To This Folder, Use drop-down list box.

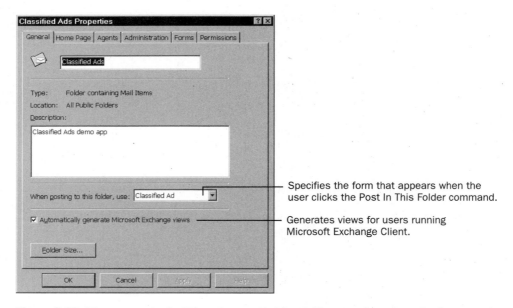

Figure 8.29 *The options in the When Posting To This Folder, Use drop-down list box specify which form appears when the New Post In This Folder command is clicked.*

To automatically generate Microsoft Exchange views

- If your organization uses both Microsoft Exchange Client and Outlook, select the Automatically Generate Microsoft Exchange Views check box. This option generates Microsoft Exchange views for the folder so the views can be seen by users of the Microsoft Exchange Client, the predecessor to Outlook.

Note This property is only available for Outlook table views.

Test Forms and Views

After you publish forms and define views for the folder, you need to test them to make sure they work as expected.

- To test the forms, open the folder in which the forms are published, and then click the menu commands that are associated with the form on the Actions menu. In the form, enter the information you want, and then click the Post button. After posting the item in the folder, double-click it to open it and make sure it shows information correctly in the form. You should test each form in the folder.

- To test views, open the folder you want to test, and then click each of the views in the Current View drop-down list box on the Advanced toolbar. If the folder has multiple forms, you should post several types of items in the folder before testing the views.

When you finish testing the forms and views, you can delete the test items you posted in the folder.

Copy the Folder to Public Folders

After adding forms, defining views, and testing their functionality, you are ready to copy your folder to Public Folders. You can then complete the folder design by designating types of items allowed in the folder, setting permissions, setting administration properties, and specifying rules. This step is necessary only if you started the folder design process with a personal folder or a mailbox folder, and not in a public folder.

Depending on the policies of your organization, you may not have permission to add a folder to Public Folders. You may be required to hand off the folder to your administrator, who then copies the folder and completes the design task according to your specifications. Perhaps you may be given permission to copy your folder to a specific public folder and then complete the task yourself. See your administrator for specific instructions.

To copy the folder to a new location

1. In the Folder List, right-click the folder, and then click Copy Folder Name on the shortcut menu.

2. Select the public folder you want to copy the folder to, and then click OK.

Specify Internet Newsgroup

The Internet News page identifies the folder as an Internet newsgroup folder. Users of Internet newsreader software within a Microsoft Exchange environment can view and post items posted in the newsgroup folder.

To set a Public Folder as a Newsgroup folder

1. In the Folder List, right-click the folder you want to identify as a newsgroup folder, and then click Properties on the shortcut menu.

2. Click the Internet News page

3. Select the Publish This Folder To Users Of Newsreader Software check box.

Note In order to access the Internet News page in the Folder Properties dialog box, you must have privileges to administer NNTP, and the Internet News Service must be established on your Microsoft Exchange Server. For additional information, see the documentation that accompanies Microsoft Exchange Server.

Set Administration Properties

After you copy a folder to a public folder, it's a good idea to restrict access to the folder while you set folder permissions and test the folder. To restrict access to the folder, you can use the This Folder Is Available To option on the Administration page, as shown in Figure 8.30.

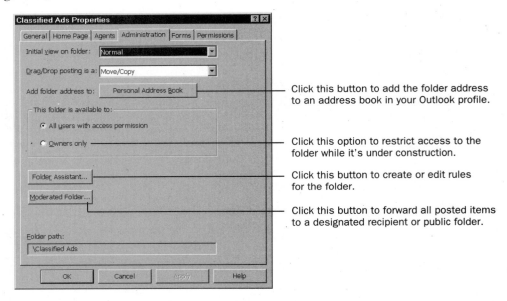

Click this button to add the folder address to an address book in your Outlook profile.

Click this option to restrict access to the folder while it's under construction.

Click this button to create or edit rules for the folder.

Click this button to forward all posted items to a designated recipient or public folder.

Figure 8.30 *Administration options for the Classified Ads folder.*

To restrict access to the folder

1. In the Folder list, right-click the folder, and then click Properties on the short-cut menu.

2. Click the Administration tab.

3. Click Owners Only.

Initial View on Folder

You use this option to specify the folder view that you want to display when the user first opens the folder. By default, this view is the Messages or Normal view, depending on the type of items the folder contains.

Drag/Drop Posting Is A

You use this option to specify how Outlook formats items that are dragged to a folder. You can specify that the drag/drop operation formats the posted item in one of the following ways:

- **Move/Copy**   This option specifies that when an item is dragged to a folder, Outlook does not reformat the item. For example, if Eric Lang drags an item sent by Clair Hector from his Inbox to the Employee Feedback folder, the item appearing in the Employee Feedback folder is shown as sent by Clair Hector.
- **Forward**   This option specifies that when an item is dragged to a folder, Outlook reformats the item to show that it has been forwarded by the user who dragged it to the folder. For example, if Eric Lang drags an Inbox item from Clair Hector to the Employee Feedback folder, the item in the Employee Feedback folder appears as though it has been forwarded by Eric Lang.

Add Folder Address To Personal Address Book

You use this option to preaddress forms. When you click the Personal Address Book button, the folder address is automatically added to an Address Book in your Exchange profile. Unlike previous versions of Outlook which would only add a public folder address to your Personal Address Book when you clicked the Personal Address Book button, Outlook 2000 will add the folder address to the Address Book selected in the Keep Personal Addresses In drop-down list box on the Addressing page of the Services dialog box for your Exchange profile. You can then use the folder address in your Address Book to preaddress a Message form to a folder or to create a rule that automatically forwards items to the folder.

Tip Another way to make the folder address available for preaddressing a form is to ask your Exchange administrator to add the folder address to the Global Address Book. Normally, public folder addresses are hidden from the Global Address Book. However, your Exchange administrator can unhide the public folder address by using the Exchange Administrator program. You can then select the folder name from the Global Address Book to preaddress a form.

More Info For more information about preaddressing a Message form to a folder address, see "To Field" in Chapter 6, "Controls, Fields, and Properties."

This Folder Is Available To

You use this option to make a folder unavailable while it's under construction.

You can click Owners Only if you are modifying or creating a folder design. This gives only those people with the Owner role permission to access the folder. After the folder is tested and ready for general use, you can click All Users With Access Permission and make the folder available for public use.

Tip The Owners Only option prevents access to the specified folder, but does not prevent access to subfolders. This way, users can post items in a subfolder while the parent folder is disabled.

Folder Assistant

You can click the Folder Assistant button to create rules that automatically process incoming folder items. Rules are described in more detail in "Design Rules" later in this chapter.

Moderated Folder

You can use a moderated folder to cause all posted items to be forwarded to a designated recipient or public folder for review. Permissions must be granted to move these items back into the folder for general viewing once they have been reviewed and approved.

Set Permissions

You assign permissions to users to define the functions they can perform in the folder. You determine who can view and use the folder by adding the user names, distribution list names, or public folder names to the Name list box on the Permissions page. After the names are added to the Name list box, you can assign roles to define the permissions for each user or distribution list, as shown in Figure 8.31.

Note Permissions can be set for folders in your Mailbox or public folders. Permissions cannot be set for personal folders.

To open the Permissions page

1. In the Folder List, right-click the folder you want to set permissions for, and then click Properties on the shortcut menu.
2. Click the Permissions tab.

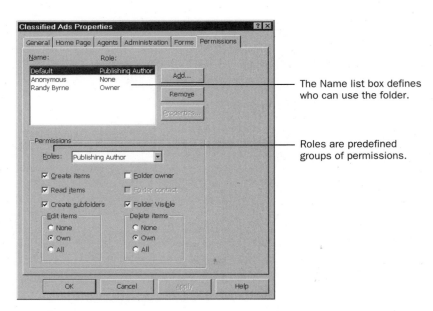

Figure 8.31 *Permissions for the Classified Ads folder.*

The Name list box defines who can use the folder.

Roles are predefined groups of permissions.

Modify the Name List

The names in the Name list box determine who can view and use the folder. If you create the folder, you are automatically given owner permissions for the folder. With owner permissions, you can add users to, and remove users from, the Name list box. You can also change permissions for selected users.

One name in the Name list box is *Default*. The permissions defined for *Default* are granted to all users who have access to the folder. If you want to give a particular user permissions other than *Default*, add the user's name to the Name list box, and then set permissions for that user.

When you test the folder, it's a good idea to set the *Default* permissions to None in the Roles drop-down list box. Then, grant access to a limited number of users. When you are sure that everything is working correctly in the folder, you can change the *Default* permissions and add names to the Name list box.

You can remove any name from the Name list box except *Default* and, if you are the sole owner of the folder, your name. If you remove *Default* or your name, they will reappear the next time you view the Permissions page.

About Distribution Lists

Distribution lists provide a convenient way to assign permissions to a group of users. For example, rather than enter 50 names in the Name list box, you can enter the distribution list name to assign permissions to all users on the list.

To add a user, distribution list, or folder name to the Name box

1. On the Permissions page, click Add.
2. Click the user, distribution list, or folder you want to add, and then click Add.
3. Click OK.

Note Public folder permissions are designed to be optimistic. Optimistic here implies the least restrictive set of permissions. The permissions that apply to the user include the set of permissions the user inherits from each of the groups the user belongs to, in addition to the explicit permissions granted directly to the user's individual account. A user's permission level is always the least restrictive of that user's explicit permissions and the permissions of any and all groups to which that user belongs.

For example, users A and B exist on a site. The Exchange administrator creates two distribution lists (DLs): Manager and Sales Team. Both user A and user B are added to the Sales Team DL; only user A is added to the Manager DL. Then, on folder X, the Manager DL is given the Owner role, and the Sales Team DL is given the Author role. User A will ultimately have owner permissions on folder X, even though user A is a member of the Sales Team DL, which has only the Author role. User B is limited to the Author role on folder X.

Assign Roles

When you set permissions for a user, you define the functions he or she can perform within the folder. You can set permissions by using predefined roles or by using custom roles:

- **Predefined Roles**   Predefined groups of permissions that are available from the Roles drop-down list box.
- **Custom Roles**   Permissions you set for the user that do not match any of the predefined roles.

To assign roles to users

1. In the Name text box on the Permissions page, click the user name you want to set permissions for.
2. In the Roles drop-down list box, click a role for the user.
3. The following table lists the roles and the predefined permissions that are assigned to each role.

Role	Description
Owner	Create, read, modify, and delete all items and files and create subfolders. As the folder owner, you can change permissions others have for the folder.
Publishing Editor	Create, read, modify, and delete all items and files and create subfolders.
Editor	Create, read, modify, and delete all items and files.
Nonediting Author	Create and read items. This person or group cannot edit, but can delete items and files you create.
Publishing Author	Create and read items and files, create subfolders, and modify and delete items and files you create.
Author	Create and read items and files, and modify and delete items and files you create.
Reviewer	Read items and files only.
Contributor	Create items and files only. The user cannot open the folder.
None	The user cannot open the folder.
Custom	Perform activities defined by the folder owner, from options selected on the Permissions page.

To assign a custom Role

1. In the Name list box, click the user name whose permissions you want to set.
2. In the Roles drop-down list box, click the role that most closely resembles the permissions you want to grant to the user.

3. Under Permissions, select the options you want. If the permissions do not match a role, you will see Custom in the Roles drop-down list box. If the permissions match a role, the role will show in the Roles drop-down list box.

Design Rules

Rules automatically process items as they arrive in a folder. A rule consists of two parts: a set of conditions that are applied to an incoming item, and the actions that are taken if the conditions are met, as shown in Figure 8.32.

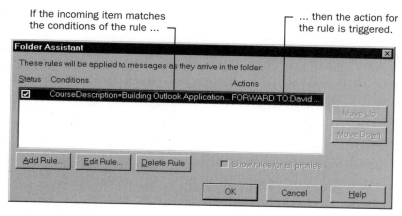

Figure 8.32 *Rules for the Training Management folder.*

You can use rules to:

- Specify that certain types of items are automatically returned to the sender
- Automatically delete items based on the specified conditions
- Automatically reply to specific kinds of items with a reply template
- Automatically forward specific types of items to another folder or user

To create rules

1. In the Folder List, right-click the folder, and then click Properties on the shortcut menu.
2. Click the Administration tab, and then click Folder Assistant.

Note Folder Assistant is only available for public folders.

Specifying Conditions of a Rule

The conditions of a rule identify the items that are to be processed by the rule. These conditions can range from very simple to relatively advanced. An example of a simple condition is From:James Allard. This condition states that if an item is submitted to the folder and the item is from James Allard, then a specified action is taken. A more advanced set of conditions is Only Messages That Do Not Match This Criteria; From:James Allard;Joe Howard;Scott Cooper. These conditions state that if the items submitted to the folder are not from James Allard, Joe Howard, or Scott Cooper, then a specified action is taken.

Rules Syntax

Before you create rules, there are a few fundamental concepts you need to know:

- A rule consists of conditions and a corresponding action. A rule can have one condition or multiple conditions. For example, From:James Allard is a single condition and From:James Allard;Subject:GG&G are two conditions. Each condition is delimited by a semicolon. A condition can consist of an argument or multiple arguments. For example, From:James Allard is a condition with a single argument and From:James Allard;Joe Howard is a condition with multiple arguments.
- Multiple conditions within a rule are logical AND values. For example, the condition From:James Allard;Subject:GG&G is *True* if the From field of the incoming items contains *James Allard* and the Subject field contains *GG&G*.
- Multiple arguments within a condition are logical OR values. For example, the condition From:James Allard;Joe Howard;Max Benson is *True* if the From field of the incoming item contains any one of the names included in the expression.

Specifying Simple Conditions

You can specify simple conditions based on the contents of the From, Sent, To, Subject, and Message fields of an incoming item.

To specify simple conditions

1. From the Folder Assistant dialog box on the Administration page, click Add Rule, or select the rule you want and then click Edit Rule.
2. Under When A Message Arrives That Meets The Following Conditions, type the criteria in the associated boxes.

Specifying Advanced Conditions

With the Advanced dialog box, you can specify a wide range of conditions, including conditions based on values in user-defined fields in the folder.

To specify advanced conditions

1. In the Folder Assistant dialog box on the Administration page, click Add Rule, or select the rule you want and then click Edit Rule.

2.   Click Advanced.

3.   Type the criteria in the appropriate boxes.

Specifying That a Rule Applies to Items That Do Not Match the Conditions

You can create rules that take actions if conditions are met and rules that take actions if the conditions are not met.

To specify that a rule applies only to items that do not match the conditions

- In the Advanced dialog box, click the Only Items That Do Not Match These Conditions check box.

Specifying Conditions with User-Defined Fields

In some cases, you may want to create conditions based on user-defined fields in the folder. For example, for the Training Management folder, you may want to create a rule that forwards a Course Offering item to a distribution list when a Course Offering item that pertains to a specific subject is posted in the folder.

To specify custom fields as conditions

1.   In the Advanced dialog box, under Show Properties Of, do one of the following:

To Show	Click
Custom fields of the currently selected forms	Forms, and then select the forms you want
Standard document fields	Document
Custom fields of the currently selected folder	Folder: *folder name*

2.   Under Properties, select the check box of the property that you want to use to create a condition.

3.   In the drop-down list or text boxes to the right of the check boxes, do one or more of the following:

- If the field to the right of the selected check box is a text box, you can type one or more values in the text box. For example, if you want to create a rule that forwards Training Management items that have the value *Building Microsoft Outlook Applications* in the CourseDescription field, then type *Building Microsoft Outlook Applications* in the text box to its right, as shown in Figure 8.33. If you specify multiple values in the text boxes, separate the values with a semicolon.

- If a drop-down list box and a text box are to the right of the check box, click the value in the list box first. Then type or click the criteria in the box to its right.

4.   Click OK.

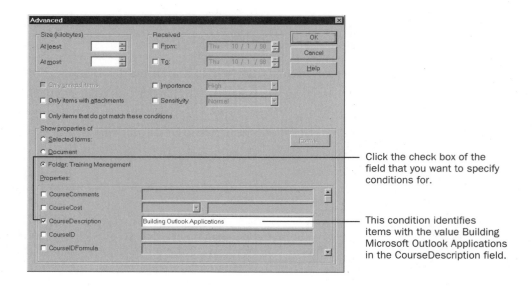

Click the check box of the field that you want to specify conditions for.

This condition identifies items with the value Building Microsoft Outlook Applications in the CourseDescription field.

Figure 8.33 *With Advanced properties, you can build conditions based on specific field values in a field.*

Specifying Actions for a Rule

Actions occur when the conditions of a rule are met. You specify an action for a rule in the Edit Rule dialog box of the Folder Assistant.

To specify an action to run when a condition is met

To Perform This Action	Click
Return the item to the sender if the conditions of the rule are met	Return To Sender.
Delete the item if the conditions of the rule are met	Delete.
Specify the Reply message that is sent if the conditions of the rule are not met	Click Reply With, click Template, and then fill out the message box of the form with the Reply message you want to send.
Forward an item if the conditions of the rule are not met	Click Forward, click To, and then select the user name, distribution list, or folder.

More Info For more information about specifying actions, see Chapter 7, "Actions."

Test and Release the Folder

After you create or modify a folder, you should test it with a few users. When testing the folder, you and the users involved in the test should compose, submit, and open items in the folder and check views, permissions, and rules to make sure they work as planned.

When you're sure the folder is working properly, you can open the Administration page in the folder's Properties dialog box and make the folder available to the general public.

To make the folder available to all users with access permission

1.   In the Folder List, right-click the folder, and then click Properties on the short-cut menu.
2.   Click the Administration page.
3.   Click All Users With Access Permission.
4.   Click OK.

If you plan to replicate the folder application between servers, have your Exchange Administrator define replication settings using the Exchange Administrator program and then test the folder on a small scale before replicating it on Exchange Servers in your organization.

When the folder is ready for public use, send out an announcement to the users who will be using the folder to let them know the folder is available. You can include a link to the folder in your announcement message so users can easily find the folder.

For More Information About	See
Setting permissions	"Set Permissions" earlier in this chapter
Distributing and maintaining folders	Chapter 12, "Distribute and Maintain Applications"
Replicating folders	The Microsoft Exchange Server documentation

Where To Go from Here

For additional information about the subjects discussed in this chapter, see the following resources.

Administering Exchange Public Folders

Microsoft Consulting Services. *Managing and Maintaining Microsoft Exchange Server 5.5*. Redmond, WA: Microsoft Press, 1998.

Microsoft Exchange Server Web site
http://www.microsoft.com/exchange/

Microsoft Support Online
http://support.microsoft.com/support/

Redmond, Tony. *Microsoft Exchange Server V5.5: Planning, Design, and Implementation*. Newton, MA: Digital Press, 1998.

Creating Views in Folders

Mosher, Sue. *The Microsoft Outlook E-mail and Fax Guide*. Loveland, CO: Duke Press, 1998.

Using Microsoft Site Server to Search Public Folders

Visit the Site Server Web site at *http://www.microsoft.com/siteserver/site/default.htm/*

Extending Web-Based Knowledge Management with Microsoft Exchange Server *http://www.microsoft.com/workshop/server/siteserver/siteexch/exchss.asp/*

Rizzo, Thomas. *Programming Microsoft Outlook and Microsoft Exchange*. Redmond, WA: Microsoft Press, 1999.

Chapter 9
Raise Events and Move to the Head of the Class

In This Chapter

Previous versions of Outlook supported a limited number of form and control level events. To write code to respond to these events in Outlook 97 and Outlook 98, you had to write VBScript code behind custom forms. New to Outlook 2000 are events at the application level that you define and program within Outlook's own Visual Basic for Applications (VBA) environment. These events let you respond to some great new Application object events, as well as events for child objects in the Outlook Object Model.

At this point, we might do well to ask what exactly an event is from a programmatic point of view. An event results from an action that is typically performed by a user, such as sending a message, switching a folder or view in an Explorer window, or changing either default or user-defined fields in an item—but the action that triggers an event can also be performed by program code, or by the system itself.

Within the context of Outlook, events occur at several different levels. The only events supported in previous versions of Outlook were primarily form-level events such as Item_Open, Item_Write, Item_Close, and a limited control-level event known as the Click event. Forms developers could write Visual Basic Scripting Edition (VBScript) event procedure code to respond to the firing of an event. You can continue to write form-level code in VBScript in Outlook 2000. Unlike previous versions of Outlook, however, you can also declare public variables using the WithEvents keyword in Outlook VBA and write code to respond to form-level events within the context of the running Outlook application. For further information on form- and control-level events, see Chapter 11, "Using VBA and VBScript with Outlook."

The primary focus of this chapter is using VBA in Outlook to respond to application-level events. For readers who are not familiar with Microsoft Visual Basic for Applications, we'll cover some of the basic functionality of the Visual Basic for Applications Editor shown in Figure 9.1 before we move on to the new events in the Outlook Object Model.

The VBA Editor

The addition of Visual Basic for Applications to Microsoft Outlook 2000 is the single most important new feature in the product from a developer's point of view. Full-featured VBA just squeaked its way into the final Outlook 2000 product specification, thanks to a commitment from members of the Outlook product team at Microsoft and the repeated requests of the Outlook developer community. Outlook 2000 supports all the functionality of Visual Basic for Applications 6.0 in Office 2000. Unlike other Office 2000 applications, where VBA is an integral component of the application, Outlook 2000 provides VBA services through an Office 2000 COM Add-in. If your company does not want to deploy Outlook VBA to every desktop, you can control the availability of Outlook VBA using the Custom Installation Wizard in the *Microsoft Office 2000 Resource Kit*.

VBA allows you to create code ranging in functionality from simple macros to complex application add-ins. Application add-ins can utilize any of the objects, properties, methods, and events in the Outlook Object Model. Moreover, you can use the VBA environment to add references to other object models, and to use Outlook as an automation controller, in addition to its traditional role as an automation server.

Launching the VBA Editor

One of the greatest features of VBA is the proximity of the design process to the application you are designing. VBA is only a few keystrokes or mouse clicks away in Outlook 2000. You have complete and immediate access to all the objects in the Outlook Object Model. Previously, you had to create advanced Outlook and MAPI functionality using C++ code. Now, you can operate in an interactive environment that lets you rapidly develop new applications. Follow these steps to open the Visual Basic for Applications Editor window, shown in Figure 9.1.

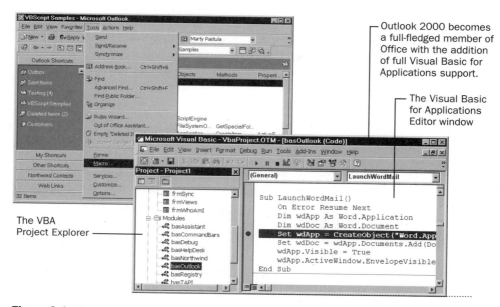

Outlook 2000 becomes a full-fledged member of Office with the addition of full Visual Basic for Applications support.

The Visual Basic for Applications Editor window

The VBA Project Explorer

Figure 9.1 *The Visual Basic for Applications Editor window in Outlook 2000.*

To open the Visual Basic for Applications Editor window

1. On the Explorer or the Inspector Tools menu, click Macro.
2. Click Visual Basic Editor command; or
3. Press Alt+F11 in an Inspector or Explorer window.

You can also customize Outlook's Standard and Advanced Outlook toolbars with a toolbar button that launches the Visual Basic Editor. To add a VBA command bar button to the Advanced toolbar for Outlook Explorer, follow these steps:

1. On the Explorer Tools menu, click the Customize command.
2. Click on Advanced Toolbar in the Toolbars drop-down list box and make sure that the Advanced Toolbar is enabled.
3. Click the Commands tab in the Customize dialog box.
4. Select Tools in the Categories list box.
5. Select Visual Basic Editor in the Commands drop-down list list box and then drag the Visual Basic Editor item from the Customize dialog box to any position on the Advanced Toolbar.
6. Click Close to close the Customize dialog box.

ThisOutlookSession Class Module

When the Outlook Visual Basic Editor opens for the first time, you will see only one object, under Project1, named ThisOutlookSession as shown in Figure 9.2. While not explicitly identified as such, ThisOutlookSession is a class module rather than a standard module. Although you cannot view its class properties, the Instancing property of ThisOutlookSession is private and the class cannot be instantiated by using *CreateObject* in another application or with VBScript code running in Outlook forms. The class represented by ThisOutlookSession is the Application object in the Outlook Object Model. The Application object is the parent of all other classes in the Outlook Object Model. All other class objects are derived from the Outlook Application object.

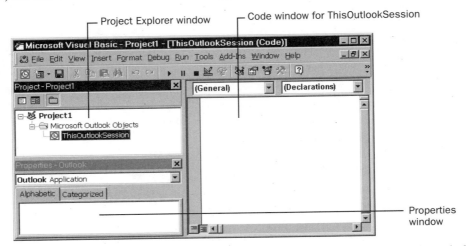

Figure 9.2 *The class module ThisOutlookSession is initially empty when you launch the Outlook Visual Basic for Applications Editor for the first time.*

Navigating in the VBA Editor

A very brief tour of the VBA Editor is helpful for developers who are new to VBA. The Project Explorer window contains a tree view of the class modules, standard modules, and UserForms in your project. The Code window shows the functions and Sub procedures for the currently selected object in the Project Explorer. The Properties window lists the design-time properties for a selected form, control, class, project, or module. The Object Browser window displays all the objects in the current project, along with their properties, methods, and events. The Immediate, Locals, Watch, and Call Stack windows are invaluable when it's time to debug your code.

Individual windows in the VBA Editor can be docked or undocked. A window is docked when it is attached or anchored to one edge of the screen, application window, or another dockable window. When you move a dockable window, it snaps to a docking position at the top, bottom, left, or right of the Editor window. Every developer will have personal preferences about configuring the window elements of their project. Here is a quick guide to keystrokes that will help you navigate the different windows in VBA.

Press	To
Ctrl+G	Display the Immediate window. You can execute statements or examine variable values in the Immediate window.
Ctrl+L	Activate the Call Stack window.
Ctrl+R	Activate the Project Explorer window.
F2	Activate the Object Browser.
F4	Activate the Properties window for the currently selected form, control, class, or module object.
F7	Activate the code window for the currently selected object in the Project Explorer.
Alt+F11	Return to the Outlook Application window.

The Outlook Application Object

The Outlook Application object is the top-level object in the Outlook Object Model. All other objects in the object model are derived from the Application object. Also, the Application object is the only object that can be created by using the *CreateObject* statement in another application. For additional information regarding the Outlook Object Model, see Chapter 11, "Using VBA and VBScript with Outlook."

From the perspective of VBA in Outlook, the Application object is directly available in the VBA Editor code window for the ThisOutlookSession object. Remember that the ThisOutlookSession object is equivalent to the Outlook Application object. When you write VBA code for Outlook, you do not have to explicitly set a reference to the Outlook object library. Figure 9.3 illustrates how both the Office and Outlook object libraries are automatically referenced in the References dialog box for your VBA project.

To view or set references for Project1

1. If the Outlook application window is active, press Alt+F11 to open the VBA Editor window.

2. On the Tools menu of the VBA Editor, select the References command.

3. Select additional object libraries to reference in your VBA project by checking the box next to the name of the object library you wish to reference in the Available References list box.

4. Click OK when you have finished selecting references.

Saving Your Outlook VBA Project

If you have written code for ThisOutlookSession or added code modules to Project1, you will be prompted to save the project when you quit Outlook. If you answer Yes to the

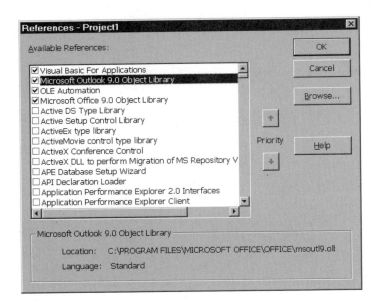

Figure 9.3 *VBA automatically sets references for both the Office and Outlook object libraries.*

alert box that prompts you to save the project, you will save the project in a file named VBAProject.otm. You cannot change the name of the file in which an Outlook VBA project is saved. Unlike project files in Visual Basic, VBAProject.otm is a binary file, and you should not attempt to edit it with a text editor. You also cannot change the folder location in which VBAProject.otm is stored. VBAProject.otm is stored in the following locations depending upon the operating system you are using:

Operating System	Location for VBAProject.otm
Windows 95 and 98 without UserProfiles	C:\Windows\Application Data\Microsoft\Outlook
Windows 95 and 98 with UserProfiles	C:\Windows\Profiles*UserName*\Application Data\Microsoft\Outlook
Windows NT 4.0 or Windows 2000	C:\Winnt\Profiles*UserName*\Application Data\Microsoft\Outlook

Securing Your Outlook VBA Project

You can secure an Outlook VBA project to protect it from unauthorized changes by others. However, you should keep in mind that an Outlook VBA project lacks the same level of security that you can achieve with an Outlook COM Add-in. The compilation of a Visual Basic COM Add-in project into an ActiveX DLL protects your source code. Only one VBA project can be associated with an Outlook application. Like their predecessor Exchange Add-ins that use .ecf files, multiple COM Add-ins can run in a single Outlook session.

Remember that Outlook VBA is more a personal development tool rather than a vehicle for deploying commercial or corporate Outlook Add-ins. If you want to protect your VBA code, you can prevent users from viewing the code unless they have a password to open the project for editing. Don't lose this password or you, too, will be prevented from viewing and editing the code for the project.

To protect an Outlook VBA project

1. If the Outlook application window is active, press Alt+F11 to open the VBA Editor window.

2. On the Tools menu of the VBA Editor, select the Project1 Properties command.

3. Check the Lock Project For Viewing check box as shown in Figure 9.4

4. Supply a password to allow viewing of project properties, and then confirm the password.

5. Click OK to accept Project1 Properties. The project is not actually locked for viewing until you quit and restart Outlook.

Note Outlook VBA projects can be digitally signed with a security certificate. On the Tools menu, select Macro, then choose the Security command to set the security level for your Outlook session. If you are developing VBA code for Outlook, it is recommended that you set the security level to Low so that you don't have to bypass the Macro Warning dialog box when Outlook launches. If you require additional information on developing solutions with security certificates, see Chapter 13, "Creating COM Add-Ins with Visual Basic."

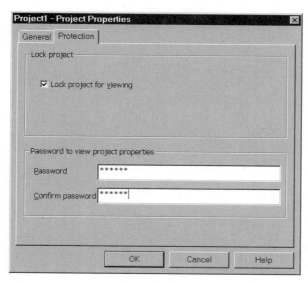

Figure 9.4 *The Protection tab of the Project Properties dialog box lets you lock your Outlook VBA project.*

Writing an Outlook Macro

Outlook 2000 supports macro code that automates repetitive tasks. Unlike some other members of the Office 2000 family, Outlook does not feature a macro recorder that will write VBA code in response to user commands and actions. From the standpoint of Outlook VBA, an Outlook macro is a public Sub procedure without arguments in a standard module. If you add arguments to your module-level Sub procedure, it will no longer be available as a macro. An Outlook macro cannot utilize a Function procedure or private Sub procedure. Also, you cannot place macro code in a class module such as ThisOutlookSession or a form module. Remember that ThisOutlookSession represents a class module rather than a standard module. If you want to write a Sub procedure that you can use as a macro, you must first insert a standard module into your Outlook project and then insert a Sub procedure into that module. Follow these steps to create a macro that launches Word 2000 and creates a Word mail message:

To create a new Outlook Macro

1. In Outlook, point to Macro on the Tools menu, and then click Visual Basic Editor.

2. On the Tools menu, click References. Use the References dialog box to set a reference to the Microsoft Word 9.0 Object Library.

3. Select Project1 in the Project Explorer. If you want to insert a new module, click Module on the Insert menu of the VBA Editor window. Otherwise, double-click the name of the module where you want to insert the macro in the Project Explorer window.

4. On the Insert menu, click Procedure.

5. In the Name box, type *LaunchWordMail* for the macro name as shown in Figure 9.5. The name cannot contain spaces.

6. Click OK.

7. The LaunchWordMail Sub procedure appears in the Code window.

8. Type the following code in the body of the Sub procedure.

```
Sub LaunchWordMail()
    On Error Resume Next
    Dim wdApp As Word.Application
    Dim wdDoc As Word.Document
    Set wdApp = CreateObject("Word.Application")
    Set wdDoc = wdApp.Documents.Add(DocumentType:=wdNewEmailMessage)
    wdApp.Visible = True
    wdApp.ActiveWindow.EnvelopeVisible = True
End Sub
```

Once you have created your macro procedure and debugged it, you'll want to customize either an Explorer or Inspector toolbar so that you can run the macro with a mouse click. In order to test the LaunchWordMail macro, you can simply insert the cursor into the LaunchWordMail Sub procedure in the Code window and select Run Sub/UserForm

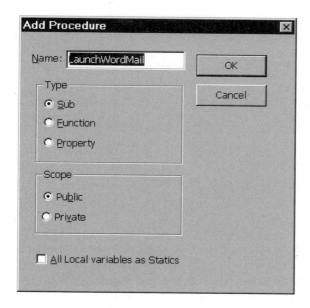

Figure 9.5 *Use the Add Procedure dialog box to create a Sub procedure for an Outlook macro.*

on the Run menu on the Visual Basic Editor toolbar. To continue with the LaunchWordMail macro example, use the following steps to create a toolbar button to run the macro:

To add an Outlook Macro to the Standard toolbar for the Explorer

1. In the Outlook Explorer, select the Customize command on the Tools menu.
2. Select Macros in the Categories drop-down list box on the Commands page.
3. Drag the LaunchWordMail macro to the position on the Standard toolbar where you want the toolbar command button to appear.
4. Right-click the Project1.LaunchWordMail toolbar button and set its properties. For example, you might want to rename the button to WordMail.

If you have created a number of Outlook macros, adding macros to the toolbar can be impractical. You can also use the Macros dialog box to run an Outlook macro.

To run an Outlook Macro using the Macros dialog box

1. Press Alt+F8 in an Outlook Explorer or Inspector window.
2. Double-click the macro name in the Macros dialog box.

Writing Code to Respond to Events

Use the WithEvents Keyword to Declare Object Variables

Outlook macros are very useful for simple repetitive tasks. However, macros are only a snack compared with the banquet of events available in the Outlook 2000 Object Model. For Visual Basic developers, the key to writing code that responds to events is learning how to use the WithEvents keyword in Visual Basic. The WithEvents keyword is used to dimension an object variable in a class module. If you attempt to use WithEvents in conjunction with an object declaration in a standard module, your code will raise an error and will not compile. By declaring an object using WithEvents, you notify Visual Basic that you want to respond to events for the instance that is assigned to that object variable. You can use the WithEvents keyword only with objects that support events, and only in a class module such as ThisOutlookSession.

> **Note** If you want to use C++ to write code supporting the new events in Outlook 2000, you should obtain Microsoft Office 2000 Developer. It comes with an Office COM Add-In template for Visual C++ that you can use to develop Outlook COM Add-ins in C++, should you so desire. This template contains complete instructions for implementing the IDTExtensibility2 interface in Microsoft C++ Version 6.0.

Since the class module ThisOutlookSession represents the Outlook Application object, you do not have to explicitly declare an Outlook Application object using the WithEvents keyword when you write Outlook VBA code. If you examine the code window for ThisOutlookSession, you'll notice that all the events for the Outlook Application object are available in the Procedures drop-down list box. Figure 9.6 shows the Application object in the code window for ThisOutlookSession.

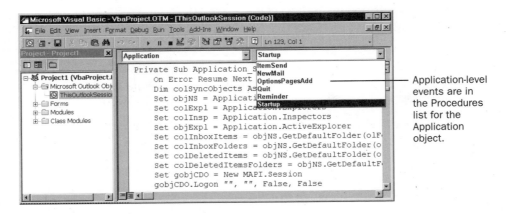

Figure 9.6 *Select an Application event from the Procedures drop-down list box to create an application-level event procedure.*

When You Must Use WithEvents to Declare the Outlook Application Object

If you are writing a COM Add-in that traps Outlook events, you must explicitly declare an Outlook Application object using the WithEvents keyword. COM Add-ins are beyond the scope of this chapter; they are discussed in depth in Chapter 13, "Creating COM Add-Ins with Visual Basic." The technique you should use to create child objects of the Application object, however, applies equally to COM Add-ins and Outlook VBA code. Many of the child objects of the Application object can also raise events. You might be wondering how you write event procedures for those child objects. The trick is to declare these objects using the WithEvents keyword and to instantiate those objects in the correct event procedures. Object-related events beget additional event-aware objects and their event procedures.

Using WithEvents for Child Objects

As discussed previously, all objects in the Outlook Object Model are child objects of the parent Application object. Not every Outlook object supports events. Consult the Object Browser in Outlook VBA or the Microsoft Outlook Visual Basic Reference Help to determine which Outlook objects raise events. The following table briefly lists new application-level events in Outlook 2000 and the objects that raise those events. Note that certain events are cancelable, meaning that you can write code to roll back the event depending on the conditions you evaluate during event processing.

Object	Event	Cancelable
Application	ItemSend	Yes
	NewMail	No
	OptionsPagesAdd	No
	Quit	No
	Reminder	No
	Startup	No
NameSpace	OptionsPagesAdd	No
Explorers	NewExplorer	No
Explorer	Activate	No
	BeforeFolderSwitch	Yes
	BeforeViewSwitch	Yes
	Close	No
	Deactivate	No
	FolderSwitch	No
	SelectionChange	No
	ViewSwitch	No
SyncObject	OnError	No
	Progress	No
	SyncEnd	No
	SyncStart	No

(continued)

(continued)

Object	Event	Cancelable
OutlookBarPane	BeforeGroupSwitch	Yes
	BeforeNavigate	Yes
OutlookBarGroup	GroupAdd	No
	BeforeGroupAdd	Yes
	BeforeGroupRemove	Yes
OutlookBarShortcut	ShortcutAdd	No
	BeforeShortcutAdd	Yes
	BeforeShortcutRemove	Yes
Folders	FolderAdd	No
	FolderChange	No
	FolderRemove	No
Inspectors	NewInspector	No
Inspector	Activate	No
	Close	No
	Deactivate	No
Items	ItemAdd	No
	ItemChange	No
	ItemRemove	No

To raise events for these child objects, you should follow these coding practices:

- **Dimension** the object as a public object variable and use the WithEvents keyword in a class module. If you are writing Outlook VBA code, declare the child object variables using WithEvents in ThisOutlookSession.

- **Instantiate** the child object variable in an appropriate event procedure or use a Sub procedure in module-level code to instantiate object variables that raise events. For example, you should instantiate the NameSpace object and the Explorers and Inspectors collection objects in the Application Startup event so that the events supported by these objects will be available throughout the life of the application. The following code fragment illustrates this technique:

```
' Place these declarations in ThisOutlookSession
Public WithEvents objNS As Outlook.NameSpace
Public WithEvents colFolders As Outlook.Folders
Public WithEvents objExpl As Outlook.Explorer
Public WithEvents colExpl As Outlook.Explorers
Public WithEvents objInsp As Outlook.Inspector
Public WithEvents colInsp As Outlook.Inspectors
Public WithEvents colInboxItems as Outlook.Items
Public WithEvents colDeletedItems As Outlook.Items

Private Sub Application_Startup()
    Set objNS = Application.GetNamespace("MAPI")
    Set colFolders = objNS.Folders
    Set colExpl = Application.Explorers
```

```
      Set colInsp = Application.Inspectors
      Set objExpl = Application.ActiveExplorer
      Set colInboxItems = objNS.GetDefaultFolder(olFolderInbox).Items
      Set colDeletedItems = _
         objNS.GetDefaultFolder(olFolderDeletedItems).Items
   End Sub
```

Where To Instantiate Child Objects Declared Using WithEvents

It's important to determine the correct event procedure when you create additional child objects. For example, if you want to raise events for an Explorer object, you can either set a reference to an Explorer object in the Application Startup event or you can use the NewExplorer event of the Explorers collection object. The NewExplorer event passes an Explorer object to the NewExplorer event procedure. Using the code example above, a reference is set to *objExpl* in the Application Startup event. This Explorer object refers to the ActiveExplorer object of the Application object when Outlook launches. Either users or code can cause multiple Explorer objects to display for a given Outlook Application object. If you want to trap events such as FolderSwitch or BeforeShortcutAdd for another instance of an Explorer, you must either create a new Explorer object that you can instantiate in the NewExplorer event or reuse the existing *objExpl* object and set *objExpl* to the Explorer object that you receive in the NewExplorer event. Many of the examples in the following section will discuss strategies and options for raising events on child objects of the application's parent object.

Observing Events in the Example VBAProject.otm

Because it writes a statement to the VBA Immediate window when an event procedure fires, the VBAProject.otm accompanying this book lets you observe events for most of the available events in the Outlook Object Model. Following the firing sequence of events in the Immediate window is an excellent way to learn about the new events in the Outlook Object Model. To observe event tracing in the VBA Immediate window, you must follow these steps:

To turn on event tracing in the example VBAProject.otm

1. Select Macro from the Tools menu.
2. Select Security from the Macro submenu.
3. On the Security Level page of the Security dialog box, click the Low option. If you click Medium, you will have to click Enable Macros in the Security Warning dialog box every time Outlook starts.
4. Click OK.
5. Press Alt+F11 to open the VBA Editor.
6. Select Project1 Properties from the Tools menu.
7. In the Conditional Compilation Arguments edit box on the General page of the Project 1 – Project Properties dialog box, enter *conDebug = 1*.
8. Click OK.

9. Press Alt+F11 to return to Outlook.

10. Select Exit And Log Off from the File menu.

11. Restart Outlook. Event tracing will be turned on, and you can observe the firing sequence of events in the VBA Immediate window.

 ## Application Events

ItemSend

The ItemSend event occurs when an item is sent either because a user clicked the Send button on the item or because code causes an item to be sent. Typically the Application ItemSend event occurs after the form-level Item_Send event and before the form-level Item_Write and Item_Close events. You should apply user-interface elements such as alert and dialog boxes with care in the ItemSend event. If you use the Cancel argument to cancel sending the item, and the item has already been sent from an open Inspector, the Inspector will remain in its previously displayed state. The item's Inspector will not close as it normally would when the Send button is clicked. The following example unobtrusively strips all attachments from outgoing mail messages:

```
Private Sub Application_ItemSend(ByVal Item As Object, Cancel As Boolean)
    Dim oAttach As Outlook.Attachment
    If Item.Attachments.Count And Item.MessageClass = "IPM.Note" Then
        Do Until Item.Attachments.Count = 0
            Set oAttach = Item.Attachments.Item(1)
            oAttach.Delete
        Loop
    End If
End Sub
```

Note The example above assumes that you are writing code directly to the explicit Application object in VBA. If you are writing a COM Add-in or using an event handler to instantiate an Outlook Application object that has been declared using WithEvents, the name of the Application object will differ but the code will remain the same.

NewMail

The NewMail event occurs when an item arrives in the Inbox of the current logged-on user. The NewMail event will not occur if an item arrives in the mailbox of a user for whom the logged-on user has delegate permissions. NewMail is a generic event that notifies you that mail has arrived in the Inbox. Unlike the ItemSend event, it does not pass an Item object representing the item or items that have arrived in the Inbox. If you want to raise an event for the arrival of a specific item in a folder, you should declare an Items collection object using WithEvents. Assign the Items collection object to the Items property of the folder that you want to monitor, and then write an event procedure for the ItemAdd event of the Items collection object. If the Explorer window is minimized, the following NewMail example causes the Explorer window to display with a normal window state.

```
Private Sub Application_NewMail()
    Dim olExplorer As Outlook.Explorer
    Dim olFolder As Outlook.MAPIFolder
    Set olFolder = _
       Application.GetNamespace("MAPI").GetDefaultFolder(olFolderInbox)
    Set olExplorer = Application.ActiveExplorer
    If olExplorer.WindowState = olMinimized Then
        If olExplorer.CurrentFolder <> olFolder Then
            olExplorer.CurrentFolder = olFolder
        End If
        olExplorer.WindowState = olNormalWindow
        olExplorer.Display
        olExplorer.Activate
    End If
End Sub
```

OptionsPagesAdd

OptionsPagesAdd is the one event in the Outlook Object Model that appears at first examination to be misnamed. This event occurs after a user selects the Options command on the Tools menu of the Outlook Explorer and before the Tools Options dialog box actually displays. Consequently, you may prefer to think of the OptionsPagesAdd event as the BeforeOptionsPagesAdd event. From the perspective of the Application object, the OptionsPagesAdd event refers to the property pages of the Tools Options dialog box. You can use this event to add custom property pages to the Tools Options dialog box. Previous versions of Outlook required complex C++ coding to add property pages to this dialog box. See Chapter 13, "Creating COM Add-Ins with Visual Basic," for a complete example of how to create an ActiveX control and use this control as a property page that stores and retrieves settings from the Windows registry.

Figure 9.7 illustrates a property page with the caption Sample Page that has been added to the Tools Options dialog box. Be aware that creating an Outlook property page requires a complete understanding of how to create ActiveX controls and how to read and save registry values. Typically, you will want to use the Windows registry to preserve user settings on controls in your property page.

The Programmatic ID of the ActiveX control that contains the controls on the property page is PPE.SamplePage. The Programmatic ID is also known as a ProgID and results from the combination of ProjectName.ClassName in the ActiveX control project that implements the property page. The syntax for using the *Add* method of the PropertyPages collection object is as follows:

```
Private Sub Application_OptionsPagesAdd(ByVal Pages As PropertyPages)
    Pages.Add "ProgID", Caption
End Sub
```

Although alternative syntaxes are proposed for the PropertyPages *Add* method in the Microsoft Outlook Visual Basic Reference, the use of the Programmatic ID and the Caption will provide the most trouble-free coding practice. Be aware that if you use the ProgID

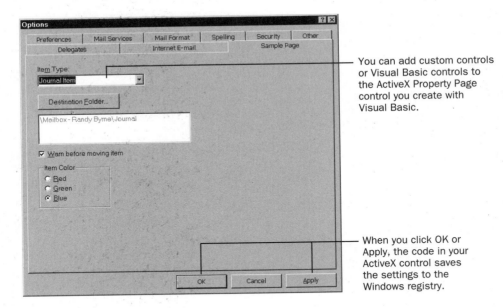

You can add custom controls or Visual Basic controls to the ActiveX Property Page control you create with Visual Basic.

When you click OK or Apply, the code in your ActiveX control saves the settings to the Windows registry.

Figure 9.7 *The Sample Page property page is added to the Tools Options dialog box.*

argument with the *Add* method, the Caption argument is mandatory rather than optional. If you omit the Caption argument, Outlook will raise an internal error.

Here is a one-line example of using the OptionsPagesAdd event to add a property page with a caption of *Sample Page* to the property pages in the Outlook Tools Options dialog box. The ActiveX control that implements the property page has been compiled so that its ProgID is PPE.SamplePage. The actual code that makes this property page behave as expected is part of the SamplePage ActiveX control.

```
Private Sub Application_OptionsPagesAdd(ByVal Pages As PropertyPages)
    Pages.Add "PPE.SamplePage", "Sample Page"
End Sub
```

Quit

The Application Quit event takes place when you exit Outlook. This event provides a location for you to clean up any objects that you have created in the Startup event. It is good programming practice to set any global object variables you have created to Nothing in the Quit event. The following code example illustrates this technique.

```
Private Sub Application_Quit()
    On Error Resume Next
    Set objNS = Nothing
    Set colExpl = Nothing
    Set colInsp = Nothing
```

```
        Set objExpl = Nothing
        Set objInsp = Nothing
    End Sub
```

Reminder

The Reminder event occurs immediately before the reminder for an item is displayed. Outlook passes a generic Item object to the Reminder event procedure. If you want to determine the type of item for which the reminder is going to be displayed, examine the Item's Class property to determine the specific Outlook item type.

```
Private Sub Application_Reminder(ByVal Item As Object)
    Select Case Item.Class
        Case olMail
        MsgBox "You are about to receive a message reminder.", vbInformation
        Case olAppointment
        MsgBox "You are about to receive an appointment reminder.", _
            vbInformation
        Case olTask
        MsgBox "You are about to receive a task reminder.", vbInformation
    End Select
End Sub
```

Startup

The Startup event fires when Outlook starts and after any Exchange or COM Add-ins have been loaded. Consequently, you can use the COMAddIns collection object to determine which COM Add-ins have been loaded on startup for the Outlook Application object. The Startup event is also the place where you'll want to create instances of other global object variables that you've declared using the WithEvents keyword. Object variables that are leading candidates for instantiation in the Startup event are the Inspectors collection object, the Explorers collection object, and the Items collection object for any folders where you want to write event procedure code when an item is added, changed, or removed in a specified folder.

The following example adds a command button to the Standard toolbar of the Outlook Explorer. Previous versions of Outlook required C++ coding to achieve the same result. This toolbar button opens the While You Were Out template located in the file system. For a more extensive discussion of programmatic control of the Outlook Bar and Command bars, see Chapter 10, "Outlook Bar, Command Bars, and the Assistant."

```
Private Sub Application_Startup()
    Dim objCB As Office.CommandBar
    Dim objCBB As Office.CommandBarButton
    Set objCB = Application.ActiveExplorer.CommandBars("Standard")
    Set objCBB = objCB.Controls.Add(msoControlButton)
    With objCBB
        .TooltipText = "Open While You Were Out Form"
        .Style = msoButtonIcon
        .FaceId = 1757
```

```
        .OnAction = "cmdWhile_Click"
    End With
End Sub

'This OnAction procedure must reside in module-level code
'rather than in ThisOutlookSession
Sub cmdWhile_Click()
    Dim objMsg As Outlook.MailItem
    Dim objInsp As Outlook.Inspector
    Set objMsg = Application.CreateItemFromTemplate _
        ("C:\Windows\My Documents\while you were out.oft")
    Set objInsp = objMsg.GetInspector
    objMsg.Display
    'You must display the message before you set WindowState
    objInsp.WindowState = olNormalWindow
End Sub
```

 ## NameSpace Events

Events that follow Application events are not available in the VBA Editor window unless you explicitly declare object variables and use the WithEvents keyword. If you look at "Using WithEvents for Child Objects" earlier in this chapter, you'll see that the NameSpace object is declared as a public variable in ThisOutlookSession using the WithEvents keyword. However, mere declaration of the variable is not sufficient. You must instantiate the NameSpace object variable in the Startup event of the Application object or use an event handler procedure to create an instance of the NameSpace object. If you don't instantiate the child object in another procedure, the event code that you write for the child object will not actually fire when the event occurs.

OptionsPagesAdd

Oddly enough, the NameSpace object supports only one event, the OptionsPagesAdd event. This event is the first cousin of the OptionsPagesAdd event for the Application object. OptionsPagesAdd for the NameSpace object occurs before a Folder Properties dialog box is displayed for a folder. The folder for which the Folder Properties dialog box is displayed is then passed as a MAPIFolder object to the event procedure for OptionsPagesAdd. You can use the OptionsPagesAdd event of the NameSpace object to add property pages to the Folder Properties dialog box for a given folder. The following example displays the property page shown in Figure 9.8.

```
Private Sub objNS_OptionsPagesAdd(ByVal Pages As PropertyPages, _
    ByVal Folder As MAPIFolder)
    Dim strCaption As String
    strCaption = Folder.Name & " Sample Page"
    Pages.Add "PPE.SamplePage", strCaption
End Sub
```

Notice that with the Folder object passed to the procedure, you can change the caption of the property page to reflect the folder name as shown in Figure 9.8.

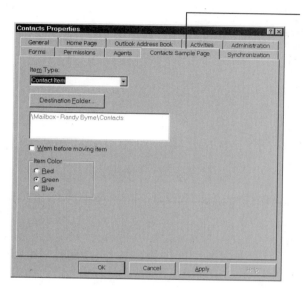

You can dynamically modify the page caption in the OptionsPagesAdd event.

Figure 9.8 *The Sample Page property page is added to the Contacts folder properties dialog box.*

Note For a complete listing of the procedures required to create an ActiveX control that serves as a container for an Outlook property page, see Chapter 13, "Creating COM Add-Ins With Visual Basic." You can also examine the source code for the Sample Page ActiveX control in the Sample Page Property Page Example folder under the Creating COM Add-Ins With Visual Basic folder in the Building Applications With Microsoft Outlook 2000 personal folders (.pst) file accompanying this book.

Explorers Collection Events

NewExplorer

The NewExplorer event fires after a new Explorer window has been created and before it is displayed. A new Explorer window can be created through a user action or through your code. If you have dimensioned an Explorer object variable using WithEvents, the NewExplorer event is the correct location to set a reference to that Explorer object. Outlook passes an Explorer object to the NewExplorer event procedure. The *cmdNewExplorer* procedure shown next runs as an Outlook macro in a VBA code module. Once the code runs, the NewExplorer event causes the Explorer window for the Contacts folder to be displayed in the upper-left corner of the display.

```
Sub cmdNewExplorer()
    Dim colExplorers As Outlook.Explorers
    Set colExplorers = Application.Explorers
    Set objFolder = Application.GetNameSpace("MAPI").GetDefaultFolder _
        (olFolderContacts)
    Set objExplorer = colExplorers.Add _
        (objFolder, olFolderDisplayNavigation)
    objExplorer.Display
End Sub

Private Sub colExpl_NewExplorer(ByVal Explorer As Explorer)
    Set objExpl = Explorer
    With objExpl
        .Left = 0
        .Top = 0
    End With
End Sub
```

 ## Explorer Events

Explorer events provide you with a great deal of control over the Outlook user interface. You can now control the size and window state of Explorer windows, respond to selection changes through the new SelectionChange event and the Selection object, and determine when the user has changed her view or the current folder. The *IsPaneVisible* and *ShowPane* methods allow you to show or hide the Folder List, Outlook Bar, and the Preview pane. The BeforeFolderSwitch and BeforeViewSwitch events are cancelable, so you can prevent the user from moving to a folder or activating a view. If you combine the Explorer events with the new events and programmatic control for the Outlook Bar and Office command bars, you have complete programmatic control over the Outlook user interface. You can customize the Outlook Explorer to suit the requirements of your organization.

Activate

The Activate event occurs when an Explorer window becomes the active window. Be careful not to overload this event procedure with code because the Activate and Deactivate events fire many times during an Outlook session. Each time a user opens an Inspector for an item, the following event sequence occurs:

Explorer Deactivate

Inspector Activate

Inspector Deactivate

Explorer Activate

The following code example shows you how to use the Activate event to make a command bar named Contacts visible or invisible, depending on the current folder in the Explorer.

```
Private Sub objExpl_Activate()
    On Error Resume Next
    If objExpl.CurrentFolder.Name = "Contacts" Then
        objExpl.CommandBars("Contacts").Visible = True
    Else
        objExpl.CommandBars("Contacts").Visible = False
    End If
End Sub
```

BeforeFolderSwitch

The BeforeFolderSwitch event occurs when the Explorer navigates to a new folder, either as a result of user action or through program code. This event is cancelable, so you can prevent users from navigating to prohibited folders. Of course, you can prevent users from opening prohibited folders through Exchange folder permissions, but with this event, you can also customize the Warning dialog box. The following code tests whether the current user is a member of a distribution list. If not, the user is prevented from switching to a public folder named Salary Guidelines.

> **Note** If *NewFolder* is a folder in the file system, then *NewFolder* is Nothing. Your code should provide for this possibility.

```
Private Sub objExpl_BeforeFolderSwitch(ByVal NewFolder As Object, _
    Cancel As Boolean)
    If NewFolder Is Nothing Then Exit Sub
    Set objAE = Application.GetNamespace("MAPI").CurrentUser
    If IsDLMember("HR Admins",objAE) = False Then
        If NewFolder.Name = "Salary Guidelines" Then
            MsgBox "You do not have permission to access this folder." _
                & vbCr & "If you believe you should have access to this folder," _
                & vbCr & "please contact your departmental HR supervisor.", _
                    vbCritical
            Cancel = True
        End If
    End If
End Sub
```

The *IsDLMember* function tests whether an AddressEntry object is a member of an Exchange distribution list. If the AddressEntry is a member, IsDLMember returns *True;* otherwise it returns *False*. This function demonstrates that you still need to use objects supplied by Collaboration Data Objects (CDO) for advanced functionality in place of similar objects in the Outlook Object Model. The Outlook Object Model still does not offer an AddressEntryFilter object that lets you create a subset of AddressEntry objects based on criteria that you add to the filter's Fields collection object.

```
Public Function IsDLMember(strDLName As String, _
    ByVal objAddressEntry As Object) As Boolean
    Dim objGAL As MAPI.AddressList
    Dim objDL As MAPI.AddressEntry
    Dim colAE As MAPI.AddressEntries
```

```
        Dim objSession As MAPI.Session
        Dim objAE As MAPI.AddressEntry
        Dim objAEFilter As MAPI.AddressEntryFilter
        Dim i As Integer
        Const CdoPR_DISPLAY_TYPE = &H39000003

        On Error Resume Next
        Set objSession = New MAPI.Session
        objSession.Logon "", "", False, False

        'Convert Outlook AE to CDO AE
        Set objAE = objSession.GetAddressEntry(objAddressEntry.EntryID)
        Set objGAL = objSession.AddressLists("Global Address List")
        Set colAE = objGAL.AddressEntries
        Set objAEFilter = colAE.Filter

        'Set fields on filter after filter is set
        dispTypeTag = CdoPR_DISPLAY_TYPE
        dispTypeVal = CdoDistList

        'Restrict colAE to Distribution Lists only
        objAEFilter.Fields.Add dispTypeTag, dispTypeVal
        Set objDL = colAE(strDLName)

        If objDL Is Nothing Then 'DL not found
            Exit Function
        End If

        For i = 1 To objDL.Members.Count
            If objDL.Members.Item(i).Address = objAE.Address Then
                IsDLMember = True 'Found member
                Exit Function
            End If
        Next
End Function
```

BeforeViewSwitch

The BeforeViewSwitch event is similar to the BeforeFolderSwitch event, except that it occurs before a view is switched to a new view, either through a user action or programmatically. If a user changes from the Contacts folder to the Tasks folder but does not explicitly change the view with the View selector, the BeforeViewSwitch event will not fire, even though the default views on the two folders have different names. This event is cancelable. The following event procedure prevents the user from switching to the view named Message Timeline if there are more than 500 items in the current folder:

```
Private Sub objExpl_BeforeViewSwitch(ByVal NewView As Variant, _
    Cancel As Boolean)
    If NewView = "Message Timeline" Then
        If objExpl.CurrentFolder.Items.Count > 500 Then
            Cancel = True
```

```
        End If
    End If
End Sub
```

Close

The Close event occurs when an Explorer object closes as a result of a user action or program code. Don't confuse this event with the *Close* method, which causes the Explorer window to close. The following example sets several Outlook Bar objects to Nothing when the Explorer window Close event fires:

```
Private Sub objExpl_Close()
    Set objPane = Nothing
    Set objContents = Nothing
    Set colOutlookBarGroups = Nothing
End Sub
```

Deactivate

The Deactivate event fires when an Explorer or Inspector window ceases to be the active window, either as a result of user action or through program code. You should treat this event with caution! If you display user interface elements such as a message box in the Deactivate event procedure, Outlook might exhibit unpredictable behavior. The following procedure simply writes a string to the VBA Immediate window when the Deactivate event occurs:

```
Private Sub objExpl_Deactivate()
    Debug.Print "Explorer Deactivate"
End Sub
```

Note You should not display a message box, dialog box, or any other user interface element during the Deactivate event of an Explorer or Inspector object. Showing a user interface element in the Deactivate event may disrupt the activation sequence and make Outlook behave unpredictably.

FolderSwitch

The FolderSwitch event occurs when the current folder changes in the Explorer, either through a user action or a programmatic change. In the following event procedures, a toolbar button is added to the Standard toolbar in the Application Startup event. If Explorer's current folder is Nwind, the FolderSwitch event makes the New Nwind CommandBarButton visible. Otherwise, the button is hidden on the Standard toolbar. This toolbar button is declared as a CommandBarButton using the WithEvents keyword in the Declarations section of ThisOutlookSession.

```
'Place these in declarations section of ThisOutlookSession
Public WithEvents objExpl As Outlook.Explorer
Public WithEvents objCBB As Office.CommandBarButton

'Instantiate objExpl and objCBB in Application Startup event procedure
```

```
Private Sub Application_Startup()
    Dim objCB As Office.CommandBar
    Set objExpl = Application.ActiveExplorer
    Set objCB = objExpl.CommandBars("Standard")
    Set objCBB = objCB.Controls.Add(Type:=msoControlButton)
    With objCBB
        .TooltipText = "New Nwind Contact"
        .Style = msoButtonIconAndCaption
        .FaceId = 1099
        .Caption = "New Nwind"
        .Visible = False
    End With
End Sub

'This event procedure hides and unhides the button
Private Sub objExpl_FolderSwitch()
    If objExpl.CurrentFolder = "Nwind" Then
        objCBB.Visible = True
    Else
        objCBB.Visible = False
    End If
End Sub

'Event handler for the button adds a new custom item to the folder
Private Sub objCBB_Click(ByVal Ctrl As Office.CommandBarButton, _
    CancelDefault As Boolean)
    Dim olNwindItem As Outlook.ContactItem
    Set olNwindItem = objExpl.CurrentFolder.Items.Add("IPM.Contact.Nwind")
    olNwindItem.Display
End Sub
```

SelectionChange

The SelectionChange event answers many requests from Outlook developers for a means to determine which items are currently selected in the Explorer. The SelectionChange event occurs when the selection changes in the current view in the active Explorer window. Be aware that this event does not fire if you iterate over a collection of items in the current folder programmatically. The event is not triggered if the current folder in the Explorer changes due to a user action or code. However, if the user then changes the selection with a mouse click or an arrow key after they change folders, the SelectionChange event occurs. When the SelectionChange event fires, use the Selection Property object of the Explorer object to return the items that are selected. The following example tests the Selection object to determine if Contact items are selected, and then displays the number of selected contacts in a message box:

```
Private Sub objExpl_SelectionChange()
    Dim intContacts As Integer
    For i = 1 To objExpl.Selection.Count
        If objExpl.Selection.Item(i).Class = olContact Then
            intContacts = intContacts + 1
        End If
```

```
        Next
        If intContacts Then
            MsgBox "You have selected " & intContacts & " contacts.", _
                vbInformation
        End If
End Sub
```

ViewSwitch

The ViewSwitch event occurs when the view in the Explorer window is switched, either through user action or programmatically. Like the FolderSwitch event, this event helps you to control the Outlook user interface by notifying you when either a view or a folder has changed. The following example uses the *ShowPane* method, a new Explorer method in Outlook 2000, to hide or display the folder list depending on the current view.

```
Private Sub objExpl_ViewSwitch()
    If objExpl.CurrentView = "Message Timeline" Then
        objExpl.ShowPane olFolderList, False
    Else
        objExpl.ShowPane olFolderList, True
    End If
End Sub
```

SyncObject Events

SyncObject events are related to the new SyncObject object in Outlook 2000. A child object of the NameSpace object, SyncObject allows you to download only a subset of the items in your mailbox and favorites folders to the offline folder file. You cannot establish a SyncObject programmatically. Both the SyncObjects collection object and the SyncObject object are read-only objects, meaning that you cannot change the properties of a SyncObject or create a new SyncObject. You can, however, create a SyncObject through the Outlook user interface.

➡️ **Follow these steps to create a SyncObject**

1. Select the Tools menu, then select the Options command to display the Tools Options dialog box.

2. Select the Mail Services tab on the Tools Options dialog box.

3. Click the Offline Folder Settings command button.

4. Click the Quick Synchronization tab on the Offline Folder Settings dialog box.

5. Click the New button and supply a name for the Quick Synchronization group. A Quick Synchronization group is equivalent to a SyncObject object in the Outlook Object Model.

6. Click the Choose Folders button to open the Offline Folder Settings dialog box shown in Figure 9.9. In this dialog box you select the folders that will be synchronized when you select the Quick Synchronization group. Alternatively,

you can set check boxes to download the offline address book, synchronize organizational forms, or download folder home pages during the synchronization.

7. Click OK to accept your choices.

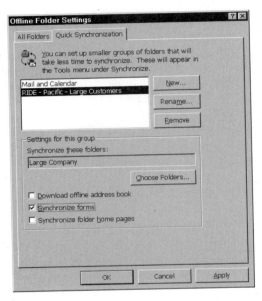

Figure 9.9 *Use the Offline Folder Settings dialog box to create a Quick Synchronization group, known programmatically as a SyncObject.*

If you need to enumerate the defined SyncObjects for the current logged-on user, use the SyncObjects collection object of the NameSpace object. Figure 9.10 illustrates a UserForm populated with Quick Synchronization groups. The following code block demonstrates how to populate a list box with SyncObjects and start synchronization when the user clicks the Start Sync command button. Notice that a default group of All Folders is defined, in addition to the Quick Synchronization groups.

```
'Place this declaration in the general section of frmSync code window
Dim colSyncObjects As Outlook.SyncObjects

Private Sub cmdCancel_Click()
    Unload Me
End Sub

Private Sub cmdStart_Click()
    Set ThisOutlookSession.objSyncObject = _
      colSyncObjects.Items(lstSync.ListIndex + 1)
    colSyncObjects.Item(lstSync.ListIndex + 1).Start
    Unload Me
End Sub
```

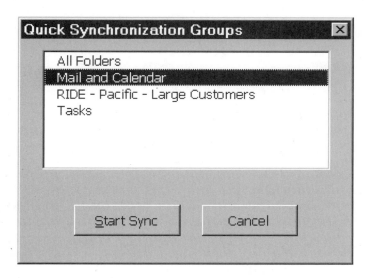

Figure 9.10 *Show a UserForm to select and start a Quick Synchronization group.*

```
Private Sub lstSync_DblClick(ByVal Cancel As MSForms.ReturnBoolean)
    Call cmdStart_Click
End Sub

Private Sub UserForm_Initialize()
    Set colSyncObjects = ThisOutlookSession.objNS.SyncObjects
    For i = 1 To colSyncObjects.Count
        lstSync.AddItem colSyncObjects.Item(i)
    Next
End Sub
```

OnError

The OnError event fires when an error occurs during synchronization of a Quick Synchronization group represented by a SyncObject. The following code example sends a message to the Help Desk when the OnError event for a SyncObject fires. Notice that *objSyncObject* is instantiated in the Quick Synchronization group's UserForm example shown earlier. When the user selects a synchronization profile in the UserForm and clicks the Start Sync command button, a reference is set to *objSyncObject* declared in ThisOutlookSession.

```
Private Sub objSyncObject_OnError(ByVal Code As Long, _
ByVal Description As String)
    Dim objMsg As Outlook.MailItem
    strText = Now() & " Sync Error " & CStr(Code) & Space(1) & Description
    Set objMsg = Application.CreateItem(olMailItem)
    With objMsg
        .Recipients.Add ("Help Desk")
        .Recipients.ResolveAll
```

```
            .Body = strText
            .Send
        End With
End Sub
```

Progress

Use the Progress event to inform a user about the completion percentage of a synchronization job for a Quick Synchronization group. Notice that the Progress event provides several values that let you provide information to the user. The *Value* variable specifies the current value of the synchronization process based on the number of items synchronized; *Max* represents the total number of items to be synchronized; and *State* identifies the current state of the synchronization process where state has one of two values representing whether synchronization has started or stopped. The following example updates the label named *lblCaption* on *frmProgress* during the synchronization process.

```
Private Sub objSyncObject_Progress(ByVal State As Outlook.OlSyncState, _
    ByVal Description As String, ByVal Value As Long, ByVal Max As Long)
    Dim strCaption As String
    If State = olSyncStarted Then
        strCaption = "Synchronization started: "
    Else
        strCaption = "Synchronization stopped: "
    End If
    strCaption = strCaption & Str(Value / Max * 100) & "% " & Description
    frmProgress.lblCaption = strCaption
End Sub
```

SyncEnd

The SyncEnd event takes place when the synchronization of a Quick Synchronization group is completed. The code example unloads a UserForm that showed the synchronization progress to the user.

```
Private Sub objSyncObject_SyncEnd()
    Unload frmProgress
End Sub
```

SyncStart

The SyncStart event takes place when the synchronization of a Quick Synchronization group begins. The code example displays a UserForm that uses the Progress event to inform the user about synchronization progress.

```
Private Sub objSyncObject_SyncStart()
    frmProgress.Show
End Sub
```

OutlookBarPane Events

Outlook 2000 provides several new events related to its programmable Outlook Bar. For a detailed discussion of the properties and methods of the OutlookBarPane, OutlookBarStorage, OutlookBarGroup, and OutlookBarShortcut objects, see Chapter 11, "Using VBA and VBScript with Outlook." You can use cancelable Outlook Bar events to prevent navigation from Outlook Bar groups or shortcuts. If you dimension the correct object variables using the WithEvents keyword, your code can raise events when Outlook Bar groups and shortcuts are added to or removed from the Outlook Bar.

If you raise events on Outlook Bar panes, groups, and shortcuts, you'll need to instantiate object variables during event procedures for other objects in the Outlook Object Model. The table below suggests event procedures where you should set a reference to the object variable.

Object	Set Object Reference in This Event Procedure
objPane	*objExplorer_Activate*
colOutlookBarGroups	*objExplorer_Activate*
colOutlookBarShortcuts	*objPane_BeforeGroupSwitch*

BeforeGroupSwitch

The BeforeGroupSwitch event occurs before Outlook switches to a different Outlook Bar group, either because of user action or a programmatic change. Because this event is cancelable, you can prevent users from changing to a prohibited group on the Outlook Bar. The following example instantiates a collection object for OutlookBarShortcuts and then prevents the user from switching to the Real Estate Division group on the Outlook Bar:

```
Private Sub objPane_BeforeGroupSwitch(ByVal ToGroup As OutlookBarGroup, _
    Cancel As Boolean)
    Set colOutlookBarShortcuts = ToGroup.Shortcuts
    If ToGroup = "Real Estate Division" Then
        MsgBox "You cannot switch to " & ToGroup.Name _
            & " on the Outlook Bar!", vbInformation
        Cancel = True
    End If
End Sub
```

BeforeNavigate

The BeforeNavigate event occurs before Outlook navigates to a folder or launches an Outlook Bar shortcut, either because of user action or program code. Because this event is cancelable, you can prevent users from navigating to folders or launching shortcut URLs or executables.

```
Private Sub objPane_BeforeNavigate(ByVal Shortcut As OutlookBarShortcut, _
    Cancel As Boolean)
    If Shortcut.Name = "RIDE" Then
        Cancel = True
    End If
End Sub
```

 ## OutlookBarGroup Events

GroupAdd

The GroupAdd event occurs after a group has been added to an Outlook Bar, either because of a user action or through program code. The following example adds shortcuts for all the members of a distribution list named Shared Calendars to a new group named Workgroup Calendars. All the members of the Shared Calendars distribution list must grant at least Reviewer permission on their calendar folders for this example to work correctly.

```
Private Sub colOutlookBarGroups_GroupAdd(ByVal NewGroup As OutlookBarGroup)
    DebugWrite "OutlookBarGroups GroupAdd " & NewGroup.Name
    Dim myFolder As Outlook.MAPIFolder
    Dim myRecip As Outlook.Recipient
    Dim myDL As Outlook.DistListItem
    On Error Resume Next
    Set myFolder = objNS.GetDefaultFolder(olFolderContacts)
    Set myDL = myFolder.Items("Shared Calendars")
    For i = 1 To myDL.MemberCount
        Set myRecip = objNS.CreateRecipient(myDL.GetMember(i).Name)
        myRecip.Resolve
        If myRecip.Resolved Then
            Set myFolder = _
            objNS.GetSharedDefaultFolder(myRecip, olFolderCalendar)
        End If
        NewGroup.Shortcuts.Add myFolder, "Calendar - " & myRecip.Name
    Next
    NewGroup.Name = "Shared Calendars"
End Sub
```

BeforeGroupAdd

The BeforeGroupAdd event occurs before a group is added to an Outlook Bar, either because of user action or through program code. This example prevents a user from adding groups to the Outlook Bar.

```
Private Sub colOutlookBarGroups_BeforeGroupAdd(Cancel As Boolean)
    Cancel = True
End Sub
```

BeforeGroupRemove

The BeforeGroupRemove event occurs before a group is removed from an Outlook Bar, either because of user action or through program code. The code in this example cancels an attempt by a user or program code to delete the Outlook Shortcuts group.

```
Private Sub colOutlookBarGroups_BeforeGroupRemove _
  (ByVal Group As OutlookBarGroup, Cancel As Boolean)
    If Group.Name = "Outlook Shortcuts" Then
        Cancel = True
    End If
End Sub
```

OutlookBarShortcut Events

ShortcutAdd

The ShortcutAdd event fires after a shortcut has been added to an Outlook Bar group, either because of user action or through program code. The following event procedure adds the name of the logged-on user to the shortcut name if the user adds a shortcut to his or her Calendar folder.

```
Private Sub colOutlookBarShortcuts_ShortcutAdd _
  (ByVal NewShortcut As OutlookBarShortcut)
    On Error Resume Next
    Dim objFolder As Outlook.MAPIFolder
    Set objFolder = NewShortcut.Target
    'Bail out if not a folder shortcut
    If Err Then Exit Sub
    'Test EntryID's to determine if folder shortcut
    'is for user's calendar folder
    If objNS.GetDefaultFolder(olFolderCalendar).EntryID = _
      objFolder.EntryID Then
        NewShortcut.Name = "Calendar - " & objNS.CurrentUser
    End If
End Sub
```

BeforeShortcutAdd

The BeforeShortcutAdd event takes place before a shortcut is added to an Outlook Bar group, either because of user action or through program code. This example prevents users from adding a shortcut to the Web Links group. Objects representing the current group on the Outlook Bar and the collection of shortcuts for the current group are instantiated in the BeforeGroupSwitch event of the Pane object.

```
Public objCurrentGroup As Outlook.OutlookBarGroup

Private Sub objPane_BeforeGroupSwitch(ByVal ToGroup As OutlookBarGroup, _
    Cancel As Boolean)
    Set colOutlookBarShortcuts = ToGroup.Shortcuts
```

```
        Set objCurrentGroup = ToGroup
    End Sub

    Private Sub colOutlookBarShortcuts_BeforeShortcutAdd(Cancel As Boolean)
        If objCurrentGroup.Name = "Web Links" Then
            Cancel = True
        End If
    End Sub
```

BeforeShortcutRemove

The BeforeShortcutRemove event takes place before a shortcut is removed from an Outlook Bar group, either because of user action or through program code. The code in this example cancels an attempt by users or program code to delete a shortcut from the Financial Services group.

```
    Private Sub colOutlookBarShortcuts_BeforeShortcutRemove(Cancel As Boolean)
        If objCurrentGroup.Name = "Financial Services" Then
            Cancel = True
        End If
    End Sub
```

 ## Inspectors Collection Events

The Inspectors collection object provides the gateway to item-level events in Outlook 2000. Although this collection object has only one event that occurs when a new Inspector is displayed through either a user action or program code, the NewInspector event lets you instantiate item-level objects declared using the WithEvents keyword. In previous versions of Outlook, the only supported events were form-level events for customized Item objects, also known as custom forms. Any form-level item for which you write VBScript code is, by definition, a custom Outlook form. VBScript code in those forms could respond to events such as Item Open, Close, Read, Send, Write, Reply, Reply All, Forward, PropertyChange, CustomPropertyChange, and CustomAction. The important departure of Outlook 2000 from previous versions is that now you can write VBA code in ThisOutlookSession or develop a COM Add-in to respond to item-level events. If you raise events using the new objects in the Outlook 2000 Object Model, you are no longer constrained by VBScript when you write code for item-level events in Outlook custom forms.

Exceptions to the NewInspector Event

Unfortunately, there are some exceptions to this rule that should be clearly explained at this point. If an item in a folder does not utilize an Inspector object, then you will not be able to write item-level event code in Visual Basic for this object. Certain e-mail editors do not support an Inspector object or the NewInspector event. For example, if you use Word as your e-mail editor and the format of the message you are composing is plain text, the NewInspector event does not fire because an Inspector object is not added to the Inspectors collection when you create the mail message. The default editor selected on the Mail Format page of the Tools Options dialog box determines whether the default MailItem with a message class of IPM.Note supports the Inspector object. The following table indicates which types of MailItems support an Inspector object, depending on your default mail editor:

Message Format	When Your E-Mail Editor is Outlook 2000	When Your E-Mail Editor is Word 2000 (Office Mail)
HTML	Supports Inspector	Does not support Inspector
Rich Text Format (RTF)	Supports Inspector	Supports Inspector
Plain Text	Supports Inspector	Does not support Inspector

There are other circumstances where you cannot instantiate an Inspector object when a user or program code creates or modifies an item in a folder. An Outlook Office Document item does not support an Inspector object. A DocumentItem object is any document—other than an Outlook item—that exists as an item in an Outlook folder. In common usage, an IPM.Document item will be an Office Document, but it may also be any type of document, an executable file, or an HTML document. Remember that Exchange folders can contain almost any type of Document item. Moreover, Office Document items can be posted or sent directly to a folder either by a user action or program code. In this instance, the DocumentItem objects do not support an Inspector object. The following table indicates when a DocumentItem object supports an Inspector object:

Document Item	Message Class	Supports Inspector for Outlook Document Item	Supports Inspector for Native Document Item
Web Page	IPM.Document.htmlfile	Not applicable	No
Word Document	IPM.Document.Word.Document.8	Yes	No
Excel Worksheet	IPM.Document.Excel.Sheet.8	Yes	No
PowerPoint Presentation	IPM.Document.PowerPoint.Show.8	Yes	No
Visio Drawing	IPM.Document.Visio.Drawing.5	No	No

If you post an Office document such as an Excel workbook or a PowerPoint presentation directly to a folder, an Inspector object will not be created. The NewInspector event will not fire when you add a native Office document to an Exchange folder. If you post or send an Office Document item, then the NewInspector event will fire. Posting any other document, whether it is an HTML document, a .zip file, a .pdf file, or any other type of document that can be posted to a public folder, will not cause the NewInspector event to fire.

If an application external to Outlook creates an Outlook Inspector object, the NewInspector event will not fire if an Inspectors collection object has been instantiated by Outlook VBA or an Outlook COM Add-in. An external application is an application that uses Simple MAPI to create an Outlook mail message. This limitation does not apply to applications that use Outlook as an ActiveX Automation Server to create Outlook items. For example, you can send a file as an attachment to an Outlook message by selecting the Mail Recipient MAPI command on the Send To menu of the file's shortcut menu. Right-click the file in Windows Explorer to display the file's shortcut menu. When you select this command, an Inspector window opens, and the file is added as an attachment to an Outlook message. However, a NewInspector event will not fire for this message. Similarly, if you use the Send Page By E-Mail or Link By E-Mail commands in Internet Explorer, a NewInspector event will not fire. The following table illustrates when a NewInspector event fires, depending on the calling application. You should realize that the exceptions regarding mail editor settings and message format discussed earlier will also determine whether the NewInspector event fires.

Calling Application	Command	NewInspector Event for Inspectors Collection object
Windows Explorer	Send To extensions such as Mail Recipient MAPI command	No
Internet Explorer	File Send Page By E-Mail or Link By E-Mail	No
Outlook	File New Mail Message	Yes, depending on default e-mail editor and message type
Outlook	Create New Item (either through user action or program code)	Yes
Word, Excel, Visual Basic, Visual C++, or any COM-compliant ActiveX automation controller application	Outlook automation through program code	Yes

NewInspector

The NewInspector event occurs when a new Inspector object is created either through a user action or program code. The NewInspector event fires before the Inspector window is displayed. If you create an item through code and do not display the item, then the NewInspector event does not occur.

As discussed earlier, the NewInspector event is the gateway to item-level events. The following code example shows how to create item-level objects depending on the class of the item returned by the CurrentItem property of the Inspector object. Once you have instantiated these form-level objects in your VBA code, you can raise events on the form-level objects in VBA as long as you have declared the form-level objects using the WithEvents keyword. All of the traditional form-level events, such as Item_Open, Item_Read, Item_Write, and Item_Send, are available for the Item object declared using WithEvents.

The importance of this approach is that these events are now available to you in VBA or in your COM Add-in, rather than in VBScript code written for a custom form.

```
'Place these declarations in the general section ThisOutlookSession
Public WithEvents objInsp As Outlook.Inspector
Public WithEvents colInsp As Outlook.Inspectors
Public WithEvents objMailItem As Outlook.MailItem
Public WithEvents objPostItem As Outlook.PostItem
Public WithEvents objContactItem As Outlook.ContactItem
Public WithEvents objDistListItem As Outlook.DistListItem
Public WithEvents objApptItem As Outlook.AppointmentItem
Public WithEvents objTaskItem As Outlook.TaskItem
Public WithEvents objTaskRequestItem As Outlook.TaskRequestItem
Public WithEvents objTaskRequestAcceptItem As Outlook.TaskRequestAcceptItem
Public WithEvents objTaskRequestDeclineItem As Outlook.TaskRequestAcceptItem
Public WithEvents objTaskRequestUpdateItem As Outlook.TaskRequestUpdateItem
Public WithEvents objJournalItem As Outlook.JournalItem
Public WithEvents objDocumentItem As Outlook.DocumentItem
Public WithEvents objReportItem As Outlook.ReportItem
Public WithEvents objRemoteItem As Outlook.RemoteItem

Private Sub colInsp_NewInspector(ByVal Inspector As Inspector)
    Dim objItem As Object
    Set objInsp = Inspector
    On Error Resume Next
    Set objItem = objInsp.CurrentItem
    Select Case objItem.Class
        Case olMail
            Set objMailItem = objItem
        Case olPost
            Set objPostItem = objItem
        Case olAppointment
            Set objApptItem = objItem
        Case olContact
            Set objContactItem = objItem
        Case olDistributionList
            Set objDistListItem = objItem
        Case olTask
            Set objTaskItem = objItem
        Case olTaskRequest
            Set objTaskRequestItem = objItem
        Case olTaskRequestAccept
            Set objTaskRequestAcceptItem = objItem
        Case olTaskRequestDecline
            Set objTaskRequestDeclineItem = objItem
        Case olTaskRequestUpdate
            Set objTaskRequestUpdateItem = objItem
        Case olJournal
            Set objJournalItem = objItem
        Case olReport
            Set objReportItem = objItem
        Case olRemote
            Set objRemoteItem = objItem
        Case olDocument
            Set objDocumentItem = objItem
```

```
        End Select
    End Sub
```

The item's class is a better guide to the type of item than the item's message class. For example, all Contact items have a class value of *olContact*. If you look up the *olContact* value in the *OlObjectClass* Enum, *olContact* has a decimal value of *40*. Any contact items, whether they are default contact items with a message class of IPM.Contact or custom contact items with a message class of IPM.Contact.MyCustomContactForm, have an item class value equal to *olContact*.

2000 Inspector Events

Activate

The Activate event for the Inspector object occurs when the Inspector window becomes the active window in Outlook. The following example makes the built-in Clipboard Command bar visible in the Inspector window if the message class of the CurrentItem is IPM.Note. When the Activate event occurs, you can return the CurrentItem property of the Inspector object to examine the properties of the item.

```
Private Sub objInsp_Activate()
    If objInsp.CurrentItem.MessageClass = "IPM.Note" Then
        objInsp.CommandBars("Clipboard").Visible = True
    Else
        objInsp.CommandBars("Clipboard").Visible = False
    End If
End Sub
```

Close

The Close event occurs when the Inspector object is closed, either through a user action or programmatically. The Close event will always occur after the Deactivate event. The following example uses the Close event to hide the Assistant. As with the Deactivate event, you cannot access the CurrentItem property of the Inspector object during the Close event.

```
Private Sub objInsp_Close()
    With Assistant
        .Visible = False
    End With
End Sub
```

Deactivate

The Deactivate event occurs when the Inspector window ceases to be the active window because of a user action or program code. The same cautions mentioned earlier regarding the Deactivate event of the Explorer window apply to the Inspector window. Do not display user interface elements in the Deactivate event procedure. The following procedure hides the built-in Clipboard Command bar. In the Deactivate event, you cannot use the CurrentItem property to return properties of the item. If you attempt to use the CurrentItem property, Outlook will generate an Object Not Found error.

```
Private Sub objInsp_Deactivate()
    objInsp.CommandBars("Clipboard").Visible = False
End Sub
```

Folders Collection Events

The Folders collection object contains all the MAPIFolder objects belonging to a parent MAPIFolder object. The NameSpace object also contains a Folders object containing all the root folders for the current logged-on user. The Folders collection object events occur when folders are added, changed, or deleted because of user action or program code. The Folders collection events give you a powerful means to control folder names, hierarchical structure, and folder contents, in addition to traditional Exchange roles and folder permissions.

Note With the proper synchronization of FolderAdd and FolderRemove events, you can actually restore deleted items and folders. Previously, this functionality was very difficult to achieve, requiring Exchange Server scripting agents.

FolderAdd

The FolderAdd event occurs when a folder is added to a Folders collection object, either through a user action or program code. The following example prevents users from deleting the Large Messages folder in their Inbox. If a user deletes this folder, a message box appears and notifies the user that the folder cannot be deleted. The folder is then moved from the user's Deleted Items folder back to the Inbox.

This example requires that you declare two collection object variables using WithEvents: *colDeletedItemsFolders* and *colInboxFolders*. When a folder is deleted from *colInboxFolders*, the FolderRemove event fires. The global variable *blnDeleteRestore* is set to *True* in the FolderRemove event procedure for *colInboxFolders*. When a folder is deleted from *colInboxFolders*, it is moved to the Deleted Items folder. The FolderAdd event procedure for the *colDeletedItemsFolders* object evaluates the *blnDeleteRestore* variable. If *blnDeleteRestore* is *True*, it moves the folder that has just been added to the Deleted Items folder back to the Inbox.

```
'Place these declarations in the general section of ThisOutlookSession
Public WithEvents colDeletedItemsFolders As Outlook.Folders
Public WithEvents colInboxFolders As Outlook.Folders
Public blnDeleteRestore As Boolean

Private Sub Application_Startup()
    Set objNS = Application.GetNameSpace("MAPI")
    Set colInboxFolders = objNS.GetDefaultFolder(olFolderInbox).Folders
    Set colDeletedItemsFolders = _
```

```
            objNS.GetDefaultFolder(olFolderDeletedItems).Folders
End Sub

Private Sub colInboxFolders_FolderRemove()
    blnDeleteRestore = True
End Sub

Private Sub colDeletedItemsFolders_FolderAdd(ByVal Folder As MAPIFolder)
    If blnDeleteRestore Then
        MsgBox "You cannot delete " & Folder.Name _
        & vbCr & "This folder will be restored to your Inbox.", vbInformation
        Folder.MoveTo objNS.GetDefaultFolder(olFolderInbox)
    End If
    blnDeleteRestore = False
End Sub
```

FolderChange

The FolderChange event occurs when a folder in a Folders collection object is changed, either through user action or program code. The FolderChange event fires if a user or program code renames a folder, or if an item in the folder is added, changed, or removed. The following code example prevents a user from renaming the Large Messages subfolder of their Inbox. Outlook 2000 uses the Large Messages subfolder to store messages above a certain size limit that a user does not want to download to their offline folders file. The *blnLargeMsgActive* global variable ensures that the code runs only if the Large Messages folder is the current folder in the Explorer. All the necessary event procedures have been included in this example so that you can see how events have to be chained together to achieve the intended result.

```
'Place these declarations in the general section of ThisOutlookSession
Public WithEvents objExpl As Outlook.Explorer
Public WithEvents colInboxFolders As Outlook.Folders
Public blnLargeMsgActive As Boolean

'Create objExpl in the Application Startup event
Private Sub Application_Startup()
    Set objExpl = Application.ActiveExplorer
End Sub

'Create colInboxFolders in BeforeFolderSwitch and set blnLargeMsgActive
Private Sub objExpl_BeforeFolderSwitch(ByVal NewFolder As Object, _
    Cancel As Boolean)
    If NewFolder.Name = "Large Messages" And _
      NewFolder.Parent.Name = "Inbox" Then
        blnLargeMsgActive = True
    Else
        blnLargeMsgActive = False
    End If
    If NewFolder.Parent.Name = "Inbox" Then
        Set colInboxFolders = NewFolder.Parent.Folders
```

```
        End If
    End Sub

    'This procedure depends upon instantiation of colInboxFolders in
    'objExpl_BeforeFolderSwitch event procedure above
    Private Sub colInboxFolders_FolderChange(ByVal Folder As MAPIFolder)
        If blnLargeMsgActive Then
            If Folder.Name <> "Large Messages" Then
                MsgBox "Can't rename Large Messages folder!", vbInformation
                objExpl.CurrentFolder.Name = "Large Messages"
            End If
        End If
    End Sub
```

FolderRemove

The FolderRemove event occurs when a folder is deleted from its Folders collection object, either through user action or program code. Unlike the FolderAdd and FolderChange
events, FolderRemove does not pass a MAPIFolder object for the folder that has been removed. This example is similar to the code examples for the FolderAdd and FolderRemove
events. It requires that you chain a FolderRemove event for the Inbox to a FolderAdd event
for the Deleted Items folder. In this instance, if a folder is deleted from the Inbox and the
deleted folder contains items, the deleted folder is displayed in an Explorer window.

> **Note** These examples are aimed at folders in a user's private information store
> where a Deleted Items folder exists. If you want to recover deleted items or fold-
> ers from public folders programmatically, you will have to write scripting agents
> and have your Microsoft Exchange Server administrator enable deleted item re-
> covery for the public information store using the Exchange Administrator program.
> You should be aware that a user can circumvent the Deleted Items folder by press-
> ing Shift+Delete to delete an item or a folder. Additional details regarding deleted
> item restoration are provided in the following articles from the Microsoft Knowl-
> edge Base on the Microsoft Support Online Web site:
>
> Q178630, "XADM: How To Recover Items That Do Not Touch The Deleted
> Items Folders" at *http://support.microsoft.com/support/kb/articles/q178/*
> *6/30.asp*
>
> Q180117, "XADM: Recovering Deleted Items from a Public Folder" at *http://*
> *support.microsoft.com/support/kb/articles/q180/1/17.asp*

```
'Place these declarations in the general section of ThisOutlookSession
Public WithEvents colDeletedItemsFolders As Outlook.Folders
Public WithEvents colInboxFolders As Outlook.Folders
Public blnDelete As Boolean

Private Sub Application_Startup()
    Set objNS = Application.GetNameSpace("MAPI")
    Set colInboxFolders = objNS.GetDefaultFolder(olFolderInbox).Folders
```

```
    Set colDeletedItemsFolders = _
        objNS.GetDefaultFolder(olFolderDeletedItems).Folders
End Sub

Private Sub colInboxFolders_FolderRemove()
    blnDelete = True
End Sub

Private Sub colDeletedItemsFolders_FolderAdd(ByVal Folder As MAPIFolder)
    If blnDelete And Folder.Items.Count Then
        Folder.Display
    End If
    blnDelete = False
End Sub
```

Items Collection Events

Like the Folders collection object, the Items collection object gives you a great deal of control over what happens in folders and with the items contained within folders. In fact, you might think of the Items collection events as a personal version of the Exchange Event Service. For a complete discussion of how you can extend Outlook with the Exchange Event Service, see Chapter 17, "Extending Outlook Using Exchange Server Scripting and Routing Objects." Like the Exchange Event Service, you can use the Items collection events to respond to message created, changed, and deleted events. The Items collection does not have a timer event like the Exchange Event Service does, although you can readily construct a timer-based COM Add-in with a Visual Basic Timer control or Windows API calls. Unlike the Exchange Event Service, Items collection events do not provide server-based scalability and process isolation. On the positive side of the ledger, your Items collection events can be delivered as a COM Add-in that is compiled rather than interpreted (the Exchange Event service uses VBScript for its code) and has obvious performance advantages over the late-bound VBScript code in the Exchange Event Service.

The following table compares the Exchange Event Service and a Visual Basic COM Add-in that uses Items collection object events:

Feature	Exchange Event Service	COM Add-In
Development language	VBScript	Visual Basic, Visual C++, or any other development tool for an ActiveX DLL
Object binding	Late-bound	Early-bound with proper declaration of variables
Variable types	Variant only	All supported types
Scalability	Yes	Limited
Process location	Server	Client
Error Logging	NT Event Service	Error log on client must be created by developer

ItemAdd

The ItemAdd event occurs when an item is added to an Items collection object, either through user action or program code. The following example creates an Items collection object for an Exchange public folder named Customers that contains Contact items. When a new customer is added to the Customers folder, a message is sent to a distribution list for the correct regional sales team. This example requires another event procedure in order to instantiate the collection object for the Customers folder. So that you can better understand the code, each of these event procedures is listed below. See Chapter 11, "Using VBA and VBScript with Outlook," for a complete listing of the *OpenMAPIFolder* function.

```
'Place these declarations in the general section of ThisOutlookSession
Public WithEvents colCustomersItems As Outlook.Items

'Instantiate collection object in Application Startup event

Private Sub Application_Startup()
    Dim strFolderPath As String
    StrFolderPath = "Public Folders\All Public Folders\" _
        & "Contact Management\Customers"
    Set colCustomersItems = OpenMAPIFolder(strFolderPath).Items
End Sub


'This event procedure sends a message to a DL
Private Sub colCustomersItems_ItemAdd(ByVal Item As Object)
Dim objContactItem As Outlook.ContactItem
Dim objMsgItem As Outlook.MailItem
Set objContactItem = Item
If objContactItem.MessageClass = "IPM.Contact.Customer" Then
    Select Case objContactItem.BusinessAddressState
        Case "CA", "NV", "WA", "OR", "AZ", "NM", "ID"
        strDL = "Sales Team West"
        Case "IL", "OH", "NE", "MN", "IA", "IN", "WI"
        strDL = "Sales Team Midwest"
        Case "ME", "NH", "NY", "NJ", "MD", "PA", "RI", "CT", "MA"
        strDL = "Sales Team East"
        Case Else
        strDL = "Sales Team National"
    End Select
    Set objMsgItem = Application.CreateItem(olMailItem)
    objMsgItem.Subject = "New Customer - " & objContactItem.CompanyName
    objMsgItem.Save
    objMsgItem.Attachments.Add objContactItem, olByValue
    objMsgItem.To = strDL
    objMsgItem.Send
End If
```

ItemChange

The ItemChange event occurs when an item in an Items collection object is changed, either by user action or program code. Continuing the example of the Customers folder described earlier, the following code writes a record to a SQL Server 7.0 database when an item changes in the Customers public folder. The *StrClean* function in the following procedure removes single quotes that could cause an error when the SQL statement executes:

```
Private Sub colCustomersItems_ItemChange(ByVal Item As Object)
    Dim objCont As Outlook.ContactItem
    Dim strSQL As String
    Const strSep = "','"
    Dim conDB As New ADODB.Connection
    Set objCont = Item
    If objCont.MessageClass <> "IPM.Contact.Customer" Then
        Exit Sub
    End If
    On Error GoTo AddContact_Error
    conDB.Open "Nwind", "sa", ""
    strSQL = "Insert Customers Values ('"
    strSQL = strSQL & StrClean(objCont.Account) & strSep
    strSQL = strSQL & StrClean(objCont.CompanyName) & strSep
    strSQL = strSQL & StrClean(objCont.FullName) & strSep
    strSQL = strSQL & StrClean(objCont.JobTitle) & strSep
    strSQL = strSQL & StrClean(objCont.BusinessAddress) & strSep
    strSQL = strSQL & StrClean(objCont.BusinessAddressCity) & strSep
    strSQL = strSQL & StrClean(objCont.BusinessAddressState) & strSep
    strSQL = strSQL & StrClean(objCont.BusinessAddressPostalCode) & strSep
    strSQL = strSQL & StrClean(objCont.BusinessAddressCountry) & strSep
    strSQL = strSQL & StrClean(objCont.BusinessTelephoneNumber) & strSep
    strSQL = strSQL & StrClean(objCont.BusinessFaxNumber) & "')"
    conDB.Execute strSQL
    conDB.Close

AddContact_Exit:
    Exit Sub

AddContact_Error:
    Utility.ErrorTrap 'Writes error to event log or file
    Resume AddContact_Exit
End Sub
```

ItemRemove

The ItemRemove event occurs when an item is removed from a specified Items collection object, either through user action or programmatically. The following example expands on the FolderRemove example described earlier to show how to undelete an item programmatically. This example undeletes a custom form with a message class of IPM.Post.ContactSettings if a user deletes the item from the Settings subfolder of the Inbox.

```
'Place these declarations in the general section of ThisOutlookSession
Public WithEvents colDeletedItems As Outlook.Items
Public WithEvents colSettingsItems As Outlook.Items
Public blnDeleteItem As Boolean
```

```
Private Sub Application_Startup()
    Set objNS = Application.GetNameSpace("MAPI")
    Set colSettingsItems = _
      objNS.GetDefaultFolder(olFolderInbox).Folders("Settings")
    Set colDeletedItems = objNS.GetDefaultFolder(olFolderDeletedItems).Items
End Sub

Private Sub colSettingsItems_ItemRemove()
    blnDeleteItem = True
End Sub

Private Sub colDeletedItems_ItemAdd(ByVal Item As Object)
    If blnDeleteItem and Item.MessageClass = "IPM.Post.ContactSettings" Then
        Set objDestFolder = _
          objNS.GetDefaultFolder(olFolderInbox).Folders("Settings")
        Item.Move objDestFolder
    End If
    blnDeleteItem = False
End Sub
```

Item Events

We've covered all the new application-level events in Outlook 2000. Do you believe that you're ready to move to the head of the class yet? You can go beyond what you've learned so far and raise item-level events in addition to application-level events. Item-level events are covered in detail in Chapter 11, "Using VBA and VBScript with Outlook," and are not discussed in detail in this chapter. You should be aware, however, that Outlook 2000 offers several new item-level events, including AttachmentAdd, AttachmentRead, BeforeAttachmentSave, and BeforeCheckNames. Following the convention established for application-level events, event names that begin with Before are subject to cancellation in the event procedure.

The important point about Outlook 2000 item-level events is that they can be controlled from ThisOutlookSession with Outlook VBA or from a COM Add-in created in Visual Basic or Visual C++. Outlook 97 and Outlook 98 did not support the declaration of item-level object variables using WithEvents in order to write event procedure code. Item-level event procedures were previously created using VBScript in Outlook custom forms. Many development projects will still require VBScript in Outlook forms. VBScript behind forms provides a simple means of enabling form-level automation and allowing that automation to travel from recipient to recipient.

In theory, an Outlook custom form could contain almost no VBScript code. The event-related behavior of this form could be controlled by item-level object variables that used Visual Basic code to create event procedures. The problem with this theoretical approach is that each client receiving your custom form would need to have your COM Add-in installed in order for the form's event procedures to function correctly. Portability of event automation is problematic when your code does not travel with the form itself. This problem becomes fatal when you try to use Outlook forms in Internet Mail Only (IMO) mode. IMO developers designing custom forms typically save their custom form definitions with the item to allow portability.

In a controlled corporate environment operating in Corporate/Workgroup(C/W) mode with Exchange Server, the theoretical proposition of item-level event code residing in COM Add-in event procedures becomes more feasible if the correct COM Add-ins are deployed consistently to every client in the organization. In fact, this is one area of event automation that lends itself perfectly to COM Add-ins or VBA code in ThisOutlookSession. If you want to create event procedures for default Outlook items such as a MailItem or ContactItem, you can do so without hesitation. A common complaint by Outlook developers is that a custom form cannot be substituted for the default mail message whose message class is IPM.Note. In Chapter 12, "Distribute and Maintain Applications," you'll learn how to make a custom form the default mail message in place of IPM.Note by changing registry settings. This ability constitutes a new hidden feature of Outlook 2000. If you don't want to resort to registry changes, you can create event procedure code that instantiates a MailItem object variable declared using WithEvents in the NewInspector event of the Inspectors collection object. You can use that MailItem object to write additional item-level event procedures.

For example, the following example requires a subject to be entered for a message before the message is sent. If the user fails to enter a subject after the initial InputBox is displayed, the Send event is canceled. This code also requires chained event procedures to accomplish the intended result. All the required event procedures and declarations in the example have been included so that you can see how object variables and events are linked.

```
'Place these declarations in the general section of ThisOutlookSession
Public WithEvents colInsp As Outlook.Inspectors
Public WithEvents objMailItem As Outlook.MailItem

Private Sub Application_Startup()
    Set colInsp = Application.Inspectors
End Sub

Private Sub colInsp_NewInspector(ByVal Inspector As Inspector)
    Dim objItem As Object
    Set objInsp = Inspector
    On Error Resume Next
    Set objItem = objInsp.CurrentItem
    Select Case objItem.Class
        Case olMail
            Set objMailItem = objItem
    End Select
End Sub

Private Sub objMailItem_Send(Cancel As Boolean)
    If objMailItem.Subject = "" Then
```

```
    objMailItem.Subject = _
    InputBox("Enter a subject for this message:", "Subject Required")
    If objMailItem.Subject = "" Then
        Cancel = True
    End If
  End If
End If
Exit Sub
```

> **Note** This functionality could also be achieved by writing code for the ItemSend event of the Application object. However, the MailItem object has a much more granular event model. Using the above example, you could write code for any one of the item-level events supported by the *objMailItem* object variable.

Firing Order of Events

For item-level events, you can clearly predict the sequence in which events will fire. Chapter 11, "Using VBA and VBScript with Outlook," contains a table illustrating the firing order of events at the item level. However, events at the application level are less predictable. You cannot guarantee that event firing will follow a specific sequence either because different events cause a unique firing sequence or because, in future versions of Outlook, the event sequence might

change. Some insights into a typical firing sequence are offered here. If you want to investigate further, it is suggested that you write Debug.Print *Object EventName* statements for each event procedure supported by a given object variable declared using the WithEvents keyword. The following list shows just such a debug sequence when a user opens a mail message, enters recipients for the message, types a subject and message body, and then sends the message. Again, don't take this sequence as invariable; it simply gives you a reasonable expectation of the event sequence when you send a mail message.

Inspectors NewInspector

MailItem Open

Explorer Deactivate

Inspector Activate

MailItem Read

MailItem PropertyChange To

MailItem PropertyChange CC

MailItem PropertyChange BCC

MailItem BeforeCheckNames

MailItem PropertyChange To

MailItem PropertyChange CC

MailItem PropertyChange BCC

MailItem PropertyChange ConversationIndex

MailItem PropertyChange ReceivedTime

MailItem PropertyChange Subject

Application ItemSend

MailItem Write

MailItem Close

Inspector Deactivate

Explorer Activate

Note You can see from the above that PropertyChange events fire for To, CC recipient, and BCC recipient before and after the BeforeCheckNames events. In fact, the message that generated the sequence above had only a single To recipient. You'll also notice that item-level events in VBA behave similarly to item-level events in VBScript. Unfortunately, a PropertyChange event does not fire when a user enters text in the message body.

Where To Go from Here

There are many resources that can help you deepen your understanding of the material in this chapter. For additional information, see the following resources.

Controlling the Use of Office Digital-Signing Features and Security Settings

Microsoft Office 2000 Resource Kit Web site
http://www.microsoft.com/office/ork/

Microsoft Office 2000 Resource Kit. Redmond, WA: Microsoft Press, 1999.

Creating and Implementing Interfaces

Microsoft Corporation. *Microsoft Visual Basic 6.0 Programmer's Guide.* Redmond, WA: Microsoft Press, 1998. An online version of this book is included with Visual Basic 6.0, and it is also available on the MSDN Online Web site at *http://msdn.microsoft.com/developer/*.

Visual Basic for Applications

Getz, Ken, and Mike Gilbert. *Visual Basic Language Developer's Handbook.* Alameda, CA: Sybex, 1999.

Microsoft Corporation. "Getting the Most Out of Visual Basic for Applications." Chapter 7 in *Microsoft Office 2000/Visual Basic Programmer's Guide.* Redmond, WA: Microsoft Press, 1999.

Microsoft Corporation. "Writing Solid Code." Chapter 3 in *Microsoft Office 2000/ Visual Basic Programmer's Guide.* Redmond, WA: Microsoft Press, 1999.

VBA Objects Web site
http://www.inquiry.com/objects/

Visual Basic for Applications Web site
http://msdn.microsoft.com/vba/

Working with Class Modules

Microsoft Corporation. "Custom Classes and Objects." Chapter 9 in *Microsoft Office 2000/Visual Basic Programmer's Guide*. Redmond, WA: Microsoft Press, 1999.

Working with Office 2000 Applications

Microsoft Corporation. "Working with Office Applications." Chapter 5 in *Microsoft Office 2000/Visual Basic Programmer's Guide*. Redmond, WA: Microsoft Press, 1999.

Working with Office 2000 Objects

Microsoft Corporation. "Understanding Office Objects and Object Models." Chapter 4 in *Microsoft Office 2000/Visual Basic Programmer's Guide*. Redmond, WA: Microsoft Press, 1999.

Chapter 10
Outlook Bar, Command Bars, and the Assistant

In This Chapter

Outlook 2000 provides new levels of programmatic control over the Outlook Bar, Inspector and Explorer window command bars, and the Office Assistant. In this chapter, we'll take a look at how you can program these elements in Outlook 2000. What does programmatic control of the Outlook Bar, command bars, and the Assistant mean to you as a developer? If you are developing a custom Outlook application, it means that you can now shape the user's experience in ways that were impossible in previous versions of Outlook. By combining control of the Outlook Bar, command bars, and the Assistant with the new events and methods of the Explorer object, developers can create customized versions of Outlook using COM Add-ins to install their customization code. Look for the following types of functionality to be wrapped in COM Add-ins that customize the Outlook user interface:

- Corporate customization and standardization of the Outlook 2000 user experience
- Vertical-market applications in the fields of Healthcare, Finance, and Transportation
- Internet Service Provider applications
- Customized rules wizards
- Sales force automation

Panes Collection Object

The Panes collection object is a property object of the Explorer object. The Panes collection object contains the three panes in the Outlook Explorer window as shown in Figure 10.1:

- The Outlook Bar Pane
- The Folder List Pane
- The Preview Pane

You can create an instance of an OutlookBarPane object only from the Panes collection. The Preview and Folder List panes are not accessible from the Outlook Object Model. When you begin to navigate an Outlook Bar's groups and shortcuts in code, you start with the Panes collection object, as demonstrated in the following code example:

```
Dim OlBarPane As Outlook.OutlookBarPane
Dim OlExplorer As Outlook.Explorer
Set OlExplorer = Application.ActiveExplorer
Set OlBarPane = OlExplorer.Panes("OutlookBar")

    'Make the Outlook Bar visible if it's hidden
    If OlBarPane.Visible = False Then
        OlBarPane.Visible = True
    End If

MsgBox "The Current Outlook Bar Group is " _
    & OlBarPane.CurrentGroup, vbInformation
```

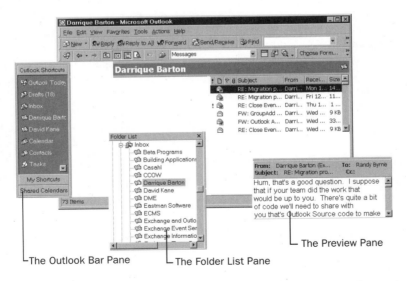

Figure 10.1 *Three Explorer panes comprise the Panes collection object.*

Determining If a Pane is Visible

You can determine whether an individual pane is visible by using the *IsPaneVisible* method of the Explorer object. If the Pane is not visible and you want to make it visible, use the *ShowPane* method. The following VBScript code unhides the Folder List if it is hidden:

```
Sub ShowFolderList
Const olFolderList = 2
Set objExpl = Application.ActiveExplorer
    If Not(objExpl.IsPaneVisible(olFolderList)) Then
        objExpl.ShowPane olFolderList, True
    End If
End Sub
```

Note You cannot size Panes programmatically in the Explorer window in Outlook 2000.

OutlookBarPane Object

The OutlookBarPane object is the only object you can instantiate from the Panes collection object. It represents the Outlook Bar and its groups and shortcuts. Generally, you'll create a reference to the OutlookBarPane on your way to its dependent child objects representing Outlook Bar groups and shortcuts. You can use the CurrentGroup property of the OutlookBarPane object to set or get the current group on the Outlook Bar. The OutlookBarPane supports two important events—BeforeNavigate and BeforeGroupSwitch—that can inform you when a user is navigating to a shortcut or a group, respectively. For additional information on writing event procedures, as well as the events supported by the OutlookBarPane, OutlookBarGroups, and OutlookBarShortcuts objects, see Chapter 9, "Raise Events and Move to the Head of the Class."

OutlookBarStorage Object

The OutlookBarStorage object is an accessor object in the Outlook object hierarchy and has no methods or events of its own. It is used to access the OutlookBarGroups collection object through its Groups property. You can access the OutlookBarStorage object by using the Contents property of the OutlookBarPane object. The following VBA code demonstrates the use of the Contents and Groups property objects:

```
Dim OlBarPane As Outlook.OutlookBarPane
Dim OlBarStorage As Outlook.OutlookBarStorage
Dim OlBarGroups As Outlook.OutlookBarGroups
Dim OlExplorer As Outlook.Explorer
Set OlExplorer = Application.ActiveExplorer
Set OlBarPane = OlExplorer.Panes("OutlookBar")
Set OlBarStorage = OlBarPane.Contents
Set OlBarGroups = OlBarStorage.Groups
'This code is more efficient
'Set OlBarGroups = OlBarPane.Contents.Groups
```

```
MsgBox "There are " & OlBarGroups.Count _
   & " groups on your Outlook Bar.", vbInformation
```

OutlookBarGroups Collection Object

The OutlookBarGroups collection object is one of the two critical collection objects used to program the Outlook Bar. Using the Groups object, you can add, modify, or delete groups on the Outlook Bar. The OutlookBarGroups object also supports three events that provide an additional level of programmatic control over Outlook Bar Groups: GroupAdd, BeforeGroupAdd, and BeforeGroupRemove. The following example creates an Outlook Bar Group named Web Links and positions the group as the last group on the Outlook Bar:

```
Dim OlBarGroups As Outlook.OutlookBarGroups
Dim OlBarGroup As Outlook.OutlookBarGroup
Set OlBarGroups = _
   Application.ActiveExplorer.Panes("OutlookBar").Contents.Groups
Set OlBarGroup = OlBarGroups.Add(Name:="Web Links", _
   Index:=OlBarGroups.Count + 1)
```

> **Note** The *Add* method shown above uses named arguments to pass the name and index arguments to the *Add* method of the OutlookBarGroups object. You can list named arguments in any order. A named argument consists of the name of the argument followed by a colon and an equal sign (:=), and the value assigned to the argument.

OutlookBarGroup

The OutlookBarGroup object represents a group on the Outlook Bar. You can manipulate the properties of the OutlookBarGroup object using its Name and ViewType properties. The ViewType property controls whether the shortcuts in the group display with a large or small icon. Use the Item property to access an existing member of an OutlookBarGroups collection object. The following example renames the Outlook Bar Group named Web Links that we created in the previous example, and changes the shortcuts to small icons. Small icons allow the user to see more icons in the group before they have to use the group scrollbar to move other shortcuts into the group viewing area.

```
Dim OlBarGroups As Outlook.OutlookBarGroups
Dim OlBarGroup As Outlook.OutlookBarGroup
Set OlBarGroups = _
   Application.ActiveExplorer.Panes("OutlookBar").Contents.Groups
Set OlBarGroup = OlBarGroups.Items("Web Links")
With OlBarGroup
    .Name = "Outlook Web Links"
    .ViewType = olSmallIcon
End With
```

OutlookBarShortcuts Collection Object

The OutlookBarShortcuts object is a property collection object for the OutlookBarGroups object. Use this collection object to add, modify, or remove shortcuts from an Outlook Bar Group. Like the OutlookBarGroups collection object, OutlookBarShortcuts also supports three events that let you write event procedure code when an Outlook shortcut is added or removed. These events are ShortcutAdd, BeforeShortcutAdd, and BeforeShortcutRemove. Continuing the Web Links example, the following code adds shortcuts to the Web Links group as shown in Figure 10.2:

```
Sub OBAddWebLinks()
Dim OlBarPane As Outlook.OutlookBarPane
Dim OlBarGroups As Outlook.OutlookBarGroups
Dim OlBarGroup As Outlook.OutlookBarGroup
Dim OlBarShortcuts As Outlook.OutlookBarShortcuts
Dim OlExplorer As Outlook.Explorer
Set OlExplorer = Application.ActiveExplorer
Set OlBarPane = OlExplorer.Panes("OutlookBar")
Set OlBarGroups = OlBarPane.Contents.Groups
    Set OlBarGroup = _
        OlBarGroups.Add(Name:="Web Links", Index:=OlBarGroups.Count + 1)

    'Show the Outlook Bar if not visible
    If OlExplorer.IsPaneVisible(olOutlookBar) = False Then
        OlExplorer.ShowPane olOutlookBar, True
    End If

    Set OlShortcuts = OlBarGroup.Shortcuts
    OlShortcuts.Add "http://www.microsoft.com/outlookdev", _
        "Microsoft Outlook Development"
    OlShortcuts.Add "http://msdn.microsoft.com/scripting", _
        "Microsoft Scripting Technologies"
    OlShortcuts.Add "http://www.outlookexchange.com", _
        "Outlook Developer Resource Center"
    OlShortcuts.Add "http://www.slipstick.com/exchange", _
        "Slipstick Systems Exchange Center"
    OlShortcuts.Add "http://www.microeye.com/outlkb.html", _
        "Micro Eye Outlook Development KB"
    Set OlBarPane.CurrentGroup = OlBarGroup
End Sub
```

OutlookBarShortcut Object

The OutlookBarShortcut object represents a shortcut on the Outlook Bar. Unlike previous versions of Outlook, a shortcut in Outlook 2000 can launch an executable file on a local or network drive, navigate to a URL, or navigate to an Outlook folder in the folder hierarchy.

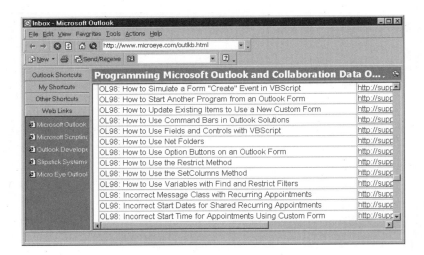

Figure 10.2 *The Web Links group provides shortcuts to Outlook development sites.*

Shortcut Function	Target Property	Example

Navigate to Outlook folder	MAPIFolder object	`Set oFolder = _`
		`objNS.GetDefaultFolder(olFolderDrafts)`
		`OlBarShortcuts.Add oFolder, "Drafts"`

Open a file system file	String file URL specification	`strTarget = "file:\\c:\my documents\foo.xls"` `OlBarShortcuts.Add strTarget, "My File"`
Open a file system folder	String folder path specification	`strTarget = "c:\my documents"` `OlBarShortcuts.Add strTarget, "My Documents"`
Open a Web page	String URL	`strTarget = "http://www.microsoft.com/outlook"` `OlBarShortcuts.Add strTarget, "Outlook"`

The Target property of the OutlookBarShortcut determines what action occurs when a user clicks a shortcut on the Outlook Bar. Oddly enough, the Target property is read-only; once you have set the Target property by adding a shortcut, you must remove the shortcut and then add it again if you want to change the Target property of an existing shortcut. The following example adds several different types of shortcuts to the My Shortcuts group on the Outlook Bar. When the user clicks the New Plan Rate shortcut, Microsoft Excel launches and opens a new workbook based on the Plan Rate template. This example also adds a shortcut to a public folder named Outlook Knowledge Base using the *OpenMapiFolder* function listed in Chapter 11, "Using VBA and VBScript with Outlook."

```
Sub OBAddShortcuts()
    Dim OlBarPane As OutlookBarPane
    Dim OlBarGroups As OutlookBarGroups
    Dim OlBarGroup As OutlookBarGroup
    Dim OlBarShortcuts As OutlookBarShortcuts
```

```
    Dim OlBarShortcut As OutlookBarShortcut
    Dim OlExplorer As Explorer
    Dim OlFolder As MAPIFolder
    Dim strTarget As String
    Set OlExplorer = Application.ActiveExplorer
    Set OlBarPane = OlExplorer.Panes("OutlookBar")
    Set OlBarGroups = OlBarPane.Contents.Groups
    Set OlBarGroup = OlBarGroups("My Shortcuts")
    Set OlBarShortcuts = OlBarGroup.Shortcuts
    'Use a URL for file and web-based URLs
    strTarget = "file://c:/program files/microsoft office/templates/plan-rate.xlt"
    OlBarShortcuts.Add strTarget, "New Plan Rate"
    'Use a path specification for executables
    strTarget = "c:\program files\microsoft office\office\winword.exe"
    OlBarShortcuts.Add strTarget, "Winword"
    'Use a path specification for folders
    strTarget = "c:\my documents"
    OlBarShortcuts.Add strTarget, "My Documents"
    'Use a MAPIFolder object as the target for an Outlook folder shortcut
    strTarget = "\Public Folders\All Public Folders\Outlook Resource Kit"
    Set OlFolder = OpenMAPIFolder(strTarget)
    OlBarShortcuts.Add OlFolder, "Outlook Resource Kit"
End Sub
```

Note If you use an *http* URL as the target of a shortcut, Outlook will open the Web page as a Web View in the Outlook Explorer window. If you want to open the Web page in a separate window, right-click the page in Outlook and select Display In Separate Window on the shortcut menu.

CommandBars Collection Object

The ability to program the Outlook Bar gives you a significant level of control over the Outlook user interface. Using the OutlookBarGroups and OutlookBarShortcuts events, you can prevent a user from removing an Outlook Bar Group or shortcut that is essential to your application. You can also dynamically add Outlook Bar Groups and shortcuts. You don't have the same flexibility, however, with Outlook Bar objects, as you do with all the objects belonging to Office command bars. Command bar and Assistant objects are actually members of the Microsoft Office 9.0 Object Model. CommandBar objects give you the opportunity to customize Outlook 2000 in a way that was impossible in previous versions of Outlook. That said, the following discussion provides you with an overview of command bars that is specific to Outlook. How you call CommandBar objects differs somewhat from other Office 2000 applications. We'll see how command bars can be used in both the Explorer and Inspector windows. Finally, we'll demonstrate an Items command bar that uses some advanced Collaboration Data Objects (CDO) code to let a user create a new custom form in a folder from a New Form combo box on the Items command bar.

> **Note** If you are writing a COM Add-in, you must explicitly add a reference to the Microsoft Office 9.0 Object Library using the appropriate command in your development tool. If you are using Outlook VBA to write code in VBAProject.otm, Outlook automatically creates a reference to the Microsoft Office 9.0 Object Model.

Overview of Command Bars

In the Outlook Object Model, both the Explorer and Inspector objects contain a CommandBars property object. The CommandBars object for both the Inspector and Explorer controls all Outlook toolbars, menu bars, and shortcut menus. The CommandBar object and its children contain all of the following items.

- Menu bars, toolbars, and shortcut menus
- Menus on menu bars and toolbars
- Submenus on menus, submenus, and shortcut menus

You can modify any built-in menu bar or toolbar, and you can create and modify custom toolbars, menu bars, and shortcut menus to deliver with your Outlook VBA project or COM Add-in application. Use command bar customization to present the features of your application as individual buttons on toolbars or as groups of command names on menus. Because toolbars and menus are both command bars, you can use the same kind of controls on both of them. Notice in Figure 10.3 how the traditional Outlook menu bar has been customized to provide a New menu before the File menu. The commands on the New menu have also been changed from their default state.

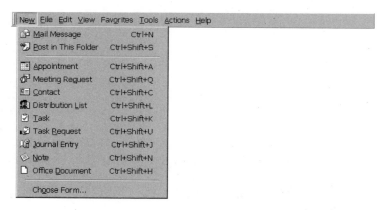

Figure 10.3 *The New menu on the standard Outlook menu bar.*

Figure 10.4 shows the Items custom command bar created by Visual Basic code that mimics the modified menu bar shown in Figure 10.3. The complete code required to build this toolbar is listed later in this chapter. Custom command bars are distinguished in part from built-in command bars because they can be deleted from the Outlook environment.

Built-in command bars can be modified by user action or by program code. However, they can be restored to their original state and default behavior by using the Reset command button on the Toolbars page of the Customize dialog box.

Figure 10.4 *The Items custom command bar.*

In Outlook, the built-in command bars are as follows:

Object	Built-In Command Bar
Explorer	Menu Bar
	Standard
	Advanced
	Remote
	Web
	Clipboard
Inspector	Menu Bar
	Standard
	Formatting
	Form Design
	Clipboard

The Items toolbar provides one-click item creation for novice Outlook users. It also offers a feature not available in either the Standard or Advanced Outlook toolbars. Whenever a user opens a folder containing custom Outlook form items published to the folder, the Items toolbar shows a New combo box at the right-hand side of the toolbar. This combo box lets the user point and click to create new custom forms in the folder. The BeforeFolderSwitch event of the Explorer object helps to refresh the combo box whenever a user switches folders. If there are no custom forms published in the folder, then the combo box is hidden.

Be aware that command bars are defined as either docked or, in the case of a floating command or menu bar, undocked. There are four command bar docks at the left, right, top, and bottom of the Outlook window. Figure 10.5 shows the Outlook menu bar undocked from its normal position at the top of the Explorer window.

If you look again at the Items command bar shown in Figure 10.4, you'll see that it contains 15 CommandBarButton objects and one CommandBarComboBox object. Although

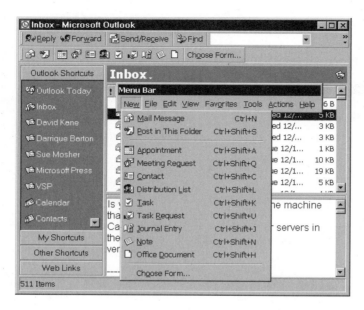

Figure 10.5 *The Outlook menu bar undocked.*

the Choose Form button doesn't appear to be a normal button, it is indeed a button with its Style property set to msoOptionCaption. CommandBarButton objects can either be iconic command bar buttons, text command bar buttons, or a combination of both an icon and text.

Outlook CommandBarButton objects represent buttons and menu items. The pop-up controls that display menus and submenus are known as CommandBarPopup objects. In Figure 10.6, the Favorites and Development controls are both pop-up controls that display a menu and a submenu, respectively. Both the menu and the submenu are unique CommandBar objects with their own sets of controls.

In addition to CommandBarButton and CommandBarPopup objects, the CommandBarControls object can contain objects known as CommandBarComboBox objects. In the Items command bar shown earlier in Figure 10.4, the New custom form combo box is a CommandBarComboBox object. CommandBarComboBox objects assume a variety of different types—edit box, drop-down list box, or drop-down combo box. Like the List Box control on Outlook forms, the CommandBarComboBox object supports both an *AddItem* method to add items to the control and a ListIndex property to retrieve the selection index.

 Personalized Menus

One of the new features of Office command bars is the appearance of personalized menus. Personalized or adaptive menus let you see a collapsed subset of the menu items that you use most often. As shown in Figure 10.7, adaptive menus are turned on by default in Office 2000.

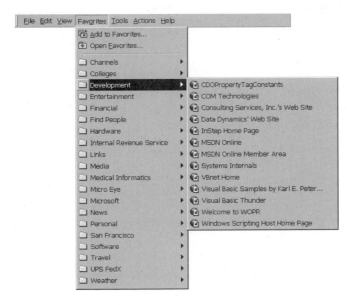

Figure 10.6 *CommandBarPopup objects are prevalent on the Favorites menu.*

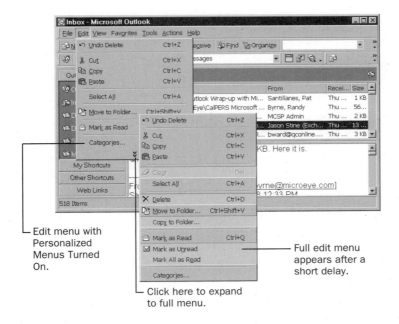

Edit menu with
Personalized
Menus Turned
On.

Click here to expand
to full menu.

Full edit menu
appears after a
short delay.

Figure 10.7 *Outlook Explorer Edit menu with personalized menus.*

⟳ To turn personalized menus on or off

1. On the View menu, select the Toolbars command.
2. Select Customize on the Toolbars submenu.
3. Click the Options tab on the Customize dialog box.
4. Check the Menus Show Recently Used Commands First box to turn on personalized menus, as shown in Figure 10.8; clear the box to turn off personalized menus. If you turn on personalized menus, you can cause full menus to appear after a short delay by checking Show Full Menus After A Short Delay.

You can control personalized menus programmatically by setting the AdaptiveMenus property of the CommandBars collection object. Be aware that, by changing this property, you will be setting AdaptiveMenus for all Office 2000 applications. The following procedure toggles the AdaptiveMenus and LargeButtons properties for the command bars in all Office applications.

```
Sub TogglePM()
    Dim colCB As CommandBars
    Set colCB = Application.ActiveExplorer.CommandBars
    'These settings are global to all Office applications
    With colCB
        .AdaptiveMenus = Not (.AdaptiveMenus)
        .LargeButtons = Not (.LargeButtons)
    End With
End Sub
```

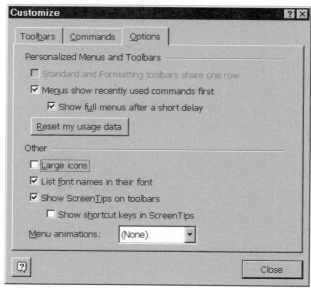

Figure 10.8 *Use the Options page in the Customize dialog box to configure personalized menus.*

You can also use the AdaptiveMenus property to detect whether personalized menus are turned on or off for a given CommandBars collection. If personalized menus are turned on, use the Priority property of the CommandBarControls object to cause a command to appear on a personalized menu. When you add a custom CommandBarControls object to a command bar, it is visible by default. If you set a control's Priority to 1, the control will always be visible. If you set the Priority to 0, the control will be visible initially, but may be hidden by Outlook if it is not used regularly. When a control is hidden, it is still available on the menu, but you must expand the menu to see it.

The AdaptiveMenus property can also set the personalized menu behavior of an individual menu within Outlook. When you set the AdaptiveMenus property for a single menu, you do not globally change the behavior of all the menus in Office 2000. The following procedure causes the File menu for the Outlook Explorer to display without personalized menu behavior, even though personalized menus are turned on for all Office applications.

```
Sub SetFileAMOff()
    Dim colCB As Office.CommandBars
    Dim objCB As Office.CommandBar
    Set colCB = Application.ActiveExplorer.CommandBars
    If colCB.AdaptiveMenus Then
        Set objCB = colCB("File")
        objCB.AdaptiveMenu = False
    End If
End Sub
```

Exploring the CommandBars Collection

One way to learn more about the CommandBars object is to write code that provides a map of the existing built-in and custom Outlook command bars. Since Outlook supports command bars for both the Explorer and Inspector windows, the following function requires a class argument that indicates whether the Inspector or Explorer command bars and controls should be output to the Debug window.

Note The following code can be found in the basCommandBars module in the VBA Samples folder.

To use the code in the VBA Samples folder

1. Using the Windows Explorer, expand the Building Microsoft Outlook 2000 Applications folder, expand the Visual Basic for Applications folder, and then expand the VBA Samples folder.

2. The code, class, and user form modules for VBAProject.otm are in the VBA Samples folder. You can double-click these items to open them in Visual Basic or you can drag them to a folder in Windows Explorer so that you can import them directly into your Outlook VBAProject.otm.

3. You can also replace your current VBAProject.otm with the VBAProject.otm on installed by the setup program on the companion CD-ROM.

To run the PrintAllCBarInfo procedure

1. Open the Visual Basic Editor by pressing Alt+F11.

2. Drag basCommandBars from the VBA Samples folder to a file system folder such as C:\My Documents.

3. Select Import File on the File menu to import basCommandBars into your Outlook VBAProject.otm.

4. Press Ctrl+G to open the Debug Window.

5. Type *?PrintAllCBarInfo(olExplorer)* and press Enter. Information on all command bars and controls in the CommandBars collection will display in the Debug window.

```
Function PrintAllCBarInfo(intClass As Integer)
    ' This procedure prints (to the Debug window)
    ' information about each command bar in the
    ' active explorer or inspector window.
    ' Use OlExplorer or OlInspector for intClass argument
    Dim cbrBar As Office.CommandBar
    Dim colCB As Office.CommandBars
    On Error Resume Next
    If intClass = OlExplorer Then
        Set colCB = Application.ActiveExplorer.CommandBars
        If Err Then
            Debug.Print "No Active Explorer found!"
            Exit Function
        End If
    Else
        Set colCB = Application.ActiveInspector.CommandBars
        If Err Then
            Debug.Print "No Active Inspector found!"
            Exit Function
        End If
    End If
    For Each cbrBar In colCB
        CBPrintCBarInfo cbrBar.Name, intClass
    Next cbrBar
End Function
```

The following function is a helper function for the *CBPrintAllCBarInfo* function shown above. It, in turn, calls two other functions that enumerate the types of command bars and command bar controls. See the code in basCommandBars for a complete listing.

```
Function CBPrintCBarInfo(strCBarName As String, intClass As Integer) _
    As Variant
    ' This procedure prints (to the Debug window) information
    ' about the command bar specified in the strCBarName argument
    ' and information about each control on that command bar.
    ' Use olExplorer or olInspector for intClass argument
```

```
    Dim cbrBar                          As CommandBar
    Dim ctlCBarControl                  As CommandBarControl
    Const ERR_INVALID_CMDBARNAME        As Long = 5
    On Error GoTo CBPrintCBarInfo_Err

    If intClass = OlExplorer Then
        Set cbrBar = Application.ActiveExplorer.CommandBars(strCBarName)
    Else
        Set cbrBar = Application.ActiveInspector.CommandBars(strCBarName)
    End If

    Debug.Print "CommandBar: " & cbrBar.Name & vbTab & "(" _
        & CBGetCBType(cbrBar) & ")" & vbTab & "(" _
        & IIf(cbrBar.BuiltIn, "Built-in", "Custom") & ")"
    For Each ctlCBarControl In cbrBar.Controls
        Debug.Print vbTab & ctlCBarControl.Caption & vbTab & "(" _
            & CBGetCBCtlType(ctlCBarControl) & ")"
    Next ctlCBarControl

CBPrintCBarInfo_End:
    Exit Function
CBPrintCBarInfo_Err:
    Select Case Err.Number
        Case ERR_INVALID_CMDBARNAME
            CBPrintCBarInfo = "'" & strCBarName & _
                "' is not a valid command bar name!"
        Case Else
            CBPrintCBarInfo = "Error: " & Err.Number _
                & " - " & Err.Description
    End Select
    Resume CBPrintCBarInfo_End
End Function
```

Listed below, you can see how the output of *CBPrintAllCBarInfo* looks when it appears in the Debug window. This excerpt shows all the controls on the Outlook Advanced toolbar.

```
CommandBar: Advanced    (Toolbar)    (Built-in)
    Outloo&k Today      (Button)
    Previous Folder     (SplitButtonPopup)
    Next &Folder        (Button)
    &Up One Level       (Button)
    Fold&er List        (Button)
    Preview Pa&ne       (Button)
    Print Pre&view      (Button)
    &Undo Delete        (Button)
    Ru&les Wizard...    (Button)
    Current &View       (Combobox)
    Group &By Box       (Button)
    Field &Chooser      (Button)
    Auto&Preview        (Button)
```

Using Images on Command Bar Buttons

Once you have explored the Outlook command bars and their controls, you will want to take a look at the images used on these buttons. In fact, if you plan to write code to create your own custom command bars, you will need to find a source for icons that will appear on the buttons. You can use the *FindControl*, *CopyFace* and *PasteFace* methods to copy and paste images from a built-in button to other custom buttons you have created. You can also supply a FaceID value for your custom command bar button that corresponds to the FaceID for a built-in icon. The following procedure creates a temporary custom toolbar that displays built-in Outlook icons as shown in Figure 10.9. If you hold your mouse pointer over the button, a tooltip will display the FaceID property.

Figure 10.9 *The ShowFaceIDs toolbar provides a palette of images to use for custom buttons.*

To run the *CBShowButtonFaceIDs* procedure

1. Open the Visual Basic Editor by pressing Alt+F11.

2. Drag basCommandBars from the VBA Samples folder to a file system folder such as C:\My Documents.

3. Select Import File on the File menu to import basCommandBars into your Outlook VBAProject.otm.

4. Press Ctrl+G to open the Debug Window.

5. Type *?CBShowButtonFaceIDs(0, 299, olExplorer)* and press Enter.

6. Press Alt+F11 to return to the Outlook application window. You should see the ButtonFaceIDs toolbar displayed over the Explorer window.

```
Function CBShowButtonFaceIDs(lngIDStart As Long, _
        lngIDStop As Long, intClass As Integer)

    ' This procedure creates a toolbar with buttons that display the
    ' images associated with the values starting at lngIDStart and
    ' ending at lngIDStop.
    ' Use olExplorer or olInspector for intClass argument
```

```
Dim cbrNewToolbar    As CommandBar
Dim cmdNewButton     As CommandBarButton
Dim intCntr          As Integer

' If the ShowFaceIds toolbar exists then delete it.
On Error Resume Next
If intClass = OlExplorer Then
    ' Delete the ShowFaceIds toolbar
    Application.ActiveExplorer.CommandBars("ShowFaceIds").Delete
    ' Create a new toolbar.
    Set cbrNewToolbar = Application.ActiveExplorer.CommandBars.Add _
        (Name:="ShowFaceIds", Temporary:=True)
Else
        ' Delete the ShowFaceIds toolbar
    Application.ActiveInspector.CommandBars("ShowFaceIds").Delete
    ' Create a new toolbar.
    Set cbrNewToolbar = Application.ActiveInspector.CommandBars.Add _
        (Name:="ShowFaceIds", Temporary:=True)
End If

' Create a new button with an image matching the FaceId property value
' indicated by intCntr.
For intCntr = lngIDStart To lngIDStop
    Set cmdNewButton = _
        cbrNewToolbar.Controls.Add(Type:=msoControlButton)
    With cmdNewButton
        ' Setting the FaceId property value specifies the appearance
        ' but not the functionality of the button.
        .FaceId = intCntr
        .Style = msoButtonIcon
        .Visible = True
        .TooltipText = "FaceId = " & intCntr
    End With
Next intCntr

' Show the images on the toolbar.
With cbrNewToolbar
    .Width = 600
    .Left = 100
    .Top = 100
    .Visible = True
End With

End Function
```

Use the ShowFaceIDs toolbar to provide icon images for your own custom toolbar buttons. Place the mouse cursor over the desired command button to learn its FaceID property. You can copy the code for the *cmdNewButton* object above and paste it into the code that your own button creates. Just substitute the actual value for the FaceID icon that you need for the *intCntr* variable.

Adding a Command Bar to the Collection

Use the *Add* method to add a command bar to either the Inspector or Explorer CommandBars collection. If you are using Visual Basic rather than VBScript, you can use named arguments when you call the *Add* method of the CommandBars collection object to add a command bar. The following example adds the Items command bar to the Explorer CommandBars collection:

```
Dim cbrNewToolbar As CommandBar
Set cbrNewToolbar = Application.ActiveExplorer.CommandBars.Add _
        (Name:="Items", Position:=msoBarTop, Temporary:=False)
```

In VBScript, all variables are declared as variants and named arguments are illegal. Here is a statement that adds an Inspector command bar:

```
Set objCommandBar= Item.GetInspector.CommandBars.Add _
        ("Command Bar Example", 1, False, True)
```

The Position property determines whether the toolbar will be docked in the Explorer or Inspector window or displayed as a floating toolbar. If you supply the msoBarPopUp value for the Position argument, you will create a shortcut menu rather than a menu bar or toolbar. The possible values for the Position property are as follows:

Constant	Description
msoBarLeft=0, msoBarTop=1, msoBarRight=2, msoBarBottom=3	Indicates the left, top, right, and bottom coordinates of the new command bar
msoBarFloating=4	Indicates that the new command bar won't be docked
msoBarPopup=5	Indicates that the new command bar will be a shortcut menu

The Temporary property indicates whether the command bar will be deleted when the Outlook application closes or when the Inspector window closes. Notice that the VBScript Command Bar Example toolbar is temporary because it appears only for a specific custom form. Generally, you don't want to create persistent Inspector toolbars.

> **Note** Once you have added the command bar to the CommandBars collection, you can set additional properties for the command bar that determine its appearance and behavior. For example, the Type property determines whether the CommandBar object behaves as a menu bar, toolbar, or shortcut menu.

Retrieving an Existing Command Bar

To retrieve an existing built-in or custom command bar, use the Items property with either an index value or the name of the command bar. Since the Items property is the default property of the CommandBars collection object, you don't actually have to use the Items property to retrieve a command bar from a collection. The two statements below are equivalent.

```
Set cbrItems = Application.ActiveExplorer.CommandBars.Items("Items")
Set cbrItems = Application.ActiveExplorer.CommandBars("Items")
```

Deleting a Command Bar

Use the *Delete* method to delete a custom command bar from the CommandBars collection. You cannot delete a built-in command bar with the *Delete* method. The *Delete* method is actually a CommandBar method rather than a CommandBars method. This function deletes a command bar and returns *True* if the command bar was successfully deleted.

```
Function CBDeleteCommandBar(strCBarName As String) As Boolean
    On Error Resume Next
    Application.ActiveExplorer.CommandBars(strCBarName).Delete
    If Err = 0 Then
        CBDeleteCommandBar = True
    End If
End Function
```

Using the OnUpdate Event

The CommandBars collection supports an OnUpdate event that fires whenever a command bar is changed. For additional information regarding Visual Basic events, the WithEvents keyword, and event procedures, see Chapter 9, "Raise Events and Move to the Head of the Class." The event is triggered by any change to a command, or the state of a bar or command bar control. These changes can result from pressing a button, or by changing text or a cell selection, just to name of few of the possibilities. Since a large number of OnUpdate events can occur during normal usage, you should be very cautious when using this event. It is strongly recommended that this event be used primarily for checking that a custom command bar has been added or removed by an Outlook COM Add-in. If you are curious how many times this event can fire, add the following code to VBAProject.otm. A statement appears in the Debug window every time the OnUpdate event fires.

```
' Place in Declarations of ThisOutlookSession
Dim WithEvents colCB As CommandBars

Private Sub Application_Startup()
    Set colCB = Application.ActiveExplorer.CommandBars
End Sub

Private Sub colCB_OnUpdate()
    Debug.Print "CommandBars OnUpdate"
End Sub
```

CommandBar Object

The CommandBar object represents a command bar for either the Outlook Explorer or Inspector window. A command bar can be either a built-in or a custom command bar. You can modify a built-in command bar through the Customize dialog box or through program code. If you are building a custom Outlook application or if you are creating a COM Add-in, you should consider providing a custom command bar or modifying the menus on the Outlook menu bar for your COM Add-in. Once you have created a command bar object programmatically, you should add controls to the command bar and cause those controls to respond to events such as Click or Change.

Properties of the CommandBar Object

The following table lists some important properties of the CommandBar object. For additional information, see properties for the CommandBar object in Microsoft Outlook Visual Basic Reference Help.

Property	Description
AdaptiveMenus	Determines whether individual command bar displays adaptive menus. *True* or *False*.
Enabled	Determines whether the command bar can be modified with the Customize dialog box. If the Enabled property is *False,* you cannot set the Visible property to *True*.
Position	Returns or sets the position of the command bar.
Type	Determines the type of command bar—menu bar, toolbar, or shortcut menu.
Visible	Determines whether the command bar is visible in the Explorer or Inspector window. *True* or *False*.

Methods of the CommandBar Object

The following methods operate on the CommandBar object. For additional information, see methods for the CommandBar object in Microsoft Outlook Visual Basic Reference Help.

Method	Description
Delete	Deletes a custom command bar.
FindControl	Finds a control on a command bar that meets specified criteria. You can search by control type, ID, or tag property based on whether a control is visible or on a submenu.
Reset	Resets a built-in command bar to its default configuration. If you have customized a built-in command bar, those customizations are removed when you call the *Reset* method.
ShowPopup	Shows the command bar as a pop-up menu at specified coordinates or at the current cursor location.

The *ShowPopup* method will work only for a command bar that has been added as a shortcut menu to the CommandBars collection. You cannot cause a built-in or custom toolbar to appear suddenly as a pop-up menu. The Outlook Inspector has a limited capacity to display shortcut menus, due to the fact that a MouseUp event is not supported using the current control container for Outlook custom forms. If you are utilizing UserForms in your VBA or COM Add-in project, use the MouseUp event of intrinsic and third-party ActiveX controls to build event procedures that display Outlook shortcut menus. The following procedure displays a pop-up menu at the current cursor location in the Explorer window:

```
Sub ExplorerPopUp()
    Dim CBCopyandPasteMenu As Office.CommandBar
    Set CBCopyandPasteMenu = Application.ActiveExplorer.CommandBars.Add _
        (Name:="Custom", Position:=msoBarPopup, Temporary:=True)
    Set Copy = CBCopyandPasteMenu.Controls.Add
    With Copy
        .FaceId = Application.ActiveExplorer.CommandBars _
            ("Menu Bar").Controls("Edit").Controls("Copy").ID
        .Caption = "Copy the selection"
    End With
    Set Paste = CBCopyandPasteMenu.Controls.Add
    With Paste
        .FaceId = Application.ActiveExplorer.CommandBars _
            ("Menu Bar").Controls("Edit").Controls("Paste").ID
        .Caption = "Paste from the Clipboard"
    End With
    CBCopyandPasteMenu.ShowPopup
End Sub
```

The next procedure uses the MouseUp event to display the Data Helper shortcut menu when the right-mouse click occurs over the lstSync control on a UserForm.

```
Private Sub lstSync_MouseUp _
    (ByVal Button As Integer, ByVal Shift As Integer, _
    ByVal X As Single, ByVal Y As Single)
On Error Resume Next
Dim cbrShortcut As CommandBar
Select Case Button
    Case vbKeyLButton 'Left
    Case vbKeyRButton 'Right
        Set cbrShortcut = _
            Application.ActiveExplorer.CommandBars("Data Helper")
        cbrShortcut.Visible = True
        cbrShortcut.ShowPopup X, Y
End Select
End Sub
```

Protecting a Command Bar from User Modification

If you develop a custom command bar, how do you protect the command bar from user modification? A user can modify your command bar either through the user interface or through program code. To prevent changes to your custom command bar, you can set the Enabled property to *False* to make the command bar invisible in the list of Outlook command bars for either the Explorer or Inspector window. Once the Enabled property equals *False*, users cannot modify your custom command bar because they will not be able to see the command bar name in the Toolbar list. You must reset the Enabled property to *True* before you can use the Visible property to display the command bar. However, the Enabled property is not the most secure means of protecting your custom command bar. The following procedure can prevent a user from using the Customize dialog box by disabling the Customize command on the Tools menu and the Toolbar list on the View menu:

```
Sub AllowExplorerCBCustomization(blnAllowEnabled As Boolean)
    ' This procedure allows or prevents access to the
    ' command bars Customize dialog box according to the
    ' value of the blnAllowEnabled argument.
    Dim colCB As CommandBars
    Set colCB = Application.ActiveExplorer.CommandBars
    colCB("Tools").Controls("Customize...").Enabled = blnAllowEnabled
    colCB("Toolbar List").Enabled = blnAllowEnabled
End Sub
```

CommandBarControls Collection Object

CommandBarControls is a collection object that represents all the controls on a command bar. Use the Controls property of a CommandBar object to refer to a control on a command bar. The Controls property is a CommandBarControls collection. If the control is of the type msoControlPopup, it also will have a Controls collection representing each control on the pop-up menu. Pop-up menu controls represent menus and submenus and can be nested several layers deep, as shown in the second example below.

In the following example, the code returns a reference to the New button on the Standard toolbar and displays the type of the control in a message box:

```
Dim ctlCBarControl As CommandBarControl
Set ctlCBarControl = Application.ActiveExplorer.CommandBars _
    ("Standard").Controls("New")
MsgBox "The type of " & ctlCBarControl.Caption _
    & " is " & CBGetCBCtlType(ctlCBarControl), vbInformation
```

Here, the code returns a reference to the Macros control on the Macro pop-up menu located on the Tools menu on the menu bar for the Explorer window:

```
Dim ctlCBarControl As CommandBarControl
Set ctlCBarControl = Application.ActiveExplorer.CommandBars("Menu Bar") _
    .Controls("Tools").Controls("Macro").Controls("Macros...")
```

Because each pop-up menu control is actually a CommandBar object itself, you can also refer to them directly as members of the CommandBars collection. For example, the following line of code returns a reference to the same control as the previous example:

```
Set ctlCBarControl = Application.ActiveExplorer.CommandBars("Macro") _
    .Controls("Macros...")
```

Once you have a reference to a control on a command bar, you can access all available properties and methods of that control.

Note When you refer to a command bar control by using the control's Caption property, you must specify the caption exactly as it appears on the menu. For example, in the previous code sample, the reference to the control caption "Macros..." requires the ellipsis (...) so that it matches how the caption appears on the menu. However, you do not have to include the ampersand that is returned in the controls Caption property when you refer to the control. `Controls("Macros...")` is equivalent to `Controls("&Macros...")` in the example above.

Use the Count property of the CommandBarControls collection to return the number of controls in the collection object. To add controls to the collection, use the *Add* method. The Item property is the default property of the CommandBarControls collection object. Since it is the default property, you do not have to use the Items property to access individual controls in the collection. `Controls("Macros...")` is the equivalent to `Controls.Items("Macros...")`.

CommandBarControl Object

The CommandBarControl object is the child object of the CommandBarControls object and represents a control on a built-in or custom command bar. If you want to refer to a control on a built-in command bar, you should dimension the control variable as a CommandBarControl object. If you want to instantiate an object on a custom command bar, use the CommandBarButton, CommandBarComboBox, or CommandBarPopup object for your item declaration in Visual Basic. If you are using VBScript in an Outlook form, the type of the object is immaterial because all objects are variants by default.

Creating the Appropriate Object Variable

If you do declare a control object as a CommandBarControl, you can still use the properties and methods of CommandBarButton, CommandBarComboBox, and CommandBarPopup objects with the CommandBarControl object. However, dimensioning the control as the correct variable type is the preferred approach. You cannot use the read-only Type property to change the type of an existing custom control. If you want to change the control type, you must delete the control and then add the control with the correct type argument in the *Add* method of the CommandBarControls object.

Adding Custom Command Bar Controls

The CommandBarControl object allows you to modify built-in controls or to add new controls on a custom command bar. Additionally, you can set the properties of the control to determine how the control will appear or what procedure will run when the user clicks the command button or selects a menu item. The difference between CommandBarControl objects is clearly demonstrated in the following step-by-step code example for a command bar named Testing, shown in Figure 10.10, that uses every type of control available for a custom command bar.

Figure 10.10 *The Testing command bar.*

The code required to create Testing is relatively straightforward. The code is presented in sections so you can clearly understand each step of the coding process. The first order of business is to instantiate a CommandBar object so that controls can be added to the command bar's CommandBarControls collection. The line below attempts to instantiate a Testing CommandBar object from the Explorer's CommandBars collection. If Testing already exists and no error occurs, the existing toolbar is deleted before the command bar is added.

```
Sub CBTestingDemo()
    Dim cbTesting As CommandBar
    Dim ctlCBarButton As CommandBarButton
    Dim ctlCBarCombo As CommandBarComboBox
    Dim ctlCBarPopup As CommandBarPopup
    On Error Resume Next
    Set cbTesting = Application.ActiveExplorer.CommandBars("Testing")
    If Err = 0 Then
        cbTesting.Delete
    End If
    Set cbTesting = Application.ActiveExplorer.CommandBars _
        .Add(Name:="Testing", Position:=msoBarTop)
```

Notice that we've added a position argument to the *Add* method in order to place the command bar in the top dock. Now we're ready to add controls to the command bar. The controls we're adding don't actually do anything when they're clicked. We'll cover the OnAction property later in the chapter. We'll add four different types of controls to Testing. The first control is a standard button control that is typical of the controls on toolbars. We've assigned the caption Color to this button and an icon that corresponds to the built-in FaceID 2167, the icon for the color palette. In order for both the icon and the caption to appear, set the button's style to msoButtonIconAndCaption. If you are using a built-in FaceID to provide an icon for a custom button, you must set the button's Visible property to *True* or the icon will not appear, even though the new button appears on the toolbar.

```
    Set ctlCBarButton = cbTesting.Controls.Add(Type:=msoControlButton)
    With ctlCBarButton
        .Caption = "Color"
        .FaceId = 2167
        .Style = msoButtonIconAndCaption
        .Visible = True
```

```
        .TooltipText = "Test color button"
End With
```

The next control to add to Testing is an Edit control. Edit controls are equivalent to edit boxes on an Outlook form. A separate object type does not exist for edit-type controls. Edit controls are actually CommandBarComboBox objects. Their Type property is msoEditBox. Edit and list box controls can show a label before the control if the Style property of the control is set to msoComboLabel. The following code adds an Edit box control to testing and sets its Text property to Red.

```
    Set ctlCBarCombo = cbTesting.Controls.Add(Type:=msoControlEdit)
    With ctlCBarCombo
        .Caption = "Color: "
        .Text = "Red"
        .Style = msoComboLabel
        .TooltipText = "Test Edit box"
    End With
```

The ComboBox control uses many of the same properties and methods of the MSForms combo box that you're familiar with from Outlook forms. You can use the *AddItem* method to add items to the list and the ListIndex property to set or to return the selected item in the list. Like the Edit box control, this combo box uses a caption to identify the value being selected by the user.

```
    Set ctlCBarCombo = cbTesting.Controls.Add(Type:=msoControlComboBox)
    With ctlCBarCombo
        .AddItem "Red"
        .AddItem "Green"
        .AddItem "Blue"
        .ListIndex = 1
        .Caption = "Test Combo box"
    End With
```

Finally, we'll add a Popup control to Testing and then make the toolbar visible. Remember that every Popup control contains a command bar object and a corresponding controls collection. If you want to add items to the Popup, use the *Add* method for the Controls property object of the CommandBarPopup object. The following code adds three button controls to the Popup control. If we added these controls as Popup controls rather than button controls, we would have submenus that, in turn, could contain additional submenus or button controls.

```
    Set ctlCBarPopup = cbTesting.Controls.Add(Type:=msoControlPopup)
    Set ctlCBarControl = ctlCBarPopup.Controls.Add(Type:=msoControlButton)
    ctlCBarControl.Caption = "Red"
    Set ctlCBarControl = ctlCBarPopup.Controls.Add(Type:=msoControlButton)
    ctlCBarControl.Caption = "Green"
    Set ctlCBarControl = ctlCBarPopup.Controls.Add(Type:=msoControlButton)
    ctlCBarControl.Caption = "Blue"
    With ctlCBarPopup
        .Caption = "Test Popup"
```

```
        End With
        cbTesting.Visible = True
End Sub
```

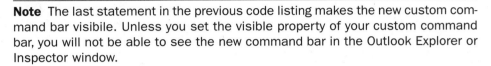

Note The last statement in the previous code listing makes the new custom command bar visibile. Unless you set the visible property of your custom command bar, you will not be able to see the new command bar in the Outlook Explorer or Inspector window.

Running a Procedure For a Control

Of course, adding controls to your custom toolbar is not very useful unless those controls help the user perform an action. In order to run a procedure when a user clicks a control button or a combo box changes, you can set the OnAction property to refer to a sub or function procedure in your project. If you are creating a custom command bar in an Outlook form using VBScript, using the OnAction property is the only way you can run a procedure for a control. If you are creating a COM Add-in, you also have the option of declaring the object variable for the control using the WithEvents keyword and running an event procedure when the control's Click event (CommandBarButton) or Change event (CommandBarComboBox) fires.

The following code from the Items toolbar example causes the *LaunchWordMail* procedure to run when a user clicks the HTML Word Mail icon on the Items toolbar.

```
Set cmdNewButton = cbrNewToolbar.Controls.Add _
    (Type:=msoControlButton) 'Custom button for Word Mail
    With cmdNewButton
        .FaceId = 42
        .BeginGroup = True
        .Visible = True
        .Style = msoButtonIcon
        .Caption = "HTML Word Mail"
        .OnAction = "LaunchWordMail"
    End With
```

Note If you have procedures with the name *LaunchWordMail* in different code modules, none of the procedures will run when the button is clicked. Outlook must be able to resolve the procedure name specified in the OnAction property for the procedure to run correctly. You cannot use traditional *basOutlook.LaunchWordMail* syntax to call a procedure in a specified module.

There is an equivalent OnAction property for CommandBarComboBox controls. Combo box controls run the OnAction procedure when a change event fires. Button controls run the OnAction procedure when a Click event fires. If the Change event causes the OnAction procedure to run, you can examine the ListIndex property of the control to determine the combo box item selected by the user.

If you have multiple controls that point to the same procedure in their OnAction property, use the Parameters property of the control to determine which control has been clicked. You should set the Parameters property of the control when you add the control to its command bar. The Action Property of the CommandBar object returns an object representing the control that has been clicked or changed. This example shows how you could use the Parameter and Action Property properties to branch code execution depending on the Parameter property.

```
Dim ctlCBarControl  As CommandBarControl
Set ctlCBarControl = Application.ActiveExplorer.CommandBars.ActionControl
If ctlCBarControl Is Nothing Then Exit Function
' Examine the Parameter property of the ActionControl to determine
' which control has been clicked
Select Case ctlCBarControl.Parameter
    Case "Next"
    ' Next code here
        olItems.GetNext
    Case "Previous"
    ' Previous code here
        olItems.GetPrevious
End Select
```

Showing and Enabling Controls

Use the Visible property of a control to show or hide the control on a command bar. Use the Enabled property to enable or disable the control on the toolbar. When a control is disabled, it is still visible, but the user cannot perform an action on the control. The following function toggles the state of a command bar control. To test this function, type *?CBCtlToggleVisible("Tools", "Services...")* in the Debug window and press Enter to toggle the Enabled property of the Services command on the Explorer Tools menu.

```
Function CBCtlToggleVisible(strCBarName As String, _
        strCtlCaption As String) As Boolean
    Dim ctlCBarControl As CommandBarControl
    On Error Resume Next

    Set ctlCBarControl = Application.ActiveExplorer _
        .CommandBars(strCBarName).Controls(strCtlCaption)
    ctlCBarControl.Visible = Not ctlCBarControl.Visible
    If Err = 0 Then
        CBCtlToggleVisible = True
    Else
        CBCtlToggleVisible = False
    End If
End Function
```

The Visible property is not the only factor that determines whether a specific menu item is visible on a given menu. If personalized menus are turned on with the AdaptiveMenus property, you can use the IsPriorityDropped property to determine if a menu item is visible on the command bar. If the control's Visible property is set to *True*, the control will not be immediately visible on a personalized menu if IsPriorityDropped is *True*.

> **Note** To determine when to set IsPriorityDropped to *True* for a specific menu item, Outlook maintains a total count of the number of times the menu item was used and a record of the number of different application sessions in which the user has used another menu item in the same menu as this menu item, without using the specific menu item itself. When this value reaches a threshold, the count is decreased. When the count reaches zero, IsPriorityDropped is set to *True.* You cannot set the session value, the threshold value, or the IsPriorityDropped property. You can, however, use the AdaptiveMenus property to disable adaptive menus for specific menus in an application.

Determining the State of a Control

The State property of a control tells you whether a button control is in a down or an up state. The State property is read-only for built-in controls. A good example of a built-in control that displays state is the Folder List control on the Advanced toolbar. When the control's state equals msoButtonDown, the button is depressed on the toolbar. If the control's state equals msoButtonUp, then the button is not depressed on the toolbar. This code examines the state of the Folder List button on the Advanced toolbar.

```
Function DisplayFolderListState()
    Dim ctlCBarButton As CommandBarButton
    Set ctlCBarButton = Application.ActiveExplorer _
        .CommandBars("Advanced").Controls("Folder List")
    Select Case ctlCBarButton.State
        Case msoButtonUp
            MsgBox "Folder List Hidden", vbInformation
        Case msoButtonDown
            MsgBox "Folder List visible", vbInformation
    End Select
End Function
```

Adding Separators Between Controls

If you want to add a separator between buttons on a command bar, set the BeginGroup property for the control to *True*. Group separators on a toolbar provide important visual clues for the user about the relationship of controls. This example adds a group separator before the Choose Form control on the Items toolbar.

```
Set cmdNewButton = cbrNewToolbar.Controls.Add _
(Type:=msoControlButton, ID:=1910) 'Choose Form...
cmdNewButton.BeginGroup = True      'Group Separator
```

Finding a Control

To find a control on a built-in or custom command bar, use the *FindControl* method. The *FindControl* method takes several arguments that facilitate your search. The following example performs a nonrecursive search of the Standard toolbar for the Find A Contact combo box. If a control with a Type of msoControlComboBox is found on the Standard toolbar and the control's caption is Find A Contact, the Text property of the combo box is set to the name of a contact. Setting the combo box Text property causes Outlook to search for the contact name as if a user had actually typed a name in the combo box. If the search completes successfully, Outlook displays the Inspector for the contact item.

```
Sub ContactFindMethod()
    Dim ctlCBarCombo As CommandBarComboBox
    Dim cbrMenuBar As CommandBar
    On Error Resume Next
    Set cbrMenuBar = Application.ActiveExplorer.CommandBars("Standard")
    Set ctlCBarCombo = _
        cbrMenuBar.FindControl (Type:=msoControlComboBox, Recursive:=False)
    If ctlCBarCombo = "Find a Contact" Then 'Caption is default property
        ctlCBarCombo.Text = "Darrique Barton"
    End If
End Sub
```

Using Control Events

Command bar controls raise two separate events, Click and Change, that you can use in place of the OnAction property to run an event procedure when a user action or program code causes an event to fire. The following table displays the control and command bar events in Outlook 2000.

Event	Source Object	Occurs
OnUpdate	CommandBars	When any change occurs to a built-in or custom command bar or to the state of a control on a command bar.
Click	CommandBarButton	When a button or menu item is clicked.
Change	CommandBarComboBox	When a user makes a selection in a drop-down list box or a combo box. The change event also occurs when text is changed in an edit box.

Caution Be aware that you cannot use control events if you are writing VBScript code in an Outlook custom form. In this case, you must use the OnAction property to specify the sub procedure in your code that runs when a toolbar button is clicked.

To write an event procedure for a Command Bar control

1. Declare an object variable using WithEvents in the declarations section of ThisOutlookSession or the class module for your COM Add-in project.

2. Select the object in the Object box of the class module's code window.

3. Select the event name in the Procedure box of the class module's code window.

4. Write event procedure code to respond to the Click or Change event.

The Items Command Bar

At this point, we'll look at the full code listing that operates the Items command bar. The Items command bar would be a trivial example if it did not use Application and Explorer events to refresh the combo box control on the toolbar. If the CustomForm combo box is visible on the toolbar, it displays all the custom forms that a user can create for the current folder. Refer to Chapter 9, "Raise Events and Move to the Head of the Class," if you need additional information about new events in Outlook 2000.

The first requirement is to declare object variables in ThisOutlookSession and instantiate the variables in the Application Startup event. You should note that Collaboration Data Objects (CDO) must be installed in order for the Items toolbar to operate correctly. CDO is not included in the default Outlook 2000 install.

```
Public WithEvents objExpl As Outlook.Explorer
Public gobjCDO As MAPI.Session

Private Sub Application_Startup()
    Set objExpl = Application.ActiveExplorer
    'Create a MAPI Session object
    Set gobjCDO = New MAPI.Session
    'Logon to the Session without displaying logon dialog
    gobjCDO.Logon "", "", False, False
End Sub
```

Once objExpl has been declared using WithEvents in ThisOutlookSession, you can write event procedure code for the BeforeFolderSwitch event. The BeforeFolderSwitch event occurs just before a user action or program code switches folders in the Explorer.

```
Private Sub objExpl_BeforeFolderSwitch(ByVal NewFolder As Object, _
    Cancel As Boolean)
    On Error Resume Next
    If NewFolder Is Nothing Then Exit Sub
    Call CBOutlookItems(NewFolder)
End Sub
```

The *CBOutlookItems* procedure creates the Items toolbar if it does not exist. Otherwise, it simply modifies the New Custom Forms combo box depending on the forms available in the current folder. If no forms are available, the combo box is hidden. The *CBOutlookItems* procedure takes a MAPIFolder object as its sole argument.

The code to create the command bar buttons on the toolbar is fairly straightforward, but it does illustrate three different approaches to adding controls to a custom command bar. A few of the buttons on the bar are built-in buttons for New Post item, Note Item, and so forth. These buttons reflect built-in commands; it is not necessary to provide an OnAction property to create the items. Simply set the ID property of the new control to the ID of a built-in Outlook command bar control. If you do not know the ID property for a built-in command, you can use the *CBGetControlID* procedure in basCommandBars to find the ID. The buttons for HTML Word, Excel, and PowerPoint mail are custom buttons; you must set the OnAction property for these buttons. The OnAction procedures used for these buttons are contained in the basOutlook module located in the VBA Samples folder described earlier. The only combo box on the form is a custom CommandBarComboBox control. We'll show you how we populate this combo box after we list the complete code for the *CBOutlookItems* procedure.

```
'***************************************************************
'Procedure: CBOutlookItems(objFolder as Outlook.MAPIFolder)
'Purpose: Update Items CB with application folder forms
'Argument: MAPIFolder object
'Usage: 'Call this procedure in objExpl_BeforeFolderSwitch
'Returns: n/a
'***************************************************************
Public Sub CBOutlookItems(ByVal objFolder As Outlook.MAPIFolder)
    Dim cbrNewToolbar   As Office.CommandBar
    Dim cmdNewButton    As Office.CommandBarButton
    Dim cmdPostButton As Office.CommandBarButton
    Dim cmdFormButton As Office.CommandBarButton
    Dim cmdNewControl As Office.CommandBarComboBox
    Dim cmdBuiltIn As Office.CommandBarButton
    Dim intCount As Integer

    ' Test if the Items toolbar already exists
    On Error Resume Next
    Set cbrNewToolbar = Application.ActiveExplorer.CommandBars("Items")
    If Err Then
        ' Create a new items toolbar.
        Set cbrNewToolbar = Application.ActiveExplorer.CommandBars.Add _
            (Name:="Items", Position:=msoBarTop, Temporary:=False)
        Set cmdNewButton = cbrNewToolbar.Controls.Add _
        (Type:=msoControlButton) 'MailItem
        With cmdNewButton
            .FaceId = 1757
            .Visible = True
            .Caption = "New Mail Message"
            .Tag = "Mail"
            .Style = msoButtonIcon
            .OnAction = "CreateMail"
        End With
        Set cmdNewButton = cbrNewToolbar.Controls.Add _
        (Type:=msoControlButton, ID:=2687) 'PostItem
        Set cmdNewButton = cbrNewToolbar.Controls.Add _
        (Type:=msoControlButton) 'Custom button for Word Mail
        With cmdNewButton
            .FaceId = 42
            .BeginGroup = True
            .Visible = True
            .Style = msoButtonIcon
```

```
        .Caption = "HTML Word Mail"
        .OnAction = "LaunchWordMail"
End With
Set cmdNewButton = cbrNewToolbar.Controls.Add _
(Type:=msoControlButton) 'Custom button for Excel Mail
With cmdNewButton
        .FaceId = 263
        .BeginGroup = False
        .Visible = True
        .Style = msoButtonIcon
        .Caption = "HTML Excel Mail"
        .OnAction = "LaunchExcelMail"
End With
Set cmdNewButton = cbrNewToolbar.Controls.Add _
(Type:=msoControlButton) 'Custom button for PPT Mail
With cmdNewButton
        .FaceId = 267
        .BeginGroup = False
        .Visible = True
        .Style = msoButtonIcon
        .Caption = "HTML PowerPoint Mail"
        .OnAction = "LaunchPowerPointMail"
End With
Set cmdNewButton = cbrNewToolbar.Controls.Add _
(Type:=msoControlButton) 'Appt
With cmdNewButton
        .FaceId = 1106
        .BeginGroup = True
        .Visible = True
        .Caption = "New Appointment"
        .Tag = "Appointment"
        .Style = msoButtonIcon
        .OnAction = "CreateAppt"
End With
Set cmdNewButton = cbrNewToolbar.Controls.Add _
(Type:=msoControlButton) 'Meeting Request
With cmdNewButton
        .FaceId = 1754
        .Visible = True
        .Caption = "Meeting Request"
        .Tag = "Meeting Request"
        .Style = msoButtonIcon
        .OnAction = "CreateMtgRequest"
End With
Set cmdNewButton = cbrNewToolbar.Controls.Add _
(Type:=msoControlButton) 'Contact
With cmdNewButton
        .FaceId = 1099
        .Visible = True
        .Caption = "New Contact"
        .Tag = "Contact"
        .Style = msoButtonIcon
```

```
        .OnAction = "CreateContact"
End With
Set cmdNewButton = cbrNewToolbar.Controls.Add _
(Type:=msoControlButton) 'Dist List
With cmdNewButton
    .FaceId = 5435
    .Visible = True
    .Caption = "Distribution List"
    .Tag = "DistList"
    .Style = msoButtonIcon
    .OnAction = "CreateDistList"
End With
Set cmdNewButton = cbrNewToolbar.Controls.Add _
(Type:=msoControlButton) 'Task
With cmdNewButton
    .FaceId = 1100
    .Visible = True
    .Caption = "New Task"
    .Tag = "Task"
    .Style = msoButtonIcon
    .OnAction = "CreateTask"
End With
Set cmdNewButton = cbrNewToolbar.Controls.Add _
(Type:=msoControlButton) 'Task Request
With cmdNewButton
    .FaceId = 2006
    .Visible = True
    .Caption = "Task Request"
    .Tag = "TaskRequest"
    .Style = msoButtonIcon
    .OnAction = "CreateTaskRequest"
End With
Set cmdNewButton = cbrNewToolbar.Controls.Add _
(Type:=msoControlButton) 'Journal Entry
With cmdNewButton
    .FaceId = 1990
    .Visible = True
    .Caption = "New Journal"
    .Tag = "Journal"
    .Style = msoButtonIcon
    .OnAction = "CreateJournal"
End With
Set cmdNewButton = cbrNewToolbar.Controls.Add _
(Type:=msoControlButton, ID:=1758) 'Note
Set cmdNewButton = cbrNewToolbar.Controls.Add _
(Type:=msoControlButton, ID:=2576) 'Office Document
Set cmdNewButton = cbrNewToolbar.Controls.Add _
(Type:=msoControlButton) 'Choose Form...
With cmdNewButton
    .Visible = True
    .Caption = "Ch&oose Form..."
    .Tag = "ChooseForm"
```

```
                .Style = msoButtonCaption
                .OnAction = "CreateForm"
            End With
            cmdNewButton.BeginGroup = True       'Group Separator
             Set cmdNewControl = cbrNewToolbar.Controls.Add _
            (Type:=msoControlDropdown)            'New Custom Form
            'GetFormDescriptions returns a variant array with
            'display name and message class for forms published
            'in the application folder. Hidden forms are not available.
            avarForms = GetFormDescriptions(objFolder.EntryID, objFolder.StoreID)
            'No custom forms published in folder
            If avarForms(0, 0) = "" Then
                cmdNewControl.Visible = False
            Else
                For i = 0 To UBound(avarForms, 1)
                    cmdNewControl.AddItem avarForms(i, 0)
                Next
                With cmdNewControl
                    .Enabled = True
                    .Visible = True
                    .BeginGroup = True
                    .Style = msoComboLabel
                    .ListIndex = 1
                    .Width = 200
                    .Caption = "New: "
                    .Tag = "New: "
                    .OnAction = "cmdCreateForm"
                End With
            End If
            'Display toolbar
            cbrNewToolbar.Visible = True
        Else
            'Modify existing toolbar
            Set cmdPostButton = cbrNewToolbar.FindControl(Tag:="Post")
            Select Case Application.ActiveExplorer.CurrentFolder.DefaultItemType
                Case olMailItem
                cmdPostButton.Visible = True
                Case olPostItem
                cmdPostButton.Visible = True
                Case Else
                cmdPostButton.Visible = False
            End Select
            'Find control on toolbar
            Set cmdNewControl = _
                cbrNewToolbar.FindControl(Type:=msoControlDropdown)
            'Clear dropdown
            cmdNewControl.Clear
            'GetFormDescriptions returns a variant array with
            'display name and message class for forms published
            'in the application folder. Hidden forms are not available.
            avarForms = GetFormDescriptions(objFolder.EntryID, objFolder.StoreID)
            'No custom forms published in folder
```

```
        If avarForms(0, 0) = "" Then
            cmdNewControl.Visible = False
            Exit Sub
        Else
            For i = 0 To UBound(avarForms, 1)
                cmdNewControl.AddItem avarForms(i, 0)
            Next
            With cmdNewControl
                .Enabled = True
                .Visible = True
                .BeginGroup = True
                .Style = msoComboLabel
                .ListIndex = 1
                .Width = 200
                .Caption = "New: "
                .Tag = "New: "
                .OnAction = "cmdCreateForm"
            End With
        End If
    End If
End Sub
```

The only missing part of the the *CBOutlookItems* procedure is the *GetFormDescriptions* procedure. This procedure returns a variant array that contains the display name and message class of every visible custom form published in the folder. If no custom forms are published in the folder, the returned array contains an empty string in its first element. When *CBOutlookItems* detects that the first element is blank, it hides the combo box control on the Items toolbar. *GetFormDescriptions* requires advanced knowledge of Collaboration Data Objects (CDO) and Exchange Server hidden messages in a folder. Suffice it to say that, when you need to probe deeper into the workings of Exchange, you must hit the books on CDO. Several Web sites are listed at the end of this chapter that will help you broaden your CDO knowledge.

Here is a brief explanation of what takes place in GetFormDescriptions. GetFormDescriptions has two arguments for the EntryID and StoreID of the folder whose custom forms you want to retrieve. First, the Outlook EntryID and StoreID properties are used to instantiate a CDO folder object with the CDO *GetFolderFromID* method. You should not confuse an Outlook MAPIFolder object with a CDO Folder object. You will raise a Type Mismatch error if you try to set a CDO folder object to an Outlook MAPIFolder object.

Custom forms published in a folder are actually hidden messages stored in the folder. You cannot retrieve these hidden messages using the Outlook 2000 Object Model. In order to determine which custom forms are available in a given folder, you use CDO to create a HiddenMessages collection object for messages that have a message class of IPM.Microsoft.FolderDesign.FormDescription. Next you iterate over the HiddenMessages collection and determine which forms in the folder are hidden using the PR_HIDDEN_FORM property. Finally, you dimension a variant array and place the form's display name and message class into the elements of the array.

```
Public Function GetFormDescriptions(strEntryID, strStoreID) As Variant
Dim objFolder As MAPI.Folder
Dim objMsgFilter As MAPI.MessageFilter
Dim colHiddenMsgs As MAPI.Messages
Dim objHiddenMsg As MAPI.Message
Dim avarArray As Variant
Dim intCount, intLoop As Integer
'MAPI Properties for FormDescription Hidden Messages
Const PR_HIDDEN_FORM = &H6803001E
Const PR_FORM_MESSAGECLASS = &H6800001E
Set objFolder = ThisOutlookSession.gobjCDO.GetFolder(strEntryID, strStoreID)
Set colHiddenMsgs = objFolder.HiddenMessages
'colHiddenMsgs.Sort CdoAscending, CdoPR_DISPLAY_NAME
If colHiddenMsgs.Count Then
    'Set a filter on messages collection
    Set objMsgFilter = colHiddenMsgs.Filter
    objMsgFilter.Type = "IPM.Microsoft.FolderDesign.FormsDescription"
    'Sort FormDescription collection on Display Name
    colHiddenMsgs.Sort CdoAscending, CdoPR_DISPLAY_NAME
    If colHiddenMsgs.Count Then
        'Count number of forms in folder excluding hidden forms
        For Each objHiddenMsg In colHiddenMsgs
            If Not (objHiddenMsg.Fields(PR_HIDDEN_FORM)) Then
                intCount = intCount + 1
            End If
        Next
        If intCount Then
            'Dimension variant array to hold forms
            ReDim avarArray(intCount - 1, 1)
            For Each objHiddenMsg In colHiddenMsgs
                If Not (objHiddenMsg.Fields(PR_HIDDEN_FORM)) Then
                    avarArray(intLoop, 0) = _
                    objHiddenMsg.Fields(CdoPR_DISPLAY_NAME)
                    avarArray(intLoop, 1) = _
                    objHiddenMsg.Fields(PR_FORM_MESSAGECLASS)
                    intLoop = intLoop + 1
                End If
            Next
            GetFormDescriptions = avarArray
        Else
            GetFormDescriptions = Empty
        End If
    Else
        GetFormDescriptions = Empty
    End If
End If
End Function
```

Once avarForms has been created for the current folder, a brief procedure called *cmdCreateForm* does the work of creating a new form using the message class of the form selected by the user in the Items toolbar combo box. This procedure uses the *Add* method of the folder's Items collection object to add a custom form and then display the form. For this procedure to operate correctly, it is necessary to dimension avarForms as a public variable in the basCommandBars module.

```
Private Sub cmdCreateForm()
    Dim objCB As Office.CommandBar
    Dim objCBB As Office.CommandBarComboBox
    Dim objFolder As Outlook.MAPIFolder
    Dim objItem As Object
    On Error Resume Next
    Set objCB = ThisOutlookSession.objExpl.CommandBars("Items")
    Set objCBB = objCB.FindControl(Type:=msoControlDropdown)
    Set objFolder = ThisOutlookSession.objExpl.CurrentFolder
    'Column 1 of array contains message class for custom form
    'objFolder.Items.Add("IPM.Note.My Custom Note")
    'avarForms is a public variable
    Set objItem = objFolder.Items.Add _
        (avarForms(objCBB.ListIndex - 1, 1))
    objItem.Display
End Sub
```

CommandBarButton Object

The CommandBarButton object represents a button control on a command bar. We have already discussed in detail many of the properties and methods of the CommandBarButton. For additional information, search for CommandBarButton in Microsoft Outlook Visual Basic Reference Help. The Outlook 2000 Explorer and Inspector command bars offer a major advancement over command bars in previous versions of Outlook. It is possible to create custom command bars for an Inspector in a previous version of Outlook if you use the Office 97 CommandBars object. However, custom command bars in Outlook 97 and Outlook 98 do not persist between Outlook sessions and cannot be created for the Explorer window. You can use the *Execute* method to cause built-in commands to run, but the functionality and customization potential of toolbars is limited in previous versions of Outlook.

Note For additional information regarding CommandBars in previous versions of Outlook, see the following Q articles in the Microsoft Knowledge Base:

Q173604, OL97: How to Use Command Bars in Outlook Solutions

Q182394, OL98: How to Use Command Bars in Outlook Solutions

CommandBarComboBox Object

The CommandBarComboBox object represents a Combo box or an Edit box control on a command bar. When you add the combo box to a command bar, you specify the type of combo box in the *Add* method. The following table lists some of the unique properties, methods, and events of a CommandBarComboBox object.

Type	Name	Description
Property	DropDownLines	Returns or sets the number of items displayed in the drop-down list box. If the number of items in the list is greater than DropDownLines, a scroll bar appears in the drop-down list box.
	DropDownWidth	Returns or sets the width in pixels of the combo box drop-down.
	ListCount	Returns the number of items in the list.
	ListIndex	Returns or sets the index of the selected item in the list.
	Text	Returns or sets the text in the edit portion of the control.
Method	AddItem	Adds an item to the list.
	Clear	Clears the items in the list.
	RemoveItem	Removes an item from the list.
Event	Change	Occurs when a user changes the selection in a combo box or the text in an edit box.

CommandBarPopup Object

The CommandBarPopup object represents a Pop-up control on a command bar. Pop-up controls are unique in that every control contains a CommandBar property object. You can use the CommandBar object to access the child controls of a CommandBarPopup object. The following example uses the CommandBar property object to add additional buttons to the Pop-up control.

```
Set ctlCBarPopup = cbTesting.Controls.Add(Type:=msoControlPopup)
Set cbTestPopup = ctlCBarPopup.CommandBar
Set ctlCBarControl = cbTestPopup.Controls.Add(Type:=msoControlButton)
ctlCBarControl.Caption = "Red"
Set ctlCBarControl = cbTestPopup.Controls.Add(Type:=msoControlButton)
ctlCBarControl.Caption = "Green"
Set ctlCBarControl = cbTestPopup.Controls.Add(Type:=msoControlButton)
ctlCBarControl.Caption = "Blue"
With ctlCBarPopup
    .Caption = "Test Popup"
End With
```

Assistant Object

The Assistant property object of the Outlook Application object represents the Office Assistant. The Assistant presents an interactive, animated character that gives the user information in an entertaining way. The Assistant can provide the finishing touches to your corporate or commercial Outlook COM Add-in. You can also program most attributes of the Assistant from VBScript in Outlook forms. The Assistant is now frameless in Office

2000 and introduces some new characters in addition to Clippit and the traditional cast of favorites. Like the CommandBars object, the Assistant object properly belongs to the Office 2000 Object Model rather than the Outlook 2000 Object Model. Figure 10.11 illustrates Clippit in the new frameless incarnation.

What would you like to do?

- Recall or replace a message you've already sent
- Make a sent message unavailable after a specified date
- Outlook features available when you use Microsoft Exchange Server
- Symbols in Microsoft Exchange Server
- None of the above, look for more help on the Web

How do I recall a message?

Options   Search

Figure 10.11   *The new Office 2000 Assistant.*

Microsoft Agent

The Assistant represents a subset of Microsoft Agent technology. If you want to add speech capabilities to your Assistant, you should consider using Microsoft Agent version 2.0 or later in place of the Assistant. You can use the Agent control in Office applications, on Web pages, on Outlook forms, or in any environment that supports ActiveX controls.

For additional information regarding Microsoft Agent, please visit:
http://www.microsoft.com/workshop/imedia/agent/default.asp/

To download Microsoft Agent, go to this URL:
http://www.microsoft.com/workshop/imedia/agent/agentdl.asp/

You can access the Assistant and its child properties by using the Assistant property of the Outlook Application object. See the Assistant Demo form in Figure 10.12. You can run the code listings relating to the Assistant by replacing your current VBAProject.otm with the VBA Project.otm on the companion CD-ROM. See the instructions under "Exploring the Command Bars Collection," discussed earlier in this chapter. You can also import only the code that is relating to the Assistant by following these instructions:

To run the Assistant samples

1. Open the Visual Basic Editor by pressing Alt+F11.
2. Drag frmAssistant, clsAssistantProperties, and clsTimer from the VBA Samples folder to a file system folder such as C:\My Documents.
3. Select Import File on the File menu to import basAssistant, frmAssistant, clsAssistantProperties, and clsTimer into your Outlook VBAProject.otm.
4. Open the Forms folder in the VBA Project Explorer window.
5. Double-click frmAssistant.
6. Select the Run Sub/UserForm button on the VBA toolbar to display the form.

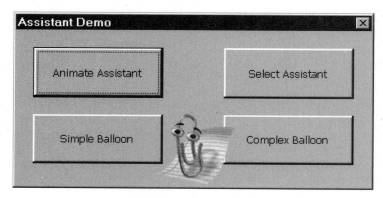

Figure 10.12 *The Assistant Demo form provides a demonstration of Assistant programming examples.*

Displaying the Assistant

Turn the Assistant on or off using the On property of the Assistant object. The On setting is global to all Office 2000 applications. If you set Outlook's Application.Assistant.On property to *False*, you will also turn off the Assistant for all other Office applications. The following procedure turns the Assistant on and makes it visible:

```
Sub ShowAssistant()
    With Application.Assistant
        If Not .On Then
            .On = True
        ElseIf Not .Visible Then
            .Visible = True
        End If
    End With
End Sub
```

Here is the same procedure adapted for use in VBScript in an Outlook form:

```
Sub ShowAssistant()
```

```
      Set oAssistant = Item.Application.Assistant
      If oAssistant.On = False Then
          oAssistant.On = True
      ElseIf oAssistant.Visible = False Then
          OAssistant.Visible = True
      End If
End Sub
```

> **Note** If you want to program the Assistant and dependent objects, it's a good idea to save the state of the Assistant before you modify settings. When your process is completed, you should restore the Assistant to its original state. A class named clsAssistantProperties in the VBA Samples folder allows you to save the current state of the Assistant and then restore the Assistant to its original state when your procedure completes execution. See the *TestSaveAssistProperties* procedure in basAssistant in the VBA Samples folder for additional details.

Changing the Assistant Character

A variety of characters are available for the Assistant. You can also change the character programmatically, if necessary. However, you should be aware that all of the Office Assistants are not installed by default. To change the character to an Assistant that has not been installed requires running the Windows Installer to install the new character. The following procedure will change the Assistant:

```
' Assistant constants in declarations section of basAssistant
Const ASST_CHAR_CHANGED    As Integer = 0
Const ASST_CHAR_SAMECHAR   As Integer = 1

Function ChangeCharacter(strCharName As String) As Integer
    With Application.Assistant
        If UCase(.FileName) = UCase(strCharName) Then
            ChangeCharacter = ASST_CHAR_SAMECHAR
            Exit Function
        End If
        .FileName = strCharName
        ChangeCharacter = ASST_CHAR_CHANGED
    End With
End Function
```

Balloon Object

The Assistant Balloon object contains text, option buttons (known as labels), check boxes, and command buttons. You can present a much more complex set of choices for an end user in an Assistant Balloon than you can using standard Visual Basic message boxes. From an object model point of view, a Balloon object contains BalloonCheckBoxes and also the BalloonLabels collection objects. These collection objects, in turn, contain BalloonCheckBox and BalloonLabel objects, respectively.

Creating a Balloon

Only one balloon can be displayed for an Assistant object. Consequently, the Balloon object does not have a parent collection object. To create a balloon, use the NewBalloon property of the Assistant object to set a reference to a Balloon object as follows:

```
Sub BasicBalloon()
    Dim balBalloon As Balloon
    Set balBalloon = Application.Assistant.NewBalloon
        With balBalloon
            ' Set Balloon properties here
            .Heading = "Basic Balloon"
            .Icon = msoIconNone
            .Text = "Hello world!"
            .Show
        End With
End Sub
```

Adding Colors to Balloon Text

You supply the text that appears in a balloon by using the Text property. You can use Visual Basic intrinsic constants such as vbCrLf to cause the text to wrap at designated locations in the text string. You can also cause the balloon text to appear in different colors or to contain underlined text. The following procedure creates a simple balloon with text colors and underlining:

```
Sub ShowSimpleBalloon()
    Dim balSimple          As Balloon
    Dim strMessage         As String
    Dim strHeading         As String
    Dim blnAssistVisible   As Boolean

    strHeading = "This is a simple balloon."
    strMessage = "When you have finished reading this message, _
        & click OK to proceed." _
        & vbCrLf & "{cf 249}This text is red." & vbCrLf _
        & "{cf 252}This text is blue." & vbCrLf _
        & "{cf 0}This text has a {ul 1}word{ul 0} that is underlined." _
        & vbCrLf & "This text is plain."
    blnAssistVisible = Application.Assistant.Visible

    Set balSimple = Application.Assistant.NewBalloon
    With balSimple
        .Text = strMessage
        .Heading = strHeading
        If Not blnAssistVisible Then
            Call ShowAssistant
        End If
        .Show
    End With
    Application.Assistant.Visible = blnAssistVisible
End Sub
```

For additional information regarding the control characters necessary to change balloon text colors, see the help for the Text property of the Balloon object in Microsoft Outlook Visual Basic Reference Help.

Running Procedures with the Callback Property

A balloon displays in either a modal or modeless state. If you set the Balloon's Mode property to msoModeModeless, the user can continue to work in Outlook while the Balloon is displayed. When the balloon's Mode property is set to msoModeModal, users must respond to the balloon before they can return to the application. Modeless balloons can use the Callback property of the balloon to specify a procedure that runs when the user selects an option label in the balloon. This procedure must be constructed with three arguments to operate successfully. The example below shows a modeless balloon that allows the user to select an Office application for an HTML mail envelope. The Assistant displays an animation indicating that mail is being sent when the user makes a selection.

```
Sub SelectHTMLMail()
    Dim blnBalloon As Balloon
    Set blnBalloon = Assistant.NewBalloon
    With blnBalloon
        .Button = msoButtonSetCancel
        .Heading = "Select HTML Mail"
        .Labels(1).Text = "Word Mail"
        .Labels(2).Text = "Excel Mail"
        .Labels(3).Text = "PowerPoint Mail"
        .BalloonType = msoBalloonTypeButtons
        .Mode = msoModeModeless
        .Callback = "ProcessHTMLMail"
        .Show
    End With
End Sub

Sub ProcessHTMLMail(bln As Balloon, lbtn As Long, lPriv As Long)
    If lbtn > 0 Then
        Assistant.Animation = msoAnimationSendingMail
    End If
    Select Case lbtn
        Case 1
            Call LaunchWordMail
        Case 2
            Call LaunchExcelMail
        Case 3
            Call LaunchPowerPointMail
    End Select
    bln.Close
End Sub
```

Using Labels for a Single-Choice Balloon

If the balloon displays modally, the user must make a choice in the balloon or use a balloon button to dismiss the balloon. If your balloon allows users to make only a single choice from a list of choices, use the BalloonLabel object to create a list of options. BalloonLabel objects appear as option buttons on the balloon by default. You can also cause the Balloon Label to appear as a number or a bullet by setting the BalloonType property. The following procedure asks the user to choose an Assistant character. If the user clicks the Cancel button at the bottom of the balloon, the Assistant is dismissed.

```
Sub TestChooseAssistant()
    Dim intRetval As Integer
    Dim strChoice As String
    Dim balBalloon As Balloon

    With Application.Assistant
        Set balBalloon = .NewBalloon
    End With
    With balBalloon
        .Button = msoButtonSetCancel
        .Heading = "Select Assistant"
        .Text = "Select one of the following " _
            & "Assistant options:"
        .Labels(1).Text = "Clippit"
        .Labels(2).Text = "Genius"
        .Labels(3).Text = "Rocky"
        ' Show the balloon.
        intRetval = .Show
    End With

    Select Case intRetval
        Case 1
            ChangeCharacter ("clippit.acs")
        Case 2
            ChangeCharacter ("genius.acs")
        Case 3
            ChangeCharacter ("rocky.acs")
    End Select
End Sub
```

Using Check Boxes for a Multiple-Choice Balloon

If you require the user to select one or more choices from a list of options, use the BalloonCheckBox object instead of the BalloonLabel object in your balloon. If you use a balloon check box, you will have to write code that iterates over the BalloonCheckBox objects in the balloon to determine which check boxes were checked. The following procedure uses check boxes to determine which safety reports should be printed:

```
Sub TestComplexBalloon()
Dim i, intPrinted As Integer
With Assistant.NewBalloon
    .Icon = msoIconAlertQuery
    .Heading = "Regional Safety Data"
    .Text = "Select the region(s) you want to print."
    For i = 1 To 4
```

```
            .Checkboxes(i).Text = "Region " & i
        Next
        .Button = msoButtonSetOkCancel
        If .Show = msoBalloonButtonOK Then
            intPrinted = 0
            For i = 1 To 4
                If .Checkboxes(i).Checked = True Then
                    ' Code to print region data.
                    intPrinted = intPrinted + 1
                    MsgBox "Region " & i & " data printed.", vbInformation
                End If
            Next
            If intPrinted = 0 Then MsgBox "No data printed.", vbInformation
        End If
    End With
End Sub
```

Where To Go from Here

For additional information about the subjects discussed in this chapter, see the following resources.

Working with Office 2000 Objects

Microsoft Corporation. "Understanding Office Objects and Object Models." Chapter 4 in *Microsoft Office 2000/Visual Basic Programmer's Guide.* Redmond, WA: Microsoft Press, 1999.

Working with Software Assistants

Microsoft Corporation. *Developing for Microsoft Agent.* Redmond, WA: Microsoft Press, 1998.

Microsoft Agent Web site
http://www.microsoft.com/workshop/imedia/agent/default.asp/

Part IV
Beyond the Basics

Chapter 11, "Using VBA and VBScript with Outlook," introduces VBScript and the Microsoft Script Editor and provides a wide variety of code examples for the most commonly performed tasks using VBA and VBScript in Outlook. Chapter 12, "Distribute and Maintain Applications," shows you how to distribute forms in folders and provides some techniques for maintaining applications. It also covers how mobile users can use offline folders, increasing the effectiveness of using applications in collecting and recording information while in the field.

Chapter 11
Using VBA and VBScript with Outlook

In This Chapter

In response to fervent requests from many Outlook developers, Outlook 2000 now supports Visual Basic for Applications (VBA) in addition to Visual Basic Scripting Edition (VBScript). This chapter addresses both VBA and VBScript from the perspective of the Outlook Object Model. For additional information on the new events supported by Outlook 2000, see Chapter 9, "Raise Events and Move to the Head of the Class," and Chapter 13, "Creating COM Add-Ins with Visual Basic."

Developers should be aware that VBA is supported only within the context of the running Outlook application. The development environment for Outlook 2000 custom forms programming remains VBScript. Outlook custom forms cannot contain VBA code. VBScript behind forms still provides a simple yet powerful way to enable form-level automation and have that automation travel between recipients.

Think of Outlook VBA, in contrast, as a personal development tool. VBA provides an integrated, high-end design environment for creating solutions at the Application level. VBA solutions can include all the new Outlook 2000 events, as well as existing Outlook 97 and Outlook 98 events at the form level. A single VBA project also can be digitally signed and distributed to users within a corporation.

The greatest significance of Microsoft's inclusion of VBA in Outlook 2000 is that programmers will be able to begin COM Add-in development using VBA, and then convert their VBA code to a compiled Visual Basic COM Add-in. COM Add-ins greatly extend the power and functionality of Outlook 2000 by taking advantage of over 30 new events in the Outlook 2000 Object Model. Supported events include NewMail, Startup, Quit, SendMail, NewInspector, FolderSwitch, ViewSwitch, and SelectionChange, just to name a few.

Microsoft intends for COM Add-ins to replace Exchange Client Extensions which require C++ as the development language and which are difficult to write and install. Developed using any COM-compliant development tool, COM Add-ins can be digitally signed with certificates for security authentication, and can be deployed to the enterprise with the Office 2000 Custom Installation Wizard. Possible COM Add-in scenarios include custom rules that fire when new mail arrives, custom and third-party applications that control the Outlook user interface to provide unique functionality, and integration of Outlook with corporate databases.

This chapter primarily addresses the use of VBScript in Outlook forms. Most of the code examples can be extended directly in Outlook VBA. Exceptions are noted accordingly. For detailed information about the use of the Visual Basic Editor and VBA in Outlook, see Chapter 9, "Raise Events and Move to the Head of the Class."

Using either VBA or VBScript in Outlook, you can create procedures that control Outlook folders, forms, items, pages, properties, actions, events, and controls. For example, you can create procedures that use code to create and send or post items. You can also use VBA or VBScript to write information from an Outlook item to a database, and you can display information from a database in an Outlook item. In addition, you can write Outlook code to automate processes. For example, you can create a procedure for a Bulk Mailer Announcement form that automatically addresses an announcement message to all users in a specified Contacts folder.

This chapter is designed to give you the fundamental skills and knowledge you need to create collaborative applications using VBA and VBScript. You'll find items demonstrating almost all the code examples in this chapter in the VBScript Samples folder. This chapter covers how to use VBA or VBScript to:

- Reference a folder collection or a folder in the Folder List
- Create, open, send, and post standard and custom items
- Open and close standard and custom forms
- Set and change field values in items
- Hide or show a form page
- Change the properties of a control on a page
- Specify the recipients of an item
- Modify Outlook events

To open the VBScript Samples folder

- In the Folder List, expand the Building Microsoft Outlook 2000 Applications folder, expand the folder 4. Beyond the Basics, expand the VBScript folder, and then click the VBScript Samples folder.

VBScript Versions

The following table lists the versions of VBScript and their relationship to the various versions of Outlook and Internet Explorer. Both Outlook 98 and Outlook 2000 require a minimal install of Internet Explorer 4.0 or later, even if another default browser is installed on the computer. Users of earlier versions of Outlook can upgrade to a later version of VBScript without upgrading their Outlook version. Most of the examples in this book assume that you are using VBScript 3.0 or later. If you are using Outlook 97 and your installed VBScript version is still 1.0, you should definitely upgrade to VBScript 3.0 or later. Any version-specific VBScript code will be noted in the examples in this chapter.

Host Application	VBScript Version				
	1.0	2.0	3.0	4.0	5.0
Microsoft Internet Explorer 3.0	X				
Microsoft Outlook 97	X				
Microsoft Internet Information Server 3.0		X			
Microsoft Internet Explorer 4.0			X		
Microsoft Windows Scripting Host 1.0			X		
Microsoft Outlook 98			X		
Microsoft Visual Studio 6.0				X	
Microsoft Internet Explorer 5.0					X

Determining the VBScript Version in Code

Use the following function to determine the current VBScript version in code. You can also open the ScriptEngine Object form containing the *GetScriptEngineInfo* function in the VBScript Samples folder. If you require a specific version of VBScript, you can use the GetScriptEngineInfo procedure to warn the user or to initiate a download that upgrades the VBScript version. Because of a memory leak in VBScript 1.0 and the greatly expanded functionality in VBScript 3.0 and later, it is strongly recommend that you install VBScript 3.0 or later for any Outlook forms application.

```
Function GetScriptEngineInfo
    Dim s
    On Error Resume Next
    ' Build string with necessary info
    s = ScriptEngine & " Version "
    If Err Then ' VBScript 1.0
        GetScriptEngineInfo = "VBScript Version 1.0"
    Exit Function
    End If
    s = s & ScriptEngineMajorVersion & "."
    s = s & ScriptEngineMinorVersion & "."
    s = s & ScriptEngineBuildVersion
    GetScriptEngineInfo = s
End Function
```

The Outlook Script Editor

With the Script Editor, which is available for each form, you can add procedures to forms to control an Outlook application or another application such as Microsoft Word or Microsoft Excel. Remember, however, that if your primary purpose is to control the Outlook application rather than an Outlook form, you should be using VBA instead of VBScript behind forms. In addition, you can create procedures to control Outlook folders, forms, items, controls, and properties in items. For example, you can create a procedure to automatically set a folder as the active folder, and then create and post an item to the folder. Or you can create a procedure that creates a collection of items in a folder based on a specified filter, and then change a field value for each item in the collection.

To view the Outlook Script Editor

1. In Inbox, click New Mail Message on the Actions menu.
2. On the Tools menu of the form, click Forms, and then click Design This Form.
3. On the Form menu of the form, click View Code.

Development Tip

Customize the Inspector standard toolbar to display toolbar buttons for the Design This Form and View Code commands. If you do a significant amount of forms development work, you'll appreciate having toolbar buttons right in front of you when you want to switch to Design mode or to inspect code behind the form. Follow these steps to customize the Standard Inspector Toolbar:

1. Open a new Mail Message by pressing Ctrl+N.
2. Select Customize from the Tools menu.
3. Click Tools in the Categories list box on the Commands page of the Customize dialog box.
4. Drag the Design This Form command from the Commands list box to the Standard toolbar.
5. Click Form Design in the Categories list box.
6. Drag the View Code command from the Commands list box to the Standard toolbar.
7. Click Close to dismiss the Customize dialog box.

An Introduction to Using the Script Editor

As an introduction to using the Script Editor, this section describes how to add code to the PropertyChange event to show a message any time you change a standard field value on a Mail Message form. The PropertyChange event is triggered whenever a standard field value changes on a form. For example, if you change the standard Importance or Sensitivity options on a Message form, the PropertyChange event is triggered because a field value has been changed.

To create and test a PropertyChange event

1. On the Script Editor Script menu, click Event Handler.
2. In the Insert Event Handler dialog box, double-click PropertyChange.
3. Add the code shown in Figure 11.1.
4. Click Close on the Script Editor File menu.
5. On the Form menu of the form, click Run This Form.

6. On the Standard toolbar of the form in Run mode, click Importance: High.

7. Click OK to close the message.

8. On the File menu of the form in Run mode, click Close.

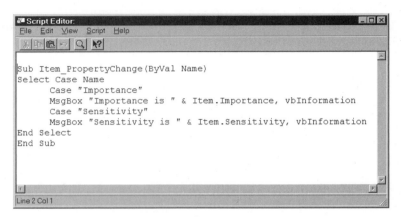

Figure 11.1 *The PropertyChange event in the Outlook Script Editor.*

If there is an error in the syntax of the code when you run the form, Outlook will display a message and immediately stops executing the code.

Note Changes you make to a script do not affect forms that are currently running. If you want to compare the effect of a code change, run one form, change the procedure you want to test, and then run a second instance of the form (from the form that is in Design mode). You can then compare the two forms in Run mode to see how the code change affects the second instance.

Jumping to a Line of Code

As you test procedures, you will see error messages referring to specific lines of code if there are errors in your code. If you use On Error Resume Next to suppress error messages, you will not see an error message unless you explicitly trap the error. The Script Editor provides a way to jump to a particular line of code.

To jump to a line of code

1. On the Script Editor Edit menu, click Go To.

2. In the Line Number text box, type the line number, and then click OK.

Troubleshooting Code Using the Microsoft Script Editor

The Microsoft Script Editor is a new tool included with Office 2000 that helps you control the execution of a script so you can observe where run-time errors occur. You can view and change the value of a variable while the script is running, which lets you observe how different values affect the execution of the script. You can see the names of all the procedures that are currently executing. The Microsoft Script Editor lets you examine the properties of all variables in the current procedure in the Watch window, including the properties and dependent property objects of the Item object itself. The Microsoft Script Editor replaces previous versions of the Internet Explorer Script Debugger used to debug VBScript behind forms for Outlook 97 and Outlook 98.

> **Note** The Microsoft Script Editor is included in the Office 2000 Web Scripting Office Tools component, which you can install after installing Outlook 2000. The Script Editor is not installed by default for a typical installation.

To install the Microsoft Script Editor

1. Insert the Office 2000 CD-ROM into your CD-ROM drive.
2. Click Start, click Settings, and then click Control Panel.
3. Double-click Add/Remove Programs.
4. On the Install/Uninstall page, click Microsoft Office 2000, and then click Add/Remove.
5. In the Microsoft Office 2000 Maintenance Mode dialog box, click Add or Remove Features.
6. Double-click the Office Tools item to expand the item in the Microsoft Office 2000: Update Features dialog box.
7. Double-click the HTML Source Editing item under Office Tools to expand the item.
8. Click the Web Scripting drop-down item and select Run From My Computer.
9. Click Update Now to complete the installation of Script Editor.

To launch the Microsoft Script Editor

1. With a form in Design mode, on the Form menu, click View Code
2. Enter a Stop statement at the point in your code where you want to halt code execution and invoke the Microsoft Script Editor (see Figure 11.2). Be certain to remove the Stop statement when you have completed the debugging process.
3. Select Run This Form from the Form menu.
4. When you see an alert box stating "An Exception Of Type 'Runtime Error' Was Not Handled. Would You Like To Debug The Application?", click Yes to open the Script Editor. Answer No to "Would You Like To Open A Project For Debugging?"

5. You can now debug your code by stepping through the code, examining variables in the immediate window, and watching expressions and variables in the Watch window. Press F11 to step through the code in the Text Editor window.

6. Close the Microsoft Script Editor when you are finished with the debugging process.

Note When the Script Editor is active, Outlook will not respond normally to Explorer or Inspector window commands. You will not be able to restore Outlook windows from the Windows Taskbar while code execution is paused in the Script Editor. You should close the Microsoft Script Editor window to return control to Outlook.

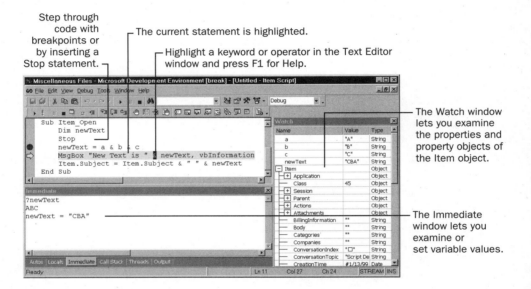

Figure 11.2 *The Microsoft Script Editor.*

Tip You can also obtain context-sensitive help when you are debugging your code. Follow these steps to receive context-sensitive help in the Microsoft Script Editor:

1. Place the insertion point under the keyword or operator for which you need help.

2. Press F1.

Note The Microsoft Script Editor allows you to view the script and copy text from it, but you cannot use the debugger to interactively edit the script in Outlook. You can, however, change the value of procedure and script variables in the Immediate window and insert breakpoints into the running script.

Controlling How a Script Executes

The Debug toolbar lets you control the execution of your script at run time. Using this toolbar, you can do any of the following:

- Set and clear breakpoints that halt execution of the script at the breakpoint.
- Step through the script, executing each line one line at a time.
- Resume normal execution after stopping for a breakpoint.

More Info For more information about controlling script execution, see Microsoft Script Editor Help.

Entering a Breakpoint

Once your script has halted execution at a Stop statement, you can enter breakpoints in the code window. In Outlook, you can only set breakpoints once code execution has halted due to a Stop statement. You can set or remove a breakpoint only at run time. When you set a breakpoint, a red dot is displayed in the selection margin of the Text Editor window next to the line containing the breakpoint. After setting breakpoints, you can run the application in the development environment. When execution reaches the first breakpoint, the code pauses and starts the debugger. The next line to be executed is indicated in the Text Editor window by a yellow arrow in the selection margin.

To set or remove a breakpoint

1. In the Text Editor window, move the insertion point to the line of code where you want to set or remove a breakpoint and click in the selection margin.

2. Move the insertion point to the line of code you want to insert a breakpoint into. From the Debug menu, choose Insert Breakpoint or press F9. To remove the breakpoint, choose Remove Breakpoint from the Debug menu or press F9.

3. Or from the Debug menu, choose the Breakpoints command to display the Breakpoints dialog box. In the Breakpoints dialog box, you can click the Properties command button and set a conditional expression for a breakpoint or specify the number of times a breakpoint should be hit before stopping code execution.

Entering Commands at Run Time

Using the Immediate window of the Script Editor, you can execute script commands any time the script is halted at a breakpoint or has stepped to another statement. The command reflects or affects the state of the script at the point where execution has halted.

To enter script commands

1. On the Debug toolbar, click the Immediate window button to activate the Immediate window or choose Immediate from the Debug windows submenu of the View menu.

2. In the Immediate window, type the command you want executed and press Enter. For example, to display the current value of the variable *Name*, type the following in the Immediate window:

```
? Name
```

To change the value of the variable, use an assignment statement, as in this example:

```
Name = "New Name"
```

Tip In addition to using ? to display the value of a variable in the Immediate window, you can also use the mouse pointer to display the value of a variable in the Text Editor. If you hover the mouse pointer over the variable whose value you want to inspect, a pop-up window will appear displaying the current value of the highlighted variable.

Viewing the Call Stack

The Call Stack window lets you see the names of all the procedures that are currently executing. This is especially useful if your script contains nested procedures; that is, procedures that are called within other procedures.

To view the call stack

- On the Debug toolbar, click Call Stack, or choose Call Stack from the Debug Windows submenu, available from the View menu.

Viewing the Locals Window

The Locals window displays local variables and their values in the current procedure. As the execution switches from procedure to procedure, the contents of the Locals window change to reflect the local variables applicable to the current procedure. If you have declared script-level variables in the code behind your form, these variables will not be visible in the Locals window. You can track the value of script-level variables in either the Immediate window or the Watch window.

The Locals window is updated only when execution is stopped. Values that have changed since the last break are highlighted. This list indicates some of the features of the Locals window:

- Drag a selected variable to the Immediate window or the Watch window.
- Double-click a variable to edit its value. When you change the value of a variable in the Locals window, its color will change to red.
- Click + or - to view or hide the member variables of an object variable or array.

To view the Locals window

- On the Debug toolbar, click Locals or choose Locals from the Debug Windows submenu, available from the View menu.

Note The Locals window displays a variable's name, value, and type. Variables are strongly typed as strings, integers, and so forth, in the Locals and Watch windows. Don't be misled by this variable typing. From the perspective of VBScript, all variables are still typed as variants.

Viewing the Watch Window

The Watch window displays the values of selected variables or watch expressions and is only updated when execution is stopped at a breakpoint or an exception. Values that have changed since the last break are highlighted. You can use the Watch window to display script-level variables, including the Item object variable that represents the custom Outlook form you are debugging. Figure 11.3 illustrates the Item object and its properties displayed in the Watch window.

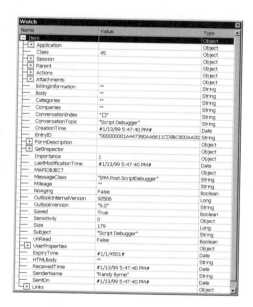

Figure 11.3 *Viewing properties of the Item object in the Watch window.*

To view the Watch window

- On the Debug toolbar, click Watch or choose Watch from the Debug window's submenu, available from the View menu.

To display the properties and property objects of the Item object

1. Type *Item* in an empty cell of the Name column of the Watch window and press Enter.

2. Click + or - to view or hide the member variables of the Item object.

How To Open an Item Containing VBScript

When you are designing and editing forms, you can prevent VBScript code from executing when you open a form by holding down the Shift key when you select the form. For example, to open a form in your Personal Forms Library, click Forms on the Outlook Tools menu, select Choose Form, select Personal Forms Library, and then hold down the Shift key and double-click the form you want to open. The form will then open, but the VBScript code will not execute. This method ensures that values are not inadvertently written to the fields in the form when the Open event fires as the form opens. It also helps to ensure that user-defined fields do not contain unwanted data when you publish the form.

Information Resources for Programming Outlook 2000

Web Resources

In the subfolder 1. Help and Web Sites in the Building Microsoft Outlook 2000 Applications folder, you can find folders containing items telling you how to install Help files or to visit Web sites. These Web sites can assist you in your Outlook programming tasks. You can get to these sites by opening the folder 1. Help and Web Sites in the Building Microsoft Outlook 2000 Applications folder, opening the Microsoft Web Sites folder, and then double-clicking the appropriate item. Here is an overview of the Web sites available in the Microsoft Web Sites folder:

- *http://msdn.microsoft.com/scripting/* The Microsoft Scripting Technologies Web site. This site contains documentation, code examples, and technical articles on all the products in the Microsoft Scripting family, including VBScript.

- *http://www.microsoft.com/outlookdev/* The Microsoft Outlook Developer Forum Web site. A sub-site of the Office Developer Forum, this site contains VBScript samples, form samples, white papers, and technical articles for creating Outlook applications.

- *http://www.microsoft.com/exchange/developers.htm/* The Microsoft Exchange Developer Web site. This site contains valuable tips and techniques for creating Outlook applications on Microsoft Exchange Server. It offers essential information on Exchange Server Scripting and Routing, Public Folder Applications, Collaboration Data Objects, Outlook Web Access, and Exchange Application development in general.

Note There are several excellent third-party sites that also focus on Exchange and Outlook development. Open the Third Party Sites folder under the folder 1. Help and Web Sites in the Building Microsoft Outlook 2000 Applications folder to see a listing of these sites.

Sample Code

The VBScript Samples folder in the folder 4. Beyond the Basics provides sample items that let you view and run VBScript code snippets.

➯ **To open the VBScript Samples folder**

1. In the Folder List, open the Building Microsoft Outlook 2000 Applications folder, and then open the folder 4. Beyond the Basics.

2. Open the VBScript Samples folder, and then open the VBScript Samples folder.

Microsoft Outlook Visual Basic Reference Help

You can use the Microsoft Outlook Visual Basic Reference Help file to view the properties, methods, and events for each object in the Outlook Object Model, as shown in Figure 11.4.

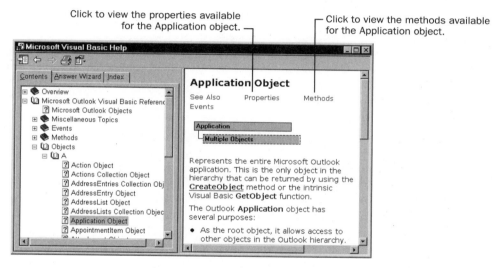

Figure 11.4 *Help for the Application object.*

➯ **To use Microsoft Outlook Visual Basic Reference Help**

1. On the Script Editor Help menu, click Microsoft Outlook Object Library Help.

2. Click the Contents page, and then double-click Microsoft Outlook Visual Basic Reference if the book is not open. (Click the Show button if the Contents, Answer Wizard, and Index tabs are not visible.)

3. Double-click Objects, and then double-click the letter for the object you want help on. You can also click the Index tab and do a keyword search, or you can click the Answer Wizard tab and perform a search using the Answer Wizard.

Note If you have installed Outlook Visual Basic Reference Help, you can also access Help by selecting the Advanced Customization book in the main Outlook Help window.

Caution You can't use context-sensitive help in the Outlook Script Editor. If you place the cursor under a keyword or operator and press F1, Outlook will not respond. However, if you select a keyword or operator and press F1 when you're debugging code in the Microsoft Script Editor, context-sensitive help will be displayed. You can also use the Object Browser in the Script Editor environment to display help for an object, property, event, or method. Unlike the Outlook Script Editor, Outlook VBA fully supports context-sensitive help.

A Caution About the Outlook Programming Environment

The code examples in Microsoft Outlook Visual Basic Reference Help were written for both Visual Basic for Applications and VBScript. In most cases, the target programming environment for the code examples is clearly identified in Microsoft Outlook Visual Basic Reference Help. Many of the code examples in this chapter, however, are written for VBScript behind Outlook forms and must be modified accordingly if you want to use them in Visual Basic or Visual Basic for Applications. There are several distinct programming environments for Outlook forms and application development. They are illustrated in the following table:

Environment	Language	Intrinsic Objects
Code behind Outlook forms	VBScript	Item
ThisOutlookSession in VBAProject.OTM	Visual Basic for Applications	Application
COM Add-in project	Visual Basic	None
Outlook Automation from another Office 2000 application	Visual Basic for Applications	None
Outlook Automation from any COM-compliant development tool	Varies	None

Clearly identify the Outlook programming environment you are using and be aware of the following issues:

- There are no implicit objects in Visual Basic code. All objects must be explicitly referenced. For example, you cannot use the implicit Item object available in VBScript in Visual Basic code. All objects must be declared and instantiated on their own.

- If you do not declare constants with the CONST statement in your VBScript code, you must replace constant names in copied VBA or Visual Basic code with their numeric values in VBScript code.

The Implied Item Object

In VBScript, when you reference the active item in Outlook, the Item object is implied. As such, you do not need to set the Item object when referencing the active item. For example, to set the value of an active item's Subject field, you can use the following statement:

```
Item.Subject = "This is a test"
```

You can also leave out the reference to the item, as shown in this example:

```
Subject = "This is a test"
```

➡ **To test this example**

1.   On the Outlook Actions menu, click New Mail Message.
2.   On the form's Tools menu, click Forms, and then click Design This Form.
3.   On the Form Design toolbar, click Control Toolbox.
4.   Resize the Message control on the form to make room for a CommandButton control.
5.   Drag a CommandButton control to the form. By default, the CommandButton control is given the name CommandButton1.
6.   On the Form Design toolbar, click View Code.
7.   In the Script Editor window, replace the current *CommandButton1_Click* procedure with the following:

```
Sub CommandButton1_Click
   Subject = "The item is implied."
End Sub
```

8.   On the form's Form menu in Design mode, click Run This Form.
9.   Click CommandButton1.
10.   In the Subject box of the form, you will see that the item is implied.

Object Libraries

An object library is a file with an .olb file extension that provides information to programs such as VBScript and Visual Basic for Applications about available objects. For example, the Microsoft Outlook 2000 Object Model (Msoutl9.olb) contains the methods, events, properties, and constants that can be used to program the available objects. Sometimes object libraries are contained within dynamic link library (.dll) files, such as Fm20.dll, which contains the Microsoft Forms 2.0 Object Library.

When you use VBScript or VBA in Outlook, there are three primary object libraries that you use.

- **The Microsoft Outlook 2000 Object Model**   This library contains the objects, properties, methods, and events for almost all the objects that you work with in Outlook, with the exception of the Forms 2.0 Object Library objects and the Microsoft Office 2000 Object Library objects.
- **The Microsoft Forms 2.0 Object Library**   This library contains the objects, methods, properties, and constants that you use to work with a Page object, a Controls collection object, and a Control object.
- **The Microsoft Office 2000 Object Model**   This library contains the objects, methods, properties, and constants you use to work with CommandBars, Assistant, COMAddIns, LanguageSettings, and AnswerWizard objects.

To view the objects available in the Microsoft Outlook 2000 Object Model and the Microsoft Forms 2.0 Object Library, you can use the Help file described earlier in this chapter, or you can use an object browser. To view the objects available in the Microsoft Office 2000 Object Model, navigate to the Microsoft Outlook Objects page in the Microsoft Visual Basic Reference Help, and then click the Office 2000 object to view help on that object.

Using an Object Browser

An object browser shows the objects, properties, and methods available from object libraries. Now that Visual Basic for Applications has been included in Outlook 2000, Outlook provides a superb object browser that you can use to view the Outlook Object Model or any other object model that you want to use. A more limited object browser is also available when you use the Object Browser command on the Script menu of an Outlook form's Script Editor. If you want to view the Forms Object Model from within Outlook's Object Browser, you must follow a few extra steps.

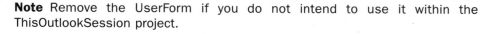

To use the Microsoft Outlook 2000 Object Browser to view the Forms Object Model

1. On the Tools menu, point to Macro, and then click Visual Basic Editor.
2. On the Insert menu, click UserForm.
3. On the View menu, click Object Browser.
4. Select MSForms from the Project/Library drop-down list box in the Object Browser window.

Note Remove the UserForm if you do not intend to use it within the ThisOutlookSession project.

Moving Around in the Outlook Object Browser

There are now two Object Browsers available in Outlook: one browser is available in the VBScript environment for use with the Script Editor, and the other browser is available for use with Visual Basic for Applications. With the Outlook VBScript Object Browser, you can browse through all the available objects in the Microsoft Outlook 2000 Object

Library and see their properties, methods, and events, as shown in Figure 11.5. In addition, you can get help for any component in the library.

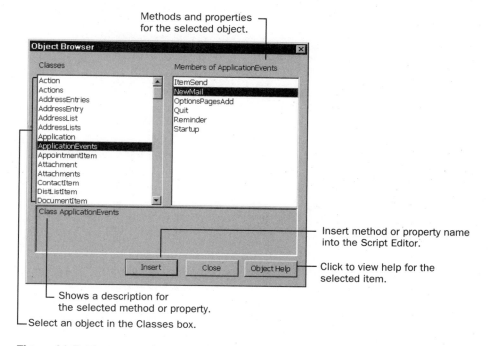

Figure 11.5 *The Microsoft Outlook VBScript Object Browser.*

To move around in the VBScript Object Browser

1. In the Classes list box, click an object to view the properties, methods, and events for the object.

2. In the Members Of Object Name list box, click a property, method, or event to view further details, as shown earlier in Figure 11.5.

To view the Outlook Visual Basic Reference Help topic for the selected item, click Help. To place the item or procedure in your code, click Insert.

For those of you who prefer premium fare over the standard variety, the Object Browser in Outlook Visual Basic for Applications is recommended. The Outlook Visual Basic for Applications Object Browser lets you view the object libraries for Outlook, VBA, Office, or any other object library for which you can set a reference using the Tools menu and the References command. This object browser is shown in Figure 11.6.

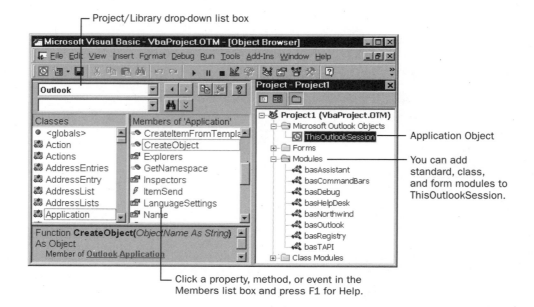

Figure 11.6 *The Microsoft Outlook Visual Basic for Applications Object Browser.*

To display the Outlook VBA Object Browser

1. Press Alt+F11 in an Inspector or Explorer window to display the Visual Basic for Applications Editor window.

2. Press F2 to display the Object Browser.

Object Models

An object model provides a visual representation of the hierarchical structure and relationship of objects in an object library, as shown in Figure 11.7. As such, it provides a way for you to quickly see how an object library is designed.

To view the Microsoft Outlook Object Model

1. On the Script Editor Help menu, click Microsoft Outlook Object Library Help.

2. Click the Contents page in the Microsoft Visual Basic Reference Help window.

3. Open the Microsoft Outlook Visual Basic Reference Help book, and then click the Microsoft Outlook Objects page. If the book is not open, double-click the book to open it.

To view the Microsoft Forms 2.0 Object Model

1. Start VBA in Outlook by pressing Alt + F11 in an Explorer window.

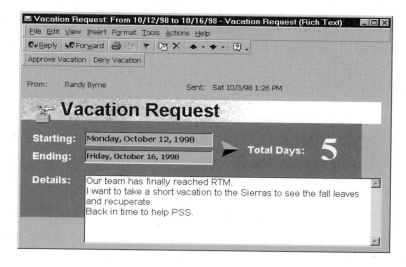

Figure 11.7 *The Microsoft Outlook Object Model.*

2. Press F2 to launch the VBA Object Browser.
3. On the Help menu of the Object Browser, click Microsoft Visual Basic Help.
4. Click the Contents tab in the Visual Basic Reference Help window.
5. Open the book named Microsoft Forms Reference.
6. Click the page named Microsoft Forms Object Model Overview.

Using the Object Hierarchy

In an object library, all objects have a unique set of methods, properties, and events. Properties are attributes of the object that define it, and methods are actions that can be performed on an object. Events occur when specific actions are performed on an object (when it is opened or clicked, for example).

To use the object model, you must often move down through the object hierarchy to reference the particular object you want. For example, assume you want to display the Outlook window, which is represented by the Explorer object. Because the Application object sits at the top of the hierarchy, you must first reference the Application object before you can reference the Explorer object. In the following procedure, the *ActiveExplorer* method of the Application object is used to return the currently active Outlook window (the Explorer object). The *Display* method of the Explorer object is then used to make the Outlook window the active window on the desktop.

```
Sub CommandButton1_Click
    Set objExplorer = Application.ActiveExplorer
    objExplorer.Display
End Sub
```

⤵ **To test the code samples in this chapter**

1. In the Folder List, open the Building Microsoft Outlook 2000 Applications folder, and then open the folder 4. Beyond the Basics.

2. Open the VBScript folder, and then open the VBScript Samples folder.

3. Double-click the item you want to open, and then click a command button to execute the sample procedure.

4. To view the sample code, click Forms on the Tools menu, click Design This Form, and then click View Code on the Form Design toolbar.

5. You can also click the Script button on the form shown in Figure 11.8. This button copies the code behind the example form and pastes it into the body of a Mail Message.

6. If you want to debug the sample code, use step 4 above to open the Script Editor window and insert a Stop statement in the procedure you wish to debug. Click Run This Form on the Form menu, and then click the command button for the procedure you are debugging.

The following example moves further down the object hierarchy and returns a Folder object. It then uses the Name property of the Folder object to display the name of the folder in a message.

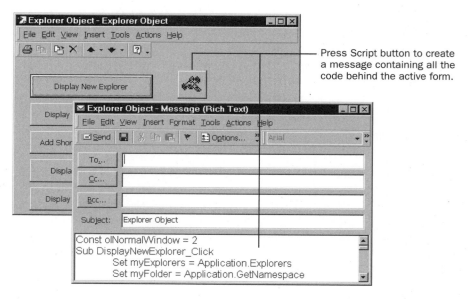

Figure 11.8 *The Script button lets you quickly inspect the code behind the example form.*

```
Sub CommandButton1_Click
    Set objFolder = Application.ActiveExplorer.CurrentFolder
    MsgBox objFolder.Name, vbInformation
End Sub
```

Getting and Setting Properties

This section covers how you either get or set the properties of an object. To get or set a property, you must reference both the object name and the property name.

Getting an Object Property

In certain cases, you want to get the properties of an object. The following procedure retrieves the text in the message box of an item and shows it in a message. Before you click CommandButton1, type some text in the message box of the form.

```
Sub CommandButton1_Click
    BodyText = Item.Body
    MsgBox BodyText
End Sub
```

Tip Notice in the preceding example that the active item is referenced without moving through the object hierarchy. In this case, the item is implied, as discussed in the section "The Implied Item Object," earlier in this chapter.

Setting an Object Property

In this example, the body text of the item is set.

```
Sub CommandButton1_Click
    Item.Body = "This text appears in the message box."
End Sub
```

Using the With Statement

If you've installed Internet Explorer 5.0 with Outlook 2000, you will be using version 5.0 of VBScript. VBScript 5.0 supports the With...End With statement, which allows you to perform a series of statements on a specified object without requalifying the name of the object. For example, the following code is now supported only in VBScript 5.0. If you use this code in a VBScript version prior to 5.0, the code will fail. The With...End With syntax is available in all current versions of VBA or Visual Basic.

```
Sub CreateContact
    Const olContactItem = 2
    Set myContact = Application.CreateItem(olContactItem)
    With myContact
        .FirstName = "Dolores"
        .LastName = "DelRio"
        .FullName = "DelRio, Dolores"
        .CompanyName = "XYZ Corporation"
        .JobTitle = "Senior Accountant"
```

```
        .EmailAddress = "ddelrio@xyz.com"
        .EmailAddressType = "SMTP"
        .Save
    End With
End Sub
```

Important Do not jump into or out of With blocks. If statements in a With block are executed, but either the With or End With statement is not executed, you may get unpredictable behavior.

Using Variables

Variable names follow the standard naming convention rules for naming objects, properties, methods, and so on, in Microsoft VBScript. A variable name:

- Must begin with an alphabetic character
- Cannot contain an embedded period
- Must not exceed 255 characters
- Must be unique in the scope in which it's declared

Generally, when you declare a variable within a procedure, only code within that procedure can reference or change the value of the variable; it has local scope and is known as a procedure-level variable. When you declare a variable outside a procedure, you make it recognizable to all the procedures in your script; it has script-level scope and is known as a script-level variable. When you're using variables in VBScript, the following limitations apply:

- There can be no more than 127 procedure-level variables (arrays count as a single variable).
- Each script is limited to no more than 127 script-level variables.

The length of time a variable exists is called its lifetime. A script-level variable's lifetime extends from the time it's declared until the time the script has finished running. A local variable's lifetime begins when its declaration statement is encountered as the procedure begins, and it ends when the procedure concludes. Local variables are ideal as temporary storage space while a procedure is running. You can have local variables with the same name in different procedures because each variable is recognized only by the procedure in which it's declared.

A variable's scope is determined by where the variable is declared. At the script level, the lifetime of a variable is always the same; it exists while the script is running. At the procedure level, a variable exists only while the procedure is running; when the procedure exits, the variable is destroyed. A global or script-level variable is available to any procedure in a form while the script is running. To set global variables, assign values to the variables before any procedures.

> **Note** The constraints listed earlier apply only to variables and procedures within VBScript code. Select the Microsoft Visual Basic Help command on the Help menu in the Outlook VBA Editor for additional information regarding variables, constants, and scope in VBA.

Using the Variant Data Type

VBScript in Outlook uses only the variant data type, which is a special kind of data type that can contain different types of information, depending on how the value is used. The Variant data type can contain several types of information—string, date and time, Boolean (True or False), currency, and numeric—with varying degrees of precision. The variant data type behaves as a number when it's used in a numeric context and as a string when it's used in a string context. If you're working with data resembling numeric data, VBScript treats it as such and processes it accordingly. If you're working with data that resembles string data, VBScript treats the data as a string. Numbers enclosed in quotation marks are also treated as strings.

The variant data type can make distinctions about the specific nature of numeric information, such as information that represents a date or time. When used with other date or time data, the result is always expressed as a date or a time. The variant data type can contain numeric information ranging in size from Boolean values to huge floating-point numbers. These various categories of information that can be contained in a variant data type are called subtypes. For a complete listing of VBScript subtypes, see "VBScript Data Types" in the VBScript documentation. Usually, you can put the type of data you want in a variant, and it will most likely behave in a way that's suited to the data it contains. You should be aware, however, of type conversion when you assign values to variables in VBScript. A classic example of a type conversion error is as follows:

```
Sub CommandButton1_Click()
    Dim A,B,C 'Variant Data Type
    A = "1" 'Assigned to string
    B = "1"
    C = A + B 'Variant result will be a string subtype
    MsgBox "The value of " & A & " plus " & B & " equals " & C & vbCr _
        & "where the subtype of C is " & TypeName(C)
    A = 1 'Assigned to integer
    B = 1
    C = A + B 'Variant result will be an integer subtype
    MsgBox "The value of " & A & " plus " & B & " equals " & C & vbCr _
        & "where the subtype of C is " & TypeName(C)
End Sub
```

> **Tip** Use the *VarType* and *TypeName* functions in VBScript to determine the subtype of *VBScript* variables. These functions can be especially useful in the Immediate window of the Script Debugger when you are attempting to debug a type conversion problem.

VBScript Naming Conventions

You will have fewer headaches in the future if you adopt a naming convention for variables in your VBScript code. Although a naming convention, in itself, will not prevent type conversion errors, the naming convention does indicate what the original programmer intended for the subtype of a given variable. While a naming convention seems superfluous in a weakly-typed language like VBScript, it will save time and reduce errors in the long run. If you are developing Outlook forms in a corporate environment, you should consult with other Visual Basic and VBScript developers. Adopt a corporate VBScript naming convention and then stick with it.

Subtype	Prefix	Example
Boolean	bln	blnSent
Byte	byt	bytRasterData
collection object	col	colHiddenMessages
Date (Time)	dtm	dtmStartDate
Double	dbl	dblTolerance
Error	err	errOrderNum
Integer	int	intQuantity
Long	lng	lngDistance
Object	obj	objMessage
Single	sng	sngAverage
String	str	strFirstName

Declaring Constants

The first version of VBScript that shipped with Outlook 97 did not support the CONST statement. The CONST statement allows you to declare constant values and improve the readability of your code. Fortunately, the CONST statement is valid in VBScript 2.0 and later and thus is operational in VBScript code that you write for Outlook 2000. The extra work of declaring constants with the CONST statement may be preferable to calling a method or setting a property with a specific value. For example, which of the following statements is more readable (and more easily debugged)?

```
Set objItem = Application.CreateItem(0)
Set objItem = Application.CreateItem(olMailItem)
```

Unlike VBA code in Outlook, constants for object models external to VBScript must be explicitly declared. You can ignore the advice about constant declarations if you are only writing VBA code for Outlook. From the perspective of VBScript, Outlook's Object Model is external to VBScript. Rather than declaring constants at the procedure level, declare constants at the script level to avoid duplication. Here is a short example.

```
Const olPostItem = 6 'Script-level constant
Sub CommandButton1_Click
    Set objItem = Application.CreateItem(olPostItem)
    objItem.Display
End Sub
```

> **Note** Versions of VBScript 2.0 and later support intrinsic constants for certain VBScript objects and functions. For example, use vbInformation or vbCritical to display icons when you use the *MsgBox* function instead of the specific values. See VBScript Constants in VBScript Help for a complete listing. Intrinsic constants also make your code easier to maintain and read.

To add Outlook CONST declarations to your VBScript code

1. Open the Outlook Constants item in the VBScript Samples folder.
2. Copy the necessary CONST declarations from the Outlook Constants item.
3. Paste the CONST declarations into your VBScript code. The CONST declarations typically should be placed at the top of your code before any other procedures. These CONST declarations have script-level scope in your code.

Assigning Objects to Variables

Object variables are assigned in a slightly different way from other variables. For example, if a variable is shared between procedures, you declare the variable as a script-level variable. In this procedure, the *ItemChanged* variable is declared as a script-level variable. *ItemChanged* is set to *True* whenever a standard property is changed in an item.

```
Dim ItemChanged   ' Script-level variable.
Sub Item_PropertyChange(ByVal Name)
    ItemChanged = True
End Sub
```

An object variable is a variable that is used to refer to an object. As shown in the following example, you don't need to declare the variable. Instead, you use the Set statement to assign an object to a variable. The first line of code in the following example assigns the object variable to the newly created item. Once you've set an object, you can then use the object's methods and properties to control the object. This example creates a new mail item, and then displays the item.

```
Sub CommandButton1_Click
    Set objItem = Application.CreateItem(0)
    objItem.Display
End Sub
```

Referencing Collections and Single Objects

Some objects in Outlook are collection objects, while others are single objects. For example, all the items in a folder can be contained in an Items collection object. However, a single item in an Items collection object may be represented by a MailItem object or a PostItem object. The following code uses the Items property to reference the collection of items in your Inbox. It then shows the number of items in the Items collection object.

```
Sub CommandButton1_Click
    Set objFolder = Application.GetNameSpace("MAPI").GetDefaultFolder(6)
    Set colItems = objFolder.Items
    MsgBox colItems.Count
End Sub
```

In the next example, the items in the Items collection object are referenced by index number. In this case, the code iterates through the Items collection and shows the text in the Message field for the first three items in the your Inbox. (Note that items in the Inbox do not necessarily appear in the order received.)

```
Sub CommandButton1_click
    Set MyFolder = Application.GetNameSpace("MAPI").GetDefaultFolder(6)
    Set MyItems = MyFolder.Items
    For i = 1 to 3
        MsgBox MyItems(i).Subject
    Next
End Sub
```

After you set a collection object, you can reference objects in the collection by index, as shown in the preceding example, or by name. For example, to reference an item in an Items collection by name, you specify the value of the Subject field. Before you run this example, do the following:

- Press Ctrl+Shift+I to make the Inbox your active folder.
- Press Ctrl+Shift+S to create a new Post in the Inbox.
- Type *VBScript Test* in the Subject box.
- Click Post.
- Press Ctrl+Shift+S to create a new Post item.
- Select Design This Form from the Forms submenu of the Tools menu.
- Click the Control Toolbox button on the Form Design toolbar.
- Drag a command button control from the Control Toolbox to (P.2) of the form.
- Type the code shown in the following example into the Script Editor window.
- Select Run This Form from the Form menu.
- Click OK in the Select Folder dialog.
- Click CommandButton1 on (P.2) of the form.

```
    Sub CommandButton1_Click
        Const olFolderInbox = 6
        Set objFolder = _
            Application.GetNameSpace("MAPI").GetDefaultFolder(olFolderInbox)
        Set colItems = objFolder.Items
```

```
        Set objItem = colItems("VBScript Test")
        objItem.Display
    End Sub
```

Generally, you don't reference an item in an Items collection by name. However, you almost always reference a field property in a UserProperties collection by name. The following example sets the name of the user-defined field called Customer Name to James Allard. Before you run this example, do the following:

1. Make sure the form is in Design mode, and then click Field Chooser on the Form Design toolbar.

2. In the Field Chooser, click New, type *Customer Name* in the Name text box, and then click OK.

3. Drag the Customer Name field from the Field Chooser to the form. Add the code shown in the example to the Script Editor.

4. Click Run This Form on the Form menu to switch to Run mode, and then click CommandButton1.

```
Sub CommandButton1_Click
    UserProperties("Customer Name") = "James Allard"
End Sub
```

The Application Object

The Application object sits at the top of the object model and represents the entire Microsoft Outlook application. The Outlook Application object has several purposes:

- As the root object, it enables you to reference other objects in the Outlook object hierarchy.

- It provides methods such as *CreateItem* and *CreateObject* so that you can create new items and reference them without moving through the object hierarchy.

- It provides methods for directly referencing the active Outlook window or form.

More Info For a complete list and description of the methods, properties, and events for the Application object, see Microsoft Outlook Visual Basic Reference Help.

Important Open the Application object item in the VBScript Samples folder to work directly with this code in Outlook.

Application Object Methods

This section covers the *ActiveExplorer*, *ActiveWindow*, *CreateItem*, *CreateObject*, and *GetNameSpace* methods.

Returning the Active Window

You can use the *ActiveWindow* method of the Application object to return the topmost active Outlook window. The *ActiveWindow* method returns either an Explorer or an Inspector object.

```
'Get the Active Outlook Window
'The ActiveWindow object is the topmost window in the running Outlook instance
Sub GetOutlookActiveWindow_Click
    If TypeName(Application.ActiveWindow) = "Inspector" Then
        MsgBox "The active window is an inspector", vbInformation
    Else
        MsgBox "The active window is an explorer", vbInformation
    End If
End Sub
```

The following example sets the MyExplorer object to the currently active Outlook Explorer window, displays a message that indicates the active window type, and then redisplays the item window when the ShowOutlookActiveExplorer control is clicked.

```
Sub ShowOutlookActiveExplorer_Click
    Set MyExplorer = Application.ActiveExplorer
    MyExplorer.Display
    GetOutlookActiveWindow_Click()
    Item.Display
End Sub
```

Creating a Standard Item

You can use the *CreateItem* method of the Application object to create and return Outlook standard items such as a Message item, a Post item, or an Appointment item. The following example creates a Message item using the default editor and displays it when CreateAMailMessage is clicked.

```
Sub CreateAMailMessage_Click
    Set MyItem = Application.CreateItem(0)
    MyItem.Display
End Sub
```

The next simple example creates an HTML message.

```
Sub CreateHTMLMessage_Click
    Const olMailItem = 0
    Set myItem = Application.CreateItem(olMailItem)
    myItem.HTMLBody = ""
    myItem.Display
End Sub
```

Since the Office Envelope will undoubtedly become a popular message container, it's useful to know that you can also create a Word Envelope message in code. This example uses the *CreateObject* method to launch Word and display a Word Envelope message. From the standpoint of the message body, Word Envelope messages are equivalent to HTML messages.

```
'Creates a Word Message item and displays it
Sub CreateAWordMessage_Click
    Const wdNewEmailMessage = 2
    Dim objApp,objMsg
    Set objApp = CreateObject("Word.Application")
    Set objMsg = objApp.Documents.Add(,,wdNewEmailMessage)
    objApp.Visible = True
    objApp.ActiveWindow.EnvelopeVisible = True
End Sub
```

The following table lists the numeric values you use as arguments for the *CreateItem* method. You can also copy the CONST declarations in the Enum OlItemType section of the Outlook Constants item in the VBScript Samples folder and paste them into your code.

Type of Item	Value
Appointment	1
Contact	2
Distribution List	7
Journal	4
Mail Message	0
Note	5
Post	6
Task	3

More Info For more information about creating custom items, see "Items Collection Methods" later in this chapter.

Creating an Automation Object

You can use the *CreateObject* method of the Application object to create Automation objects, such as Microsoft Excel, Microsoft Access, or Microsoft Word objects. You can also use the *CreateObject* method to create instances of custom ActiveX DLLs that extend the functionality of Outlook. See Chapter 16, "Using ActiveX DLLs and Microsoft Transaction Server with Outlook." The following example uses the *CreateObject* method to create an instance of Excel, adds a workbook, and then renames the first sheet in the workbook to Outlook CreateObject Example:

```
'Launch Excel with CreateObject
Sub LaunchExcel_Click
    Dim xLApp 'As Excel.Application
    Dim xLSheet 'As Excel.Worksheet
    Set xLApp = CreateObject("Excel.Application")
    If Err Then
        MsgBox "Could not create Excel Application", vbCritical
        Exit Sub
    End If
```

```
      xLApp.Workbooks.Add
      Set xLSheet = xLApp.Sheets(1)
      xLSheet.Name = "Outlook CreateObject Example"
      'Make the Excel Application window visible
      xLApp.Visible = True
End Sub
```

Tip When you are writing Automation code for VBScript in Outlook forms, you can expedite the development process by using the VBA Editor in Word or Excel to write the code and then pasting the code into VBScript. As noted in the example above, you must place comment marks before the As keyword in the object type declarations, or VBScript will raise an error. The beauty of this approach is that you have all the IntelliSense features of the VBA Editor at your disposal, including auto list members, syntax checking, parameter info, quick info, and code formatting. Before you begin, set references to the appropriate object libraries by using the Tool menu's References command in the VBA Editor window. Figure 11.9 illustrates the *LaunchExcel* procedure code in the Word VBA Editor.

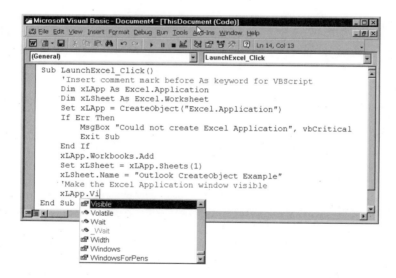

Figure 11.9 *Use the VBA Editor to simplify the writing of Automation code for VBScript.*

Returning a MAPI NameSpace Object

You can use the *GetNameSpace("MAPI")* method of the Application object to return the MAPI message store.

In the following example, the *GetNameSpace* method returns the NameSpace object. The CurrentUser property of the NameSpace object is then used to show your name in a message box.

```
Sub CommandButton1_Click
    Set MyNameSpace = Application.GetNameSpace("MAPI")
    MsgBox MyNameSpace.CurrentUser, vbInformation
End Sub
```

> **Important** The only data source currently supported is MAPI, which allows access to all Outlook data stored in MAPI. For this reason, the *GetNameSpace* method must always appear in Outlook as *GetNameSpace("MAPI")*.

Creating Office Objects

The Application object has several child objects that are actually members of the Office 2000 Object Model. For example, the Application object contains member objects for the Office 2000 AnswerWizard, Assistant, COMAddIns, and LanguageSettings objects. The following code example uses an animated Assistant to display the LanguageID settings for the Outlook Application object.

```
'Display the LanguageSettings
Sub DisplayLanguageSettings_Click
    Const msoLanguageIDInstall = 1, msoLanguageIDUI = 2, msoLanguageIDHelp = 3
    Const msoAnimationListensToComputer = 26
    Const msoModeModal = 0, msoButtonSetOK = 1, msoIconTip = 3
    On Error Resume Next
    Dim oa 'As Office.Assistant
    Dim bln 'As Office.Balloon
    strMsg = "The following locale IDs are registered " _
        & "for this application:" & vbCr & "Install Language - " & _
        Application.LanguageSettings.LanguageID(msoLanguageIDInstall) _
        & vbCr & "User Interface Language - " & _
        Application.LanguageSettings.LanguageID(msoLanguageIDUI) _
        & vbCr & "Help Language - " & _
        Application.LanguageSettings.LanguageID(msoLanguageIDHelp)
    Set oa = Application.Assistant
    oa.On = True 'Assistant not available
    If Err Then
        MsgBox strMsg, vbInformation
    Else
    oa.Visible = True
    Set bln = oa.NewBalloon
        bln.Heading = "Language Settings"
        bln.Mode = msoModeModal
        bln.Button = msoButtonSetOK
        bln.Icon = msoIconTip
        bln.Text = strMsg
        bln.Show
    oa.Animation = msoAnimationListensToComputer
    End If
End Sub
```

The NameSpace Object

In Outlook, the NameSpace object represents the MAPI message store. The NameSpace object provides methods for logging on or off Outlook, referencing a default folder, and returning objects directly by ID. In addition, the NameSpace object provides access to a variety of methods and properties that are not normally available with the Application object.

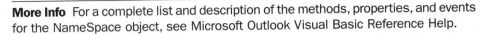 **More Info** For a complete list and description of the methods, properties, and events for the NameSpace object, see Microsoft Outlook Visual Basic Reference Help.

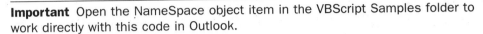 **Important** Open the NameSpace object item in the VBScript Samples folder to work directly with this code in Outlook.

NameSpace Object Methods

This section covers the *GetDefaultFolder* method of the NameSpace object.

Returning a Default Folder

You can use the *GetDefaultFolder* method of the NameSpace object to access folders in the root folder, also known as the Mailbox. To reference a folder in the Mailbox, you can either specify a numeric value as the argument in the *GetDefaultFolder* method or copy the OlDefaultFolders constants from the Outlook Constants item in the VBScript Samples folder and paste them into your code. The following table lists these numeric values:

Folder	Value
Deleted Items	3
Outbox	4
Sent Items	5
Inbox	6
Calendar	9
Contacts	10
Journal	11
Notes	12
Tasks	13
Drafts	16

The following example uses the *GetDefaultFolder* method of the NameSpace object to return the Contacts folder and then display it.

```
Sub CommandButton1_Click
    Set MyFolder = Application.GetNameSpace("MAPI").GetDefaultFolder(10)
    MyFolder.Display
End Sub
```

Properties of the NameSpace Object

The NameSpace object provides two properties that you use quite often. These are the CurrentUser and Folders properties.

Returning the Name of the Current User

You can use the CurrentUser property of the NameSpace object to return the name of the currently logged-on user. The following example shows the current user's name in the message box when the CommandButton1 control is clicked:

```
Sub CommandButton1_Click
    Set MyNameSpace = Application.GetNameSpace("MAPI")
    MsgBox MyNameSpace.CurrentUser
End Sub
```

Referencing a Folder Collection

You can use the Folders property of the NameSpace object to reference the collection of folders in the MAPI NameSpace.

The following example displays the number of subfolders in the Building Microsoft Outlook 2000 Applications .pst file:

```
Sub ReferenceAFolderCollection_Click
    Set MyNameSpace = Application.GetNameSpace("MAPI")
    set objFolder = _
        MyNameSpace("Building Microsoft Outlook 2000 Applications")
    Set colFolders = objFolder.Folders
    MsgBox "There are " & colFolders.Count & " subfolders" _
        & vbCr & "in " & objFolder.Name, vbInformation
End Sub
```

Selecting a Folder

You can use the *PickFolder* method of the NameSpace object to return a MAPIFolder object. The *PickFolder* method displays a dialog box for the user to select a folder from all available folders in the current profile. The following example displays the Select Folders dialog box and also displays an alert dialog box if the user clicks Cancel. If the user selects a folder, then the folder is displayed in an Explorer window.

```
Sub PickAFolder_Click()
On Error Resume Next
Set MyNameSpace = Application.GetNameSpace("MAPI")
Set objFolder = MyNameSpace.PickFolder
    If objFolder Is Nothing then
        MsgBox "User Pressed Cancel!", vbInformation
    Else
        objFolder.Display
    End If
End Sub
```

The Outlook Window (Explorer Objects)

The Explorer object represents the window in which the contents of a folder are displayed. The Explorers object is the parent collection object for Explorer objects. The following sections cover some of the methods and properties for the Explorer and Explorers objects.

Figure 11.10 illustrates elements of the Outlook user interface viewed from an object model perspective. This illustration is not meant to be all-inclusive; it shows just a few of the objects in the Outlook Object Model that you can manipulate programmatically.

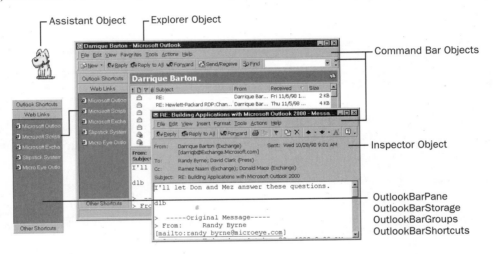

Figure 11.10 *Object model components of the Outlook user interface.*

More Info For a complete list and description of the properties, methods, and events for the Explorer and Explorers objects, see Microsoft Outlook Visual Basic Reference Help.

Important Open the Explorer object item in the VBScript Samples folder to work directly with this code in Outlook.

Explorer Methods

Creating a New Explorer Window

Outlook 2000 supports a new Explorers collection object. You can use the Explorers object to add a new Explorer window for a specific folder. Use the *Display* method to present the new Explorer window. The following example creates a new Explorer window for the Drafts folder by using the *Add* method, and then shows it on the desktop in a normal window state.

```
Const olNormalWindow = 2
Sub DisplayNewExplorer_Click
    Set myExplorers = Application.Explorers
    Set myFolder = Application.GetNameSpace("MAPI").GetDefaultFolder(16)
    Set myOlExpl = myExplorers.Add(myFolder, 2)
    myOlExpl.Display
    myOlExpl.WindowState = olNormalWindow
End Sub
```

Explorer Properties

Returning the Active Folder

You can use the CurrentFolder property of the Explorer object to return the active folder in the Outlook window. The following example shows the name of the active folder in the message box when the DisplayTheCurrentFolder control is clicked:

```
Sub DisplayTheCurrentFolder_Click
    Set myExplorer = Application.ActiveExplorer
    MsgBox "The current folder in the Explorer is: " _
        & myExplorer.CurrentFolder.Name, vbInformation
End Sub
```

Obtaining the Current View for the Active Explorer

You can use the CurrentView property of the Explorer object to return or set the current view for the Active Explorer window.

The following example displays the name of the current view for the Active Explorer window:

```
Sub DisplayTheExplorerView_Click
    Set myExplorer = Application.ActiveExplorer
    MsgBox "The current Explorer view is: " & vbCr _
        & myExplorer.CurrentView, vbInformation
End Sub
```

Adding Shortcuts to the Outlook Bar

You can add both groups and shortcuts to the Outlook Bar by using the Panes collection object. Use the *IsPaneVisible* and *ShowPane* methods of the Explorer object to show the Outlook Bar in the Explorer. The Panes object lets you access the OutlookBarGroups and OutlookBarShortcuts collection objects. You can also set the current group in code and use VBA code to respond to Outlook Bar events such as GroupAdd, BeforeGroupAdd, BeforeGroupRemove, ShortcutAdd, BeforeShortcutAdd, and BeforeShortcutRemove. The following example adds an Outlook Bar group named Web Links and then adds five shortcuts to the group:

```
Sub AddOutlookBarShortcuts_Click
    Dim MyOLBar 'As OutlookBarPane
    Dim MyOLGroup 'As OutlookBarGroup
```

```
Dim MyExplorer 'As Explorer
Set MyExplorer = Application.ActiveExplorer

'Show the Outlook Bar if not visible
If MyExplorer.IsPaneVisible(1) = False Then
    MyExplorer.ShowPane 1, True
End If

Set MyOLBar = MyExplorer.Panes("OutlookBar")
Set MyOLBarStorage = MyOLBar.Contents
Set MyOLBarGroups = MyOLBarStorage.Groups

MyOLBar.Contents.Groups.Add "Web Links", MyOlBarGroups.Count + 1

Set MyOLGroup = myOLBarGroups("Web Links")
Set myOLShortcuts = MyOLGroup.Shortcuts

myOLShortcuts.Add "http://www.microsoft.com/outlookdev", _
    "Microsoft Outlook Development"
myOLShortcuts.Add "http://msdn.microsoft.com/scripting", _
    "Microsoft Scripting Technologies"
myOLShortcuts.Add "http://www.outlookexchange.com", _
    "Outlook Exchange Developer Resource Center"
myOLShortcuts.Add "http://www.slipstick.com/exchange", _
    "Slipstick Systems Exchange Center"
myOLShortcuts.Add "http://www.microeye.com/outlkb.html", _
    "Micro Eye Outlook Development KB"

Set MyOLBar.CurrentGroup = MyOLGroup
End Sub
```

2000 Determining Which Items are Selected in the Explorer

Outlook developers will be relieved to know that a Selection collection object has been added to the Explorer object in Outlook 2000. The Selection object, in turn, contains an Items collection that lets you iterate over selected items. If you are writing VBA code, you can respond to the SelectionChange event of the Explorer object. The following example displays the number of selected items in the Active Explorer and then asks if the user wants to display the item:

```
Sub DisplaySelectedItems_Click
    DisplayNewExplorer_Click
    Set mySelection = Application.ActiveExplorer.Selection
    MsgBox "The number of selected items in the Explorer is " _
        & mySelection.Count, vbInformation
    If MsgBox ("Display selected items?", vbYesNo+vbQuestion) = vbNo Then
        Exit Sub
    End If
    For i = 1 to mySelection.Count
        Set myItem = mySelection.Item(i)
        myItem.Display
    Next
End Sub
```

The AddressLists Collection Object

Important Open the AddressLists collection object, AddressEntries collection object, and the AddressEntry object items in the VBScript Samples folder to work directly with this code in Outlook.

Outlook users often have several address books from which they can select recipients for a message. The AddressLists collection object contains all the address books available to a user. Using the AddressLists object, you can reference one or more AddressList objects, each of which represents a single address book.

The AddressLists collection object is always referenced from the NameSpace object.

AddressLists Collection Methods

This section covers the *Item* method of the AddressLists collection object.

Iterating Through a Collection of Address Lists

You can use the *Item* method of the AddressLists collection object to iterate through a collection of address books. The following example uses the Count property of the AddressLists collection object to determine the number of AddressList objects referenced by the collection. It then uses the *Item* method of the AddressLists collection object to return and display the name of each address book.

```
Sub ShowAddressLists_Click
    Set MyNameSpace = Application.GetNameSpace("MAPI")
    Set MyAddressLists = MyNameSpace.AddressLists
    MsgBox "There are " & MyAddressLists.Count & " address lists.", _
        vbInformation
    For i = 1 to MyAddressLists.Count
        Set MyAddressList = MyAddressLists.Item(i)
        MsgBox MyAddressList.Name & " is " & i & " of " _
            & MyAddressLists.Count, vbInformation
    Next
End Sub
```

The AddressList Object

The AddressList object represents a single Outlook address book that contains a set of AddressEntry objects. The AddressEntry objects, in turn, can be accessed through the AddressEntries property of the AddressList object.

The AddressEntries Collection Object

The AddressEntries collection object is provided by the AddressEntries property of the AddressList object. It provides access to each of the AddressEntry objects contained within a given address book.

AddressEntries Collection Methods

This section covers the *Add* and *Item* methods of the AddressEntries collection object.

Adding an Address Entry

You can use the *Add* method of the AddressEntries collection object to create a new item in an address book. The following example uses the *Add* method to create a new entry in the Personal Address Book. The *Update* method of the AddressEntry object is required to commit the new item to the address book.

```
Sub AddAddressEntry_Click
    On Error Resume Next
    Set MyNameSpace = Application.GetNameSpace("MAPI")
    Set MyAddressList = MyNameSpace.AddressLists("Personal Address Book")
    If MyAddressList Is Nothing Then
        MsgBox "Personal Address Book Unavailable!", vbExclamation
        Exit Sub
    End If
    Set MyEntries = MyAddressList.AddressEntries
    Set myEntry = MyEntries.Add _
        ("SMTP","James Allard","jamesallard@microsoft.com")
    myEntry.Update
End Sub
```

Iterating Through a Collection of Address Entries

You can use the *Item* method of the AddressEntries collection object to iterate through the items in an address book. The following example uses the Count property of the AddressEntries collection object to return the number of items in the user's Personal Address Book. It also uses the *Item* method of the AddressEntries collection object to return each item in the address book and then display its name.

```
Sub ShowAddressEntries_Click
    On Error Resume Next
    Set MyPage = Item.GetInspector.ModifiedFormPages _
        ("AddressEntries Collection")
    Set ListBox1 = MyPage.Controls("ListBox1")
    Set MyNameSpace = Application.GetNameSpace("MAPI")
    Set MyAddressList = MyNameSpace.AddressLists("Personal Address Book")
    If MyAddressList Is Nothing Then
        MsgBox "Personal Address Book Unavailable!", vbExclamation
        Exit Sub
    End If
    Set MyAddressEntries = MyAddressList.AddressEntries
```

```
        For i = 1 to MyAddressEntries.Count
            Set MyEntry = MyAddressEntries.Item(i)
            ListBox1.AddItem MyEntry.Name
        Next
    End Sub
```

The AddressEntry Object

The AddressEntry object represents an individual item in an address book. The AddressEntry object contains information about one or more individuals or processes to which the messaging system can send messages. If the AddressEntry object represents a distribution list (that is, if its DisplayType property is set to olDistList or olPrivateDistList), it can contain additional AddressEntry objects that can be accessed through its Members property.

AddressEntry Object Methods

This section covers the *Details*, *Update*, *Delete*, and *GetFreeBusy* methods of the AddressEntry object.

Displaying Details of an Address Entry

The *Details* method of the AddressEntry object displays a modal dialog box that lets a user see (and, if permissions allow, change) the information stored in the Address Book item represented by the object.

The following example steps through the items in a user's Personal Address Book, using the *Details* method to display the information contained in each item. If the user clicks OK in the dialog box, the next entry is displayed. If the user clicks the Cancel button in the dialog box, an error is produced. For this reason, an On Error statement is included to prevent the routine from exiting immediately, and the *Err global* variable is tested to determine if it is not zero (which would indicate that the user clicked Cancel or that an error had occurred).

```
Sub DisplayEntryDetails_Click
    On Error Resume Next
    Set MyNameSpace = Application.GetNameSpace("MAPI")
    Set MyAddressList = MyNameSpace.AddressLists("Personal Address Book")
    If MyAddressList Is Nothing Then
        MsgBox "Personal Address Book Unavailable!", vbExclamation
        Exit Sub
    End If
    Set MyAddressEntries = MyAddressList.AddressEntries
    On Error Resume Next
    For i = 1 to MyAddressEntries.Count
        Set MyEntry = MyAddressEntries.Item(i)
        MyEntry.Details
        If err <> 0 Then Exit Sub
    Next
End Sub
```

Changing an Address Entry

If you have the appropriate permissions, you can change the Address, Name, and Type properties of an AddressEntry object. To commit the change to the address book, you use the object's *Update* method. The following example converts the Name property of an AddressEntry object to all uppercase characters:

```
Sub ChangeAddressEntry_Click
    On Error Resume Next
    Set MyNameSpace = Application.GetNameSpace("MAPI")
    Set MyAddressList = MyNameSpace.AddressLists("Personal Address Book")
    If MyAddressList Is Nothing Then
        MsgBox "Personal Address Book Unavailable!", vbExclamation
        Exit Sub
    End If
    Set MyEntries = MyAddressList.AddressEntries
    Set MyEntry = MyEntries.Item(1)
    MyEntry.Name = Ucase(MyEntry.Name)
    MyEntry.Update
End Sub
```

Deleting an Address Entry

The *Delete* method of the AddressEntry object removes an item from the address book. The following example steps through the items in the Personal Address Book and deletes the first item where the type is set to Sample:

```
Sub DeleteAddressEntry_Click
    On Error Resume Next
    Set MyNameSpace = Application.GetNameSpace("MAPI")
    Set MyAddressList = MyNameSpace.AddressLists("Personal Address Book")
    If MyAddressList Is Nothing Then
        MsgBox "Personal Address Book Unavailable!", vbExclamation
        Exit Sub
    End If
    Set MyEntries = MyAddressList.AddressEntries
    MsgBox "Adding a sample entry...", vbInformation
    Set MyEntry = MyEntries.Add ("SAMPLE","Sample Entry","sampleentry")
    MyEntry.Update
    MyEntry.Details
    Set MyEntry = MyEntries.GetFirst
    Do While TypeName(MyEntry) <> "Nothing"
        If MyEntry.Type = "SAMPLE" Then
            MsgBox "Deleting "& MyEntry, vbCritical
            MyEntry.Delete
        Exit Sub
        End If
        Set MyEntry = MyEntries.GetNext
    Loop
    MsgBox "No sample entries found.", vbInformation
End Sub
```

Getting Free/Busy Information for a User

You can determine whether someone is available at a given time using the *GetFreeBusy* method of the AddressEntry object. This method returns a string representing 30 days of free/busy information starting at midnight on a specified date. Each character in the string is a digit that indicates whether the person is available during a specified time period. You can specify that the string should indicate only whether the person is available, or you can specify that you want the string to indicate whether a busy time is marked as tentative or out of office.

For example, the following code example returns a string 1,440 characters long (48 half-hour periods over 30 days) containing 0 for each half-hour period the person is free, 1 for each period the person has a busy time marked tentative, 3 for each period the person has a busy time marked out of office, and 2 for other busy periods:

```
MyStatus = MyAddressEntry.GetFreeBusy("7/1/98",30,True)
```

The following code example returns a string 720 characters long (24 one-hour periods over 30 days) containing 0 for each hour the person is free and 1 for each hour the person is busy, regardless of how the busy periods are designated:

```
MyStatus = MyAddressEntry.GetFreeBusy("7/1/98",60,False)
```

The following example displays the next time a person is busy. In addition to Outlook objects and methods, it uses the following VBScript functions:

- **InputBox**   to prompt the user for the name of the person whose first busy time is to be checked
- **Date**   to retrieve the current date
- **FormatDateTime**   to convert the retrieved date to the format required by GetFreeBusy
- **InStr**   to determine the location (offset) of the first 1 character in the string returned by GetFreeBusy

```
Sub GetFreeBusyInformation_Click
    On Error Resume Next
    Set MyNameSpace = Application.GetNameSpace("MAPI")
    Set MyAddressList = MyNameSpace.AddressLists("Global Address List")
    If MyAddressList Is Nothing Then
        MsgBox "Global Address List Unavailable!", vbExclamation
        Exit Sub
    End If
    Set MyEntries = MyAddressList.AddressEntries
    MyName = InputBox("Find first busy time for:")
    If MyName <> "" then
        Set MyEntry = MyEntries(MyName)
        If Err Then
            MsgBox "Could not find " & MyName, vbCritical
        Exit Sub
        End If
```

```
            StartDate = FormatDateTime(Date,2)
            MyBusyTime = MyEntry.GetFreeBusy(StartDate,60)
            MsgBox MyEntry.Name & " is busy " & InStr(MyBusyTime,"1")-1 _
                & " hours after 12:00 am " & StartDate
        End If
End Sub
```

AddressEntry Properties

You can use such properties as Name, Address, Members, Type, and Manager to retrieve useful information contained in the item.

More Info For a complete list and description of the methods and properties for the AddressEntry object, see Microsoft Outlook Visual Basic Reference Help.

The following example uses the Members, Name, and Address properties of the AddressEntry object to display the name and address of each member of a private distribution list named Department:

```
Sub DisplayListMembers_Click
    On Error Resume Next
    Set MyNameSpace = Application.GetNameSpace("MAPI")
    Set MyAddressList = MyNameSpace.AddressLists("Personal Address Book")
    If MyAddressList Is Nothing Then
        MsgBox "Personal Address Book Unavailable!", vbExclamation
        Exit Sub
    End If
    MyName = InputBox("Display entries in this Personal Distribution List:")
    If MyName <> "" Then
        Set MyDistList = MyAddressList.AddressEntries(MyName)
        If Err Then
            MsgBox "Could not find " & MyName, vbCritical
            Exit Sub
        End If
        Set MyAddressEntries = MyDistList.Members
        For i = 1 to MyAddressEntries.Count
            Set MyEntry = MyAddressEntries.Item(i)
            MsgBox MyEntry.Name & " " & MyEntry.Address
        Next
    End If
End Sub
```

Using CDO to Obtain Recipients

Collaboration Data Objects (CDO) is an object model that assists in building messaging and collaboration applications. CDO serves as a complementary object model to manipulate MAPI folders and items from Visual Basic or VBScript code. In future versions of Outlook, CDO and the Outlook Object Model are expected to merge into a common object model. At this point, however, you can use CDO to access messaging objects which are not available in the Outlook Object Model. For example, the Address procedure shown next lets you present an AddressBook dialog box to the user. When the user makes recipient selections from the AddressBook dialog box, the resolved recipient names are stored in the user-defined field CDORecipients on the AddressEntry object example form in the VBScript Samples folder.

```
Sub GetRecipients_Click()
    Address "CDORecipients", "Recipients"
End Sub

Sub Address(strUDFieldName, strShortName)
    Dim i
    Dim strRecip
    On Error Resume Next
    strDialogCaption = "Select " & strUDFieldName
    Set objCDO = Application.CreateObject("MAPI.Session")
    'Piggyback on existing Outlook session
    objCDO.Logon "", "", False, False, 0
    If Err Then
        MsgBox "Could not establish CDO session!", vbCritical
    End If
    Set Recips = objCDO.AddressBook(Nothing, _
        strDialogCaption, False, True, 1, strShortName, "", "", 0)
    'These recipients have been resolved by forceResolution argument above
    If Not Err Then
        For i = 1 To Recips.Count
            strRecip = strRecip & Recips(i).Name & "; "
        Next
        If strRecip <> "" Then
            strRecip = Left(strRecip, Len(strRecip)-2)
            Userproperties(strUDFieldName) = strRecip
        End If
    End If
    objCDO.Logoff
End Sub
```

Installing Collaboration Data Objects

Unfortunately, CDO is not installed by default with Outlook 2000. This decision reverses Microsoft's default CDO installation for Outlook 98. Moreover, the location of cdo.dll has also changed from previous versions of Outlook. CDO provides functionality for many of the examples in this book and must be installed for the examples to operate correctly. The setup program for the companion CD automatically installs CDO, or it can be done manually.

To install Collaboration Data Objects

1. Insert the Office 2000 CD-ROM into your CD-ROM drive.
2. Click Start, click Settings, and then click Control Panel.
3. Double-click Add/Remove Programs.

4. On the Install/Uninstall page, click Microsoft Office 2000, and then click Add/Remove.

5. In the Microsoft Office 2000 Maintenance Mode dialog box, click Add or Remove Features.

6. Double-click the Microsoft Outlook For Windows item to expand the item in the Microsoft Office 2000: Update Features dialog box.

7. Click the Collaboration Data Objects item under Microsoft Outlook For Windows to expand the item.

8. Select Run From My Computer.

9. Click Update Now to complete the installation of Collaboration Data Objects.

More Info For additional information on Collaboration Data Objects properties and methods, see the Collaboration Data Objects Online Help (cdo.chm) file. For your convenience, cdo.chm can be found in the Collaboration Data Objects self-extracting zip file located in the Help folder in the Building Microsoft Outlook 2000 Applications personal folders (.pst) file accompanying this book.

The Folders Collection Object

The Outlook 2000 Object Model provides two folder objects: a Folders collection object and a MAPIFolder object. The Folders collection object represents multiple folders. The MAPIFolder object, covered later in this chapter, represents a single folder.

The Folders collection object can contain single or multiple folders. The Folders collection object is always referenced from the NameSpace object.

More Info For a complete list and description of the properties, methods, and events for the Folders collection object, see Microsoft Outlook Visual Basic Reference Help.

Folders Collection Methods

This section covers the *Add* and *Item* methods of the Folders collection object.

Adding a Folder to the Folder List

You can use the *Add* method of the Folders collection object to add a folder to the Folder List. The following example uses the *Add* method of the Folders collection object to add a folder called My New Folder to the Building Microsoft Outlook 2000 Applications personal folder (.pst) file.

```
Sub CommandButton1_Click
    Set MyNameSpace = Application.GetNameSpace("MAPI")
    Set MyFolder = MyNameSpace.Folders _
        ("Building Microsoft Outlook 2000 Applications")
```

```
        Set MyNewFolder = MyFolder.Folders.Add("My New Folder")
    End Sub
```

Iterating Through a Collection of Folders

You can use the *Item* method of the Folders collection object to iterate through a collection of folders. The following example uses the uses the Count property of the Folders collection object to return the number of folder items in the folders collection. It also uses the *Item* method of the Folders collection object to return each folder in the collection and then display its name. You can also use the For Each...Next syntax to iterate over the objects in a collection object.

```
Sub IterateThroughAFolderCollection_Click
    Set myNameSpace = Application.GetNameSpace("MAPI")
    set myFolders = myNameSpace.Folders _
        ("Building Microsoft Outlook 2000 Applications")
    Set MyCollection = myFolders.Folders
    For i = 1 to MyCollection.Count
        set MyFolder = myCollection.Item(i)
        MsgBox MyFolder.Name, vbInformation
    Next
    'For Each...Next provides alternative syntax
    'For Each MyFolder in MyCollection
        'MsgBox MyFolder.Name, vbInformation
    'Next
End Sub
```

> **Note** When iterating through a collection of folders or items, the folders or items are not always ordered in the collection based on the date they are received in the folder. If your code depends on a particular order in the collection, use the *Sort* method of the collection object to control the order of the collection.

The MAPIFolder Object

The MAPIFolder object represents a single Outlook folder. A MAPIFolder object can contain other MAPIFolder objects, as well as Outlook items. This section explains how to move through the Folder List by using the MAPIFolder object and its Folders property.

> **More Info** For a complete list and description of the properties, methods, and events for the MAPIFolder object, see Microsoft Outlook Visual Basic Reference Help.

> **Important** Open the MAPIFolder object item in the VBScript Samples folder to work directly with this code in Outlook.

MAPIFolder Object Methods

This section covers the *CopyTo* and *Display* methods of the MAPIFolder object.

Copying a Folder

You can use the *CopyTo* method of the MAPIFolder object to create a copy of a folder in another folder. The following example copies the Notes folder to the Inbox:

```
Sub CommandButton1_Click
    Set MyNameSpace = Application.GetNameSpace("MAPI")
    Set MyInboxFolder = MyNameSpace.GetDefaultFolder(6)
    Set MyCurrentFolder = MyNameSpace.GetDefaultFolder(12)
    Set MyNewFolder = MyCurrentFolder.CopyTo(MyInboxFolder)
End Sub
```

Displaying a Folder

You can use the *Display* method of the MAPIFolder object to display the folder represented by the MAPIFolder object.

```
Sub DisplayAFolder_Click
    On Error Resume Next
    Set MyNameSpace = Application.GetNameSpace("MAPI")
    Set MyFolder = MyNameSpace.Folders("Public Folders")
    If MyFolder Is Nothing Then
        MsgBox "Public Folders folder not found", vbCritical
            Exit Sub
    End If
    MyFolder.Display
End Sub
```

MAPIFolder Object Properties

This section covers the DefaultMessageClass, Folders, Items, Parent, Child, EntryID, StoreID, UnReadItemCount, and WebViewURL properties. The Folders property is useful for accessing a folder in the folder list. The Items property is useful for retrieving a collection of items in the folder.

Referencing a Folder in the Folder List

You can use the Folders property with the MAPIFolder object to return another MAPIFolder object. The *OpenMAPIFolder* function shown below is a more efficient way to return a folder in the folder list, compared with the folder-by-folder method illustrated here. In the following procedure, the Folders property is used to move through the various branches of a personal folders list:

```
Sub ReferenceAFolder_Click
    Set MyNameSpace = Application.GetNameSpace("MAPI")
    Set MyFolder = MyNameSpace.Folders _
        ("Building Microsoft Outlook 2000 Applications")
    Set BeyondFolder = MyFolder.Folders("4. Beyond the Basics")
    Set VBScriptFolder = BeyondFolder.Folders("VBScript")
    MsgBox VBScriptFolder.Name, vbInformation
End Sub
```

Iterating Through a Collection of Items in a Folder

You can use the Items property of the MAPIFolder object to return a collection of items in the folder.

The following example uses the Items property of the MAPIFolder object to return the collection of items in the Inbox folder. It then shows the Subject value of the first five items in the Items collection.

```
Sub IterateThroughACollectionofItems_Click()
  On Error Resume Next
  Set MyNameSpace = Application.GetNameSpace("MAPI")
  Set MyInboxFolder = MyNameSpace.GetDefaultFolder(6)
  Set MyItems = MyInboxFolder.Items
  For i = 1 to 5
      Set MyItem = MyItems(i)
      Msgbox MyItem.Subject, vbInformation
  Next
End Sub
```

The EntryID and StoreID Properties

The EntryID and StoreID properties of the MAPIFolder object can be used to identify a folder in Outlook. The EntryID property corresponds to the MAPI property PR_ENTRYID. When an object is created, MAPI systems assign a permanent, unique ID string which does not change from one MAPI session to another. The EntryID and StoreID properties, which are analogous to primary keys in a database table, let you identify both Folder and Item objects in the MAPI subsystem. Once you have these values, you can use the *GetFolderFromID* method to return a MAPIFolder object.

The following example displays the value of the MAPI EntryID and StoreID for the current folder in a message box, displays another message box showing the folder's UnReadItemCount, DefaultMessageClass, and WebViewURL, and then uses the *GetFolderFromID* method to re-instantiate the Folder object and display the folder:

```
Sub ShowFolderInfo_Click
    Set MyNameSpace = Application.GetNameSpace("MAPI")
    Set MyFolder = MyNameSpace.PickFolder
    If MyFolder Is Nothing Then
        MsgBox "User pressed cancel.", vbInformation
        Exit Sub
    End If
    MsgBox "The Entry ID for the selected folder is:" & vbCr _
        & MyFolder.EntryID & vbCr & vbCr _
        & "The Store ID for the selected folder is:" & vbCr _
        & MyFolder.StoreID, vbInformation
    MsgBox MyFolder.UnReadItemCount & " of " & MyFolder.Items.Count _
        & " items are unread." & vbCr _
        & "The folder default message class is: _
        " & MyFolder.DefaultMessageClass & vbCr _
        & "The folder URL is: " & MyFolder.WebViewURL, vbInformation
```

```
        Set MyFolder = MyNameSpace.GetFolderFromID _
            (MyFolder.EntryID, MyFolder.StoreID)
        MyFolder.Display
    End Sub
```

Returning a Folder from a Folder Path

The OpenMAPIFolder procedure allows you to return a MAPIFolder object if you supply a folder path as an argument. A folder path is expressed as follows:

```
Set objFolder = OpenMAPIFolder _
  ("\Public Folders\All Public Folders\Sales\Q499")

Function OpenMAPIFolder(ByVal strPath) 'As MAPIFolder
    Dim objFldr 'As MAPIFolder
    Dim strDir 'As String
    Dim strName 'As String
    Dim i 'As Integer
    On Error Resume Next
    If Left(strPath, Len("\")) = "\" Then
        strPath = Mid(strPath, Len("\") + 1)
    Else
        Set objFldr = Application.ActiveExplorer.CurrentFolder
    End If
    While strPath <> ""
        i = InStr(strPath, "\")
        If i Then
            strDir = Left(strPath, i - 1)
            strPath = Mid(strPath, i + Len("\"))
        Else
            strDir = strPath
            strPath = ""
        End If
        If objFldr Is Nothing then
            Set objFldr = Application.GetNameSpace("MAPI").Folders(strDir)
            On Error Goto 0
        Else
            Set objFldr = objFldr.Folders(strDir)
        End If
    Wend
    Set OpenMAPIFolder = objFldr
End Function
```

Note The type declarations have been commented out in the *OpenMAPIFolder* and *GetFolderPath* functions. If you want to use these functions in VBA or Visual Basic code, remove the comment marks.

Returning a Folder Path from a Folder

The GetFolderPath function allows you to return a string representing a folder path if you supply a MAPIFolder object as an argument.

```
Function GetFolderPath(ByVal objFolder) 'As String
    On Error Resume Next
    Dim strFolderPath 'As String
    Dim objChild 'As MAPIFolder
    Dim objParent 'As MAPIFolder
    strFolderPath = "\" & objFolder.Name
    Set objChild = objFolder
    Do Until Err <> 0
        Set objParent = objChild.Parent
        If Err <> 0 Then
            Exit Do
        End If
        strFolderPath = "\" & objParent.Name & strFolderPath
        Set objChild = objParent
    Loop
    GetFolderPath = strFolderPath
End Function
```

Displaying a Folder Web View

One of the exciting new features of Outlook 2000 is the ability to display Web views in the Explorer View pane. The following example sets the WebViewURL for your Drafts folder to the Microsoft Outlook Home Page and then displays the Web view of the folder. The WebViewOn property is then set to *False* to restore the default view on the folder.

```
Sub DisplayFolderWebView_Click
    On Error Resume Next
    Set MyNS = Application.GetNameSpace("MAPI")
    Set MyFolder = MyNS.GetDefaultFolder(16) 'Drafts folder
    MyFolder.WebViewURL = "http://www.microsoft.com/outlook"
    MyFolder.WebViewOn = True
    MyFolder.Display
    MsgBox "Click OK to Reset Web View", vbInformation
    MyFolder.WebViewOn = False 'Reset
    'Re-instantiate the MAPIFolder object
    Set MyFolder = MyNS.GetDefaultFolder(16) 'Drafts folder
    MyFolder.Display
End Sub
```

The Items Collection Object

Items are the discrete packages of information represented by a Mail Message, a Post item, a Contact item, a Distribution List item, a Document item, a Journal item, a Meeting Request, a Note, or a Task item. You use the Items property to return the Items collection of a MAPIFolder object. The single item object is represented by the following objects:

- AppointmentItem object—an Appointment item
- ContactItem object—a Contact item
- DistListItem object—a Distribution List item

- DocumentItem object—a Document item
- JournalItem object—Journal item
- MailItem object—a Mail Message item
- MeetingItem object—a Meeting item
- NoteItem object—a Note item
- PostItem object—a Post item
- ReportItem object—a Mail-delivery report item
- TaskItem object—a Task item
- TaskRequestAcceptItem—an item sent to accept a Task request
- TaskRequestDeclineItem—an item sent to decline a Task request
- TaskRequestItem—an item sent to assign a Task
- TaskRequestUpdateItem—an item sent to update a Task request

This section covers some of the methods and properties of the Items collection object. Sections that follow this section cover the methods and properties of specific Item objects.

More Info For a complete list and description of the properties, methods, and events for the Items collection object, see Microsoft Outlook Visual Basic Reference Help.

Important Open the Items collection object item in the VBScript Samples folder to work directly with this code in Outlook.

Items Collection Methods

This section covers the *Add*, *Find*, and *Restrict* methods of the Items collection object.

Creating a Custom Item

With Outlook, there are two basic methods of creating items. Standard items such as Message items (IPM.Note), Post items (IPM.Post), and Contact items (IPM.Contact) are created using the *CreateItem* method of the Application object, as discussed earlier in this chapter.

To create custom items, however, such as an IPM.Post.Product Idea item, you use the *Add* method of the Items collection object. For example, to create a Product Idea item (IPM.Post.Product Idea) for the Product Ideas folder, you must first return the Items collection object, and then use the *Add* method of the Items collection object to add the new item to the collection. The custom item has the methods and properties of the item upon which is it based. For example, an item with the message class IPM.Post.Product Idea contains the methods and properties of the PostItem object, in addition to the custom UserProperties defined for IPM.Post.Product Idea. If you create an item with the message class IPM.Note.Orders, you use the MailItem object.

Important Before you can create a custom item, the form associated with the item must exist in the forms library of the folder in which the item is created. For example, to create a Product Idea item, the Product Idea form must exist in the Product Ideas Folder forms library or in the Personal or Organizational Forms Libraries.

The following example references the Product Ideas folder, and then creates a Product Idea item and displays it. Note that the Product Idea form exists in the Product Ideas folder forms library.

```
Sub CreateACustomItem_Click()
    Set MyNameSpace = Application.GetNameSpace("MAPI")
    Set BldFolder = MyNameSpace.Folders _
    ("Building Microsoft Outlook 2000 Applications")
    Set QuickFolder = BldFolder.Folders("2. Quick Guide")
    Set ProductIdeasFolder = QuickFolder.Folders("Product Ideas")
    Set MyItems = ProductIdeasFolder.Items
    Set MyItem = MyItems.Add("IPM.Post.Product Idea")
    MyItem.Subject = "VBScript Test"
    MyItem.Body = "This is a test"
    MyItem.Display
End Sub
```

Important Note that in the preceding procedure, the Body property of the single Item object corresponds with the Message field on the form. For more details about the properties of standard items, see "MailItem and PostItem Objects Properties" later in this chapter.

Finding an Item in a Folder

You can use the *Find* method of the Items collection object to find an item in a folder based on the conditions you specify. The following example uses the *Find* method of the Items collection object to return the first item in the Product Ideas folder with the value Boating in the Product Category field:

```
Sub FindAnIteminAFolder_Click ()
    Set MyNameSpace = Application.GetNameSpace("MAPI")
    Set BldFolder = MyNameSpace.Folders _
        ("Building Microsoft Outlook 2000 Applications")
    Set QuickFolder = BldFolder.Folders("2. Quick Guide")
    Set ProductIdeasFolder = QuickFolder.Folders("Product Ideas")
    Set MyItem = ProductIdeasFolder.Items.Find _
        ("[Product Category] = 'Boating'")
    MyItem.Display
End Sub
```

Important If you are using user-defined fields as part of a restriction argument of a *Find* or *Restrict* method, the user-defined fields must exist in the folder; otherwise, the code will raise an error and the *Find* or *Restrict* method will fail. You can add a field to a folder by displaying the Field Chooser and clicking New.

Creating a Filtered Collection of Items from a Folder

You can use the *Restrict* method of the Items collection object to create filters that return only those items in a folder matching the conditions you specify.

> **More Info** For more information about constructing filter expressions, see *Find* Method and *Restrict* Method in Microsoft Outlook Visual Basic Reference Help.

The following example returns the collection of items from the Product Ideas folder, and then creates a filtered collection of items with only the value Boating in the Product Category field:

```
Sub CreateAFilteredCollection_Click
    Set MyNameSpace = Application.GetNameSpace("MAPI")
    Set BldFolder = MyNameSpace.Folders _
        ("Building Microsoft Outlook 2000 Applications")
    Set QuickFolder = BldFolder.Folders("2. Quick Guide")
    Set ProductIdeasFolder = QuickFolder.Folders("Product Ideas")
    Set MyItems = ProductIdeasFolder.Items
    Set MyFilter = MyItems.Restrict("[Product Category] = 'Boating'")
    MsgBox "There are " & MyFilter.Count & " Boating items.", vbInformation
End Sub
```

> **Note** The *Restrict* method does not offer optimal performance for a large collection of items in a folder. If you need to iterate over hundreds or thousands of items in a folder, use the *SetColumns* method to cache specified properties and increase performance. Only certain Item properties can be cached with the *Restrict* and *SetColumns* methods. User-defined properties cannot be cached with *SetColumns*. See *Restrict* Method and *SetColumns* Method in Microsoft Outlook Visual Basic Reference Help for additional information.

Sorting the Items in a Filtered Collection

If you want to sort the items in the Items collection, use the *Sort* method. Currently, the *Sort* method only supports sorting on built-in properties for the Item. The example below creates a restricted collection of Contacts in your mailbox that have an Email1Address value. After the restriction has been created, the *Sort* method is used on the filtered Items collection object. Finally, the first item is the Sorted Items collection is displayed.

```
Sub SortAFilteredCollection_Click
    On Error Resume Next
    olFolderContacts = 10
    Set MyNameSpace = Application.GetNameSpace("MAPI")
    Set myFolder = MyNameSpace.GetDefaultFolder(olFolderContacts)
    Set MyItems = myFolder.Items
    'Create the Filter first and then sort
    Set MyFilter = MyItems.Restrict("[Email1Address] <> ''")
    'Sort by LastName in descending order
    MyFilter.Sort "[LastName]", True
```

```
        'Display the first item in the filter
        MyFilter.Item(1).Display
End Sub
```

Important The *Sort* method will return an error if you attempt to sort for built-in multi-valued properties such as Companies and Categories. You also cannot sort by a user-defined field unless the user-defined field is defined in the folder. The *Sort* method is effective, from a performance standpoint, only for small collections of items.

Deleting the Items in a Collection

If you want to delete items from an Items collection object, you can't use the *For i = 1 to MyItems.Count...MyItems.Item(i).Delete...Next* routine or the *For Each myItem in MyItems...myItem.Delete...Next* routine you would normally use to iterate over the items in the collection. The following example is a generic function that will delete all the items in the Items collection passed as an argument to the function:

```
Function DeleteAllItems(myItems) 'MyItems is an Items collection object
    On Error Resume Next
    Do Until MyItems.Count = 0
        MyItems.Remove 1
    Loop
End Function
```

Items Collection Object Properties

This section explains how to use the Count property.

Returning the Count of Items in the Items Collection

You can use the Count property of the Items collection object to return the number of items in the Items collection. This provides an easy way to loop through collections to process a large number of items, as shown in the previous example. The following example returns the number of items in the Inbox and shows the number in a message box:

```
Sub CommandButton1_Click()
    On Error Resume Next
    Set MyFolder = Item.Application.GetNameSpace("MAPI").GetDefaultFolder(6)
    Set MyItems = MyFolder.Items
    MsgBox "You have " & MyItems.Count _
        & " items in your Inbox.", vbInformation
End Sub
```

The PostItem Object

The PostItem object represents a message posted in a public folder. Unlike a MailItem object, a PostItem object is not sent to a recipient. This section covers some of the methods of the PostItem object. Properties of the PostItem object are similar to the properties of the MailItem object, so they are discussed together in "MailItem and PostItem Objects Properties" later in this chapter.

PostItem Object Methods

The PostItem object provides a variety of methods that you can use to control the actions of an item. This section covers the *Copy*, *Move*, *Delete*, *Display*, and *Post* methods.

Copying and Moving an Item

You can use the *Copy* method of the PostItem object to create a copy of an item. You can then use the *Move* method to move the copied item to a new location.

The following example returns the first item in the Product Ideas folder with the value Boating in the Product Category field. It then uses the *Copy* method to create a copy of the item returned from the Product Ideas folder. If the user selects Yes in the message box, the *Move* method copies the item from the Product Ideas folder to the Drafts folder. If you want to move rather than copy the item, use the *Delete* method and place a MyItem.Delete statement after the MyItem.Copy statement.

```
Sub CopyAndMove_Click
    Set MyNameSpace = Application.GetNameSpace("MAPI")
    Set BldFolder = MyNameSpace.Folders _
        ("Building Microsoft Outlook 2000 Applications")
    Set QuickFolder = BldFolder.Folders("2. Quick Guide")
    Set ProductIdeasFolder = QuickFolder.Folders("Product Ideas")
    Set MyItem = ProductIdeasFolder.Items.Find _
        ("[Product Category] = 'Boating'")
    If MyItem Is Nothing Then
        MsgBox "Could not find an item.", vbInformation
    Else
        strQuestion = "Copy " & MyItem.Subject & " to Drafts?"
        If MsgBox(strQuestion, vbQuestion+vbYesNo) = vbYes Then
            Set MyCopiedItem = MyItem.Copy
            'MyItem.Delete if a move instead of copy
            Set DestinationFolder = MyNameSpace.GetDefaultFolder(16)
            myCopiedItem.Move DestinationFolder
            MsgBox MyItem.Subject & " copied to Drafts.", vbInformation
        End If
    End If
End Sub
```

Creating and Displaying a Custom Post Item

You can use the *Display* method of the PostItem object to display an item on the desktop. As discussed earlier, you use the *Add* method of the Items collection object to create a new custom Post item. The following example returns the Product Ideas folder, and then creates a new custom PostItem object by using the *Add* method of the Items collection object. It then displays the item in the Product Idea form. If you click the Post button on the form, the item is posted in the Product Ideas folder.

```
Sub CreateAndDisplay_Click()
    Set MyNameSpace = Application.GetNameSpace("MAPI")
    Set BldFolder = MyNameSpace.Folders _
        ("Building Microsoft Outlook 2000 Applications")
    Set QuickFolder = BldFolder.Folders("2. Quick Guide")
    Set ProductIdeasFolder = QuickFolder.Folders("Product Ideas")
    Set MyItem = ProductIdeasFolder.Items.Add("IPM.Post.Product Idea")
    myItem.Subject = "Handlebar polish"
    myItem.UserProperties("Product Category") = "Cycling"
    myItem.Body = "For cyclists who want their bikes to gleam in the wind."
    MyItem.Display
End Sub
```

Posting an Item

You can use the *Post* method of the PostItem object to post an item in a folder. The following example sets the folder to the Product Ideas folder. It then creates a new item with the message class IPM.Post Product Idea, which is added to the Product Ideas Items collection. In this procedure, the object returned to MyItem by the *Add* method has a base message class of IPM.Post so you can use the *Post* method. The Subject and Body properties of the MyItem object are set, and then the item is posted to the Product Ideas folder.

```
Sub PostanItem_Click
    Set MyNameSpace = Application.GetNameSpace("MAPI")
    Set BldFolder = MyNameSpace.Folders _
        ("Building Microsoft Outlook 2000 Applications")
    Set QuickFolder = BldFolder.Folders("2. Quick Guide")
    Set ProductIdeasFolder = QuickFolder.Folders("Product Ideas")
    Set myItem = ProductIdeasFolder.Items.Add("IPM.Post.Product Idea")
    myItem.Subject = "VBScript is versatile"
    myItem.Body = "Let's develop new products using this technology."
    myItem.Post
    MsgBox myItem.Subject & _
        " has been posted in the Product Ideas folder.", vbInformation
End Sub
```

The MailItem Object

The MailItem object represents a message in a mail folder. This section also covers some of the methods and properties of the PostItem object. Properties of the PostItem object are similar to the properties of the MailItem object, so they are discussed together.

> **Important** Open the MailItem object and PostItem object items in the VBScript Samples folder to work directly with this code in Outlook.

MailItem Object Methods

This section covers the *Send*, *Reply*, and *Close* methods of the MailItem object.

Sending a Message

You can use the *Send* method of the MailItem object to send a message to a recipient. The following example creates a Mail Message item, sets the Subject and message Body fields, and then sets the To field to your name. You can retrieve the ScriptText property of the FormDescription object for the item to set the Body property of the message. It then uses the *Send* method to send the item to the specified recipient.

> **Note** The Body property of the item only lets you set plain text as the message text. If you want to format the Body programmatically, use the HTMLEditor property discussed below.

```
Sub SendAMessage_Click
    Set MyItem = Application.CreateItem(olMailItem)
    MyItem.Subject = "VBScript Code for MailItem object"
    Set MyForm = Item.FormDescription
    MyItem.Body = MyForm.ScriptText
    MyItem.To = Application.GetNameSpace("MAPI").CurrentUser
    MyItem.Send
End Sub
```

Replying to a Message

You can use the *Reply* method of a MailItem object to return a Reply item. The following example creates a Reply item based on the current item, and then returns the Reply item represented by the MyReply object. The Reply item is then displayed. To run this example, you must first put a CommandButton1 control on the Read page of a Mail Message form. Exit Design mode and send the item to your Inbox, and then open the item in the Inbox and click CommandButton1. The Reply item is displayed.

```
Sub CommandButton1_Click
    Set MyFolder = Application.GetNameSpace("MAPI").GetDefaultFolder(6)
    Set MyItem = MyFolder.Items.Item(1)
    Set MyReply = MyItem.Reply
    MyReply.Display
End Sub
```

Closing an Item

You can use the *Close* method of the MailItem object to close an item. When you close the item, you also close the item's associated form. The following example closes the current item when the CloseAnItem button is clicked. Note that if the *blnIsDirty* script-level variable is *True*, then the user is prompted to save changes. If *blnIsDirty* is *False*, then the item is closed and changes are not saved. You could modify this procedure to automatically save changes to a dirty form. This example also illustrates how you can write event procedures in the code for your custom form to control how and when the form is saved.

```
Dim blnIsDirty

Sub Item_PropertyChange(ByVal Name)
    blnIsDirty = True
End Sub

Sub Item_CustomPropertyChange(ByVal Name)
    blnIsDirty = True
End Sub

Function Item_Write()
    blnIsDirty = False
End Function

Sub CloseAnItem_Click
    Const olSave = 0
    Const olDiscard = 1
    Const olPromptForSave = 2
    If blnIsDirty = True Then
        Item.Close olPromptForSave
    Else
        Item.Close olDiscard
    End If
End Sub
```

You can use one of the following arguments with the *Close* method or use CONST declarations as shown in the preceding example.

Save Option	Value
Save all changes without prompting	0
Discard all changes without prompting	1
Prompt to save or discard all changes	2

Note Unlike previous versions of Outlook, Outlook 2000 allows you to write VBA or VB code to respond to all the events that are raised in a Message item. For additional information, see Chapter 9, "Raise Events and Move to the Head of the Class," and Chapter 13, "Creating COM Add-Ins with Visual Basic."

MailItem and PostItem Objects Properties

This section covers the GetInspector, Body, HTMLBody, To, and SenderName properties of the MailItem and PostItem objects.

Using GetInspector To Reference the Form

You can use the GetInspector property of the MailItem object or the PostItem object to reference the form associated with an item. You can then reference the page on the form, and then the controls on the page. The following example uses the GetInspector property of the MailItem object to return the form associated with the item. It references the Message page on the form, and then sets the Visible property of the TextBox1 control to *False*.

Before you run this example, do the following:

1. If you don't have a TextBox1 control on the form, click Design This Form from Forms on the Tools menu to switch to Design mode.

2. Drag a TextBox control from the Control Toolbox to the form.

3. Click Run This Form on the Form menu to switch to Run mode, and then click CommandButton1 to hide the TextBox1 control.

```
Sub CommandButton1_Click
    Set MyPage = GetInspector.ModifiedFormPages("Message")
    MyPage.TextBox1.Visible = False
End Sub
```

Setting the Message Text of an Item

You can use the Body property of a MailItem object or a PostItem object to specify the text that appears in the Message control of a Mail Message.

The following example creates a Reply item, enters text in the Message control of the Reply item, and then sends the form. To run this example, you must first put a CommandButton1 control on the Read page of a Mail Message form. Then switch to Run mode and send the item to your Inbox. Open the item in your Inbox and click Enable Macros in the Macro Warning dialog box. Click CommandButton1 when the form opens. The Reply item appears.

```
Sub CommandButton1_Click
    Set MyReply = Item.Reply
    MyReply.Body = "Let's go to the Napa Valley next weekend."
    MyReply.Display
End Sub
```

Note The Body property does not support Rich Text Format (RTF) or HyperText Markup Language (HTML).

You can also use the HTMLBody property of a MailItem or PostItem object to specify formatted text in the Message control. When you set this property, Outlook automatically sets the EditorType property of the associated Inspector object to olEditorHTML(2).

The following example displays the current editor type, sets the HTMLBody property of the item, and then displays the new editor type. Open the HTMLBody object form in the VBScript Samples folder to see a more sophisticated example of using the HTMLBody property. You can create HTML dynamically in the VBScript code behind a form and then present that HTML in the body of an Item.

```
Sub CommandButton1_Click
    MsgBox "EditorType = " & Item.GetInspector.EditorType
    Item.HTMLBody = "<H1>This is HTML text.</H1>"
    MsgBox "EditorType is now = " & Item.GetInspector.EditorType
End Sub
```

> **Note** Setting the Body property of the item causes Outlook to reset the editor type as the user's default.

Setting the To Field of an Item

You can use the To property of the MailItem object to set the value of a To field. The following example creates a new item, and then sets the To field and Subject field values of the item:

```
Sub CommandButton1_Click
    Set MyItem = Application.CreateItem(0)
    MyItem.To = "James Allard"
    MyItem.Subject = "How to set the To field"
    MyItem.Display
End Sub
```

Getting the Sender Name of an Item

You can use the SenderName property of the MailItem object to return the name of the person who sent the message. This example gets the first item in the Inbox and sets the *Recip* variable to the value of the SenderName property. It then creates a new Message item and sets its To field to the value of the *Recip* variable. When the item is displayed, the value of the SenderName property shows in the To box of the form.

```
Sub GetTheSenderName_Click
    Set MyFolder = Application.GetNameSpace("MAPI").GetDefaultFolder(6)
    Set MyItem = MyFolder.Items(1)
    Recip = MyItem.SenderName
    Set MyNewItem = Application.CreateItem(0)
    MyNewItem.To = Recip
    MyNewItem.Display
End Sub
```

> **Note** In the preceding example, the name in the To field is not resolved. To resolve a name, the name must be added to the Recipients collection object. For more information, see "The Recipients Collection Object" later in this chapter.

Getting the Sender Address of an Item

The Outlook Object Model does not provide a means to obtain the e-mail address of the item's sender. To obtain the e-mail address of the sender, you can use CDO to create a Sender object for the MAPI Message object. The Sender object exposes several useful properties, one of which is the Address property. The following VBA code displays a message box containing the e-mail address for the sender of the first item in the Inbox:

```
Sub GetSender()
    Dim objCDO As MAPI.Session
    Dim objMsg As MAPI.Message
    Dim objSender As MAPI.AddressEntry
    Dim oMsg As Outlook.MailItem
    Dim strMsg As String
    On Error Resume Next
    Set oMsg = Application.ActiveExplorer.Selection.Item(1)
    Set objCDO = CreateObject("MAPI.Session")
    objCDO.Logon "", "", False, False
    Set objMsg = objCDO.GetMessage(oMsg.EntryID)
    Set objSender = objMsg.Sender
    strMsg = "Subject: " & objMsg.Subject & vbCrLf _
        & "Sender Name: " & objSender.Name & vbCrLf _
        & "Sender e-mail: " & objSender.Address & vbCrLf _
        & "Sender type: " & objSender.Type
    MsgBox strMsg, vbInformation
End Sub
```

Adding Attachments to an Item

You can add attachments to an item programmatically by using the *Add* method of the Attachments collection object. VBScript's FileSystemObject lets you write and read from a file programmatically. Therefore, you can write to a file and then attach the file to a message in code. Open the FileSystemObject item in the VBScript Samples folder to see this code in action.

```
Sub WriteandAttachFile_Click()
    Const ForReading = 1, ForWriting = 2, ForAppending = 8
    Const olByValue = 1, olByReference = 4, olEmbeddeditem = 5, olOLE = 6
    Dim fso
    Set fso = CreateObject("Scripting.FileSystemObject")
    strPath = GetTempDir & "\FSObject.txt"
    Set objFile = fso.OpenTextFile(strPath, ForAppending, True)
    strLine = Now & " - " & "This file demonstrates use " _
        & "of the FileSystemObject to write to a text file."
    objFile.Write(strLine)
    objFile.Close
    Set objMsg = Application.CreateItem(0)
    Set colAttachments = objMsg.Attachments
    colAttachments.Add strPath, olByValue, 1, "FileSystemObject Attachment"
    objMsg.Subject = "FileSystemObject Object"
    objMsg.Display
End Sub
```

```
Function GetTempDir
    Const TemporaryFolder = 2, SystemFolder = 1, WindowsFolder = 0
    On Error Resume Next
    Dim fso, tfolder
    Set fso = CreateObject("Scripting.FileSystemObject")
    Set tfolder = fso.GetSpecialFolder(TemporaryFolder)
    If Err then
        GetTempDir = "Could not obtain temporary folder path."
        Exit Function
    End If
    GetTempDir = lcase(tFolder.Path)
End Function
```

The DocumentItem Object

The DocumentItem object represents an assortment of different items that can be stored in Outlook folders. To clarify what a DocumentItem object represents, the terms extrinsic and intrinsic DocumentItems need to be defined. A DocumentItem object can be a file that is dragged to an Outlook folder from Windows Explorer. It can also result from a file posted to an Exchange public folder from a source application such as Microsoft Word, Excel, or PowerPoint. These items are extrinsic DocumentItem objects, meaning that they were created by an application extrinsic to Outlook. An extrinsic DocumentItem has the following characteristics:

- The DocumentItem was created by its native application or an object model supported by its native application.
- The item does not support Outlook DocumentItem properties, methods, and events.
- You cannot create a custom Outlook form from an extrinsic DocumentItem.

Because extrinsic DocumentItem objects do not support Outlook Inspector properties and events, you cannot automate these items easily within the container of an Outlook folder. For example, you cannot write an *Item_Open* event procedure for an extrinsic DocumentItem object. Some applications—most notably Microsoft Excel—still support a native Open event that fires when a user opens the document. This event fires whether the Excel document exists in an Outlook folder or in the file system. For example, the TimeCard template (in the Time Card Application folder under the 6.Sample Applications folder) uses the *Workbook_Open* event to complete a timecard based on information stored in a user's Tasks folder.

A DocumentItem object can also be an Outlook DocumentItem that wraps an Inspector object around an Office 2000 document. A user creates an Outlook Office Document Item by selecting the Office Document command from the New submenu of the File menu in Outlook Explorer. There are only four types of Outlook DocumentItems that you can create from within Outlook: Word Documents, Excel Charts, Excel Worksheets, and PowerPoint Presentations. These DocumentItems are known as intrinsic DocumentItems. An intrinsic DocumentItem object has the following characteristics.

- They support Outlook DocumentItem properties, methods, and events.
- They can be either a Post-type or Send-type DocumentItem. When you design an Outlook DocumentItem, you will see a dialog box asking you if you want to send the document to someone or post the document in this folder. Whatever your choice, Outlook does not distinguish between a Post or Send DocumentItem in the message class of the custom form.
- You can create a custom Outlook form from an intrinsic DocumentItem. This custom form will have a base message class equivalent to the message class of the extrinsic DocumentItem. If you create a custom DocumentItem named Sales Analysis from a Word DocumentItem, the message class of the custom form will be IPM.Document.Word.Document.8.Sales Analysis.
- You can write VBScript code behind the DocumentItem custom form.

These Outlook DocumentItems have the same base message class as extrinsic DocumentItems. In all cases, DocumentItems are actually attachments to a message container with a message class of IPM.Document. The following table lists some important types of DocumentItems that can be placed in an Outlook folder:

Document Item	Message Class	Outlook DocumentItem with Inspector	Custom Form Built on Item	Document Open Event
Web Page	IPM.Document.htmlfile	No	No	Use DHTML to create window onload event.
Word Document	IPM.Document.Word.Document.8	Yes	Yes	No. See workaround below.
Excel Worksheet	IPM.Document.Excel.Sheet.8	Yes	Yes	Yes.
PowerPoint Presentation	IPM.Document.PowerPoint.Show.8	Yes	Yes	No.
Adobe Acrobat Document	IPM.Document.AcroExch.Document	No	No	No.
Visio Drawing	IPM.Document.Visio.Drawing.5	No	No	No.
Other Document Types	IPM.Document.<Document Class>	No	No	Depends on the object model and VBA support in the source application.

Creating a Word DocumentItem

You can create a Word Document Item programmatically in a folder as long as you have Word installed. Creating a DocumentItem programmatically is a two-step process. First, create a DocumentItem with the correct message class in the target folder. To complete the process, use the Attachments collection of the DocumentItem to add an appropriate attachment to the DocumentItem. The following VBA example uses Word Automation to create a Word document in the temporary folder. The Word document is then attached to a Word DocumentItem created in the user's Inbox. Finally, the Word document in the temporary folder is deleted. The same basic sequence would be followed if you wanted to create an Excel workbook instead of a Word document.

```
Sub AddDocumenttoInbox()
    Dim objWordDoc As DocumentItem
    Dim wdApp As Word.Application
    Dim wdDoc As Word.Document
    Dim objFolder As MAPIFolder
    On Error Resume Next
    Set objFolder = _
        Application.GetNameSpace("MAPI").GetDefaultFolder(olFolderInbox)
    Set objWordDoc = objFolder.Items.Add("IPM.Document.Word.Document.8")
    Set wdApp = CreateObject("Word.Application")
    Set wdDoc = wdApp.Documents.Add
    With wdApp.Selection
        .TypeText "Microsoft Outlook 2000"
        .TypeParagraph
        .TypeText "A great tool for communication and collaboration!"
    End With
    'GetTempDir returns trailing \
    strPath = GetTempDir() & "O2KTest.doc"
    wdDoc.SaveAs strPath
    wdDoc.Close
    'Save the DocumentItem with wdDoc attachment
    With objWordDoc
        .Subject = "Microsoft Outlook 2000"
        .Attachments.Add (strPath)
        .Save
    End With
    'Delete wdDoc in temp folder
    Kill strPath
End Sub
```

Firing the Word Document Open Event

One problem with intrinsic DocumentItems based on Microsoft Word is that the *Document_Open* event does not fire when the DocumentItem is opened from an Outlook folder. If you build an application based on a Word DocumentItem, you'll want to be able to use the *Document_Open* event so that code can assign values to bookmarks, insert and format text, and fill tables from an external database, if necessary. In short, the *Document_Open* event is the gateway to automating your custom DocumentItem form from Word VBA code embedded in the DocumentItem, rather than from VBScript code in the *Item_Open* event.

You'll find a workaround for this problem in the Word *Document_Open* item located in the VBScript Samples folder. The workaround uses the VBScript GetObject function to return a reference to the Word Application object. Since the document embedded in the DocumentItem object represents the ActiveDocument in the Word Application object, you can instantiate a Word Document object and use the *AutoRunMacro* method on that object to fire the *Document_Open* event. In this example, the *Document_Open* event displays a message box indicating the word count for the document:

```
Sub Item_Open()
    On Error Resume Next
    'Get CurrentUser
    strUser = Application.GetNameSpace("MAPI").CurrentUser
    Set objWord = GetObject(, "Word.Application")
    ' Use Word TypeText to insert some sample text
    strText = "The CurrentUser is: " & strUser
    objWord.Selection.TypeText strText
    objWord.Selection.TypeParagraph
    'Run the Document_Open procedure with RunAutoMacro method
    Set objDoc = objWord.ActiveDocument
    Const wdAutoOpen = 2
    objDoc.RunAutoMacro wdAutoOpen
    Item.Subject = "DocumentItem Word Document_Open Workaround"
    'Use Built-in properties to set subject and author
    Const wdPropertySubject = 2
    Const wdPropertyAuthor = 3
    objDoc.BuiltinDocumentProperties(wdPropertySubject) = _
        "Document_Open Workaround"
    objDoc.BuiltinDocumentProperties(wdPropertyAuthor) = strUser
    'Optional: Use CustomDocumentProperties to set additional fields
End Sub

Private Sub Document_Open()
    Dim strMsg As String
    strMsg = "This document contains " _
        & ThisDocument.BuiltInDocumentProperties(wdPropertyWords) _
        & " words."
    MsgBox strMsg, vbInformation, "Document Open Event"
End Sub
```

Using DocumentProperties with DocumentItem Objects

One of the great, but little known, features of Outlook is the ability to place documents in folders and expose both the BuiltInDocument properties and CustomDocumentProperties objects of the document in folder views. The DocumentProperties object is exposed for all applications in the Office 2000 suite, except Outlook 2000. Each DocumentProperty object represents a built-in or custom property of a container document. DocumentProperties are, in turn, divided into BuiltInDocumentProperties and CustomDocumentProperties. Each Office application exposes a subset of the BuiltInDocumentProperties collection object. If you are building an application around a folder containing DocumentItems, you can add BuiltInDocumentProperties to folder views.

To add Built-in Document Properties to a Folder View

1. Navigate to the folder where you want to establish the view.
2. On the Advanced toolbar, click the Field Chooser icon.
3. Select All Document Fields in the drop-down list box at the top of the Field Chooser window.
4. Drag appropriate fields to the folder View.

More Info For additional information about the DocumentProperties collection object, see DocumentProperties in the Microsoft Office Visual Basic Reference Help.

To use Custom Document Properties in a folder view, you must add the CustomDocumentProperties fields to the folder as user-defined fields in the folder. The following example assumes that you have installed the Expense Statement template for Excel 2000. (If you have not installed the Expense Statement template, it will demand to be installed the first time you attempt to create a workbook based on that template.)

To create an Expense Statement Document

1. Launch Excel 2000.
2. Select New from the File menu.
3. Double-click Expense Statement on the Spreadsheet Solutions page of the New dialog box.
4. Complete the Expense Statement template by clicking the Select Employee button and adding expense report information.
5. Select Send To from the File menu and then select Exchange Folder from the Send To submenu. If you are operating in Internet Mail Only (IMO) mode, you can save the file to a file system folder and then drag the Expense Statement workbook from the file system to an Outlook folder.

To add Custom Document Properties to a Folder View

1. In the folder where you placed the Expense Statement report, click the Field Chooser icon on the Advanced toolbar.
2. Select User-Defined Fields In Folder in the drop-down list box at the top of the Field Chooser window.
3. Click the New button to create a new user-defined field in the folder.
4. Enter Employee Name as the name of the user-defined field and click OK.
5. Drag the Employee Name field into the folder view.
6. In the Field Chooser, click New again.
7. Enter Total Reimbursement/Payment as the name of the user-defined field.
8. Select Number in the Type drop-down list box.

9. Click OK.

10. Drag the Total Reimbursement/Payment field into the folder view.

11. You should now see the values of the Custom Document Property fields displayed in the view in the folder.

The AppointmentItem Object

An AppointmentItem object represents an appointment in the Calendar folder. An AppointmentItem object can represent a one-time appointment, a meeting, or recurring appointments and meetings. A meeting usually involves more than one person, and is created when an AppointmentItem is sent to other users, who then receive it in the form of a MeetingItem object in their respective Inbox folders.

An appointment or meeting can be recurring—that is, set to occur more than once on a regular or repetitive basis. When this occurs, a RecurrencePattern object is created for the AppointmentItem object. An instance of a recurring appointment can be changed or deleted. This creates an exception to the recurrence pattern, and this exception is represented by an Exception object. All Exception objects associated with a given AppointmentItem object are contained in an Exceptions collection object associated with the AppointmentItem.

This section covers working with recurring appointments, including how to create a recurring appointment and how to deal with exceptions to the recurrence pattern. The section that follows covers creating a meeting from an appointment.

Important Open the AppointmentItem object in the VBScript Samples folder to work directly with this code in Outlook.

Working with Recurring Appointments

Creating a Recurring Appointment

A recurring appointment is represented by an AppointmentItem object with the IsRecurring property set to *True*. However, you cannot set this property directly. Instead, you create a recurring appointment by calling the *GetRecurrencePattern* method of the AppointmentItem object and then saving the item. The following example illustrates how to create an appointment named Test Appointment and then call the *GetRecurrencePattern* method to make it a recurring appointment:

```
Sub CreateRecurringAppointment_Click
    Set MyItem = Application.CreateItem(1)
    MyItem.Subject = "Test Appointment"
    Set MyPattern = MyItem.GetRecurrencePattern
    MyItem.Save
End Sub
```

The *GetRecurrencePattern* method returns a RecurrencePattern object. You can change the recurrence pattern of the appointment by setting properties of the appointment's RecurrencePattern object.

Setting the Recurrence Pattern of an Appointment

When a new recurring appointment is created, it inherits a default recurrence pattern based on the time the appointment was created. To change the recurrence pattern of an appointment, set the appropriate properties of the appointment's RecurrencePattern object.

More Info For more information about the properties of the RecurrencePattern object affecting the recurrence pattern, see Microsoft Outlook Visual Basic Reference Help.

The following example shows how to create a one-hour recurring appointment that occurs at noon on the second Tuesday of each month for two months, starting July, 1998:

```
Sub SetRecurrencePattern_Click
    Set MyItem = Application.CreateItem(1)
    MyItem.Subject = "Monthly Appointment"
    Set MyPattern = MyItem.GetRecurrencePattern
    MyPattern.RecurrenceType = 3 ' Monthly, on a specific weekday
    MyPattern.Interval = 1 ' Every month (2 would be every other month)
    MyPattern.DayOfWeekMask = 4 ' Which day of week (Tuesday)
    MyPattern.Instance = 2 ' Which instance (second Tuesday)
    MyPattern.StartTime = "12:00 pm" ' Time each appointment begins
    MyPattern.EndTime = "1:00 pm" ' Time each appointment ends
    MyPattern.PatternStartDate = #7/1/1998# ' Earliest date appt can occur
    MyPattern.PatternEndDate = #9/1/1998# ' Latest date appt can occur
    MyItem.Save
End Sub
```

Working with a Single Appointment in a Series

To determine whether an instance of a recurring appointment occurs at a particular time, use the *GetOccurrence* method of the RecurrencePattern object. This method returns an AppointmentItem object representing the instance of the recurring appointment.

Important The *GetOccurrence* method will produce an error if an instance of the recurring appointment does not start at the date and time you provide. If it is possible that your script can supply a date and time that does not match an instance of a recurring appointment (because of user input, for example), the script should be able to handle the error appropriately. Otherwise, the script procedure will fail and Outlook will display an error message.

The following example illustrates how to use the *GetOccurrence* method to determine whether a recurring appointment (created by the code in the previous section) starts on a date and time provided by the user. The On Error Resume Next statement ensures that the procedure will continue if the user enters anything that does not match the start date and time of an instance of the recurring appointment. After calling the *GetOccurrence* method, the script tests the *MyAppointment* variable to determine whether it is set to Nothing, indicating that the method failed and did not return an AppointmentItem object.

```
Sub CheckOccurrence_Click
    Set MyNameSpace = Application.GetNameSpace("MAPI")
    Set MyCalendarFolder = MyNameSpace.GetDefaultFolder(9)
    Set MyItem = MyCalendarFolder.Items("Monthly Appointment")
    Set MyPattern = MyItem.GetRecurrencePattern
    On Error Resume Next
    MyDate = InputBox ("Enter a date and time (m/d/yy hh:mm): ")
    Do While MyDate <> ""
        Set MyAppointment = Nothing
        Set MyAppointment = MyPattern.GetOccurrence(MyDate)
        If TypeName(MyAppointment) <> "Nothing" Then
            MsgBox "This instance of " & MyAppointment.Subject _
                & " occurs on " & MyAppointment.Start
        Else
            MsgBox MyItem.Subject & " does not occur on " & MyDate
        End If
        MyDate = InputBox ("Enter another date and time (m/d/yy hh:mm):")
    Loop
End Sub
```

Once you retrieve the AppointmentItem object representing an instance of a recurring appointment, you can delete or change the appointment instance. When this happens, Outlook creates an Exception object. The properties of this object describe the changes that were made to the instance. All of the Exception objects for a recurring appointment are contained in an Exceptions collection object associated with the appointment's RecurrencePattern object.

The AppointmentItem property of the Exception object returns the AppointmentItem object that constitutes the exception to the original recurrence pattern of the recurring appointment. You can use the methods and properties of the AppointmentItem object to work with the appointment exception. The following example changes the subject of an instance of the recurring appointment created by the script in the previous section. It then uses the AppointmentItem property of the resulting Exception object to change the start time of the appointment exception.

```
Sub CreateException_Click
    Set MyNameSpace = Application.GetNameSpace("MAPI")
    Set MyCalendarFolder = MyNameSpace.GetDefaultFolder(9)
    Set MyItem = MyCalendarFolder.Items("Monthly Appointment")
    Set MyPattern = MyItem.GetRecurrencePattern
    Set MyInstance = MyPattern.GetOccurrence(#8/11/98 12:00 pm#)
    MyInstance.Subject = "Monthly Pattern (exception)"
    MsgBox MyInstance.Subject & " starts on " & MyInstance.Start
    MyInstance.Save
    Set MyNewPattern = MyItem.GetRecurrencePattern
```

```
      Set MyException = MyNewPattern.Exceptions.Item(1)
      Set MyNewInstance = MyException.AppointmentItem
      MyNewInstance.Start = (#8/11/98 1:00 pm#)
      MsgBox MyNewInstance.Subject & " now starts on " & MyNewInstance.Start
      MyNewInstance.Save
   End Sub
```

The following two sections describe how to use the Exception object to work with changed or deleted instances of a recurring appointment.

Determining the Original Date of an Exception

The OriginalDate property of the Exception object returns the start date and time of the changed appointment before it was changed. The following example uses the OriginalDate property to retrieve the original start date of the appointment exception created in the previous section. In addition, it uses the Start property of the AppointmentItem associated with the Exception object to provide the new start date of the appointment.

```
Sub ShowOriginalDate_Click
   On Error Resume Next
   Set MyNameSpace = Application.GetNameSpace("MAPI")
   Set MyCalendarFolder = MyNameSpace.GetDefaultFolder(9)
   Set MyItem = MyCalendarFolder.Items("Monthly Appointment")
   Set MyPattern = MyItem.GetRecurrencePattern
   Set MyException = MyPattern.Exceptions.Item(1)
   MsgBox "The changed appointment originally occurred on " _
       & MyException.OriginalDate & Chr(13) & "It now occurs on "_
       & MyException.AppointmentItem.Start, vbInformation
End Sub
```

Determining Whether an Appointment Instance Was Deleted

When an appointment in a recurring series is deleted, an Exception object representing the deleted appointment is created, and the Deleted property of the Exception object is set to *True*. The following example uses the *Delete* method of the AppointmentItem object to delete the appointment instance changed in the previous section. It then tests the value of the Deleted property of the Exception object representing the deleted appointment to determine whether the appointment was actually deleted.

```
Sub CheckIfDeleted_Click
   Set MyNameSpace = Application.GetNameSpace("MAPI")
   Set MyCalendarFolder = MyNameSpace.GetDefaultFolder(9)
   Set MyItem = MyCalendarFolder.Items("Monthly Appointment")
   Set MyPattern = MyItem.GetRecurrencePattern
   Set MyAppointment = MyPattern.GetOccurrence(#8/11/98 1:00 pm#)
   MyAppointment.Delete
   Set MyException = MyPattern.Exceptions.Item(1)
   If MyException.Deleted Then MsgBox "The appointment was deleted."
End Sub
```

The MeetingItem Object

Important Open the MeetingItem object in the VBScript Samples folder to work directly with this code in Outlook.

A MeetingItem object represents a request for a meeting received in a user's Inbox mail folder. You cannot create a MeetingItem object directly. Instead, Outlook creates a MeetingItem object in each recipient's Inbox folder when a user sends an AppointmentItem object with its MeetingStatus property set to olMeeting(1). The following example shows how to create an appointment and then send the appointment as a meeting request to a required attendee and an optional attendee:

```
Sub SendMeetingRequest_Click
    Set myItem = Application.CreateItem(1) ' Create an appointment
    myItem.MeetingStatus = 1 ' Appointment is a meeting
    myItem.Subject = "Marketing Strategy Meeting"
    myItem.Location = "Conference Room B"
    myItem.Start = #9/24/98 1:30:00 PM#
    myItem.Duration = 90
    myAttendee = InputBox ("Enter name of Required Attendee")
    If myAttendee <> "" then
        Set myRequiredAttendee = myItem.Recipients.Add(MyAttendee)
        myRequiredAttendee.Type = 1 ' Required
    End If
    myAttendee = InputBox ("Enter name of Optional Attendee")
    If myAttendee <> "" then
        Set myOptionalAttendee = myItem.Recipients.Add(MyAttendee)
        myOptionalAttendee.Type = 2 ' Optional
    End If
    myItem.Send
End Sub
```

The MeetingItem object replaces the MeetingRequestItem object provided by Outlook 97.

Working with Meeting Requests

Most often, you will not work directly with a MeetingItem object. For example, you do not use the MeetingItem object to accept or decline the meeting. Instead, you use the appointment associated with the meeting request.

The *GetAssociatedAppointment* method of the MeetingItem object returns an AppointmentItem object that you can use to accept or refuse the meeting request or to directly add the meeting (as an appointment) to the Calendar folder.

You can also directly access an AppointmentItem that has its MeetingStatus property set to olMeeting(1) to determine which recipients have accepted or declined the meeting request. The following sections illustrate how to work with a meeting request through the appointment associated with the meeting.

Retrieving the Associated Appointment of a Meeting

The MeetingItem object is a message containing a request to add an appointment to the recipient's calendar—it is not the appointment itself. To access the appointment associated with the meeting request, you use the *GetAssociatedAppointment* method of the MeetingItem object. This method requires a Boolean argument that specifies whether the appointment is added to the user's Calendar.

The following example calls the *GetAssociatedAppointment* method of each MeetingItem in the user's Inbox and then uses the returned AppointmentItem object's *Display* method to open the appointment. Note that the argument of GetAssociatedAppointment is set to *False* so that the appointment is not added to the user's Calendar.

```
Sub DisplayMeetingRequests_Click
    Set myNameSpace = Application.GetNameSpace("MAPI")
    Set myFolder = myNameSpace.GetDefaultFolder(6)
    Set myItems = myFolder.Items
    Set myMeetingRequest = _
        myItems.Find("[MessageClass] = 'IPM.Schedule.Meeting.Request'")
    Do While TypeName (myMeetingRequest)<> "Nothing"
        myMeetingRequest.GetAssociatedAppointment(False).Display
        Set myMeetingRequest = myItems.FindNext
    Loop
End Sub
```

Responding to a Meeting Request

To respond to a meeting request, you use the *GetAssociatedAppointment* method of the MeetingItem object to obtain the AppointmentItem object associated with the meeting request. You then use the *Respond* method of the AppointmentItem object to notify the meeting organizer whether the meeting has been accepted, declined, or tentatively added to the receiving user's Calendar.

The *Respond* method allows you to send the notification without user intervention, or it can allow the user to edit the response before sending it. The *Respond* method accepts three parameters: The first specifies the actual response (accept, decline, or tentative), while the second two are Boolean values that determine whether the user will be given the opportunity to edit the response.

To send the notification without requiring action by the user, you call the *Respond* method with the second parameter set to *True*, and then send the AppointmentItem as shown in the following example:

```
Sub AutoAcceptMeetingRequest_Click
    Set myNameSpace = Application.GetNameSpace("MAPI")
    Set myFolder = myNameSpace.GetDefaultFolder(6)
    Set myMtgReq = _
        myFolder.Items.Find("[MessageClass] = 'IPM.Schedule.Meeting.Request'")
```

```
        If TypeName(myMtgReq) <> "Nothing" Then
            Set myAppt = myMtgReq.GetAssociatedAppointment(True)
            myAppt.Respond 3, True
            myAppt.Send
            MsgBox "The " & myAppt.Subject & " meeting on " & myAppt.Start _
                & " has been accepted."
        Else
            MsgBox "You have no meeting requests in your Inbox."
        End If
End Sub
```

If you want to allow the user to choose how to respond (that is, whether to send a response and whether to edit the body of the response before sending), call the *Respond* method with the second parameter set to *False* and the third parameter set to *True*, as shown below:

```
Sub PromptUserToAccept_Click
    Set myNameSpace = Application.GetNameSpace("MAPI")
    Set myFolder = myNameSpace.GetDefaultFolder(6)
    Set myMtgReq = _
        myFolder.Items.Find("[MessageClass] ='IPM.Schedule.Meeting.Request'")
    If TypeName(myMtgReq) <> "Nothing" Then
        Set myAppt = myMtgReq.GetAssociatedAppointment(True)
        myAppt.Respond 3, False, True
    Else
        MsgBox "You have no meeting requests in your Inbox."
    End If
End Sub
```

In the following example, the *Respond* method displays a dialog box that gives the user three choices:

- Edit The Response Before Sending.
- Send The Response Now.
- Don't Send A Response.

Outlook immediately sends the AppointmentItem to the meeting organizer if the user chooses Send The Response Now. If the user chooses Edit The Response Before Sending, Outlook opens the item to allow the user to change recipients, the subject, or the body text before sending the response.

Instead of giving the user the choice of how to respond, you can call the *Respond* method with the second and third parameters both set to *False*. The result is the same as when the user chooses Edit the response before sending.

Determining the Status of a Recipient of a Meeting Request

An AppointmentItem object created from a MeetingItem object has an associated Recipients collection object. You can use the MeetingResponseStatus property of the Recipient objects in this collection to determine whether a given recipient has accepted or declined the requested meeting.

The script in the following example retrieves each meeting that the user has requested and then checks the MeetingResponseStatus property for each recipient of the meeting. A description of the status for each recipient is added to a text string that is displayed in a message box once the status of all the recipients has been checked.

```
Sub CheckRecipientStatus_Click
    Set myNameSpace = Application.GetNameSpace("MAPI")
    Set myFolder = myNameSpace.GetDefaultFolder(9)
    Set myItems = myFolder.Items
    Set myMeeting = myItems.Find("[MeetingStatus] = 1")
    Do While TypeName(myMeeting) <> "Nothing"
        TextStr = "The following is the status of recipients for " _
            & MyMeeting.Subject & " on " & MyMeeting.Start & ":" & chr(13)
        Set myRecipients = myMeeting.Recipients
        For x = 1 To myRecipients.Count
            TextStr = TextStr & chr(13)& myRecipients(x).Name
            Select Case myRecipients(x).MeetingResponseStatus
                Case 0
                    TextStr2 = " did not respond."
                Case 1
                    TextStr2 = " organized the meeting."
                Case 2
                    TextStr2 = " tentatively accepted."
                Case 3
                    TextStr2 = " accepted."
                Case 4
                    TextStr2 = " declined."
            End Select
            TextStr = TextStr & TextStr2
        Next
        If MsgBox(TextStr,1) = 2 then Exit Sub ' Use OK/Cancel; exit if Cancel
        Set myMeeting = myItems.FindNext
    Loop
End Sub
```

More Info For more information about the MeetingResponseStatus property and the values it returns, see Microsoft Outlook Visual Basic Reference Help.

The TaskItem Object

The TaskItem object represents a single item in the user's Tasks folder. A task is similar to an appointment in that it can be sent to others (much like a meeting request) and can be a recurring task. Unlike an appointment, however, an uncompleted recurring task has only a single instance. When an instance of a recurring task is marked as complete, Outlook creates a second instance of the task for the next time period in the task's recurrence pattern.

This section shows you how to work with a TaskItem object.

 Important Open the TaskItem object and TaskRequestItem object items in the VBScript Samples folder to work directly with this code in Outlook.

TaskItem Object Methods

This section covers the *GetRecurrencePattern* and *Assign* methods of the TaskItem object.

Creating a Recurring Task

You can use the *GetRecurrencePattern* method of the TaskItem object to create a recurring task, in much the same manner as creating a recurring appointment (for more information, see "Creating a Recurring Appointment" earlier in this chapter). The following example shows how to create a task and then call the *GetRecurrencePattern* method to make the task a recurring task:

```
Sub CreateRecurringTask_Click
    Set MyItem = Application.CreateItem(3)
    MyItem.Subject = "Test Task"
    Set MyPattern = MyItem.GetRecurrencePattern
    MyItem.Save
End Sub
```

As with a recurring meeting, you use the RecurrencePattern object associated with the task to specify how often and when the task will recur. Unlike a recurring appointment, however, a recurring task does not have multiple occurrences. Instead, when a recurring task is marked as completed, Outlook creates a copy of the task for the next date in the recurrence pattern. Consequently, the RecurrencePattern object of a task does not support the *GetOccurrence* method or the Exceptions property.

Delegating a Task

In much the same way as you can invite others to a meeting by sending them an AppointmentItem object, you can delegate a task to others by sending them a TaskItem object. Before sending the object, however, you must first use the *Assign* method to create an assigned task. The following example shows how to create and delegate a task using the *Assign* and *Send* methods:

```
Sub AssignTask_Click
    Set myItem = Application.CreateItem(3)
    myItem.Assign
    Set myDelegate = myItem.Recipients.Add("James Allard")
    myItem.Subject = "Develop order confirmation form"
    myItem.DueDate = #6/12/99#
    myItem.Send
End Sub
```

When a task is assigned and sent to another user, the user receives a TaskRequestItem object. You can use this object to access the task associated with the request and to respond to the task request.

The TaskRequestItem Object

A TaskRequestItem object represents a request to assign a task in the Inbox of the user to whom the task is being assigned. The following example displays a message box containing the subject of each task request in the user's Inbox folder:

```
Sub ShowTaskRequests_Click
    Set myNameSpace = Application.GetNameSpace("MAPI")
    Set myFolder = myNameSpace.GetDefaultFolder(6)
    Set myItems = myFolder.Items
    Set myTaskRequest = _
        myItems.Find("[MessageClass] = 'IPM.TaskRequest'")
    Do While TypeName (myTaskRequest)<> "Nothing"
        myMessage = myMessage & chr(13) & myTaskRequest.Subject
        Set myTaskRequest = myItems.FindNext
    Loop
    If myMessage = "" then
        MsgBox "You have no pending task requests"
    Else
        MsgBox "Your pending task requests are:" & chr(13) & myMessage
    End If
End Sub
```

Working with Task Requests

As with a MeetingItem object, usually you will not work directly with a TaskRequestItem object. For example, you do not use the TaskRequestItem object to accept or decline the task. Instead, you use the task associated with the task request.

The *GetAssociatedTask* method of the TaskRequestItem object returns a TaskItem object that you can use to accept or refuse the task.

Retrieving the Associated Task of a Task Request

Using the *GetAssociatedTask* method, you can access the task associated with a TaskRequestItem. Properties of the TaskItem returned by this method contain additional information about the assigned task, such as its due date.

Important Before you call the *GetAssociatedTask* method for a TaskRequestItem object, you must first process the TaskRequestItem object. By default, this is done automatically (unless the user has cleared the Process Requests And Responses On Arrival check box on the Advanced E-Mail Options dialog box available through the Options dialog box). You can also process a TaskRequestItem object by calling its *Display* method. Note that when a TaskRequestItem object is processed, its associated task is added to the user's Tasks folder.

The following code example displays a message box containing the subject and due date of every task request in the user's Inbox. This example is identical to the one in the previous section, but uses the *GetAssociatedTask* method to access the DueDate property of the task associated with the task request. Note that this example assumes that the TaskRequestItem objects have already been processed.

```
Sub ShowAssociatedTasks_Click
    Set myNameSpace = Application.GetNameSpace("MAPI")
    Set myFolder = myNameSpace.GetDefaultFolder(6)
    Set myItems = myFolder.Items
    Set myTaskRequest = _
    myItems.Find("[MessageClass] = 'IPM.TaskRequest'")
    Do While TypeName (myTaskRequest)<> "Nothing"
        myMessage = myMessage & chr(13) _
            & myTaskRequest.Subject & " due on " _
            & myTaskRequest.GetAssociatedTask(False).DueDate
        Set myTaskRequest = myItems.FindNext
    Loop
    If myMessage = "" then
        MsgBox "You have no pending task requests"
    Else
        MsgBox "Your pending task requests are:" & chr(13) & myMessage
    End If
End Sub
```

Responding to a Task Request

To accept, decline, or modify a task request, use the *Respond* method of the TaskItem object returned by the *GetAssociatedTask* method of a TaskRequestItem object. The following example retrieves the first TaskRequestItem in the user's Inbox and accepts it:

```
Sub AcceptTaskRequest_Click
    Set myNameSpace = Application.GetNameSpace("MAPI")
    Set myFolder = myNameSpace.GetDefaultFolder(6)
    Set myItems = myFolder.Items
    Set myTaskRequest = _
    myItems.Find("[MessageClass] = 'IPM.TaskRequest'")
    If TypeName(myTaskRequest) <> "Nothing" then
        Set myTask = MyTaskRequest.GetAssociatedTask(False)
        myTask.Respond 2, True,False
        myTask.Send
        msgbox "Accepted: " & MyTask.Subject, vbInformation
    Else
        MsgBox "You have no pending task requests", vbInformation
    End If
End Sub
```

Note that if you set the second parameter of the *Respond* method to *True*, you must call the *Send* method of the TaskItem.

When the *Respond* method is used to respond to a task request, the initiating user receives a TaskRequestAcceptItem, TaskRequestDeclineItem, or TaskRequestUpdateItem object, depending on the type of response. You work with these objects in much the same way as a TaskRequestItem object in that you use the object's *GetAssociatedTask* method to retrieve the TaskItem object associated with the request and then call the methods and access the properties of the TaskItem object.

The ContactItem and DistListItem Objects

The ContactItem welcomes two important new collection objects in Outlook 2000. One of the most important new objects in the Outlook 2000 Object Library—the Links object—lets you link child ContactItem objects to parent Item objects. In Outlook 2000, only ContactItem objects can perform as child objects of a parent MailItem, PostItem, AppointmentItem, DocumentItem, JournalItem, TaskItem, DistListItem, or ContactItem object. Another great feature of the Links object is that Link object members do not have to live in the same folder as the parent item object.

The second new collection object that pertains to the ContactItem is the DistListItem. A DistListItem acts as a container for ContactItem objects and, as the name implies, is a means of creating distribution lists in both your mailbox Contacts folder and in public folders. Because the Outlook ContactItem is such a rich form with over 100 properties that support Personal Information Management (PIM), the DistListItem is also a rich container and can be manipulated programmatically by your application.

> **More Info** For a complete list and description of the properties, methods, and events for the ContactItem and DistListItem objects, see Microsoft Outlook Visual Basic Reference Help.

> **Important** Open the ContactItem object item in the VBScript Samples folder to work directly with this code in Outlook.

ContactItem Object Methods

Sending the Contact as a vCard

This example uses the *ForwardAsvCard* method to forward a vCard attachment for a Contact in a Mail Message. A vCard attachment provides a common format for exchanging contact information over the Internet.

```
Sub SendAsvCard_Click
    Const olContactItem = 2
    On Error Resume Next
    Set myContact = Application.CreateItem(olContactItem)
```

```
        myContact.FirstName = "Becky"
        myContact.LastName = "Liou"
        myContact.FullName = "Liou, Becky"
        myContact.CompanyName = "XYZ Corporation"
        myContact.JobTitle = "Senior Analyst"
        myContact.Department = "ITSD"
        myContact.EmailAddress = "bliou@xyz.com"
        myContact.EmailAddressType = "SMTP"
        myContact.Display
        Set myMsg = myContact.ForwardasvCard
        myMsg.Display(True) 'Forces modal display
    End Sub
```

ContactItem Object Properties

Adding Items to the Links Collection

Use the Links collection to add Contacts to an existing item. You can add Link items to any Item type. The following example shows you how to use the *Add* method of the Links collection object to add the last three LastNames in your Contacts folder to a Contact item that was created programatically. Only items with a base message class of IPM.Contact can be added as a member of the Links collection for an item. You cannot add a Distribution List Item to the Links collection.

```
Sub AddItemstoLinks_Click
    Const olContactItem = 2, olFolderContacts = 10
    Set objContact = Application.CreateItem(olContactItem)
    objContact.FirstName = "Jane"
    objContact.LastName = "Smith"
    objContact.FullName = "Smith, Jane"
    objContact.CompanyName = "XYZ Corporation"
    objContact.JobTitle = "Senior Analyst"
    objContact.Department = "ITSD"
    objContact.EmailAddress = "jsmith@xyz.com"
    objContact.EmailAddressType = "SMTP"
    Set colLinks = objContact.Links
    'Add the last three names in your contacts folder to links
    Set objNS = Application.GetNameSpace("MAPI")
    Set objFolder = objNS.GetDefaultFolder(olFolderContacts)
    Set colContacts = objFolder.Items
    colContacts.Sort "[LastName]", True 'Descending
    For Each myContact in colContacts
        'Can only add Contacts to Links collection
        If Instr(myContact.MessageClass,"IPM.Contact") Then
            If myContact.EmailAddress <> "" Then
                colLinks.Add(myContact)
                intAdded = intAdded + 1
            End If
    End If
        If intAdded = 3 Then Exit For
    Next
```

```
       'Contact must be saved for links to work
       objContact.Save
       objContact.Display
End Sub
```

Adding Contacts to a DistListItem

The following example shows you how to programmatically add members to a DistListItem object. The trick is to create a temporary mail item and instantiate a Recipients collection item for that Mail item. Once you have added recipients to the Recipients collection, use the *AddMembers* method of the DistListItem to add the recipients to the Distribution List. For additional information on the Recipients object, see "The Recipients Collection Object" later in this chapter.

```
Sub AddContactstoDistListItem_Click
    On Error Resume Next
    Const olMailItem = 0, olDistributionListItem = 7, olFolderContacts = 10
    Set objDL = Application.CreateItem(olDistributionListItem)
    'Create a temporary mail item
    Set objMsg = Application.CreateItem(olMailItem)
    Set colRecips = objMsg.Recipients
    'Add the first three names in your contacts folder to links
    Set objNS = Application.GetNameSpace("MAPI")
    Set objFolder = objNS.GetDefaultFolder(olFolderContacts)
    Set colContacts = objFolder.Items
    colContacts.Sort "[LastName]"
    For Each myContact in colContacts
        'Can only add Contacts with E-mail Address
        If myContact.Email1Address <> "" Then
            colRecips.Add MyContact.Email1Address
            intAdded = intAdded + 1
        End If
        If intAdded = 3 Then Exit For
    Next
    objDL.AddMembers colRecips
    objDL.Subject = "Test DL"
    objDL.Display
End Sub
```

The JournalItem Object

The JournalItem object provides a convenient way to record activity in relationship to any Outlook item. A journal entry can be as simple as the record of a phone call or as complex as recording the number of times a specific Word document has been edited.

JournalItem Object Methods

Since the JournalItem object records activities in time, the two most important methods of the JournalItem object are the *StartTimer* and *StopTimer* methods. The following example creates a Journal Item from a contact, creates a link to the contact for the Journal Item, and then starts the Journal Item timer with the *StartTimer* method:

```
Sub LinkJournalItemtoContact_Click
    Const olContactItem = 2, olJournalItem = 4
    On Error Resume Next
    Set myContact = Application.CreateItem(olContactItem)
    myContact.FirstName = "Friedman"
    myContact.LastName = "Fern"
    myContact.FullName = "Friedman, Fern"
    myContact.CompanyName = "XYZ Corporation"
    myContact.JobTitle = "Senior Analyst"
    myContact.Department = "ITSD"
    myContact.EmaillAddress = "ffriedman@xyz.com"
    myContact.EmaillAddressType = "SMTP"
    'Save the contact before you create a link
    myContact.Save
    Set myJournal = Application.CreateItem(olJournalItem)
    myJournal.Companies = myContact.CompanyName
    myJournal.Subject = myContact.Subject
    Set colLinks = myJournal.Links
    colLinks.Add myContact
    myJournal.Display
    myJournal.StartTimer
End Sub
```

More Info For a complete list and description of the properties, methods, and events for the JournalItem object, see Microsoft Outlook Visual Basic Reference Help.

Important Open the JournalItem object item in the VBScript Samples folder to work directly with this code in Outlook.

The Item Window (Inspector Objects)

The Inspector object represents the window in which an Outlook item is displayed. The Inspectors object is the parent collection object for Inspector objects. The following sections cover some of the methods and properties for the Inspector and Inspectors objects.

More Info For a complete list and description of the properties, methods, and events for the Inspector and Inspectors objects, see Microsoft Outlook Visual Basic Reference Help.

Important Open the Inspector object in the VBScript Samples folder to work directly with this code in Outlook.

Inspector Object Methods

This section covers the *SetCurrentFormPage*, *HideFormPage*, and *ShowFormPage* methods of the Inspector object.

Setting the Current Form Page

You can use the *SetCurrentFormPage* method of the Inspector object to set the current form page of a form. The following example shows the Details page as the current form page of a Contact form when you click CommandButton1. (To use this example, you must add a command button to a Contact form in Design mode; add the code in the Script Editor, and then run the form.)

```
Sub SetTheCurrentFormPage_Click
    Set MyNameSpace = Application.GetNameSpace("MAPI")
    Set MyFolder = MyNameSpace.Folders _
        ("Building Microsoft Outlook 2000 Applications")
    Set BeyondFolder = MyFolder.Folders("4. Beyond the Basics")
    Set VBScript = BeyondFolder.Folders("VBScript")
    Set VBScriptSamples = VBScript.Folders("VBScript Samples")
    Set MyItem = VBScriptSamples.Items.Add("IPM.Post.Test")
    set MyInspector = MyItem.GetInspector
    MyInspector.SetCurrentFormPage("Test")
    MyItem.Display
End Sub
```

Hiding and Showing a Form Page

You can use the *HideFormPage* and *ShowFormPage* methods of the Inspector object to hide and show a form page. In the following example, the Test page of the Test form is hidden.

```
Sub HideTheTestPage_Click
    Set MyNameSpace = Application.GetNameSpace("MAPI")
    Set MyFolder = MyNameSpace.Folders _
        ("Building Microsoft Outlook 2000 Applications")
    Set BeyondFolder = MyFolder.Folders("4. Beyond the Basics")
    Set VBScript = BeyondFolder.Folders("VBScript")
    Set VBScriptSamples = VBScript.Folders("VBScript Samples")
    Set MyItem = VBScriptSamples.Items.Add("IPM.Post.Test")
    Set MyInspector = MyItem.GetInspector
    MyInspector.HideFormPage("Test")
    MyItem.Display
End Sub
```

Caution Using the *HideFormPage* and *ShowFormPage* methods in your code will cause a custom form to become "one-offed." For example, if you use *HideFormPage* on a custom contact form with a message class of IPM.Contact.Hot Prospect and save the form, the item based on your custom form will open the next time you open it as if the message class of the form is IPM.Contact. The symptom of the dreaded "one-offed form disease" is that users experience the Macro Warning dialog box even though the form has been published in an appropriate forms registry. For a detailed discussion of how forms become one-offed, search for article Q207896 at *http://support.microsoft.com/support/*.

Inspector Object Properties

This section covers the ModifiedFormPages and CommandBars properties of the Inspector object. The ModifiedFormPages property returns the entire collection of pages for a form. The CommandBars object—a member of the Office 2000 Object Model—lets you create and modify command bars programmatically. The Pages collection object is covered in more detail in the next section.

Referencing a Form Page and Its Controls

You can use the ModifiedFormPages property of the Inspector object to return the Pages collection representing the pages on a form that have been modified. Note that standard pages on a form, such as a Message page, are also included in the collection if the standard pages can be customized. You must use the Pages collection object to switch to the page, which then allows you to gain access to controls on the page. The following example uses the ModifiedFormPages property of the Inspector object to return the Inspector object page in the Pages collection object. It then uses the Controls property of the Page object to reference the HideandShow toggle button control. When the HideandShow control is down (its value equals *True*), the HideandShowLabel control is visible. When the toggle button is up, the HideandShowLabel control is not visible.

```
Sub HideAndShow_Click
    Set myInspector = Item.GetInspector
    Set myPage = myInspector.ModifiedFormPages("Inspector Object")
    Set myControl = myPage.Controls("HideAndShow")
    If myControl.value = True Then
        myPage.Controls("HideAndShowLabel").Visible = True
    Else
        myPage.Controls("HideAndShowLabel").Visible = False
    End If
End Sub
```

Working with the CommandBars Object

The CommandBars property collection object is an extrinsic object from the viewpoint of the Outlook Object Model. The CommandBars object is actually a member of the Office 2000 Object Model and contains all of the menus and toolbars for either an Inspector or an Explorer object. Every Inspector object has a CommandBars collection object property that you can use to customize menus and toolbars for your Inspector. Outlook 2000 now supports customization of both Inspector and Explorer CommandBar objects though the use of VBA code or COM Add-ins. For additional information on the properties and methods of the CommandBars object and its child objects, see Chapter 10, "Outlook Bar, Command Bars, and the Assistant," and Chapter 13, "Creating COM Add-Ins with Visual Basic."

The following example creates a toolbar named Command Bar Example and adds command bar buttons that allow the user to create Outlook items. In this example, the CommandBarButton action code is contained in a VBScript procedure that is attached to the custom form. If you need to call the Windows API, run external programs, or have performance concerns, use VBA or a COM Add-in to create Inspector CommandBar objects. For purposes of economy, all the code in the example is not reproduced here. Open the Inspector object item in the VBScript Samples folder to examine the code in detail.

```
Sub CreateCommandBar_Click
    Set objCommandBar = Item.GetInspector.CommandBars.Add _
        ("Command Bar Example", 1, False, True)
    Call CreateButton(objCommandBar, _
        "Mail", 1757, "Create Message", "cmdMail_Click")
    Call CreateButton(objCommandBar, _
        "Contact", 1099 , "Create Contact", "cmdContact_Click")
    Call CreateButton(objCommandBar, _
        "Journal", 1990, "Create Journal", "cmdJournal_Click")
    Call CreateButton(objCommandBar, _
        "Appointment", 1106, "Create Appointment", "cmdAppt_Click")
    Call CreateButton(objCommandBar, _
        "Task", 1100, "Create Task", "cmdTask_Click")
    objCommandBar.Visible = True
End Sub

Sub CreateButton (cmdBar, Caption, FaceId, ToolTip, Action)
    Dim objButton
    Const msoControlButton = 1
    Const msoButtonIconAndCaption = 3
    On Error Resume Next
    Set objButton = cmdbar.Controls.Add(msoControlButton)
    objButton.Style = msoButtonIconAndCaption
    objButton.Caption = Caption
    objButton.FaceId = FaceId
    objButton.TooltipText = ToolTip
    objButton.Visible = True
    objButton.OnAction = Action
End Sub
```

The Pages Collection Object

To reference a page or controls on a page, you use the ModifiedFormPages property of the Inspector object to reference the Pages collection object, and then reference the individual page by name or number. The following procedure uses the ModifiedFormPages property of the Inspector object to return the number of modified form pages in the Pages collection. Note that the pages are not added to the collection until the page is clicked at design time.

```
Sub ShowModifiedFormPagesCount_Click
    Set PagesCollection = Item.GetInspector.ModifiedFormPages
    MsgBox "The number of modified form pages in the Pages collection is " _
        & PagesCollection.Count & "."
End Sub
```

Important Open the Page object item in the VBScript Samples folder to work directly with this code in Outlook.

The Page Object

Important The Page object is contained in the Microsoft Forms 2.0 Object Library. To view the methods and properties for the Page object, use the Microsoft Excel 2000 Object Browser or consult Control Reference in Microsoft Outlook Visual Basic Reference Help.

You can use the ModifiedFormPages property to return the Pages collection from an Inspector object. Use ModifiedFormPages*(index)*, where *index* is the name or index number, to return a single page from a Pages collection. The following example references the Message page, and then references the CommandButton1 control on the page. When clicked, the CommandButton1 control moves to the right.

```
Sub CommandButton1_Click
    Set MyPage = GetInspector.ModifiedFormPages("Message")
    Set MyControl = MyPage.CommandButton1
    MyControl.Left = MyControl.Left + 20
End Sub
```

The Controls Collection Object

To access controls on Outlook forms, you use the Controls collection object. The Controls collection object contains the collection of controls on a form page. To access an individual control in the Controls collection, you use the index value of the control or the name of the control. The Controls collection object is contained in the Microsoft Forms 2.0 Object Library. This section discusses how to reference control collections and controls on a form.

Important Open the Control object item in the VBScript Samples folder to work directly with this code in Outlook.

Methods of the Controls Collection Object

The Controls collection object offers a variety of methods that let you manipulate the controls on a form. For example, you can use the *Move* method to move all the controls on a page, or you can use the *SendToBack* method to send the controls in the Controls collection to the back layer of the page.

You can use the Controls property to return the Controls collection from a Page object. Use Controls*(index)*, where *index* is the name or index number, to return a control from a Controls collection.

Adding a Control to the Form Page

You can use the *Add* method of the Controls collection object to add a control to the form. The following example uses the *Add* method to add a new CommandButton control to the ControlObject page:

```
Sub AddAControlToAPage _Click
    Set MyPage = GetInspector.ModifiedFormPages("Control Object")
    If MyPage.Controls.Count < 3 then
        Set MyControl = MyPage.Controls.Add("Forms.CommandButton.1")
        MyControl.Left = 18
        MyControl.Top = 150
        MyControl.Width = 175
        MyControl.Height = 20
        MyControl.Caption = "This is " & MyControl.Name
    Else
        MsgBox "You can only add one command button.", vbInformation
    End If
End Sub
```

More Info For more information about using the *Add* method of the Controls collection object, see Control Reference in Microsoft Outlook Visual Basic Reference Help.

Controls Collection Object Properties

The Controls collection object provides only the Count property. With the Count property, you can use the For...Next statement to loop through the controls in a collection. The following example returns the collection of controls on the Controls collection object page. It then displays the name of each control contained on the page.

```
Sub ShowtheControlsCollectionCount_Click
    Set Page = Item.GetInspector.ModifiedFormPages("Control Object")
    Set MyControls = Page.Controls
    For i = 0 to MyControls.Count - 1
        MsgBox MyControls(i).Name, vbInformation
    Next
End Sub
```

Important Notice that the For...Next statement starts at 0. You must use 0 to reference the first item in the collection. However, Outlook returns a Count of 3. Therefore, you must specify Count -1 as the upper limit in the argument of the For...Next statement.

The Control Object

Important The Control object and the individual control objects, such as CheckBox and TextBox, are contained in the Microsoft Forms 2.0 Object Library. To view the methods and properties for this library, use the Outlook 2000 Object Browser and select MSForms in the library drop-down list box. You can also press F1 in Outlook VBA and open the book entitled Microsoft Forms Reference.

In the Visual Basic Forms Object Model, the control objects are generically represented by a Control object. Further, they are individually represented by the objects that represent the names of the individual control components, such as TextBox, CheckBox, and so on. As discussed in the preceding section, to reference a control, use the Controls property to return the Controls collection from a Page object, and then use Controls*(index)*, where *index* is the name or index number, to return a control from a Controls collection.

Unlike controls on VBA or Visual Basic forms, the control object in VBScript must be explicitly instantiated before you can access the properties and methods of the control. You must explicitly reference the control object regardless of whether the control is an intrinsic Outlook Forms control or an extrinsic custom or third-party ActiveX control. The following line of code shows you how to set a reference to a control object:

```
Set TextBox1 = Item.GetInspector.ModifiedFormPages("P.2").Controls("TextBox1")
```

A shorter alternative syntax is as follows:

```
Set TextBox1 = GetInspector.ModifiedFormPages("P.2").TextBox1
```

Setting Control References at the Script Level

If you inspect the code behind the Control object example form, you'll see that some control objects have been dimensioned as script-level variables. The *Item_Open* procedure then sets a reference to each control dimensioned as a script-level variable, and the control object has a script-level lifetime. If you follow this convention, you do not have to instantiate a control object reference in every procedure where you want to get or set control properties and call control methods. Dimension the controls as script-level variables using the same name as the control, and then instantiate those control variables in the form's *Item_Open* procedure. Don't use an alias for the control object. Name the control object on the left side of the Set statement with the same name as the actual control. This practice makes your code more readable, since the name of the control in VBScript code is the same as the control name in Design mode.

Properties of Control Objects

The properties available for a control will differ for each type of control. This section covers the Value property for the CheckBox control and the Enabled property for the TextBox and Label controls.

Setting the Enabled Property of a Control

The following example uses a CheckBox control called EnableTextBox and a TextBox control called TextBox1. When the EnableTextBox control is clicked, the procedure evaluates the state of EnableTextBox. If the value of EnableTextBox is *True*, then TextBox1 and Label1 are enabled; otherwise, they are not enabled.

```
Sub EnableTextBox_Click
    Set MyPage = Item.GetInspector.ModifiedFormPages("Control Object")
    Set MyControls = MyPage.Controls
    If MyControls("EnableTextBox").Value = True then
        MyControls("Label1").Enabled = True
        MyControls("TextBox1").Enabled = True
    Else
        MyControls("TextBox1").Enabled = False
        MyControls("Label1").Enabled = False
    End If
End Sub
```

Setting the PossibleValues Property of a ComboBox or ListBox

Rather than use the *AddItem* method to add items to a ListBox or ComboBox control, you can use the PossibleValues property. Note that the PossibleValues property is an undocumented property. In this example, the PossibleValues property is used to add the values Red, Green, and Blue to the ComboBox1 control when CommandButton1 is clicked.

```
Sub CommandButton1_Click
    Set MyPage = Item.GetInspector.ModifiedFormPages("Message")
    MyPage.ComboBox1.PossibleValues = "Red;Green;Blue"
End Sub
```

Using the List Property to Populate a ListBox or ComboBox

The most powerful method to add values to a ListBox or ComboBox control is the List property. The List property populates a ListBox control or ComboBox control with a single statement. By assigning the control object's List property to a variant array, you can create a single- or a multi-column list in the control. If you are populating controls with the results of an ADO recordset, the List property and the recordset *GetRows* method (which returns a variant array) are perfect partners. For additional information on using ADO to populate controls on Outlook forms, see Chapter 16, "Using ActiveX DLLs and Microsoft Transaction Server with Outlook." The following example from the *Item_Open* event in the Control object form creates a variant array and then assigns the array to the List property of the ListBox1 and ComboBox1 controls:

```
Sub Item_Open
    'Instance script-level control objects
    Set ListBox1 = GetInspector.ModifiedFormPages _
        ("Control Click Events").ListBox1
    Set ComboBox1 = GetInspector.ModifiedFormPages_
        ("Control Click Events").ComboBox1
```

```
        'Create a variant array to hold values
        Redim varArray(2)
        varArray(0) = "Red"
        varArray(1) = "Blue"
        varArray(2) = "Green"
        'Populate ListBox1 and ComboBox1
        ListBox1.List = varArray
        ComboBox1.List = varArray
    End Sub
```

Hiding Columns in a ComboBox

You can hide a column in a ComboBox control by using the ColumnWidths property. The following example presents a typical problem for the designer of a mutli-column combo box. You want to present recognizable names, such as the full name of a state, but you only want to store the state's abbreviation. The PopulateStates procedure in the Control object form populates the cmbStates combo box with the abbreviation and full name for several vacation states. The ColumnWidths property is set so that the state abbreviation does not appear in the drop-down portion of the list. However, the TextColumn property is set so that the abbreviation appears in the ComboBox control when the user selects an item from the list. If you are binding the control to a user-defined field, you should also set the BoundColumn property so that the bound field uses the specified column as its value source. The *cmbStates_Click* procedure utilizes the Text, ListIndex, and Column properties of the combo box to create a message box that informs the user about their selection.

```
Sub PopulateStates
    Dim varStates()
    Set cmbStates = GetInspector.ModifiedFormPages("Control Object").cmbStates
    ReDim varStates(6,1)
    varStates (0,0) = "AZ"
    varStates (0,1) = "Arizona"
    varStates (1,0) = "CA"
    varStates (1,1) = "California"
    varStates (2,0) = "HI"
    varStates (2,1) = "Hawaii"
    varStates (3,0) = "ID"
    varStates (3,1) = "Idaho"
    varStates (4,0) = "NV"
    varStates (4,1) = "Nevada"
    varStates (5,0) = "OR"
    varStates (5,1) = "Oregon"
    varStates (6,0) = "WA"
    varStates (6,1) = "Washington"
    cmbStates.List = varStates
    cmbStates.ColumnCount = 2
    cmbStates.ColumnWidths = "0 in ; 1 in" 'Hide col 0
    cmbStates.TextColumn = 1
    cmbStates.BoundColumn = 1
End Sub
```

```
Sub cmbStates_Click
    MsgBox "You selected the state of " & cmbStates.Text _
        & vbCr & "Enjoy your vacation in " _
        & cmbStates.Column(1, cmbStates.ListIndex), vbInformation
End Sub
```

Tip When you set TextColumn or BoundColumn in a ListBox or ComboBox control, remember that the Column property is zero-based so that Column 1 is referenced as Column(0).

Resizing a Control Vertically and Horizontally

Quite often, you want controls on a form to adjust horizontally and vertically when the form is resized. To do this, you must set an invisible property called LayoutFlags. This example sets the LayoutFlags property for the TextBox1 control when you click CommandButton1.

To run this example, do the following:

1. In Design mode, add a TextBox1 control to the (P.2) page of a form.

2. Resize the control so that its bottom border is near the bottom border of the form and its right border is near the right border of the form. Don't obscure the CommandButton1 control.

3. Add the following code for the CommandButton1 control.

4. Switch to Run mode, resize the form, and notice what happens.

5. Then click CommandButton1 and resize the form. After the LayoutFlags property is set, the controls adjust to the size of the form.

```
Sub CommandButton1_Click
    Item.GetInspector.ModifiedFormPages("P.2").TextBox1.LayoutFlags = 68
End Sub
```

After you set the LayoutFlags property, you can delete the procedure from the Script Editor.

Resizing a Control Vertically

In some situations, you want controls on the form to vertically resize when the form is vertically resized. To do this, set the LayoutFlags property to 65.

To run this example, do the following:

1. Delete the TextBox1 control from the (P.2) page and then add a new TextBox1 control.

2. Resize the control so that its bottom border is near the bottom border of the form. Don't obscure the CommandButton1 control.

3. Add the following code for the CommandButton1 control.

4. Switch to Run mode, and resize the form vertically. Then click CommandButton1, and vertically resize the form again.

```
Sub CommandButton1_Click
    Item.GetInspector.ModifiedFormPages _
        ("P.2").TextBox1.LayoutFlags = 65
End Sub
```

After you set the LayoutFlags property, you can delete the procedure from the Script Editor.

Binding a Control to a Field at Run Time

You can use the hidden ItemProperty property to bind a control to a field at run time. To run this example, do the following:

1. Add a new TextBox1 control (or use the existing one if it's already on the form) to the (P.2) page of the form.

2. Add the following code for the CommandButton1 control.

3. Switch to Run mode, click the Message tab, and type *Test* in the Subject box.

4. Then click CommandButton1. Notice that the value in the Subject box appears in the TextBox1 control because the control is now bound to the Subject field.

```
Sub CommandButton1_Click()
    Item.GetInspector.ModifiedFormPages _
        ("P.2").TextBox1.ItemProperty = "Subject"
End Sub
```

Note If you create a control by dragging a plain text field to a form, you cannot bind the control to a field of a different type. For example, you cannot drag a TextBox control to a form and then bind it programmatically to a field containing an E-mail recipient type (such as the To field).

Responding to the Click Event

The Click event is the only event raised by controls on Outlook forms. You must define the Click event procedure for a control in the Script Editor as follows:

```
Sub ControlName_Click
'Event code goes here
End Sub
```

The Click event fires without exception for the Label, Image, CommandButton, ToggleButton, and Frame controls. Open the Control object item in the VBScript Samples folder and click the Control Click Events page for a practical demonstration of control Click events. However, there are many exceptions to the Click event:

- Right-clicking a control does not fire a Click event.
- Not every third-party or custom ActiveX control will fire a Click event in the Outlook forms container.
- The following controls do not respond to Click events in Outlook 2000: TabStrip, SpinButton, ScrollBar, TextBox, MultiPage

- The following controls only respond to Click events when they are populated with items and an item in the list is selected: ComboBox, ListBox
- The following controls respond to a Click event based on a change in their Value property: OptionButton, CheckBox

An alternative to using a Click event is to write a CustomPropertyChange or *PropertyChange* event procedure for the bound field of the control. For example, the following procedure mimics the Buddy control available in Visual Basic by binding a SpinButton control to a user-defined field. When the user clicks the spin button, the value of TextBox2 changes. You can see this example in action on the page named "Using Control Values" in the Control Object item in the VBScript Samples folder.

```
Sub Item_CustomPropertyChange(ByVal Name)
Select Case Name
    Case "SpinButton2"
    TextBox2.Value = SpinButton2.Value
End Select
End Sub
```

The UserProperties Collection Object

The UserProperties collection object represents the custom fields contained in an item. To return a collection of user-defined fields for an item, you can use the UserProperties property of the MailItem object, the PostItem object, and so on. The UserProperty object represents a single field in the item.

More Info For a complete list and description of the properties and methods for the UserProperties collection object, see Microsoft Outlook Visual Basic Reference Help.

Note Standard properties in Outlook, such as Subject, To, and Body, are properties of the individual Item object. For more information, see "MailItem and PostItem Objects Properties" earlier in this chapter.

UserProperties Collection Object Methods

This section covers the *Find* method of the UserProperties collection object.

Getting and Setting the Value of a User Property

You can use the *Find* method of the UserProperties collection object to get or set the value of a user-defined field in an item as follows:

```
MsgBox "The value of the Customer Name field is " _
        & Item.UserProperties.Find("Customer Name").Value & "."
```

The syntax, however, can be shortened by three dots to increase performance and readability. Because the *Find* method is the default method of the UserProperties object and the Value property is the default property of the UserProperty object, the following statement is equivalent to the one above:

```
MsgBox "The value of the Customer Name field is " _
       & UserProperties("Customer Name") & "."
```

To set the value of a UserProperty object, simply reverse the statement as follows:

```
UserProperties("Customer Name") = "Microsoft Corporation"
```

The Recipients Collection Object

The Recipients collection object represents the names that appear in the To field of the MailItem, MeetingRequestItem, and TaskRequestItem objects.

Recipients Collection Object Methods

This section covers the *Add* and *ResolveAll* methods of the Recipients collection object.

More Info For a complete list and description of the properties and methods for the Recipients collection object and the Recipient object, see Microsoft Outlook Visual Basic Reference Help.

Adding Recipients to the Collection

You can use the *Add* method of the Recipients collection object to add recipient names to the Recipients collection.

The following example creates a new Message item, and then uses the Recipients property of the MailItem object to return the Recipients collection object that, in this case, is empty. It then adds two names to the Recipients collection object, uses the *ResolveAll* method to resolve the recipient names, and then displays the Message form. For this example, you can replace the names Sangita Gulati and Jim Reitz with names of people in your organization.

```
Sub AddRecipientsToCollection_Click
    Set MyItem = Application.CreateItem(0)
    Set MyRecipient = MyItem.Recipients
    MyRecipient.Add("Sangita Gulati")
    MyRecipient.Add("Jim Reitz")
    MyRecipient.ResolveAll
    MyItem.Display
End Sub
```

Automatically Addressing an Item to All Contacts in a Contacts Folder

The following example uses the *Add* method and the *ResolveAll* method to show how you can use the Recipients collection object to create a procedure that allows you to automatically address a message to all the users in the Contacts folder in your Mailbox. In this procedure, the Contact's e-mail addresses are added to the Recipients collection object.

```
Sub AddresstoAllContacts_Click
    On Error Resume Next
    Set MyNameSpace = Application.GetNameSpace("MAPI")
    Set MyFolder = MyNameSpace.GetDefaultFolder(10)
    Set MyItems = MyFolder.Items
    Set MySendItem = Application.CreateItem(0)
    Set MyRecipients = MySendItem.Recipients
    For i = 1 To MyItems.Count
        If MyItems(i).EMailAddress <> "" Then
            MyRecipients.Add MyItems(i).EMailAddress
        End If
    Next
    MyRecipients.ResolveAll
    MySendItem.Display
End Sub
```

Events

There are several types of events in Outlook 2000: Item events, Application events, and Control events. An event lets you respond to an action initiated by a user or by another process. For additional information on Outlook Application Events, see Chapter 9, "Raise Events and Move to the Head of the Class," and Chapter 13, "Creating COM Add-Ins with Visual Basic."

By using the Script Editor, you can add code to Outlook Item events to modify the event's behavior. For example, for the Open event, you can add code to specify the current form page, or you can add code to load a ComboBox control with a recordset from a database. For the Click event, you can create a procedure that creates a custom item, includes an attachment to the current item, and then posts the item in a folder. Item events are available for all Outlook item types except for the NoteItem object. Certain events are cancelable; you can prevent them from completing by writing appropriate code. The following table summarizes the Item Events in Outlook:

Event	Cancelable	Description
AttachmentAdd	No	Occurs when an attachment has been added to the item
AttachmentRead	No	Occurs when an attachment has been opened for reading
BeforeAttachmentSave	Yes	Occurs before an attachment in an item is saved
BeforeCheckNames	Yes	Occurs before Outlook starts resolving names in the Recipients collection of the item
Close	Yes	Occurs before Outlook closes the Inspector displaying the item
CustomAction	Yes	Occurs before Outlook executes a custom action of an item

(continued)

Event	Cancelable	Description
CustomPropertyChange	No	Occurs when a custom Item property has changed
Forward	Yes	Occurs before Outlook executes the Forward action of an item
Open	Yes	Occurs before Outlook opens an Inspector to display the item
PropertyChange	No	Occurs when an Item property has changed
Read	No	Occurs when a user opens an item for editing
Reply	Yes	Occurs before Outlook executes the Reply action of an item
ReplyAll	Yes	Occurs before Outlook executes the Reply To All action of an item
Send	Yes	Occurs before Outlook sends the item
Write	Yes	Occurs before Outlook saves the item in a folder

Note Item events are not raised exclusively at the item level in Outlook 2000. A COM Add-in application event handler can also use the WithEvents declaration to raise Item-level events and write Item event procedure code in VBA or Visual Basic. However, if you want the events code to travel with the form, you should use Item-level event procedures written in VBScript.

To add or modify an event

1. With the form in Design mode, click View Code on the Form Design toolbar.
2. On the Script Editor Script menu, click Event Handler.
3. In the Insert Event Handler list box, double-click the event you want.

With an event procedure, the word Item refers to the current Outlook item associated with the form. For example, the following Item_PropertyChange procedure sets the value of the Subject field in the item when the value in the Sensitivity drop-down list box in the Message Options dialog box is changed.

```
Sub Item_PropertyChange(ByVal PropertyName)
    Select Case PropertyName
    Case "Sensitivity"
        Item.Subject = "The sensitivity value has changed."
    End Select
End Sub
```

To test the preceding example code

1. On the Outlook Actions menu, click New Mail Message.
2. On the form Tools menu, select Forms, and then click Design This Form.
3. On the Form Design toolbar, click View Code.
4. Add the preceding sample code to the Script Editor window.

5. On the form's Form menu, click Run This Form.

6. Click the Options button on the Standard toolbar, and then click a new value in the Sensitivity drop-down list box.

7. Close the Message Options dialog box; the text is now added to the Subject box.

The Firing Sequence of Events

When an Outlook form is opened to compose an item or to read an item, events are fired in the sequences described in the following table:

Events	When
Open	A form is opened to compose an item.
Send, Write, Close	An item is sent.
Write, Close	An item is posted.
Write	An item is saved.
Close	An item is closed.
Read, Open	An item is opened in a folder.
Reply	A user replies to an item's sender.
ReplyAll	A user replies to an item's sender and all recipients.
Forward	The newly-created item is passed to the procedure after the user selects the Forward action for an item.
PropertyChange	One of the item's standard properties is changed.
CustomPropertyChange	One of the item's custom properties is changed.
CustomAction	A user-defined action is initiated.
AttachmentAdd	Occurs when an attachment is added to a message; occurs before the BeforeAttachmentSave event.
AttachmentRead	Occurs when an attachment is read.
BeforeAttachmentSave	Occurs when an attachment is saved in a message; occurs after the Send event and before the Write event.
BeforeCheckNames	Occurs when recipient names are resolved; occurs before the Send event.

Note An item's events fire whether the item is created through program code (VBScript or VBA) or through the Outlook user interface.

Caution The order in which Outlook calls event handlers might change depending on other events that might occur, or the order might change in future versions of Outlook.

When You Create a New Item

When you create a new item, the *Item_Open* event is fired. In Outlook, you generally create a new item by opening a form. However, for certain folders, such as the Tasks folder, you can create a new item by clicking the New Item row in the folder. In either case, the *Item_Open* event is fired.

When You Send an Item

When you send an item, the *Item_Send* event is fired, followed by the *Item_Write* event, and the *Item_Close* event.

When You Post or Save an Item

In Outlook, posting an item performs the same task as saving an item. When you post or save an item, the *Item_Write* event is fired. There are several cases in which an *Item_Write* event may occur. For example, a Post item is created and the Post button is clicked on the form; a Contact item is created and the Save And Close button is clicked on the form; a Task item is created by clicking the New Item row, and then the item is saved when the user clicks outside the New Item row. When you post or save an item, the *Item_Write* event is fired, followed by the *Item_Close* event.

When You Open an Existing Item

In Outlook, an item can be opened in a couple of ways. If the item exists in a view that allows in-cell editing, simply clicking the item in the view will open the item. An existing item can also be opened by double-clicking the item and viewing it in a form. In either case, the *Item_Read* event is fired. If the item is viewed in a form, the *Item_Read* event is followed by the *Item_Open* event.

> **Note** There are circumstances where you do not want the *Item_Open* event to fire when an item is opened by simply clicking the item in a view with in-cell editing or through another process. Outlook does not provide an *Item_New* event as opposed to an *Item_Open* event. The following *Item_Open* procedure provides an escape hatch that exits the procedure if the item is not a new item:

```
Sub Item_Open
    ' 1/1/4501 represents a date field with no value.
    ' If the item is not new, exit sub
    If Item.CreationTime <> #1/1/4501# Then
        Exit Sub
    End If
    ' Continue Item_Open code here
End Sub
```

When You Close an Item

When you close an item, the *Item_Close* event is fired. If changes have been made to the item when you attempt to close it, you are asked if you want to save the item. If you click Yes, the *Item_Write* event is fired, followed by the *Item_Close* event.

Preventing Events from Firing

In some cases, you may want to prevent events from occurring. For example, you may want to add code for a Reply event that opens a custom form rather than the default Message form. To achieve this functionality, you must first prevent the default behavior from occurring. To prevent the default behavior, assign *False* to the function value. The actual Event procedure must be declared as a Function procedure instead of a Sub procedure so you can cancel an Item event with an *Item_EventName = False* statement.

VBScript and VBA use different syntax to cancel events. In VBScript code, you write the event procedure as a function and set the function value to *False* in order to cancel the event. In VBA or Visual Basic code, the event procedure contains a Cancel argument. Set the Cancel argument to *True* to cancel the event. The following VBScript example prevents the standard Reply event from occurring in a Mail Message form. Instead, it opens a custom Orders form when the Reply button is clicked.

```
Function Item_Reply(ByVal Response)
    Item_Reply = False
    Set MyFolder = Application.GetNameSpace("MAPI").GetDefaultFolder(6)
    Set MyItem = MyFolder.Items.Add("IPM.Note.Orders")
    MyItem.To = Item.To
    MyItem.Subject = "RE: " & MyItem.Subject
    MyItem.Display
End Function
```

The following example is the same code located in an application-level event procedure in VBA. Unlike previous versions of Outlook, you can raise events for form-level events using the correct WithEvents declarations. For additional information on writing event procedures in VBA , see Chapter 9, "Raise Events and Move to the Head of the Class."

```
Public WithEvents objMailItem As Outlook.MailItem
' Additional code to instantiate objMailItem object as Inspector.CurrentItem
Private Sub objMailItem_ReplyAll(ByVal Response As Object, Cancel As Boolean)
    Cancel = True
    Set objFolder = _
        objApp.GetNameSpace("MAPI").GetDefaultFolder(olFolderInbox)
    Set objItem = objFolder.Items.Add("IPM.Note.Orders")
    objItem.To = objMailItem.To
    objItem.Subject = "RE: " & objItem.Subject
    objItem.Display
End Sub
```

Form-level events that can be canceled include:

- Item_BeforeAttachmentSave
- Item_BeforeCheckNames
- Item_Close
- Item_CustomAction
- Item_Forward

- Item_Open, Item_Reply
- Item_ReplyAll
- Item_Send
- Item_Write.

Note Many other cancelable events are available at the application level. If you want to respond to application-level events, you must write either VBA code in ThisOutlookSession or create a COM Add-in.

The AttachmentAdd Event

The AttachmentAdd event occurs when an attachment is added to an item either through a user action or a procedure that uses code to add an Attachment object. The following VBScript example checks the size of the item after an embedded attachment has been added and displays a warning if the size exceeds 250,000 bytes:

```
Sub Item_AttachmentAdd(ByVal NewAttachment)
    Const olByValue = 1
    If NewAttachment.Type = olByValue Then
        If Item.Size > 250000 Then
        MsgBox "Warning: Item size is now " _
            & Item.Size & " bytes.", vbCritical
        End If
    End If
End Sub
```

The AttachmentRead Event

The AttachmentRead event occurs when an attachment in an item has been opened for reading. If the Attachment Security option on the Security page of the Outlook Options dialog box is set to High, the AttachmentRead event occurs after the Security Warning dialog box appears to the user. The following example saves a copy of the attachment into the My Documents folder when the user opens the attachment:

```
Sub Item_AttachmentRead(ByVal ReadAttachment)
    Const olByValue = 1
    If ReadAttachment.Type = olByValue Then
    IntResponse = MsgBox("Save to c:\my documents?", vbQuestion + vbYesNo)
        If IntResponse = vbYes Then
            ReadAttachment.SaveAsFile "c:\my documents\" _
            & ReadAttachment.DisplayName
        End If
    End If
End Sub
```

The BeforeAttachmentSave Event

The BeforeAttachmentSave event occurs just after the *Item_Send* event and just before the *Item_Write* event. It always occurs after the AttachmentAdd event. The BeforeAttachmentSave event is cancelable. If you cancel the BeforeAttachmentSave event, you will also cancel the *Item_Write* event if you are sending an item that contains an attachment. The following example prevents the user from saving an .exe file as an attachment:

```
Function Item_BeforeAttachmentSave(ByVal SaveAttachment)
    Const olByValue = 1
    If SaveAttachment.Type = olByValue Then
        If Instr(SaveAttachment.FileName, ".exe") Then
            MsgBox "Cannot save this attachment!", vbCritical
            Item_BeforeAttachmentSave = False
        End If
    End If
End Function
```

The BeforeCheckNames Event

The BeforeCheckNames event occurs just before Outlook starts resolving names in the Recipient collection for an item. This event will always fire before the *Item_Send* event fires. If you cancel the BeforeCheckNames event, the *Item_Send* event will also be canceled.

The Click Event

The Click event occurs when a user clicks a control, such as a command button, on a form. You can create as many Click procedures as you have controls on the form.

Important The Click event is the only VBScript control event supported in Outlook.

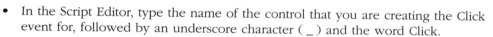

To create a Click event procedure

- In the Script Editor, type the name of the control that you are creating the Click event for, followed by an underscore character (_) and the word Click.

The following example creates an item and displays the standard Message form when CommandButton1 is clicked on the form:

```
Sub CommandButton1_Click
  Set MyItem = Application.CreateItem(0)
  MyItem.Subject = "This is a test."
  MyItem.To = "Darrique Barton"
  MyItem.Display
End Sub
```

More Info For more information about the Click event, see "Responding to the Click Event" earlier in this chapter.

The Close Event

The Close event occurs when the form associated with the item is being closed. When the Close event occurs, the form is still open on the desktop. You can prevent the form from closing by setting the function value to *False*.

The CustomAction Event

The CustomAction event occurs when a custom action defined in the form is carried out. You define custom actions on the Action page of a form by creating a new action. When a CustomAction event is fired, both the name of the custom action being carried out and the newly created response item are passed to the CustomAction event. You can prevent the custom action from occurring by setting the function value to *False*. The following example shows a CustomAction event procedure that is used in the Assigned Help Task form in the Help Desk Application, which is covered in E-Chapter 1 in the 6.Sample Applications folder. In this case, the Discussion action is created at design time with the Form Action Properties dialog box. The action is triggered when the user clicks the Discussion button on the Assigned Help Task form.

```
Function Item_CustomAction(ByVal MyAction, ByVal MyResponse)
    Select Case MyAction.Name
        Case "Discussion"
            MyResponse.Body = "For more information about this ticket, " _
                & "double-click the link." & Chr(10)
            MyResponse.Display
    End Select
End Function
```

To trigger an action from a command button, you can use the *Execute* method of the Action object. For example, when the Discussion button is clicked on the Assigned Help Task form, the custom Discussion action is triggered.

```
Sub Discussion_Click
    Item.Save
    Item.Actions("Discussion").Execute
End Sub
```

More Info For more information about how this event works, go to The Help Desk Application folder under the 6.Sample Application folder in the Building Microsoft Outlook 2000 Applications personal folders (.pst) file on the companion CD-Rom.

Tip You can also use the CustomAction event as a custom method. For example, you can set the CustomAction event to *False* so that the response form is not loaded. You can then add code to the *CustomAction* event procedure to accomplish the desired task. For example, you can add code to the CustomAction event to automatically create an announcement message and send it to a distribution list.

The CustomPropertyChange Event

The CustomPropertyChange event occurs when the value changes in one of the item's user-defined fields. The field name is passed to the procedure, so you can create a Select Case statement to determine which field value has changed. The following example is used in the Help Desk Application. In this example, the field name is passed as an argument to the ChangeProperty parameter. The Select Case statement is then used to evaluate the field that is changed. Depending on the user-defined field that changes, other user-defined fields are assigned values in the custom form.

```
Sub Item_CustomPropertyChange(ByVal ChangeProperty)
Dim Start
Dim Span
    Select Case ChangeProperty
    Case "Software"
        If Item.UserProperties("Software")="Outlook" Then
        Item.UserProperties("Software Version") = Item.Application.Version
        End If
    Case "Task Priority"
        'Preset start and end times based on priority
        Select Case UserProperties("Task Priority")
        Case "Normal"
            Start = DateAdd("d",1,Now())  'start one day after today
            Span = 2            'finish within two days of that
        Case "Work Stoppage"
            Start = DateAdd("h",4,Now())  'urgent; start within 4 hours
            Span = 1/6          'complete within 4 hours of that (day/6)
        Case "Immediate Deadline"
            Start = Now()       'start immediately
            Span = 1/6          'complete within 4 hours (day/6)
        Case "Executive"
            Start = Item.SentOn     'set start equal to request date
            Span =  1/3         'complete within 8 hours  (day/3)
        End Select
        Item.UserProperties("Start by") = Start
        Item.UserProperties("Close Date") = DateAdd("d",Span,Start)
    Case "Work Stoppage"
        If UserProperties("Work Stoppage") Then
        Item.Importance = 2
        Item.UserProperties("Task Priority") = "Work Stoppage"
        End If
    End Select
End Sub
```

The Forward Event

The Forward event occurs when the user initiates the Forward action on a form—usually by clicking the Forward button. You can prevent the default Forward behavior from occurring by setting the function value to *False*. In the following example, the Forward event is prevented from firing if the message is confidential.

```
Function Item_Forward(ByVal MyForwardItem)
    If Item.Sensitivity = 3 Then
        MsgBox "This message is confidential and cannot be forwarded.", _
            vbCritical
        Item_Forward = False
    End If
End Function
```

The Open Event

The Open event occurs when an Outlook form is opened either to compose an item or read an item. When the Open event occurs, the form is initialized but not yet displayed. You can prevent the form from opening by setting the function value to *False*.

The following example checks the ReceivedTime property of a message to determine whether the form is in Compose or Read mode. If the ReceivedTime property is not set, then the Message page is shown. If the ReceivedTime property is set, then the (P.2) page is shown so the person processing the order can view the order. Before you run this example, do the following:

1. Add a Message field to the (P.2) page.
2. Add this example code in the Script Editor, and then click Publish Form As on the Form Design toolbar.
3. In the Display Name text box, type *TestEvent*, and then publish the form to the Personal Forms Library.
4. On the Outlook File menu, select New, and then click Choose Form.
5. Select the TestEvent form in the Personal Forms Library. Notice that the Message page is shown.
6. Address the form to yourself and click Send.
7. Double-click the sent item in your Inbox. Notice that the (P.2) page is shown.

```
Function Item_Open()
    If Item.ReceivedTime <> "1/1/4501" Then
        Item.GetInspector.SetCurrentFormPage("P.2")
        Item.GetInspector.HideFormPage("Message")
    Else
        Item.GetInspector.SetCurrentFormPage("Message")
        Item.GetInspector.HideFormPage("P.2")
    End If
End Function
```

Important Note in the preceding example that the If statement checks to see whether the ReceivedTime field is set to 1/1/4501. In Outlook, Date fields that show None in the field will return a value of 1/1/4501.

The PropertyChange Event

The PropertyChange event occurs when one of the item's standard fields, such as Subject, To, Importance, or Sensitivity, is changed. The field name is passed to the procedure, so you can use the Select Case statement to determine which field value has changed.

In the following example, a message box shows the value of the Importance or Sensitivity field if the values in the fields are changed. To test this example, add the following code to the Script Editor, exit Design mode, and then change the values in the Importance and Sensitivity drop-down list boxes in the Message Options dialog box:

```
Sub Item_PropertyChange(ByVal FieldName)
    Select Case FieldName
    Case "Importance"
        MsgBox "The value of the Importance field is " _
            & Item.Importance & "."
    Case "Sensitivity"
        MsgBox "The value of the Sensitivity field is " _
            & Item.Sensitivity & "."
    End Select
End Sub
```

The Read Event

The Read event occurs when an existing Outlook item is opened for editing by a user. The Read event differs from the Open event in that the Read event occurs whenever a user selects the item in a view that supports in-cell editing, as well as when the item is being opened in an Inspector. The Read event is fired before the Open event. In this example, the value of the Date Opened user-defined field is set when the submitted item is first opened.

Before you run this example, do the following:

1. Click New in the Field Chooser, and then type *Date Opened* in the Name text box.

2. In the Type drop-down list box, click Date/Time, and then click OK.

3. Drag the Date Opened field to the Message page, and then click Edit Read Page on the Form Design toolbar.

4. Resize the Message control to make room for the Date Opened control, and then drag the Date Opened field from the Field Chooser to the Read page.

5. Click Publish Form As and publish the form in your Personal Forms Library.

6. On the Outlook File menu, select New, click Choose Form, and then select the form. Address the form to yourself and click Send.

7. Double-click the sent item in your Inbox. Notice that the current date is now in the Date Opened field.

```
Function Item_Read()
    If UserProperties("Date Opened") = "1/1/4501" Then
        UserProperties("Date Opened") = Now
    End If
End Function
```

The Reply Event

The Reply event occurs when a user clicks the Reply button on the form. When the Reply event occurs, the newly created Reply item is passed to the procedure. You can prevent the item from being sent by setting the function value to *False*. The following example prevents the standard Reply event from occurring, and creates an item with a custom Task form. It then copies the values from the item's Subject and To fields to the Task Response item.

```
Function Item_Reply(ByVal Response)
    Item_Reply = False
    Set MyFolder = Application.GetNameSpace("MAPI").GetDefaultFolder(13)
    Set MyItem = MyFolder.Items.Add("IPM.Task.Test")
    MyItem.To = Item.To
    MyItem.Subject = "RE: " & MyItem.Subject
    MyItem.Display
End Function
```

The ReplyAll Event

The ReplyAll event occurs when a user clicks the Reply To All button on a form. When a user clicks ReplyAll, the response is sent to the sender and to all recipients in the To and Cc boxes on the form. You can prevent the item from being sent by setting the function value to *False*. The following example reminds the user that he or she is replying to all the original recipients of an item, and makes it possible for the user to cancel the action:

```
Function Item_ReplyAll (ByVal MyResponse)
    MyResult = MsgBox("Do you really want to send this reply to all " _
        & "the recipients in the To and Cc boxes? ", _
        vbQuestion + vbYesNo + vbDefaultButton2, "Flame Protector")
    If MyResult = vbYes Then
        Item_ReplyAll = True
    Else
        Item_ReplyAll = False
    End If
End Function
```

The Send Event

The Send event occurs when a user sends an item. You can prevent the item from being sent by setting the function value to *False*. If you prevent the event from occurring, the form remains open. The following example automatically sets the expiration date on the item when the item is sent.

```
Function Item_Send()
    Item.ExpiryTime = Date + 7
End Function
```

The Write Event

The Write event occurs when the user sends, posts, or saves an item.

You can prevent an item from being saved by setting the function value to *False*. The following code prevents a form from changing its message class after either the *HideFormPage* or *ShowFormPage* method is called:

```
Function Item_Write
    Set objForm = Item.FormDescription
    Item.MessageClass = objForm.MessageClass
End Function
```

Automation

In addition to using VBScript to program Outlook objects, you can use it to program Outlook objects remotely. You use Automation when you want to control an entire session. For example, you may want to automatically send a message from within a Visual Basic or Microsoft Excel application.

To automate Outlook from another application, such as Visual Basic or Microsoft Excel, you must first reference the Microsoft Outlook 2000 Object Model. You can then use the GetObject function to automate a session that's already running, or the CreateObject function to open a new Outlook session. After the Outlook Application object is returned, you can then write code that uses the objects, properties, methods, and constants in the Outlook 2000 Object Model. The following example creates a Mail item from a Microsoft Excel 2000 worksheet when the MailSalesReport button is clicked:

```
Sub MailSalesReport_Click
    Set MyOlApp = CreateObject("Outlook.Application")
    Set MyItem = MyOlApp.CreateItem(olMailItem)
    MyItem.Subject = "Sales Results - " & Now()
    MyItem.Body = " Click the icon to open the Sales Results." & Chr(13)
    Set MyAttachments = MyItem.Attachments
    MyAttachments.Add "C:\My Documents\Q499.xls", OlByReference, 1, _
        "Q4 1999 Results Chart"
    MyItem.To = "Sales"
    MyItem.Display
End Sub
```

Note As shown in the preceding example, the constants in the Outlook 2000 Object Model are valid when used in Visual Basic or Visual Basic for Applications.

Where To Go from Here

For additional information about the subjects discussed in this chapter, see the following resources:

Collaboration Data Objects

CDO Live Web site at *http://www.cdolive.com/*

Microsoft Exchange Developers Forum at *http://www.microsoft.com/exchange/developers/*

Programming Microsoft Outlook and Collaboration Data Objects at *http://www.microeye.com/outlkb.html/*

Office 2000 Document Properties

Microsoft Corporation. "Working with Shared Office Components." Chapter 6 in *Microsoft Office 2000/Visual Basic Programmer's Guide*. Redmond, WA: Microsoft Press, 1999.

Scripting Technologies

Microsoft Scripting Technologies Web site at *http://msdn.microsoft.com/scripting/*

Working with Office 2000 Objects

Microsoft Corporation. "Understanding Office Objects and Object Models." Chapter 4 in *Microsoft Office 2000/Visual Basic Programmer's Guide*. Redmond, WA: Microsoft Press, 1999.

Chapter 12
Distribute and Maintain Applications

In This Chapter

The process of distributing and maintaining Microsoft Outlook applications varies with each organization. In some organizations, the application designer develops the application and then submits it to an administrator, who is then responsible for its distribution, maintenance, and security. In other organizations, the application designer both develops the application and serves as its administrator.

This chapter covers basic concepts and procedures an administrator can use for distributing and maintaining Outlook applications within an organization.

Distribute Forms

This section provides information, strategies, and instructions for distributing forms in your organization. It covers how to:

- Make forms available in the Organizational Forms Library, the Personal Forms Library, or a Folder Forms Library.
- Send a form to an administrator or to another user.
- Distribute forms in a personal folder (.pst) file.
- Make forms available for offline use.
- Use Folder Home Pages and Web views to install Outlook application components.

Make Forms Available in the Organizational Forms Library

Most often, the types of forms contained in the Organizational Forms Library are general purpose Message forms that you want to make available to the entire organization. The Organizational Forms Library is located on Microsoft Exchange Server, so access to the forms in this library is determined by the structure and configuration of your Microsoft Exchange Server system.

Usually, there are two types of Message forms published in the Organizational Forms Library:

- General purpose Message forms, such as the While You Were Out form and Vacation Request form, which are used to send messages from one user to another
- Message forms that make it possible for users to submit information to a public folder

Note Non-message forms such as Post, Contact, and Task forms are contained in the Forms Library within the folder. If the folder is a public folder, the forms contained in the folder's Forms Library are made available to all users who have access to the folder.

Submit the Form to an Administrator

In most organizations, only administrators have permission to publish forms in the Organizational Forms Library. As such, application designers who want forms published in the Organizational Forms Library must submit the forms to the administrator.

When a form is published in a forms library such as the Organizational Forms Library, the form definition (and the ability to view the form) is accessible to everyone with access to the library. Thus, when the form is published, you do not also need to send the form definition with the item (the Send Form Definition With Item check box on the form's Properties page should be cleared).

To submit a form to an Administrator

1. With the form in Design mode, click Save As on the File menu.
2. In the Save In drop-down list box, click the Outlook default template folder, such as C:\Program Files\Microsoft Office\Templates\Outlook.
3. In the File Name text box, type the form name.
4. In the Save As type drop-down list box, select Outlook Template (.oft).
5. Click Save.
6. On the form's Actions menu, click New Mail Message.
7. On the Insert menu, click File.
8. In the Look In drop-down list box, click the folder where you saved the .oft file.
9. Select the file name you entered in step 3 and click the Insert button.

10. In the To text box, type the administrator's name, or click the To button and then select the administrator's name from the list.

11. Click Send.

Check the Form for Viruses and Harmful Code

The administrator is responsible for making sure the form is free of viral infection and harmful code.

Publish the Form

If the administrator finds the form to be free of viruses and harmful code, he or she clears the Send Form Definition With Item check box on the Properties page of the form and publishes the form in the Organizational Forms Library. You must have Owner permissions to publish in the Organizational Forms Library. Contact your Exchange Administrator to obtain the correct permissions.

➔ To clear the Send Form Definition With Item check box

1. With the form in Design mode, click the Properties tab.

2. Clear the Send Form Definition With Item check box.

More Info For more information about the Send Form Definition With Item option, see "About the Send Form Definition With Item Check Box" later in this chapter.

➔ To publish the form in the Organizational Forms Library

1. With the form in Design mode, select Forms from the Tools menu, and then click Publish Form As.

2. In the Look In drop-down list box, click Organizational Forms Library.

3. Type the form name into both the Display Name and the Form Name text boxes.

4. Click Publish.

Tip If your custom form contains ActiveX controls other than the Forms 2.0 controls provided with Outlook, or if it uses ActiveX components that do not ship with Office 2000, you will need to run a setup program for these components before the custom form will run correctly on the target machine. The following alternatives apply if you are using ActiveX controls directly on your custom forms or ActiveX components that are called by VBScript's *CreateObject* function. You can install your ActiveX controls using any of the following methods (this list is not meant to be inclusive):

- Distribute the ActiveX component or control setup program as an attachment in an e-mail message. This method is practical only if a relatively small number of users will use your custom form. You can write custom code in the message that will cause the control to install automatically when the user opens the message from his Inbox.

- Use the Visual Studio 98 Package and Deployment Wizard to create either a standard setup program or a Web-based installation and make that installation available to users on your corporate intranet.

- Create a Folder Home Page that uses CODEBASE tags to install the required ActiveX components automatically when a user navigates to the Folder Home Page. For a detailed explanation of this alternative, see Chapter 14, "Customizing Folder Home Pages."

- Use an enterprise management tool, such as Microsoft Systems Management Server, to install the components.

Make Forms Available in the Personal Forms Library

There are three good reasons to publish a form in the Personal Forms Library:

1. You want to limit the number of people who have access to a form.

2. You want to publish a form in your Personal Forms Library so that you are the only person who can use the form. For example, you may want to create a customized announcement form for communicating with a specific group of customers.

3. You want to test a form that will be published later in the Organizational Forms Library. In this case, you can test the form in the Personal Forms Library before you submit it to an administrator for publishing in the Organizational Forms Library.

About the Send Form Definition With Item Check Box

If you are distributing forms to users who will install the form in their Personal Forms Libraries, or you are publishing a form to your own Personal Forms Library, you should clear the Send Form Definition With Item check box.

To clear the Send Form Definition With Item check box

1. With the form in Design mode, click the Properties tab.

2. Clear the Send Form Definition With Item check box.

By default, the Send Form Definition With Item check box is cleared. When the form is published, however, the user is prompted to either select the check box or leave it cleared. When users have access to the forms library, you do not need to send the form definition along with the item. In this case, select No to keep the Send Form Definition With Item check box clear and to minimize the size of the item.

Note If you check the Send Form Definition With Item check box for a custom form with a base message class of IPM.Post, you will create a copy of the code behind the form for every item you create that uses this form. If you have thousands of custom items stored in an Exchange folder, containing 30 KB of code overhead, you will increase your Exchange Server folder size by 30 KB times the number of items in the folder. If you store 5,000 custom items—each with 30 KB of code—in a folder, you would add almost 150 MB to the size of the folder.

Distribute a Form for Publishing in a Personal Forms Library

Quite often, you want to distribute a form to a specific group of users and give them instructions about how to publish the form in their Personal Forms Libraries. The following instructions describe how to do this.

Save the Form as an .oft File

First, save the form as an .oft file so you can distribute it to other users.

To submit a form to an administrator

1. With the form in Design mode, select Save As on the File menu.
2. In the Save In drop-down list box, select the default Outlook template folder, such as C:\Program Files\Microsoft Office\Templates.
3. In the File Name text box, type the form name.
4. In the Save As type drop-down list box, select Outlook Template (.oft).
5. Click Save.

Insert a Form (.oft) File as an Attachment in a Message

To make a form accessible to a specific workgroup, the form must be published in the Personal Forms Library of each person who needs to use the form. The easiest way to do this is to save the form as an .oft file and then insert the .oft file into the message box of a message.

To insert a form (.oft) file as an attachment in a message

1. On the form's Actions menu, click New Mail Message.
2. On the Insert menu, click File.
3. In the Look In drop-down list box, click the folder you saved the .oft file in.
4. Select the file name of the .oft file and click the Insert button.
5. In the To text box, type the names of the people you want to receive the attached .oft file, or click the To button and then select the names from the list. Click OK.
6. In the message box, include the instructions listed in the following section to publish the attached form in the users' Personal Forms Libraries.
7. Click Send.

Include Instructions About How To Publish the Form

Along with the form's .oft file, include these instructions explaining to users how to publish the attached form in their Personal Forms Libraries.

To publish the attached form in a Personal Forms Library

1. Double-click the attachment.
2. If the Macro Warning dialog box appears, click Disable Macros.
3. On the Tools menu, select Forms, and then click Publish Form As.
4. In the Look In drop-down list box, click Personal Forms Library, and then click OK.
5. Type the form name into both the Display Name and the Form Name text boxes.
6. Click Publish.
7. Click No to keep the Send Form Definition With Item check box clear. When items are published, and they are then run from the folder where they are published, they do not need embedded form definitions. This will only slow down form loading time.

Publish a Form in Your Personal Forms Library

In some cases, you may want to create a form and then publish it in your Personal Forms Library. If the form will be sent to people who do not have the form, you may want to leave the Send Form Definition With Item check box enabled.

To publish a form in your Personal Forms Library

1. On the form's Tools menu, select Forms, and then click Publish Form As.
2. In the Look In drop-down list box, click Personal Forms Library, and then click OK.
3. Type the form name into both the Display Name and the Form Name text boxes.
4. Click Publish.
5. Click No to keep the Send Form Definition With Item box clear. When items are published, and they are then run from the folder where they are published, they do not need embedded form definitions. This will only slow down form loading time.

Make Forms Available in a Folder Forms Library

Folder forms libraries are containers for forms. Each folder contains a unique forms library. As such, a forms library can exist on the server or on the user's hard disk, depending on the location of the folder. There are several good reasons for publishing forms to the folder's forms library:

- Most often, the forms stored in the library of a folder are used to post or save information in a folder. Such forms may include a standard or custom Post,

Contact, or Task form. In some cases, however, Message forms are installed in the forms library of the folder so that users can send items from the folder.

- Another reason to publish forms in the folder's forms library is to transport the forms in a personal folder (.pst) file. You can use the personal folder (.pst) file for storing and distributing forms. Making forms available in a personal folder (.pst) file is described in "Distribute Forms in a Personal Folder (.pst) File" later in this chapter.

- Forms in a folder's Forms Library are available for storage in an offline folder (.ost) file and can be used when the user is offline from Microsoft Exchange Server.

To publish a form in a folder forms library

1. On the form Tools menu, select Forms, and then click Publish Form As.

2. In the Look In drop-down list box, select Outlook Folders and then click the Browse button to locate the folder forms library to which you want to publish the form. Outlook also maintains a list of recently used folder names in the Look In drop-down list box.

3. Type the form name in both the Display Name and the Form Name text boxes.

4. Click Publish.

5. Select No to keep the Send Form Definition With Item check box cleared on the Properties page of the form. Select Yes to enable the reader of your item to have a complete and self-contained form with definition, which allows the form to be viewed without publishing.

Changing the Standard IPM.Note Messsage

Outlook 2000 makes it possible to change IPM.Note, the standard read and compose message form for reading, composing, and sending a message. These forms can contain VBScript code in addition to Forms 2.0 controls. Changes in the standard message form are accomplished through changes in the Windows registry. Outlook 2000 is engineered to look up a set of registry keys whenever an item is opened. It uses the message class identified in the registry to open, compose, or send a form.

Be aware that once you make these changes, the default IPM.Note will not be available for the customized mode of reading, composing, and sending. If you want to roll out customized forms that replace the default IPM.Note, you should publish the forms to the Organizational Forms Library and be certain that you have a means of pushing the required registry settings down to each desktop in your organization.

The locations in the registry where the standard forms can be changed is listed in the following table. Take the appropriate precautions, including a full backup of the entire system before you make any changes to the Windows registry. These changes should only be made after careful and extensive testing of the substitute forms.

Standard Message Mode	Registry Location
Compose and Send	HKEY_CURRENT_USER\Software\Microsoft\Office\9.0\Outlook\Custom Forms\Compose\<MESSAGE CLASS>
Read	HKEY_CURRENT_USER\Software\Microsoft\Office\9.0\Outlook\Custom Forms\Read\<MESSAGE CLASS>

Figure 12.1 lists the registry entries that are necessary to change the standard Read message form. For the registry settings shown, IPM.Note.Foobar Read replaces IPM.Note as the standard Read message.

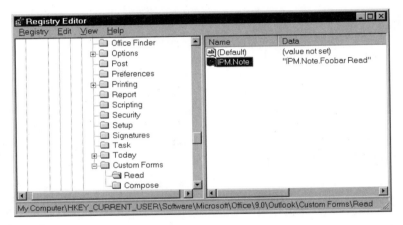

Figure 12.1 *The Read key in the Windows registry causes IPM.Note.Foobar Read to become the default Read message.*

To makes these changes for all the Outlook clients in your organization, you can create an .INF file, a .REG file, or use VBA or Visual Basic code to make the registry changes programmatically. You can also push the changes to the desktop using the Office 2000 Custom Installation Wizard or Microsoft Systems Management Server. If you want to make these registry changes manually, the following procedure outlines the required steps.

To change the default Read message

1. Click the Windows Start menu and select the Run command.
2. Type *regedit* in the Open edit box and click OK.
3. In the Windows registry editor, select the Outlook key under HKEY_CURRENT_USER\Software\Microsoft\Office\9.0.
4. Select New from the Edit menu and then select Key from the New submenu.
5. Type *Custom Forms* in place of New Key#1 and press Enter.
6. Select New from the Edit menu and then select Key from the New submenu.

7.   Type *Read* in place of New Key#1 and press Enter.

8.   Select New from the Edit menu and then select String Value from the New submenu.

9.   Type *IPM.Note* and press Enter.

10. Select the Modify command from the Edit menu.

11. Type *IPM.Note.My Custom Name.* Replace My Custom Name with the actual name of your custom form and click OK.

The Compose key has a special syntax so that you can set a replacement default message for both the Compose and Send modes of a standard message form. You can set both Compose and Send forms respectively by separating the custom Compose message class from the custom Send message class with a Null character. The exact syntax is:

```
IPM.Note.Compose Form<vbNull>IPM.Note.Send Form<vbNull><vbNull>
```

If necessary, you can write this string value with a Visual Basic program. Otherwise, if you only need to change the standard Compose message, you can set a replacement Compose message class for IPM.Note in the Compose key just as you did above for the Read key. The changes you make in the registry are reflected in Outlook instantly.

Use the Send Form Definition With Item Check Box To Send a Form to Another User

In some cases, you need to use a Message form to send items to users who do not have access to the form associated with the item. For example, you may want to send a Product Announcement form to a customer. To ensure that the item appears in the form it was created with, you select the Send Form Definition With Item check box on the Properties page of the form when the form is in Design mode. You then publish the form in a forms library, as described earlier in this chapter. When you publish, select Yes when you are prompted to Send Form Definition With Item.

This results in a larger file size, but the form is self-contained and can be viewed, even if the user does not have access to the forms library.

Distribute Forms in a Personal Folder (.pst) File

If you want to distribute one or more forms using a floppy disk, a CD-ROM, or a network drive, publish the form to the Forms Library of a folder that is located in a personal folder (.pst) file. You can then make a copy of the .pst file and use it for distribution. For more information about distributing a .pst file, see "Distribute a Folder in a Personal Folder (.pst) File" later in this chapter.

Make Forms Available for Offline Use

Users can set up Outlook so they can work offline with forms and folders.

⊃   **To set up Outlook for offline use**

1.   If you have not already done so, set up Microsoft Outlook on the computer you want to work with offline. If the prompt Do You Travel With This Computer? appears when you create your user profile, click Yes.

2.   On the Tools menu, click Services.

3.   In the The Following Information Services Are Set Up In This Profile list box, click Microsoft Exchange Server.

4.   Click Properties, and then click the Advanced tab.

5.   Click Offline Folder File Settings.

6.   In the File box, type the path to the file you want to use as the offline folder file.

7.   If you are not already connected to the network, connect by using a dial-up connection. You can specify a dial-up connection from Outlook.

8.   On the Tools menu, point to Synchronize, and then click Download Address Book. If you will be using the security feature for sealed messages while working offline, be sure you download the Address Book with security details information.

9.   Add the public folders you want to work with offline to your Public Folders Favorites folder (see "Adding a Folder to Favorites," next). On the File menu, point to Folder, and then click Add To Public Folder Favorites.

10.   Specify the folders you want to be available for offline use (see "Specifying Folders for Offline Use," later in this section).

11.   Synchronize the offline folders.

12.   Set Outlook to start offline.

13.   Quit Outlook, and then start Outlook again from an offline location.

When a user's computer is set up for offline use, Outlook creates an .ost file on the user's hard disk. The .ost file contains the following items:

- The Inbox, Outbox, Deleted Items, Sent Items, Calendar, Contacts, Tasks, Journal, Notes, and Drafts folders are automatically made available offline when you set up offline folders.

- Any other folders in the user's Mailbox are designated as offline folders.

- Folders in the user's Favorites folder are designated as offline folders.

- Forms used to compose and read items in the offline folders are made available for offline use.

Adding a Folder to Favorites

You can drag a folder in the Folder List to the Favorites folder to add it to Favorites and make it available for offline use. You can also use Outlook menus and gain additional control over the process.

To add a folder to Favorites

1. If the Folder List is not visible, click the View menu, and then click Folder List.
2. Click Public Folders, and then click the public folder you want to add to the Favorites folder.
3. On the File menu, point to Folder, and then click Add To Public Folder Favorites.
4. To change the name of the public folder that appears in your Favorites folder, type a new name in the Favorite Folder Name box.
5. To add subfolders of this public folder, click Options, and then select the options you want. Figure 12.2 illustrates how you can use the Add To Favorites dialog box to enhance the process of adding folders to Favorites by adding subfolders and automatically adding new folders.
6. For help on an option, click Help.
7. Click Add.

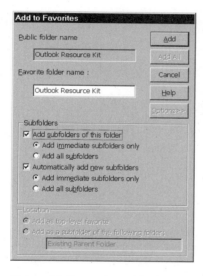

Figure 12.2 *Use the Add To Favorites dialog box to add folders to Favorites.*

Specifying Folders for Offline Use

To use offline folders in addition to the automatic folders (such as Inbox, Sent Items, Calendar, Contacts, and so forth), you must explicitly identify those folders for use offline.

To specify folders for offline use

1. On the Tools menu, click Options, and then click the Mail Services tab.
2. Select the Enable Offline Access check box, and then click the options you want. For Help on an option, click the question mark, and then click the option.

3. Click Offline Folder Settings. You will see the Offline Folder Settings dialog box illustrated in Figure 12.3.

4. Select the folders you want to use offline in addition to your default folders.

5. If you want to apply a filter to a specific folder, click the folder, and then click Filter Selected Folder.

6. If you want to limit the size of messages to download when you synchronize folders, click Download Options, and then click the options that you want.

7. If you want to download Folder Home Pages, check Synchronize folder home pages.

8. If you want to download custom forms from the Organizational Forms Library for offline use, check Synchronize forms.

9. Click the Quick Synchronization tab to select folders to synchronize as a group.

10. Click OK twice, and then synchronize offline folders.

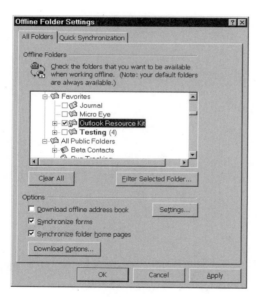

Figure 12.3 *Use the Offline Folder Settings dialog box to add Quick Synchronization Groups and establish other settings for offline use.*

How Forms Are Made Available for Offline Use

Any form associated with an Item in the user's offline folder file is automatically made available for offline use when the user selects Synchronize on the Tools menu and then clicks a choice. When the user selects Synchronize and then clicks on a choice, Outlook searches the items in each offline folder and copies any forms associated with the items to the offline folder (.ost) file (if the forms are not already in the .ost file).

For example, suppose a Weekly Schedule item is sent to a user's Inbox and the user's computer is set up for offline use. When the user synchronizes offline folders, the Weekly Schedule form, which is the form associated with the Weekly Schedule item, is copied to the user's offline folder file and is available for offline use.

How Form Conflicts Are Resolved

Changes made to forms while the user is working offline are not transferred back to Microsoft Exchange Server. Any changes made to forms on Microsoft Exchange Server, however, are automatically reflected in the user's .ost file when the user synchronizes folders.

Make Forms Available for Remote Use

Users in remote locations with dial-up connections to Microsoft Exchange Server can use forms just as if they were connected directly to the server. Before users can work with a dial-up connection, however, they must prepare their computers for dial-up work. The recommended way to work with a dial-up connection is to use offline folders. Users can then work with items in offline folders exactly as they work with items in folders on the server.

Manage Forms

This section describes how to copy and delete forms and change form properties using the Forms Manager. It also provides some strategies and tricks for making changes to forms.

The Forms Manager

With the Forms Manager, shown in Figure 12.4, you can copy and delete forms and change form properties.

⮕ **To open the Forms Manager**

1. Select Options on the Tools menu, and then click the Other tab.
2. Click Advanced Options under General, and then click Custom Forms.
3. Click Manage Forms

The Forms Manager dialog box allows you to manage forms in the Personal and Organizational Forms libraries simultaneously with the forms libraries of folders.

⮕ **To copy a form**

1. Click the left Set button to choose the forms library from which you want to copy forms.
2. In the left list box, select the forms you want to copy.
3. Click the right Set button to choose the forms library to which you want to copy forms.
4. Click Copy.

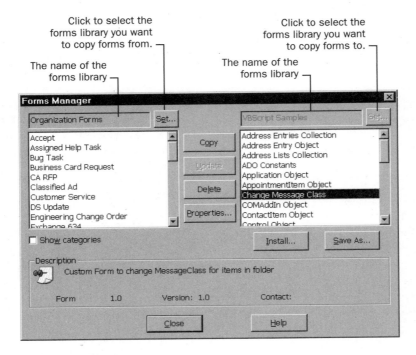

Click to select the forms library you want to copy forms from.

The name of the forms library

Click to select the forms library you want to copy forms to.

The name of the forms library

Figure 12.4 *The Forms Manager dialog box.*

To set form properties

1. In the right list box, select the form whose properties you want to set.
2. Click Properties.
3. Select the options you want.

To delete a form

1. In the right list box, click the forms you want to delete.
2. Click Delete.

To synchronize one form with an updated version, select the one you wish to update. For the update process to work, the form must be visible in both forms libraries (in both the right and left list boxes).

To update forms published in different forms libraries

- In the right list box, click the form, and then click Update. Although you won't see an action, the forms will now be updated.

Note The Install and Save As buttons are used to install and save forms developed for Microsoft Exchange Client.

Modify Forms

Quite often, changing a form can affect other forms or folders. When modifying a form, here are some things to consider:

- If a view or rule is based on a particular field and you remove or modify that field name, the view or rule must be updated to reflect the change.
- If fields are renamed on an existing form, their associated field values in items created using a previous version of the form do not appear on the new form.
- If the form contains VBScript code, any changes you make to the form components, such as the controls or fields, must also be changed in the Script Editor if the components are referenced in script.
- If you add new fields to an existing form, publish the modified form in a forms library, and then open old items with the new form, the new fields on the form will be blank or show the initial value for the field, if there is one.
- Forms with the same name, but with different contents, may cause unpredictable results. It is recommended that you use unique names or update the form in all the forms libraries in which it is published. For more information, see "The Forms Manager" in the preceding section, or see "How Folders are Synchronized" later in this chapter.

Making Changes to a Form's Message Class

There are circumstances under which you will need to reset the message class of forms that have already been created in a folder. In this case, you can use the Change Message Class form that is included in the VBScript Samples folder under the folder 4. Beyond the Basics in the personal folders (.pst) file that accompanies this book. Changing the message class of a form will alter both the behavior and appearance of the form. Be aware that you should test the change thoroughly before you make changes to production items stored on your Microsoft Exchange Server. Figure 12.5 illustrates the Change Message Class form.

To change the message class of existing forms in a folder

1. Use the Folder List to navigate to the VBScript Samples folder in the personal folders (.pst) file accompanying this book.

2. Double-click the Change Message Class item in the VBScript Samples folder to open the form.

3. Click Pick Folder to select a folder where you want to change the message class.

4. Select the From Message Class in the drop-down combo box. You can also type a built-in message class such as IPM.Post in the From combo box.

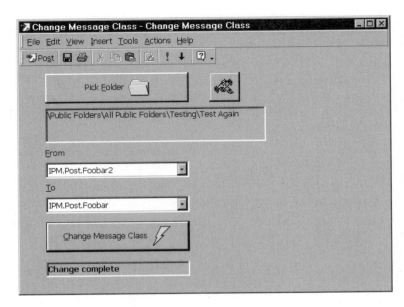

Figure 12.5 *The Change Message Class form changes the message class of existing items in a folder.*

5. Select the To Message Class in the drop-down combo box. You can also type a built-in message class such as IPM.Post in the To combo box.

6. Click Change Message Class to change the message class for all forms with the From message class in the selected folder.

Note The Change Message Class form uses Collaboration Data Objects (CDO) to populate the From and To combo boxes with the list of available message classes and custom forms in a folder. You can click the View Script button on the Change Message Class form to see the code that makes the form work.

Manage Changes to Forms

Let's assume you make changes to a form in an application that has been in use for several months. Rather than remove the old form, you can keep the old form in the forms library and set its Hidden property. This way, users can't create new items with the form, but they can view existing items with the form the items were created with.

To set the Hidden property of a form

1. In the Folder List, right-click the folder that contains the form you want to change. For the Organizational and Personal Forms libraries, you can right-click Inbox.

2. On the shortcut menu, click Properties.

3. Click the Forms tab, and then click Manage.

4. The Forms Manager shows the forms in the active folder's Forms Library in the right list box, as shown earlier in Figure 12.4.

5. Click the right Set button to choose the forms library containing the forms for which you want to set the Hidden property.

6. In the right list box, click the form you want to set the Hidden property for, and then click Properties.

7. Select the Hidden check box, and then click OK.

Note Another way to set the Hidden property for a form is to select the Use Form Only For Responses check box on the Properties page of a form.

Install Forms Programmatically

It is not possible to perform a completely unattended form installation using the Outlook 2000 Object Model if the form has not been published in a Personal Folder, or an Organizational Forms Library. If you attempt to create an item using the *CreateItemFromTemplate* method of the Application object, the Macro Warning dialog box will always appear for the .oft file if the form template contains VBScript code. It is possible, however, to automate a complex form installation over an extensive subfolder hierarchy using the *PublishForm* method of the FormDescription object. The *PublishForm* method can publish custom forms into one or more of the following form registries: Personal Forms, Organizational Forms, or active Folder Forms. Every Outlook custom form contains a FormDescription object that contains the form's general properties. You can use the Hidden property of the FormDescription object to hide the form, if necessary.

More Info For more information about the FormDescription object and its properties and methods, see Microsoft Outlook Visual Basic Reference Help.

The following procedure uses the *AddStore* method of the NameSpace object to add a personal folder (.pst) file to the current profile. The Foobar form has already been published to the Foobar container folder in the foobar.pst file. Because the Foobar form is already a trusted form in the Foobar container folder, you can obtain the form description for a new Foobar form and use the *PublishForm* method to publish the form to another forms library in the current profile. The following example installs the Foobar form to a public folder named Testing Permission. For this example to work correctly, you need to copy the OpenMAPIFolder procedure from basOutlook in the VBA Samples folder into a code module in your form installation project. After the form has been installed successfully, the *RemovePST* method of the NameSpace object removes Foobar.pst from the current profile. *RemovePST* is a hidden method of the NameSpace object.

```
Sub TestPublishForm()
    Dim oNS As Outlook.NameSpace
    Dim oFormDesc As Outlook.FormDescription
    Dim oMsg As Outlook.PostItem
```

```
Dim oSource As Outlook.MAPIFolder
Dim oSourceRoot As Outlook.MAPIFolder
Dim oTarget As Outlook.MAPIFolder

On Error Resume Next
Set oNS = Application.GetNameSpace("MAPI")
'Add store with published form
oNS.AddStore "d:\exchange\foobar.pst"
Set oSource = OpenMAPIFolder("\Foobar\Foobar Container")
Set oSourceRoot = oSource.Parent
Set oMsg = oSource.Items.Add("IPM.Post.Foobar")
Set oFormDesc = oMsg.FormDescription
Set oTarget = OpenMAPIFolder("\Public Folders\ _
    & All Public Folders\Test Permission")
oFormDesc.PublishForm olFolderRegistry, oTarget
If Err Then
    MsgBox Err.Description, vbCritical
End If
oNS.RemoveStore oSourceRoot 'Remove store
End Sub
```

The Forms Cache

The forms cache is a local file system folder that serves as a forms storage location. The forms cache improves the load time of a form because commonly used forms are loaded from the hard disk rather than downloaded from Microsoft Exchange Server. When a form is activated for the first time, the form definition file is copied from its forms library to the user's Forms folder. The forms cache keeps a temporary copy of the form definition in a subfolder whose name roughly matches the name of the form. The Forms folder can be found in the following locations, depending on the operating system you are using.

Operating System	Location for Forms Cache
Windows 95 and 98 without UserProfiles	C:\Windows\Local Settings\Application Data\Microsoft\Forms
Windows 95 and 98 with UserProfiles	C:\Windows\Profiles*UserName*\Local Settings\Application Data\Microsoft\Forms
Windows NT 4.0 or Windows 2000	C:\Winnt\Profiles*UserName*\Local Settings\Application Data\Microsoft\Forms

Note The location of the forms cache has changed from previous versions of Outlook. The previous Forms folder might still be present on the local hard disk, but it no longer stores the forms cache for Outlook 2000.

The form table, Frmcache.dat, is also located in the Forms folder, and is used to locate a form and to prevent multiple instances of the same form from being loaded in the cache.

When a form is activated, Outlook checks to see whether a form with the same message class is already in the cache. If not, it copies the form definition to the cache. In addition, if a change has been made to a form, Outlook copies the new form definition to the cache.

The user can determine the size of the forms cache. The default size of the forms cache is 2048 KB. If a user changes the size of the forms cache to 0, no custom forms can be opened on the user's system.

To specify the amount of disk space allocated for forms

1. Click Options on the Tools menu.
2. Click the Other tab, and then click Advanced Options.
3. In the Advanced Options dialog box, click the Custom Forms button.
4. Specify the disk space under Temporary storage for forms.

Clearing the Forms Cache

There are circumstances where the Outlook forms cache can become corrupted. If the forms cache is corrupted, users could experience one or more of the following conditions when they attempt to open a custom form:

- A user receives a "Cannot Create The Item" error message when the user opens an item.
- Forms suddenly do not behave properly.
- A user receives a message about a problem with the Frmcache.dat file.
- A user receives a "The Object Could Not Be Found" error message appears when the user opens an item or clicks on a mailto: link.

Clearing the forms cache does not always resolve a corrupted form problem. Sometimes, the form definition is actually corrupted on Exchange Server. In this case, you will need to delete the form using the Manage Forms dialog box described earlier in this chapter. Then, you will need to republish the form from an .oft file in order to rebuild the damaged message containing the custom form description. Although the possibility of a damaged form description message in the Exchange store is small, it could occur. Consequently, you have one more reason to back up custom forms to an .oft file stored on a network or local drive which is backed up regularly.

To clear the forms cache in Outlook 2000

1. Quit Outlook by selecting the Exit And Logoff command from the File menu.
2. On the Windows taskbar, click Start, point to Programs, and then click Windows Explorer.
3. In Windows Explorer, move to the Forms folder on the hard drive of the problem system. See the Location for Forms Cache table shown earlier to determine the correct location of the Forms folder.

4. On the Edit menu of Windows Explorer, choose the Select All command.

5. Press the Delete key. Answer Yes when prompted:

   ```
   Are you sure you want to remove these <number> items
   to the Recycle Bin?
   ```

6. Restart Outlook. A new Frmcache.dat file will be created.

Using Windows Scripting Host to Clear the Forms Cache

The forms cache can be cleared automatically if you use a Windows Scripting Host script. Windows Scripting Host provides an easy way to automate administrative tasks using Microsoft scripting technologies. If you have installed Windows Scripting Host, the following procedure will clear the forms cache automatically. For the complete Windows Scripting Host file, open ClearFormsCache.vbs in the VBScript Samples folder.

```vbscript
Sub ClearCache()
    Dim intDoIt 'As Integer
    Dim strLocalPath 'As String
    Dim oFS 'As Scripting.FileSystemObject
    Dim oFile 'As Scripting.File
    Dim oFolder 'As Scripting.Folder
    Dim oFolderForms 'As Scripting.Folder
    Dim colFolderForms 'As Scripting.Folders
    Dim WSHNetwork 'As Wscript.Network
    Dim strUserName 'As String

    intDoIt = MsgBox("Clear the Outlook 2000 Forms Cache?", _
                     vbYesNo + vbQuestion)
    If intDoIt = vbYes Then
        On Error Resume Next
        Set WSHNetwork = WScript.CreateObject("WScript.Network")
        strUserName = WSHNetwork.UserName
        Set oFS = WScript.CreateObject("Scripting.FileSystemObject")
        Const WindowsFolder = 0
        Set oFolder = oFS.GetSpecialFolder(WindowsFolder)
        strLocalPath = "\Local Settings\Application Data\Microsoft\Forms"
        Set oFolderForms = oFS.GetFolder(oFolder.Path & strLocalPath)
        If Err Then 'UserProfile
            Err.Clear
            strLocalPath = "\Profiles\" & strUserName & strLocalPath
            Set oFolderForms = oFS.GetFolder(oFolder.Path & strLocalPath)
            If Err Then
                MsgBox "Could not find " _
                    & vbCr & oFolder.Path & strLocalPath, _
                    vbCritical
                Exit Sub
            End If
        End If
        Set colFolderForms = oFolderForms.SubFolders
        'Delete all subfolders in Forms folder
```

```
        For Each oFolder In colFolderForms
            oFolder.Delete
        Next
        'Delete frmcache.dat
        Set oFile = oFolderForms.Files.Item("frmcache.dat")
        oFile.Delete
        MsgBox "Cleared Outlook 2000 Forms Cache.", vbInformation
    End If
End Sub
```

Caution Because Outlook caches forms, you should avoid having more than one form with the same name in—or publishing the same form to—more than one forms library. If you do publish forms with the same name to more than one forms library (for example, a public folder and a folder in a personal folders file), you might experience forms cache corruption. Symptoms of forms cache corruption include Outlook displaying an alert message telling you that your custom form could not be opened. To reset the Outlook forms cache, you must shut down Outlook and then follow the procedures outlined earlier to clear the forms cache.

Forms used in a folder-based solution should be published only in the application folder. If you're developing a solution based on mail message forms, you can temporarily publish the forms in your Personal Forms Library. Once the form is finalized, you should publish the form to the Organizational Forms Library on the Microsoft Exchange Server and then delete the form from your Personal Forms Library after making a backup of the form. If, for some reason, you need to publish a form in more than one location, you should be sure to keep all forms libraries up-to-date with the current version of the form.

Form Activation

A form is activated when the user selects a form to compose an item, or when the user performs an operation on a existing item. For example, the user double-clicks an existing item in a folder to open it. Outlook uses the following form-caching sequence to activate forms:

1. **Standard Forms Library**   Checks for standard forms, such as Note, Post, Contact, Distribution List, Task, Journal, and Appointment.

2. **Cached Forms**   Checks for a form in the forms cache.

3. **Active Folder Library**   Checks for a form in the forms library of the active folder.

4. **Personal Forms Library**   Checks for the form definition in the Personal Forms Library. If it is found, Outlook opens the form.

5. **Organizational Forms Library**   Checks the form definition in the Organizational Forms Library. If it is found, Outlook opens the form.

Distribute Folders

After a folder is designed, you can copy it to a Mailbox folder, Personal Folders, or Public Folders.

This section discusses the different methods for making a folder available for use. It also discusses offline folder issues and offers references for archiving and aging folders.

> **Important** Do not attempt to distribute folders using the Outlook Import and Export Wizard. The Import and Export Wizard is designed for importing and exporting data, not for distributing folders.

Make a Folder Available to All Users in Your Organization

You can make a folder available to all users in your organization by creating the folder in, or copying the folder to, Public Folders. Then, it is up to the administrator to determine whether the folder is replicated throughout the organization. You or the administrator can set permissions for who has access to the folder and to what extent those users can work in the folder.

> **Note** To copy a folder to Public Folders, you must have permission to create subfolders for that portion of the Microsoft Exchange Server folder hierarchy.

Based on the policies of your organization, you may not have permission to copy a folder to Public Folders. You may be required to hand off the folder to your administrator, who then copies the folder and completes the design tasks according to your specifications. Alternatively, you may be given permission to copy your folder to a specific public folder and then complete the task yourself. See your administrator for specific instructions.

To create a folder in Public Folders

1. In Public Folders, right-click the folder in which you want to create the subfolder, and then click New Folder on the shortcut menu.

2. In the Name text box, type a name for the folder.

3. Select the options you want.

4. If prompted, select a choice about creating a shortcut on the Outlook Bar, and then click OK.

To copy a folder to Public Folders

1. In the Folder List, right-click the folder you want to copy, and then click Copy *folder name* on the shortcut menu, where *folder name* is the folder name you used in item 2 above.

2. Click the public folder you want to copy the folder to, and then click OK.

Set Permissions for the Folder

When you set permissions on the folder, you determine who has access to the folder and what functions they can perform in the folder.

To set permissions for the folder

1. In the Folder List, right-click the folder you copied to Public Folders, and then click Properties on the shortcut menu.
2. Click the Permissions page.
3. Set permissions for the folder.

> **More Info** For more information about setting permissions, see "Set Permissions" in Chapter 8, "Folders."

If the folder is replicated to other servers, make sure you set the permissions so that all users who need access to the folder have the appropriate permissions.

Make a Folder Available for Personal Use

Private folders are stored in the user's Mailbox folder or in a personal folder (.pst) file. There are three good reasons for storing a folder in a personal folder file:

1. Users have exclusive rights to the folder. For example, many users keep a list of personal contacts in their Contacts folder.
2. Users can access information in the folder even when they are not logged on to Microsoft Exchange Server. This can be especially useful for people who travel, because they can access information in a personal folder on a laptop without a live connection to the server.
3. Users can easily distribute the folder in personal folder (.pst) files. For example, many of the applications in this book were tested in public folders on a test Exchange Server. After testing, they were copied to the Building Microsoft Outlook 2000 Applications folder so they could be distributed in a .pst file.

> **More Info** If you have not yet created a Personal Folder file, see "Create a Personal Folder (.pst) File" later in this chapter.

To create a folder in your Mailbox or in a personal folder (.pst) file

1. In the Folder List, right-click the Mailbox folder or personal folder you want to create the subfolder in, and then click New Folder on the shortcut menu.
2. In the Name text box, type a name for the folder.
3. Select the options you want.

To copy a folder to your Mailbox or personal folder (.pst) file

1. In the Folder List, right-click the folder you want to copy, and then click Copy *folder name* on the shortcut menu, where *folder name* is the folder name you used in item 2 above.

2. Click the Mailbox folder or personal folder you want to copy the folder to, and then click OK.

Distribute a Folder in a Personal Folder (.pst) File

A personal folder (.pst) file provides a convenient way to distribute applications using a floppy disk, a CD-ROM, or a network drive. For example, you can create folders on your Microsoft Exchange Server system in either public or personal folders. When you are ready to distribute the folders, you can create a personal folder file and then copy the folders to the file.

Create a Personal Folder File

To create a personal folder (.pst) file

1. On the File menu, click New, and then click Personal Folders File (.pst).

2. On the Save In drop-down list box, specify the location for your personal folder (.pst) file.

3. In the File Name text box, enter a name for the personal folder (.pst) file.

4. Click Create.

5. In the Create Microsoft Personal Folders dialog box, select the options you want, and then click OK.

Copy Folders to a Personal Folder File

To copy a folder to a personal folder (.pst) file

1. In the Folder List, right-click the folder you want to copy, and then click Copy *folder name* on the shortcut menu, where *folder name* is the folder name you used in step 3 above.

2. Click the personal folder you want to copy the folder to, and then click OK.

Distribute the Personal Folder File

To distribute the personal folder (.pst) file, open Windows Explorer and copy the .pst file to a floppy disk, a network drive, or a CD-ROM drive.

Install a Personal Folder File Programmatically

You can now install a personal folder (.pst) file programmatically if you use the *AddStore* method of the NameSpace object. If the .pst file does not exist, a new .pst file will be created using the file specification provided. The following procedure adds a .pst file named appwzd.pst located in the D:\Exchange folder.

```
Sub AddPST()
    Set oNS = Application.GetNameSpace("MAPI")
    oNS.AddStore "d:\exchange\appwzd.pst"
End Sub
```

Make an Existing Personal Folder File Available on Your Microsoft Exchange System

⮕ **To make an existing personal folder (.pst) file available on your Microsoft Exchange System**

1. On the File menu, select Open, and then click Personal Folders File (.pst).
2. Specify the location you want, and then double-click the personal folder (.pst) file you want.
3. The file appears in your Folder List.

Making Changes to a Folder

If you are responsible for maintaining an application, you are often asked to make changes to the forms or folders that make up the application. For example, users may ask for enhancements to a form, for additional folder views, or for permissions.

If the changes to the folder are substantial, you should copy the design of the folder to another folder, make the necessary changes to the folder, and then copy the design back to the original folder. If the changes are minor, such as adding a permission or a view, you can modify the folder directly. To make changes to a folder, you must have Owner permission for the folder.

More Info For more information about how to modify a folder, see Chapter 8, "Folders."

Make Folders Available for Offline Use

To work offline or with a dial-up connection, the user's computer should be prepared for offline and dial-up work. Once the computer is set up, the task of setting up folders for offline use is simple.

More Info For more information about setting up a computer and Outlook with a dial-up connection or setting up offline folders, see Outlook Help or Windows Help.

To make a folder available for offline use, the user designates the folder as an offline folder. The following folders can be designated as offline folders:

- Inbox, Outbox, Sent Items, Drafts, Contacts, Calendar, Tasks, Notes, Journal, and Deleted Items are Outlook folders in the user's Mailbox that are selected by default for offline use.
- Any folder in the user's Mailbox that the user created.
- Any folder in the user's Favorites folder.

How Folders Are Made Available for Offline Use

When the user sets up a computer for offline use, an offline folder (.ost) file is created on the user's hard disk. The offline folder file contains a replica of folders the user works with offline.

Once the folders are set up for offline use, they must be synchronized by the user so the offline folders contain the same information as the folders on the server. To synchronize folders, the user selects Synchronize on the Tools menu and then clicks the desired choice. Outlook 2000 provides Quick Synchronization settings that allow a user to establish a filter on a set of synchronized subfolders.

More Info For specific procedures, see "Set Outlook to Start Offline" and "Synchronize Offline Folders" in Outlook Help, and see "Specifying Folders for Offline Use," earlier in this chapter.

How Folders Are Synchronized

While a user is working offline, the contents of both the offline folder and the folder on the server can change. For example, the user may post items in a Contacts folder while offline. At the same time, users connected to the server may also post items to the Contacts folder.

To make sure the contents of offline folders match the contents of folders on the server, the user selects the Synchronize command on the Tools menu, and then clicks the desired choice. Offline folders can be synchronized individually or all at once. When the user synchronizes folders, the changes made in the server folder are reflected in the offline folder, and the changes made in the offline folder are reflected in the server folder.

When a user of offline folders reconnects to Microsoft Exchange Server, any changes made in the offline folders are reflected in the folders on the server. However, changes made in the folder on Microsoft Exchange Server while the user was offline are not reflected in the offline folders until the user synchronizes the folders.

Synchronizing Folder Home Pages

You must have Microsoft Internet Explorer 5.0 or later installed on your computer to view Folder Home Pages offline.

To synchronize a Folder Home Page

1. On the Tools menu, point to Synchronize, and then click Offline Folder Settings.
2. Select the check box next to the folder with the home page that you want to view offline.
3. Under Options on the All Folders page of the Offline Folder Settings dialog box, select the Synchronize Folder Home Pages check box, and then click OK.
4. In the Folder List, right-click the folder, and then click Properties on the shortcut menu.

5. Click the Home Page tab, and then click Offline Web Page Settings. If you have not enabled the folder for use offline, you will not see the Offline Web Page settings command button. When you click Offline Web Page Settings, you will see the dialog box shown in Figure 12.6.

6. On the Schedule and Download tabs, select the options you want. For help on an option, click the question mark and then click the option.

7. Click OK twice.

8. On the Tools menu, point to Synchronize, and then select This Folder to synchronize the folder and its Folder Home Page.

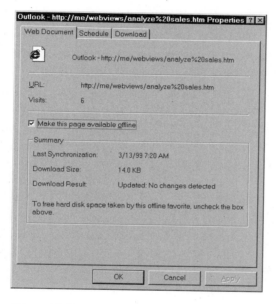

Figure 12.6 *Use this dialog box to establish settings for Folder Home Page synchronization.*

Folder Replication Issues

Replication is the process by which Microsoft Exchange Server keeps folders that are in different locations synchronized. Generally, folder replication is handled by Microsoft Exchange Server administrators and involves careful planning and coordination between site administrators.

If you are an application designer, here are a few issues you should be aware of regarding folder replication:

- If a folder contains critical data that must be refreshed immediately in all locations when new data is received, the folder should not be replicated.

- Replicate applications from a central location. It often makes sense to store all applications on one server and perform all replication and updates to the application from this central location.
- Make sure each site that needs to replicate the application has appropriate permissions to support replication.

Age and Archive Folders

You can have Outlook automatically remove items of a specified age and transfer them to an archive file.

To turn on AutoArchiving for Outlook

1. On the Tools menu, select the Options command.
2. Click the AutoArchive button on the Other page of the Tools Options dialog box.
3. Check the AutoArchive Every <*number*> Days check box.

To turn AutoArchiving on for a specific folder

1. Select the folder you want to AutoArchive in the Folder List.
2. On the File menu, select Folder, and then select Folder Properties.
3. Click the AutoArchive page of the Folder Properties dialog box.
4. Check the Clean Out Items Older Than <*number*> <*weeks,days,months*> check box.

Where To Go from Here

For additional information about the subjects discussed in this chapter, see the following resources.

Installing Forms on Microsoft Exchange Server

Microsoft Corporation. Rizzo, Thomas. *Programming Microsoft Outlook and Microsoft Exchange*. Redmond, WA: Microsoft Press, 1999.

Windows Scripting Host

Microsoft Corporation. Dan Gookin. *Introducing Windows Scripting Host for Microsoft Windows 98*. Redmond, WA: Microsoft Press, 1999.

Microsoft Scripting Technologies Web site
http://www.msdn.microsoft.com/scripting/

Windows Scripting Host Web site
http://wsh.glazier.co.nz/

Part V
Advanced Topics

The Advanced Topics chapters are primarily for developers who want to use Visual Basic to extend Outlook in a corporate environment where Microsoft Exchange Server is installed. Chapter 13, "Creating COM Add-Ins with Visual Basic," provides you with practical templates for Visual Basic COM Add-in component creation and discusses some of the security issues associated with COM Add-ins. You'll also learn how to use Visual Basic to create an ActiveX control that serves as a property page in the Outlook Tools Options dialog box. Chapter 14, "Customizing Folder Home Pages," gives you a quick tour of the forthcoming Team Folder Wizard and then introduces you to a Visual Basic DHTML application that serves as the Folder Home Page for the Customers folder in the Northwind Contact Management application. In Chapter 15, "Outlook Data Access Strategies," we'll look at several options you can use to bring external data into Outlook. Chapter 16, "Using ActiveX DLLs and Microsoft Transaction Server with Outlook," considers how you can use remote components and MTS to your advantage when you attempt to scale your Outlook application to hundreds or thousands of users. Finally, Chapter 17, "Extending Outlook Using Exchange Server Scripting and Routing Objects," offers a practical example Using VBScript and Visual Basic of bilateral data synchronization between a SQL Server database and the Customers public folder in the Northwind Contact Management application.

Chapter 13
Creating COM Add-Ins with Visual Basic

In This Chapter

Outlook 2000 COM Add-ins provide an abundance of exciting new opportunities for Outlook developers. In the past, Outlook development took place primarily in the forms arena. Modification of the Outlook application environment—toolbars, dialog boxes, and property pages—required costly development of Exchange Client Extensions authored in C++. The costs associated with the C++ and MAPI development cycle discouraged the building of components that extended Outlook or fostered vertical market applications using Outlook and Exchange.

Outlook 2000 changes all that with the appearance of COM Add-ins. A COM Add-in is an ActiveX component packaged in a dynamic-link library (DLL) that is specially registered so that it can be loaded by Outlook 2000. COM Add-ins are also known as Office Pluggable Components. We'll avoid the marketing terminology and stick with COM Add-ins, a term that is more meaningful to developers familiar with COM and ActiveX components. You can create Outlook 2000 COM Add-ins with either Visual Basic 5.0 or 6.0. Visual Basic 5.0 requires some gymnastics on your part to get a COM Add-in to register correctly, so this chapter will focus instead on the use of Visual Basic 6.0 to create COM Add-ins. In fact, you can use any COM compliant development tool, including Microsoft Visual C++, Microsoft Visual J++, or a tool from a vendor other than Microsoft—as long as that tool can create ActiveX DLLs. In this chapter, we'll show you how to convert the code behind the Northwind Contact Management application into a COM Add-in. Along the way, we'll cover the techniques you must be aware of when you create COM Add-in solutions.

> **Note** COM Add-ins can also be created using an ActiveX .exe file, but this approach is not recommended for Outlook COM Add-ins. Since ActiveX .exe components operate out of process, you'll incur a performance penalty if you create an ActiveX .exe COM Add-in.

Tools Needed to Create COM Add-Ins

To create an Outlook COM Add-in, you should obtain Visual Studio 98 Professional Edition or Visual Basic 5.0 Professional Edition. Visual Studio 98 is the preferred development tool because you can use Visual InterDev 6.0 to customize Folder Home Pages, as well as Visual Basic 6.0 to create COM Add-ins. You can also create COM Add-ins for Outlook with Microsoft Office 2000 Developer. If you don't have Office Developer, you can develop a project using ThisOutlookSession and Outlook VBA, but a solution based on ThisOutlookSession will have several limitations, including Outlook's inability to run more than one ThisOutlookSession project in a given Outlook session. If you install a custom VBAProject.otm (the project that contains ThisOutlookSession), you will overwrite the existing VBAProject.otm for the current user. On the other hand, multiple COM Add-in solutions can run in a given Outlook session. The following table outlines the solutions you can create with the development tools mentioned, as well as listing the pros and cons of each tool.

Tool	Solution Created	Intellectual Property Protection	Deployment	Multiple Solutions in an Outlook Session
Microsoft Office 2000 Developer	COM Add-in ActiveX DLL built with VBA 6.0	Compiled ActiveX DLL	Package and Deployment Wizard	Yes
Microsoft Visual Basic 5.0 Professional or Enterprise Edition	COM Add-in ActiveX DLL built with VB 5.0. Extra steps required because VB 5.0 does not support Add-in Designers	Compiled ActiveX DLL	Setup Wizard with extra steps required	Yes
Microsoft Visual Basic 6.0 Professional or Enterprise Edition	COM Add-in ActiveX DLL built with VB 6.0	Compiled ActiveX DLL	Package and Deployment Wizard	Yes

> **Note** You can use Microsoft Visual C++ or Microsoft Visual J++ to create COM Add-ins for Office 2000 applications. You can also use any development tool capable of creating an ActiveX DLL, as long as you meet the special requirements of Office 2000 COM Add-Ins.

The COMAddIns Collection Object

Before we cover the steps required to create a COM Add-in, you should realize that COM Add-ins are exposed in the Office 2000 Object Model through the COMAddIns collection object and its member COMAddIn objects. You can determine which COM Add-ins are available in a given Outlook application session by iterating over the items in the COMAddIns collection object. The COMAddIns collection object is available as a property object of the Outlook Application object. Although the COMAddIns collection object is available as a property object for each Application object in the Office 2000 suite, the COMAddIns collection object is application-specific, meaning that you can obtain the COMAddIns collection only for the Outlook Application object. The COMAddIns collection object supports only two methods, the *Update* method and the *Items* method. The *Items* method lets you access a COMAddIn object from the collection by index or by the COMAddIn's COM ProgID. The *Update* method refreshes the COMAddIns collection from the COM Add-ins that are registered in the Windows registry. Figure 13.1 illustrates a UserForm that displays the friendly names of Outlook COM Add-Ins, whether the COM Add-in is loaded in the current Outlook session, and the ProgID of the Add-in.

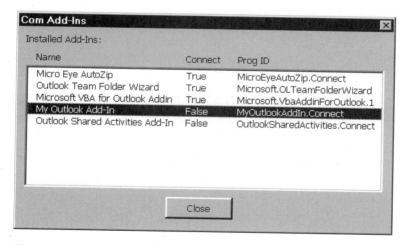

Figure 13.1 *The COM Add-Ins dialog box displays the members of the COMAddIns collection that are registered.*

COMAddIn Object

The COMAddIn object lets you determine the friendly name of a COM Add-in, whether the COM Add-in is loaded, and the ProgID of the COM Add-in. You can cause a COM Add-in to programmatically load or unload by setting its Connect property. If you are worried about a performance penalty in loading your COM Add-in during Outlook startup, you should consider loading and unloading your Add-in through program code instead. A more typical approach is to let the user install COM Add-ins through a setup program, and then use the Outlook COM Add-Ins dialog box to determine which COM Add-ins are loaded. The following code populates the list box shown in Figure 13.1. To create a multi-column list box, create a variant array and then fill the array with the Add-in's friendly name, connect state, and ProgID. When the array is populated, assign the array to the List property of the list box.

```
Private Sub UserForm_Initialize()
Dim avarArray
Dim intCount As Integer
Dim intAddIns As Integer
Dim objAddIn As Office.COMAddIn
Dim colAddIns As Office.COMAddIns
Set colAddIns = Application.COMAddIns
intAddIns = colAddIns.Count
If intAddIns Then
    ReDim avarArray(intAddIns - 1, 2)
    For intCount = 1 To intAddIns
        Set objAddIn = colAddIns.Item(intCount)
        avarArray(intCount - 1, 0) = objAddIn.Description
        If objAddIn.Connect = True Then
            avarArray(intCount - 1, 1) = "True"
        Else
            avarArray(intCount - 1, 1) = "False"
        End If
        avarArray(intCount - 1, 2) = objAddIn.ProgId
    Next
    lstAddIns.List = avarArray
End If
End Sub
```

Displaying the List of COM Add-Ins

Outlook's COM Add-Ins dialog box is buried deep in the Tools Options dialog box. If you are developing COM Add-ins, you'll want to customize your Standard or Advanced Explorer toolbar and place a command bar button on the toolbar to provide a shortcut to the COM Add-Ins dialog box.

To display the Outlook COM Add-Ins dialog box

1. Select the Options command on the Tools menu.
2. Click the Other page on the Tools Options dialog box.
3. Click the Advanced Options command button.
4. Click the COM Add-Ins command button on the Advanced Options dialog box.

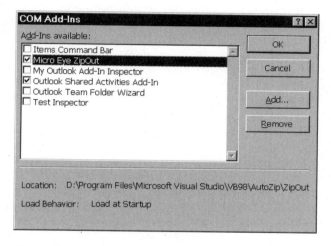

Figure 13.2 *The Outlook COM Add-Ins dialog box lets you control the connection state of registered COM Add-ins.*

To add a toolbar button for the COM Add-Ins dialog box

1. Select the Customize command on the Tools menu.
2. Click the Commands page.
3. In the Categories list, click Tools.
4. In the Commands list, click COM Add-Ins. You may have to scroll through the list to find it.
5. Drag the COM Add-Ins command to the Standard or the Advanced Explorer toolbar.
6. Close the Customize dialog box.

To Load or Unload a COM Add-In

You can load a COM Add-in by checking the box next to the friendly name of the Add-in in the COM Add-Ins dialog box. Depending on the load behavior of the COM Add-In, the COM Add-in will either load immediately, or it will load the next time you launch Outlook. There are circumstances in which you will want to unload a COM Add-in to debug the COM Add-in directly in Visual Basic in run mode. See "The Debugging Process" later in this chapter.

To Add a COM Add-In

If you install a COM Add-in by using its setup program, it will automatically register and appear in the list box of the COM Add-In dialog box shown in Figure 13.2. However, you can also add an unregistered COM Add-in by clicking Add in the COM Add-Ins dialog box and selecting the correct ActiveX DLL in the Add Add-In dialog box. If the ActiveX DLL you select is a valid Outlook 2000 COM Add-in, it will be registered and loading by Outlook the next time it starts.

> **Note** If you select an ActiveX DLL that is not an Office 2000 COM Add-in, Outlook will alert you and decline to load the Add-in. You cannot load other application-specific Add-ins (such as an Excel Add-in) with the Outlook COM Add-Ins dialog box.

To Remove a COM Add-In

To remove a COM Add-in, select it in the COM Add-Ins dialog box and click Remove. Removing an Add-in deletes the registry key containing the Add-in's name and load behavior. The registry contains information about COM Add-ins under HKEY_CLASSES_ROOT and HKEY_CURRENT_USER. Like any other DLL, the Add-in's ActiveX DLL is registered as a unique object in the system under HKEY_CLASSES_ROOT. In addition, information about the Add-in is placed under HKEY_CURRENT_USER\Software\Microsoft\Office\Outlook\Addins to notify Outlook that the Add-in exists. If you remove a COM Add-in from the list of installed Add-ins, the subkey identifying the COM Add-in is removed from the registry, but the AcitveX DLL itself remains registered. If you add the Add-in to the list again, the Add-in's informational subkey is re-created in the registry.

Creating an Outlook COM Add-In Project in Visual Basic

The companion CD-ROM includes a template project—Outlook COM AddIn.vbp—for creating an Outlook COM Add-In using Visual Basic 6.0. This template project is available in the Outlook COM Add-In Template folder. It provides an easy-to-use template that lets you create Outlook COM Add-Ins with a minimum of confusion. We'll assume that you have already installed Visual Basic 6.0 and that you want to add the Outlook COM Add-In to your development environment. The first sequence of steps will show you how to move the files for the Outlook COM Add-In template from the personal folders (.pst) file that accompanies this book to the projects folder for your Visual Basic 6.0 installation. Any project placed in the Visual Basic 6.0 Projects folder is available as a new project when you select New Project on the File menu in Visual Basic.

To install the Outlook COM Add-In project in your Visual Basic 6.0 Projects folder

1. Expand the subfolder 5. Advanced Topics in the Building Microsoft Outlook 2000 Applications personal folders (.pst) file.

2. Expand the Creating COM Add-Ins Using Visual Basic folder and click the Outlook COM Add-In Template folder.

3. Select all the files in the Outlook COM Add-In Template folder.

4. Launch Windows Explorer and navigate to the Projects folder for Visual Basic 6.0. If you've selected the default installation, the Projects folder is located in C:\Program Files\Microsoft Visual Studio\VB98\Template\Projects.

5. Drag the files you selected in step 3 to the Projects folder in Windows Explorer. In case you have problems dragging and dropping files, we've also included a self-extracting .zip file containing all the Outlook COM Add-In Template files in the Outlook COM Add-In Template folder. Just double-click the file named Outlook COM AddIn.exe and extract the files to the folder listed in step 4.

To open a new Outlook COM Add-in project in Visual Basic 6.0

1. Launch Visual Basic 6.0.

2. Select New Project from the File Menu.

3. Select Outlook COM AddIn in the New Project dialog box, as shown in Figure 13.3.

4. Click OK.

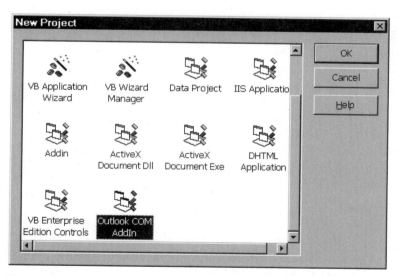

Figure 13.3 *Use the Visual Basic New Project dialog box to create a new Outlook COM Add-In project after you have installed the Outlook COM AddIn project template.*

Note Once you've opened a new Outlook COM Add-In project, you should rename the project and the base class to names you choose. These names will determine how your COM Add-in appears in the Outlook COM Add-Ins dialog box, and they will form the basis of its programmatic identifier in the Windows registry.

To add your identity to the Outlook COM Add-In project

1. Press CTRL+R to open the Visual Basic Project Explorer.

2. Click MyOutlookAddIn in the Project Explorer window.

3. Press F4 to open the Visual Basic Properties window.

4. Use the Properties window to rename the project from MyOutlookAddIn to a name that describes your project. The project name cannot contain spaces. The project name that you supply will serve as the first part of the programmatic identifier for your project.

5. Rename the Class module OutAddIn, if necessary. The class module name serves as the second part of the programmatic identifier of the class object in the Windows registry. If you compiled the MyOutlookAddIn project without changing any names, the compiled ActiveX DLL would have a ProgID of *MyOutlookAddIn.OutAddIn* in the Windows registry.

6. Rename the Connect Add-In Designer, if necessary. The Add-In Designer name also serves as the second part of the programmatic identifier for the Add-in Designer object in the Windows registry. If you compiled the MyOutlookAddIn project without changing any names, the compiled COM Add-in would have a ProgID of *MyOutlookAddIn.Connect* in the Windows registry.

7. Select Save Project As from the File Menu. Save your new project in a folder other than the VB98 folder. We suggest you click the New Folder icon on the Save As dialog box, supply a new folder name for your project, and save all the files in the project into that folder.

8. You're now ready to begin the work of adding code to both the Add-In Designer and the class module for the COM Add-in. (See Figure 13.4)

The Outlook COM Add-In Project Template

The Outlook COM AddIn.vbp template serves as the foundation for your own COM Add-ins and provides you with the following:

- An Add-In Designer. An Add-In Designer is a component that helps you create and register a COM Add-in. This Add-In Designer is created specifically for Outlook COM Add-Ins.

- A reference to the Microsoft Add-In Designer Object Library. The Visual Basic 6.0 Outlook COM Add-In template project sets a reference to the Microsoft Add-In Designer Object Library contained in the file msaddndr.dll. When you set a reference to the Microsoft Add-In Designer, you can implement the IDTExtensibility2 Type Library, which supplies the events you can use to run code when your Add-in is connected to or disconnected from its hosting Outlook application.

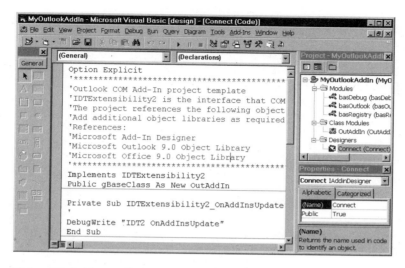

Figure 13.4 *The Outlook COM Add-In project in the Visual Basic 6.0 development environment.*

- A reference to both the Microsoft Outlook 9.0 and the Microsoft Office 9.0 Object Libraries. You need to reference the Office 9.0 Object Library to create custom toolbars for Outlook Explorer and Inspector objects.
- Object variables declared WithEvents so that you can write event procedures in the OutAddIn class module in the MyOutlookAddIn project.
- Standard modules that allow you to debug your project and that contain common Outlook functions.
- A standard module that allows you to get and set Windows registry settings.
- A standard module that lets you create and manipulate Office command bar controls from a COM Add-in.

Moving ThisOutlookSession Code to a COM Add-In

The Outlook COM Add-In project does not actually contain working code. We'll examine a working COM Add-in project later in this chapter. If you've worked with Outlook VBA and developed code that you'd like to port to a COM Add-in, you might be wondering how you accomplish this conversion. Here is some good news and some bad news: Contrary to early rumors and speculation during the public beta of Office 2000, there is no VBA ThisOutlookSession-to-COM Add-In conversion tool shipping with Office 2000 Developer or with Outlook 2000. This does not prohibit third parties from developing such a tool. The good news is that you don't have to completely reconstruct your Outlook VBA code to change it into a COM Add-in. We'll discuss the problems you will encounter with conversion later in this chapter, when we cover how to convert the Create Shared Activities toolbar used in the Northwind Contact Management application into a COM Add-in. You'll also see a very practical introduction to problems associated with the conversion process.

What Is a COM Add-In?

As stated at the beginning of this chapter, a COM Add-in is a special type of ActiveX DLL that communicates with Outlook 2000. The Outlook COM Add-In project template provided with this book gives you a cookie-cutter tool for creating Outlook COM Add-ins. The one essential requirement for a COM Add-in is that it must contain code to implement the IDTExtensibility2 Type Library that provides the programming interface for integrating COM Add-ins with their host applications. The examples included with this book use two classes, rather than one, to build a COM Add-in. The reason for this approach is so that you can separate the code into two separate class modules when you build your COM Add-in. The first class derives from the Add-In Designer that must be added to a COM Add-in project in order to create a COM Add-in. The second class actually does the work of implementing the functionality of your COM Add-in. We'll call this class the base class of your COM Add-in. Figure 13.5 illustrates the COM interfaces of the Outlook COM Add-In project template. Refer to books and Web sites on COM listed at the end of this chapter for a complete understanding of the theoretical aspects of COM objects. You should realize that you could construct your COM Add-in from only one class if you so desire. The two-class approach makes it easier to plug another base class into a standard Connect class module that handles the unique events of the IDTExtensibility2 Type Library.

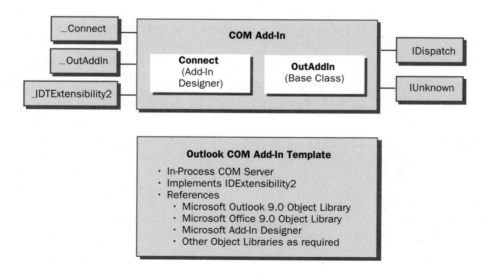

Figure 13.5 *The COM interfaces of the Outlook COM Add-In project.*

From the more practical rather than theoretical perspective of this chapter, the important point to remember is that the Outlook COM Add-in project supplied with this book supports at least two public classes. The Connect class is the umbilical cord between your COM Add-in and Outlook 2000. Without the Connect class, your COM Add-in is just a garden variety ActiveX DLL looking for a client object to instantiate it. If you wanted to load this garden variety ActiveX DLL whenever Outlook started, you'd have some difficult obstacles to overcome before you could create a reliable solution. The Connect class that Implements IDTExtensibility2 solves this problem for you. It provides a means for Outlook to instantiate your COM Add-in automatically when Outlook launches, either through a user action or program code. The Connect class for the MyOutlookAddIn project has no public methods or properties.

Note If your COM Add-in is set to launch on startup, the COM Add-in will run if a user opens Outlook from the Start menu, or if program code in an Automation controller application launches Outlook to send a mail message. If you've set your COM Add-in's initial load behavior to Load On Startup, your COM Add-in will run whenever Outlook runs.

The base class of your COM Add-in actually does the work of the COM Add-in. The base class has been isolated from the Add-In Designer Connect class so that you can plug different base classes into your Connect class. Although the OutAddIn class in the Outlook COM Add-In project template does not expose any properties or methods, you could expose public properties and methods in the base class of your COM Add-in. Those public properties and methods would then be available to any other Automation controller that can instantiate your COM Add-in base class object. Later, you will see how you can use this approach to make a public method in a COM Add-in available to VBScript code in an Outlook form.

Building a COM Add-In

Now that we have a template project available in Visual Basic 6.0, we can walk through the steps of building a COM Add-in. After you have created and saved a new project using the Outlook COM Add-In template, you need to save some settings that control the load behavior of your COM Add-in. The Add-In Designer for the Outlook COM Add-In project is a class module with a user interface that lets you set properties for the Add-in. Figure 13.6 shows the AddInDesigner dialog box for Connect.dsr in the Outlook COM Add-In template. Remember that this dialog box appears only when you are in Design mode in Visual Basic; this dialog box is not exposed to the user who actually uses your COM Add-in.

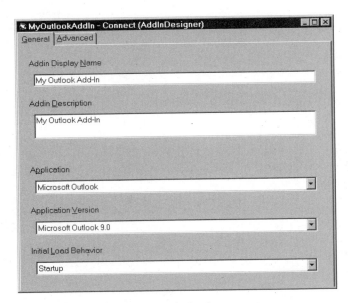

Figure 13.6 *AddInDesigner dialog box.*

Setting AddInDesigner Properties

Using the AddInDesigner Dialog Box

The properties you set in the AddInDesigner dialog box control the initial load behavior of your COM Add-in and the friendly name a user sees in the COM Add-Ins dialog box. The following table lists the available settings in the AddInDesigner dialog box's General page.

Option	Description
Addin Display Name	The name that will appear in the COM Add-Ins dialog box in Outlook. The name you supply should be descriptive to the user. The Addin Display Name is equivalent to the Description property of the COMAddIn object. In the Windows registry, the Addin Display Name is stored in the FriendlyName key. If the name is to come from a resource file specified in the Satellite DLL Name box on the Advanced page, it must begin with a number sign (#), followed by an integer specifying a resource ID within the file.
Addin Description	In the Windows registry, the Addin Description is stored in the Description key. This name is not available as a property of a COMAddIn object. If the description is to come from a resource file specified in the Satellite DLL Name box on the Advanced page, it must begin with a number sign (#), followed by an integer specifying a resource ID within the file.

(continued)

(continued)

Option	Description
Application	The application in which the Add-in will run. This list displays applications that support COM Add-ins.
Application Version	The version of the application in which the Add-in will run.
Initial Load Behavior	The way the Add-in will load in Outlook 2000. The list of possible settings comes from the registry.

The Advanced page of the AddInDesigner dialog box allows you to specify a file containing localized resource information for the Add-in and to specify additional registry data in the Windows registry. The following table describes the options available on the Advanced page:

Option	Description
Satellite DLL Name	The name of a file containing localized (translated) resources for an Add-in. The file must be located in the same directory as the Add-in's registered DLL.
Registry Key For Additional Addin Data	The registry subkey to which additional data is to be written.
Addin Specific Data	The names and values to be stored in the registry subkey. Only String and DWORD type values are permitted.

Determining the ProgID for Your COM Add-In

If you change the Add-In Designer name in the Properties window of the Visual Basic Project Explorer, you will change the class name from Connect to the name you enter in the Properties window. The class name of the Add-In Designer is used to create the programmatic identifier—or ProgID—for your COM Add-in. The ProgID derives from the combination of the Visual Basic project name and the Add-In Designer name. If your Visual Basic project name is MyProjectName and the name of your Add-In Designer is MyConnect, then the ProgID for your COM Add-in would be *MyProjectName.MyConnect*.

Where Outlook COM Add-Ins Are Registered

Outlook COM Add-Ins are registered in the Windows registry under the following key:

HKEY_CURRENT_USER\Software\Microsoft\Office\Outlook\Addins

Each COM Add-in has a subkey under the Addins key based on its ProgID. If you are using Visual Basic 6.0 to create your Add-in, the ProgID subkey and some essential key values are automatically created for you when you compile your Add-in project or when a user installs a COM Add-in. Figure 13.7 shows the Addins key in the Windows Registry Editor.

> **Note** If your install program registers your Add-in under HKEY_LOCAL_MACHINE instead of HKEY_CURRENT_USER, the Add-in will be available for every user who logs

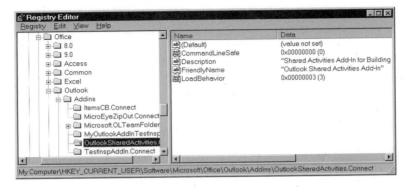

Figure 13.7 *COM Add-in settings in the Windows Registry Editor.*

on to the machine. If you examine HKEY_LOCAL_MACHINE\Software\Microsoft\ Office\Outlook\Addins, you'll see that Microsoft has added an Add-in key for Outlook VBA. Outlook VBA is registered under HKEY_LOCAL_MACHINE as a demand-loaded Outlook COM Add-In.

Controlling Initial Load Behavior

You control the initial load behavior of your COM Add-in by setting the Initial Load Behavior drop-down list box on the General page of the AddInDesigner dialog box. If you are not using a Visual Basic 6.0 Add-In Designer to create your COM Add-in, you can set the initial load behavior directly by assigning the correct DWORD value to the LoadBehavior key in the Windows registry. Notice in the table below that a value of *0x01* is added to the LoadBehavior value if the Add-in is connected.

Initial Load Behavior Setting	LoadBehavior DWORD	Behavior Description
None	*0x00* *0x01* (Connected)	The COM Add-in is not loaded when Outlook boots. It can be loaded in the COM Add-Ins dialog box, or by setting the Connect property of the corresponding COMAddIn object.
Startup	*0x02* *0x03* (Connected)	The Add-in is loaded when Outlook boots. Once the Add-in is loaded, it remains loaded until it is explicitly unloaded.
Load On Demand	*0x08* *0x09* (Connected)	The Add-in is not loaded until the user clicks the button or menu item that loads the Add-in, or until a procedure sets its Connect property to *True*. In most cases, you won't set the initial load behavior to Load On Demand directly; you'll set it to Load At Next Startup Only, and it will automatically be set to Load On Demand on subsequent boots of Outlook.

(continued)

(continued)

Initial Load Behavior Setting	LoadBehavior DWORD	Behavior Description
Load At Next Startup Only	*0x10* (Reverts to *0x09* on next boot)	After the COM Add-in has been registered, it loads as soon as the user runs Outlook for the first time, and it creates a button or menu item for itself. The next time the user boots Outlook, the Add-in is loaded on demand; that is, it doesn't load until the user clicks the button or menu item associated with the Add-in.

COM Add-In Load Behavior and Boot Performance

Be careful to test your Add-in under different hardware and software configurations before you release your COM Add-in. If you have set the Initial Load Behavior setting so that your Add-in is loaded on startup and your Add-in does extensive processing or makes a database connection, you will incur an unacceptable performance penalty when Outlook launches. Users of your COM Add-in will soon be knocking at your door. Outlook's Object Model is single-threaded and does not return control to a calling application until its thread of execution has completed.

IDTExtensibility2 Event Procedures

The next step in creating your Outlook COM Add-In is to write code for the event procedures exposed by the IDTExtensibility2 Type Library. If you use the Outlook COM Add-In the template supplied on the companion CD, the *IDTExtensibility2* event procedures have already been created for you. If you examine the code listing below from the Connect Add-In Designer in the Outlook COM Add-In project, you'll see an Implements IDTExtensibility2 statement in the declarations section of the code listing. The Visual Basic Implements statement can appear only in the declarations section of a class module, and it indicates that the specified interface that follows the Implements keyword will be implemented in the class module in which the Implements statement appears. To function correctly, all of the public methods of the interface specified by the Implements statement must be available in the class module. To make the public event procedures of *IDTExtensibility2* available in the Connect class module, you have to expose them by selecting IDTExtensibility2 in the Object drop-down list box in the Code window, and then clicking each procedure name for IDTExtensibility2 in the Visual Basic Procedure drop-down list box. Even if you are not writing code for the event procedure, it's a good idea to add a Visual Basic comment marker (a single apostrophe) inside each event procedure.

More Info For additional information on the Implements statement and classes in general, see the Visual Basic 6.0 on-line documentation.

```
Option Explicit
'****************************************************************************
'Outlook COM Add-In project template
```

```vba
'IDTExtensibility2 is the interface that COM Add-Ins must implement.
'The project references the following object libraries:
'Add additional object libraries as required for your COM Add-In.
'References:
'Microsoft Add-in Designer
'Microsoft Outlook 9.0 Object Library
'Microsoft Office 9.0 Object Library
'*******************************************************************
Implements IDTExtensibility2
Private gBaseClass As New OutAddIn

Private Sub IDTExtensibility2_OnAddInsUpdate(custom() _
    As Variant)
'
    DebugWrite "IDT2 OnAddInsUpdate"
End Sub

Private Sub IDTExtensibility2_OnBeginShutdown(custom() _
    As Variant)
'
    DebugWrite "IDT2 OnBeginShutdown"
End Sub

Private Sub IDTExtensibility2_OnConnection(ByVal _
    Application As Object, ByVal ConnectMode As _
    AddInDesignerObjects.ext_ConnectMode, ByVal _
    AddInInst As Object, custom() As Variant)
    'Create and Initialize a base class
    gBaseClass.InitHandler Application, AddInInst.ProgId
    DebugWrite "IDT2 OnConnection"
End Sub

Private Sub IDTExtensibility2_OnDisconnection(ByVal RemoveMode _
    As AddInDesignerObjects.ext_DisconnectMode, custom() _
    As Variant)
    'Tear down the class
    'IMPORTANT: This event will not fire when
    'RemoveMode = ext_dm_HostShutdown
    'It will fire when RemoveMode = ext_dm_UserClosed
    'Instead objExpl_Close in OutAddIn class module calls UnInitHandler
    gBaseClass.UnInitHandler
    Set gBaseClass = Nothing
    DebugWrite "IDT2 OnDisconnection"
End Sub

Private Sub IDTExtensibility2_OnStartupComplete(custom() _
    As Variant)
'
    DebugWrite "IDT2 OnStartupComplete"
End Sub
```

OnAddInsUpdate Event

The OnAddInsUpdate event occurs when the collection of loaded COM Add-ins changes. When an Add-in is loaded or unloaded, the OnAddInsUpdate event occurs in any other loaded Add-ins. For example, if Add-ins A and B are both currently loaded, and Add-in C is subsequently loaded, the OnAddInsUpdate event fires in Add-ins A, B, and C. If Add-in C is unloaded, the OnAddInsUpdate event occurs again in Add-ins A and B.

If you have an Add-in that depends on another Add-in, you can use the *OnAddInsUpdate* event procedure in the dependent Add-in to determine whether the other Add-in has been loaded or unloaded. Examine the Connect property of the other Add-ins to determine whether or not they are loaded. If the Connect property is *True*, then the Add-in is loaded. The following example prints the friendly name and the connect state of the COMAddIns Collection to the immediate window when the OnAddInsUpdate event occurs. This code uses a global Outlook Application object, golApp, that is instantiated during the *InitHandler* procedure called by code in the *OnConnection* event procedure.

```
Private Sub IDTExtensibility2_OnAddInsUpdate(custom() As Variant)
    Dim oAddIn As Office.COMAddIn
    For Each oAddIn In golApp.COMAddIns
        Debug.Print oAddIn.Description, oAddIn.Connect
    Next
End Sub
```

Note The OnStartupComplete, OnBeginShutdown, and *OnAddInsUpdate* event procedures each provide only a single argument, the *custom()* argument, which is an empty array of Variant type values. You can ignore this argument for COM Add-ins for Office 2000 applications.

OnBeginShutdown

The OnBeginShutdown event occurs when Outlook begins its shutdown, but only in the case where Outlook closes while the COM Add-in is still loaded. If the Add-in is not currently loaded when Outlook closes, the OnBeginShutdown event does not fire. When this event does occur, it occurs before the OnDisconnection event.

OnConnection

The OnConnection event occurs when the COM Add-in is loaded through the user-interface or when program code sets the Add-in's Connect property to *True*. An Add-in can be loaded in one of the following ways:

Action	ConnectMode
The user starts Outlook and the Add-in's load behavior is specified to load when Outlook starts	ext_cm_Startup

(continued)

(continued)

Action	ConnectMode
The user loads the Add-in in the COM Add-Ins dialog box	ext_cm_AfterStartup
The Connect property of the corresponding COMAddIn object is set to *True*	ext_cm_AfterStartup

If you revisit the OnConnection event code listing for the Outlook COM Add-In template, you'll see that an *InitHandler* procedure is called in the OnConnection event. The *InitHandler* procedure instantiates event-ready object variables in the OutAddIn class module so that you can write event procedure code using the new events in the Outlook 2000 Object Model. It's worth taking a moment to discuss what happens in the *InitHandler* procedure. First, look at the parameters passed to the *InitHandler* procedure. An Outlook application variable is passed, which is a copy of the *Application* object passed to the *IDTExtensibility2_OnConnection* procedure. The *olApp* variable that is passed to the *InitHandler* procedure creates two Outlook application variables, *objOutlook* and *golApp*. The first application variable, *objOutlook*, is declared WithEvents in the OutAddIn class module so that you can raise application-level Outlook events in OutAddIn. A string variable is passed that contains the ProgID of the COM Add-in, which is useful for setting the OnAction property of custom CommandBarButtons.

The *InitHandler* procedure also instantiates *NameSpace, Explorers, Inspectors,* and other object variables declared WithEvents in the OutAddIn class module. The Friend keyword is used to make the *InitHandler* procedure available to other form and class modules in the project. However, the Friend keyword prevents the *InitHandler* procedure from being exposed as a public method of the OutAddIn class. Friend makes the procedure visible throughout the project, but not to a controller of an instance of the object. Another important aspect of the *InitHandler* procedure is that we instantiate a global Application variable, *golApp*. To be public to all code modules in the project, *golApp* must be declared in a standard module (basOutlook) rather than in a class module. Unlike Outlook VBA where a global Application object is always available, you must explicitly declare a global Outlook Application object in a COM Add-in. The *InitHandler* procedure in the OutAddIn class module is listed below:

```
'Object variables for Event procedures declared in OutAddIn class module
Private WithEvents objOutlook As Outlook.Application
Private WithEvents objNS As Outlook.NameSpace
Private WithEvents objExpl As Outlook.Explorer
Private WithEvents colExpl As Outlook.Explorers
Private WithEvents objInsp As Outlook.Inspector
Private WithEvents colInsp As Outlook.Inspectors
Private WithEvents objMailItem As Outlook.MailItem
Private WithEvents objPostItem As Outlook.PostItem
Private WithEvents objContactItem As Outlook.ContactItem
Private WithEvents objDistListItem As Outlook.DistListItem
Private WithEvents objApptItem As Outlook.AppointmentItem
Private WithEvents objTaskItem As Outlook.TaskItem
```

```
Private WithEvents objJournalItem As Outlook.JournalItem
Private WithEvents objDocumentItem As Outlook.DocumentItem

'Use gstrProgID to set the OnAction property of CB buttons
Private gstrProgID As String
'Declare CommandBar, CommandBarButton, and CommandBarComboBox
'object variables here
'Private WithEvents CBBMyButton As Office.CommandBarButton

Friend Sub InitHandler(olApp As Outlook.Application, strProgID As String)
    'Declared WithEvents
    Set objOutlook = olApp
    'Instantiate a public module-level Outlook application variable
    Set golApp = olApp
    'Declared WithEvents
    gstrProgID = strProgID
    Set objNS = objOutlook.GetNameSpace("MAPI")
    Set colExpl = objOutlook.Explorers
    Set colInsp = objOutlook.Inspectors
    Set objExpl = objOutlook.ActiveExplorer
End Sub
```

OnDisconnection

The OnDisconnection event occurs when the COM Add-in is unloaded. You can use the *OnDisconnection* event procedure to run code that restores any changes made to Outlook by the Add-in and to perform general clean-up operations.

An Add-in can be unloaded in one of the following ways:

Action	ConnectMode
Outlook closes. If the Add-in is currently loaded when Outlook closes, it is unloaded. If the Add-in's initial load behavior is set to Startup, it is reloaded when Outlook starts again.	ext_dm_HostShutdown
The user clears the check box next to the Add-in in the COM Add-Ins dialog box.	ext_dm_UserShutdown
The Connect property of the corresponding COMAddIn object is set to *False*.	ext_dm_UserShutdown

The *RemoveMode* argument of the OnDisconnection event lets you determine how the Add-in was unloaded, either by a user action (user shutdown) or by Outlook closing (host shutdown). The following code example writes a string to the Visual Basic Immediate window indicating the mode with which the COM Add-in was removed:

```
Private Sub IDTExtensibility2_OnDisconnection(ByVal RemoveMode _
    As AddInDesignerObjects.ext_DisconnectMode, custom() As Variant)
    'Tear down the class
    gBaseClass.UnInitHandler
```

```
        Set gBaseClass = Nothing
        Dim strMode As String
        If RemoveMode = ext_dm_HostShutdown Then
            strMode = "Host Shutdown"
        Else
            strMode = "User Shutdown"
        End If
        Debug.Print "IDT2 OnDisconnection " & strMode
    End Sub
```

The important task in the OnDisconnection event is to tear down the base class and other object variables before the COM Add-in is removed from memory. If you do not clean up your object variables, you might find that Outlook continues to remain in memory, even though the user has selected the Exit And Log off command from the Outlook File menu. The OnDisconnection event in the Outlook COM Add-in project calls the *UnInitHandler* procedure in the OutAddIn class module. The *UnInitHandler* procedure sets object variables to Nothing. Remember that if you declare a public Outlook Application variable in a standard module, you should use the *UnInitHandler* procedure to clean up that object reference. Otherwise, Outlook will remain in memory and your COM Add-in will not behave as expected.

```
Friend Sub UnInitHandler()
    'You must dereference all objects in this procedure or
    'Outlook will remain in memory
    'If you have created an objMailItem variable,
    'be sure to Set objMailItem = Nothing in this procedure
    Set objInsp = Nothing
    Set objExpl = Nothing
    Set colInsp = Nothing
    Set colExpl = Nothing
    Set objNS = Nothing
    Set golApp = Nothing
    Set objOutlook = Nothing
End Sub
```

Special Disconnection Considerations for Outlook 2000

If you are using Outlook in Corporate/Workgroup mode, you must consider that the messaging spooler can cause anomalous behavior that will prevent Outlook from shutting down cleanly when your COM Add-in is unloaded. For example, you might declare *objOutlook* as an Outlook Application object in the declarations of your base class module. You then instantiate that object, an Explorer object, and a global Outlook Application object for use in the code listed below. If you do not dereference these object variables, you will find that Outlook remains in memory due to your COM Add-in.

```
Private WithEvents objOutlook As Outlook.Application
Private WithEvents objExpl as Outlook.Explorer

Friend Sub InitHandler(olApp As Outlook.Application, strProgID As String)
    'Declared WithEvents
```

```
      Set objOutlook = olApp
      'Instantiate a public module-level Outlook application variable
      Set golApp = olApp
      'Set additional object references as required
      Set objExpl = objOutlook.ActiveExplorer
End Sub
```

A symptom of an incomplete shutdown is when Outlook remains in memory after a user selects the Exit And Log Off command from the File menu. You should carefully test your COM Add-in to determine whether Outlook remains in memory after you quit Outlook. Don't trust the behavior of your Add-in in debug mode, because events are proxied by the debugger and the Disconnection event will fire, whereas it might not fire when your compiled COM Add-in is running. To determine if Outlook has remained in memory, start the Windows Task Manager by pressing Ctrl+Alt+Delete, or run a process viewer tool such as the Process Viewer Application that ships with Visual Basic 6.0.

Disconnection Event Workaround

There is a workaround for the problem of Outlook remaining in memory, and it is strongly suggested that you implement it in your COM Add-in. Both the Inspector and the Explorer objects support a Close event that you should use to remove references to all objects in your application. Use the Close event to remove the reference to all Outlook object variables when you are certain that Outlook is shutting down. For example, you can check the Explorers collection object's Count property. If the Count property is equal to 1 during the Close event, you can be certain that Outlook's Explorer is shutting down.

The following code sets all object variables in the COM Add-in to Nothing by calling the *UnInitHandler* procedure in the Explorer object Close event. See the *UnInitHandler* listing earlier in this chapter to see how this procedure removes references to object variables.

```
Private Sub objExpl_Close()
    If objOutlook.Explorers.Count = 1 Then 'Host shutdown
        Call UnInitHandler
    End If
End Sub
```

OnStartupComplete Event

The OnStartupComplete event occurs when Outlook completes its startup, but only in the case where the COM Add-in has an Initial Load Behavior setting that forces load at startup. If the Add-in is not loaded when Outlook starts up, the OnStartupComplete event does not fire, even when the user loads the Add-in the COM Add-Ins dialog box. When this event does occur, it occurs after the OnConnection event.

You can use the *OnStartupComplete* event procedure to run code that interacts with the application and shouldn't be run until the application has finished loading. For example, if you want to display a dialog box that gives users a choice of items to create when they start Outlook, you can put that code in the *OnStartupComplete* event procedure.

Adding Property Pages

Installing the Sample Page Project

Custom property pages allow you to add your own page to either the Outlook Tools Options dialog box or the Folder Properties dialog box. Figure 13.8 shows the Sample Page property page in the Tools Options dialog box. The Sample Page example is useful because it shows you how to use common Visual Basic controls on an Outlook property page. A group of option buttons has been placed in a frame as well as a text box, a command button, a drop-down combo box, and a check box on the User Form. You'll learn how the Sample Page works and how you can add custom property pages to your COM Add-in. If you need to maintain persistent user settings for your COM Add-in, you should consider adding a custom property page .ocx to your COM Add-in project. You implement Outlook property pages as an ActiveX control created in Visual Basic or another ActiveX control creation tool. First, you will learn how to create a property page ActiveX control, and then you will learn how to load that control in your COM Add-in. Before we discuss the creation of Outlook property pages, you must first install the Sample Page project from the companion CD.

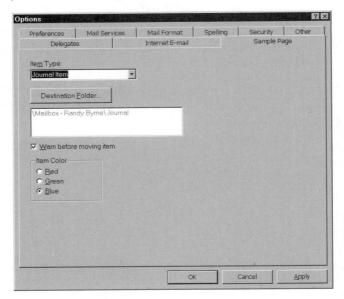

Figure 13.8 *The Sample Page property page in the Tools Options dialog box.*

To install and open the Sample Page project

1. Expand the subfolder 5. Advanced Topics in the Building Microsoft Outlook 2000 Applications personal folders (.pst) file.

2.   Expand the Creating COM Add-Ins with Visual Basic folder and click the Sample Page Property Page Example folder.

3.   Select all the files in the Sample Page Property Page Example folder.

4.   Launch Windows Explorer and create a folder named Sample Page Property Page under the VB98 folder for Visual Basic 6.0. If you've selected the default installation, the VB98 folder is located in C:\Program Files\Microsoft Visual Studio\VB98.

5.   Drag the files you selected in step 3 to the Sample Page Property Page folder in Windows Explorer. If you have problems dragging and dropping files, we've also included a self-extracting .zip file that contains all the files in the Sample Page Property Page Example folder. Just double-click the file SampleOptionsPage.exe and extract the files to the folder listed in step 4.

6.   Launch Visual Basic and open the SampleOptionsPage project in the folder you created in step 4.

Creating a custom property page in Visual Basic is actually quite straightforward, once you get the hang of it. Figure 13.9 shows the SampleOptionsPage project loaded in the Visual Basic 6.0 development environment. The most basic rule of property page creation is that the code module for the UserControl must contain *Implements Outlook.PropertyPage* in its declarations section. An Outlook property page is an abstract object in the Outlook Object Model. You can't actually instantiate a property page object in the way that you can create a MailItem object, for example. However, the Implements keyword lets you access the properties and methods of the PropertyPage class in the same way that *Implements IDTExtensibility2* lets you access the methods of the IDTExtensibility2 class. Here is the declarations section of the SamplePage UserControl.

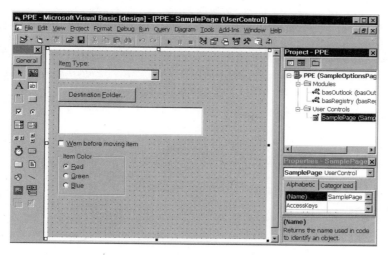

Figure 13.9 *The Sample Page property page in the Visual Basic 6.0 development environment.*

```
'***********************************************************************
'Outlook Property Page Example
'PropertyPage is the interface that property pages must implement.
'The project references the following object libraries:
'Add additional object libraries as required for your control.
'References:
'Microsoft Outlook 9.0 Object Library
'***********************************************************************
Implements Outlook.PropertyPage
Dim objSite As Outlook.PropertyPageSite
Dim gblnDirty As Boolean
Dim IsLoading As Boolean
```

Loading the Page and Persisting Settings in the Registry

Two module-level variables, *gblnDirty* and *IsLoading*, help to ensure that the property page is not marked as dirty when the control is loading. Typically, you would have the values for the constituent controls persist on your Property page in the Windows registry. When the user clicks OK or Apply on the Property page, you save the values represented by the controls on that page to the registry. When the user invokes the Property page by selecting the Outlook Tools Options command, you have to retrieve the values you stored in the registry and set the controls on your Property page accordingly. Consequently, the *InitProperties* procedure listed below sets the initial values of the controls on the Property page. An extensive discussion about programming the Windows registry is beyond the scope of this chapter. Suffice it to say that *GetKeyValueEx* and *SetKeyValue* are functions included in basRegistry that let you set and get registry values.

Notice in the listing below that if the values retrieved from the registry are not blank, the registry value in each of the constituent controls of the Property page is set. If the registry value is an empty string, then the default values of the controls are used on the page. By setting *IsLoading = True* at the beginning of the procedure, the *SetDirty* procedure is prevented from setting gblnIsDirty to *True*. Once the values of controls have been set in the *InitProperties* procedure, *IsLoading* is set to *False*. This means that any changes to the controls on the page will set gblnIsDirty to *True*, and the user will be able to click the Apply button on the property page to save their changes.

```
Private Sub UserControl_InitProperties()
    On Error Resume Next
    Dim strType as String, strFolderPath as String
    Dim strWarn as String, strOption As String
    Set objSite = Parent
    'Set IsLoading to False so that setting controls will not dirty form
    IsLoading = True
    cmbType.Clear
    cmbType.AddItem "Appointment Item"
    cmbType.AddItem "Contact Item"
    cmbType.AddItem "Journal Item"
    cmbType.AddItem "Mail Item"
```

```
        cmbType.AddItem "Task Item"
        'Set controls based on registry values
        strType = GetKeyValueEx(HKEY_CURRENT_USER, _
            "Software\Microsoft\Office\9.0\Outlook\Options\SamplePage", _
            "ItemType")
        If strType <> "" Then
            cmbType.Text = strType
        End If
        strFolderPath = GetKeyValueEx(HKEY_CURRENT_USER, _
            "Software\Microsoft\Office\9.0\Outlook\Options\SamplePage", _
            "FolderPath")
        If strFolderPath <> "" Then
            txtFolder = strFolderPath
        End If
        If GetKeyValueEx(HKEY_CURRENT_USER, _
            "Software\Microsoft\Office\9.0\Outlook\Options\SamplePage", _
            "Warn") = "1" Then
            chkWarn.Value = vbChecked
        Else
            chkWarn.Value = vbUnchecked
        End If
        strOption = GetKeyValueEx(HKEY_CURRENT_USER, _
            "Software\Microsoft\Office\9.0\Outlook\Options\SamplePage", _
            "ColorOption")
        Select Case strOption
            Case "1"
            optRed = True
            Case "2"
            optGreen = True
            Case "3"
            optBlue = True
        End Select
        IsLoading = False
        gblnDirty = False
    End Sub
```

Marking the Page as Dirty

The *SetDirty* procedure does the work of marking the page as dirty when a user changes the value of one of the controls on the page. The *gblnDirty* variable is set to *True* so that the *Apply* procedure can reset *gblnDirty* to *False* when it completes its work. The *SetDirty* procedure notifies Outlook that a Property page has changed by calling the *OnStatusChange* method of the PropertyPageSite object. The PropertyPageSite object represents the container of a custom Property page. You must call the *SetDirty* procedure in the Change event for the controls on the page. For some controls like the combo box named cmbType, you should also use the DropDown event (or a CloseUp event if supported by the control) to call *SetDirty*.

```
Private Sub SetDirty()
    If Not objSite Is Nothing Then
        If Not (IsLoading) Then
```

```
            gblnDirty = True
            objSite.OnStatusChange
        End If
    End If
End Sub
```

Applying Changes

Once the *OnStatusChange* method has notified Outlook that the page is dirty, the Apply button on the property page changes from disabled to enabled, as shown in Figure 13.10. The user can click the Apply button to apply changes or the OK button to apply the changes and dismiss the dialog box where the property page appears. Notice in the *Apply* procedure below that the *SetKeyValue* function is called in basRegistry to maintain the persistent settings for each of the controls to the Windows registry.

```
Private Sub PropertyPage_Apply()
    'User clicked Apply or OK so save changes to registry
    SetKeyValue HKEY_CURRENT_USER, _
        "Software\Microsoft\Office\9.0\Outlook\Options\SamplePage", _
        "ItemType", cmbType.Text, REG_SZ
    SetKeyValue HKEY_CURRENT_USER, _
        "Software\Microsoft\Office\9.0\Outlook\Options\SamplePage", _
        "FolderPath", txtFolder, REG_SZ
```

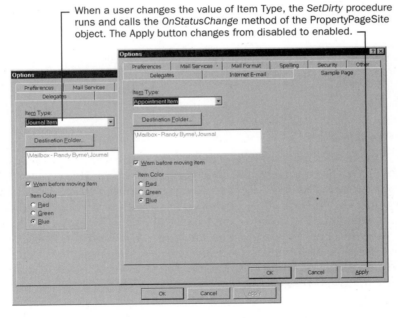

When a user changes the value of Item Type, the *SetDirty* procedure runs and calls the *OnStatusChange* method of the PropertyPageSite object. The Apply button changes from disabled to enabled.

Figure 13.10 *When a user changes a value on the Property page, the Apply button is available.*

```
    If chkWarn.Value = vbChecked Then
        SetKeyValue HKEY_CURRENT_USER, _
            "Software\Microsoft\Office\9.0\Outlook\Options\SamplePage", _
            "Warn", "1", REG_SZ
    Else
        SetKeyValue HKEY_CURRENT_USER, _
            "Software\Microsoft\Office\9.0\Outlook\Options\SamplePage", _
            "Warn", "0", REG_SZ
    End If
    If optRed Then
        SetKeyValue HKEY_CURRENT_USER, _
            "Software\Microsoft\Office\9.0\Outlook\Options\SamplePage", _
            "ColorOption", "1", REG_SZ
    ElseIf optGreen Then
        SetKeyValue HKEY_CURRENT_USER, _
            "Software\Microsoft\Office\9.0\Outlook\Options\SamplePage", _
            "ColorOption", "2", REG_SZ
    ElseIf optBlue Then
        SetKeyValue HKEY_CURRENT_USER, _
            "Software\Microsoft\Office\9.0\Outlook\Options\SamplePage", _
            "ColorOption", "3", REG_SZ
    End If
    'Set dirty to false
    gblnDirty = False
End Sub
```

Compile and Distribute the ActiveX Control

Once you've completed designing and debugging the ActiveX control for your Property page, you should compile the control. Your control will compile to an ActiveX .ocx control. Remember that when you distribute your COM Add-in, you must include the ActiveX .ocx control for your custom property page in your COM Add-in distribution package.

> **More Info** For additional information on the creation, compilation, and distribution of ActiveX controls, see "Component Tools Guide" in the Visual Basic 6.0 online documentation.

Displaying the Property Page

To display your custom Property page, you only have to insert a single line of code in the OptionsPagesAdd event of either the Application object (for Tools Options property pages) or the NameSpace object (for Folder Properties property pages). Chapter 9, "Raise Events and Move to the Head of the Class," discusses how the OptionsPagesAdd event lets you display property pages. However, that discussion occurs in the context of Outlook VBA. If you want to display a Property page in a COM Add-in, you need to dimension an object variable WithEvents for an Outlook Application object and/or an Outlook NameSpace object. For example, in the sample Outlook COM Add-In project, *objOutlook* is declared WithEvents in the OutAddIn class module. If you add the following code to the *objOutlook_OptionsPagesAdd* event procedure, the Sample Page property page will be visible in the Outlook Tools Options dialog box when your compiled COM Add-in is loaded. When you create your own COM Add-in, change the ProgID of *PPE.SamplePage* in the example below to a ProgID that matches the ProgID of the ActiveX control supplying the property page for your COM Add-in.

```
Private Sub objOutlook_OptionsPagesAdd(ByVal Pages As _
    Outlook.PropertyPages)
        Pages.Add "PPE.SamplePage", "Sample Page"
End Sub
```

Modifying Command Bars

Developing a Property page is one way to add a user-interface to your Outlook COM Add-In. The other (and perhaps more common) way to provide a user interface is to modify the command bars for the Outlook Explorer and Inspector windows. If you want to modify command bars, you must be certain to set a reference to the Microsoft Office 9.0 Object Library with the Visual Basic Project References command. The Outlook COM Add-In template project has set this reference for you. If you've reviewed the material in Chapter 10, "Outlook Bar, Command Bars, and the Assistant," you'll know that the OnAction property is used to set the procedure that runs when a user clicks a CommandBarButton object. If you want a CommandBarButton to respond to a Click event on the Explorer toolbar, for example, you must code a call to the event procedure for a COM Add-in differently than you would in Outlook VBA.

Basic Techniques

Two procedures you should follow when you create command bar buttons for Explorer or Inspector command bars are:

- The first basic technique is to dimension object variables using the WithEvents keyword for the CommandBarControls on your toolbar, and then write code in the Click event for each CommandBarButton object. Instanitate object variables for the event-ready CommandBarButton objects in the *InitHandler* procedure of your COM Add-in.

- You should also set the OnAction property for a CommandBarButton or CommandBarComboBox with a string that contains the ProgID for your COM Add-in. This string is prefixed by <! and ends with >. You can obtain the ProgID for your COM Add-in by setting the ProgID property of the AddInInst object passed in the OnConnection event to a public variable. Following the example of the Outlook Add-In sample project, you can also pass the ProgID to the *InitHandler* procedure in the base class of the Add-in. The exact syntax is as follows:

```
objCommandBarButton.OnAction = "<!" & gstrProgID & ">"
```

The OutlookSharedActivities Project

Let's turn to the example code in the OutlookSharedActivities project to illustrate these two basic techniques. If you've examined E-Chapter 3, "The Northwind Contact Management Application," in the E-Chapters folder on the companion CD, you should be familiar with the Create Shared Activities toolbar. This Explorer toolbar lets users create shared items in the subfolders of the Customers folder in the Northwind Contact Management application. The original code for this toolbar can be found in the VBAProject.otm file accompanying this book. This code, principally found in the basNorthwind module of VBAProject.otm, has been converted to a COM Add-in. Once the code for the Northwind Contact Management application is lifted out of the ThisOutlookSession module, you can run the Northwind Contact Management application independently of the book's VBAProject.otm. Install the OutlookSharedActivities COM Add-In project if you want to load the code into Visual Basic.

To install the OutlookSharedActivities COM Add-In project

1. Expand the folder 5. Advanced Topics in the Building Microsoft Outlook 2000 Applications personal folders (.pst) file.

2. Expand the Creating COM Add-Ins with Visual Basic folder and click the Shared Activities COM Add-In Project folder.

3. Select all the files in the Shared Activities COM Add-In Project folder.

4. Launch the Windows Explorer and create a folder named Shared Activities under the VB98 folder for Visual Basic 6.0. If you've selected the default installation, the VB98 folder is located in C:\Program Files\Microsoft Visual Studio\VB98

5. Drag the files you selected in step 3 to the Shared Activities folder in Windows Explorer. If you have problems dragging and dropping files, we've also included a self-extracting .zip file containing all the files in the Shared Activities COM Add-In Project folder. Just double-click the file SharedActivities.exe and extract the files to the folder listed in step 4.

6. Launch Visual Basic and open the OutlookSharedActivities project in the folder you created in step 4.

The *InitHandler* procedure in the base class for the OutlookSharedActivities project calls the *CBSharedItems* procedure to create the Create Shared Items toolbar for the Outlook Explorer. *CBSharedItems* instantiates object variables that represent each of the custom command buttons on the toolbar. Notice that the ProgID for the Add-in is passed to the procedure so that *strProgID* can, in turn, be passed to the *CreateAddInCommandBarButton* procedure.

```
Friend Sub CBSharedItemsCreate(strProgID As String)
    On Error Resume Next
    Set objCommandBar = objExpl.CommandBars("Create Shared Items")
    If Err Then
        Set objCommandBar = objExpl.CommandBars.Add _
```

```
            (Name:="Create Shared Items", Position:=msoBarTop, Temporary:=False)
    End If
    Set CBBDial = CreateAddInCommandBarButton(strProgID, objCommandBar, _
        "Dial Phone", "Dial Phone", "Dial Customer/Contact", 1982, False)
    Set CBBMail = CreateAddInCommandBarButton(strProgID, objCommandBar, _
        "Shared Mail", "Shared Mail", "Create Shared Mail", 1757, True)
    Set CBBContact = CreateAddInCommandBarButton(strProgID, objCommandBar, _
        "Shared Contact", "Shared Contact", "Create Shared Contact", 1099, False)
    Set CBBJournal = CreateAddInCommandBarButton(strProgID, objCommandBar, _
        "Shared Journal", "Shared Journal", "Create Shared Journal", 1990, False)
    Set CBBAppt = CreateAddInCommandBarButton(strProgID, objCommandBar, _
        "Shared Appointment", "Shared Appointment", "Create Shared Appointment", _
        1106, False)
    Set CBBTask = CreateAddInCommandBarButton(strProgID, objCommandBar, _
        "Shared Task", "Shared Task", "Create Shared Task", 1100, False)
End Sub
```

The *CreateAddInCommandBarButton* function handles the creation of command bar buttons if the button does not exist. If the button does exist, this function sets a reference to the CommandBarButton object and returns that object reference as the return value of the function. Both the *CreateAddInCommandBarButton* function and the *CreateAddInCommandBarComboBox* function can be found in the basCommandBars module in the OutlookSharedItems project.

```
Public Function CreateAddInCommandBarButton _
    (strProgID As String, objCommandBar As CommandBar, _
    strCaption As String, strTag As String, strTip As String, _
    intFaceID As Integer, blnBeginGroup As Boolean) _
    As Office.CommandBarButton

    On Error Resume Next
    ' Test to determine if button exists on command bar.
    Set ctlBtnAddIn = objCommandBar.FindControl(Tag:=strTag)
    If ctlBtnAddIn Is Nothing Then
        ' Add new button.
        Set ctlBtnAddIn = objCommandBar.Controls.Add _
        (Type:=msoControlButton, Parameter:=strTag)
        ' Set button's Caption, Tag, Style, and OnAction properties.
        With ctlBtnAddIn
            .Caption = strCaption
            .Tag = strTag
            .FaceId = intFaceID
            .Style = msoButtonIconAndCaption
            .TooltipText = strTip
            .BeginGroup = blnBeginGroup
            ' Set the OnAction property with ProgID of Add-In
            .OnAction = "<!" & strProgID ">"
        End With
    End If
    ' Return reference to new commandbar button.
    Set CreateAddInCommandBarButton = ctlBtnAddIn
End Function
```

Converting ThisOutlookSession Code to a COM Add-In

If you examine the code for OutlookSharedActivities and compare it to the code in basNorthwind in the VBAProject.otm accompanying this book, you'll find that straightforward modifications are required to convert the code. If you modularize the code as you develop in the Outlook VBA environment, you'll have an easier time when it comes to converting your code to a COM Add-in. If you have developed UserForms in your VBA project, you can export those forms as .frm files from your VBAProject.otm and then import them into your COM Add-in project as Designer objects. Follow these steps to add VBA forms to your Visual Basic COM Add-in project:

1. Export the UserForm by selecting the form in the Project Explorer, and then select the Export File command from the VBA File menu.

2. Import the UserForm by selecting the Add File command on the Project menu in Visual Basic.

3. The imported form will be listed under the Designers node in the Visual Basic Project Explorer.

Once the object variables for CommandBarButton objects have been set, you can write event procedure code that runs when a user clicks the toolbar button. In this case, the Click event calls exactly the same code that you'll find in basNorthwind in VBAProject.otm that ships with this book. You can, in fact, move code from a solution developed in Outlook VBA to a COM Add-in with minimum modification.

```
Private Sub CBBAppt_Click(ByVal Ctrl As Office.CommandBarButton, _
    CancelDefault As Boolean)
        Call basNorthwind.cmdAppointment_Click
End Sub

Private Sub CBBContact_Click(ByVal Ctrl As Office.CommandBarButton, _
    CancelDefault As Boolean)
        Call basNorthwind.cmdContact_Click
End Sub

Private Sub CBBDial_Click(ByVal Ctrl As Office.CommandBarButton, _
    CancelDefault As Boolean)
        Call basNorthwind.cmdDial
End Sub

Private Sub CBBJournal_Click(ByVal Ctrl As Office.CommandBarButton, _
    CancelDefault As Boolean)
        Call basNorthwind.cmdJournal_Click
End Sub

Private Sub CBBMail_Click(ByVal Ctrl As Office.CommandBarButton, _
    CancelDefault As Boolean)
        Call basNorthwind.cmdMail_Click
End Sub
```

```
Private Sub CBBTask_Click(ByVal Ctrl As Office.CommandBarButton, _
    CancelDefault As Boolean)
        Call basNorthwind.cmdTask_Click
End Sub
```

Step-By-Step Summary for COM Add-In Command Bars

To create an Explorer command bar button in an Outlook COM Add-in

1.   In the Add-In Designer's module or the class module for the base class, use the WithEvents keyword to declare a module-level variable of type CommandBarButton. This creates an event-ready CommandBarButton object.

2.   In the same module, create the *Click* event procedure stub for the CommandBarButton object by clicking the name of the object variable in the Object box and then clicking Click in the Procedure box.

3.   Write code within the event procedure stub.

4.   In the *OnConnection* event procedure or in the *InitHandler* procedure for your base class, check to see whether the command bar control already exists, and return a reference to it if it does. If it doesn't exist, create the new command bar control and return a reference to it. You need to check whether the command bar control exists so that you don't create a new control each time your code runs.

5.   When you create the new command bar control, set the Tag property for the CommandBarButton object to a unique string. The Tag property lets you easily find the control using the *FindControl* method.

6.   When you create the new command bar control, set the OnAction property for the command bar control if the COM Add-in is to be demand-loaded. If you fail to set the OnAction property, the command bar button will load the Add-in the first time Outlook starts, but will not load the Add-in when Outlook is closed and re-opened.

7.   Within the *OnConnection* event procedure or in the *InitHandler* procedure for your base class, assign the reference to the command bar control to the event-ready CommandBarButton object variable.

8.   Add code to the OnDisconnection event or to the *UnInitHandler* procedure in the base class to remove the command bar control when the Add-in is unloaded.

Adding Dialog Boxes

Dialog boxes in COM Add-ins follow the same guidelines as dialog boxes in any other Visual Basic project, with one precaution: do not attempt to show a modal dialog box directly from your COM Add-in. Outlook (and for that matter, any other Office 2000 application) cannot display a modal dialog box when that dialog box is displayed directly from a COM Add-in or an ActiveX DLL component. Figure 13.11 illustrates a Visual Basic About dialog box displayed from a COM Add-in. By displaying Visual Basic modeless dialog boxes, you can add a wealth of functionality to your COM Add-in application. If you are connected to your network, you can display information from corporate databases, provide data entry forms, or enable users to create settings that might otherwise not be available on a custom Tools Options property page. An enormous number of third-party ActiveX custom controls are available for your dialog boxes, in addition to the intrinsic and extrinsic ActiveX controls that ship with Visual Basic.

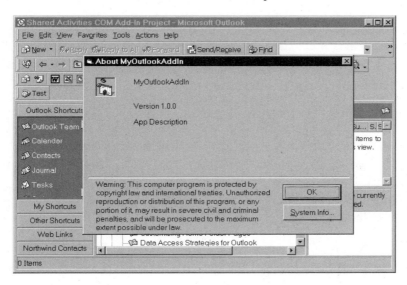

Figure 13.11 *A Visual Basic dialog box displays when the user clicks the Test command bar button.*

Caution Do not display modal dialog boxes directly from your COM Add-in. You can, however, display a modal Visual Basic dialog box from a modeless dialog box that is displayed from COM Add-in code. For example, assume you have Form1 and Form2 in your COM Add-in. You can place a Form1.Show statement in the Click event for a toolbar button, but you cannot write Form1.Show vbModal in the Click event without hanging either your COM Add-in or Outlook. However, you can place a command button on Form1 that executes Form2.Show vbModal without a problem.

Visual Basic Forms

Adding dialog boxes to your COM Add-in is simple once you've designed and debugged the dialog box. It is advisable to design and test the dialog box in a standard .exe project before you move the dialog box to your COM Add-in.

 To add a Visual Basic form to a COM Add-in

1.   Select the Add Form command from the Visual Basic Project menu.

2. Add controls and code to your form.

3. Display the form from your COM Add-in by adding *FormName.Show* to an event procedure for a CommandBarButton on an Explorer or Inspector command bar.

Forms 2.0 Forms

You can also add Microsoft Forms 2.0 forms to your COM Add-in project. Microsoft Forms 2.0 provides the familiar form design environment of Outlook custom forms. You are not, however, limited to a single Click event and a reduced property set when you use Forms 2.0 in the Visual Basic environment. If you've developed forms in Outlook VBA, you can also directly import those forms without modification into your COM Add-in.

➡ **To add a Forms 2.0 form to a COM Add-in**

1. Select the Components command from the Visual Basic Project menu.

2. Click the Designers page on the Components dialog.

3. Check the Microsoft Forms 2.0 Form box in the Designers list box.

4. Select Add Microsoft Forms 2.0 Form on the Project menu.

5. Add controls and code to your form with the Forms 2.0 control toolbox. You cannot add Visual Basic intrinsic controls to your Forms 2.0 form. You must display the Forms 2.0 Control Toolbox before you can drag controls onto your form. Right-click the Forms 2.0 form and check the Toolbox command on the context menu.

6. If you want to add Visual Basic extrinsic or third-party ActiveX controls to your Forms 2.0 form, you must do so by adding the controls to the Forms 2.0 Control Toolbox rather than the Visual Basic toolbox. Right-click the Forms 2.0 Control Toolbox and select the Additional Controls command to add controls to the Forms 2.0 Control Toolbox.

7. Display the form from your COM Add-in by adding *FormName.Show* to an event procedure for a CommandBarButton on an Explorer or Inspector command bar.

Displaying a Dialog Box with a Public Method

You have more options for your COM Add-in than simply displaying a dialog box when a command bar button is clicked. Because a COM Add-in is a special form of ActiveX DLL component, you can also add public methods and properties to your component. The beauty of this approach is that you can then instantiate your COM Add-in component from VBScript and call the *ShowMyForm* method of your component. If you look at the OutlookSharedActivities project, you'll observe a public procedure in the OutAddIn class. Since this procedure is public, it is exposed as a method of the OutAddIn class. Figure 13.12 below shows the *DialPhone* method of the OutAddIn class in the object browser in Outlook.

The following code example shows how you call the *DialPhone* method from VBScript to display the Dial Phone dialog box. The *DialPhone* procedure is also shown.

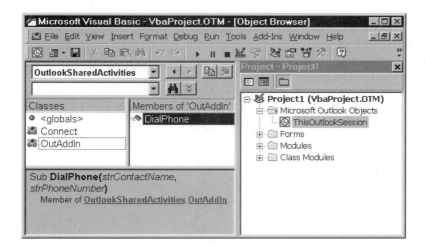

Figure 13.12 *The DialPhone method in the Outlook Object Browser.*

```
'DialPhone is public in order to expose it as a method
'for OutlookSharedActivities.OutAddIn
'Can be called from VBScript as follows:
Sub CommandButton1_Click()
    Dim objOutAddIn
    Set objOutAddIn = CreateObject("OutlookSharedActivities.OutAddIn")
    objOutAddIn.DialPhone "800 Information", "1--800--555--1212"
End Sub

Public Sub DialPhone(strContactName, strPhoneNumber)
    On Error Resume Next
    With frmDial
        .txtContactName.Enabled = True
        .txtContactName = strContactName
        .cmbNumber = strPhoneNumber
        .chkJournal.Visible = False
        .cmdOpen.Visible = False
        .Show
    End With
End Sub
```

The Debugging Process

You can debug a COM Add-in by opening your COM Add-in project in Visual Basic and placing the project into Run mode. When you set breakpoints or watches in your code, you can interactively debug your COM Add-in. Figure 13.13 shows the OutlookSharedActivities project in debug mode. A watch has been added for the *RemoveMode* variable in the *OnDisconnection* event procedure in the Connect code module.

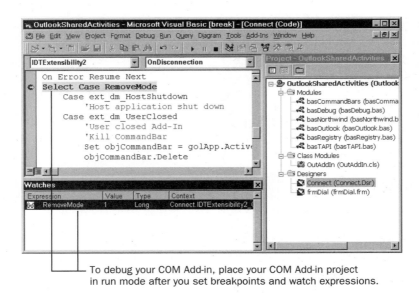

To debug your COM Add-in, place your COM Add-in project
in run mode after you set breakpoints and watch expressions.

Figure 13.13 *Debugging a COM Add-in in Visual Basic 6.0.*

To debug a COM Add-in Visual Basic 6.0

1. Open the Add-In project in Visual Basic 6.0.

2. Place any desired breakpoints, Stop statements, or watches in the code.

3. On the Run menu, click Start With Full Compile or press Ctrl+F5. This action compiles your project, alerts you to any compilation errors, and then puts the project into run mode.

4. Launch Outlook. If you've set the Add-in's load behavior to Startup or Load At Next Startup Only, the Add-in loads as soon as you start Outlook. If the Add-in's Initial Load Behavior is set to None or Load On Demand, open the COM Add-Ins dialog box and select the check box next to your Add-in to load it.

Note When your COM Add-in stops at a breakpoint, you might not be able to activate the running Outlook application until you complete code execution.

Troubleshooting Debug Mode

You might find that you have problems forcing your COM Add-in to enter Debug mode even after you've set breakpoints or watch expressions in your code. Here are a few suggestions that will help you debug your Add-in.

- Make sure that you've set the Version Compatibility option for your project in the Visual Basic Project Options dialog Component page to Project Compatibility or Binary Compatibility. If Version Compatibility is set to No Compatabilty,

> you might discover that Outlook cannot locate your COM Add-in component and you can't enter Debug mode.
>
> - If you've already loaded your compiled COM Add-in in Outlook, you will have to unload the Add-in using the COM Add-Ins dialog box. Use the COM Add-Ins dialog box again and reload the COM Add-in until your Add-in enters debug mode in Visual Basic. Set a breakpoint in the *OnConnection* event procedure to ensure that you're in Debug mode.
>
> - Make sure that your Add-in is actually in Run mode. I've had occasion to wonder why my Add-in was not entering Debug mode, only to discover that I had not placed my Visual Basic COM Add-In project in Run mode. The project was still in Design mode. You can't debug your component in Design mode.

Compiling Your COM Add-In

Once you've completed the debugging process, you can compile your COM Add-in and create an ActiveX DLL. This ActiveX DLL, along with any required ActiveX controls for custom Property pages or for UserForms and dialog boxes, will be distributed to users of your COM Add-in.

To compile a COM Add-in in Visual Basic 6.0

1. Open the Add-in project in Visual Basic 6.0.

2. Select the *<ProjectName>* Properties command on the Project menu. Make sure that you've entered the correct company, version, and copyright information on the Make page of the Project Properties dialog box. Click OK to accept changes you've made to project properties.

3. On the File menu, select the Make *<ComponentName>*.dll command.

Add-In Registration

When you compile your COM Add-in in Visual Basic 6.0, you have actually registered the COM Add-in in the correct location in the Windows registry. When you deploy your COM Add-in, the Package and Deployment wizard handles registration automatically on the target installation system. If you are using Visual Basic 5.0 to create your COM Add-in, you must create registry entries for the COM Add-in programmatically. If you are using Visual Basic 5.0, a registry key with the ProgID of your COM Add-in and three required subkeys for the COM Add-in must be created in the following location:

HKEY_CURRENT_USER\Software\Microsoft\Office\Outlook\Addins

These subkeys under the ProgID of the Add-in are required for correct operation of your COM Add-in.

Name	Type	Value
Description	String	A descriptive string that is not exposed by the COMAddIn object. If you need to, you can retrieve this string from the Windows registry.
FriendlyName	String	Name in COM Add-Ins dialog box. Equivalent to COMAddIn object Description property.
LoadBehavior	DWORD	Integer indicating load behavior: *0* (None), *3* (Startup), *9* (Load On Demand), or *16* (Load At Next Startup Only). These are decimal values.

Providing Security

In this section, we'll look at security from the perspectives of both the developer and the user of the COM Add-in. From the developer's perspective, COM Add-ins provide protection from anyone who wants to steal or tamper with the source code. Because COM Add-ins are compiled, source code is unavailable to anyone but the developer of the Add-in. In this regard, COM Add-ins offer a comfortable level of security for your intellectual property. Outlook VBA solutions do not provide the same level of intellectual property protection because a password for the project can be hacked, lost, or stolen.

Securing Your Intellectual Property

Let's consider what your options are as a developer if you want to offer a solution to other users. First, you can develop your solution in Outlook VBA. You might want to test an Outlook VBA solution before you move your code to a COM Add-in. So, you should be aware of how you provide security for an Outlook VBA solution. Outlook VBA solutions gain security for the developer from password protection of the Outlook VBA project.

To lock an Outlook VBA project for viewing

1. Start Outlook on the computer that contains the VBA project you want to protect.
2. Open the Visual Basic Editor by pressing Alt+F11.
3. On the Tools menu, select the <ProjectName> Properties command.
4. On the Protection page of the Project Properties dialog box, select the Lock Project For Viewing check box, enter and confirm the password, and then click OK.

Important VBA project passwords are case-sensitive. To view a locked VBA project, you must use the exact case you used when you initially set the password. If you lose or forget the password, there is no way to view the locked VBA project. When password-protecting a VBA project, be sure to write down the password and keep it in a physically secured location.

> **Note** If you unlock a VBA project for editing by supplying the project password, you must re-lock the project when you've completed your modifications. Otherwise, your project will no longer be protected when you save it.

Securing the User from Malicious Code

If you've decided to move beyond Outlook VBA to a COM Add-in solution, your concern will shift from providing security for yourself to providing security for the user of your solution. Before discussing how you can assure users that they can trust your solution, it's important to discuss how Add-in security is implemented in Outlook 2000. Outlook 2000 COM Add-in and VBA project security is set on a user-by-user basis by using the Security command under Macro on the Tools menu. Figure 13.14 illustrates the Security dialog box, which allows a user to set the security level. As a side note, you should not confuse code or macro security with Outlook message-level security provided by either S/MIME or Exchange. They are completely separate and distinct areas of concern.

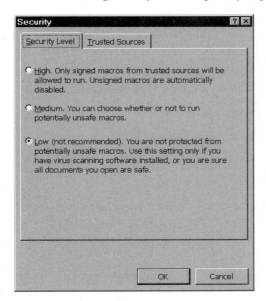

Figure 13.14 *The Security dialog box.*

> **Note** If you are responsible for rolling out Outlook 2000 with an automated installation process, you can set registry settings with the Custom Installation Wizard, which will move control of security from the user to the administrator. Users will not be able to display the Security dialog box and change their security settings.

The following table summarizes the three security levels in Outlook 2000.

Type of Solution and Verification Result	High	Medium	Low
No VBAProject or COM Add-ins.	N/A	N/A	N/A
Unsigned VBAProject.	Outlook VBA macros are automatically disabled without notification and Outlook application starts.	User is prompted to enable or disable Outlook VBA macros. Outlook VBA code is then demand-loaded.	No prompt. Outlook VBA code is demand-loaded.
Signed Outlook VBAProject from a trusted source. Verification succeeds.	Macros are automatically enabled and Outlook application starts.	Macros are automatically enabled and Outlook application starts.	No prompt or verification. Macros are enabled.
Signed Outlook VBAProject from an unknown author. Verification succeeds.	A dialog box is displayed with information about the certificate. Macros can be enabled only if the user chooses to trust the author and certifying authority by selecting the Always Trust Macros From This Author check box in the Security Warning dialog box. A network administrator can lock the trusted sources list and prevent the user from adding the author to the list and enabling Outlook VBA project's macros.	A dialog box is displayed with information about the certificate. The user is prompted to enable or disable macros. Optionally, the user can choose to trust the author and certifying authority by selecting the Always Trust Macros From This Author check box in the Security Warning dialog box.	No prompt or verification. Macros are enabled.
Signed macros from any author. Verification fails, possibly due to a virus.	User is warned of a possible virus. Macros are automatically disabled.	User is warned of a possible virus and macros are automatically disabled.	No prompt or verification. Macros are enabled.
Signed macros from any author. Verification not possible because public key is missing or incompatible encryption methods were used.	User is warned that verification is not possible. Macros are automatically disabled.	User is warned that verification is not possible. User is prompted to enable or disable macros.	No prompt or verification. Macros are enabled.
Signed macros from any author. The signature was made after the certificate had expired or been revoked.	User is warned that the signature has expired or been revoked. Macros are automatically disabled.	User is warned that the signature has expired or been revoked. User is prompted to enable or disable macros.	No prompt or verification. Macros are enabled.

Obtaining a Digital Certificate

A digital certificate is a digital ID card that guarantees users that your COM Add-in emanates from a trusted source. You can sign an Outlook VBA Project or a COM Add-in with a digital certificate. There are several sources for digital certificates that provide security for your COM Add-in:

- Selfcert.exe, included on the Office 2000 CD-ROM, creates a personal certificate. A personal certificate lets you certify your own macro code to yourself if you've set the Outlook security settings to High.

- You can obtain a certificate from your organization's internal certification authority. Some organizations may elect to produce in-house digital certificates by using tools such as Microsoft Certificate Server. In effect, this option lets you act as your own organizational certification authority.

- You can obtain a commercial Class 2 or Class 3 certificate from a commercial certificate authority. For a listing of certificate authorities, visit *http://backoffice.microsoft.com/securitypartners/default.asp/*. Use this option if you plan to distribute your COM Add-in commercially or to the public at large.

Signing an Outlook VBA Project

If you want to set security settings to High and run your own Outlook VBA code, you need to install the personal certificate that ships with Office 2000. This process installs selfcert.exe in the same folder where you've installed Office 2000.

To install the Create Digital Certificate utility

1. In the Control Panel, double-click Add/Remove Programs.
2. On the Install/Uninstall page, click Microsoft Office 2000, and then click Add/Remove.
3. In the Microsoft Office 2000 Maintenance Mode dialog box, click the Add Or Remove Features button.
4. Expand Office Tools and set Digital Signature For VBA Projects To Run From My Computer.
5. Click Update Now.
6. Once you've installed selfcert.exe, you need to actually add a digital signature to your Outlook VBA project. First create your personal certificate by double-clicking selfcert.exe. You'll be asked to enter your name to identify your personal certificate. That's all there is to it. Next you actually sign your Outlook VBA project.

To digitally sign a VBA project

1. If user profiles are in use, log on to Windows as the user whose Outlook VBA project you want to sign. Start Outlook.

2. Open the Visual Basic Editor by pressing Alt+F11.

3. On the Tools menu, click Digital Signatures.

4. Do one of the following:

- If you haven't previously selected a digital certificate, or want to use another one, click Choose, select the certificate, and click OK twice.

- Click OK to use the current certificate.

Signing a COM Add-In

Before you sign a COM Add-in, you need to download signcode.exe, which ships with the Microsoft Internet Client SDK. For information about downloading the SDK, see *http://msdn.microsoft.com/developer/sdk/inetsdk/*. You also need to obtain a digital certificate that will authenticate your COM Add-in. Once your COM Add-in has been signed, its ActiveX DLL file will contain a digital signature. If you examine the COM Add-in DLL in Windows Explorer, the Properties page for the file will display a Digital Signatures page containing information about the certificate. Figure 13.15 shows Properties pages for a digitally signed version of shareact.dll that contains the COM Add-in for the Create Shared Activities toolbar.

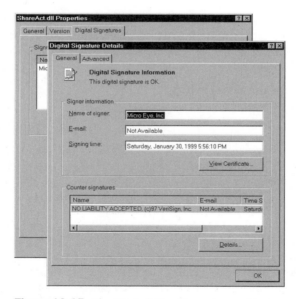

Figure 13.15 *The Digital Signatures page appears on the Properties dialog box for a signed COM Add-in.*

More Info For additional information about obtaining a digital certificate, signing code with signcode.exe, and using command line switches for signcode.exe, see the Internet Client SDK.

Note Outlook macro security differs from other Office 2000 applications in one important respect: If you examine the Trusted Sources page of the Security dialog box in Word, you'll see a check box for Trust All Installed Add-Ins And Templates. If you clear that check box in Word, COM Add-ins will not be trusted by default. Outlook 2000 has no such check box on the Trusted Sources page. All COM Add-ins are trusted by default. If you want to apply security checks to COM Add-ins for Outlook, you must add a DontTrustInstalledFiles DWORD value under the Security key for Outlook in the Windows registry and set the value of DontTrustInstalledFiles to *1*.

Deploying Your COM Add-In

The Package and Deployment Wizard

Once you have developed, debugged, and secured your COM Add-in, you can create an installation setup program with either the Setup Wizard, if you are using Visual Basic 5.0, or the Package and Deployment Wizard if you are using Visual Basic 6.0. If you use the Visual Basic 5.0 Setup Wizard, you must add code to the setup program to ensure that the correct registry settings will be created for your Add-in. See "Add-In Registration" earlier in this chapter for the correct registry key names and values for a COM Add-in. If you use Visual Basic 6.0 and the Package and Deployment Wizard, all the registration chores are handled for you automatically. The discussion that follows assumes that you will use the Visual Basic 6.0 Package and Deployment Wizard to package your Add-in.

Setup Checklist

Before you begin the package and deployment process, be certain that you have completed the following steps:

- Debug and test your COM Add-in under different operating systems and in different Outlook modes—Corporate/Workgroup and Internet Only.
- If required, ensure that your Add-in has been digitally signed with a digital certificate.
- Make sure that you have added any required property page ActiveX controls and also third-party or extrinsic ActiveX controls required by your Add-in.
- If your Add-in requires object libraries that are not part of Office 2000, make sure that you have the right to distribute those object libraries and that you've identified all the dependencies for your COM Add-in.
- Test the setup program under a variety of circumstances. Don't assume that because the COM Add-in installs on your development machine that it will install on a machine that only has Office 2000 installed.

The Visual Studio 98 Package and Deployment Wizard

The Package and Deployment Wizard lets you create either a standard setup package or a Web-based setup package using Active setup with Internet Explorer. There are a number of ways to start the Package and Deployment Wizard:

- You can launch the Package and Deployment Wizard as a stand-alone application. In this case, you must select the Visual Basic project that you want to package and deploy.
- If you have loaded the Package and Deployment Wizard as an Add-in, it is available from within the Visual Basic Development environment. In this case the default project to package will be the current project.

Standard Setup Package

A standard setup package uses setup.exe to bootstrap the setup process. Setup.exe in turn calls setup1.exe, which contains the main setup program for your COM Add-in. Unlike the Setup Wizard that shipped with previous versions of Visual Basic, the Visual Basic 6.0 Package and Deployment Wizard places the ActiveX DLL and all dependent files into a single cabinet (.cab) file. When installation occurs, the application component and its dependent files are extracted from the cabinet file and moved to the correct folder on the local drive. A standard setup package can create a floppy, CD, or network-share type of setup. If you want the end-user of your COM Add-in to be able to uninstall your COM Add-in, you should select the standard setup package option in the Package and Deployment Wizard.

Web-Based Setup

In a Web-based setup, the Package and Deployment Wizard creates a cabinet file and a Web page so that your COM Add-in component can be downloaded from the Internet or a corporate intranet. When a user accesses the Web page that hosts your COM Add-in package, the system downloads the ActiveX DLL component and dependent files to the user's computer. Internet Component Download, a feature of Internet Explorer 3.0 and higher, causes the package to be verified for safety, unpacked, registered, installed, and then activated. The downloading occurs in the background and is controlled by the browser. User intervention is kept to a minimum or is nonexistent, depending on the security settings in the user's browser.

The most compelling feature of a Web-based setup is that it lends itself to use with Folder Home Pages. You could design a Folder Home Page for the top-level folder in an Exchange public folder application. When users navigate to that folder, they could read instructions for using the application, and a Web-based setup would automatically install all the COM Add-in or other ActiveX components required for the application. For additional information on this technique, see Chapter 14, "Customizing Folder Home Pages."

> **More Info** For additional information on the Visual Basic 6.0 Package and Deploy-
> ment Wizard, see the book *Distributing Your Applications* in the Visual Basic on-
> line documentation.

Where To Go from Here

For additional information about the subjects discussed in this chapter, see the following resources.

Creating ActiveX Controls

Appleman, Dan. *Developing COM/ActiveX Components with Visual Basic 6.0
—A Guide for the Perplexed.* Indianapolis, IN: Macmillan Computer Publishing,
1998.

Creating Add-Ins and DLLs in Microsoft Visual Basic

Appleman, Dan. *Developing COM/ActiveX Components with Visual Basic 6.0
—A Guide for the Perplexed.* Indianapolis, IN: Macmillan Computer Publishing,
1998.

Microsoft Corporation. *Microsoft Visual Basic 6.0 Programmer's Guide.*
Redmond, WA: Microsoft Press, 1998. An online version of this book is included with Visual Basic 6.0, and is also available on the MSDN Online Web
site at *http://msdn.microsoft.com/developer/*.

Microsoft Corporation. McKinney, Bruce. *Hardcore Visual Basic, Second Edition.* Redmond, WA: Microsoft Press, 1997.

Cornell, Gary, and Dave Jezak. *Core Visual Basic 6.* Upper Saddle River, NJ:
Prentice Hall PTR, 1998.

Creating COM Add-Ins with Visual C++ and Visual J++

MSDN Online Web site
http://msdn.microsoft.com/developer/

Deploying Templates and Add-Ins

Downloading Code on the Web
http://www.microsoft.com/workshop/components/downcode.asp/

Installing Windows Applications via the Web with Visual Studio 6.0
http://www.microsoft.com/workshop/components/vsappinstall/install.asp/

Microsoft Corporation. "Designing and Deploying Office Solutions," Chapter 2
in *Microsoft Office 2000/Visual Basic Programmer's Guide.* Redmond, WA:
Microsoft Press, 1999.

Office 2000 COM Add-Ins

Microsoft Corporation. "Add-Ins, Templates, Wizards, and Libraries," Chapter 11 in *Microsoft Office 2000/Visual Basic Programmer's Guide*. Redmond, WA: Microsoft Press, 1999.

Securing VBA Projects and Working with Digital Signatures

Microsoft Corporation. "Securing Office Documents and Visual Basic for Applications Code," Chapter 2 in *Microsoft Office 2000/Visual Basic Programmer's Guide*. Redmond, WA: Microsoft Press, 1999.

Working with Office 2000 Objects

Microsoft Corporation. "Working with Shared Office Components," and "Custom Classes and Objects," Chapters 6 and 9 in *Microsoft Office 2000/Visual Basic Programmer's Guide*. Redmond, WA: Microsoft Press, 1999.

Chapter 14
Customizing Folder Home Pages

In This Chapter

As a developer, you might be wondering what use, if any, you can make of the new Folder Home Page feature in Outlook 2000. Some Outlook developers—especially those who concentrate their efforts on form development—might be puzzled by the importance and significance of Folder Home Pages. What are they for and why would anyone use them? This chapter will try to provide you with answers to these questions. Folder Home Pages are a complementary technology to COM Add-ins; they let you customize the Outlook environment and shape a user's experience of a public folder application.

What Folder Home Pages Are

Folder Home Pages help promote features of your application directly to the user. You can replace nested menu commands, which many users will ignore, with command buttons that appear front and center on a Folder Home Page. The concept of bringing all the commands and features of your application to a single Folder Home Page is known as enhancing discoverability. Those of us who make a living through our development work enjoy exploring the nooks and crannies of applications. However, many end users are interested only in the point-and-click approach to application discovery. Typically, they are too busy with their everyday work to learn about hidden features in an application. This might be termed the reality of application design: "If you don't put it right in front of them, they will ignore it." Folder Home Pages let you present all the important commands and data for your application in the view pane of the Outlook Explorer. Figure 14.1 illustrates a Folder Home Page created for the Northwind Contact Management Application in E-Chapter 3 on the companion CD. We'll examine the Visual Basic 6.0 DHTML project used to create this Folder Home Page later in the chapter. As you can see from the Customers Folder Home Page, a great deal of functionality is placed on a single Folder Home Page. You might say that everything but the kitchen sink is in there, yet, at the same time, the user experience has been streamlined and simplified. The sales personnel who will use this application will enjoy its simplicity and its straightforward approach in design.

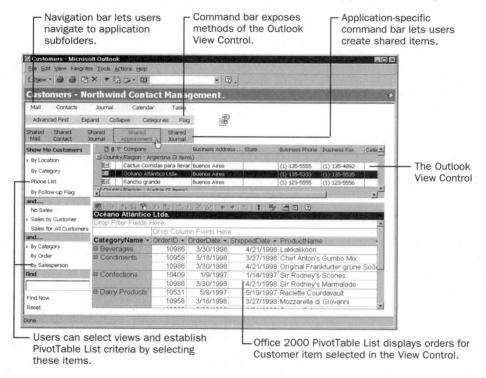

Figure 14.1 *A customized Folder Home Page for the Northwind Contact Management Customers folder.*

What Folder Home Pages Are Not

It's also important to understand what Folder Home Pages are not. Folder Home Pages should not be confused with Outlook Web Access. Outlook Web Access allows users to open their private mailbox from any browser that supports frames. Outlook Web Access is a cross-platform technology that lets mobile users read their mail from a system that is independent of the Outlook client. You don't need to have an Outlook client installed to read your mail from Outlook Web Access. The simplicity of Outlook Web Access also comes with several limitations. For example, Outlook Web Access cannot render Task or Journal items at this time. The performance of Outlook Web Access is generally less than optimal. It can render items in public folders, but you must typically use the Outlook HTML Form Converter to convert custom forms to Outlook Web Access forms. The Outlook HTML Form Converter does not convert the VBScript behind your custom form. If you want to replace the code behind your custom form, you would turn to Exchange Server Scripting to duplicate some of the functionality of your custom form code. Finally, Outlook Web Access cannot render Contact, Calendar, Task, or Journal forms in public folders.

Folder Home Pages Compared to Outlook Web Access

The following table illustrates some of the differences between Folder Home Pages and Outlook Web Access.

Technology	Outlook Web Access	Folder Home Pages
Browser neutral (requires the ability to render frames)	Yes	No. Internet Explorer 4.x or later.
Client	Outlook 97, 98, 2000, and Outlook for the Macintosh	Outlook 2000 only.
Client-side scripting	No	Yes.
Server-side scripting	Yes	Not typical when using Outlook View Control. However, Folder Home Pages can also execute as ASP pages on a server.
Supports event procedures	Only if combined with Exchange scripting agents	Yes, using events in Outlook 2000 Object Model.
Supports Outlook View Control	No	Yes.
Windows NT/2000 and Windows 95/98 computers only	No	Yes.

Placeholder Folders and Active Folder Home Pages

In Chapter 8, "Folders," Folder Home Pages were briefly discussed, and you were presented with some scenarios for their use in placeholder folders. The Northwind Contact Management Application in E-Chapter 3 on the companion CD uses an Access 2000 Data Access Page as a Folder Home Page for the root folder of the application. Although the root folder does not contain Outlook items (and thus it is a placeholder to the active subfolders that do contain custom forms), it does host a Folder Home Page that lets a user examine sales data in a Pivot Table List for current Northwind customers. Typically, a placeholder Folder Home Page does not let the user open items directly in the placeholder folder. A placeholder home page certainly qualifies as a Folder Home Page, but it just scratches the surface of what is possible with this technology. In this chapter, you'll see examples of what I'll describe as an active Folder Home Page. An active Folder Home Page lets the user directly manipulate the items contained in the folder hosting the home page. To start our tour of Folder Home Page development opportunities, we'll first take a look at the tools you can use to create active Folder Home Pages.

The Outlook Today Page

Like its predecessor Outlook 98, Outlook 2000 provides an Outlook Today page that is customizable. You might think of the Outlook Today page in Outlook 2000 as a customized Folder Home Page at the root of your private information store. Unlike the Outlook Today page that is implemented by a custom .dll and databinding code to an object known as a RENSTATICTABLE, Folder Home Pages are exposed as straightforward HTML pages and are comparatively easy to customize using Visual InterDev or the editor of your choice. Outlook Today sports some minor enhancements in Outlook 2000, most notably the ability to enforce browser security within the Outlook Today view. In Outlook 98, browser security was always disabled in the Outlook Today view, no matter what URL was being viewed. Outlook 2000 offers an enhanced security model that turns on browser security as soon as the user navigates away from the default URL.

End users can customize their Outlook Today page by clicking the Customize Outlook Today link in the page header. Developers can customize Outlook Today to brand the page with a corporate identity or to modify the page for use within different departments in an organization. You can also change the layout of the page and add links to pages on your corporate intranet. Developer customization of the Outlook Today view in Outlook 2000 is beyond the scope of this chapter. A technical article that discusses advanced customization techniques for Outlook Today will be available on the Web at *http://www.microsoft.com/office/ork/* after Office 2000 ships.

Tools To Create Folder Home Pages

To create Folder Home Pages, you can use any of tools listed next. If you become a serious Folder Home Page developer, you will use a combination of these tools or a third-party authoring tool not listed in the following table. If you want to customize your Folder Home Pages, you should look at Visual Studio 98 Professional or Enterprise edition as the tool of choice. Since Visual Studio ships with both Visual Basic and Visual InterDev in the box, you have the two essential tools for Folder Home Page customization in your toolkit. In this chapter, we'll examine a DHTML Visual Basic 6.0 application in detail. You can modify this DHTML application to suit your specific requirements. You can also modify the client-side scripts in the HTML pages that accompany the Team Folder Wizard using either Visual InterDev 6.0 or FrontPage 2000.

Tool	Solution Created	Skill Set	Outlook View Control	Code and Debug Environment
Microsoft Word 2000	HTML-based page	Basic to Intermediate	No	Microsoft Script Editor
Microsoft FrontPage 2000	HTML-based page	Intermediate	No	Microsoft Script Editor
Microsoft Visual Basic 6.0	VB 6.0 DHTML project combining ActiveX DLL and HTML-based page	Intermediate to Advanced	Yes	Visual Basic 6.0
Microsoft Visual InterDev 6.0	HTML-based page with client-side script or Active Server Page for server-side deployment in IIS 4.0 or later	Advanced	Yes	Visual InterDev 6.0 using VBScript or JavaScript

The Outlook Team Folder Wizard

The Outlook Team Folder Wizard contains a set of turnkey applications for common collaborative scenarios using Outlook and Exchange Public Folders. Implemented as an Outlook 2000 COM Add-in, the Team Folder Wizard lets end users create their own collaboration applications with the wizard. Since the Team Folder Wizard is a COM Add-in, you can only use the Team Folder Wizard if you have installed Outlook 2000. From the perspective of Outlook development, the Folder Home Pages created by the wizard offer a great starting point for the customization of your own Folder Home Pages. Figure 14.2 shows the home page for the FAQ folder in a Team Folder Project Application.

Obtaining the Team Folder Wizard

The Team Folder Wizard will be available on the Web shortly after the public release of Outlook 2000. Look for the Team Folder Wizard at the following URL:

http://officeupdate.microsoft.com/outlook/

Team Folder Wizard Basics

The basic steps in using the Team Folder Wizard are covered in this section. For additional information on the Outlook Team Folder Wizard installation and customization, visit the URL listed in the previous section and download additional documentation and white papers on the Team Folder Wizard.

The Team Folder Wizard essentially uses a series of personal folders (.pst) files to create one or more subfolders in your public folders. The personal folders file contains custom forms for administration of the folders and for issue tracking and frequently asked ques-

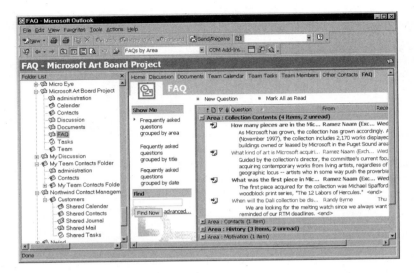

Figure 14.2 *The FAQ Folder Home Page created by the Team Folder Wizard.*

tions (FAQ). The Team Folder Wizard also handles permissions so that users can establish groups with different Exchange permissions for subfolders established by the Team Folder Wizard. Once the folders have been established in your public folders, the wizard publishes the appropriate HTML pages to a server on your intranet so that Folder Home Page links can be established between the Team Folder folders and the correct Folder Home Page in a virtual directory on your Web server.

Types of Team Folder Applications

You can create several different types of applications using the Team Folder Wizard. The following table lists the discussion applications you can create without any customization of the folders or Folder Home Pages supplied by the wizard.

Application	Subfolders	Description
Team Project	Administration, Calendar, Contacts, Discussion, FAQ, Documents, Tasks, Team	A team project is a complete set of folders for a collaboration project.
Team Calendar	Administration, Calendar	Team folder for managing group calendars.
Team Contacts	Administration, Contacts	Team folder for managing group contacts.
Team Tasks	Administration, Tasks	Team task management folder.

(continued)

(continued)

Application	Subfolders	Description
Discussion	Administration, Discussion	Discussion forum with several custom views and an easy-to-use discussion filter.
Document Library	Administration, DocLib	Folder for tracking shared documents
Frequently asked questions (FAQ)	Administration, FAQ	Discussion forum for frequently asked questions.

Running the Wizard

Follow the instructions that download with the Team Folder Wizard to install the Team Folder COM Add-in and supporting files. Before you run the Team Folder Wizard, you should ensure that the Team Folder Wizard has installed correctly. The Team Folder Wizard runs as an Outlook 2000 COM Add-in. Figure 14.3 illustrates the Outlook Team Folder Wizard loaded as a COM Add-in and the Team Folder command that the COM Add-in provides is at the bottom of the New submenu.

To verify that the Team Folder Wizard is loaded as a COM Add-in

1. Select Options from the Tools menu.
2. Click the Other tab on the Tools Options dialog box.
3. Click the Advanced Options button.
4. Click the COM Add-Ins button on the Advanced Options dialog box.
5. The Outlook Team Folder Wizard COM Add-In box should be checked.
6. Click OK.

Once you're certain the Team Folder Wizard is loaded as a COM Add-in, you can proceed to run the wizard. Before you start the Team Folder Wizard, you should complete the following checklist:

- What type of application do you want to create? (See the list of supported application types shown previously).
- What will you name the application?
- Where will you deploy the application? You need to identify one of the following locations:
  - A public folder where you have permissions to create a subfolder. The logged-on Outlook user who runs the Team Folder Wizard will own the Team Folder application folder and its subfolders. Consult your Microsoft Exchange Server administrator if you have questions about public folder administration and permissions.

- A folder on an intranet Web server or a folder on a shared directory on your file server. All the members of your team who will be using the application must have sufficient access rights to those resources.

- Which members of your team have which Exchange permissions (reviewer, author, editor, and so forth) in the Team Folder application? You can set permissions for individual users or members of a Distribution List in the last step of the wizard.

After you've completed the answers to the questions above, you can launch the wizard and create your application in a few easy mouse clicks. The following steps are numbered consecutively so that you can be sure you didn't omit a step. Of course, the wizard won't let you skip a step, even if you want to.

To launch the Outlook Team Folder Wizard

1. Select New from the Explorer File Menu.
2. Select Team Folder from the New submenu, as shown in Figure 14.3.

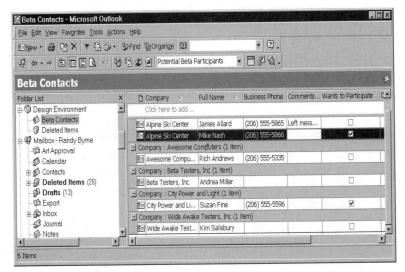

Figure 14.3 *The Outlook Team Folder Wizard COM Add-in enables the Team Folder Wizard within Outlook 2000.*

To select the type of Team Folder Application you want to create

1. Select the Team Folder Application type from the list box on the first dialog box of the Team Folder Wizard, as shown in Figure 14.4.
2. Click Next.

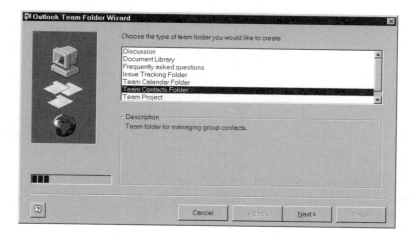

Figure 14.4 *Selecting an application type in the Team Folder Wizard.*

To name your Team Folder Application

1. Enter the name of your Team Folder application in the second dialog box of the Team Folder Wizard, as shown in Figure 14.5. This name will be used to create the root or home folder of your Team Folder application.

2. Click Next.

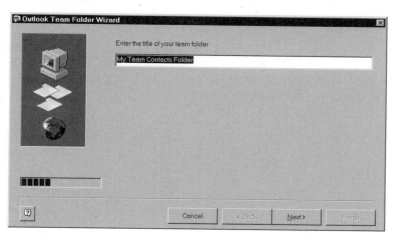

Figure 14.5 *Name your Team Folder Application.*

Pick a location for your Team Folder folders and home pages

1. Click the Choose Folder button to select a location for your Team Folder application and its subfolders. You will need sufficient permissions to create folders

in this location. Consult your Microsoft Exchange Server administrator if you do not have sufficient permissions.

2. Select the correct publishing protocol in the Protocol drop-down list box, as shown in Figure 14.6. If you have installed the Web Publishing extensions, you can publish the Folder Home Page HTML files associated with your Team Folder application to a Web server on your intranet. If you have sufficient permissions, you can also publish to a shared directory on a file server in your organization. Select the file:// protocol to publish to a shared directory on a file server. Click the Browse button to locate the shared directory, if necessary.

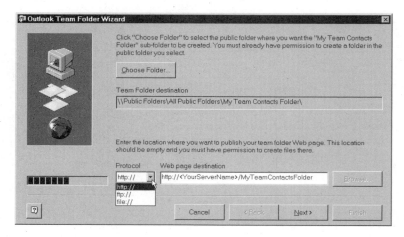

Figure 14.6 *Set locations for Team Folder application folders and Folder Home Pages.*

3. Enter the server name of your Web server, assuming that you are publishing to a Web server in your organization.

4. Click Next.

Add members to the Team Folder application and establish permissions

1. The logged-on Outlook user who creates the Team Folder application will be the owner of the Application folder and its subfolders. See Chapter 8, "Folders," for additional information on Exchange Public Folder roles and permissions.

2. Add additional users with specified permissions. Click the Add button to add user names or Exchange Distribution Lists to the member list box on the Outlook Team Folder Wizard dialog box. Notice in Figure 14.7 that a distribution list named ExAdmin has been added as an owner of the Application. Owners receive system messages concerning the folder and its subfolders. To simplify administration, the example in Figure 14.7 shows that a distribution list named N CA Sales Team has received author permissions for the application.

3. Click Next.

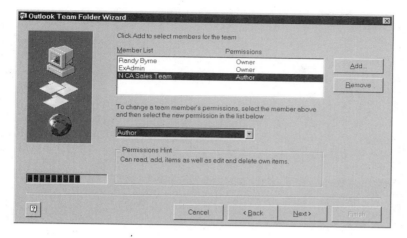

Figure 14.7 *Add members to the Team and set their permissions.*

➔ **Review your choices and click Finish to create your Team Folder application**

1. The Team Folder Wizard will present you with a summary of the choices you have made in its final dialog box, shown in Figure 14.8. You can click the Back button if you need to make changes.

2. Click Finish.

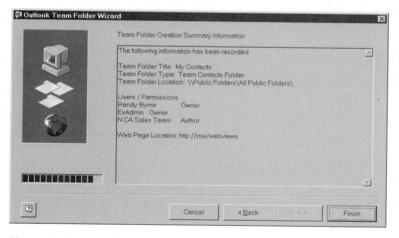

Figure 14.8 *The Team Folder Wizard Summary dialog box.*

Once you've created your Team Folder application, you are ready to complete a set of administration tasks that will help you customize the Folder Home Pages for your application.

Administration Tasks

The Team Folder Wizard uses a set of messages in the Administration folder, shown in Figure 14.9, to store information that provides a customized look to your Team Folder application. This technique of using messages in folders to create persistent application settings is one that you should add to your developer's bag of tricks. Think of these messages in the Administration folder as a sort of Exchange-based registry for your application. You can't use the registry on individual user machines to support your application. Messages in an administration folder (to which other users don't have permissions higher than Reviewer) provide a convenient means of storing settings for your application.

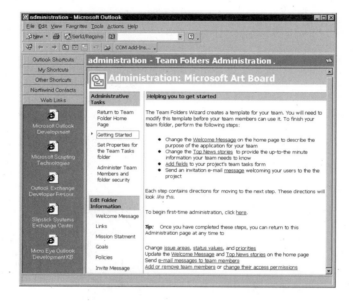

Figure 14.9 *The Team Folder Administration page lets you determine application settings.*

You will need to complete the following administrative tasks on the Folder Home Page for the Administration folder.

Task	Description
Set Welcome Message	Change the Welcome Message on the home page to describe the purpose of the application for your team.
Set Top News	Change the Top News Stories to provide up-to-the minute information your team needs to know.
Add Fields	Add fields to your project's team tasks form.
Send Message	Send an invitation e-mail message welcoming your users to the project.

Your Team Folder application is complete. Once the users of your application receive their invitation to use your Team Folder application, they can begin to contribute items to the application and collaborate with coworkers.

Modifying Team Folder Pages

The Team Folder HTML pages installed by the wizard are fully customizable. In fact, they were designed with developer customization in mind, even though the Team Folder Wizard appears to be an end-user tool. Since the main focus of this chapter is a Visual Basic DHTML Folder Home Page application, we won't dwell extensively on the customization possibilities of Team Folder HTML pages.

To customize a Team Folder HTML page, you should open it with Visual InterDev 6.0 or a Web scripting editor of your choice. Figure 14.10 illustrates default.htm, the Folder Home Page for the Team Folder application opened in Visual InterDev.

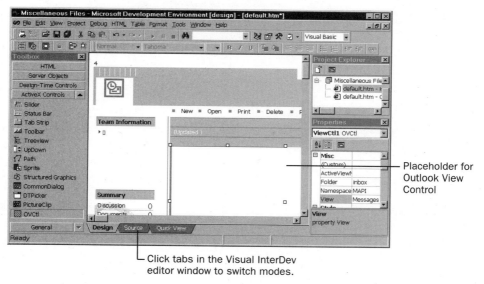

Figure 14.10 *The Team Folder default.htm file opened in Design mode in Visual InterDev.*

⟳ To open a Team Folder HTML page in Visual InterDev

1. Launch Visual InterDev. If Visual InterDev displays the New Project dialog box when it starts, click Cancel or press Esc.

2. Select Open File on the File menu.

3. Click Existing Page in the File Open dialog box and locate the team Folder Home Page that you wish to modify. This file could be located on a Web server or in a shared directory on a file server in your organization.

4.   Click OK to open the HTML page.

Switching Modes

There are three modes available in the Visual InterDev HTML editor window. You can switch from Design View mode to Source View mode to Quick View mode simply by clicking the appropriate tab in the HTML editor window. Figure 14.11 shows the HTML editor in Source View mode.

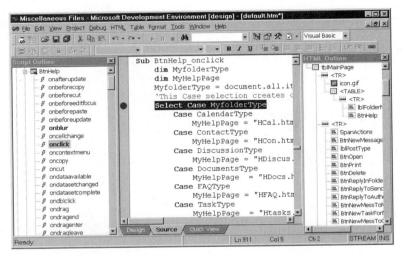

Figure 14.11 *Use Source View mode to write VBScript procedures for your Folder Home Page.*

- **Design View**   The editor displays text with character and paragraph formatting, much like a word processor. You can drag and drop ActiveX and HTML controls directly onto the page from the Toolbox window.

- **Source View**   The editor shows HTML tags, text, and script, and highlights the HTML tags and text. VBScript code appears with color coding much as it does in Visual Basic or VBA. The Visual InterDev code window supports the same IntelliSense features such as AutoComplete that you enjoy in Visual Basic.

- **Quick View**   The editor displays .htm files as they will appear in Internet Explorer. You should test and display Folder Home Pages in Outlook itself rather than in Quick view.

Using the Index in the Source

In order to help you find your way through the source code for the Folder Home Page, Team Folder Home Pages contain an inline index to help you find the code procedures you would like to change. This index is shown next.

```
'############################
'Index for this page
'If you would like to make modifications to any part
'of this page, this index will help you locate the correct
'place in the code to make your changes.
'LOC --> Localizable Areas
'FNP --> Folder Name Properties
'PCV --> Page Characteristic Variables
'NBP --> Navigation Bar Properties
'VTP --> View Tab Properties
'DVT --> Default View Tab
'TBB --> Navigation Buttons
'VCT --> View Control Tabs
'############################
```

To find a segment of code by its Index

1. Click the Source tab in the HTML Editor window.

2. Select the Find And Replace command from the Edit menu or press Ctrl+F.

3. Enter the appropriate index string in the Find combo box of the Find dialog box and click Find.

Note The collection of HTML pages created by the Team Folder Wizard really consists of only three sources. The file css.css is the style sheet for the application, admin.htm is the administration page for the application, and all the other files are based on the source code found in default.htm. The HTML is written in a way that makes the same page take on different faces depending on what purpose it's serving. These HTML files have different names, but they share a common code base found in default.htm.

Changing the Name of a Folder in the Navigation Bar

Let's assume, for example, that you want to change the name of a folder in the Navigation bar of a Folder Home Page for FAQ. The Navigation bar is shown in Figure 14.12. It sits at the top of the Team Folder Home Page and lets the user navigate to different folders in the application. Remember that the Navigation bar code in the Team Folder Home Page is causing the source folder for the Outlook View control to change; it is not actually causing the Explorer Object's CurrentFolder property to change to a different Outlook folder in the public folder hierarchy.

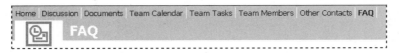

Figure 14.12 *The FAQ Team Folder Home Page Navigation bar.*

Folder navigation buttons can be modified with relative ease. Each Folder navigation button has five properties which are set in the Navigation Button properties (search for NBP) in the Source view for the page:

- .style.display
- .innerHTML
- .setAttribute "FolderPath", [MyFolderPath]
- .setAttribute "FolderType", [FolderType]
- .setAttribute "DefaultTab", [DefaultTabName]

.style.display

Syntax:

```
[MyFolderButton].style.display = "[inline | none]"
```

The .style.display property takes a string value. It determines whether the button displays when the page is rendered. It's value can either be none or inline. None will hide the button completely, and inline will show the button. If you don't want one of the buttons to show up—if you've decided to delete one of your subfolders, for instance—simply setting this value to none will prevent any of your users from trying to navigate to that nonexistent folder.

.innerHTML

Syntax:

```
[MyFolderButton].innerHTML = "[Button Face Text]"
```

The innerHTML property for any given button determines what text will show up on the face of the button when you assign a string value to the property value. The value of this parameter has no real effect on the workings of the page; it can be any string value you desire. If you want to change the name of a folder to something you know would make more sense to the user, but you don't want to make fundamental changes to the code, you can simply rename the Calendar button, for example, to Appointments by changing the innerHTML property, thus avoiding having to make any additional changes to the code or the application itself.

.setAttribute "FolderPath", [MyFolderPath]

Syntax:

```
[MyFolderButton].setAttribute "FolderPath", [MyFolderPath]
```

The FolderPath property of a button tells the page which child folder the Outlook View control should use to gather its information when that button is clicked. This property takes one of the Folder Name variables in place of [MyFolderPath]. If, for instance, you want the View control to access the Tasks folder when a button is clicked, you would set this property as follows:

```
FolderBtnN.setAttribute "FolderPath", L_folderNameTasks_Text
```

.setAttribute "FolderType", [FolderType]

Syntax:

```
[MyFolderButton].setAttribute "FolderType", [CalendarType | ContactType
| DiscussionType | DocumentsType | FAQType | TaskType |
AdministrationType | TeamType]
```

The FolderType property tells the Outlook View control what type of folder it will be accessing when a button is clicked. This option is provided so that you can name any type of folder anything you want. As long as you set this property correctly, the page can make the necessary adjustments to deal with that folder's contents.

.setAttribute "DefaultTab", [DefaultTabName]

Syntax:

```
[MyFolderButton].setAttribute "DefaultTab", [DefaultTabName]
```

Default tabs are the tab buttons that let a user switch the views on the Outlook View control. When you set the DefaultTab property, you indicate which tab is the default tab within the context of the page. If you have created your own views for a subfolder in a Team Folder application, you can go to the View Tab properties section of code and modify the views that appear in the default tab for the page (search for VTP).

Button Change Example

Let's assume that you would like the seventh button in the Folder Navigation bar of the FAQ page to read Customer Contacts. When this button is clicked, you want the Outlook View control to navigate to a folder called Customer Contacts, which contains Contact items. Follow the steps below to change the button's display text and its functionality.

To change a Navigation bar button's display text and its linked folder

1. Rename the target folder in the Outlook Folder List. In this case, rename the Contacts subfolder to Customer Contacts.

2. Launch Visual InterDev.

3. Select the Open File command from the File menu and open faq.htm on a Web server or in a shared directory on a file server.

4. Select the Find And Replace command from the Edit menu.

5. Enter FNP in the Find combo box and click Find twice to locate the Folder Name properties (FNP) in the Source page of faq.htm.

6. Change `L_folderNameContact_Text = "Contacts"` to read `L_folderNameContact_Text = "Customer Contacts"`.

7. Select the Find And Replace command from the Edit menu.

8. Enter *FolderBtn7* in the Find combo box and click Find once to locate the assignment statements for FolderBtn7 on the navigation bar. You will see the code shown below.

```
'FolderBtn7 Properties
    FolderBtn7.style.display = "inline"
```

```
FolderBtn7.innerHTML = "Contacts"
FolderBtn7.setAttribute "folderPath",L_folderNameContact_Text
FolderBtn7.setAttribute "folderType",ContactType
FolderBtn7.setAttribute "DefaultTab","OtherContactsTab1"
```

9.   Change the FolderBtn7.innerHTML = "Contacts" statement to read as follows:

```
FolderBtn7.innerHTML = "Customer Contacts"
```

10.   Select the Save FAQ.htm command on the File menu to save the page.

11.   To see the results of your changes, navigate to the FAQ folder in the Outlook Folder List. If the Contacts Navigation bar button has not changed to Customer Contacts, display the Web toolbar using the Toolbars command on the View menu and click the Refresh Current Page button on the Web toolbar. You should see a modified FAQ navigation bar similar to the one illustrated in Figure 14.13.

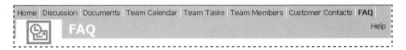

Figure 14.13 *Modified FAQ Team Folder Home Page Navigation bar.*

Additional changes to the Team Folder Home Pages are beyond the scope of this chapter. Because you have complete access to the HTML documents published by the Team Folder Wizard, you can change almost any aspect of these pages, including title, background color, images on the page, and the views named in the DefaultTab for the page. You can also extend the page with completely new functionality if you so desire.

More Info For additional information on HTML page customization, see the Team Folder Wizard documentation available at *http://officeupdate.microsoft.com/outlook/*.

Team Folder Extensibility

Developers who wish to distribute their own custom Team Folder Wizard application can extend the Team Folder Wizard by using its extensibility model. Planned extensibility features include the ability to add your own Wizard pages after the Permissions page and before the Summary page. The extensibility model of the Team Folder Wizard was still under development at the time of this writing. The following extensibility features will be available when the Wizard ships:

- Add templates to the list of available Team Folder Wizard applications
- Deliver folder contents, form definitions, and pre-existing views
- Deliver customized Folder Home Pages
- Provide custom pages (dialog boxes) for the Team Folder Wizard

The Outlook View Control

The Outlook View Control gives an Outlook Folder Home Page the ability to display the contents of an Outlook folder, to control folder views, and to create, open, print, and delete items in the source folder. It is implemented as an ActiveX control (in a .dll file rather than as an .ocx file) that can be added to a Web page, an Outlook form, a VBA UserForm, or a Visual Basic form. The View control allows Folder Home Pages to operate with the speed and versatility that they exhibit. Unlike Outlook Web Access pages which must convert folder items to HTML, the View control encapsulates the view pane that you see in the Outlook Explorer window and makes it portable.

Adding the View Control to a Form

Figure 14.14 illustrates the Outlook View control placed on a UserForm. This UserForm is included in the VBAProject.otm accompanying this book. Before discussing the use of the View Control on HTML pages, it would be helpful to examine how the View control is used on the frmViews UserForm.

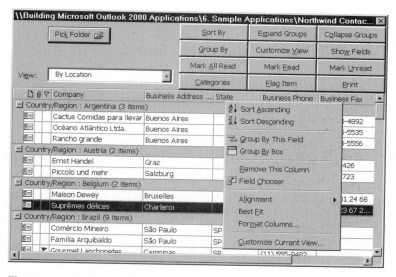

Figure 14.14 *The Outlook View control on a VBA UserForm.*

To open the Outlook View Control UserForm

1. Press Alt+F8 to open the Macro dialog box.
2. Select ShowViewControlForm in the Macro Name list box.
3. Click Run.

This form demonstrates many of the features of the Outlook View control. On first inspection, you'll notice that this control exposes a full-featured Outlook view in the dialog box or UserForm on which it has been placed. If you right-click on the View control, all the normal shortcut menus of a standard Outlook view are available, including the ability to customize the view from the shortcut menu. You can drag and drop fields on the view. You can select a view from the View drop-down list box and the view in the View control will change. You can also use the command buttons on the form to demonstrate some of the methods of the control. If you double-click on an item in the view, the item opens. The beauty of this control is that it's fast and relatively lightweight. The shipping version of the control will be signed for use in a secured browser environment.

Let's take a look at how the Outlook View Control UserForm is implemented. Before you can add a View control to a UserForm or an Outlook form, you must add it to the list of available controls in your Control Toolbox. The steps below assume that you're adding the control to the Control Toolbox in VBA. The steps are essentially the same if you're adding the control to a Control Toolbox in Visual Basic or Visual InterDev.

To add the Outlook View control to your Control Toolbox

1. Press Alt+F11 to open the Visual Basic editor.
2. Select UserForm from the Insert menu.
3. If the Control Toolbox is not visible, select Toolbox from the View menu.
4. Right-click the Control Toolbox and select the Additional Controls menu.
5. Check Microsoft Outlook View Control in the list of available controls in the Additional Controls dialog box, as shown in Figure 14.15.

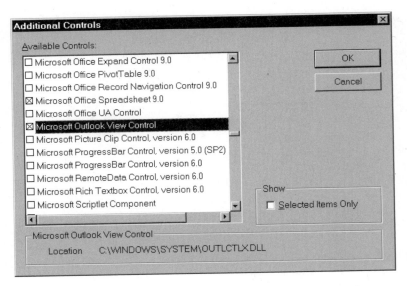

Figure 14.15 *Add the Outlook View control to your Control Toolbox.*

To add the Outlook View control to your form

1. Drag the View control from the Control Toolbox to your form. The default name of the Outlook View Control is OVCtl.

2. The View control will default to showing the contents of your Inbox.

Programmatic control of the Outlook View control is straightforward. The control exposes many methods that are equivalent to Outlook menu commands. The two most important properties exposed by the View control are the Folder and the View properties. These properties let you set or get the current folder and view that is displayed in the control. Both the View and the Folder properties are strings. While you might expect the Folder property to be a MAPIFolder object, it is a string value that indicates the full path to the target folder. You can see the Folder property in the caption of the UserForm, as shown previously in Figure 14.14. If you want to set the Folder property for the View control when you only have a MAPIFolder object (such as the MAPIFolder object returned by the *PickFolder* method of the NameSpace object), you must use the *GetFolderPath* function listed in Chapter 11, "Using VBA and VBScript with Outlook."

Note The *GetFolderPath* function returns a folder path with one leading backslash instead of two leading backslashes. The View Control will accept either one or two leading backslashes when you set the Folder property for the control. When the View control returns its Folder property string, it will always contain two leading backslashes. For example, if you obtain the View control Folder property when the control points to your Inbox, the Folder property will be \\Mailbox - <UserName>\Inbox.

Outlook View Control Properties

The following table lists the properties of the Outlook View control:

Property	Type	Description
ActiveFolder	Object	Returns an ActiveFolder object for use when the control is hosted in a Web page.
Folder	String	Returns or sets the path of the folder displayed by the control.
NameSpace	String	Returns or sets the NameSpace property of the control. The NameSpace property represents an abstract root object for any data source. This property can be set to MAPI (the default), representing the Outlook data source, or FAT representing the Windows file system.
OutlookApplication	Object	Returns an Outlook Application object for use when the control is hosted in a Web page.

(continued)

(continued)

Property	Type	Description
Restriction	String	Applies a filter to the items displayed in the control, displaying only those items that contain the string in the filter. Note that the behavior of the control's Restriction property differs from the *Restrict* method in the Outlook Object Model. See Restrict in the Microsoft Outlook Help Reference for additional details on logical and comparison operators.
View	String	Returns or sets the name of the view in the control. Setting this property to a value that does not match a view name listed above does not cause the view to change, although this property will subsequently return the invalid view name.

Outlook View Control Methods

The following table lists the methods of the Outlook View control:

Method	Description
AddressBook	Displays the Outlook Address Book dialog box.
AddToPFFavorites	Adds the folder displayed in the control to the user's Favorites folder. Does not display the Add To Favorites dialog box.
AdvancedFind	Displays the Outlook Advanced Find dialog box.
Categories	Displays the Outlook Categories dialog box for the item or items currently selected in the control, allowing the user to select categories for the current item or to modify the master category list.
CollapseAllGroups	Collapses all displayed groups in the control. If the view displayed in the control does not group items, this method has no effect.
CollapseGroup	Collapses the currently selected group in the control. If the view displayed in the control does not group items or if an item in the view is selected, this method has no effect.
CustomizeView	Displays the Outlook View Summary dialog box, allowing the user to customize the current view in the control.
Delete	Deletes the currently selected groups or items in the control. If one or more groups are selected, the groups and all items in the groups will be deleted.
ExpandAllGroups	Expands all displayed groups in the control. If the view displayed in the control does not group items, this method has no effect.
ExpandGroup	Expands the currently selected group in the control. If the view displayed in the control does not group items or if an item in the view is selected, this method has no effect.

(continued)

(continued)

Method	Description
FlagItem	Displays the Outlook Flag For Follow Up dialog box for the selected item.
ForceUpdate	Refreshes the view in the control.
Forward	Executes the Forward action for the selected item or items in the control.
GoToToday	Sets the displayed day in the control to the current day. This method affects only views of Calendar folder and Timeline views in the Inbox and Task folders.
GroupBy	Displays the Outlook Group By dialog box, allowing the user to group items in the current view. This method has no effect if the current view does not display grouped items.
MarkAllAsRead	Marks all items as read in the folder displayed in the control. The user is prompted for confirmation before any change is made.
MarkAsRead	Marks all selected items as read in the control. The user is prompted for confirmation before any change is made.
MarkAsUnread	Marks all selected items as unread in the control. The user is prompted for confirmation before any change is made.
MoveItem	Displays the Outlook Move Items dialog box for the items selected in the control.
NewAppointment	Creates and displays a new appointment.
NewContact	Creates and displays a new contact. If the control is displaying a Contacts folder, when the new contact is saved, it is saved in the folder displayed in the control. Otherwise, the contact is saved in the user's default Contacts folder.
NewDefaultItem	Creates and displays a new Outlook item. The item type is the default item type for the folder displayed in the control.
NewForm	Displays the Outlook Choose Form dialog box, allowing a user to create a new Outlook item by selecting a form from a forms library.
NewJournalEntry	Creates and displays a new Journal entry. If the control is displaying a Journal folder, when the new journal entry is saved, it is saved in the folder displayed in the control. Otherwise, the journal entry is saved in the user's default Journal folder.
NewMeetingRequest	Creates and displays a new meeting request. If the control is displaying a Calendar folder, when the meeting request is sent, the corresponding appointment is saved in the folder displayed in the control. Otherwise, the appointment is saved in the user's default Calendar folder. Responses to the meeting request are tallied only if the appointment is saved in the user's default Calendar folder.
NewMessage	Creates and displays a new e-mail message.

(continued)

(continued)

Method	Description
NewOfficeDocument	Displays the Outlook New Office Document dialog box. This method prompts the user to select the type of Office document to create, and then asks the user whether the document is to be sent as a mail message or posted to the folder displayed in the control.
NewPost	Creates and displays a new post item. When the user posts the message, it is posted to the folder displayed in the control. This method has no effect if the folder displayed in the control does not support messages.
NewTask	Creates and displays a new task. If the control is displaying a Tasks folder, when the new task is saved, it is saved in the folder displayed in the control. Otherwise, the task is saved in the user's default Tasks folder.
NewTaskRequest	Creates and displays a new task request.
Open	Opens the item or items currently selected in the control.
OpenSharedDefaultFolder	Displays a specified user's default folder in the control. This method takes two arguments. These arguments are the same as the arguments for the *GetSharedDefaultFolder* method of the Namespace object in the Outlook object model. An error occurs if the user running the control does not have permission to access the specified folder.
PrintItem	Prints the currently selected items in the control. If a group is selected, the items in the group are selected and printed. The Print dialog box is displayed to allow the user to specify how the items are to be printed.
Reply	Executes the Reply action for the selected item or items in the control.
ReplyAll	Executes the ReplyAll action for the selected item or items in the control.
ReplyInFolder	Creates a Post item for each currently selected message in the control. The Post item contains the text of the message it is replying to and has the same conversation topic.
SaveAs	Saves the selected items in the control as a file. The Save As dialog box is displayed to allow the user to select the location and format of the resulting file. If more than one item is selected, the items are concatenated and saved as a text file; otherwise, the user is allowed to choose from several file formats.
SendAndReceive	Sends messages in the Outbox folder and checks for new messages.
ShowFields	Displays the Outlook Show Fields dialog box, allowing the user to select the fields to be displayed in the current view in the control.
Sort	Displays the Outlook Sort dialog box, allowing the user to sort the contents of the control using multiple criteria.
SynchFolder	Synchronizes the displayed folder in the control for off-line use.

Obtaining Views For the Active Folder

One important piece of code behind the Outlook View Control user form is the *GetFolderViews* procedure. *GetFolderViews* returns a variant array that contains the views available in the folder displayed in the control. When a user clicks the Pick Folder button, she or he can select a different folder in the folders available to the current logged-on Outlook user.

The Advanced Explorer toolbar contains a control named Current View containing a list of the custom and built-in views available for a folder. First assign an object variable named *objCBCombo* to the object returned by objCB.Controls("Current View"), where *objCB* is an object variable referring to the Advanced toolbar. To obtain a variant array to return as *GetFolderViews*, iterate over the List property object of the *objCBCombo* variable to obtain each view name and assign that name to an element of the array. Once you have the variant array of folder views, you can assign that array in the List property of the cmbViews combo box on the form. The following listing shows you the *cmdPickFolder_Click* procedure and the supporting *GetFolderViews* function.

```
Private Sub cmdPickFolder_Click()
    On Error Resume Next
    Dim objNS As Outlook.NameSpace
    Dim objFolder As Outlook.MAPIFolder
    Set objNS = Application.GetNamespace("MAPI")
    Set objFolder = objNS.PickFolder
    If objFolder Is Nothing Then
        Exit Sub 'If user pressed cancel
    End If
    Set Application.ActiveExplorer.CurrentFolder = objFolder
    'Prevents cmbView_Change event from firing
    blnViewChange = True
    cmbView.Clear
    'Use GetFolderPath to convert MAPI folder to string
    OVCtl1.Folder = GetFolderPath(objFolder)
    Me.Caption = OVCtl1.Folder
    'Get views in the new folder
    cmbView.List = GetFolderViews(objFolder)
    If cmbView.List(0) = "" Then 'Handles error condition or no views
        cmbView.Value = ""
    Else
        cmbView.Value = OVCtl1.View
        If Err = 380 Then 'Invalid property assignment
            'View Control Active View Name is incorrect
            cmbView.Value = cmbView.List(0)
            OVCtl1.View = cmbView.List(0)
        End If
    End If
    'Done - allow cmbView_Change to fire
    blnViewChange = False
End Sub
```

```
Function GetFolderViews(objFolder As MAPIFolder) As Variant
    On Error Resume Next
    Dim objExpl As Explorer
    Dim objCB As CommandBar
    Dim objCBCombo As CommandBarComboBox
    Dim avarArray
    Set objExpl = Application.Explorers.Add(objFolder)
    Set objCB = objExpl.CommandBars("Advanced")
    Set objCBCombo = objCB.Controls("Current View")
    ReDim avarArray(objCBCombo.ListCount - 1)
    For i = 1 To objCBCombo.ListCount
        avarArray(i - 1) = objCBCombo.List(i)
    Next
    GetFolderViews = avarArray
End Function
```

Using the View Control in an HTML Page

One special feature of the Outlook View Control is that you can use it on an HTML page as well as on the page of an Outlook form. The control can be used in any of the environments listed in the table below. To use the control, Outlook 2000 must be installed on the target system. When the control is running purely within Internet Explorer, its scriptability is limited for security reasons. When you host the control within an HTML page with Internet Explorer as the container application, you will not be able to access the full Outlook Object Model programmatically.

Environment	Outlook 2000 Object Model Exposed
HTML Page in Internet Explorer 4.x or later running outside Outlook	No
HTML Page in Outlook 2000 Folder Home Page running in an Outlook Web View	Yes
Outlook 2000 Custom Form	Yes
Office 2000 UserForm	Yes
Visual Basic Form	Yes
Visual Basic DHTML Project	Yes

 The Northwind DHTML Application

While the Team Folder Wizard provides HTML pages that you can customize for a Team Folder application, you own application requirements might dictate that you create a customized Folder Home Page from scratch. Of course, this is somewhat of a misnomer because many of us know that part of being a good developer relates to knowing where to look for example code. All the code for the Northwind Folder Homepage DHTML

Project is included in a subfolder of the Customizing Folder Home Pages folder in the personal folders (.pst) file accompanying this book.

If you are comfortable with Visual Basic programming, you won't experience a difficult transition when you modify this DHTML project to satisfy your own needs. The Folder Home Page created by the DHTML project allows users of the Customers folder in the Northwind Contact Management Application to view Customer items in the Outlook View Control. Additionally the user can track sales by customer directly on the Folder Home Page and view order information in the Office 2000 PivotTable List by product category, order ID, or salesperson. This Folder Home Page responds to Outlook events (a selection change in the Outlook View Control) and provides an easy-to-navigate interface for folder users. Once you complete a DHTML project, you may be pleasantly surprised at how friendly the environment turns out to be.

What Is a DHTML Application?

A DHTML application is a Visual Basic application that uses a combination of Dynamic HTML and compiled Visual Basic code in an interactive, browser-based application. You compile your DHTML project into an ActiveX DLL that must be installed on each client system that runs your application. In contrast to a server-based Active Server Page (ASP) that executes within the process space of Internet Information Server, a DHTML application resides on the browser machine, where it interprets and responds to actions the end user performs in the browser. Since Outlook is an application that resides on the client and consumes client resources, a client-based DHTML application, the Outlook View Control, and Outlook 2000 are well matched. Here are some of the characteristics and requirements of DHTML applications used for Outlook 2000 Folder Home Pages:

- Requires Internet Explorer 4.x or later. This is generally not a problem since Internet Explorer 4.x or later is a required element of your Outlook 2000 installation.

- Supports use of the new Outlook View Control.

- Supports use of the new Office 2000 Web Components.

- Provides full access to the Outlook 2000 Object Model, including all the new events discussed in Chapter 9, "Raise Events and Move to the Head of the Class."

- Provides full access to the Dynamic HTML Object Model, including the events supported by DHTML.

- Installs with a Web-based setup provided by the Package and Installation Wizard.

If you compare the modification of an HTML-based Team Folder Home Page in Visual InterDev 6.0 or later with the modification of the Northwind Folder Home Page DHTML project in Visual Basic 6.0 or later, you'll appreciate the convenience and productivity inherent in the Visual Basic environment. A page designer in a Visual Basic DHTML project is analogous to the Connect Designer in a COM Add-in project or a class module in an ActiveX DLL. You can declare Outlook object variables using the WithEvents keyword in the code window of your page designer and use those object variables to respond to Outlook Application events.

> **More Info** See "The Dynamic HTML Object Model in Visual Basic" in the chapter entitled "Writing Code Using Dynamic HTML" in the Visual Basic 6.0 documentation for more information on the objects available in DHTML applications and their properties, methods, and events.

In addition to writing Visual Basic code integrated with a DHTML Web page, you can use a Visual Basic page designer to create Web pages that act as the user interface for your application. You can also import an existing HTML page into a Visual Basic DHTML project and use that page as the basis for your application. In fact, the DHTML page used for the Northwind DHTML Project was based on the design of the Folder Home Pages used in the Team Folder Wizard. Figure 14.16 shows the CMHomepage Folder Home Page project in the Visual Basic Editor.

> **Note** Due to some HTML editing limitations in the Visual Basic 6.0 Page Designer, it is recommended that you use another HTML editor such as FrontPage 2000 or Visual InterDev 6.0 to design the page. Once you have designed the page, you can import the HTML page into the Visual Basic Page Designer.

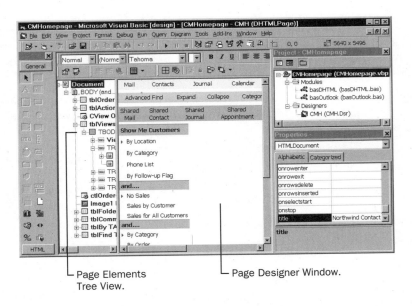

Page Elements Tree View.   Page Designer Window.

Figure 14.16 *CMHomepage Folder Home Page project in the Visual Basic Editor.*

Installing the Northwind DHTML Project

Before you install the Northwind DHTML project, you must install Visual Basic 6.0 Professional or Enterprise edition. You cannot load a DHTML project in Visual Basic 5.0.

To install and open the Northwind Folder Homepage DHTML project

1. Expand the folder 5. Advanced Topics of the Building Microsoft Outlook 2000 Applications personal folders (.pst) file.

2. Expand the Customizing Folder Home Pages folder and click the Northwind Folder Homepage DHTML folder.

3. Select all the files in the Northwind Folder Homepage DHTML folder.

4. Launch Windows Explorer and create a folder named Northwind Folder Homepage DHTML under the VB98 folder for Visual Basic 6.0. If you've selected the default installation, the VB98 folder is located in C:\Program Files\Microsoft Visual Studio\VB98.

5. Drag the files that you selected in step 3 to the Northwind Folder Homepage DHTML folder in the Windows Explorer. If you have problems dragging and dropping files, we've also included a self-extracting .zip file containing all the files in the Northwind Folder Homepage DHTML folder. Just double-click the CMHomepage.exe file and extract the files to the folder listed in step 4.

6. Launch Visual Basic and open the CMHomepage project in the folder you created in step 4.

Testing the Folder Home Page

Register CMHomepage.dll

To test the Folder Home Page for the DHTML Folder Home Page application properly, you must first register CMHomepage.dll using one of the options listed below. You must complete one of these options before you can establish a Folder Home Page for the Customers folder.

- You can load the CMHomepage project in Visual Basic 6.0 and compile CMHomepage.dll on your computer. This will register CMHomepage.dll in the registry on your system.

- You can run the regsvr32 utility to register CMhomepage.dll on your computer. This option assumes that you have Visual Basic 6.0 Professional or Enterprise edition installed on your computer.

- If you don't have Visual Basic 6.0 installed on your computer, you can run the Setup program included in the CMHomepage Setup folder under the Customizing Folder Home Pages folder. This Visual Basic 6.0 setup program will install the Contact Management Homepage.htm file and supporting .dll files into the CMHomepage directory on your computer. To use this option, you must drag the files in the CMHomepage setup folder to an empty folder on your hard disk.

Run the Setup program from this folder on your hard disk to set up the CMHomepage application. Do not attempt to run Setup from inside the folder in the Building Microsoft Outlook 2000 Applications personal folders (.pst) file.

Download the Microsoft Outlook View Control

Download the latest version of the Microsoft Outlook View control from *http://officeupdate.microsoft.com/outlook/*. If the View control is not installed on your computer, the Contact Management Homepage will not function correctly.

Install the Microsoft Office 2000 Web Components

The Contact Management Homepage requires the installation of the Office 2000 Web Components, which install by default in a typical Office 2000 installation. If the PivotTable List does not appear on the Contact Management Homepage when you load the page as a Folder Home Page, you must install the Web Components.

To install the Office 2000 Web Components

1. Insert the Office 2000 CD-ROM into your CD-ROM drive.
2. Click Start, click Settings, and then click Control Panel.
3. Double-click Add/Remove Programs.
4. On the Install/Uninstall page, click Microsoft Office 2000, and then click Add/Remove.
5. In the Microsoft Office 2000 Maintenance Mode dialog box, click Add Or Remove Features.
6. Double-click the Office Tools item to expand the item in the Microsoft Office 2000: Update Features dialog box.
7. Click the Office Web Components item under Office Tools to expand the item.
8. Select Run from My Computer.
9. Click Update Now to complete the installation of Web Components.

Set the Folder Home Page For the Customers Folder

Assuming that you've followed the instructions above to install the correct components on your computer, you can set the Folder Home Page for the Customers folder. The instructions below assume that you will set the Folder Home Page for the Customers folder in the Building Microsoft Outlook 2000 Applications personal folders (.pst) file. Test the Folder Home Page locally before you attempt to establish a Folder Home Page for the Northwind Contact Management application in public folders on your Microsoft Exchange Server.

To set a Folder Home Page for the Customers Folder

1. In the Folder List, right-click the Customers folder in the Northwind Contact Management folder under folder 6. Sample Applications, and then click Properties on the shortcut menu.

2. Click the Home Page tab.

3. Check the Show Home Page By Default For This Folder box.

4. Enter the URL for the Folder Home Page in the Address edit box. If you installed the CMHomepage application using the setup program, click the Browse button and look in the C:\Program Files\CMHomepage folder for a file named Contact Management Homepage.htm. If you installed the Northwind DHTML project into a different folder, you'll need to use the Browse button to locate Contact Management Homepage.htm in a different folder.

5. Click OK.

Navigate to the Customers Folder

You should now be able to navigate to the Customers folder and see the Contact Management Homepage HTML page displayed in an Outlook Web view. Here are some features of the application that you'll want to test.

Using the View Control

- Double-clicking an item in the Outlook View control will open the item
- Right-clicking the Outlook View control will display shortcut menus

Using the Command Buttons

- Clicking the buttons on the Navigation bar (at the top of the page) will bring you to a subfolder of the Customers folder. For example, clicking the Journal button brings you to the Shared Journal folder. To return to the Customers folder, click the Previous Folder button (left-pointing arrow) on Outlook Explorer's Advanced toolbar.

- Click the commands in the Command bar (second from the top of the page) to carry out the command. For example, select a customer in the View control and then click the Flag button to flag a customer for follow-up.

- Click the commands in the Shared Items bar (third from the top of the page) in order to carry out the command. For example, select a customer and then click the Shared Journal button to create a Shared Journal Item for the selected customer.

Working the PivotTable List To Display Customer Sales Information

- If you select a customer in the View control, you can click Sales By Customer in the left frame of the page and the Office 2000 PivotTable List will appear and display sales information for the selected customer. If you click any of the different ordering options for the PivotTable List (By Category, By Order, or By Salesperson), the control will display data for the selected customer using the order you specified.

- If you click Sales By All Customers in the upper And... list, the PivotTable List will display data for all customers using the ordering option specified in the Order By list (the lower And... list). Click the No Sales option to redisplay the Outlook View Control.

Finding Items

- Enter a find string in the edit box above the Find and Reset buttons to display a subset of customers in the View control. The string you type in the Find edit box imposes a Contains restriction on the View control when you click the Find button, which is applied against the Customer company name. For example, if you enter the word *The* in the edit box and then click Find, all customer names containing that word will appear in the View control.

- Click the Reset button to display all the items in the current view in the Customers folder.

Running the Project in Visual Basic

You should open the CMHomepage project in Visual Basic before you go over this section of the chapter. If DHTML application concepts are foreign to you, going over the code in the project step-by-step will help understand how a DHTML project is built and what you can do with this type of application. As you can see from the Project Explorer window shown in Figure 14.16, the CMHomepage project consists of two code modules, basOutlook and basDHTML, and one Designer, CMH.dsr. The Designer is where most of the action is from a programming perspective. In DHTML applications, there are two top-level objects analogous to the Application and Document objects in the Word 2000 Object Model. Equivalent top-level DHTML objects are the BaseWindow and Document objects.

The BaseWindow Object

The BaseWindow object represents an instance of Internet Explorer and is used to display the Document object. Important events for the BaseWindow object are the onload and onunload events. The following code hides the PivotTable List and initializes global variables during the BaseWindow onload event. The onresize event is also a key event. It's analogous to the Form_Resize event for Visual Basic Forms. When this event occurs, you can reposition elements on the page, depending on the size of the Document window.

```
Private Sub BaseWindow_onload()
    Set gobjView = Document.All("CView")
    Set gobjOrders = Document.All("ctlOrders")
    'Hide PivotTable List
    gobjOrders.Style.display = "None"
    'Establish global settings
    gintView = 1
    gintBy = gByCategory
    gintState = gStateNoSales
    Call BaseWindow_onresize
End Sub
```

Note Most events in the Dynamic HTML Object Model are similar to the events in the Visual Basic programming model. Event names are different in one important respect. All event names in Dynamic HTML are preceded by the word *on*. For additional differences, see the "Document Object Model" in the Dynamic HTML section of the Internet Client SDK for a complete listing of the properties, methods, and events available in an HTML page through the Microsoft HTML Object Library.

Caution When the BaseWindow object unloads and the DHTMLPage onunload event fires, you should set all object variables to Nothing to prevent Outlook from remaining in memory.

The Document Object

The Document object represents the HTML page you view in the browser. You use events in the Document object to access the Dynamic HTML Object Model and handle user actions in the browser. In the sample project, the two important Document events are onmouseout and onmouseover. These events help to set a style for an element on the page by toggling the class name of the element. For example, when you move your mouse over a command button, the text in the button turns red because the classname changes from Action to ActionMOver. This highlighting occurs due to the different styles defined in the Contact Management Homepage HTML page.

If you assign style names to a classname property, you can change all the style attributes of the given element by toggling classnames. If you elect to store your styles in the Page Designer page rather than in an external cascading style sheet (.css) file, you can edit the styles in FrontPage 2000. Figure 14.17 shows the Style dialog box in FrontPage 2000. FrontPage provides HTML editor capabilities not found in the Visual Basic Page Designer.

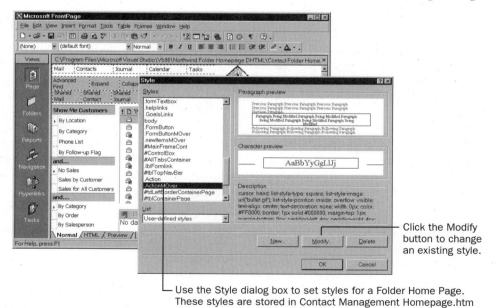

Click the Modify button to change an existing style.

Use the Style dialog box to set styles for a Folder Home Page. These styles are stored in Contact Management Homepage.htm rather than in an external .css file.

Figure 14.17 *Use the FrontPage 2000 Editor to modify styles in your Folder Home Page.*

> **More Info** For more information on the Style collection or other style-related properties in Dynamic HTML, see "Dynamic HTML" in the Internet Client SDK available on MSDN at *http://msdn.microsoft.com/developer/*.

```
Private Sub Document_onmouseout()
    Select Case BaseWindow.event.srcElement.className
        Case "ActionMOver"
            BaseWindow.event.srcElement.className = "Action"
        Case "ViewButtonMOver"
            BaseWindow.event.srcElement.className = "ViewButton"
        Case "FormButtonMOver"
            BaseWindow.event.srcElement.className = "FormButton"
    End Select
End Sub

Private Sub Document_onmouseover()
    Select Case BaseWindow.event.srcElement.className
        Case "Action"
            BaseWindow.event.srcElement.className = "ActionMOver"
        Case "ViewButton"
            BaseWindow.event.srcElement.className = "ViewButtonMOver"
        Case "FormButton"
            BaseWindow.event.srcElement.className = "FormButtonMOver"
    End Select
End Sub
```

The DHTMLPage Object

The DHTMLPage object is contained by the Document object, and represents a run-time utility that links the page to its Visual Basic code in CMHomepage.dll when the application runs. The DHTMLPage object provides load, unload, initialize, and terminate events for your HTML pages. You cannot access the DHTMLPage object directly through the Document object. In the CMHomepage project, the DHTMLPage Load and Unload events are used to create and destroy two important Outlook objects, gobjOutlook and gobjActiveExplorer. These objects correspond to an Outlook Application and Explorer object, respectively. The gobjActiveExplorer object is declared WithEvents in the declarations section of the CMH Designer module. Once you've declared gobjActiveExplorer using WithEvents, you can write Outlook event procedure code to respond to the full gamut of Explorer object events.

The other noteworthy piece of code in the DHTML_Load procedure shown next is the assignment of the View control's Folder property to the folder path of the current folder for the ActiveExplorer object. Since the View control is hosted in a Folder Home Page, the current folder is, in fact, the folder hosting the Folder Home Page. If you don't set a Folder property for the View control, it will display the contents of your Inbox instead of the target folder. Rather than hard-coding the folder path into the application, this technique lets you retrieve the current folder path with the familiar *GetFolderPath* function and assign the folder path string to the View control's Folder property.

> **More Info** For additional information on Outlook events, see Chapter 9, "Raise Events and Move to the Head of the Class."

```
Private Sub DHTMLPage_Load()
    On Error Resume Next
    Set gobjOutlook = CView.OutlookApplication
    Set gobjActiveExplorer = gobjOutlook.ActiveExplorer
    'Use GetFolderPath to retrieve path of current folder
    'This assumes that this page will only be viewed when
    'user navigates to Customers folder
    'Relative rather than absolute path
    CView.Folder = GetFolderPath(gobjActiveExplorer.CurrentFolder)
    CView.View = "By Location"
End Sub

Private Sub DHTMLPage_Unload()
    Set gobjView = Nothing
    Set gobjOrders = Nothing
    Set gobjActiveExplorer = Nothing
    Set gobjOutlook = Nothing
End Sub
```

> **More Info** For additional information about the sequence and significance of load and unload events in a DHTML application, see the page entitled "Key Events in DHTML Applications" in Visual Basic 6.0 Help.

Writing Outlook Event Procedures in a DHTML Project

The SelectionChange event lets you respond to a change in the selected item in the Outlook View control. Note that you can only use the Explorer SelectionChange event to determine the selected item when the Outlook View control is hosted in a Folder Home Page Web view in Outlook. If you are using the View control in an Outlook form or a VBA UserForm, it is impossible to determine the selected item. The selected item in the Outlook ActiveExplorer can differ from the selected item in the Outlook View control. Unfortunately, the Outlook View control does not expose a Selection property object of its own. This limitation makes the control less versatile than the Outlook development community would have hoped. In the example below, the PivotTable List is refreshed with customer-specific data whenever the user changes their Customer selection in the View control. This type of dynamic link between database information and data stored in public folders gives Folder Home Pages a special and unique appeal. You can quickly create a rich, versatile DHTML page for every folder in your application where the combined display of RDBMS and MAPI data is appropriate.

```
Private Sub gobjActiveExplorer_SelectionChange()
    Dim ActView As PivotView
    Dim fldSets As PivotFieldSets
    Dim item As ContactItem
    Dim Tot As GroupingDef
    On Error Resume Next
```

```
            If gobjActiveExplorer.selection.Count <> 1 Then
                'Can't deal with multiple selection
                Exit Sub
        End If
        'Get selected item in View Control
        'You should only assume that the ActiveExplorer
        'will return the selected item when the View control
        'is hosted by a Folder Home Page.
        Set item = gobjActiveExplorer.selection.item(1)
        If Not gintState = gStateNoSales Then
            If gobjActiveExplorer.selection.Count = 1 Then
                'Create dynamic SQL string with Customer Account
                ctlOrders.CommandText = gstrSQL _
                    & "  WHERE Orders.CustomerID = '" _
                    & item.Account & "'"
                Set ActView = ctlOrders.ActiveView
                ActView.TitleBar.Caption = item.CompanyName
                Set fldSets = ActView.FieldSets
                Set item = Nothing
                Select Case gintBy
                    Case gByCategory
                        'Group by Category
                        Call ActView.RowAxis.InsertFieldSet(fldSets("CategoryName"))
                        'Row data
                        Call ActView.DataAxis.InsertFieldSet(fldSets("OrderID"))
                        Call ActView.DataAxis.InsertFieldSet(fldSets("OrderDate"))
                        Call ActView.DataAxis.InsertFieldSet(fldSets("ShippedDate"))
                        Call ActView.DataAxis.InsertFieldSet(fldSets("ProductName"))
                        Call ActView.DataAxis.InsertFieldSet(fldSets("Quantity"))
                        Call ActView.DataAxis.InsertFieldSet(fldSets("Total"))
                    Case gByOrder
                        'Group by OrderID
                        Call ActView.RowAxis.InsertFieldSet(fldSets("OrderId"))
                        'Row data
                        Call ActView.DataAxis.InsertFieldSet(fldSets("OrderDate"))
                        Call ActView.DataAxis.InsertFieldSet(fldSets("ProductName"))
                        Call ActView.DataAxis.InsertFieldSet(fldSets("UnitPrice"))
                        Call ActView.DataAxis.InsertFieldSet(fldSets("Quantity"))
                        Call ActView.DataAxis.InsertFieldSet(fldSets("Discount"))
                        Call ActView.DataAxis.InsertFieldSet(fldSets("Total"))
                    Case gBySalesperson
                        'Group by Salesperson LastName
                        Call ActView.RowAxis.InsertFieldSet(fldSets("LastName"))
                        'Row data
                        Call ActView.DataAxis.InsertFieldSet(fldSets("OrderID"))
                        Call ActView.DataAxis.InsertFieldSet(fldSets("OrderDate"))
                        Call ActView.DataAxis.InsertFieldSet(fldSets("ShippedDate"))
                        Call ActView.DataAxis.InsertFieldSet(fldSets("ProductName"))
                        Call ActView.DataAxis.InsertFieldSet(fldSets("Quantity"))
                        Call ActView.DataAxis.InsertFieldSet(fldSets("Total"))
                End Select
                'Add a total
```

```
            fldSets("Total").Fields(0).NumberFormat = "Currency"
            Set Tot = ActView.AddTotal _
                ("Total ", fldSets("Total").Fields.item(0), _
                ctlOrders.Constants.plFunctionSum)
            Call ActView.DataAxis.InsertTotal(Tot)
        End If
      Else
      Set item = Nothing
    End If
End Sub
```

> **Note** Before you respond to events for Outlook-based object variables in your
> DHTMLPage code, you must be certain that you use the References command
> on the Visual Basic Project menu to set a reference for the Microsoft Outlook 9.0
> Object Library.

Writing Code for DHTML Events

Writing code for DHTML events is very similar to writing code for Visual Basic events, in fact, it's almost the same process. Unlike the pure DHTML environments in Visual InterDev or the Microsoft Script Editor, you are writing event procedures in Visual Basic rather than VBScript. The DHTMLPage object knows which elements have been placed on your HTML page and creates object variables in the Designer code window that correspond to the ID properties of the elements on the page. Unlike Visual Basic, the ID property—rather than the name property—uniquely identifies an element in a DHTML application.

The Contact Management Homepage displays a Help button in the upper-right corner of the page. When a user clicks this button for help, another Explorer window opens to display the Help page. You should not attempt to navigate from within the Folder Home Page itself. Use the BaseWindow *Open* method to open a separate Internet Explorer window to display help. The code below shows you how to open a Help window when a user clicks a button on the page. The Help window illustrated in Figure 14.18 has been created without a toolbar, navigation buttons, and status bar. The important concept is to keep things clean and simple.

```
Private Function btnHelp_onclick() As Boolean
    Dim strFeatures As String
    strFeatures = "toolbar = no, location = no, status = no, " _
        & "width = 400, height = 400, resizable= yes, scrollbars = yes"
    Document.open "CMHelp.htm", "HelpWindow", strFeatures
End Function
```

Using Tables To Contain Command Buttons

Another interesting feature of the Contact Management Homepage HTML page is the use of an HTML table element to contain command buttons. In a sense, these table containers are analogous to the CommandBar object that represents an Office toolbar. If you need to add additional commands to the table, you can add additional columns to the table either at Design time or run time. With the exception of the Dial Phone button, the Create Shared

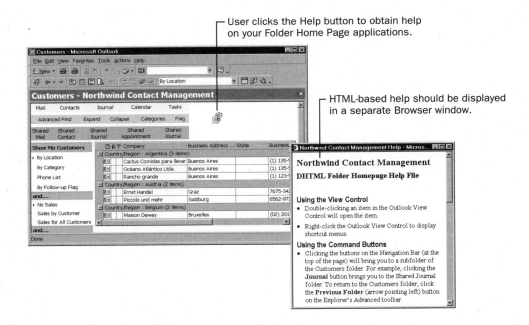

User clicks the Help button to obtain help on your Folder Home Page applications.

HTML-based help should be displayed in a separate Browser window.

Figure 14.18 *Open a Folder Home Page Help window in a separate browser window.*

Items toolbar that serves as a COM Add-in example from Chapter 13, "Creating COM Add-Ins with Visual Basic," has been duplicated here. This code uses a Select statement to examine the innerHTML property (equivalent to a Visual Basic Caption or Text property) and then calls the appropriate procedure to execute the command.

```
Private Function tblActions_onclick() As Boolean
    Select Case BaseWindow.event.srcElement.innerHTML
        Case "Shared Contact"
            Call ButtonClick(olContactItem)
        Case "Shared Mail"
            Call ButtonClick(olMailItem)
        Case "Shared Journal"
            Call ButtonClick(olJournalItem)
        Case "Shared Appointment"
            Call ButtonClick(olAppointmentItem)
        Case "Shared Task"
            Call ButtonClick(olTaskItem)
    End Select
End Function
```

To leverage the existing code for the Northwind Contact Management Application, I've copied the code almost in its entirety from the Outlook VBA modules described in E-Chapter 3, "The Northwind Contact Management Application" on the companion CD, to the CMHomePage project. That code won't be reproduced here because it has been covered in previous chapters. The ease of conversion should alert you to the power of Outlook VBA as a prototyping environment for both COM Add-in and DHTML applications.

> **Caution** If you copy code from one Outlook programming environment to another, be certain that you reference the top-level Application object consistently or adjust your code to account for different names. For example, the CMHomepage project uses gobjOutlook to refer to the Outlook Application object. The basNorthwind module uses the intrinsic Outlook Application object. Like a COM Add-in, there is no intrinsic Outlook Application object available in a DHTML project. You must create your own Outlook Application object variable.

Using Methods and Properties of the Outlook View Control

The Outlook View control is Outlook's surrogate in a Folder Home Page. It contains many more methods than properties so that you can execute safe Outlook commands from within the HTML page. One of the interesting properties of the View control is the Restriction property. This corresponds to the *Restrict* method in the Outlook object model. The View control is somewhat unique in that its Restrict property acts as a "like" clause in a SQL statement. Instead of testing for equivalence, the Restriction property creates a subset of items that meet the condition specified in the restriction. Figure 14.19 shows the results of applying a restriction for the word *The* to the customer items in the Customers folder of the Northwind Contact Management application. To reset the View control back to all the items displayed in the current view, assign the empty string to the Restriction property. The code below demonstrates these techniques.

```
Private Function BtnFind_onclick() As Boolean
    Dim Myfield As String
    Dim strRestrict As String
    On Error Resume Next
    Myfield = "[CompanyName]"
    If txtSearchString.Value = "" Then
        strRestrict = ""
    Else
        strRestrict = Myfield & " = " & txtSearchString.Value
    End If

    Cview.Restriction = strRestrict
End Function

Private Function BtnShowAll_onclick() As Boolean
    Cview.Restriction = ""
    txtSearchString.Value = ""
End Function
```

Maintaining State in a DHTML Application

Like all browser-based applications, DHTML applications do not maintain state. This means that if a user navigates away from your Folder Home Page using the Folder List and then

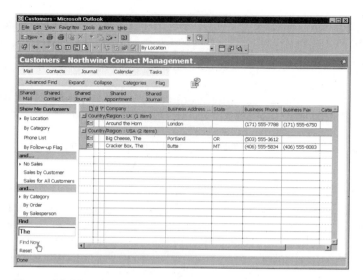

Figure 14.19 *Restrict causes a subset of items to be displayed in the Outlook View Control.*

returns to the folder that hosts your page, the page must be reloaded and no state is maintained between the initial display and redisplay of the page. For example, let's say that your application design requires that the DHTML application remember the user's preference in the Orders table. If the user leaves the page with a view that shows Sales By Customer (meaning that both the Outlook View control and the PivotTable List are displayed simultaneously), how can you recreate the state of the page when a user returns to your Folder Home Page? The answer is found in cookies. A client-side cookie helps your DHTML application to maintain state. A cookie represents a small packet of information used to store persistent state information on the hard disk of a user's computer. Use the *GetProperty* and *SetProperty* functions in the basDHTML module to set and get state values. This is one piece of code that is not included in the CMHomepage project.

Compiling Your DHTML Application

Our tour of the CMHomepage application has come to an end. You should consult the DHTML application help for additional information regarding testing and debugging techniques for a DHTML application. You should develop and debug the Outlook portion of your code in Outlook VBA before you move it to a Folder Home Page DHTML application. If you decide to modify the existing CMHomepage application, you will need to recompile the ActiveX DLL that supports the Page Designer HTML page.

To compile your DHTML application

1. If the project is in Run mode, click the End button to return to Design mode.
2. Set the BuildFile property to the full path and file name to which you want to build the project. By default, the BuildFile property is set to the value of the

SourceFile property. Click the DHTML Page Designer Properties button on the toolbar of the Page Designer window to set BuildFile and SourceFile properties in the Properties window.

3. On the File menu, click Make CMHomepage.dll to open the Make Project dialog box. Click OK to make the DLL file.

Deploying Your Folder Home Page

The Package and Deployment Wizard

Once you have developed, debugged, and secured your DHTML application, you can create an installation setup program with the Visual Studio 6.0 Package and Deployment Wizard. When you use Visual Basic 6.0 and the Package and Deployment Wizard, all registration chores for your DHTML application are handled for you automatically. There are, however, some unique considerations that apply to DHTML application deployments on your Web.

Web-Based Setup

When a user accesses the Web page associated with your DHTML application, she might not have the required components to run the application installed on her system. The solution to this problem is to use a Web-based setup that works in conjunction with the HTML page specified as the Folder Home Page for the application folder. Using a Web-based setup, the system downloads ActiveX components and dependent files to the user's computer. Internet Component Download—a feature of Internet Explorer 3.0 or later—causes the package to be verified for safety, unpacked, registered, installed, and then activated. The downloading occurs in the background and is controlled by the browser. User intervention is kept to a minimum or is nonexistent, depending on Internet Explorer security settings. The most compelling feature of a Web-based setup is that it lends itself to use with Folder Home Pages. You can design a Folder Home Page for the top-level folder in an Exchange Public Folder application. When a user navigates to that folder, she reads instructions for using the application and Web-based setup automatically installs all the COM Add-ins, ActiveX controls, or DHTML Page Designer components required for the application.

Packaging a Folder Home Page Application

To create a Web-based setup, use the Visual Studio 6.0 Package and Deployment Wizard. The wizard will create a cabinet-based setup that you can then deploy to a shared directory on your network or to a Web server on your intranet.

To package a Folder Home Page application

1. Launch the Visual Studio 6.0 Package And Deployment Wizard from the Microsoft Visual Studio Tools folder under Microsoft Visual Studio 6.0 from Programs on the Start menu.

2. Click the Package icon on the Package And Deployment Wizard Startup dialog box shown in Figure 14.20.

3. Select Internet Package in the Package Type list box. Click Next.

4. Choose the folder where the package will be assembled. Click Next.

5. Select files to be included in your package. Click Next. You must select the DHTML Application ActiveX component and mshtmpgr.dll, in addition to any additional ActiveX controls required by your Folder Home Page application. If you inspect Figure 14.21, you'll see that outlctlx.dll (the Microsoft Outlook View control) is also selected for download. The Microsoft Outlook 9.0 Object Library (msooutl9.olb) and the Microsoft Office Web Components 9.0 Object Library (msowc.dll) are deselected because these components will install by default in a typical installation of Outlook 2000. They do not need to be reinstalled by your Web-based setup. Click Next.

6. Determine which files will be packaged in the .cab file created by the wizard and which files will be downloaded from alternate sites. When you package a Folder Home Page application, it is strongly suggested that you download all components from your own intranet rather than going to a remote site where Internet traffic might delay or disrupt the download. For example, the wizard will default to downloading VB6 run-time files from a Microsoft site. Figure 14.22 shows the File Source dialog box for the wizard. Because you already have the latest versions of these run-times (keep downloading those Service Packs) on your development machine, you should let the wizard package the

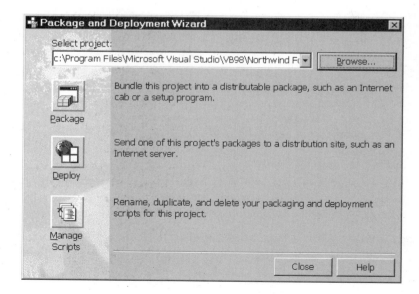

Figure 14.20 *The Visual Studio 6.0 Package And Deployment Wizard.*

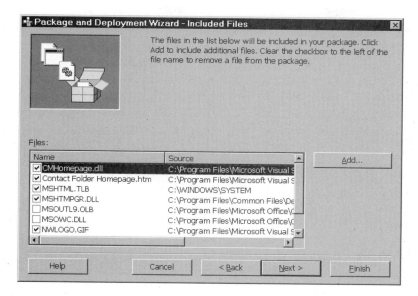

Figure 14.21 *Selecting DHTML Folder Home Page Application files with the Visual Studio 6.0 Package And Deployment Wizard.*

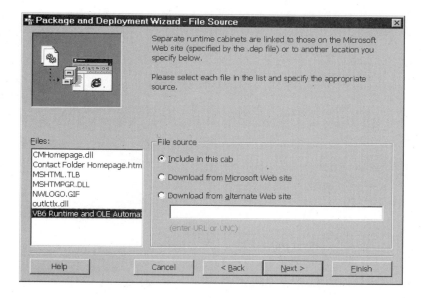

Figure 14.22 *The Package And Deployment Wizard File Selection dialog box.*

VB6 run-time files to your .cab file, rather than downloading them on the Web. Click Next.

7. Create safety settings for your DHTML Application. Because you will use the Folder Home Page application on your intranet, mark the component safe for scripting and safe for initialization. Click Next.

8. Provide a script name or accept the default in the wizard's final dialog box. Click Finish to create your Web-based installation package.

9. Once you have created the .cab file for your package, you should digitally sign the package to guarantee to Internet Explorer that the package is secure.

More Info For additional information on signing the .cab file created by the Package And Deployment Wizard, see the Internet Client SDK on MSDN or visit *http://msdn.microsoft.com/developer/*.

Adding a CODEBASE Tag

In a Web-based setup, the Package And Deployment Wizard creates a cabinet file and a Web page so that your DHTML component can be downloaded from your corporate intranet. The Package And Deployment Wizard usually creates a CODEBASE tag in a separate HTML page when it creates a Web-based setup package for an ActiveX component such as a COM Add-in. This is not the case when you package a DHTML application; the Package And Deployment Wizard does not create a separate HTML page with a CODEBASE tag. It inserts the correct CODEBASE tag into the Page Designer HTML page when you create and deploy your package with the wizard. The following CODEBASE tag was inserted into Contact Management Homepage.htm when the CMHomepage project was packaged into CMHomepage.CAB:

```
<BODY bottomMargin=0 leftMargin=0 rightMargin=0 topMargin=0>
<!--METADATA TYPE="MsHtmlPageDesigner" startspan-->
<OBJECT codebase=CMHomepage.CAB#Version1,0,0,1 id="DHTMLPage2"
classid="clsid:BA083848-CB62-11D2-A1B3-0080C70ED36E" width=0 height=0>
</object><!--METADATA TYPE="MsHtmlPageDesigner" endspan-->
```

Before Deploying a Folder Home Page Application

There are some prerequisite steps you must follow before you deploy a Folder Home Page application. These steps assume that you have already developed, debugged, and published the Outlook custom forms that you will use in your application.

More Info For additional information on installing Outlook custom forms, see Chapter 12, "Distribute and Maintain Applications."

➔ **Complete these steps before you deploy your Folder Home Page**

1. Set the appropriate Exchange Public Folder permissions for users of your application.

2. Identify the virtual directory or network file share where you will place the Contact Management Homepage.htm file and its associated .cab file created by the Package And Deployment Wizard in the steps below.

3. Set the Folder Home Page URL on the Home Page tab of the Folder Properties dialog box and check the Show Home Page By Default For This Folder check box.

The Folder Home Page URL set on the Home Page tab in the Folder Properties dialog box is not an administrative setting from an Exchange Server perspective. Individual users can access the Home Page tab and turn off a Folder Home Page or erase the URL by clicking the Restore Defaults button on the Home Page tab. If you don't want the user to be able to turn off the Folder Home Page for your application folder, you can write a COM Add-in that uses the BeforeFolderSwitch event to set the WebViewURL and WebViewOn properties of your application folder to the desired settings. Unlike a Folder Home Page, you can lock down COM Add-ins with system policies and the Office 2000 Custom Installation Wizard to prevent users from disabling or changing COM Add-ins.

Deploying a Folder Home Page Application

At this point you should have packaged your application with the Package And Deployment Wizard. The final step is to actually deploy the Web-based setup package to a Web server or to a shared directory on your network.

To deploy a Folder Home Page application

1. Launch the Package And Deployment Wizard.

2. Click the Deploy icon on the Package And Deployment Wizard Startup dialog box shown in Figure 14.20.

3. Select the Package To Deploy. The Package name should correspond to the package name you supplied in step 8 under "Packaging a Folder Home Page Application." Click Next.

4. Select a Deployment method. You can deploy to a Web site or to a network file share. In either case, you will have to identify the Web site or the shared directory that you identified under step 2 of "Before Deploying a Folder Home Page Application." Click Next.

5. If you've selected a folder-based deployment, select the shared folder where you will deploy the Folder Home Page and the .cab file. You can click Finish to complete a folder-based deployment at this time. The following steps apply only to a Web-based deployment

6. Select the Items To Deploy. Click Next.

7. Select Additional Items To Deploy. If you have any .gif or .jpeg images that require deployment, select them in this step. Click Next.

8. Enter a destination URL and select a publishing protocol in the Web Publishing dialog box. Click Next.

9. Enter a name for your deployment package and click Finish. Your Folder Home Page application will be deployed using the method you selected.

Checking Browser Security Settings and Testing the Installation Package

It's now time to test your Folder Home Page application on a clean machine before you roll the application out to users.

More Info For information on establishing a clean machine for testing purposes, see "Testing Component Download on Clean Machines" in the chapter entitled "Building Internet Applications" in the Visual Basic on-line documentation.

Before you test the application, you should make sure that Internet Explorer security settings on the client are set correctly. You don't want a flurry of alert messages and dialog boxes to appear when a user navigates to the public folder containing your Folder Home Page application.

To check browser security settings

1. Select Options from the Outlook Tools menu.
2. Click the Security page in the Tools Options dialog box.
3. Click the Zone Settings button on the Security page.
4. Click the Local intranet icon and then click the Custom Settings button. If you have not signed your Folder Home Page .cab file, then you should click the Enable option for Download Unsigned ActiveX Controls. See Figure 14.23 for an illustration of the Custom Settings and Security dialog boxes.
5. Click OK three times to dismiss all the dialog boxes.

To test a Folder Home Page application on a clean machine

1. Start Outlook.
2. Open the Folder List by clicking the Folder List button on the Advanced toolbar.
3. Navigate to the application folder for your Folder Home Page in the Folder List. All the components required to display the Folder Home Page should download to the client computer and the Folder Home Page should display.

Note Some components might post a message indicating that the system must be restarted in order to complete the installation. Your testing should include a determination whether rebooting is required to correctly install all components for your Folder Home Page application.

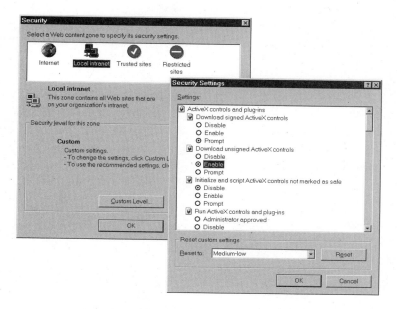

Figure 14.23 *Checking Internet Explorer Security Settings.*

Where To Go from Here

For additional information about the subjects discussed in this chapter, see the following resources.

Creating ActiveX Components in Microsoft Visual Basic

Appleman, Dan. *Developing COM/ActiveX Components with Visual Basic 6.0 —A Guide to the Perplexed.* Indianapolis, IN: Macmillan Computer Publishing, 1998.

Creating PivotTable Reports

Microsoft Corporation. "Retrieving and Analyzing Data," Chapter 15 in *Microsoft Office 2000/Visual Basic Programmer's Guide.* Redmond, WA: Microsoft Press, 1999.

Deploying Components

Downloading Code on the Web
http://www.microsoft.com/workshop/components/downcode.asp/

Installing Windows Applications via the Web with Visual Studio 6.0
http://www.microsoft.com/workshop/components/vsappinstall/install.asp/

Microsoft Corporation. "Designing and Deploying Office Solutions," Chapter 2 in *Microsoft Office 2000/Visual Basic Programmer's Guide.* Redmond, WA: Microsoft Press, 1999.

DHTML

Isaacs, Scott. *Inside Dynamic HTML*. Redmond, WA: Microsoft Press, 1997.

HTML Reference Help (C:\Program Files\Microsoft Visual Studio \Common\IDE\IDE98\MSE\1033\Htmlref.chm).

Microsoft Corporation. "Custom Classes and Objects," Chapter 9 in *Microsoft Office 2000/Visual Basic Programmer's Guide*. Redmond, WA: Microsoft Press, 1999.

Microsoft Site Builder Workshop Web site *http://www.microsoft.com/workshop/default.asp/*.

Simpson, Alan. *Official Microsoft Internet Explorer 4 Site Builder Toolkit*. Redmond, WA: Microsoft Press, 1998.

Working with Visual InterDev and DHTML

Duthie, Andrew G. *Microsoft Visual InterDev 6.0 Enterprise Developer's Workshop*. Redmond, WA: Microsoft Press, 1998.

Evans, Nicholas D; Miller, Ken; Spencer, Ken. *Programming Microsoft Visual InterDev 6.0*. Redmond, WA: Microsoft Press, 1999.

Understanding DHTML, Cascading Style Sheets, and Scripting

Microsoft Corporation. "Using Web Technologies," Chapter 12 in *Microsoft Office 2000/Visual Basic Programmer's Guide*. Redmond, WA: Microsoft Press, 1999.

Chapter 15
Outlook Data Access Strategies

In This Chapter

Data storage, retrieval, and manipulation constitute an enormous subject. A comprehensive, up-to-date review of this topic is available in the *Microsoft Office 2000/Visual Basic Programmer's Guide,* which devotes some excellent chapters to the discussion of database design concepts and the current data access tools available to you as an Office 2000 developer. The examples discussed here cover basic techniques for data retrieval and display in Outlook forms and introduce some options that are new to Outlook 2000. The intention is to provide some answers to one of the most frequently asked questions in the Outlook newsgroups: How do I handle data in Outlook?

Whether the Outlook application you build is simple or complex, early in the design process you may need to consider how to incorporate external data. You might want to display a simple client list or look up values for a location based on the postal code the user enters. Perhaps the information you need is static; possibly it changes at regular and predictable intervals; or it could be constantly in flux. In some cases, the information changes in response to your application. In this chapter, we will examine some techniques for handling external data in Outlook/Exchange applications.

Connecting with Data Sources

Before getting into the details of some of the available options, we need to review some of the constraints in Outlook applications that affect your design decisions.

Design Trade-Offs

A Balance of Speed, Power, and Agility

The standard Outlook forms you will be using to build any application are very light, and they load quickly. This is obviously desirable in terms of performance and storage requirements. It takes careful planning to avoid bloating your custom forms or stretching out load times in the process of bringing in external data. Users won't be happy waiting for a grid to fill with ten years of sales data when they just use the form to check phone numbers.

That's Great, But Does It Work Offline?

The demand for data in an Outlook application often correlates directly with the number of disconnected users the application must serve. The fact that this is a common problem doesn't make it easy to solve. We'll cover a few ways to address this later on. It's very important to stress this issue early in the design process, so you don't waste many hours on a very cool way to import data that breaks your application for the users who will need it most.

It's Got Data in It—Is It a Database?

A word of caution: you should avoid trying to use Outlook as a front-end for a database. The Outlook client is designed to interface with the unstructured storage of an Exchange Server or personal folders file information store, and it does that very well. There are many ways, as we will see, to display data within Outlook to enhance its effectiveness. Trying to make an Outlook solution conform to the requirements of a relational database management system does not usually produce a successful application.

Basic Methods of Displaying Data in a Form

Before we get into external data sources, let's cover some of the most basic ways to display data in an Outlook form.

Populating Lists

The most straightforward way to populate a list is simply to type in a semicolon-delimited string of values on the Properties page of the combo or list box (see Figure 15.1). Once the list exceeds three or four items, this approach can become very tedious, and with large lists, it's easy to make mistakes because you can't see all the items at once.

One solution is to use the *AddItem* method of the combo box or list box control, and input the values in Visual Basic Scripting Edition (VBScript) code. If the list remains constant, you will only have to load it once—during the form's Item_Open event. It's not unusual for the list values in one control to be determined by the selected value in another control; in these cases, you will need to dynamically reload the list. The Library Materials form illustrated in Figure 15.2 uses this technique, and is also shown in the *Item_CustomPropertyChange* procedure on page 594.

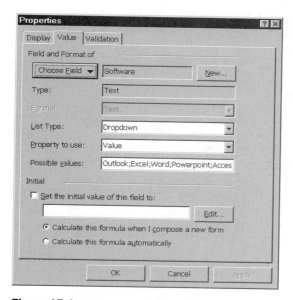

Figure 15.1 *Enter a semicolon-delimited list in the Possible Values text box on the Value tab of the Properties dialog box.*

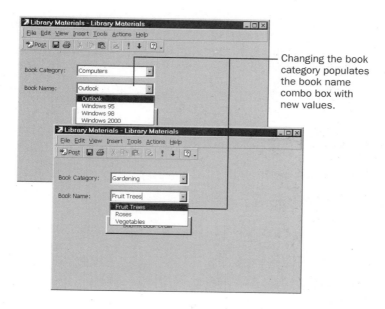

Figure 15.2 *The items in a list change based on the selection in another list.*

```
Sub Item_CustomPropertyChange(ByVal Name)
    Set MyPage = GetInspector.ModifiedFormPages("Orders")
    Set MyControl = MyPage.Controls("BookName")
    If Name = "Book Category" Then
        Select Case Userproperties("Book Category")
            Case "Computers"
                MyControl.Clear
                MyControl.AddItem "Outlook"
                MyControl.AddItem "Windows 95"
                MyControl.Additem "Windows 98"
                MyControl.AddItem "Windows 2000"
                MyControl.ListIndex = 0
            Case "Gardening"
                MyControl.Clear
                MyControl.AddItem "Fruit Trees"
                MyControl.Additem "Roses"
                MyControl.AddItem "Vegetables"
                MyControl.ListIndex = 0
        End Select
    End If
End Sub
```

Populating a List with Hidden Fields

Rather than adding items to the list one item at a time, you can set the list equal to an array that holds your data. The Control Object form located in the VBScript Samples folder uses this technique to load a combo box with a list of U.S. states. In this case, the array is static and hard-coded in the procedure, but an array retrieved from a separate data source works the same way. The combo box shown in Figure 15.3 has two columns, only one of which is displayed. In this case, the hidden column holds state name abbreviations, but it could also contain some unique identifier for the friendly name that appears in the list. The History list box of the Assigned Help Task form in the Help Desk application covered in E-Chapter 3, "The Northwind Contact Management Application," in the E-Chapters folder on the companion CD, uses this method to hide the item's EntryID and StoreID—not the kind of thing your average user likes to deal with, but essential for locating items in the Exchange information store.

```
Sub PopulateStates
Dim varStates()
Set cmbStates = GetInspector.ModifiedFormPages("Control Object").cmbStates
ReDim varStates(6,1)
varStates (0,0) = "AZ"
varStates (0,1) = "Arizona"
varStates (1,0) = "CA"
varStates (1,1) = "California"
varStates (2,0) = "HI"
varStates (2,1) = "Hawaii"
varStates (3,0) = "ID"
varStates (3,1) = "Idaho"
varStates (4,0) = "NV"
```

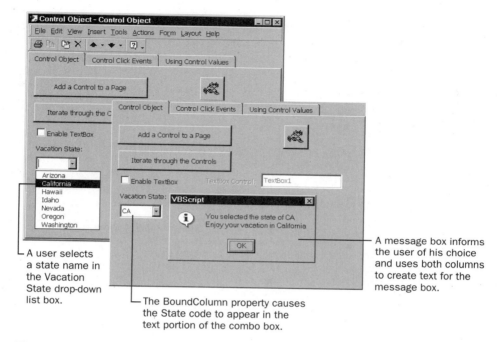

A user selects a state name in the Vacation State drop-down list box.

The BoundColumn property causes the State code to appear in the text portion of the combo box.

A message box informs the user of his choice and uses both columns to create text for the message box.

Figure 15.3 *A drop-down list box contains additional data in hidden columns.*

```
varStates (4,1) = "Nevada"
varStates (5,0) = "OR"
varStates (5,1) = "Oregon"
varStates (6,0) = "WA"
varStates (6,1) = "Washington"
cmbStates.List = varStates
cmbStates.ColumnCount = 2
'Set column 0 to 0 width to hide the column
cmbStates.ColumnWidths = "0 in ; 1 in"
cmbStates.TextColumn = 1
cmbStates.BoundColumn = 1
End Sub
```

Loading Data into a Grid

When it is important to show a number of different information fields for each item of data, you may want to use a grid. ActiveX Grid controls are included in Office 2000 Developer, and a number of additional ActiveX Grid controls are available from third-party vendors. As a rule, there are many properties, methods, and events associated with each of these controls, and a corresponding learning curve, as well. Therefore, developers tend to find one data grid that they prefer and they stick with it.

A grid can be loaded from an array. Most have one or more methods that permit them to connect directly to a data source. You can also load the data row by row using an unbound *AddItem* method. The Customers form in the Northwind Contact Management application discussed in E-Chapter 3 on the companion CD uses this method to dynamically fill a Microsoft MSFlexGrid control with data from items in an Exchange public folder.

```
'If the link item does not exist remove it.
'Otherwise, retrieve and store in Grid.
Do While i <= intorigcount
    If Not IsObject(Item.Links.Item(i).Item) Then
        Item.Links.Remove(i)
        intorigcount = intorigcount - 1
    Else
        Set objLContact = Item.Links.Item(i).Item
        strAdd = "" & vbTab & objLContact.FullName & vbTab _
            & objLContact.JobTitle & vbTab & objLContact.CompanyName _
            & vbTab & objLContact.BusinessTelephoneNumber & vbTab _
            & objLContact.MobileTelephoneNumber
        ctlContactGrid.AddItem strAdd
        ctlContactGrid.Row = i
        ctlContactGrid.Col = 0
        Set ctlContactGrid.CellPicture = P1.Picture
        i = i + 1
    End If
Loop
```

Accessing the Data in Exchange/Outlook

Information in personal folders—and in public folders if you are connected to a Microsoft Exchange Server—is available to other members of the Office 2000 suite (or any application that supports ActiveX Automation), as well as to Outlook. A personal Outlook Contacts folder, for instance, is one of the standard data source options for a mail merge in a Word 2000 document. You can use the Link Outlook/Exchange Wizard in Access 2000 to link or import data from public or private folders to a table in an Access 2000 database. You can also use the Outlook Import And Export Wizard to export data from Outlook to other applications.

If your data import and export requirements are complex, you will have to write code in Visual Basic to create a data pump between Exchange/Outlook and your external source of data. Accessing data in Exchange/Outlook is not confined to moving this data between applications. You also need to access information within Exchange and Outlook. Finally, you might also want to access data in other folders for use in your custom forms. We'll cover some basic ways to move data between Exchange/Outlook and other applications, and then move on to some advanced techniques for accessing folder and message information in Outlook custom forms.

Using the Access 2000 Link Outlook/Exchange Wizard

Access 2000's Link Outlook/Exchange Wizard offers a quick means of linking or importing information in Outlook public or private folders. However, linking a table in Access to a public folder with thousands of items will not yield acceptable performance. Use this approach only when you have a manageable number of items in a folder.

To start the Outlook/Exchange Wizard in Access 2000

1. Launch Access 2000.

2. Select New from the File menu and double-click Database in the General tab of the New dialog box to open a new Access database.

3. Select the Get External Data command from the File menu, and then select Link Tables or Import, depending on whether you want to link or import Outlook data. The steps below assume that you will link tables rather than import data.

4. In the Link dialog box, select Outlook in the Files of type combo box at the bottom of the dialog box.

5. Log on to Outlook if the Choose Profile dialog box appears.

6. Select the folder you want to link to in the Exchange/Outlook Wizard dialog box, and then click Next.

By using Get External Data from the File menu and selecting Exchange or Outlook as the data source, it is a simple matter to extract a Contact list or create a report on the volume and sources of incoming messages to a particular folder or group of folders. The wizard can access any folders for which your MAPI profile has permission, but only certain standard fields are available. User-defined fields in a custom item are available as long as those fields are included in the current view. Unfortunately, working with the Exchange/Outlook Wizard can be frustrating because fields are not always imported or linked correctly. You can achieve quicker and more accurate results by just dragging items from a folder into Microsoft Excel.

Dragging Items in a View to Excel 2000

One of the easiest ways to export data from Outlook is to drag items from a view and drop them into an Excel worksheet. For example, you might want to export the Contact items in the Customers folder of the Northwind Contact Management application in E-Chapter 3 on the companion CD. A simple drag operation from Outlook to Excel will export the items in a jiffy. However, you must arrange the fields you want to export in the current view on the folder. Use the Field Chooser to add appropriate fields to the view and remove other fields—such as the Paper Clip icon—that are not appropriate for Excel. Figure 15.4 illustrates the Northwind Contact Management application Customer items after they have been dragged to an empty Excel worksheet.

To drag items from Outlook to Excel 2000

1. Launch Excel 2000, and then minimize Excel so that it appears on the Windows taskbar.

2. Navigate to the folder you want to export using the Folder List.

3. Customize the current view so that all the fields you want to export appear in the view. Use the Field Chooser to customize the current view, or select View

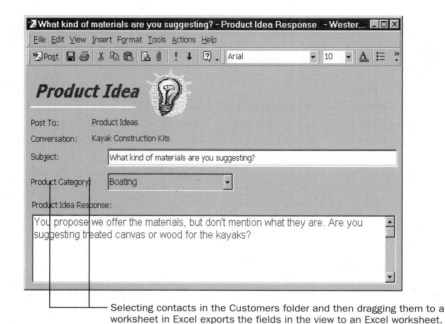

Selecting contacts in the Customers folder and then dragging them to a worksheet in Excel exports the fields in the view to an Excel worksheet.

Figure 15.4 *Drag items from Outlook to Excel to export the fields in a view to a worksheet.*

from the View menu and click on Customize Current View to modify the current view. You can also establish a filter to display only a subset of items in the view. If you have any groups in the view, remove them at this time.

4.   Press Ctrl+A to select all the items in the view, or select a subset of the items in the view.

5.   Click the selected items in the view and hold down the left mouse button. Do not release the mouse button until you have completed the drag operation. Drag the selected items down to the Excel icon on the Windows taskbar and continue to hold down the left mouse button.

6.   After a brief pause, the Excel application window will open. Do not release the left mouse button yet. Move the drag pointer from over the Excel taskbar icon to over cell A1 on the Excel worksheet.

7.   Release the left mouse button and all selected Outlook items will be dropped into the Excel worksheet.

8.   If you want to define the items in Excel as a database, you can press Ctrl+F3 while all the dropped cells are still selected and type *Database* in the Names In Workbook edit box of the Define Name dialog box. Click the Add button and then press OK.

9.   Save the workbook with an appropriate descriptive name for the imported Outlook items.

Using the Outlook Import/Export Wizard

The Outlook Import/Export Wizard provides another way to move data between applications as long as your needs are relatively simple. The Import/Export Wizard in Outlook 2000 is a major improvement over previous versions of the wizard because you can map fields in the Outlook 2000 Export/Import Wizard. One limitation of the Outlook Import/Export Wizard is that it will not export information from public folders. Its use is restricted to personal information store (.pst) files in your profile and the folders in your private mailbox. You can overcome this limitation by copying information from a public folder to a personal folders (.pst) file if you have the correct permissions for the public folder.

⟳ **To export items using the Outlook Import/Export Wizard**

1. Select Import And Export from the Outlook File menu.
2. Select Export To A File in the Choose An Action To Perform list box. Click Next.
3. Select Microsoft Access in the Create A File Of Type list box. You can select a different export format if required in this step. Click Next.
4. Select a folder in the Select Folder To Export From listing of folders. Click Next.
5. Type a filename and path in the Save Exported File As edit box. Click Next.
6. The last dialog box in the wizard has a Map Custom Fields button. If you want to map custom fields, click this button.
7. The Map Custom Fields dialog box, shown in Figure 15.5, lets you create mappings between the fields in an Outlook item and the proposed fields in the output file or database. Drag and drop fields to create a mapping that suits your requirements. Click OK when you've completed the mapping.
8. Click Finish to complete the export operation.

Data Access Using the Outlook Object Model

To retrieve data from Outlook/Exchange information stores with the best performance for a large number of items, you can turn to the Outlook Object Model and, if necessary, Collaboration Data Objects (CDO). Use CDO when you need to retrieve messages or address book fields that are not available in the Outlook Object Model. In most instances, the Outlook 2000 Object Model provides you with direct access to the properties, methods, and events for all Outlook objects. There are some instances when Outlook's object model falls short, most notably in regard to the Exchange directory. A combination approach using both CDO and the Outlook Object Model can solve almost all development tasks. Microsoft plans, in the not-too-distant future, to combine CDO and Outlook into a unified object model for accessing all the data stored on Microsoft Exchange Server or in offline store (.ost) or personal folder (.pst) files.

Displaying Outlook Data in a Custom Form

One of the most common questions posed by a beginning Outlook developer is how to retrieve the items in a folder and display those items to a user in a custom form. The

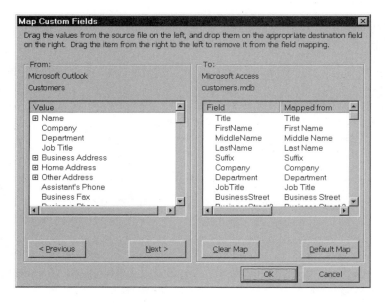

Figure 15.5 *You can map fields between Outlook and your exported data with the Outlook 2000 Import/Export Wizard.*

following custom Post form named Outlook/Exchange Data shows you two ways to solve this problem. We'll discuss the pros and cons of each approach.

➥ **To open the Outlook Exchange Data example form**

1. Expand subfolder 5. Advanced Topics of the Building Microsoft Outlook 2000 Applications personal folders (.pst) file.

2. Expand the Outlook Data Access Strategies folder and double-click the Outlook/Exchange Data item in the folder.

Iterating Over the Items Collection

The Items and Folders objects are collection objects, meaning that they contain a collection of individual items or folders. When you iterate over the collection of items in the Items collection, you can retrieve both the default properties and user-defined fields for an item and use those values to add to a list or combo box, as shown in Figure 15.6.

If you click the command button labeled Populate Combo Box With Contacts Using Restrict And Sort, you'll execute code that does exactly what is advertised. A reference to your default Contacts folder is set using the *GetDefaultFolder* method of the NameSpace object. This statement creates a Folder object variable that represents your Contacts folder. However, it's the items in the folder—rather than the folder itself—we're interested in. The Items collection object of the MAPIFolder object contains every item in the Contacts

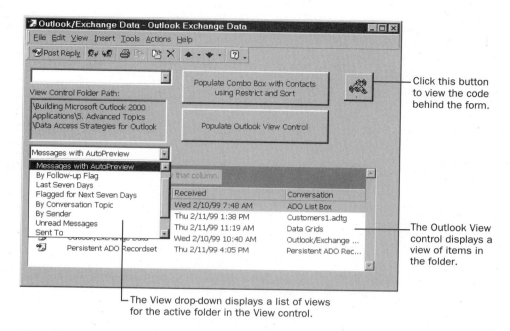

The View drop-down displays a list of views for the active folder in the View control.

Click this button to view the code behind the form.

The Outlook View control displays a view of items in the folder.

Figure 15.6 *The Outlook/Exchange Data Sample Form.*

folder. The statement Set MyItems = MyContacts.Items creates a *MyItems* object variable you can use to obtain all the items in the collection.

What happens if you don't want to retrieve all the items in the MyItems collection? You should use the *Restrict* method of the Items collection object to create a subset of items. Using the *Restrict* method is the programmatic equivalent of setting a filter on an Outlook view. In the case of the *cmdPopulateList_Click* procedure below, we don't want to retrieve any names from the Contacts folder that do not have an e-mail address. Therefore, the *Restrict* condition is set to exclude any contact items that do not contain a value in the Email1Address property of the ContactItem object. The *RestrictedContactItems* object variable is also an Items collection object, but with a subset of the original *MyItems* collection. If you were to populate the cmbContacts combo box with *RestrictedContactItems*, you'd find that the items were not sorted. To make the combo box position correctly when a user types the first letter of the contact's last name, *RestrictedContactItems* has been sorted using the *Sort* method. Notice that you must enclose the field name arguments in brackets for the *Restrict* and *Sort* methods to work correctly. Once you've retrieved a sorted and filtered Items collection, you can populate the cmbContacts combo box with items in the collection. A For...Each statement is used to iterate over the items in the *RestrictedContactItems* collection, and the *AddItem* method of the Forms 2.0 combo box is used to add items in sorted sequence.

```
Sub cmdPopulateList_Click
    Const olContactsFolder = 10
    Set MyContacts = _
        Application.GetNameSpace("MAPI").GetDefaultFolder(olContactsFolder)
    Set MyItems = MyContacts.Items
    Set RestrictedContactItems = MyItems.Restrict("[EmailAddress] <> ''")
    'Sort by LastName in ascending order
    RestrictedContactItems.Sort "[LastName]"
    For Each MyItem in RestrictedContactItems
            cmbContacts.AddItem MyItem.FileAs
    Next
    IsLoading = True
    cmbContacts.ListIndex = 0
    IsLoading = False
End Sub
```

Once you've loaded the cmbContacts combo box, the user can select an item from the combo box, and you can display the item or use its properties to create another item. In this case, a Mail Message is created and addressed to the e-mail address stored in the Email1Address property of the contact. Figure 15.7 shows a selection made in the drop-down portion of the combo box. Selecting an item in a populated combo box causes the Click event to fire for the combo box. The *cmbContacts_Click* procedure shown below contains three lines of code that create, address, and display the mail message.

```
Sub cmbContacts_Click
    If Not(IsLoading) Then
        Set MyItem = Application.CreateItem(0)
        MyItem.To = RestrictedContactItems _
            (cmbContacts.ListIndex + 1).Email1Address
        MyItem.Display
    End If
End Sub
```

You should recognize one important trick in the *cmbContacts_Click* procedure: the *RestrictedContactItems* variable is dimensioned as a script-level variable so that it is available to all procedures in the VBScript code. The ListIndex property of the cmbContacts combo box serves as an index into the *RestrictedContactItems* collection object. Remember that you can access items in an Items collection either by name or by numerical index. An Items collection is 1-based, whereas the ListIndex of a combo box is 0-based. Consequently, if you add 1 to *cmbContacts.ListIndex*, you can retrieve the correct item from the *RestrictedContactItems* collection.

If you actually try out this example in the Outlook/Exchange Data sample form, you'll find that the performance is less than stellar if you have only a moderate number of items in your Contacts folder. Even if you port this code to a UserForm in Outlook VBA and use early-bound variables instead of VBScript's late-bound variables, you'll find that the performance is still not what you'd expect. It seems that the combination of *Restrict* and *Sort* methods leads to speed problems. If you have to load the cmbContacts combo box during the Item_Open event of the form because of the design requirements of your ap-

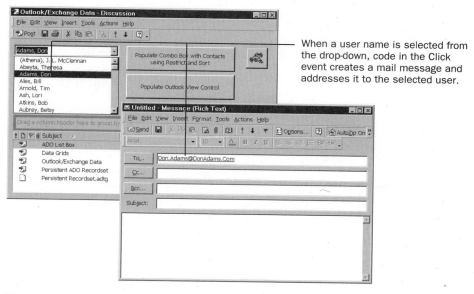

When a user name is selected from the drop-down, code in the Click event creates a mail message and addresses it to the selected user.

Figure 15.7 *Selecting an item in the drop-down portion of the combo box fires the Click event.*

plication, you won't be a happy camper. The overhead imposed by the *Restrict* and *Sort* methods will cause an unacceptable delay when your form opens.

The Outlook View Control

The Outlook View control is an ActiveX control that ships with the Outlook Team Folder Wizard and allows you to place Explorer-like views on Web pages or on the pages of an Outlook custom form. We've included a beta version of the Outlook View control on the CD-ROM accompanying this book. Once you've used the Outlook View control, you'll wonder how you lived without it. The Outlook View control, shown earlier in Figures 15.6 and 15.7, is displayed at the bottom of the form. Step-by-step instructions for adding an Outlook View control to the page of a custom form are given next, even though the control is already on the Outlook/Exchange data sample form.

To add an Outlook View control to an Outlook form page

1. Open a form in Design mode by selecting Forms on the Tools menu and then selecting Design A Form.
2. Click a blank page on the form.
3. Click the Control Toolbox on the Forms Design toolbar.
4. Right-click the Control Toolbox and select the Additional Controls command.
5. Check Microsoft Outlook View Control in the list of available controls, as shown in Figure 15.8.

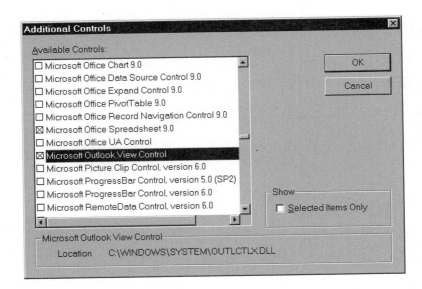

Figure 15.8 *Check the Microsoft Outlook View Control in the Additional Controls dialog box.*

6. Click OK.
7. Drag the Outlook View control from the Control Toolbox to an empty page on your form.

If you simply place the control on a form page, you'll find that it shows the messages in your Inbox by default. However, the control has a programmatic interface that lets you control the folder whose messages are rendered in the control, as well as the view for that folder. For purposes of instruction, a command button that lets you select the folder displayed in the View control has been added to the form. Code has been added to show you how to populate a combo box with the available views for the folder. When a user selects a view from the combo box, the View property for the Outlook View control is set, and the View control refreshes the view accordingly. The following code listing shows how you set the Folder property of the View control, depending on which folder is selected by a user in the Pick Folder dialog box. To refresh your memory, you display the Pick Folder dialog box by calling the *PickFolder* method of the NameSpace object.

The Folder property of the View control is somewhat misleading at first. If you set the Folder property to a MAPIFolder object, the assignment will fail. The View control is looking for a folder path expressed as a string instead of a folder object. The *GetFolderPath* function introduced in Chapter 11, "Using VBA and VBScript with Outlook," is used in the following code example. The final two statements in this procedure also bear examination. The *GetFolderViews* function obtains all the available views for a given folder. In essence, *GetFolderViews* steals the views from the Current View combo box on the Advanced Toolbar in the Outlook Explorer.

```
Sub cmdPopulateOVCtl_Click
    On Error Resume Next
    Set objNS = Application.GetNameSpace("MAPI")
    Set objFolder = objNS.PickFolder
    If objFolder Is Nothing Then
        Exit Sub
    End If
    Item.UserProperties("OVCtlFolder") = GetFolderPath(objFolder)
    OVCtl1.Folder = GetFolderPath(objFolder)
    cmbView.List = GetFolderViews(objFolder)
    cmbView.Text = OVCtl1.View
End Sub


'***************************************************************
'Custom procedure: GetFolderViews(ByVal objFolder)
'Purpose: Return available views for a MAPIFolder
'Argument: MAPIFolder object
'Usage: Used to populate a combo box containing views
'Returns: One-dimensional variant array
'***************************************************************

Function GetFolderViews(ByVal objFolder)
    Dim objExpl 'As Explorer
    Dim objCB 'As CommandBar
    Dim objCBCombo 'As CommandBarComboBox
    Dim avarArray
    Set objExpl = Application.Explorers.Add(objFolder,2)
    'Must use Item syntax in VBScript
    Set objCB = objExpl.CommandBars.Item("Advanced")
    Set objCBCombo = objCB.Controls("Current View")
    ReDim avarArray(objCBCombo.ListCount)
    For i = 1 To objCBCombo.ListCount
        avarArray(i - 1) = objCBCombo.List(i)
    Next
    GetFolderViews = avarArray
    Set objExpl = Nothing
End Function
```

Once you've populated the cmbView combo box with the available views, you need to set the Text property of the combo box to create the selected item in the list. The View control's View property contains the name of the active view in the folder. You then set the text property of the cmbView control to the View property of the Outlook View control. When a user changes the value in the cmbView control, you simply reverse the assignment and set the View property to the combo box Text property as follows:

```
Sub Item_CustomPropertyChange(ByVal Name)
    If Name = "OVCtlView" Then
        OVCtl1.View = Item.UserProperties("OVCtlView")
    End If
End Sub
```

The View and Folder properties of the View control are bound to user-defined fields in the Outlook/Exchange Data custom form. Consequently, if you change the View control Folder and View and then save the form, the View control will persist those settings for Folder and View the next time you open the form. Here is how to handle the persistence in the Item_Open event of the form: If the user-defined field named OVCtlFolder is not a blank string, set the Folder property of the View control to the value of the user-defined field. The Folder property of the View control takes a folder path as its argument, rather than a MAPIFolder object. The final step is to refresh the cmbView list with the views for the MAPIFolder object returned by the Folder property of the View control. If you want to obtain a MAPIFolder object for the folder path returned by the View control's Folder property, then you must use the *OpenMAPIFolder* function listed in Chapter 11, "Using VBA and VBScript with Outlook."

```
Function Item_Open()
Const olFolderInbox = 6
On Error Resume Next
Set cmbContacts = Item.GetInspector.ModifiedFormPages("Outlook/Exchange Data") _
    .Controls("cmbContacts")
Set cmbView = Item.GetInspector.ModifiedFormPages("Outlook/Exchange Data") _
    .Controls("cmbView")
Set OVCtl1 = Item.GetInspector.ModifiedFormPages("Outlook/Exchange Data") _
    .Controls("OVCtl1")
If Item.UserProperties("OVCtlFolder") <> "" Then
    OVCtl1.Folder = Item.UserProperties("OVCtlFolder")
    strFolderPath = OVCtl1.Folder
    If Left(strFolderPath, 2) = "\\" Then
        strFolderPath = Right(strFolderPath, Len(strFolderPath) - 1)
    End If
    If strFolderPath <> Item.UserProperties("OVCtlFolder") Then
        Item.UserProperties("OVCtlFolder") = strFolderPath
    End If
    cmbView.List = GetFolderViews(OpenMAPIFolder(strFolderPath))
    cmbView.Text = OVCtl1.View
Else
    Set objFolderInbox = _
            Application.GetNameSpace("MAPI").GetDefaultFolder(olFolderInbox)
    OVCtl1.Folder = GetFolderPath(objFolderInbox)
    Item.UserProperties("OVCtl1Folder") = OVCtl1.Folder
    cmbView.List = GetFolderViews(objFolderInbox)
    cmbView.Text = OVCtl1.View
End If
End Function
```

Using the View control is preferable to iterating over a collection in order to populate a Forms 2.0 control with Outlook items. The View control is speedy, easy to use, and supports all the interface elements, such as double-clicking an item, that are familiar to users. If you elect to use the Outlook View control in your application, however, be aware that because the Outlook View control is not an intrinsic control that installs with Outlook, you will have to distribute the control to your application users. For additional information on distributing controls in your application, see Chapter 12, "Distribute and Maintain Applications."

More Info For additional information on the properties and methods of the Microsoft Outlook View control, see Chapter 14, "Customizing Folder Home Pages."

Using Universal Data Access in Outlook

The sources of electronic data available today are numerous and diverse: relational databases, semi-structured and unstructured storage such as spreadsheets and flat files, messages on the Web, and more. The permutations and combinations seem endless. The number and kinds of sources continue to multiply as quickly as the need to extract, transform, and analyze the data they contain. Microsoft's current strategy for utilizing this data across the enterprise is called Universal Data Access. This framework is based on specifications with wide industry support and works with all major database platforms. At the heart of Universal Data Access is OLE DB, a specification for a set of data access interfaces designed to enable a multitude of data stores of all types and sizes to work seamlessly together. OLE DB provides a way for any type of data store to expose its data in a standard, tabular form. OLE DB expands beyond the boundaries of ODBC, which is limited to relational databases. A number of OLE DB providers are included in Data Access Components as part of Office 2000. These OLE DB providers significantly expand the range of data sources available to you as an Outlook developer. Microsoft's eventual plan is for OLE DB to encompass all types of data in the enterprise, including Exchange and Outlook data. At some point in the not-too-distant future, there will be an OLE DB provider that lets you query Exchange and Outlook data, as well as RDBMS and Active Directory data.

The Data Source Name (DSN)

The high-level interface to these numerous data providers is ActiveX Data Objects (ADO), also included with Data Access Components. ADO functions at the application level to permit data consumers (such as your Outlook form) to communicate with a wide variety of data providers through OLE DB. It combines the best features of—and will eventually replace—Remote Data Objects (RDO) and Data Access Objects (DAO). ADO's familiar conventions and simplified semantics make it comparatively easy to learn. Because it uses OLE DB, the effort involved in learning ADO can be leveraged over a wide variety of potential data sources.

The examples that follow all incorporate some feature that is new to Outlook 2000. They do not cover every means available to interact with external data sources in an Outlook application. The subject is vast, and you will find articles on the Web at the Microsoft Office Developer site (*http://www.microsoft.com/officedev/*) and elsewhere that demonstrate a wide variety of valid techniques. The purpose of these examples is to demonstrate what is possible. Every method has advantages and disadvantages that should be evaluated in the context of your application requirements.

Connecting to a Data Source

If your form needs to look up postal codes or get a list of orders linked by supplier and shipping date, it will probably be getting the data from a relational database such as Access or SQL Server. A number of different options are available to create the necessary connection to that data source. It's possible to use ADO to connect directly to a specific database on a local or shared drive. The connection can also be made via an ODBC Data Source Name (DSN), or you can use the new OLE DB-based Universal Data Link, both of which are discussed below.

Data Source Name (DSN)

A Data Source Name contains the information necessary to connect to an ODBC-compliant data source. The requirements for different systems vary, but at a minimum, they include the ODBC driver to use and the name of the database. ODBC drivers exist for SQL Server, Access, Paradox and Oracle relational database management systems (RDBMS), and drivers exist for Excel and for certain text file formats, as well.

As shown in Figure 15.9, there are three types of DSN: User, System, and File.

- A User DSN is only available to the user profile under which it was created.
- A System DSN is available to any user with appropriate privileges on the local machine. Both User and System DSNs are stored as registry settings; as such, they can be retrieved programmatically from the registry, and a new DSN can be created by similar methods.
- A File DSN is stored in the file system, and can be created on a network share, available to all users with the required driver installed.

You will need a DSN for the Northwind Sample Database for some of the examples that follow, so let's create one now.

The Northwind Sample Database

To test the functionality of the example forms in this chapter, you need to have a copy of the Northwind Sample Database installed on a local or shared drive. This database is included in Office 2000 but is not installed by default. Follow the steps outlined below to install the Northwind Sample Database.

To install the Northwind Sample Database

1. Insert the Outlook 2000 CD-ROM into your CD-ROM drive.
2. Click Start, click Settings, and then click Control Panel.
3. Double-click Add/Remove Programs.

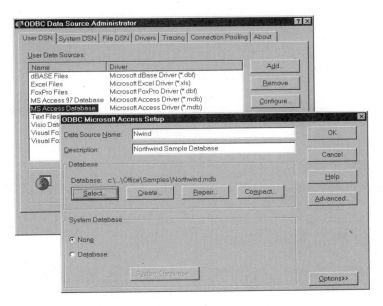

Figure 15.9 *Creating a DSN.*

4. On the Install/Uninstall page, click Microsoft Office 2000, and then click Add/Remove.

5. In the Microsoft Office 2000 Maintenance Mode dialog box, click Add Or Remove Features.

6. Double-click the Microsoft Access for Windows item to expand the item in the Microsoft Office 2000: Update Features dialog box.

7. Double-click the Sample Databases item under Microsoft Access for Windows to expand the item.

8. Click the Northwind Database drop-down item and select Run From My Computer.

9. Click Update Now to complete the installation of the Northwind Sample Database.

To create a User DSN for the Northwind Sample Database

1. Click Control Panel and then double-click the ODBC Data Sources icon.

2. Click the User DSN tab.

3. Click Add.

4. Select Microsoft Access Driver from the list of drivers.

5. Click Finish.

6. In the Data Source Name edit box, type Nwind.

7. In the Description edit box, type Northwind Sample Database.

8. Click Select and use the Select Database dialog box to select the Northwind.mdb file. Northwind.mdb should be located in the Samples subdirectory under the Office subdirectory where you installed Office 2000. The default folder for the Northwind Sample Database is C:\Program Files\Microsoft Office\Office\Samples.

9. Click OK to accept your addition, and then click OK to close the ODBC Data Source Administrator dialog box.

The Universal Data Link

Universal Data Access introduces a new way to store data connection information. The Universal Data Link (UDL) is the OLE DB equivalent of a File DSN. A UDL can be created anywhere on your local or network drives. To test the code in some of the example forms, you will need a UDL for the Northwind Sample Database.

To create a UDL for the Northwind Sample Database

1. A Universal Data Link can be created and located anywhere you choose. For this example, you will use the default search directory for the ADO Data control, which will be covered later. This folder is automatically created the first time you browse for it from the ADO Data control, but not before, so you will need to create it. Navigate to C:\Program Files\Common Files\System\Ole DB and create a new folder named Data Links.

2. Right-click within the folder, or select File from the folder menu, select New and then select Microsoft Data Link, as shown in Figure 15.10.

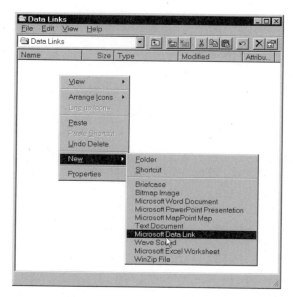

Figure 15.10 *Creating a Universal Data Link.*

3. Double-click the New Microsoft Data Link.udl file to open its Properties page. The Connection page will open for an ODBC Data Source by default.

4. Click the Provider tab and select Microsoft Jet 4.0 OLE DB Provider, as shown in Figure 15.11. Notice the list of available OLE DB Providers. Click Next.

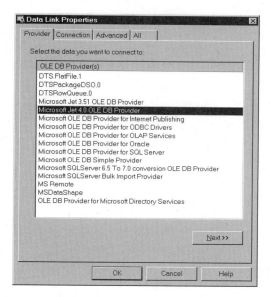

Figure 15.11 *Select a Data Provider.*

5. Use the ellipsis button (…) to navigate to the location of Northwind.mdb and select it. Be sure to use the Test Connection button.

6. Select OK. Rename the new data link to Northwind.udl.

Creating Recordsets with ADO

Within the Data Access Strategies for Outlook subfolder of the Building Microsoft Outlook 2000 Applications.pst file are some demonstration forms that use ADO to bring data into Outlook. Let's take a look at the first page of the Data Grids form shown in Figure 15.12. This illustrates a method that requires minimal code through the use of the ADO Data Control.

The Building Microsoft Outlook 2000 Applications .pst file

In order to test the demonstration forms accompanying this chapter, you must have previously installed the Building Microsoft Outlook 2000 Applications.pst file included on the CD-ROM accompanying this book. If you have not already done so, refer to the instructions in the Introduction.

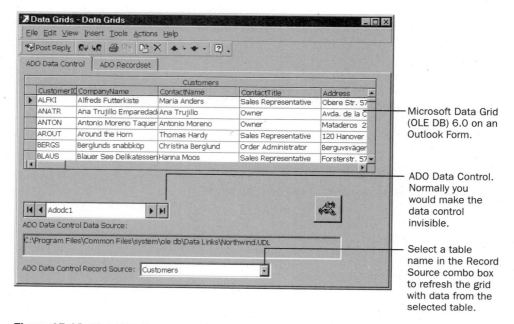

Microsoft Data Grid (OLE DB) 6.0 on an Outlook Form.

ADO Data Control. Normally you would make the data control invisible.

Select a table name in the Record Source combo box to refresh the grid with data from the selected table.

Figure 15.12 *The ADO Data control page of the Data Grids Form.*

The ADO Data Control

The ADO Data control is the simplest way to bring the data from an OLE DB provider onto an Outlook form. This ActiveX control establishes a data connection for the form. The ADO Data control provides a recordset that can function as the data source for other OLE DB-capable controls on the form, such as the Microsoft Data Grid used in the example. The ADO Data control itself includes record selectors that can be used to navigate through the recordset. Since you can also select records directly with the Data Grid, it would make more sense to hide the ADO Data control behind the grid if this were a production form.

The connection parameters for the ADO Data control are set in its Properties page. Let's take a look at the steps involved in placing this control on a form and configuring it.

Note To use the ADO Data control and the Microsoft Data Grid control in Design mode, you must install either Microsoft Office 2000 Developer or Microsoft Visual Studio 98. Run-time versions of these controls are included on the CD-ROM accompanying this book.

Adding an ADO Data control and Data Grid to a form

1. Select the Design a Form command on the Forms submenu of the Tools menu.
2. Select Post Form from the Standard Forms Library in the Design Forms dialog box.

3. In Design Mode, click the form's second page (P.2).

4. Use the crossed tools button on the toolbar to open the Control Toolbox.

5. Right-click the Toolbox and select Additional Controls from the context menu.

6. Scroll down the list of additional controls and select Microsoft ADO Data Control, Version 6.0 (OLE DB). At this point, you should also select the Microsoft DataGrid Control, version 6.0 (OLE DB) as shown in Figure 15.13.

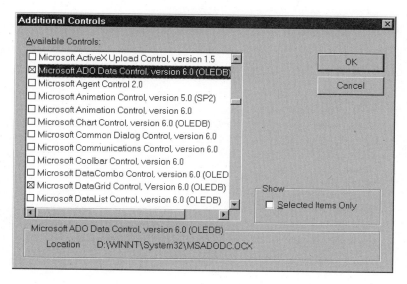

Figure 15.13 *Adding the ADO Data control and Data Grid control to the Control Toolbox.*

7. Place an ADO Data control on the form and right-click it to bring up the context menu. Select ADODC Properties.

8. The General page of the ADODC Properties dialog box includes three options for the Source of Connection. For this example, choose Use Data Link File. When you click Browse, the dialog box should open to the Data Links folder you created earlier, which contains the Northwind.udl. If it doesn't, locate Northwind.udl in your file system and select it.

9. If you have installed security for the Northwind Sample Database, you should include a valid user name and password on the Authentication page.

10. On the RecordSource page, select adCmdTable as the Command Type. Select Customers from the Table Or Stored Procedure Name drop-down list box.

11. Click OK.

12. Drag a Microsoft OLE DB Data Grid control to the form and size it appropriately.

At this point, the ADO Data control is configured to deliver a recordset from the Customers table to other controls on your form. However, the DataSource property of the Data Grid has not been connected to the Data control yet. The surprise here is that you cannot make this connection in the Advanced Properties window of the Data control. You must set the DataSource property for the Data Grid in the Item_Open event of the form. You need to add three lines of code to instantiate form objects, and one line of code to make the Data Grid live. The relevant lines from the Data Grids sample form are located in the Item_Open event:

```
Set ADODCpage = Item.GetInspector.ModifiedFormPages("ADO Data Control")
Set adodc1 = ADODCpage.adodc1
Set DataGrid1 = ADODCpage.DataGrid1
Set DataGrid1.DataSource = adodc1
```

The other interesting feature of the ADO Data control in the Data Grids example form is the use of the *OpenSchema* method of ADO to obtain a list of the tables in the Northwind Sample Database. When a user selects a table from the Record Source combo box on the form, the grid is refreshed with data from that table. To use the *OpenSchema* method, we first need to clone the ADO Connection object used in the ADO Data control.

The following code creates a clone of the Data control's connection by using its ConnectionString property to open another ADODB Connection object. The *OpenSchema* method is then used on the Connection object to obtain a recordset that contains all the tables, views, and system tables for the Connection object. If the TABLE_TYPE field equals TABLE, then the table name is added to the cmbRecordSource combo box.

```
'Fill cmbRecordSource with tables in Northwind using GetSchema method
Set cnnClone = CreateObject("ADODB.Connection")
cnnClone.ConnectionString = adodc1.ConnectionString
cnnClone.Open
Set rstSchema = cnnClone.OpenSchema(adSchemaTables)
Do Until rstSchema.EOF
    If rstSchema.Fields("TABLE_TYPE") = "TABLE" Then
        cmbRecordSource.AddItem rstSchema.Fields("TABLE_NAME")
    End If
    rstSchema.MoveNext
Loop
rstSchema.Close
cnnClone.Close
```

As you can see, the ADO Data control is a fairly painless way to connect to a data source. You have flexibility in the type of connection created and in the form of the recordset that is returned. Choosing adCmdUnknown or adCmdText for the RecordSource enables you to input a SQL query string that will be used to generate the ADO Data control's recordset. These properties and others can also be set programmatically, if you choose.

More Info To delve deeper into the capabilities of the ADO Object Model, refer to the ADO documentation and the Office 2000 Programmers' Guide. ADO 2.1

installs with Office 2000. The default location for the ADO Help and program files is C:\Program Files\Common Files\System\Ado. The ADO documentation can be found in Help file ado210.chm located in the ADO folder.

Creating ADO Connection and Recordset Objects

The ADO Data control requires almost no code, and there isn't really a lot more required to manipulate the ADO Object Model directly. The ADO Recordset page of the Data Grid form is intended to give you a feel for the parameters required to supply data to a grid using only code.

When the ADO Recordset page first opens, the grid will be empty. Clicking the Create Recordset button creates an ADO connection, using the OLE DB Provider, User ID, Password, and Data Source parameters displayed in the text boxes. Once the connection to the data source has been opened, a recordset is created using the SQL string in the Query drop-down list box. Finally, the data source of the grid is set to the recordset, which populates the grid, as shown in Figure 15.14.

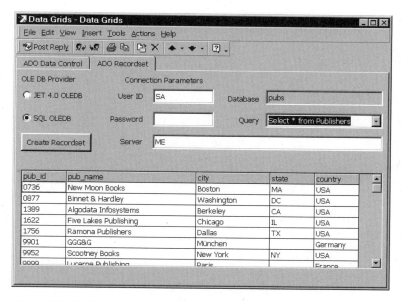

Figure 15.14 *The ADO Recordset page of the Data Grids form.*

In order to use the Microsoft SQL OLE DB Provider for SQL Server, you must be able to connect to a running SQL Server, either the desktop (if you are using SQL Server 7.0) or server edition. You will need to enter the appropriate user ID, password, and server name to create the connection. To simplify the coding, the form does not permit changing the default database, but a connection could be made to any valid database on the target server.

Once a connection has been created, you can change the recordset returned by selecting a different query string, or by entering another query directly into the combo box. As an example, try the following:

1. Select the Jet 4.0 OLEDB Provider option using the default values, and click Create Recordset.

2. Change the string in the Query combo box to read:

    ```
    Select * from Customers Where City = 'London'
    ```

3. Click the Create Recordset command button.

The grid used for this page is the MS Hierarchical Flex Grid. Other than setting its width in the Item_Open event, no attempt has been made to adjust the grid's formatting or use the special features of the grid. For a production form, considerably more attention could be paid to the way the grid looks and how the data is presented.

The significant code for the ADO Recordset page is found in the *cmdRecordset_Click* procedure. Because this form is intended as a demonstration tool, there is actually a lot more code than would be necessary to simply get data and fill the grid. In this procedure, the Provider, User ID, Password, and Data Source are set as separate properties of the Connection object, and then the connection is opened in a separate step. It would work just as well to simply create the Connection object in one line and open it in the next line, supplying all the required properties in a single connection string. Once the connection has been opened and the Recordset object has been created, a new recordset is opened using the SQL query from the combo box.

```
Sub cmdCreateRecordset_Click()
On Error Resume Next
'Create the Connection object if it doesn't exist; close it if it is open
If IsEmpty(adoCNN) Then
    Set adoCNN= Application.CreateObject("ADODB.Connection")
Else
    If adoCNN.state = adStateOpen Then adoCNN.Close
End If
adoCNN.Provider = UserProperties("Provider")
If UserProperties("User ID")<>"" Then
    adoCNN.Properties("User ID")= UserProperties("UserID")
Else
    MsgBox "You must enter a User ID to create a recordset.", _
        vbInformation, "Missing Data Source or Server"
    Exit Sub
End If
adoCNN.Properties("Password") = UserProperties("Password")
If UserProperties("DataSource")<>"" Then
    adoCNN.Properties("Data Source") = UserProperties("DataSource")
Else
    MsgBox "You must enter a Server Name (SQL OLEDB) "_
        or Access Database " (JET OLEDB) to create a recordset.", _
        vbInformation, "Missing Data Source or Server"
    Exit Sub
```

```
End If
Err.Clear
'Open the Connection
adoCNN.open
If Err Then
    MsgBox Err.Description,vbInformation,"Could Not Open Connection"
    MSHFlexGrid1.Clear
    Exit Sub
End If
'For SQL connection, the correct database should be specified
If UserProperties("Provider") = "SQLOLEDB" Then
    adoCNN.DefaultDatabase = UserProperties("DefaultDB")
End If
'Create the Recordset object if it doesn't exist; close it if it is open
If IsEmpty(adoRST) Then
    Set adoRST= Application.CreateObject("ADODB.Recordset")
Else
    If adoRST.State = adStateOpen Then adoRST.Close
End If
Err.Clear
'Open a recordset using the selected query
adoRST.Open ComboBox1.Value, adoCNN, adOpenKeyset
If Err Then
    Msgbox Err.Description, vbInformation, "Could not open Recordset"
    MSHFlexGrid1.Clear
    Exit Sub
End If
'Reset the grid, then load it
MSHFlexGrid1.ClearStructure
Set MSHFlexGrid1.DataSource = adoRST
End Sub
```

Populating List and Text Boxes with an ADO Recordset

Once you have created an ADO recordset, populating a data grid from it is a one-step maneuver. In the next example, we'll cover the somewhat more time-consuming process of displaying that data in list and text boxes.

Any time you distribute a form that relies on an external data source, you need to be sure the form can find the data source from every client machine. One option—if the data is fairly constant—is to install a copy of the database locally on every client. As the database or the number of installed clients grows in size, or the data's rate of change increases, this rapidly becomes impractical. If all the clients are connected to a LAN and the database is on a SQL Server or equivalent RDBMS, one possibility is a UDL file. Once you have created the UDL file and tested the connection, a copy of the file can be installed in the Data Links directory (or any other directory) on each client. If the data is not held in a server, but, rather, in a specific file such as an Access database, all clients would have to share the same drive mapping in order to use the identical UDL file. Otherwise, a separate UDL file would need to be created on each client.

The ADO list box form demonstrates the creation of an ADO connection using a UDL. The first step in the Item_Open event is the creation of a FileSystemObject, which is used to search likely directories for the Northwind.udl created earlier in this chapter. Once the UDL is located, the Connection object is created and then opened with two lines of code, followed by the creation and opening of the Recordset object. After the form controls are instantiated, iterating through the recordset fills the list box, as shown in Figure 15.15.

```
Function Item_Open()
    Set FSO = Application.CreateObject("Scripting.FileSystemObject")
    If FSO.FileExists("C:\My Documents\Northwind.udl") Then
      strUDLpath = "C:\My Documents\Northwind.udl"
      Set FSO = Nothing
    Elseif FSO.FileExists _
      ("C:\Program Files\Common Files\system\ole db\" _
        & "Data Links\Northwind.udl") Then
      strUDLpath = "C:\Program Files\Common Files\system\ole db\" _
        & "Data Links\Northwind.udl"
      Set FSO = Nothing
    Else
      Set FSO = Nothing
      Msgbox "The Northwind.udl was not found - this form will not " _
        & " function properly!" & vbCr & _
        "Please create the Northwind.udl in:" & _
        vbcr & vbTab & "C:\My Documents" & _
        vbCr & vbTab & "or" & _
        vbCr & vbTab & "C:\Program Files\Common Files\system\ole db\Data Links", _
        vbExclamation,"Missing Data Link"
      Exit Function
    End If
    Set cnnNWind = Application.CreateObject("ADODB.Connection")
    'Open ADO connection using the UDL
    cnnNWind.Open "File Name=" & strUDLpath
    If Err Then
      Msgbox Err.Description, vbInformation, "Unable to Open ADO Connection"
      Exit Function
    End If
    'Create and open the ADO recordset
    Set rstCust = Application.CreateObject("ADODB.Recordset")
    rstCust.Open "Select * from Customers", cnnNWind, adOpenKeyset
    'Instantiate the page and controls
    Set ListPage = GetInspector.ModifiedFormPages("List Box")
    Set ListBox1=ListPage.ListBox1
    Set ListBox1 = ListPage.ListBox1
    'Step through the recordset to fill the list box
    i = 0
    Do Until rstCust.EOF
      ListBox1.AddItem
      ListBox1.Column(0,i) = rstCust.Fields("CustomerID")
      ListBox1.Column(1,i) = rstCust.Fields("CompanyName")
      i=i+1
      rstCust.MoveNext
```

```
    Loop
    rstCust.MoveFirst
    'If a value exists for the Company Name field on the form,
    'select that value in the list box
    If UserProperties("CustomerID")<>"" Then
        'prevent moving recordset again in CustomPropertyChange event
        IsLoading = True
        ListBox1.Value = UserProperties("CustomerID")
        'set the bookmark to the current position
        ListBookmark = ListBox1.ListIndex
        'move to the selected value in the recordset
        rstCust.Move ListBookmark
        IsLoading = False
    Else
        ListBox1.Listindex = 0
    End If
End Function
```

Each time a selection is made in the text box, the corresponding record is located in the ADO recordset, and the various fields are then displayed in the text boxes. The form behaves as if the text boxes are bound to those fields, but it is important to recognize that they are not. The list box and the text boxes are bound to user-defined fields on the form. When the form closes, the Recordset and Connection objects are closed. When the form re-opens, the list box and text boxes are set to the value of the user-defined fields, and then the recordset cursor is moved to match the value of the list box. This behavior is intentionally made more obvious in the next form, where the ADO connection is not made during the form's Item_Open event.

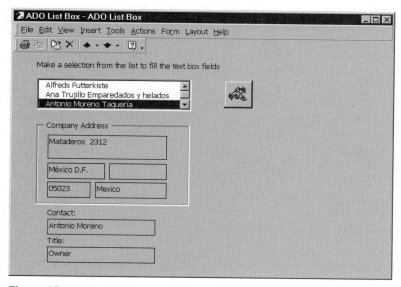

Figure 15.15 *The ADO List Box form.*

Accessing Data with a Persistent Recordset

The conflict between incorporating external data and serving disconnected users was mentioned earlier in this chapter (see "That's Great, But Does It Work Offline?"). The Persistent ADO Recordset form incorporates a possible solution for some applications using a Persisted ADO Recordset. The MSPersist OLE DB Provider supports saving recordset data and metadata as a string in the Advanced Data TableGram (ADTG) file format. The recordset can be recreated later from the persisted file. In this case, the recordset is saved as a DocumentItem in the Outlook Data Access Strategies folder. Although this example stores the persisted recordset in the personal folders (.pst) file folder that accompanies this book, there is no reason why you couldn't store the ADTG file in a public folder so that both on-line and offline users have access to the data in the file. The Persistent ADO Recordset form retrieves the ADTG file from the folder, recreates the original recordset, and uses it as a data source. This example solves one of the thornier problems Outlook developers face when they try to integrate database information with a custom form application: Where do we store the data? In this case, you store the data in an ADTG file in the folder where your application resides. For most situations, this solution is much more effective than using either Access 2000 or SQL Server in a database replication environment.

In practice, this solution would require some process to keep the persisted recordset in the public folder synchronized with its source database. Connected users would always access that updated copy. Offline users would pick up changes to the persisted recordset each time they synchronized their offline store. The Persistent ADO Recordset form shows both how to save and how to recreate the recordset, although the two parts would normally occur separately.

As you can see in Figure 15.16, the Persistent ADO Recordset form has the same fields as the previous form. It creates a connection to Northwind.mdb in the Item_Open event to create a persistent recordset. To see how this works, we'll examine the critical code in the *SaveRstPersist* and *cmdOpenPersist_Click* procedures.

Saving a Persistent Recordset

The persisted recordset will initially be saved to the temporary directory as Customers1.adtg. The FileSystemObject is used to locate the path to the local temporary directory and delete any previous versions of the file. The current version of the persisted recordset is created using the *Save* method of the ADO Recordset object. The next step is to delete any copies of the persisted recordset DocumentItem from the target folder. Following this deletion, a new DocumentItem is created in the folder and saved, and then the ADTG file is attached to the item which is saved again. Finally, the persisted recordset file is deleted from the temporary directory. The following code listing shows you how to save a datagram or persisted recordset in an Outlook folder:

```
Sub SaveRstPersist()
    'save a persistent recordset
    Dim FSO, strPath, flr, rstItem, i
    'save the recordset in advanced datagram format in the Temp directory
```

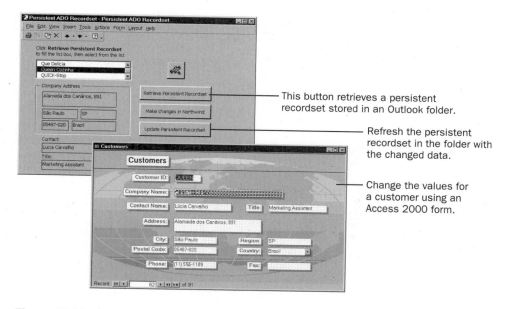

Figure 15.16 *The Persistent ADO Recordset form.*

```
Set FSO = CreateObject("Scripting.FileSystemObject")
strPath = "\Customers1.adtg"
strPath = GetTempDir & strPath
If FSO.FileExists(strPath) Then
    FSO.DeleteFile (strPath)
End If
'Make sure the reference recordset is current
rstCust.Requery
rstCust.Save strPath
'if a copy of the recordset already exists in the folder, delete it
strFolderPath = "\Building Microsoft Outlook 2000 Applications\" _
    & "5. Advanced Topics\Data Access Strategies for Outlook"
Set flr = OpenMAPIFolder(strFolderPath)
i = 1
Do While i < flr.Items.Count + 1
    If flr.Items(i).Subject = "Customer Recordset.adtg" Then
        flr.Items(i).Delete '
    i = i - 1
    End If
    i = i + 1
Loop
'create a new document item for the persistent recordset
Set rstItem = flr.Items.Add("IPM.Document.*adtg")
rstItem.Subject = "Customer Recordset.adtg"
rstItem.Save
'add the persistent recordset as an attachment to a new document item
rstItem.Attachments.Add strPath, 1
```

```
    rstItem.Save
    'delete the copy in the temp directory
    FSO.DeleteFile (strPath)
End Sub
```

Opening a Persisted Recordset

The *cmdOpenPersist_Click* procedure basically mirrors the *Save* procedure in reverse. The target folder is searched to locate the persisted recordset DocumentItem with a subject of Customer Recordset.adtg. If this item is found in the folder, the attachment is saved as Customer2.adtg in the user's temporary directory after any existing copy of the file is deleted. To open the ADTG file as a recordset, we use the *Open* method of the ADO Recordset object (it should be noted that the rstPersist object is independent of any other ADO objects). The rstPersist recordset is then used to fill the list box. The beauty of this approach is that the recordset lives in a MAPIFolder rather than in a RDBMS or on a local drive. If you synchronize this folder for offline use, the latest copy of the disconnected recordset will be downloaded to the user's offline store (.ost) file.

```
Sub cmdOpenPersist_Click()
    Dim strPath, myItem, myFile, OldFile, FSO, blnFound, flr, i
    'Locate the Document item with the persistent recordset attached
    strFolderPath = "\Building Microsoft Outlook 2000 Applications\" _
        & "5. Advanced Topics\Data Access Strategies for Outlook"
    Set flr = OpenMAPIFolder(strFolderPath)
    For i = 1 To flr.Items.Count
        Set myItem = flr.Items(i)
        If InStr(myItem.subject, "Customer Recordset.adtg") Then
            'Delete any previous copy of the file from the Temp directory
            strPath = GetTempDir & "\Customers2.adtg"
            Set FSO = CreateObject("Scripting.FileSystemObject")
            If FSO.FileExists(strPath) Then
                FSO.DeleteFile (strPath)
            End If
            'Save the attachment as a persistent recordset in Temp
            Set myFile = myItem.Attachments(1)
            myFile.SaveAsFile strPath
            blnFound = True
            Exit For
        End If
    Next
    'If a persistent recordset wasn't found, prompt the user to create one
    '(This is for the purposes of this demonstration form only)
    If Not blnFound Then
        If MsgBox("A Persistent ADO Recordset was not found in " & _
            vbCrLf & Application.ActiveExplorer.CurrentFolder & _
            vbCrLf & "Do you want to create one now?", _
            vbYesNo, "ActiveX Data Objects") = vbYes Then
                Call SaveRstPersist
                Call cmdOpenPersist_Click
                Exit Sub
        Else
```

```
        Exit Sub
    End If
End If
'Create an ADO recordset object, if there isn't one already.
If IsEmpty(rstPersist) Or TypeName(rstPersist) = "Nothing" Then
    Set rstPersist = Application.CreateObject("ADODB.Recordset")
End If
'Use it to open the persistent recordset
If rstPersist.State = adStateOpen Then rstPersist.Close
rstPersist.Open strPath
Set FSO = Nothing
'load the recordset data into the list box
ListBox1.Clear
i = 0
Do Until rstPersist.EOF
    ListBox1.AddItem
    ListBox1.Column(0, i) = rstPersist.Fields("CustomerID")
    ListBox1.Column(1, i) = rstPersist.Fields("CompanyName")
    i = i + 1
    rstPersist.MoveNext
Loop
rstPersist.MoveFirst
ListBookmark = 0
'if the form has a value for CustomerID, select that value in the list
If UserProperties("CustomerID") <> "" Then
    ListBox1.Value = UserProperties("CustomerID")
Else
    ListBox1.ListIndex = 0
End If
End Sub
```

Refreshing Data in the Form

You navigate through the rstPersist recordset by selecting a customer name in the list box on the form. If you close and then reopen the Persisted ADO Recordset form after making a selection from the list box, you will notice the text boxes are filled with information from the recordset, even though the list box is empty. The text boxes are displaying the values of the user-defined fields to which they are bound. The list box is also bound to a user-defined field named CustomerID, but because there are no items in the list, it can't display the value. Once you re-open the persisted recordset, the list box will be refilled and the bound value of the list box will be used to move to the corresponding record in the rstPersist. A script-level variable named *ListBookmark* holds the pointer to the current record in the rstPersist recordset.

```
Sub Item_CustomPropertyChange(ByVal Name)
If Name = "CustomerID" and Not IsLoading Then
    'Company Name changes when the list box selection changes
    'ListBookmark holds the last position in the list
    'use the difference between list index and last position
    'to move to the correct record in the recordset
    rstPersist.Move (ListBox1.ListIndex - ListBookmark)
```

```
    UserProperties("Contact Name")= _
        CheckForNull(rstPersist.Fields("ContactName"))
    UserProperties("Contact Title")= _
        CheckForNull(rstPersist.Fields("ContactTitle"))
    UserProperties("Address")=CheckForNull(rstPersist.Fields("Address"))
    UserProperties("CompanyCity")=CheckForNull(rstPersist.Fields("City"))
    UserProperties("Region")=CheckForNull(rstPersist.Fields("Region"))
    UserProperties("Company Postal Code")= _
        CheckForNull(rstPersist.Fields("PostalCode"))
    UserProperties("Company Country")= _
        CheckForNull(rstPersist.Fields("Country"))
    'reset the bookmark to the new position
    ListBookmark = ListBox1.ListIndex
End If
```

You can test the persisted recordset example by clicking the command buttons on the form in top-to-bottom sequence as follows:

1. Retrieve the data in the persisted recordset in the folder by clicking the Retrieve Persistent Recordset button.

2. Change data in the source database by clicking the Make Changes In Northwind button. Using Access Automation in VBScript, the Customers form in the Northwind database is opened to the record which is current in the disconnected recordset. Make changes to the current record and then either close the Access application window or use the record selector to move off the current record and update the database with your changes.

3. Click the Update Persistent Recordset button to update the persistent recordset in the folder with the latest data from the Northwind database. The changes you made in step 2 are reflected in the data retrieved from the datagram and displayed on the form.

Some final remarks are in order regarding disconnected ADO recordsets stored as ADTG Document items in folders. This approach will only work as long as the datagram contains current information from the source database. If you are using SQL Server as the data source of the ADTG file, you can write a trigger or use an agent process that recreates the disconnected recordset in the folder when data in the source table changes. Avoid placing dynamic data that constantly changes in an ADTG file. The ADTG disconnected recordset is best used for static data that changes infrequently and which is read-only to the user. Tables are often used in an application as lookups (for example, chart of accounts tables). They are infrequently updated and are read-only. Instead of rereading this data from the server every time your custom Outlook form is opened, the form can simply load the data from a locally persisted recordset.

Office 2000 Web Components

Office 2000 Web Components provides a way to bring database information into your Outlook application. The following table lists the Web Components that are available for use as ActiveX controls on pages of an Outlook custom form:

Component	Function
Pivot Table	The PivotTable component enables users to analyze information by sorting, grouping, filtering, outlining, and pivoting. The data can come from a spreadsheet range, a relational database such as Microsoft Access or Microsoft SQL Server, or any OLAP (On Line Analytical Processing) data source that supports OLE DB for OLAP, such as Microsoft's OLAP Services for SQL Server.
Chart	The Chart component graphically displays information from the spreadsheet, the PivotTable, or the data source component. Because it is bound directly to other controls on the page, it updates instantly in response to user interaction with the other components.
Spreadsheet	The Spreadsheet component provides a recalculation engine, a full-function library, and a simple spreadsheet user interface.
Data Source	The Data Source component is the reporting engine behind Data Access Pages and the PivotTable component. It manages communication with back-end database servers and determines what database records are available for display on the page.

Although the Office Components controls were designed with Web-based functionality in mind, they are also appropriate for Outlook custom forms. The Customers form in the Northwind Contact Management application in E-Chapter 3 on the companion CD uses the Pivot Table control to display customer order information.

> **More Info** For additional information on writing code for the Pivot Table control in an Outlook form, see E-Chapter 3, "The Northwind Contact Management Application," in the E-Chapters folder on the companion CD.

Strategic Considerations

Now that you've seen some of the ways that both extrinsic and intrinsic data can be incorporated into Outlook applications, let's summarize how these various options fit into a strategic picture of Outlook application development.

The following table discusses some of the approaches outlined in this chapter. This table focuses only on approaches for Outlook custom form development; it does not consider some of the other development avenues available, such as Outlook Web Access or Exchange Server Scripting and Routing. Although it is not meant to be all-inclusive or appropriate for every scenario, this table will give you an idea of some of the tradeoffs you must consider when you begin to design your Outlook application. You should consider all alternatives and make a choice that is best for your application before you begin to design forms and write VBScript code behind the forms. Otherwise, choices you make in the design phase can come back to bite you later. Keep in mind, of course, that your final decision might well include a combination of the approaches listed here.

Approach	C/W	IMO	Mobile Users	Advantages	Disadvantages
Build data into forms using PossibleValues and Keywords fields	Yes	Yes	Yes	Easy to build and no controls or type libraries to install.	Works only when a small number of unchanging values are associated with a user-defined field.
Supply lookup and dynamic data to intrinsic or extrinsic ActiveX controls on forms using ADO, DAO, or RDO	Yes	Yes, if data is supplied in a local database	Only when connected to network	Easier to maintain updates to lookup tables. ADO and DAO install by default. Fast and versatile object libraries.	Must install and maintain extrinsic ActiveX controls on user machine. Slow network or mobile connections adversely affect form load performance. Local error trapping and debugging.
Supply lookup data with persistent recordsets stored in folder	Yes	N/A	Yes	Works well with static lookup tables that must be available for mobile users.	Must use agent to update persistent recordset in folder.
Middle-tier components built as ActiveX DLLs in Microsoft Transaction Server*	Yes	N/A	Only when connected to network	Scales to hundreds and thousands of users with code executing on remote server. Errors tracked in NT Event log on server. Encapsulates business logic in middle tier. Works with diverse data sources, including Mainframe, RDBMS, Unix, etc.	Requires higher level of development skills. Not well suited to applications with mobile users.

*See Chapter 16, "Using ActiveX DLLs and Microsoft Transaction Server with Outlook."

A Word of Caution

Before you get too carried away with visions of all the cool tricks you can perform with data, take a little time to think about deployment and maintenance. One of the great things about Outlook is the power it offers for disconnected applications. Offline storage allows remote users to extract what they need from your Exchange information store and take it with them. Filtered synchronization allows those users to stay current with minimal connect times. If the application you build will serve remote users, you need to consider how much data they can effectively access without a network connection, or how much connect time will be required to keep their data up-to-date.

Where To Go from Here

ActiveX Data Objects (ADO)

Microsoft Corporation. *Microsoft Jet Database Engine Programmer's Guide, Third Edition*. Redmond, WA: Microsoft Press, 1999.

Microsoft Universal Data Access Web site
http://www.microsoft.com/data/

Microsoft ActiveX Data Objects Web site
http://www.microsoft.com/data/ado/

Office 2000 Programmer's Guide

Microsoft Corporation. *Microsoft Office 2000/Visual Basic Programmer's Guide*. Chapter 12, "Using Web Technologies," Chapter 14, "Working with the Data Access Components of an Office Solution," Chapter 15, "Retrieving and Analyzing Data," and Chapter 16, "Multiuser Database Solutions." Redmond, WA: Microsoft Press, 1999.

OLE DB

Microsoft Corporation. *Microsoft OLE DB 2.0 Programmer's Reference and Data Access SDK*. Redmond, WA: Microsoft Press, 1998.

Microsoft OLE DB Web site
http://www.microsoft.com/data/oledb/

Using ActiveX Data Objects with MDB Files and the Microsoft Jet Database Engine

Microsoft Corporation. *Microsoft Jet Database Engine Programmer's Guide, Third Edition*. Redmond, WA: Microsoft Press, 1999.

Henry, Alyssa. "Migrating from DAO to ADO (Using ADO with the Microsoft Jet OLE DB Provider)." Microsoft ActiveX Data Objects Web site at *http://www.microsoft.com/data/ado/*

Using ActiveX Data Objects with SQL Server

Vaughn, William R. *Hitchhiker's Guide to Visual Basic and SQL Server, Sixth Edition*. Redmond, WA: Microsoft Press, 1998.

Microsoft Corporation. *SQL Server Books Online*, "Building SQL Server Applications." An online version of this book is included with SQL Server 7.0, and is also available on the MSDN Online Web site at *http://msdn.microsoft.com/developer/*.

Using ActiveX DLLs and Microsoft Transaction Server with Outlook

In This Chapter

Why Use ActiveX DLL Components?

This chapter is aimed toward Outlook developers who are looking for an alternative to writing all of their form-level code in Visual Basic Scripting Edition (VBScript). ActiveX DLL components offer an alternative to developing and debugging your code in VBScript. As you learned in Chapter 13, "Creating COM Add-Ins with Visual Basic," you can create add-ins that expose public properties and methods. While COM Add-ins provide great advantages for Outlook 2000 development, they do not work as add-ins in previous versions of Outlook. If your application needs to access data stored on a remote server, then modularizing your code and creating ActiveX DLL components offers a very attractive alternative to writing data access code, for example, in VBScript. Many advanced Outlook forms applications require retrieval of data from external data sources—a chart of accounts, a list of approved suppliers, and so forth. These data sources might live in very disparate locations on your network.

This chapter shows you how to add a middle tier to a Corporate/Workgroup Outlook application using ActiveX DLL components and Microsoft Transaction Server. Microsoft Transaction Server (MTS) is a middleware object broker that ships as part of the NT 4.0 Option Pack. It offers process isolation, transaction control, security, and resource pooling for ActiveX components running on your network. MTS is one of the cornerstones of Microsoft's vision of DNA—also known as the Distributed interNet Architecture—which is based on COM and COM+. This chapter includes an example ActiveX component running within MTS that retrieves data to populate a multi-column list box or combo box on an Outlook form. This example might seem trivial at first, but scalability is a serious issue that must be addressed when you attempt to deploy your Outlook form to thousands of users in an organization.

This chapter is not meant to provide a complete and detailed presentation of all the nuances of ActiveX component design and MTS package deployment. Sources that offer knowledgeable in-depth information on these issues are listed at the end of this chapter. Think about Outlook applications from the perspective of N-tiered application development. Commonly Outlook applications are considered in terms of the Outlook client and the Exchange back-end. As collaboration applications become more sophisticated, you will need to think more about scalability, reliability, and the cost of development and deployment. Once you move down this path, you'll find that creating a middle tier for your collaborative application makes a lot of sense. Figure 16.1 illustrates the three-tiered approach we'll be covering in this chapter. The idea is to transfer some of the coding chores from the VBScript environment to the more robust environment of MTS running ActiveX components.

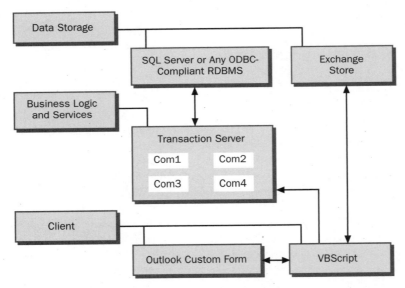

Figure 16.1 *Three-tier architecture for collaboration applications.*

Corporate/Workgroup Mode Only

The material covered here can only be used for a Corporate/Workgroup installation of Outlook 2000. If you want to run the example code, you must have Distributed COM (DCOM) installed on the client side and Microsoft Transaction Server 2.0 and SQL Server 6.5 or later installed on an NT server in your network. You will also need Visual Basic 6.0 Professional edition to run the sample List Server ADO project. If you want to create an ActiveX component that runs on a remote server, you will need Visual Basic 6.0 Enterprise edition.

Integrating Enterprise Data with Outlook Applications

As companies develop workflow applications using the rich messaging and forms development environment of Microsoft Exchange, some of these applications will require integration with other corporate data stores. Enterprise data stores reside in a variety of relational database management systems (RDBMS)—from LAN-based file data to mainframe data.

Applications based on Outlook and Exchange store their data in MAPI data stores. While MAPI data stores are perfectly adequate for most workflow applications, more sophisticated applications require additional links to data on the corporate network. Currently, MAPI data stores do not lend themselves to relational database design; one-to-many relationships cannot be easily modeled in a hierarchy of MAPI folders.

For example, you might design a billing and time-tracking application using the Outlook Contacts and Tasks folders. What happens when the design specification calls for adding general ledger codes to specific tasks so that the billing for these tasks can be sent to a corporate invoicing application? If you are the application designer, you know that it is not practical to add chart of accounts codes and descriptions to the PossibleValues property of a Forms 2.0 combo box. You'll have to retrieve the general ledger codes and descriptions from a departmental or corporate database and then load the data into your combo box. Once you have crossed the bridge into the complex world of departmental and corporate data, you'll need to consider issues relating to security, performance, data integrity, and scalability. The design alternatives that initially confront you might seem somewhat daunting. The choice you will finally make depends on the scope of your project and the depth of your programming resources.

The ListServerADO Project

The ListServerADO project creates a simple ActiveX DLL that exposes no properties and only two methods, *GetList* and *ExecSQL*. These methods retrieve and change information in any OLE DB or ODBC-compliant database, respectively. The *GetList* method returns a variant array used to populate a multi-column Forms 2.0 list box or combo box. The *ExecSQL* method runs an action query or a stored procedure against a database. Both *GetList* and *ExecSQL* require that you pass a Connect and a SQL string as method arguments. Of course, you can accomplish both of these tasks by writing VBScript code directly in your Outlook custom form. If your application requires you to support a small number of users (fewer than 50, for example), then writing code in VBScript using ActiveX Data Objects (ADO) works from the standpoint of development cost, performance, and scalability.

Consider an alternative situation when you're contemplating the rollout of an Outlook time card approval application to thousands of users. If your custom form will be heavily used during a time period, you need to test the scalability of your application against diverse load conditions before you move it into production. Having hundreds of users of your custom form attempting to make a database connection simultaneously may cause unacceptable performance levels. If you move interpreted code that executes in the VBScript forms environment to compiled Visual Basic code packaged as a component running under Microsoft Transaction Server on a remote server, you'll gain the advantage of a three-tiered collaborative application design described in the following table:

Benefit	Description
Component scalability	Your component runs on a single server within the protected process space of Microsoft Transaction Server, rather than on diverse clients. Requires installation of DCOM on the client where Outlook is running.
Component security context	The MTS Context object determines the DirectCaller, OriginalCaller, DirectCreator, and OriginalCreator user names. You can write those names to the NT Event log when an error occurs. MTS lets you manage component security and define security roles. You can define authorization for each component and component interface by assigning roles based on NT users and groups.
Database connection pooling	Pooling improves performance when you open Outlook forms that must populate list and combo boxes with lookup data.
Enhanced debugging to NT Event log	Component errors are trapped and recorded at the server level, rather than at the client level. The component writes errors to a central and secure NT Event log for distributed users of the component.
Implicit transaction support	Transaction Server uses Microsoft Distributed Transaction Coordinator (MS DTC), a system service that coordinates transactions. Work can be committed as an atomic transaction even if it spans multiple resource managers, potentially on separate computers.

As you'll see when we walk through the sample project, ActiveX components also offer ease of development and improved error tracking once you've deployed your application. Before you proceed, be certain you have the required software installed on both a test server and test client machine.

Client System
- Windows 98 or Windows NT Workstation with DCOM support. If you want to use Microsoft Windows 95 clients, install DCOM for Windows 95.
- Outlook 2000 and the Building Microsoft Outlook 2000 Applications personal folders (.pst) file on the CD-ROM accompanying this book.

Server System
- Windows NT Server Service Pack 3 or later
- Microsoft Transaction Server 2.0 Service Pack 1 or later

- ActiveX Data Objects (ADO) 2.1 or later
- Microsoft SQL Server 6.5 Service Pack 3 or later with upsized Northwind database, or SQL Server 7.0 with the sample Northwind database
- Microsoft Distributed Transaction Coordinator service
- Microsoft Visual Basic 6.0 Enterprise edition (optional) to modify and compile the ListServerADO project

Installing the Sample ListServerADO Project

To install the ListServerADO project

1. Expand the folder 5. Advanced Topics of the Building Microsoft Outlook 2000 Applications personal folders (.pst) file.

2. Expand the Using ActiveX DLLs and Microsoft Transaction Server folder and click the ListServerADO Project folder.

3. Select all the files in the ListServerADO Project folder.

4. Launch Windows Explorer and open Network Neighborhood. Select the computer that Transaction Server is installed on and create a folder named ListServerADO on that computer.

5. Drag the files you selected in step 3 to the ListServerADO folder in Windows Explorer. If you have problems dragging and dropping files, a self-extracting .zip file is located in the ListServerADO folder containing all the files in the ListServerADO Project folder. Just double-click the ListServerADO.exe file and extract the files in the .zip file to the folder listed in step 4.

Once you have installed the ListServerADO project, you can begin to install the ListServerADO.dll component on the computer where you are running Microsoft Transaction Server. Of course, the following discussion assumes that you have installed MTS. To install MTS, you must install the Windows NT 4.0 Option Pack or Windows 2000. Although you can install MTS on a Windows 98 system, it is recommended that you test MTS on a system running Windows NT 4.0 Service Pack 3 or later. The Transaction Server Explorer window shown in Figure 16.2 lets you create a Transaction Server package. A package is a collection of ActiveX DLL components that run in the same process. You can create an empty package and then add components, or you can install a pre-built package. We'll go through the steps of creating an empty package and then adding ListServerADO.dll to the package in the next section.

More Info For additional information regarding Visual Basic development strategies and the administration of MTS, see the on-line help that accompanies Microsoft Transaction Server.

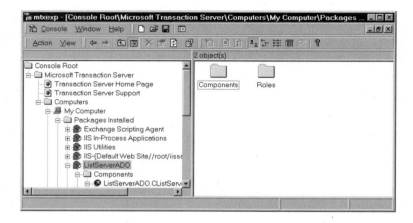

Figure 16.2 *Microsoft Transaction Server Explorer window.*

Creating a Package on Microsoft Transaction Server

Creating an Empty Package

You can either create an empty package or import an existing package if you have an MTS package (.pak) file. The following steps will show how to create an empty package and then import the compiled ListServerADO component.

To create an empty package

1. In the left pane of MTS Explorer, select the computer for which you want to create a package.

2. Open the Packages Installed folder for that computer.

3. On the Action menu, click New. You can also select the Packages Installed folder and either right-click and select New and then Package from the shortcut menu, or click the Create A New Object button on the MTS toolbar.

4. Click the Create An Empty Package button in the Package Wizard, as shown in Figure 16.3.

5. Type *ListServerADO* as the name for the new package, and click Next.

6. Specify the package identity in the Set Package Identity dialog box, and then click the Finish button. The default selection for package identity is Interactive User. The interactive user is the user that logged on to the server computer on which the package is running. You can select a different user by selecting the This User option and entering a specific Windows NT user in the User edit box.

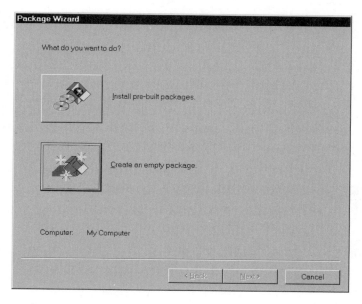

Figure 16.3 *Microsoft Transaction Server Package Wizard.*

Adding a Component

The next step in the process is to import the compiled ActiveX DLL component you placed into the ListServerADO folder on the computer where you are running Transaction Server. Follow these steps to install the ActiveX DLL component into the ListServerADO package:

To add a component to an empty package

1. In the left pane of MTS Explorer, select the computer on which you want to install the component.
2. Open the Packages Installed folder, and select the ListServerADO package.
3. Open the Components folder.
4. On the Action menu, click New.
5. Click the Install New Component(s) button in the Component Wizard.
6. In the dialog box that appears, click Add Files to select the files you want to install. You should select the ListServerADO.dll component that you copied to the folder C:\ListServerADO. Make sure that in Windows NT Explorer, the Hidden Files option is set to Show All Files. If this option is set to hide files with the .dll extension, you will not see ListServerADO.dll in the Select files To Install dialog box.
7. In the dialog box that appears, select ListServerADO.dll and click Open.

8. After you add the file, the Install Components dialog box shown in Figure 16.4 displays the file or files you have added and their associated components.

9. Click the Finish button to install the component. Note that installing a component allows you to view the interfaces and methods on that component. Figure 16.5 illustrates the interfaces and methods of the ListServerADO component shown in the Transaction Server Explorer. Notice that the component's two public methods, *ExecSQL* and *GetList,* are shown in the Methods folder under the Interfaces folder. The other so-called methods shown in this window are COM interfaces that cannot be directly called from Visual Basic or VBScript code.

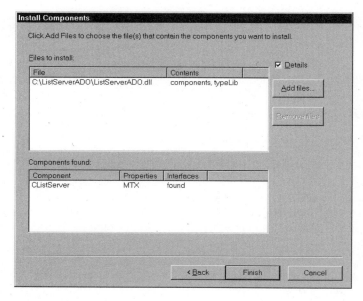

Figure 16.4 *The Component Wizard Install Components dialog box.*

Exporting the Package

That's all there is to creating an empty package and installing the ListServerADO component into the package. The final step, before you install the component in the registry of client systems, is to export the package. Exporting MTS packages will create package files that you can drag to another MTS machine to replicate the package, and it also creates a package installation program for client systems in a folder named Client.

To export the ListServerADO package

1. In the left pane of MTS Explorer, select the computer to which you want export the package.

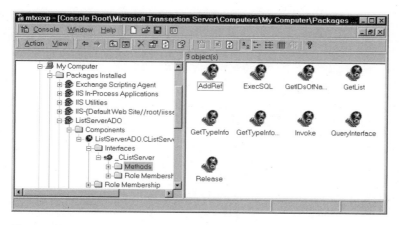

Figure 16.5 *Interfaces and methods for the ListServerADO component.*

2. Open the Packages Installed folder, and select the ListServerADO package.

3. On the Action menu, click Export.

4. In the Export Package To File dialog box that appears, click the Browse button to locate a folder to export your package to. If you export packages to C:\MTSExport, then point the Export Package To File dialog box to that folder and type *ListServerADO.pak* in the File Name edit box. Click Save.

5. Click Export to export the package and create an executable client installation.

6. Copy the client installation executable ListServerADO.exe in the Clients folder under the folder where you exported the package to a shared folder on your network so that you can install this package on client systems. Figure 16.6 shows the executable client installation in the Windows Explorer ready for installation on client systems.

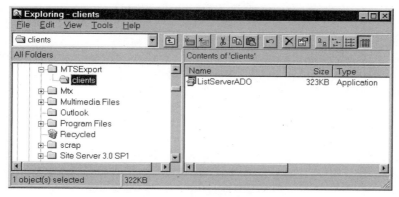

Figure 16.6 *The executable client installation for ListServerADO in Windows Explorer.*

Caution Do not run the client executable file on the server computer that is running MTS. Running the client executable on the server computer removes the registry entries required to run the server package. If you make this mistake, you must remove the application using the Add/Remove Programs utility in the Control Panel. Then delete and re-install the package using the MTS Explorer.

Important If a component's class ID (CLSID), type library identifier (TypeLibId), or interface identifier (IID) changes because you have recompiled the ActiveX DLL after you have exported the package, you must export the package again.

MTS Executables for Client Computers

Using the MTS Explorer, you can generate an application executable that installs and configures a client computer to access a remote server application. When you exported the ListServerADO package, you also created the MTS client executable file. The client computer that installs the executable must have DCOM installed, but it does not require any MTS server files, other than the executable, to access a remote MTS application. Executables generated by exporting a package will configure a client computer to access the deployment server on which the executable was generated.

MTS Client Executable

On the client system, the executable automates the following steps:

- It copies to a temporary directory on the client or server machine and then extracts the necessary client-side files, including type libraries and custom component DLLs. When the application installation is complete, files in the temporary directory are deleted.

- It transfers type libraries and component DLLs for the server application to the Remote Applications folder of the Program Files folder (all remote applications are stored in the Remote Applications folder). Each remote application has an individual directory named by the package's globally unique identifier (GUID).

- It updates the system registry with entries that enable clients to use the server application remotely (including information that is related to application, class, programmatic interface, and library identifiers), or that enable the server application to run on the server computer. Figure 16.7 shows the installed ListServerADO component installed in the Windows registry on the client machine, set to run remotely on a server named ME.

- It registers the application so that users can use the Add/Remove Programs icon in the Control Panel to remove it at a later date. All remote applications are prefaced with Remote Application so you can easily find the ListServerADO application in the list of installed components. Figure 16.8 shows the ListServerADO remote component on the Install/Uninstall page of the Control Panel Add/Remove Programs dialog box. Notice that you can only uninstall the ListServerADO remote application.

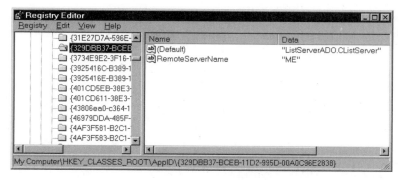

Figure 16.7 *The ListServerADO component in the registry of a client machine after installation with the MTS client executable.*

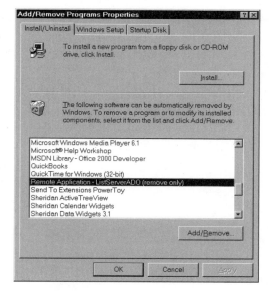

Figure 16.8 *You can uninstall Remote Applications from the list of installed components.*

Client Installation

To install the client executable for ListServerADO

1. Launch Windows Explorer on the client system and locate ListServerADO.exe in the Client's folder under the MTSExport folder you created earlier.

2. Double-click ListServerADO.exe in Windows Explorer to install the client executable.

More Info For additional information on installing ActiveX components with Outlook applications, see Chapter 12, "Distribute and Maintain Applications."

The client installation executable handles the registry settings that enable a calling application on the client computer to run the ListServerADO component on a remote computer. Normally, you should not have to run dcomcnfg.exe on the client computer to check DCOM settings. If the ListServerADO component does not function properly, check the impersonation and authentication levels on the client computer using dcomcnfg.exe. MTS works properly using the default values for these settings: Identify For Impersonation Level and Connect For Authentication Level.

⟳ To run the Distributed COM Configuration utility

1. Click the Start button, select Run, and enter *dcomcnfg.exe* in the Open edit box.

2. Click OK.

3. Click the Default Properties tab in the Distributed COM Configuration Properties dialog box, as shown in Figure 16.9.

4. Check Enable Distributed COM On This Computer check box.

5. Set the Default Authentication Level to Connect.

6. Set the Default Impersonation Level to Identify.

7. Click OK.

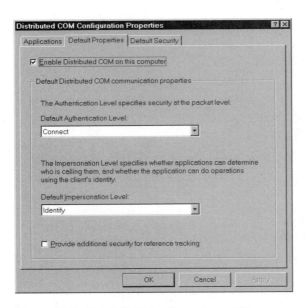

Figure 16.9 *The DCOM Configuration utility.*

Running the List Server Example Outlook Form

Once the ListServerADO client executable has installed the MTS component on your system, you can run the sample form that tests ListServerADO running remotely on an MTS computer. This Outlook form, which is shown in Figure 16.10, is just a basic example of what you can do with ListServerADO. It contains a Suppliers combo box that is populated with a recordset from the Suppliers table in the Northwind SQL Server database. When you click a command button on the form, you can populate the cmbSuppliers combo box with suppliers in ascending or descending order, depending on the SQL query passed to the *GetList* method of the component. You can also trigger an error condition in the remote component by clicking the Raise Error command button. In this instance, a bad DSN is passed in the Connect string argument for the *GetList* method. The NT Event log on the Microsoft Transaction Server computer records important information about the error when an error occurs.

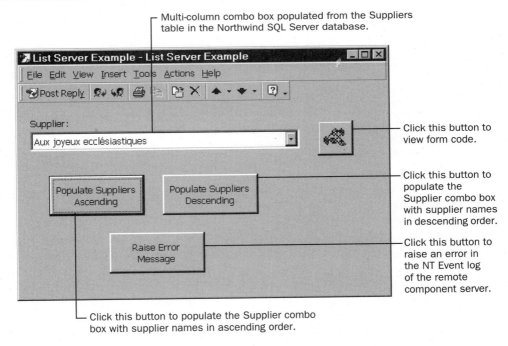

Figure 16.10 *The List Server Example form.*

⟳ **To open the List Server Example form**

1. In the Outlook 2000 Folder List, expand the folder Using ActiveX DLLs And Microsoft Transaction Server folder under the Folder 5. Advanced Topics.

2. Click the ListServerADO Example folder.

3.   Double-click the existing List Server Example item in the folder, or select New List Server Example from the Actions menu.

The code behind the List Server Example form appears in the following example. In a real application, you would populate combo boxes and list boxes during the Item_Open event of the form. The first form opened by a user will incur a slight performance penalty because the component on the remote server must be created in the process space of MTS. Also, a database connection must be made, and making this connection can require additional time depending on your network configuration. Once the first component is created at the server level, however, subsequent calls to the remote component running under MTS are almost instantaneous.

The VBScript code for the List Server Example dimensions two script-level variables. The *cmbSuppliers* object variable refers to the Suppliers combo box on the form. Because it is a script-level variable, you only have to set a reference for the variable once during the Item_Load event.

```
Dim cmbSuppliers 'Script-level declaration
Dim IsLoading 'Prevents cmbSuppliers Click event from firing during load

Sub Item_Open
    On Error Resume Next
    Set cmbSuppliers = Item.GetInspector.ModifiedFormPages _
        ("ListServerADO Object").Controls("cmbSuppliers")
    'If you bind the cmbSuppliers to a UD field,
    'Add code to populate cmbSuppliers in Item_Open event
    'cmdAscending_Click
End Sub
```

In the various button Click events, the *IsLoading* variable is set to *True* so that the cmbSuppliers_Click event will not fire when the List Index of the combo box is set. You should notice that well-designed remote components should allow error trapping on the client as well as on the server. The ListServerADO component writes error messages to the NT Event log on the machine where MTS is installed, and also passes an error back to the calling code in VBScript. You can trap this error in your code and raise a message box to the user, or you can elect not to raise errors directly in the client application. The *cmdAscending_Click* procedure loads the cmbSuppliers combo box with supplier names and phone numbers. One simple assignment statement loads the multi-column combo box by using the Column property of the combo box. If you set the Column property to the variant array returned by the *GetList* method of the ListServerADO.CListServer object, the combo box is populated in a single statement. The cmbSuppliers combo box has its ColumnCount property set to 3; the third column's width is set to 0 in the ColumnWidths property. To set the ColumnCount and ColumnWidths properties, use the Advanced Properties dialog box in Design mode.

```
Sub cmdAscending_Click
    Dim objLS 'As ListServerADO.CListServer
    Dim strSQL, strConnect
```

```
    On Error Resume Next
    IsLoading = True
    cmbSuppliers.Clear
    Set objLS = CreateObject("ListServerADO.CListServer")
    If Err Then
        MsgBox "Could not create ListServerADO object.", vbCritical
        Exit Sub
    End If
    strConnect = "DSN=NwindSQL"
    strSQL = "Select CompanyName, Phone, SupplierId " _
        & "from Suppliers ORDER BY CompanyName ASC"
    cmbSuppliers.Column = objLS.GetList(strConnect, strSQL)
    If Err Then
        MsgBox Err.Description, vbCritical
    End If
    cmbSuppliers.ListIndex = 0
    IsLoading = False
End Sub
```

The *cmdDescending_Click* procedure clears the cmbSuppliers combo box and repopulates the control with supplier names in descending order.

```
Sub cmdDescending_Click
    Dim objLS 'As ListServerADO.CListServer
    Dim strSQL, strConnect
    On Error Resume Next
    IsLoading = True
    cmbSuppliers.Clear
    Set objLS = CreateObject("ListServerADO.CListServer")
    If Err Then
        MsgBox "Could not create ListServerADO object.", vbCritical
        Exit Sub
    End If
    strConnect = "DSN=NwindSQL"
    strSQL = "Select CompanyName, Phone, SupplierId " _
        & "from Suppliers ORDER BY CompanyName DESC"
    cmbSuppliers.Column = objLS.GetList(strConnect, strSQL)
    If Err Then
        MsgBox Err.Description, vbCritical
    End If
    cmbSuppliers.ListIndex = 0
    IsLoading = False
End Sub
```

The *cmdRaiseError_Click* procedure lets you test error trapping in the remote component. A bad DSN is passed in the strConnect argument and causes the database connection to fail in the remote component. The error is passed back down to the calling application from the remote component and is also posted to the NT Event log on the MTS server where the component is running. Figure 16.11 shows an entry created in the NT Event log when the *cmdRaiseError_Click* procedure runs.

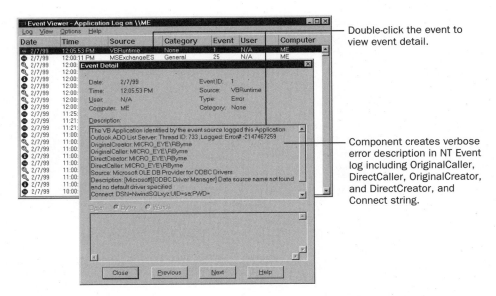

Double-click the event to view event detail.

Component creates verbose error description in NT Event log including OriginalCaller, DirectCaller, OriginalCreator, and DirectCreator, and Connect string.

Figure 16.11 *One of the many benefits of remote components is a centralized repository for error messages in the NT Event log of the MTS server where the component is packaged.*

```
Sub cmdRaiseError_Click
    Dim objLS 'As ListServerADO.CListServer
    Dim strSQL, strConnect
    On Error Resume Next
    IsLoading = True
    cmbSuppliers.Clear
    Set objLS = CreateObject("ListServerADO.CListServer")
    If Err Then
        MsgBox "Could not create ListServerADO object.", vbCritical
        Exit Sub
    End If
    'Pass an invalid DSN
    strConnect = "DSN=NwindSQL101"
    strSQL = "Select CompanyName, Phone, SupplierId " _
        & "from Suppliers ORDER BY CompanyName ASC"
    cmbSuppliers.Column = objLS.GetList(strConnect, strSQL)
    If Err Then
        MsgBox Err.Description, vbCritical
    End If
    cmbSuppliers.ListIndex = 0
    IsLoading = False
End Sub
```

Finally, the *cmbSuppliers_Click* procedure shows you how to retrieve a value in the hidden column of the combo box. Once the user selects a value in a populated combo box, the Click event fires for the control. The following example displays a message box informing the user of their selection and the hidden SupplierID value.

```
Sub cmbSuppliers_Click
    On Error Resume Next
    If Not(IsLoading) Then
        MsgBox "You selected " & cmbSuppliers.Column(0) & vbCrLf _
        & "Supplier ID: " & cmbSuppliers.Column(2), vbInformation
    End If
End Sub
```

Object Creation with Microsoft Transaction Server

Package Activation

When you test the ListServerADO component, you will notice that the first instantiation of the object takes a few seconds, whereas creating subsequent instances is almost instantaneous. There are two reasons for the initial delay when a component is first created. A component is created because a client application has executed the following statement:

```
Set objLSCreateObject = ("ListServerADO.CListServer")
```

Depending on the package activation type, MTS creates a process environment for the component code to execute. MTS can create two types of packages: library packages and server packages. You set the package type for a MTS package on the Activation page of the Package Properties dialog box. The Activation page for the ListServerADO package is shown in Figure 16.12.

Figure 16.12 *The Package Properties Activation page.*

A Library package runs in the process environment of the client that invokes a component in the package so long as the calling application also resides on the computer where MTS is installed. Library packages offer no component tracking, role checking, or process isolation. A Server package runs in the process environment of the NT Server where MTS is installed. MTS actually creates a separate application instance of MTS in order to run a Server package. Server packages offer all the benefits of component tracking, role checking, and process isolation. It is highly recommended that you select the Server package option when you package your own components in MTS.

Let's assume that the ListServerADO component has been created for the first time and the ListServerADO package is set to run as a Server package. At this point, MTS creates a separate instance of itself to run the ListServerADO package. The processing type required for this first-time instantiation is noticeable at the client machine when you first create a ListServerADO object. When the component is called again from either the same base client or another base client, you'll see the benefits of just-in-time activation in MTS. Although MTS releases the resources for the ListServerADO component when the *GetList* or the *ExecSQL* method completes execution, MTS still maintains a reference to the ListServerADO object as long as the idle time for the object has not expired. The separate application instance of MTS for your Server package also continues to run as long as the idle time has not expired. You set the idle time for a MTS package object on the Advanced page of the Package Properties dialog box shown in Figure 16.13.

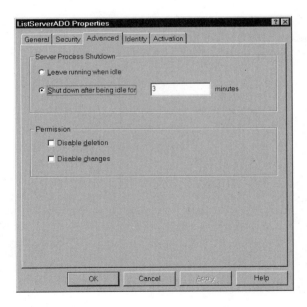

Figure 16.13 *The Package Properties Advanced page.*

If another component reference is created from a base client before the idle time has expired, MTS activates the component from its resource pool and the code in the component method executes. In MTS parlance, this feature is known as just-in-time activation. From a practical perspective, it means that MTS processes component requests from the calling client quickly and efficiently. Although calling the remote component from the base client requires COM marshaling across process boundaries, the net performance effect is not noticeable, given normal network bandwidth. You'll see the real benefit when hundreds or thousands of users call the component simultaneously.

Connection Pooling

One other point needs to be made about the benefits of using MTS. Database connections are pooled by MTS, so a database connection does not have to be made for every call to the *GetList* or *ExecSQL* method of the ListServerADO object. Connection pooling is not a unique feature of MTS. In fact, connection pooling is available on client systems running the version of ODBC and OLE DB shipping with Office 2000. Without going into a complex discussion of MTS component and package security—as well as database security issues (both of which can affect connection pooling)—connection pooling is automatic in MTS when a component packaged in a Server package makes a call to a database through ADO. As long as the idle time for a package running as a Server package has not expired and the time-out for the specific driver has not expired, the database connection will remain alive. Subsequent connection requests will recycle the existing database connection.

Opening the ListServerADO Project in Visual Basic

The List Server Example Outlook form lets you test the performance and behavior of VBScript code that calls a remote ActiveX component to accomplish its work. At this point, we'll examine the Visual Basic code for the ListServerADO project.

To open the ListServerADO project

1. Launch Visual Basic 6.0 from the Windows Start menu.
2. Select Open Project from the File menu.
3. On the Existing page of the Open Project dialog box, set the Look In drop-down list box to look in the ListServerADO folder that you created when you moved the sample code from the Building Microsoft Outlook 2000 Applications personal folders (.pst) file to a folder in the file system.
4. Double-click ListServerADO.vbp in the ListServerADO folder to open the project.

Setting Project References

The code in the ListServerADO project is, again, very simple and straightforward. Only two public methods are available in this component: *GetList* and *ExecSQL*. In a component you create for your own application, you will probably have methods that enforce business rules or interact with a database in more complex ways. Whatever properties and methods you create in your component, you must take some additional steps when you create a component for MTS. Before you create a component for MTS, you must first add a reference to the Microsoft Transaction Server Type Library, as shown in Figure 16.14.

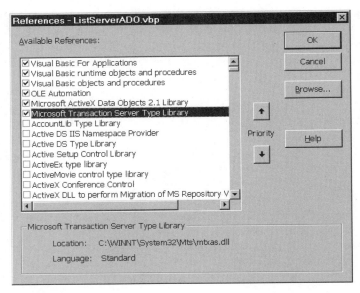

Figure 16.14 *Setting a reference to the Microsoft Transaction Server Type Library.*

➲ To set Project References for an MTS-enabled ActiveX component

1. Select the References command from the Visual Basic Project menu.

2. In the Available References list box, check the Microsoft Transaction Server Type Library reference. Be sure to add any additional required object library references at this point.

3. Click OK.

Note Don't confuse the MTS 2.0 Admin Type Library with the Microsoft Transaction Server Type Library. The Microsoft Transaction Server Type Library lets you create transactional components in Visual Basic for use in MTS. The MTS 2.0 Admin Type Library lets you administer MTS through a type library that is exposed to VBScript running in Windows Scripting Host, for example. You can also control MTS administration by including a reference to this object library in a Visual Basic application. When you write code for the MTS 2.0 Admin Type Library, you are automating commands that you would normally select in the MTS Explorer.

Threading Model

Next, you need to set project properties for your component relating to the component's threading model. The threading model determines how the component behaves with regard to COM concurrency. ListServerADO uses the apartment threading model. If possible, avoid creating single-threaded (also known as main-threaded) components for use in MTS. Single-threaded components do not scale effectively, and are subject to deadlocks.

To set project properties for an MTS-enabled ActiveX component

1. Select the *<Project Name>* Properties command from the Visual Basic Project menu.

2. On the General page of the Project Properties dialog box, make sure you've set the Threading Model drop-down list box to Apartment Threaded. See Figure 16.15 for an illustration of the Project Properties dialog box. Single-threaded ActiveX components are not recommended for packaging in Microsoft Transaction Server.

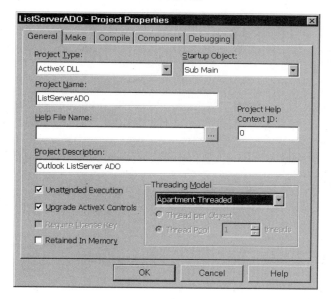

Figure 16.15 *Use the Project Properties dialog box to set the threading model.*

3. If your component does not expose user interface elements such as message or dialog boxes, be sure to check the Unattended Execution check box.

4. Make sure that the Startup object for your project is set correctly. ListServerADO uses an empty Sub Main as its startup object.

5. Click OK.

Class Properties

The next step is to set the Instancing property for classes in your component. Use the Properties window for the class to set the Instancing property. Figure 16.16 shows the class property settings for CListServer, which is the only class of ListServerADO. The Instancing property determines whether you can create instances of a public class outside a project, and, if so, how the class will behave. The Instancing property for CListServer is set to MultiUse, which allows other applications to create multiple objects from the class. One instance of the ListServerADO component can provide any number of objects created in this way.

If you want to use the transactional support of MTS, you should also set the MTSTransactionMode property in the Properties window for the class. The MTSTransactionMode for CDataServer is set to Uses Transactions. Even if you will not use MTS transactions in every method of your component, you should set MTSTransactionMode to Uses Transactions to use the MTS ObjectContext object in your component.

The MTS ObjectContext Object

In MTS, an ObjectContext object refers to the current object's context in MTS. Context contains information about the object's execution environment, including the identity of the object's creator and, optionally, the MTS transaction encompassing the work of the object. ListServerADO can always determine the NT identity of the object's creator and uses this identity for error logging. An object's context represented by the ObjectContext object is similar in concept to the process context that an operating system maintains for an executing program. You should be aware that setting MTSTransactionMode to Uses Transactions does not require that you actually use MTS Transactions in your component. Although it's easy to get confused about what constitutes a transaction in MTS, you shouldn't mistake a database transaction for an MTS transaction. MTS transactions can act as database transactions and, in fact, they do act as a set of database transaction commands for the *ExecSQL* method in ListServerADO. The *GetObjectContext*, *SetComplete*, and *SetAbort* methods that apply to MTS transactions provide the same functionality as the *BeginTrans*, *CommitTrans*, and *RollbackTrans* methods in ADO.

More Info For additional information about the properties and methods of the ObjectContext object, see the on-line help that accompanies Microsoft Transaction Server.

➲ To set Instancing and MTSTransactionMode properties for a class

1. Select the Class object in the Visual Basic Project Explorer window. Press Ctrl+R to display the Project Explorer window in Visual Basic.

2. Open the Properties window, as shown in Figure 16.16, by pressing F4.

3. Set the Instancing property to Multiuse, and set the MTSTransactionMode property to Uses Transactions.

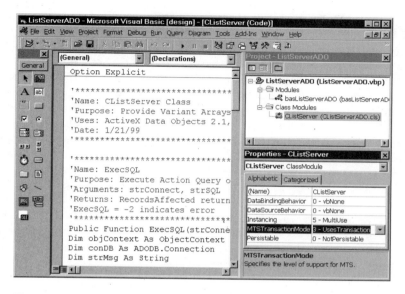

Figure 16.16 *Set MTS-related properties in the Properties window for the class.*

Once you've set class and project properties, you can get down to the work of creating methods and properties for your class. As a general rule of remote component creation, you want to minimize the number of cross-process calls to property procedures. If you can, make the properties of the component into arguments for the method calls. For example, in the following code listing for the ListServerADO class, you'll notice that strConnect and strSQL are passed as arguments to both the *GetList* and *ExecSQL* methods. The Connect string and SQL string could have been object properties, but then we would have three times as many trips across process boundaries to make a single method call such as *ExecSQL*. Instead, you pass these property strings as arguments to the method and economize on cross-process communication.

Both the *ExecSQL* and *GetList* methods are listed next. What you should notice in the almost identical code for both of these methods is the use of the MTS ObjectContext object to control the transactional state of the ListServerADO.CListServer object. An *objContext* object variable representing an MTS ObjectContext object is instantiated as the first executable statement in the procedure. After an ADO database connection has been created, the ADO *Execute* method is called for the database connection object in the *ExecSQL* procedure. If no error occurs, then the MTS *SetComplete* method commits the object's transaction. Because MTS uses the Microsoft Distributed Transaction Coordinator, the action query executed by the *ExecSQL* method is also committed as a database transaction. You don't need to add Transact-SQL Begin Tran, Commit Tran, and Rollback Tran statements to your query; MTS handles all the transactions for you.

Error Trapping in a Remote Component

Both *ExecSQL* and *GetList* have more code in their error handler than they do in the procedure itself. If an error occurs during the execution of the SQL statement, ADO will raise an error that is trapped, in turn, by the error handling code in the *ExecSQL* method. The error handler *Error_ExecSQL* obtains the NT identity for the caller of the object by using the Security property object for objContext. With the Security property of the ObjectContext object, you can obtain the name of the object creator in many guises. All of these security identities—plus the SQL and Connect strings passed to the method—are written to the NT Event log. The *LogEvent* method of the Visual Basic Application object writes *strMsg* to the NT Event log. Once the error has been recorded in the Event log, the *SetAbort* method is called to instruct MTS to roll back pending transactions. Finally, like any well-behaved component, the error handler also passes an error to the base client by using the *Raise* method of the Err object. If you refer back to the VBScript code for the List Server Example form, you'll see that the VBScript code uses in-line error trapping to raise an error message to the end user of your form. Some developers might elect to remove the client-level error trapping and consolidate all their error events in the NT Event log.

```
'*******************************************************************************
'Name: ExecSQL
'Purpose: Execute Action Query or Stored Procedure
'Arguments: strConnect, strSQL
'Returns: RecordsAffected returned by query
'ExecSQL = -2 indicates error
'*******************************************************************************
Public Function ExecSQL(strConnect As Variant, strSQL As Variant) As Variant
      Dim objContext As ObjectContext
      Dim conDB As ADODB.Connection
      Dim strMsg As String

      On Error GoTo Error_ExecuteSQL
      Set objContext = GetObjectContext()
      Set conDB = CreateObject("ADODB.Connection")
      conDB.Open strConnect
      conDB.Execute strSQL, ExecSQL        'ExecSQL=RecordsAffected
      objContext.SetComplete                      'No errors, SetComplete

Exit_ExecuteSQL:
    Exit Function

Error_ExecuteSQL:
    'Prepare error message for NT Event log
    strMsg = "Error# " & Err.Number & vbCrLf _
    & "OriginalCreator: " & objContext.Security.GetOriginalCreatorName _
      & vbCrLf _
    & "OriginalCaller: " & objContext.Security.GetOriginalCallerName & vbCrLf _
    & "DirectCreator: " & objContext.Security.GetDirectCreatorName & vbCrLf _
    & "DirectCaller: " & objContext.Security.GetDirectCallerName & vbCrLf _
    & "Source: " & Err.Source & vbCrLf _
    & "Description: " & Err.Description & vbCrLf
```

```vb
        strMsg = strMsg & "Connect: " & strConnect & vbCrLf _
        & "SQL: " & strSQL
        'Write error message to NT Event log
        App.LogEvent strMsg, vbLogEventTypeError
        ExecSQL = -2  'Error
        objContext.SetAbort
        'Raise an error for the caller
        Err.Raise vbObjectError + ERR_EXEC, Err.Source, Err.Description
        Resume Exit_ExecuteSQL

End Function

'****************************************************************************
'Name: GetList
'Purpose: Returns variant array to base client
'Arguments: strConnect, strSQL
'Returns: Variant Array populated with resultset created by strSQL
'****************************************************************************
Public Function GetList(ByVal strConnect As String, ByVal strSQL As String) _
        As Variant
        Dim rstADO As ADODB.Recordset
        Dim conDB As ADODB.Connection
        Dim objContext As ObjectContext
        Dim strMsg As String
        Dim avarList As Variant
        Dim intRows As Integer

        On Error GoTo Error_GetList
        Set objContext = GetObjectContext()
        Set conDB = CreateObject("ADODB.Connection")
        Set rstADO = CreateObject("ADODB.Recordset")
        conDB.Open strConnect
        rstADO.Open strSQL, conDB, adOpenForwardOnly
        'Notice that with ADO redim of array is not required
        avarList = rstADO.GetRows()
        intRows = UBound(avarList, 2) + 1
        GetList = avarList
        'This handles the exception when recordset is empty
        If intRows = 0 Then
            ReDim avarList(0, 0)
            GetList = avarList
        End If
        objContext.SetComplete

Exit_GetList:
    Exit Function

Error_GetList:
    ReDim avarList(0, 0)
    GetList = avarList 'Return empty
    'Prepare error message for NT Event log
    strMsg = "Error# " & Err.Number & vbCrLf _
```

```
                    & "OriginalCreator: " & objContext.Security.GetOriginalCreatorName & vbCrLf _
                    & "OriginalCaller: " & objContext.Security.GetOriginalCallerName & vbCrLf _
                    & "DirectCreator: " & objContext.Security.GetDirectCreatorName & vbCrLf _
                    & "DirectCaller: " & objContext.Security.GetDirectCallerName & vbCrLf _
                    & "Source: " & Err.Source & vbCrLf _
                    & "Description: " & Err.Description & vbCrLf
                strMsg = strMsg & "Connect: " & strConnect & vbCrLf _
                    & "SQL: " & strSQL
                'Write error message to NT Event log
                App.LogEvent strMsg, vbLogEventTypeError
                objContext.SetAbort
                'Raise an error for the caller
                Err.Raise vbObjectError + ERR_GETLIST, Err.Source, Err.Description
                Resume Exit_GetList
    End Function
```

Putting the Component to Work

If you want to expand the functionality of ListServerADO, use this project as a template for your own ActiveX component integrated with an Outlook/Exchange application. If you need to perform several database lookups to populate controls on forms during the Item_Open event, you'll discover that packaging components in MTS makes a lot of sense, especially when you must scale your application for hundreds or thousands of users. However, remote components do not fit every Outlook application requirement. Test your components by running them both locally and remotely in MTS before you commit to a design choice. If you do decide to keep your components local, remember that you can move a great deal of your code from VBScript behind Outlook forms into fully compiled, strongly-typed, and early-bound code in ActiveX DLLs that run on either the local machine or on a remote server.

Where To Go from Here

Additional Transaction Server Information

"COM Security in Practice"
http://msdn.microsoft.com/developer/news/feature/010598/mts/securecom.htm/

"DCOM: A Technical Overview"
http://www.microsoft.com/ntserver/appservice/techdetails/overview/dcomtec.asp/

"Developing a Visual Basic Component for IIS/MTS"
http://www.microsoft.com/sitebuilder/workshop/server/components/vbmtsiis.asp/

"Microsoft Transaction Server FAQ: Databases and Transactions"
http://msdn.microsoft.com/developer/news/feature/010598/mts/transfaq.htm/

Creating ActiveX Components with Microsoft Visual Basic

Appleman, Dan. *Developing COM/ActiveX Components with Visual Basic 6.0 — A Guide for the Perplexed*. Indianapolis, IN: Macmillan Computer Publishing, 1998.

Kurata, Deborah. *Doing Objects in Microsoft Visual Basic 6.0*. Indianapolis, IN: Macmillan Computer Publishing, 1998.

McKinney, Bruce. *Hardcore Visual Basic, Second Edition*. Redmond, WA: Microsoft Press, 1997.

Microsoft Corporation. *Microsoft Visual Basic 6.0 Programmer's Guide*. Redmond, WA: Microsoft Press, 1998. (An online version of this book is included with Visual Basic 6.0 and is also available on the MSDN Online Web site at *http://msdn.microsoft.com/developer/*.)

Pattison, Ted. *Programming Distributed Applications with COM and Visual Basic 6.0*. Redmond, WA: Microsoft Press, 1998.

Microsoft Transaction Server

Homer, Alex, and David Sussman. *Professional MTS MSMQ with VB and ASP*. Birmingham, United Kingdom: Wrox Press Ltd., 1998.

Visual Basic Web Sites

Advanced Visual Basic
http://vb.duke.net/

Carl & Gary's Visual Basic Home Page
http://www.cgvb.com/

Microsoft Visual Basic Web Sites
http://www.msdn.microsoft.com/vbasic/
http://www.microsoft.com/msj/0198/mtscom/mtscomtop.htm/

Chapter 17
Extending Outlook Using Exchange Server Scripting and Routing Objects

In This Chapter

The Server Side of Outlook 2000

Up to this point, we have focused on application development for Outlook 2000 from the client side. In this chapter we look at a different type of Outlook application, using a feature of Exchange Server available in version 5.5. The Exchange Event Service opens up new possibilities for developers of collaborative solutions. It offers a way to run event scripts in a server-based process, rather than running Visual Basic Scripting Edition (VBScript) code in the Outlook client application. Event Service scripts use Collaboration Data Objects (CDO) to instantiate messaging objects available to the script code. Because CDO provides support for calendaring as well as traditional messaging functions, scripting applications can be developed that automate appointment scheduling and replies to meeting requests.

To provide scalability and process isolation, the Event Service scripting engine can be configured to run as a package in Microsoft Transaction Server. An added benefit, from a developer's perspective, is the ability to instantiate custom ActiveX components in Event Service code that can perform many tasks not typically associated with Outlook/Exchange applications. Such tasks include database reporting for disconnected remote users using ActiveX Data Objects (ADO), account creation using Active Directory Services Interface (ADSI), or transaction-based messaging using Microsoft Message Queue Server (MSMQ).

The Event Service is a real workhorse provided there is a multi-processor CPU and enough memory on the server side. Event scripts function at the server level, and are therefore very powerful and flexible. For the same reason, they are not nearly as straightforward or forgiving as Outlook form-based scripts. This chapter will lead you through setting up the Event Service on your server and, in the process, briefly discuss its architecture. Next, we will cover the creation and installation of sample scripts, touching on some ideas for collaborative solutions using Event Service Scripting.

Corporate/Workgroup Mode Only

Most of the previous chapters contain information that is useful no matter how you are using Outlook 2000. The material covered here can only be used for a Corporate/Workgroup installation of Outlook 2000, and requires Exchange Server version 5.5 or later. To set up the Event Service initially, you must be a member of the Exchange Administrators group, although rights at that level will not be required to install or edit scripts in individual folders.

What Is the Event Service?

The Exchange Event Service is an NT service that monitors activity within the Exchange Information store on a folder-by-folder basis. If an item is added to, changed, or deleted from a folder—or if a specified timer event has elapsed—the service causes the script action associated with that event in that folder to fire. As a simple example, a public folder named Job Applications has an associated agent named Prelim Route. When a new message arrives in the Job Applications folder, the Event Service runs the *Folder_OnMessageCreated* procedure of the Prelim Route script. This procedure parses the subject line of the new message and routes a copy to the appropriate person in the Human Resources department, depending on the presence or absence of particular values in the subject string. For simple routing like this, it might make more sense to use a Folder Assistant in the Job Applications folder; however, the event script is potentially much more powerful. The *Folder_OnMessageCreated* procedure could include searching the Human Resources database for previous messages or actions connected to the sender of this message, and attaching that information to the forwarded message.

Because event scripts run on the server, an active Outlook session is not required. Agents can be created in dedicated private mailboxes to handle specific tasks; as long as the server is up, the agents continue to function. It is important to note that folder events and the Event Service response are not synchronous. The Event Service traps all the events for all items in all folders, and then processes them in sequence; depending on the number of items in the folders, an item could be added to a folder and then deleted by a user before the New Message event has fired.

The Event Service is automatically installed for a new installation of Exchange Server 5.5. If you upgrade from a previous Exchange version, however, the Event Service is not added by default. Once the service is installed, there are a number of components you must configure correctly before you can successfully create an application using event scripting. We will take a look at the system architecture to help you understand how those pieces fit together.

Installing and Configuring the Event Service

Installation of the Event Service is straightforward, but the configuration of its various pieces requires some care and coordination. Follow these steps to install during an upgrade:

Installing the Event Service

1.   Run Exchange setup and click the Add/Remove Components command button.

2.   Select Microsoft Exchange Server in the Options list box in the Complete/Custom dialog box and click the Change Option button.

3.   Check the Microsoft Exchange Event Service option and then click OK to install the Event Service.

Event Service Architecture

Figure 17.1 illustrates a view of the significant components of this service and how it interacts with the Exchange information store. The base process for the Exchange Event Service is provided by events.exe, which runs as an NT service. Typically, events.exe is installed in the C:\Exchsrvr\Bin folder. You can use the Services utility in the Control Panel to stop, start, and assign a service account to the Event Service application.

Normally, the Event Service will run under the same security context as the Microsoft Exchange System Attendant Service. However, there are instances when you will want the Event Service to run under a service account that can access network or database resources. If you plan to call ActiveX components from within your script code, you must carefully consider the service account assigned to the Event Service. As shown in Figure 17.2, any account you assign as the Log On As service account must have Log On As A Service privileges.

Assign the Event Service an NT Account

Follow these steps to add Log On As A Service privileges to an existing NT account:

To add Log On As A Service privileges to an NT account

1.   Start User Manager, click the user name or group you want to change, and select the User Rights command from the Policies menu.

2.   Check the Show Advanced User Rights check box.

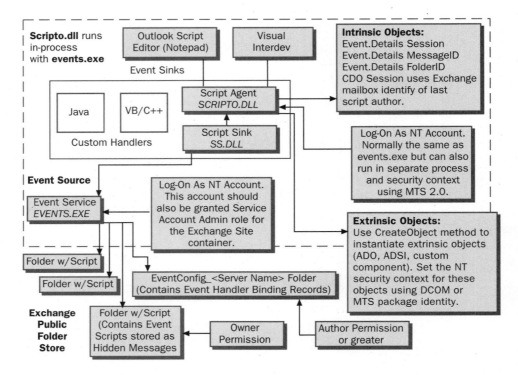

Figure 17.1 *In this version of the architecture, the script agent runs in the same process as the Event Service. Use Microsoft Transaction Server to allow the script agent to run in a separate process, with security context running from the Event Service.*

Figure 17.2 *Assign a Log On As user account to the Event Service using the Startup button in the Services utility of the Windows Control Panel. Be certain that any user account you assign as the Log On As Account actually has privileges to log on as a service account.*

3.   Select Log On As A Service in the Rights drop-down list box and then use the Add button to add a user or group.

4.   Click OK to confirm the addition.

NT Security and Exchange Roles

You cannot pick an arbitrary NT service account for the Event Service. The account you pick must have log-on permissions for all potential mailboxes and public folders that you will use to install scripts. By default, the Exchange Service account has this permission for all mailboxes and folders. However, if you select another NT account as the Event Service NT service account, you must explicitly grant permission to this account at either the folder or the mailbox level if you want to create scripts in the folder, or implicitly grant permission by assigning this account to the Service Account Administrator Role in the Exchange site, as shown in Figure 17.3.

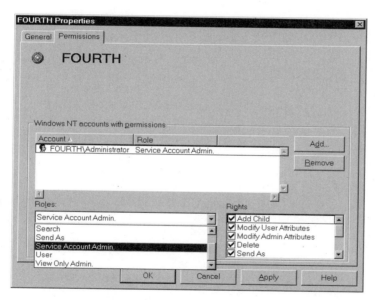

Figure 17.3 *Use the Permissions page in the Site container to assign the Service Account Admin role to the same NT service account used for the Event Service.*

The reason you must carefully consider NT security and Exchange Roles is that a pre-logged-on MAPI session object is created for each folder or mailbox involved in Event Scripting. The designated NT account must have the ability to log on to these Exchange resources. Any NT account that is given permission on a folder resource must have Mailbox Owner and Send As permissions for the resource. By default, the NT account assigned to the Service Account Administrator role for the site has these permissions for all resources in the site.

Setting Folder Permissions

Once you have installed the Event Service and used the Services utility in the Control Panel to ensure that the Event Service is running, you should use the Exchange Administrator application to assign permissions on both the source folder and a hidden system folder. If you do not assign the correct permissions, you will not be able to see the Agents tab on the Folder Properties dialog box for the folder in which you want to establish scripts. Figure 17.4 illustrates the use of the Exchange Administrator to set permissions on the EventConfig folder.

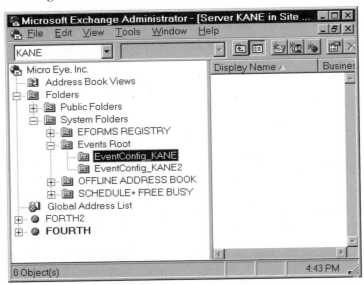

Figure 17.4 *Locate EventConfig_<ServerName> under Events Root under System Folders. If you cannot see this folder in the Exchange Administrator, it's likely that you have not installed the Event Service.*

This folder's permissions must be set using the Exchange Administrator application. Permissions for EventConfig_*<ServerName>* cannot be set using the Outlook client. To set the permissions on the EventConfig_*<ServerName>* folder, follow these steps:

➲ **Granting permissions on the EventConfig_*<ServerName>* folder**

1. Log on to your computer with an NT account having Administrative privileges on your Exchange server. Use the Windows Start menu to launch the Exchange Administrator program.

2. Expand the Folders item in the site so that you can see the EventConfig_*<ServerName>* folder under Events Root under System Folders. Remember that *<ServerName>* will be replaced with the actual name of your Exchange Server.

3. Highlight the EventConfig_<*ServerName*> folder and select the Properties command on the File menu.

4. Click the Client Permissions command button on the General page of EventConfig_<*ServerName*> Properties dialog box.

5. Assign a role of Author or greater using the Client Permissions dialog box. Click the Add button to add either individual mailbox accounts or a Distribution List. Distribution Lists are useful when you want to add a group of script developers whose membership might vary over time. Make sure that the role assigned to the account is at least Author. Exercise caution in assigning the Owner role to untrusted accounts.

6. Click OK when you have assigned accounts and roles to EventConfig_<*ServerName*>.

Once you have assigned permissions on EventConfig_<*ServerName*>, you can begin to create scripts in either public folders or an individual user's mailbox subfolders. To create a script in a folder, you must have Owner permissions on that folder (see Figure 17.5). If you have less than Owner permissions, or if the Exchange Server Scripting Add-in has not been installed, you will not see the Agents tab when you view the Folder Properties dialog box.

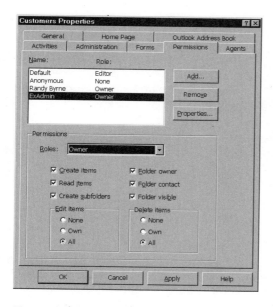

Figure 17.5 *Make sure that you have Owner permissions on a folder before you attempt to add event scripting to the folder.*

To check your permissions, follow these steps in the Outlook client.

To verify your permissions on the EventConfig folder

1. Open Outlook 2000 and select Options from the Tools menu.

2. Click the Other tab on the Options dialog box and click the Advanced Options button to open the Advanced Options dialog box.

3. Click the Add-In Manager command button. Make sure that Server Scripting is checked in the list of add-ins. You will have to locate and install the scrptxtn.ecf add-in if it is not in the list.

4. Click OK twice.

5. Navigate to the folder where you want to establish a script in either the Outlook Shortcut bar or the Folder List. Single-click the folder.

6. Select Folder on the File menu and then select the Properties For <FolderName> command, or right-click the folder and select the Properties command on the shortcut menu.

7. If you see the Agents tab, you will be able to attach event scripts to the folder. If you are the folder owner and wish to add a user or Distribution List as additional owners of your folder, click the Permissions tab and then click the Add button to add these accounts in the Owner role.

8. Click OK to accept your changes.

Note: Use the Exchange Administrator to add trusted script developers as individual users or a global group with Inherited Permissions to either the Site or the Recipients container. These users will be able to open mailboxes that will run Event Service scripts without requiring explicit permissions on the folders in the mailbox. Remember that when you add user permissions to a site, server, or container, you are adding users or groups based on NT security accounts. Unlike the Permissions page for a folder that sets permissions based on mailbox accounts or membership in Distribution Lists in the Global Address List, these permissions can only be set using the Exchange Administrator application.

Writing Scripts

After installing the Event Service and setting up permissions correctly, it's a good idea to familiarize yourself with the sample scripts that ship with Exchange before you actually write code. The sample scripts are located on the Exchange 5.5 CD-ROM in folders under the Server\Support\Collab\Sampler\Scripts folder. Also consult the Help file agents.hlp located in the same scripts folder. The following steps provide a general outline of the steps you must follow to create a script agent:

To create a script agent

1. Start Outlook.

2.   Navigate to the folder where you want to establish a script in either the Out-look Shortcut bar or the Folder List. Single-click the folder.

3.   Select Folder on the File menu and engage the Properties For <FolderName> command or right-click the folder and select the Properties command on the shortcut menu.

4.   Click the Agents tab on the Folder Properties dialog box to display the Agents property page. If you cannot see the Agents tab, you are not the owner of the folder where you intend to establish a script agent, or you do not have Author or higher permissions on the EventConfig folder. Ask your System Administra-tor to check your permissions on the EventConfig_<ServerName> folder.

5.   If you are creating a new script, select New to display the New Agent dialog box. If you are editing an existing script, select the script in the Agents For This Folder list box and click the Edit button.

6.   Give the agent a name, such as Sales Agent. You can also provide a date for the agent script in the Agent Name list box.

7.   Select the events to be monitored in the When The Following Events Occur list box. See Figure 17.6 for an illustration of the Agent dialog box.

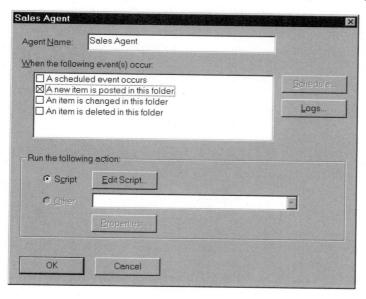

Figure 17.6 *The Agent dialog box lets you determine which events are monitored by the Event Service. You can also view a log that records errors in your script.*

8.   Choose an agent for the event. To use the default script agent, choose the Script Option button and go to step 9.

Note Notice in Figure 17.6 that the Schedule button is dimmed unless you select A Scheduled Event Occurs option in the list box. If you check A Scheduled
Event Occurs, you will cause the Folder_OnTimer procedure to fire in your folder.
You can specify intervals from 15 minutes to weekly, with day and time restrictions. Use the timer event judiciously to prevent server overload. See Figure 17.7
for an example of the Scheduled Event dialog box.

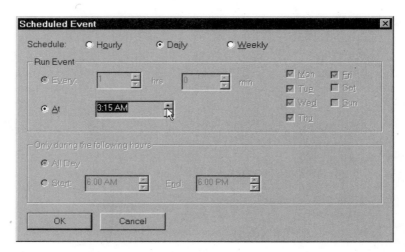

Figure 17.7 *Use the Scheduled Event dialog box to fire folder-level events at a
specified interval.*

Note If you write code in an event procedure, the event must be checked in the
When The Following Events Occur list box before the event will actually fire. Conversely, if you check the event but don't supply code to the stubs that appear in
a default script, nothing will happen when the event fires.

9.   Choose Edit Script to launch Notepad. Notice that a temporary file name is vis-
     ible in the title bar of the Notepad application. If you are creating a new script,
     a default script opens that contains stubs for the four events supported in the
     Event Service. See the table on page 668 for a list of the supported events. If a
     script already exists, clicking the Edit Script command button will open the ex-
     isting script in your editor. Figure 17.8 illustrates a script open for editing. You
     must explicitly save the script in the Editor window to save changes.

10. If custom agents are available, they are listed in the drop-down list box below
     the Edit Script command button. Custom agents are ActiveX components that
     implement the IExchangeEventHandler interface. See the Help file agents.hlp
     for detailed information about creating and installing custom event handlers. If

you select a custom agent that is also an ActiveX control, choose the Properties button to set the properties of the control in the Properties dialog box.

11. Be sure to approve the Agent dialog box by clicking OK. If you attempt to close the Agent dialog box while you have an open editing session, you will be warned that you must close the session before continuing.

12. Remove all Stop statements used in debugging your code before putting the script into production. Test your scripts thoroughly on a test server before you move them into a production environment.

```
'Division ID is concatentation of GroupID and DivisionID
strGroupID= Left(msgTarget.Text,8)
strDivID=Mid(msgTarget.Text,9,4)
objDS.GetPlanRate strDivision,strGroupID, strDivID
If Err.Number = 0 Then
        strSubject = msgTarget.Subject
        strBody = ""
        strFileName = objDS.ExcelFileName
        strPathName = objDS.ExcelFilePath
        If strPathName <> "" then
                MakeResponseMessage strSubject, strBody, strFil
                objDS.KillFile strPathName
        Else
                strResponse = "GetPlanRate Internal Error: " &
                strBody = "Internal Error. Sales Agent could no
                RaiseError strResponse, strBody
                Set ObjDS = Nothing
                Exit Sub
        End If
Else
        Script.Response = "GetPlanRate Method Failed " & Err.De
End If
```

Figure 17.8 *An open editing session. This script uses* CreateObject *to create an instance of a custom ActiveX DLL component written in Visual Basic that automates the creation of Excel workbooks containing data stored in Microsoft SQL Server. The Event Script code attaches the workbook to a response message and sends the attached workbook back to the originator of the message.*

Event Service Event Model

The following table lists the four events supported by the Exchange Event Service. One of the strengths of the Event Service is that the events are independent of the client that creates the message in the event-ready folder. Exchange Event Service events are folder-based, not client-based. For example, your Exchange Server could host a public folder discussion application that allows anonymous users to post messages to a public folder using Outlook Web Access. If your Exchange Administrator has enabled Outlook Web Access on your server, users can access their private information stores and public folders through a browser. Anonymous users can also contribute to public folder discussions. The Post form in the folder could also be an Outlook custom form that was converted with the Outlook HTML Form Converter that ships with Exchange 5.5. If an anonymous user posts to the target public folder, an Exchange scripting agent can apply application logic to the messages posted to the folder, regardless of whether they were posted by a client running Outlook for Windows, Outlook for the Macintosh, Netscape Navigator, or Internet Explorer.

Event Type	VBScript Sub Name	Applies To	Frequency
New	Folder_OnMessageCreated	Folder/Message	Asynchronous.
Change	Message_OnChange	Message of any item type (IPM.Note, etc.)	Asynchronous.
Delete	Folder_OnMessageDeleted	Folder/Message	Asynchronous.
Timer	Folder_OnTimer	Folder only	Minimum 15 minute interval. Hourly, daily, or weekly with day and time restrictions.

Using Collaboration Data Objects

Collaboration Data Objects (CDO) provides the intrinsic object model for Event Service Scripting. CDO is thread-safe and provides a robust environment for scripting in a server environment. You might wonder why you can't create a reference to an Outlook Application object in your event script, since Outlook's Object Model contains objects and properties that are not available in CDO. It is strongly recommended that you avoid instantiating an Outlook Application object in an event script on your Exchange server. Outlook's Object Model is single-threaded and can display user-interface elements such as Explorer or Inspector windows that are likely to hang either your script or your server in unanticipated ways. In the event you need to retrieve fields in Outlook custom forms within your script, we'll discuss some tricks to help you accomplish this functionality later in the chapter. In its former incarnation, CDO was known as Active Messaging. For more information on CDO, sample scripts, and knowledge base articles, visit the CDO Live Web site at *http://www.cdolive.com/*.

Here are the main features that CDO offers to Exchange Server scripting:

- Scalable and tuned to the server environment
- Thread-safe
- Supports multiple code pages for multiple language applications
- Supports server-side caching for increased performance
- Provides a comprehensive object model that lets you access folders, messages, and user-defined fields in items

- Provides AppointmentItem and MeetingItem objects to enhance scripting in folders that contain Calendars .
- Compatible with scripting code written in VBScript or JScript

If you refer to the Event Service Architecture diagram shown earlier in Figure 17.1, you will see that CDO provides the intrinsic objects for Event Service code. All objects in CDO derive from the Session object. The Session object is conveniently preloaded into the scripting agent as an object referenced by EventDetails.Session. It's helpful if you then assign this Session object to a global session object known as objCDO. Use a consistent naming convention in your scripts to increase readability and facilitate debugging. The following table lists the intrinsic objects in the agent script and the equivalent object in the Outlook Object Model:

Intrinsic Object	CDO Object	Outlook Object Model Equivalent
EventDetails.Session	Session object	Outlook.NameSpace
EventDetails.MessageID	Message.ID property	Item.EntryID
EventDetails.FolderID	Folder.ID property	Folder.EntryID

Pre-Loaded CDO Session Assumes Identity of Last Editor

It's critical to recognize that the CDO Session object is pre-loaded in the agent script environment. For security reasons, this CDO Session uses the mailbox identity of the last Exchange user to save the script in a given folder. The mailbox identity of the script editor is determined by the mailbox name you entered in the General page of the Microsoft Exchange Server Properties dialog box in the Mail utility of the Windows Control Panel. In the object terminology of CDO, the CurrentUser object property of the CDO Session returned by EventDetails.Session corresponds to the mailbox name of the Exchange user identified in the profile used during the last editing of the script.

This distinction is essential when you attempt to write scripts in a mailbox where you want to create appointments, for example. If your profile is registered under *Your Name* and you create a script in the Inbox of the mailbox for Conference Room 101, any Appointment items created in the script will be placed in the Calendar folder for the *Your Name* mailbox, rather than being placed in the Conference Room 101 mailbox. To circumvent this identity convention, create a Conference Room 101 profile for the Conference Room 101 mailbox, log on to Outlook using this profile, and finally edit and save the script in the Conference Room 101 Inbox. When this script executes, the CurrentUser property of the Session object will return Conference Room 101 as the CurrentUser rather than *Your Name*. Do not attempt to instantiate a CDO object using a different Logon identity. You also should never call a *Logon* method that will display a Logon dialog box or an alert box within an event script. Remember that scripts are designed for unattended execution.

A Choice of Programming Languages

You can author scripts in either Visual Basic Scripting Edition (fondly known as VBScript) or JScript. The examples in this chapter use VBScript as the programming language of choice. See the Help file agents.hlp for additional details on using both languages in one script.

When using VBScript, remember that enumerated constants in a called object model such as ActiveX Data Objects (ADO) are not available intrinsically. You must use the CONST statement in the global declarations section of your code to declare these constants. Be aware that constants and variables are scoped by position in VBScript code. This means that any variables or constant declarations that precede pre-defined script event procedures—or other function or sub procedures in your code—are global by position. Here are some suggestions and examples you will want to consider when writing VBScript code for event scripts:

- Use Option Explicit to enforce variable declaration.
- Don't type your variables; all variables in VBScript code have a type of variant.
- Use a consistent naming convention to improve readability.
- Use the *CreateObject("ProgID")* method in your script code to create an instance of other object components. Make sure you have NT account permissions to create an instance of any object you create in this manner. Use DCOM to check object permissions for a given NT account or group. The following code example obtains the number of records in the Authors table in the pubs database in SQL Server and prepares a response message:

```
Set objConn = CreateObject("ADODB.Connection")
objConn.Open ("DSN=Pubs;UID=sa;PWD=")
strSQL = "Select Count(*) from Authors"
Set objRS = objConn.OpenResultset(strSQL)
MakeResponseMsg "Record Count", "There are " _
& objRS(0) & " records in authors", "", ""
```

- Use in-line error trapping in your code with On Error Resume Next. Since the Event Service environment is not interactive, liberally use the *DebugAssert* procedure to pinpoint the source of an error. Use the *Script.Response* method to write error messages to the Script log. See Code Example 1 for a detailed piece of code that uses in-line error trapping to send a response message with an optional attachment.
- If you use *CreateObject* to create additional objects, don't attempt to raise dialog boxes or forms from the extrinisic object library.
- Use the Fields collection to access the Outlook user-defined fields collection object in a message item.

Code Example 1. **Use extensive in-line error trapping in event script code to pinpoint the source of an error**

```
'**************************************************************************
'    Name: MakeResponseMsg
'    Description: Sends message and optional attachment
'    Arguments: Subject, Body Text, Attachment Name, Attachment Path
'**************************************************************************
Private Sub MakeResponseMsg(strSubj, strBody, strName, strPath)
Dim objCDO                'Session Object
Dim objMsgResponse        'Response Message Object
Dim objFolder             'Current Folder Object
Dim objFolderOutbox        'Outbox Folder Object
Dim objMsgTarget          'Target Message Object
Dim objRec                'Recipients Object

On Error Resume Next      'In-line error trapping

Set objCDO = EventDetails.Session
DebugAssert "EventDetails.Session"

Set objFolderOutbox = objCDO.Outbox
DebugAssert "objCDO.Outbox"

Set objFolder = objCDO.GetFolder(EventDetails.FolderID, Null )
DebugAssert "objCDO.GetFolder"

Set objMsgTarget = objCDO.GetMessage(EventDetails.MessageID, Null )
DebugAssert "objCDO.GetMessage"

Set objMsgResponse = objFolderOutbox.Messages.Add(strSubj, strBody)
If Err.Number = 0 Then
        'Must have both strName and strPath to add to attachments
    If Len(strName) and Len(strPath) Then
        objMsgResponse.Attachments.Add strName, 0, 1, strPath
        If Not Err.Number = 0 then
            DebugAssert "objMsgResponse.Attachments.Add"
        End If
    End If
    Set objRec = objMsgResponse.Recipients
    objRec.Add "", "", 1, objMsgTarget.Sender.ID
    If Err.Number = 0 Then
        objRec.Resolve(False)
        If objRec.Resolved = True Then
            objMsgResponse.Send
            If Not Err.Number = 0 Then
                DebugAssert "objMsgResponse.Send"
            End If
        Else
            DebugAssert "objRec.Resolve"
        End If
```

```
        Else
            DebugAssert "objRec.Add"
        End If
    Else
        DebugAssert "objFolderOutbox.Messages.Add"
    End If
End Sub
'*********************************************************************************
'   Name: DebugAssert
'*********************************************************************************
Private Sub DebugAssert(strMsg)
Dim strDebug
if err.number <> 0 then
        strDebug = strMsg & " Failed. Error " _
    & cstr(err.number) & " Desc: " & err.description
        err.clear
    Script.Response = strDebug
end if
End Sub
```

Debugging Scripts

Script errors are inevitable, and script developers must have a means of debugging them. Depending on the software installed on your Microsoft Exchange Server, you have the following debugging options:

- Microsoft Script Debugger available with the NT 4.0 Option Pack and Internet Explorer 4.x.

- Microsoft Visual InterDev 6.0 Script Editor available with Visual Studio 98.

- Microsoft Script Editor available with Office 2000. The Microsoft Script Editor is not included in the default installation of Office 2000. See Chapter 11, "Using VBA and VBScript with Outlook," for additional information on installing and using the Microsoft Script Editor.

Note If you have both Visual InterDev 6.0 Script Editor and Microsoft Script Editor that accompanies Office 2000 installed on your Exchange server, Microsoft Script Editor will operate as the default debugger for Exchange scripting agents.

Using Visual InterDev 6.0 Script Editor with the Event Service

When it comes to debugging Exchange Event Service scripts, you can struggle along with the Script Debugger available with Internet Explorer 4.x or you can use the superior Script Editor that ships with Visual InterDev 6.0. The Visual InterDev 6.0 Script Editor offers the following debugging features for Exchange Event Service script developers.

- Although script debugging is not interactive (you cannot modify the script while your code is running), you can obtain context-sensitive help using MSDN Library by placing the cursor under a keyword and pressing F1.
- The Script Editor provides Step Into, Step Over, Step Out commands.
- The Locals window lets you observe the value of all variables in the currently executing procedure.

Caution One limitation of the Event Service is that you must use a debugger on the actual machine where you are running the event script, as shown in Figure 17.9. You cannot debug event scripts remotely, so dress warmly and wear comfortable shoes if your Exchange Server is mounted on a rack in a climate-controlled machine room!

The accepted way to cause the debugger to fire is to insert a Stop statement (VBScript) or a Debugger statement (JScript) at the appropriate point in your code. Keep the following tips in mind when you use either debugger:

- You must log on to your NT Server using the same service account under which the Event Service is running. You will have unpredictable results if you are using different NT accounts for the current logged-on user and the service account for the Event Service.
- Use the immediate window to examine variable values while the code is running. You can also execute statements from the immediate window.

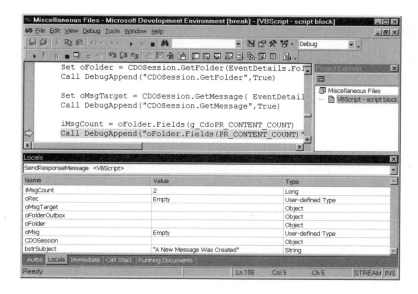

Figure 17.9 *The Visual InterDev 6.0 Script Editor allows you to step through code execution and observe variables in the Locals window.*

- To step through your code after the Stop statement, use F8 for the Script Debugger, and F11 if you are using the Script Editor.

- Remember that neither debugger is interactive. If you discover errors, press F5 to complete execution. You will then need to edit your script and retest it.

- If your code hangs within the Script Debugger or causes a protection error, you will probably need to use the Task Manager to kill events.exe. For a more graceful recovery, attempt to stop and restart the Exchange Event Service using the Services utility in the Windows Control Panel. See the Exchange readme.doc for additional precautions when debugging scripts on a production server.

- To get around the limitations of Notepad as your code editor, you can copy and paste your code into other tools that you may have available. To check for syntax errors, for example, you can copy your VBScript code and paste it into a form in a dummy Visual Basic project. Obviously, this technique will work only for code written in VBScript. After commenting out the <SCRIPT RunAt=Server Language=VBScript> and </SCRIPT> tags enclosing the code in the Event Service editor, use Run To Start With Full Compile to check for syntax errors. Correct the code, uncomment the <SCRIPT> tags, and then paste it back into the script editor window.

- You can also use a third-party tool such as Micro Eye Script Director to create, edit, and catalog scripting agents. Script Director lets you edit scripts using the Script Editor in Visual InterDev 6.0 instead of the Notepad editor (also known sardonically as Visual InterNotepad), which is the default editor for the Agents page.

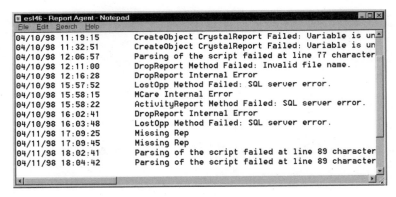

Figure 17.10 *The Script Execution Log appears in the Notepad.*

Scripting Error Logs

In addition to the Script Debugger, you can use the *Script.Response* method to write debugging strings to the scripting error log. See the DebugAssert function in Code Example 1, shown earlier in this chapter, for an example of this technique. You do not need to add the time and date stamp to your debug string; these will be added automatically when you call *Script.Response*. This execution log, shown in Figure 17.10 earlier, is limited, by default, to 32 KB of text, and is specific to the folder in which you've created the event script. Older items are overwritten on a first-in/first-out basis. A log is maintained for each agent script contained in the folder. Unlike the Script Debugger, which can only run locally on your Exchange server, the *Script.Response* method lets you perform remote debugging by clicking the Logs button on the Agent dialog box in the Outlook client.

The NT Event Log

Certain scripting errors will cause a failure in events.exe, the event source for the Event Service. If an error occurs, you'll find a message in the application error log. Use the NT Event Viewer to browse these messages. Event Service log events will appear under Source name of MSExchangeES. Use the View Filter Events command in the Event Viewer to view only those events that pertain to the Event Service.

Scripting Tips and Techniques

Registry Settings for the Event Service

You can control the number of events recorded in the NT Event log by changing the Logging Level value in the Windows registry for your Exchange server box. A value of 5 causes verbose logging of Events Service events to the NT Event log. Be certain that you have backed up your system completely before you make changes to the registry. The HKLM\System\CurrentControlSet\MSExchangeES\Parameters key contains values that control the following aspects of the Exchange Event Service:

DWORD Value	Possible Values	Description
Logging Level	0–5	Controls logging level in NT Event Log. 0=default value 5=maximum logging
Maximum execution time for scripts in seconds	900 default	Scripts will time out if they exceed this value. Increase the value for long running scripts and decrease for debugging.
Maximum size for agent log in KB	32 KB default	Size of agent log in KB. Agent log is maintained on a per folder basis.

Tools for Event Scripting

Our experience in the trenches with event scripts made it abundantly clear that the need existed for enterprise-level tools to create, distribute, and maintain script agents. This led directly to the development of Micro Eye Script Director. We believe that Script Director is an essential tool for developers who are working with Exchange Server Scripting and Routing Agents. Script Director also simplifies the installation and administration of custom Outlook forms in your public folder hierarchy. For additional information, or to obtain an evaluation copy, visit:

http://www.microeye.com/scriptdirector/

Using *CreateObject* Within Your Event Script

You can use the *CreateObject* method within your agent script to instantiate other ActiveX Automation components and call their properties and methods. Extending your scripts with *CreateObject* offers you a greatly expanded range of functionality—database access using ADO, secure message delivery with MSMQ, directory management via ADSI, or document creation using any of the Office 2000 Object Models. You can either call these object models directly from Event Service code, or you can create your own ActiveX components with any ActiveX component creation tool, such as Visual Basic or Visual C++. For purposes of scalability and performance, it is preferable to use the Event Service to instantiate the component and then let the component do most of the heavy lifting in your application. If you create composite components (components which, in turn, instantiate remote COM components), be sure that the security account under which you are running the Event Service has the capability of instantiating these objects. Use dcomcnfg.exe located in the Winnt\System32 folder to ensure that launch permissions are available for the service account that has Log On As permission for the Exchange Event Service.

Accessing Fields in Outlook Items

One of the snafus in Exchange Server scripting is the fact that the Collaboration Data Objects Object Model supports only a limited set of properties for built-in Message and Appointment items. From the perspective of the Outlook Object Model, all default properties on the other Outlook item types—Contact, Journal, Task, Document, and custom forms built on the base Outlook form classes—are not available in CDO. Workarounds have been published on newsgroups and on some Web sites, but Microsoft has advised that these solutions may break in future versions of Exchange Server. For example, you might want to use the Account field in a Contact item to look up the customer account in a SQL Server database.

Unfortunately, there is no easy way to access the Account property of a Contact item through CDO. First, no Contact item exists in the CDO Object Model. Even if the item did exist, the Account property might not be exposed to CDO. Microsoft has promised that future versions of CDO will support all the intrinsic Outlook item types and their properties. Be that as it may, there is a workaround that will let you access properties of Outlook items in a custom form. You should realize that this workaround applies only to a custom form created from a built-in form such as IPM.Contact. To get around the limitations of CDO with regard to default properties, you can proxy the property through a user-defined field. User-defined fields, unlike the built-in fields of an Outlook item, are accessible through the Fields collection object in CDO. Use the PropertyChange event in your custom form to assign the value of a user-defined field to a default field in your form. For example, assume that you need to determine the Account property of a Contact item that you obtain in one of the event procedures in a scripting agent. The following code from the Customer form in the Northwind Contact Management application in E-Chapter 3 in the E-Chapters folder on the companion CD converts the Account property to a user-defined field named Customer ID.

```
Sub Item_PropertyChange(ByVal Name)
    Select Case Name
        Case "Account"
            Item.UserProperties("CustomerID") = Item.Account
        Case "Links"
            LoadContact
    End Select
End Sub
```

When you write an event script that attempts to determine the value of the Customer form's Account field, you can use objMessage.Fields("CustomerID") to determine the value of Account, because any change in Account always changes the user-defined field named CustomerID. The following event script uses the CustomerID field to write data to a change table in a SQL Server database when a user modifies a Customer item in the Customers folder.

Code Example 2. The *Message_OnChange* event procedure in the Customers folder of the Northwind Contact Management application

```
Public Sub Message_OnChange()
    Dim strSQL, strCID, objConn, strConnect
    On Error Resume Next    'In-line error trapping
    Set objCDO = EventDetails.Session
    DebugAssert "EventDetails.Session"
    Set objFolder = objCDO.GetFolder(EventDetails.FolderID, Null)
    DebugAssert "objCDO.GetFolder"
    Set objMsgTarget = objCDO.GetMessage(EventDetails.MessageID, Null)
    DebugAssert "objCDO.GetMessage"
    'Only process messages of a certain message class
    If objMsgTarget.Type = "IPM.Contact.Customer" Then
        'These items are in process
        'Next Item_Write in form resets this UserDefined Field
        If objMsgTarget.Fields("Nwind Agent") Then
            Exit Sub
        End If
        'Create an ADO connection object
        Set objConn = CreateObject("ADODB.Connection")
        DebugAssert "CreateObject('ADODB.Connection')"
        'Open the connnection
        strConnect = "DSN=NwindSQL;UID=sa;PWD="
        objConn.Open strConnect
        DebugAssert "objConn.Open " & strConnect
        'Use fields collection to retrieve primary key
        strCID = objMsgTarget.Fields("CustomerID")
        'Prepare an insert SQL statement
        strSQL = "Insert tUpdate "
```

```
        strSQL = strSQL & "(UpdCid,UpdOpCd,UpdType,"
        strSQL = strSQL & "UpdEntryID,UpdFolderID,UpdStoreID) Values ("
        If strCID <> "" Then
            strSQL = strSQL & "'" & strCID & "','"
        Else
            strSQL = strSQL & "Null,'"
        End If
        'Use U to indicate Update
        strSQL = strSQL & "U','" & objMsgTarget.Type & "','" _
            & objMsgTarget.ID & "','"
        strSQL = strSQL & objFolder.ID & "','" _
            & objFolder.StoreID & "')"
        objConn.Execute strSQL
        DebugAssert "objConn.Execute " & strSQL
        objConn.Close
        DebugAssert "objConn.Close"
    End If
End Sub
```

When To Consider Event Scripting

Selecting a Routing or Agent Process

In evaluating the possibilities that Exchange and Outlook offer you as a developer, you have a variety of options for workflow applications. These applications typically require a set of Routing rules for either the default message types or for custom forms developed in Outlook. You need to weigh the advantages and disadvantages of each of the Routing or Agent processes described below.

Event Service for Private Mailboxes or Public Folders

Advantages

- Server-based logic, execution, and administration.
- Client independence.
- Scalability dependent on server memory and configuration.
- High level of security, since only permitted users can develop, install, and debug scripts.
- Tied to a specific folder.
- Works whether user is on-line or off-line. Exchange Incremental Change Synchronization (ICS) ensures that message events are always recorded, even if the Event Service is down or stopped.
- Granular events model—new, update, delete, and timer.
- Improved error handling and reporting. Handles exceptions through either NT Event log or agent-based scripting log.
- Facilitates debugging of complex event scripts with Visual InterDev Script Editor.

- Permits hiding Agent mailboxes or public folders from Global Address List.
- Useful for other types of workflow applications, in addition to Routing-based workflow.
- *CreateObject("ProgID")* can be used to instantiate other object models and provide additional functionality. If you create ActiveX DLL components in Visual Basic or Visual C++, you can package these components in Microsoft Transaction Server in order to provide process isolation and security. Components provide a way to modularize your Event Script code. They also offer a development environment superior to VBScript, with better performance because composite components can be early-bound to their dependent object models.

Disadvantages

- Requires experienced developer using VBScript or JScript.
- Interactive coding environment is not available.
- Should not be installed on a large number of mailboxes with extensive mail traffic.
- Difficult to administer because scripts must be installed in each folder where they operate. There is no centralized script administration tool in the Exchange Administrator application. If you install the same script in a large number of folders in a public folder application, you will face a considerable administrative burden if you modify the script. Third-party applications can provide relief in this area.
- Does not work well in conjunction with folders monitored by Rules Wizard or Folder Assistant.

COM Add-Ins for Private Mailbox or Public Folders

Advantages

- All the new events in the Outlook 2000 Object Model are available to COM Add-ins, including Items collection Add, Change, and Remove events, which are similar to the folder-level events for Exchange scripting agents.
- Client-dependent (Win32 only).
- Full access to other object models, such as ADO, ADSI, MSMQ, and Office 2000.
- Fully interactive development environment in Visual Basic 5.0 or 6.0.
- Robust error handling compared to VBScript.
- Easy to package and deploy to many users.

Disadvantages

- Executes on client machine. If the client machine fails, your process fails.
- Lacks server scalability and durability of Incremental Change Synchronization on server.
- Can be turned off by user, either deliberately or accidentally.
- Exceptions are created locally and thus are more difficult to debug.

Folder Assistant for Public Folders

Advantages

- Server-based execution.
- Scalability dependent on server memory and configuration.
- Available to owner of public folder.
- Profile-specific.
- Installed by default.
- User-defined and configurable.
- Minimal training required.
- In the File menu, click Folders and Copy Folder Design to copy rules from source folder to target folder.

Disadvantages

- Cannot handle complex routing logic.
- Should not be installed on large number of public folders with extensive message traffic.
- Cannot call other processes through ActiveX automation; use launcher for custom action.

Rules Wizard

Advantages

- Rules can execute on server or on client.
- Available to any Exchange recipient or to any Outlook user, even those not connected to Exchange server.
- Installed by default.
- Applies to any folder in recipient mailbox.
- User-defined and configurable.
- Minimal training required.

Disadvantages

- Not scalable.
- Complex routing is difficult to achieve.
- Exceptions are created locally and thus are more difficult to debug.
- Difficult to administer because each Exchange user defines rules.
- Cannot call other processes through ActiveX automation; use launcher for custom action.

Northwind SQL Agent

The Northwind Contact Management application featured in E-Chapter 3 in the E-Chapters folder on the companion CD demonstrates how you can track shared activities in public folders. To fully extend the example of the Northwind Contact Management application, this section discusses how to create bilateral synchronization between Customer items in a public folder and customer records in the Northwind database. The conversion program listed in E-Chapter 3 converts customer records in the Access 2000 sample Northwind database to Customer Contact items in the Northwind application folder hierarchy. The Northwind SQL Agent presented in this chapter requires the Northwind sample database that ships with SQL Server 7.0 or an upsized Northwind sample database in SQL Server 6.5. SQL Server serves as the back-end database for this example for two reasons. First, you must install triggers on the Customers table to write a record to a change table in the Northwind database when a record is added, changed, or deleted in the Customers table. Second, a SQL Server database is more likely to replicate a real-world application for users who want to synchronize Exchange public folders with external corporate data.

Bilateral Synchronization Between Exchange Public Folders and SQL Server

Bilateral synchronization between Exchange and SQL Server means that changes in the SQL Server database automatically synchronize with items in the Customers public folders, and vice versa. There are many different approaches to bilateral synchronization between Exchange data and RDBMS data. The design used here creates a synchronization table in SQL Server that contains records of changes to either SQL Server data in the Customers table or Customer Contact items in the Customers public folder. On the Exchange side, the Event Service writes a record to the tUpdate table in SQL Server when a Customer item is added, changed, or deleted. On the SQL Server side, the triggers on the Customer table in the Northwind database write a record to tUpdate when a customer database record is added, changed, or deleted. Periodically, a Visual Basic application named NwindSQLAgent launches and uses the records in the tUpdate table to synchronize data in the Customers public folder and the Customers table in the Northwind SQL Server database. If you want to extend this application, you could design NwindSQLAgent to run as an NT Service. This functionality is beyond the scope of this book, but you can find articles on running a Visual Basic application as an NT Service in the Visual Basic knowledge base at *http://support.microsoft.com/support/* and in the Visual Basic documentation. NwindSQLAgent.exe is designed to run as a scheduled job in the SQL Server Agent Manager. Figure 17.11 illustrates the conceptual design of the bilateral synchronization process.

Installing the Sample Application

Several steps are required to set up the bilateral synchronization between the Northwind SQL Server database and the Customers public folder. The steps required to get the application going are listed next, followed by a discussion of the code that makes the synchronization operate. The operating assumption here is that you will be testing this

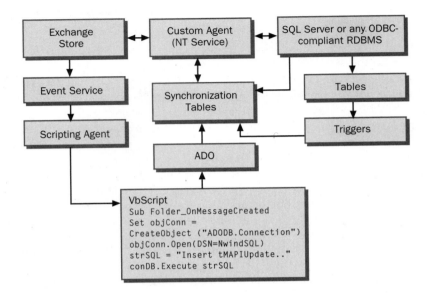

Figure 17.11 *Conceptual design of bilateral synchronization between Exchange and SQL Server.*

application on a test Exchange Server running in conjunction with a test SQL Server 7.0 system. Do not attempt to run this application on a production system. Exchange Server and SQL Server 7.0 can be running on the same system or on separate systems.

To install the NwindSQLAgent project

1. Expand the Folder 5. Advanced Topics subfolder of the Building Microsoft Outlook 2000 Applications personal folders (.pst) file.

2. Expand the Extending Outlook Using Exchange Server Scripting And Routing Objects folder and click the NwindSQLAgent Project folder.

3. Select all the files in the NwindSQLAgent Project folder.

4. Launch Windows Explorer and create a folder named NwindSQLAgent under the VB98 folder for Visual Basic 6.0. If you've selected the default installation, the VB98 folder is located in C:\Program Files\Microsoft Visual Studio\VB98.

5. Drag the files that you selected in step 3 to the NwindSQLAgent folder in Windows Explorer. If you have problems dragging and dropping files, we've also included a self-extracting .zip file that contains all the files in the NwindSQLAgent Project folder. Just double-click the NwindSQL.exe file and extract the files in that file to the folder listed in step 4.

To create synchronization tables and triggers in the Northwind database

1. Make sure that SQL Server 7.0 client utilities have been installed on your system.

2. Launch the SQL Server Query Analyzer and open NwindTrigger.sql in the folder you created in step 4 above. Execute this SQL script in the Northwind database. This script will create two additional tables in the Northwind database named tUpdate and tMAPICustRel. It will also create triggers for the Customers table.

3. Launch the ODBC Data Sources utility in the Windows Control Panel and create a DSN on your system named NwindSQL to point to the Northwind sample database on SQL Server.

To create DSN on Exchange Server

1. Make sure that ActiveX Data Objects (ADO) 2.1 or later is installed on the Exchange Server.

2. Launch the ODBC Data Sources utility in the Windows control panel and create a DSN named NwindSQL on the Exchange Server machine to point to the Northwind sample database on SQL Server. The SQL Server machine name might differ from the machine where Exchange server is running.

To convert the Northwind customers table into Customer forms

1. Follow the steps outlined in "Copying the Application folders to Public Folders" from E-Chapter 3, "The Northwind Contact Management Application," to copy the Northwind Contact Management application from the personal folders file that accompanies this book to Exchange public folders.

2. Use Visual Basic 6.0 to open the NwindMAPI project in the NwindSQLAgent project folder.

3. Run the NwindMAPI project to convert Northwind customers into IPM.Contact.Customer custom items. If you have existing Customer and Customer Contact items in your public folders, this process will delete those items and replace them with items that derive from customer records in the Northwind SQL Server database.

Install the Nwind Agent script

1. Select the Customers public folder and then right-click for Folder Properties.

2. Click the Agents tab and then click the New button.

3. Enter *Nwind Agent* in the Agent Name box.

4. Check the New Item, Changed Item, and Deleted Item check boxes.

5. Click the Edit Script button, and then select the Select All command from the Edit menu.

6. Right click the NwindSQL.vbs script file in the NwindSQLAgent folder in Windows Explorer and select Edit to open it in a separate Notepad window. The

scripting agent installed with this sample application uses a User ID of SA and a blank password. Change these values to match the correct User ID and password for the Northwind database on your SQL Server.

7. Select the Select All command from the Edit menu and then select the Edit Copy command from the Edit menu in the notepad opened in step 6.

8. Select the Paste command on the Edit menu in the Script Editor Notepad to replace the default contents of your script with the code that you copied in step 7.

9. Select the Save command on the File menu in the Script Editor Notepad and then close the Notepad window.

10. Click OK in the Nwind Agent dialog box, and then click OK to close the Folder properties dialog box.

Use SQL Server Agent to run NWindSQLAgent.exe as a scheduled job

1. NwindSQLAgent.exe synchronizes the public folder Contact items with customer records in the Northwind database. NwindSQLAgent.exe is located in the folder you created in "Install the Nwind Agent script."

2. Install NwindSQLAgent.exe as a scheduled job under the SQL Server Agent service for SQL Server 7.0. Figure 17.12 shows the NwindSQLAgent job in the SQL Server Enterprise Manager window. For help on creating a new job, see the documentation that accompanies SQL Server 7.0. Schedule an appropriate frequency for the job; every 15 minutes is a good place to start.

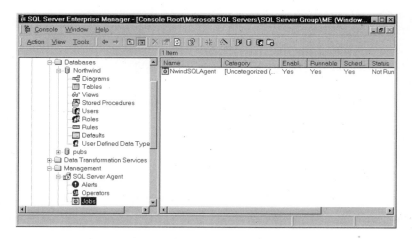

Figure 17.12 *NwindSQLAgent.exe runs as a scheduled job and synchronizes the Customers folder with the Northwind Customers table.*

⊃   **Test the application**

1. Select the Customers folder in the public folder hierarchy and then open one of the Customer items in the folder. Make a change to the address, for example, and then click the Save and Close button.

2. Install the Northwind SQL project file from the Office 2000 CD. To install the Northwind SQL project file, follow the steps outlined to install the Northwind sample database outlined in Chapter 15, "Outlook Data Access Strategies." In addition to selecting the Northwind database, select Northwind SQL Project File from Sample Databases under Microsoft Access For Windows and set this item to Run From My Computer.

3. After the NwindSQLAgent process runs, use the Customers form in the NorthwindCS project to view the customer contact that you modified in step 1 above. If you installed it in step 2 above, the NorthwindCS project (NorthwindCS.adp) is located in the same samples folder (typically C:\Program Files\Microsoft Office\Office\Samples) that contains Northwind.mdb. Link the tables in this database to the tables in the Northwind database on SQL Server 7.0. If the agent script has fired and the NwindSQLAgent.exe has run, you will see the changes reflected in the Northwind database.

4. Conversely, you can change customer records in the Northwind database and those changes will be reflected in the Customers public folder.

NwindSQLAgent Project

There are two Visual Basic projects in the NwindSQLAgent folder. The NwindMAPI project converts records in the Customers table of the SQL Server Northwind database to Customer items in a public folder. Since the code for this application is almost identical to the code behind frmNorthwind in the Northwind Contact Management application discussed in E-Chapter 3 on the companion CD, it does not bear re-examination here. The heart of the Northwind SQL Agent application lies in the code for the NwindSQLAgent project. NwindSQLAgent does not have a user interface. If errors occur during code execution, they are written to the NT Event log.

Sub Main

The startup object for the application is Sub Main located in basMAPINorthwind. The code in Sub Main examines the records in the tUpdate table in SQL Server. If changes (insert, update, or delete) have occurred in the SQL Server Northwind database, the triggers on the Customers table write a record into the tUpdate table. If a change (add, change, or remove) occurs in the Customers public folder, the Nwind Agent scripting agent installed on the Customers public folder writes a record into the tUpdate table. Each row in tUpdate has a unique ID and identifies whether the change comes from SQL Server or from an

Exchange Public Folder. Code Example 3 shows the listing from *Sub Main* in the NwindSQLAgent project.

Code Example 3. The Sub Main procedure in NWindSQLAgent

```
Sub Main()
    Dim flr As Outlook.MAPIFolder
    Dim strEntryID As String, strFolderID As String, strStoreID As String
    Dim strMC As String, strCID As String, strTable As String
    Dim strSQL As String
    Dim lngID As Long, N As Long
    Dim MyRS As New ADODB.Recordset
    Dim MapiRs As New ADODB.Recordset
    Dim avarArray As Variant

    On Error GoTo Main_Error
    'Create an Outlook Application object
    If Not CreateOutlookInstance() Then
        End
    End If
    'Open ADO Connection to Northwind DB  - Change UID and PWD if necessary
    conDB.Open "NwindSQL", "sa", ""
    'Static resultset returns recordcount
    MyRS.Open "Select * from tUpdate order by UpdID Asc", conDB, adOpenStatic
    If MyRS.EOF Then
        'no records to process
        GoTo Main_Exit
    End If
    'This array holds UpdID and True or False for Delete or Retain
    ReDim avarArray(MyRS.RecordCount - 1, 2)
    Do Until MyRS.EOF
        strEntryID = CheckNull(MyRS!UpdEntryID)
        strFolderID = CheckNull(MyRS!UpdFolderID)
        strStoreID = CheckNull(MyRS!UpdStoreID)
        strMC = CheckNull(MyRS!UpdType)
        lngID = MyRS!UpdID
        strCID = CheckNull(MyRS!UpdCid)
        avarArray(N, 0) = lngID
        If strMC = "IPM.Contact.Customer" Then
            If MyRS!UpdOpCd = "U" Then
                If UpdateContact(strEntryID, strFolderID, strStoreID) Then
                    'Delete the item
                    avarArray(N, 1) = True
                End If
            ElseIf MyRS!UpdOpCd = "I" Then
                If AddContact(strEntryID, strFolderID, strStoreID) Then
                    'Delete the item
                    avarArray(N, 1) = True
                End If
            ElseIf MyRS!UpdOpCd = "D" Then
                'This represents a special case since there is no longer
                'an item in the Exchange folder
```

```
                        'EventDetails.MessageID does return a partial Message ID
                        'and that ID can be used to retrieve the CustomerID from
                        'the tMapiCustRel table
                        If DeleteContact(strEntryID, strFolderID, strStoreID) Then
                            'Delete the item
                            avarArray(N, 1) = True
                        End If
                    End If
                ElseIf strMC = "" Then 'These items are moving from SQL to MAPI
                    strTable = CheckNull(MyRS!UpdTblNm)
                    If strTable = "Customers" Then
                        If MyRS!UpdOpCd = "U" Then
                            If UpdateContactMAPI(strCID) Then
                                'Delete the item
                                avarArray(N, 1) = True
                            Else
                                avarArray(N, 1) = True
                            End If
                        ElseIf MyRS!UpdOpCd = "I" Then
                            If AddContactMAPI(strCID) Then
                                'Delete the item
                                avarArray(N, 1) = True
                            End If
                        ElseIf MyRS!UpdOpCd = "D" Then
                            'DeleteContactMAPI always returns True
                            If DeleteContactMAPI(strCID) Then
                                'Delete the item
                                avarArray(N, 1) = True
                            End If
                        End If
                    End If
                End If
            End If
            MyRS.MoveNext
            N = N + 1
        Loop
        'Switch to On Error Resume Next to delete as many rows as possible
        On Error Resume Next
        For N = 0 To UBound(avarArray)
            If avarArray(N, 1) Then
                strSQL = "Delete from tUpdate where UpdID = " & avarArray(N, 0)
                conDB.Execute strSQL
                If Err Then
                    Utility.ErrorTrap
                End If
            End If
        Next

    'Set global objects to nothing and close connection

Main_Exit:
    On Error Resume Next
    Set gobjNameSpace = Nothing
```

```
    Set gobjOutlook = Nothing
    conDB.Close
    Exit Sub

Main_Error:
    Utility.ErrorTrap
    Resume Main_Exit
End Sub
```

To simplify the explanation of this code, we'll walk through one condition only. Let's assume that a user has modified a customer record in the Customers table. The trigger on the Customers table writes a record to the tUpdate table that indicates a record has changed and identifies the changed record with its primary key, CustomerID. It also adds the code U to the record to indicate that a changed record must be updated in the Exchange store. Let's assume that the change was applied to The Hungry Coyote Import Store with a CustomerID equal to HUNGC.

When the NwindSQLAgent runs, it finds the change record in the tUpdate table. It adds this record to a variant. Depending on whether the change emanates from the Customers public folder in Exchange or the Customer table in SQL Server, either the *UpdateContact* procedure or the *UpdateContactMAPI* procedure runs. *UpdateContact* updates the customer record in SQL Server from an item in Exchange and *UpdateContactMAPI* updates a Customer item in the public folder from the Customer record in SQL Server. *UpdateContactMAPI* is reproduced in Code Example 4 so that you can observe how a customer item in the Customers folder is obtained from a record in the tUpdate table.

UpdateContactMAPI Function Procedure

The key to finding an item in the Exchange store is to use its EntryID and StoreID as arguments for the *GetItemFromID* method of the NameSpace object. Where did we find the EntryID and StoreID for the customer item? When the item was created in the NwindMAPI project, a record was written to a SQL Server table named tMAPICustRel. This table stores the primary key for the record (its CustomerID) along with the EntryID and StoreID for the newly created item in the Customers folder. Since we know the CustomerID for the changed record (passed as the argument strCID in the *UpdateContactMAPI* procedure), we can obtain the StoreID and the EntryID by running a select query against the tMAPICustRel table. Once we have the StoreID and EntryID, we instantiate an Outlook ContactItem object representing the Customer item in the Customers folder and update all of its properties with the current values for the Customer record in SQL Server.

Code Example 4. The UpdateContactMAPI Function

```
Function UpdateContactMAPI(strCID As String) As Boolean
    Dim objCont As Outlook.ContactItem
    Dim RsMapi As New ADODB.Recordset
    Dim rsNwind As New ADODB.Recordset
    Dim strSQL As String, strEntryID As String, strStoreID As String
```

```
    On Error GoTo UpdateContactMAPI_Error
    'Get MAPI data, if exists, from tMAPICustRel
    strSQL = "Select EntryID, StoreID from tMAPICustRel where Cid = '" _
        & strCID & "'"
    RsMapi.Open strSQL, conDB
    'If no MAPI data, exit cleanly
    If RsMapi.EOF Then
        GoTo NoItem
    End If
    strEntryID = CheckNull(RsMapi!EntryID)
    strStoreID = CheckNull(RsMapi!StoreID)
    RsMapi.Close

    strSQL = "Select * from Customers where CustomerId = '" _
        & strCID & "'"
    rsNwind.Open strSQL, conDB

    If Not rsNwind.EOF Then
        On Error Resume Next
        Set objCont = gobjNameSpace.GetItemFromID(strEntryID, strStoreID)
        'Handle errors
        If objCont Is Nothing Then
            If AddContactMAPI(strCID) Then
                GoTo NoItem
            Else
                GoTo UpdateContactMAPI_Exit
            End If
        End If
        On Error GoTo UpdateContactMAPI_Error
        'Update fields in contact item
        With objCont
            .CompanyName = CheckNull(rsNwind!CompanyName)
            .BusinessAddressStreet = CheckNull(rsNwind!Address)
            .BusinessAddressCity = CheckNull(rsNwind!City)
            .BusinessAddressState = CheckNull(rsNwind!Region)
            .BusinessAddressPostalCode = CheckNull(rsNwind!PostalCode)
            .BusinessAddressCountry = CheckNull(rsNwind!Country)
            .Account = rsNwind!CustomerID
            .UserProperties("CustomerID") = rsNwind!CustomerID
            .BusinessTelephoneNumber = CheckNull(rsNwind!Phone)
            .BusinessFaxNumber = CheckNull(rsNwind!Fax)
            'Setting this UD property to True prevents event service
            'from creating an entry in tUpdate table
            .UserProperties("Nwind Agent") = True
            .Save
        End With
    End If
    UpdateContactMAPI = True

NoItem:
    UpdateContactMAPI = True
```

```
UpdateContactMAPI_Exit:
    Exit Function

UpdateContactMAPI_Error:
    Utility.ErrorTrap
    On Error Resume Next
    UpdateContactMAPI = False
    Resume UpdateContactMAPI_Exit
End Function
```

Cleanup and Exit

If the UpdateContactMAPI procedure completes without an error, it returns *True*. The Boolean result of *UpdateContactMAPI* is stored in a variant array in *Sub Main* named *avarArray*. If a record is marked as updated in avarArray, then the change record in the tUpdate table is deleted and the update process is complete. One hidden trick in this application requires a special user-defined field on the custom Customer form. The Customer form contains a user-defined field named Nwind Agent. The default value of this field is *False*. When the NwindSQLAgent application changes the Outlook item representing Hungry Coyote Import Store, it causes a change event to fire in the Customers folder. We don't want the Event Service to recognize this synchronization event as a change in the Outlook item that must be propagated back to SQL Server. Why not? If we write a change to tUpdate, we'll wind up in an endless loop and our application will fail. If you examine the scripting agent code in Code Example 2, you'll see that the *Message_OnChange* procedure skips any items in the folder where the user-defined field Nwind Agent is *True*. The next time a user opens the Customer form, the Item_Write event in the form resets the Nwind Agent user-defined field to *False*. Since the Nwind Agent user-defined field is *False,* and, presumably, the item has changed because a user has saved the item, the Nwind Agent script in the Customers folder will now create a new change record in the tUpdate table.

```
Function Item_Write()
    'Resets Nwind Agent boolean so that continuous loop is avoided
    If Item.UserProperties("Nwind Agent") and Len(Item.Account) Then
        Item.UserProperties("Nwind Agent") = False
    End If
End Function
```

Once the *Sub Main* procedure completes execution, the NwindSQLAgent process quits and removes itself from memory until the next time it is scheduled to run. While we've only covered the update process in the NwindSQLAgent application, you are encouraged to examine the other procedures in the application that are called when an item is added or deleted.

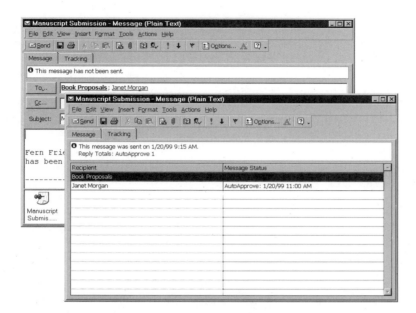

Figure 17.13 *The Manuscript Approval Routing Object application moves documents through serial or parallel routes and tracks voting responses.*

Exchange Routing Objects

First released in Exchange 5.5 Service Pack 1, Routing objects allow you to construct both serial and parallel Routing applications with sophisticated levels of complexity, compared with the Routing available with Server Scripting alone. Figure 17.13 shows a simple Outlook Post form designed to track manuscript approval through a financial and legal review process. The Routing Objects Object Model defines Routing primitives known as Intrinsic Actions. Examples of intrinsic actions are Wait, Terminate, OrSplit, AndSplit, and GoTo. Each activity that controls a message as it moves through the Routing table is known as a row in the item's Process Map. Routing objects also allow for extrinsic functions customized by the developer for a specific workflow application. These extrinsic actions are known as Script Actions. The Routing objects agent is a noteworthy example of a Custom Script Handler developed for the Exchange Event Service. An extensive discussion of Exchange Routing Objects is beyond the scope of this chapter. See "Where To Go from Here" at the end of this chapter for additional resources on Exchange Routing Objects.

In Summary

The Exchange Event Service expands the range of application development possibilities for Outlook and Exchange application developers. Use the Event Service to develop complex Exchange and Outlook applications, especially when your application requires integration of Exchange data with backend corporate databases. Event script code runs in a secure server-based process that is centrally administered. Locating your code on the server can result in significantly fewer installation and deployment problems compared with code that runs in a client application. There are some application scenarios where you can code application logic into the event script, rather than using VBScript behind forms. At this point, we've come a long way from simple applications that use built-in Outlook forms to create discussion applications. When you apply the techniques outlined in NwindSQLAgent to a collaboration application like the Northwind Contact Management application, you can create very powerful applications that combine corporate data with the flexibility of the Exchange store and the rapid development cycle of Outlook custom forms. We hope that you've enjoyed your journey and that your imagination is open to the great potential of Outlook and Exchange application development.

Where To Go from Here

Additional Exchange Information

For the latest information on Microsoft Exchange, visit the Exchange Web site at *http://www.microsoft.com/exchange/*.

Visit the Exchange Application Farm at *http://technet.microsoft.com/reg/download/exchange/*.

The best source of information for Collaboration Data Objects and Exchange Server Scripting Agents is CDO Live at *http://www.cdolive.com/*.

The premier privately maintained site for Exchange information is Sue Mosher's Exchange Center at *http://www.slipstick.com/exchange/*.

A good example of a sophisticated and widely used scripting agent is the revised AutoAccept script, available from the Exchange Code Exchange at *http://exchangecode.com/*.

See *http://msdn.microsoft.com/developer/* for updated white papers and technical articles on the Exchange Event Service and Exchange Application Development.

Programming Applications on Microsoft Exchange Server

Rizzo, Thomas, *Programming Microsoft Outlook and Microsoft Exchanges.* Redmond, WA: Microsoft Press, 1999

Index

A

Randy Byrne A veteran Outlook developer, Randy Byrne is the President and CEO of Micro Eye, Inc., a Microsoft Solution Provider specializing in collaborative application development using Microsoft Exchange and Outlook. As a Microsoft Most Valued Professional (MVP) for Outlook, he has extensive experience with the concerns of the Outlook development community. He received his Bachelor's degree from Yale University and a graduate degree from the University of California at Berkeley. He has presented on Outlook and Exchange programming topics at Microsoft Tech Ed and contributes regularly to the Outlook newsgroups. Micro Eye, Inc. is located in the Sacramento area of Northern California.

The manuscript for this book was prepared and galleyed using Microsoft Word 97. Pages were composed by Black Hole Publishing Services using Adobe PageMaker 6.52 for Windows, with text in Garamond and display type in Franklin Gothic. Composed pages were delivered to the printer as electronic prepress files.

Cover Designer:	Tim Girvin Design, Inc.
Cover Illustrator:	Glenn Mitsui
Interior Graphic Designer:	James D. Kramer
Principal Compositor:	Jo-Anne H. Rosen
Principal Proofreader:	Jeffrey Barash
Indexer:	Eugene Ahn

There's no *substitute* for **experience.**

Now you can apply the best practices from real-world implementations of Microsoft technologies with *Notes from the Field.* Based on the extensive field experiences of Microsoft Consulting Services, these valuable technical references outline tried-and-tested solutions you can use in your own company, right now.

Deploying Microsoft® Office 2000 (Notes from the Field)		Deploying Microsoft SQL Server™ 7.0 (Notes from the Field)		Optimizing Network Traffic (Notes from the Field)		Managing a Microsoft Windows NT® Network (Notes from the Field)	
U.S.A.	**$39.99**	**U.S.A.**	**$39.99**	**U.S.A.**	**$39.99**	**U.S.A.**	**$39.99**
U.K.	£37.49	U.K.	£37.49	U.K.	£37.49 [V.A.T. included]	U.K.	£37.49 [V.A.T. included]
Canada	$59.99	Canada	$59.99	Canada	$59.99	Canada	$59.99
ISBN 0-7356-0727-3		ISBN 0-7356-0726-5		ISBN 0-7356-0648-X		ISBN 0-7356-0647-1	

Microsoft Press® products are available worldwide wherever quality computer books are sold. For more information, contact your book or computer retailer, software reseller, or local Microsoft Sales Office, or visit our Web site at mspress.microsoft.com. To locate your nearest source for Microsoft Press products, or to order directly, call 1-800-MSPRESS in the U.S. (in Canada, call 1-800-268-2222).

Prices and availability dates are subject to change.

Microsoft®

mspress.microsoft.com

http://mspress.microsoft.com/reslink/

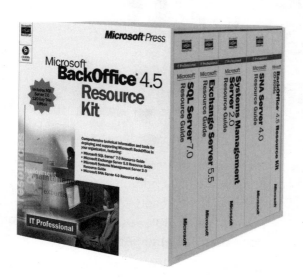

ResourceLink—your online IT library!

Access the full line of Microsoft Press® Resource Kits for the Windows® and BackOffice® families, along with MCSE Training Kits and other IT-specific resources at mspress.microsoft.com/reslink/. Microsoft Press ResourceLink is the essential online information service for IT professionals. Get Microsoft Press training resources, technical updates, support alerts, insider tips, and downloadable utilities—direct from Microsoft. If you evaluate, deploy, or support Microsoft® technologies and products, the information you need to optimize their performance—and your own—is on line and ready for work at ResourceLink.

For a complimentary 30-day trial CD packed with Microsoft Press
IT products, or for a no-cost, 15-day trial membership,
visit: mspress.microsoft.com/reslink/

Microsoft®

mspress.microsoft.com

Practical, *portable* guides for **troubleshooters**

For hands-on, immediate references that will help you troubleshoot and administer Microsoft Windows NT Server 4.0, Microsoft SQL Server 7.0, or Microsoft Exchange 5.5, get the:

Microsoft® Windows NT® 4.0 Administrator's Pocket Consultant
ISBN 0-7356-0574-2 $29.99 ($44.99 Canada)

Microsoft SQL Server™ 7.0 Administrator's Pocket Consultant
ISBN 0-7356-0596-3 $29.99 ($44.99 Canada)

Microsoft Exchange 5.5 Administrator's Pocket Consultant
ISBN 0-7356-0623-4 $29.99 ($44.99 Canada)

Ideal at the desk or on the go, from workstation to workstation, these fast-answers guides focus on what needs to be done in specific scenarios to support and manage these mission-critical IT products. Great software and great learning solutions: Made for each other. Made by Microsoft.

Microsoft Press® products are available worldwide wherever quality computer books are sold. For more information, contact your book or computer retailer, software reseller, or local Microsoft Sales Office, or visit our Web site at mspress.microsoft.com. To locate your nearest source for Microsoft Press products, or to order directly, call 1-800-MSPRESS in the U.S. (in Canada, call 1-800-268-2222).

Prices and availability dates are subject to change.

Microsoft®
mspress.microsoft.com

Microsoft Press Resource Kits— powerhouse resources to minimize costs while maximizing performance

Microsoft® Windows NT® Server 4.0 Resource Kit
ISBN   1-57231-344-7
U.S.A. $149.95
U.K.   £140.99 [V.A.T. included]
Canada $201.95

Microsoft Windows NT Workstation 4.0 Resource Kit
ISBN   1-57231-343-9
U.S.A. $69.95
U.K.   £64.99 [V.A.T. included]
Canada $94.95

Microsoft Internet Information Server Resource Kit
ISBN   1-57231-638-1
U.S.A. $49.99
U.K.   £46.99 [V.A.T. included]
Canada $71.99

Microsoft Windows® 2000 Resource Kit
ISBN   1-7356-0555-6
U.S.A. $59.99
U.K.   £??.99 [V.A.T. included]
Canada $89.99

Microsoft Internet Explorer Resource Kit
ISBN   1-57231-842-2
U.S.A. $49.99
U.K.   £46.99 [V.A.T. included]
Canada $71.99

Microsoft BackOffice® Resource Kit, Second Edition
ISBN   1-57231-632-2
U.S.A. $199.99
U.K.   £187.99 [V.A.T. included]
Canada $289.99

Direct from the Microsoft product groups, the resources packed into these bestselling kits meet the demand for hardcore use-now tools and information for the IT professional. Each kit contains precise technical documentation, essential utilities, installation and rollout tactics, planning guides, and upgrade strategies. Use them to save time, reduce cost of ownership, and maximize your organization's technology investment.

mspress.microsoft.com

Microsoft Press® products are available worldwide wherever quality computer books are sold. For more information, contact your book or computer retailer, software reseller, or local Microsoft Sales Office, or visit our Web site at mspress.microsoft.com. To locate your nearest source for Microsoft Press products, or to order directly, call 1-800-MSPRESS in the U.S. (in Canada, call 1-800-268-2222).

Prices and availability dates are subject to change.

MICROSOFT LICENSE AGREEMENT

Book Companion CD

IMPORTANT—READ CAREFULLY: This Microsoft End-User License Agreement ("EULA") is a legal agreement between you (either an individual or an entity) and Microsoft Corporation for the Microsoft product identified above, which includes computer software and may include associated media, printed materials, and "on-line" or electronic documentation ("SOFTWARE PRODUCT"). Any component included within the SOFTWARE PRODUCT that is accompanied by a separate End-User License Agreement shall be governed by such agreement and not the terms set forth below. By installing, copying, or otherwise using the SOFTWARE PRODUCT, you agree to be bound by the terms of this EULA. If you do not agree to the terms of this EULA, you are not authorized to install, copy, or otherwise use the SOFTWARE PRODUCT; you may, however, return the SOFTWARE PRODUCT, along with all printed materials and other items that form a part of the Microsoft product that includes the SOFTWARE PRODUCT, to the place you obtained them for a full refund.

SOFTWARE PRODUCT LICENSE

The SOFTWARE PRODUCT is protected by United States copyright laws and international copyright treaties, as well as other intellectual property laws and treaties. The SOFTWARE PRODUCT is licensed, not sold.

1. **GRANT OF LICENSE.** This EULA grants you the following rights:

   a. **Software Product.** You may install and use one copy of the SOFTWARE PRODUCT on a single computer. The primary user of the computer on which the SOFTWARE PRODUCT is installed may make a second copy for his or her exclusive use on a portable computer.

   b. **Storage/Network Use.** You may also store or install a copy of the SOFTWARE PRODUCT on a storage device, such as a network server, used only to install or run the SOFTWARE PRODUCT on your other computers over an internal network; however, you must acquire and dedicate a license for each separate computer on which the SOFTWARE PRODUCT is installed or run from the storage device. A license for the SOFTWARE PRODUCT may not be shared or used concurrently on different computers.

   c. **License Pak.** If you have acquired this EULA in a Microsoft License Pak, you may make the number of additional copies of the computer software portion of the SOFTWARE PRODUCT authorized on the printed copy of this EULA, and you may use each copy in the manner specified above. You are also entitled to make a corresponding number of secondary copies for portable computer use as specified above.

   d. **Sample Code.** Solely with respect to portions, if any, of the SOFTWARE PRODUCT that are identified within the SOFTWARE PRODUCT as sample code (the "SAMPLE CODE"):

      i. **Use and Modification.** Microsoft grants you the right to use and modify the source code version of the SAMPLE CODE, *provided* you comply with subsection (d)(iii) below. You may not distribute the SAMPLE CODE, or any modified version of the SAMPLE CODE, in source code form.

      ii. **Redistributable Files.** Provided you comply with subsection (d)(iii) below, Microsoft grants you a nonexclusive, royalty-free right to reproduce and distribute the object code version of the SAMPLE CODE and of any modified SAMPLE CODE, other than SAMPLE CODE (or any modified version thereof) designated as not redistributable in the Readme file that forms a part of the SOFTWARE PRODUCT (the "Non-Redistributable Sample Code"). All SAMPLE CODE other than the Non-Redistributable Sample Code is collectively referred to as the "REDISTRIBUTABLES."

      iii. **Redistribution Requirements.** If you redistribute the REDISTRIBUTABLES, you agree to: (i) distribute the REDISTRIBUTABLES in object code form only in conjunction with and as a part of your software application product; (ii) not use Microsoft's name, logo, or trademarks to market your software application product; (iii) include a valid copyright notice on your software application product; (iv) indemnify, hold harmless, and defend Microsoft from and against any claims or lawsuits, including attorney's fees, that arise or result from the use or distribution of your software application product; and (v) not permit further distribution of the REDISTRIBUTABLES by your end user. Contact Microsoft for the applicable royalties due and other licensing terms for all other uses and/or distribution of the REDISTRIBUTABLES.

2. **DESCRIPTION OF OTHER RIGHTS AND LIMITATIONS.**

   - **Limitations on Reverse Engineering, Decompilation, and Disassembly.** You may not reverse engineer, decompile, or disassemble the SOFTWARE PRODUCT, except and only to the extent that such activity is expressly permitted by applicable law notwithstanding this limitation.

   - **Separation of Components.** The SOFTWARE PRODUCT is licensed as a single product. Its component parts may not be separated for use on more than one computer.

   - **Rental.** You may not rent, lease, or lend the SOFTWARE PRODUCT.

   - **Support Services.** Microsoft may, but is not obligated to, provide you with support services related to the SOFTWARE PRODUCT ("Support Services"). Use of Support Services is governed by the Microsoft policies and programs described in the user manual, in "on-line" documentation, and/or in other Microsoft-provided materials. Any supplemental software code provided to you as part of the Support Services shall be considered part of the SOFTWARE PRODUCT and subject to the terms and conditions of this EULA. With respect to technical information you provide to Microsoft as part of the Support Services, Microsoft may use such information for its business purposes, including for product support and development. Microsoft will not utilize such technical information in a form that personally identifies you.

- **Software Transfer.** You may permanently transfer all of your rights under this EULA, provided you retain no copies, you transfer all of the SOFTWARE PRODUCT (including all component parts, the media and printed materials, any upgrades, this EULA, and, if applicable, the Certificate of Authenticity), **and** the recipient agrees to the terms of this EULA.
- **Termination.** Without prejudice to any other rights, Microsoft may terminate this EULA if you fail to comply with the terms and conditions of this EULA. In such event, you must destroy all copies of the SOFTWARE PRODUCT and all of its component parts.

3. **COPYRIGHT.** All title and copyrights in and to the SOFTWARE PRODUCT (including but not limited to any images, photographs, animations, video, audio, music, text, SAMPLE CODE, REDISTRIBUTABLES, and "applets" incorporated into the SOFTWARE PRODUCT) and any copies of the SOFTWARE PRODUCT are owned by Microsoft or its suppliers. The SOFTWARE PRODUCT is protected by copyright laws and international treaty provisions. Therefore, you must treat the SOFTWARE PRODUCT like any other copyrighted material **except** that you may install the SOFTWARE PRODUCT on a single computer provided you keep the original solely for backup or archival purposes. You may not copy the printed materials accompanying the SOFTWARE PRODUCT.

4. **U.S. GOVERNMENT RESTRICTED RIGHTS.** The SOFTWARE PRODUCT and documentation are provided with RESTRICTED RIGHTS. Use, duplication, or disclosure by the Government is subject to restrictions as set forth in subparagraph (c)(1)(ii) of the Rights in Technical Data and Computer Software clause at DFARS 252.227-7013 or subparagraphs (c)(1) and (2) of the Commercial Computer Software—Restricted Rights at 48 CFR 52.227-19, as applicable. Manufacturer is Microsoft Corporation/One Microsoft Way/Redmond, WA 98052-6399.

5. **EXPORT RESTRICTIONS.** You agree that you will not export or re-export the SOFTWARE PRODUCT, any part thereof, or any process or service that is the direct product of the SOFTWARE PRODUCT (the foregoing collectively referred to as the "Restricted Components"), to any country, person, entity, or end user subject to U.S. export restrictions. You specifically agree not to export or re-export any of the Restricted Components (i) to any country to which the U.S. has embargoed or restricted the export of goods or services, which currently include, but are not necessarily limited to, Cuba, Iran, Iraq, Libya, North Korea, Sudan, and Syria, or to any national of any such country, wherever located, who intends to transmit or transport the Restricted Components back to such country; (ii) to any end user who you know or have reason to know will utilize the Restricted Components in the design, development, or production of nuclear, chemical, or biological weapons; or (iii) to any end user who has been prohibited from participating in U.S. export transactions by any federal agency of the U.S. government. You warrant and represent that neither the BXA nor any other U.S. federal agency has suspended, revoked, or denied your export privileges.

6. **NOTE ON JAVA SUPPORT.** THE SOFTWARE PRODUCT MAY CONTAIN SUPPORT FOR PROGRAMS WRITTEN IN JAVA. JAVA TECHNOLOGY IS NOT FAULT TOLERANT AND IS NOT DESIGNED, MANUFACTURED, OR INTENDED FOR USE OR RESALE AS ON-LINE CONTROL EQUIPMENT IN HAZARDOUS ENVIRONMENTS REQUIRING FAIL-SAFE PERFORMANCE, SUCH AS IN THE OPERATION OF NUCLEAR FACILITIES, AIRCRAFT NAVIGATION OR COMMUNICATION SYSTEMS, AIR TRAFFIC CONTROL, DIRECT LIFE SUPPORT MACHINES, OR WEAPONS SYSTEMS, IN WHICH THE FAILURE OF JAVA TECHNOLOGY COULD LEAD DIRECTLY TO DEATH, PERSONAL INJURY, OR SEVERE PHYSICAL OR ENVIRONMENTAL DAMAGE. SUN MICROSYSTEMS, INC. HAS CONTRACTUALLY OBLIGATED MICROSOFT TO MAKE THIS DISCLAIMER.

DISCLAIMER OF WARRANTY

NO WARRANTIES OR CONDITIONS. MICROSOFT EXPRESSLY DISCLAIMS ANY WARRANTY OR CONDITION FOR THE SOFTWARE PRODUCT. THE SOFTWARE PRODUCT AND ANY RELATED DOCUMENTATION ARE PROVIDED "AS IS" WITHOUT WARRANTY OR CONDITION OF ANY KIND, EITHER EXPRESS OR IMPLIED, INCLUDING, WITHOUT LIMITATION, THE IMPLIED WARRANTIES OF MERCHANTABILITY, FITNESS FOR A PARTICULAR PURPOSE, OR NONINFRINGEMENT. THE ENTIRE RISK ARISING OUT OF USE OR PERFORMANCE OF THE SOFTWARE PRODUCT REMAINS WITH YOU.

LIMITATION OF LIABILITY. TO THE MAXIMUM EXTENT PERMITTED BY APPLICABLE LAW, IN NO EVENT SHALL MICROSOFT OR ITS SUPPLIERS BE LIABLE FOR ANY SPECIAL, INCIDENTAL, INDIRECT, OR CONSEQUENTIAL DAMAGES WHATSOEVER (INCLUDING, WITHOUT LIMITATION, DAMAGES FOR LOSS OF BUSINESS PROFITS, BUSINESS INTERRUPTION, LOSS OF BUSINESS INFORMATION, OR ANY OTHER PECUNIARY LOSS) ARISING OUT OF THE USE OF OR INABILITY TO USE THE SOFTWARE PRODUCT OR THE PROVISION OF OR FAILURE TO PROVIDE SUPPORT SERVICES, EVEN IF MICROSOFT HAS BEEN ADVISED OF THE POSSIBILITY OF SUCH DAMAGES. IN ANY CASE, MICROSOFT'S ENTIRE LIABILITY UNDER ANY PROVISION OF THIS EULA SHALL BE LIMITED TO THE GREATER OF THE AMOUNT ACTUALLY PAID BY YOU FOR THE SOFTWARE PRODUCT OR US$5.00; PROVIDED, HOWEVER, IF YOU HAVE ENTERED INTO A MICROSOFT SUPPORT SERVICES AGREEMENT, MICROSOFT'S ENTIRE LIABILITY REGARDING SUPPORT SERVICES SHALL BE GOVERNED BY THE TERMS OF THAT AGREEMENT. BECAUSE SOME STATES AND JURISDICTIONS DO NOT ALLOW THE EXCLUSION OR LIMITATION OF LIABILITY, THE ABOVE LIMITATION MAY NOT APPLY TO YOU.

MISCELLANEOUS

This EULA is governed by the laws of the State of Washington USA, except and only to the extent that applicable law mandates governing law of a different jurisdiction.

Should you have any questions concerning this EULA, or if you desire to contact Microsoft for any reason, please contact the Microsoft subsidiary serving your country, or write: Microsoft Sales Information Center/One Microsoft Way/Redmond, WA 98052-6399.

System Requirements

To use the *Building Applications with Microsoft Outlook 2000* CD-ROM, you need a computer equipped with the following minimum configuration:

- Pentium or higher processor

- Microsoft Windows 95, Windows 98, Windows NT 4.0, or later

- At least 12 MB of RAM on Windows 95, 16 on Windows 98 or Windows NT 4.0

- 25 MB of available hard disk space

- CD-ROM drive

- Mouse or other pointing device (recommended)

- Microsoft Office 2000

Register Today!

Return this
*Building Applications with Microsoft® Outlook® 2000
Technical Reference*
registration card today

Microsoft®Press
mspress.microsoft.com

OWNER REGISTRATION CARD   0-7356-0581-5

Building Applications with Microsoft® Outlook® 2000
Technical Reference

FIRST NAME _____   MIDDLE INITIAL _____   LAST NAME _____

INSTITUTION OR COMPANY NAME _____

ADDRESS _____

_____

CITY _____   STATE _____   ZIP _____

E-MAIL ADDRESS _____   ( ) _____
                                                 PHONE NUMBER

U.S. and Canada addresses only. Fill in information above and mail postage-free.
Please mail only the bottom half of this page.

**For information about Microsoft Press®
products, visit our Web site at
mspress.microsoft.com**

Microsoft·Press

BUSINESS REPLY MAIL
FIRST-CLASS MAIL   PERMIT NO. 108   REDMOND WA

POSTAGE WILL BE PAID BY ADDRESSEE

MICROSOFT PRESS
PO BOX 97017
REDMOND, WA 98073-9830

NO POSTAGE
NECESSARY
IF MAILED
IN THE
UNITED STATES